SHAREPOINT® 2010 SIX-IN-ONE

Continues

SharePoint® 2010

SIX-IN-ONE

Chris Geier
Cathy Dew
Becky Bertram
Raymond Mitchell
Wes Preston
Ken Schaefer
Andrew Clark

WILEY

Wiley Publishing, Inc.

SharePoint® 2010 Six-in-One

Published by
Wiley Publishing, Inc.
10475 Crosspoint Boulevard
Indianapolis, IN 46256
www.wiley.com

ISBN: 978-0-470-87727-2
ISBN: 978-1-118-05943-2 (ebk)
ISBN: 978-1-118-05826-8 (ebk)
ISBN: 978-1-118-05827-5 (ebk)

Manufactured in the United States of America

10 9 8 7 6 5 4 3 2 1

For general information on our other products and services please contact our Customer Care Department within the United States at (877) 762-2974, outside the United States at (317) 572-3993 or fax (317) 572-4002.

Wiley also publishes its books in a variety of electronic formats. Some content that appears in print may not be available in electronic books.

Library of Congress Control Number: 2010941219

ABOUT THE AUTHORS

 CHRIS GEIER is a 15-year veteran of the technology industry and specializes in all things Microsoft. He was introduced to SharePoint 2001 while working for Microsoft services. Chris is a participant in, and advocate for, the SharePoint community, as well as a regular participant/speaker at SharePoint Saturday and other grass-roots events. When not twiddling with the latest gadgets, software, and technology, you'll find Chris cheering his budding baseball and gymnastic stars. Chris and his wife, Sara, have four kids and live in suburban Chicago.

 BECKY BERTRAM is an independent consultant living in the St. Louis area. She has more than a decade of experience building web content management solutions for clients, using the Microsoft platform. She and her husband, Ryan, are looking forward to the birth of their first child. Becky posts frequently to her blog, www .beckybertram.com. You can also follow Becky on Twitter, at @beckybertram.

 **ANDREW CLARK** is a senior SharePoint consultant based in the Chicago area. A graduate in finance from North Central College, his background is mainly ASP.NET web application development, with an emphasis on security. His focus for the last three years has been entirely on SharePoint. He is an MCTS with WSS 3.0 Configuration, WSS 3.0 Application Development, MOSS 2007 Configuration, and MOSS 2007 Application Development. When not behind a computer screen, he can be found at the nearest basketball court.

CATHY DEW (MCTS) is a senior consultant and graphic designer for Summit 7 Systems in Huntsville, Ala. With an advertising agency and graphic design background, her focus is on user interface design and user experience with sites. She has worked primarily with SharePoint installations to brand SharePoint and make it look "not like SharePoint." She helped found the Birmingham SharePoint User Group and is the communications VP for the Women in SharePoint Group. She has presented at user groups and conferences.

 **RAYMOND MITCHELL** is a senior consultant in Minneapolis, and has worked with SharePoint since 2001. He is a frequent speaker at the Minnesota SharePoint User Group, and has also spoken before the Wisconsin, Iowa, Nebraska, and St. Louis user groups, as well at several SharePoint Camps/Saturdays. He blogs at www.iwkid.com on information worker technologies, including SharePoint and Office development.

WES PRESTON is a SharePoint consultant and Microsoft MVP, and works primarily as a SharePoint product specialist, solution designer, and IT pro, helping align business needs with the SharePoint platform and guiding organizations through the use of best practices. A technology evangelist for 15 years, he has been an organizer and frequent speaker at the Minnesota SharePoint User Group and Twin City SharePoint Saturdays. He blogs at www.idubbs.com/blog. Outside the office, he spends time with his wife and two boys.

 KEN SCHAEFER, MBA, is a senior consultant in the Chicago area, and has worked in technology for 20 years, focusing for the past five on SharePoint-based solutions. He was a contributing author for *Professional SharePoint 2010 Development* (Wrox) where he wrote on web content management. Ken has presented at user groups and conferences on a variety of technical and business topics, and he blogs at www.sharepointy.net. He can be reached at ken@sharepointy.net.

ABOUT THE TECHNICAL EDITOR

FABIO CLAUDIO FERRACCHIATI is a senior consultant and a senior analyst/developer. He works for Brain Force (www.brainforce.com) in its Italian branch (www.brainforce.it). He is a Microsoft Certified Solution Developer for .NET, a Microsoft Certified Application Developer for .NET, and a Microsoft Certified Professional. Over the past 10 years he has written articles for Italian and international magazines, and co-authored more than 10 books on a variety of computer topics.

CREDITS

ACQUISITIONS EDITOR
Paul Reese

PROJECT EDITOR
William Bridges

TECHNICAL EDITOR
Fabio Claudio Ferracchiati

PRODUCTION EDITOR
Rebecca Anderson

COPY EDITOR
Kim Cofer

EDITORIAL DIRECTOR
Robyn B. Siesky

EDITORIAL MANAGER
Mary Beth Wakefield

FREELANCER EDITORIAL MANAGER
Rosemarie Graham

ASSOCIATE DIRECTOR OF MARKETING
David Mayhew

PRODUCTION MANAGER
Tim Tate

VICE PRESIDENT AND EXECUTIVE GROUP PUBLISHER
Richard Swadley

VICE PRESIDENT AND EXECUTIVE PUBLISHER
Barry Pruett

ASSOCIATE PUBLISHER
Jim Minatel

PROJECT COORDINATOR, COVER
Katie Crocker

PROOFREADER
Sheilah Ledwidge, Word One New York

INDEXER
J & J Indexing

COVER DESIGNER
Michael E. Trent

COVER IMAGE
© kycstudio/istockphoto.com

CONTENTS

PART IV: BUSINESS CONNECTIVITY SERVICES

FOREWORD

It is nearly impossible to give a short, coherent answer to a SharePoint novice when I'm asked "What is SharePoint?" SharePoint has grown from simple portal software that includes search and content management capabilities, into a complex enterprise platform used for everything from managing collaboration on departmental projects all the way to handling hundreds of thousands of transactions a day for banks, hospitals, pharmaceutical companies, government agencies, the military, and major corporations.

SharePoint has become so large and so complex that no one can profess to be a master of the entire platform. How do you describe it to someone?

Chris Geier has taken up the challenge of answering that question by putting together a team of authors, each of whom is an expert in a specific area of SharePoint. The authors Chris has chosen are the same subject matter experts I look to when I need help with a thorny business issue that might be solved with SharePoint.

As a SharePoint evangelist, I personally know each of the authors through their contributions to the SharePoint community. They "pay it forward" by freely giving their time and expertise through participation in conferences, user groups, blogs, and SharePoint Saturdays. They have firsthand knowledge and experience with the most important aspects of utilizing SharePoint in real-world situations.

It is a long, treacherous road to becoming an expert in any specific aspect of SharePoint, whether it is branding, workflow, search capabilities, connecting to legacy data systems, or server administration. Other piecemeal alternatives are available as enterprise-level content management and knowledge management systems, but SharePoint is the foundation most companies choose when they make the final selection for managing their most important processes and information. Knowing this, you have the advantage of being able to choose which aspect of SharePoint interests you the most.

Use this book wisely by glancing through each section to see what interests you and then choose a subject for a deep dive. Become proficient at that one aspect, and the knowledge gained will flow into other areas of the platform, helping you to gain a broader understanding as to how SharePoint works and what it can do. But don't stop there.

The complexity of the business world makes it necessary to continue your discovery process by keeping in mind the problems your business is trying to solve. SharePoint is a platform for developing solutions to those business problems. Keeping that uppermost in mind will help you choose the right path when selecting which corner of SharePoint to investigate.

Read through each chapter with confidence, knowing you are being led by the people the SharePoint community recognizes as experts. Better yet, join the SharePoint community by participating on Twitter, blogs, forums, and SharePoint wikis.

This book is your launch pad into SharePoint 2010. Choose your subject and take the jump. Five years down the road you'll be glad you did.

—MARK MILLER,
Founder and Editor, EndUserSharePoint.com
Chief Communication Officer and SharePoint Evangelist, Global 360

INTRODUCTION

On a weekly basis, some poor IT workers — both IT pros and developers — are saddled with new projects and or technology they know nothing about and are asked to run with them. They're expected to be successful with little guidance, direction, or training. They're also expected to pull off these tremendous feats of IT power with little to no leeway time.

In the IT world those to whom this happens are the unsung heroes. They are the backbone of every IT organization. Fortunately, in today's connected world numberless resources are available for you to read, download, and use to further your knowledge and answer your questions. But these resources can only help if you know what you're looking for. If you're new to a platform like SharePoint 2010, you'll find it has hundreds of new and improved features. You have new terminology and new concepts; without knowing at least a little you may be lost in a sea of blogs, wikis, and search results. If you've picked up this book because you fall into this category, you're in luck. If you are looking at SharePoint 2010 and do not even know where to begin, or if you're overwhelmed by all the features and pieces that make up SharePoint 2010, rest assured that the authors of this book have picked the some of the key features you should understand to get you going.

WHOM THIS BOOK IS FOR

This book is designed to get you started with SharePoint 2010. The authors have picked some of the most important areas of 2010 in order to arm you with knowledge of those areas that can make the biggest impact on the success of your SharePoint 2010 deployment. This book is not intended to provide you with a step-by-step process for installing, configuring, and deploying SharePoint 2010. Nor will it walk you through all the different configuration options for a SharePoint farm. However, it will expose you to key features of SharePoint 2010, explain them, strive to show their value, and show how their use can contribute to your success in your SharePoint implementation. Microsoft has provided tremendous resources for your planning and installation of SharePoint 2010. For starters, see the planning guide on TechNet at http://technet.microsoft.com/en-us/library/ee667264.aspx.

At the end of this book you probably won't be a SharePoint expert. You will, however, be well on your way to having a good understanding of the platform that is SharePoint. You should also have an appropriate amount of information to feel more confident in going out and implementing SharePoint in your organization. Once you're done reading, we hope you'll follow the book's guidance in your SharePoint implementation. You should be in a position to understand what features or technology areas within SharePoint you need to dig into. Your organization may need to take your use of SharePoint search to a much deeper level; if so, you may need to get a book, or even several books, dedicated to search. Technical depth is not the goal of this book; rather, the goal is to get you started with SharePoint with a focus on some of the most important pieces available.

WHAT THIS BOOK COVERS

This book is all about SharePoint; however, it is not everything you need to know. It covers the following topics:

- ➤ SharePoint introductions and basics
- ➤ SharePoint branding (look and feel)
- ➤ SharePoint development
- ➤ Business Connectivity Services (BCS)
- ➤ SharePoint social features
- ➤ SharePoint workflow
- ➤ SharePoint search

The last six of these are distinctive areas within SharePoint — hence, the title of this book: *SharePoint 2010 Six-in-One*. These areas were felt to be of vital importance to getting true value from your SharePoint deployment. They are a start on your journey, after which you can chose to dive in deeper or move on down a different path. Either way, the sections about these six areas should be a great beginning.

HOW THIS BOOK IS STRUCTURED

This book is broken down into sections. Each section addresses a specific topic chosen by the authors because that topic is important to your success with SharePoint.

In the first section you are introduced to the basics of SharePoint, and then you will be empowered to customize the look and feel of your implementation to gain greater use and adoption.

Next you are given insight into the developer mind as well as an introduction to how development within SharePoint works. From there, you are introduced to a new and powerful feature within SharePoint called Business Connectivity Services (BCS).

After this it's time to take a softer approach to SharePoint and think about social communications and how your users can journey into social networking, MySite communication, tagging, and ratings.

An area within SharePoint 2010 that has gotten wide attention is workflow. The next section walks you through the basics of workflow to give you a better general understanding of this subject. You are also introduced to all of your options and given advice on planning your workflow strategy.

Once you have all this down, it's time to journey into the world of search, which opens up your SharePoint implementation to a greater degree, allowing users to find content they are looking for anywhere in the SharePoint farm or even beyond.

Finally, you are given information that ties all these topics together and gives you references to help you with your next steps.

WHAT YOU NEED TO USE THIS BOOK

We hope you're planning on following along, experimenting with examples, and trying different approaches on your own. To do this you'll need to have SharePoint 2010 installed and working. Some sections may allow you to use SharePoint Foundation, but most of the real power comes with SharePoint Server Standard or Enterprise.

For a full list of features broken down by edition, see the following link: `http://sharepoint.microsoft.com/en-us/buy/Pages/Editions-Comparison.aspx`.

To take full advantage of all sections you may also need SharePoint Designer, which is a free utility from Microsoft. To download this go to the following link: `http://sharepoint.microsoft.com/en-us/product/related-technologies/pages/sharepoint-designer.aspx`.

For getting in and developing solutions for SharePoint 2010 you will also need to get Visual Studio 2010, which you can find at the following site: `www.microsoft.com/visualstudio/en-us/`.

CONVENTIONS

To help you get the most from the text and keep track of what's happening, we've used several conventions throughout the book. Two of the most frequent are shown here:

> *Boxes with a warning icon like this one hold important, not-to-be-forgotten information that is directly relevant to the surrounding text.*

> *The pencil icon indicates notes, tips, hints, tricks, or asides to the current discussion.*

As for styles in the text:

- We *highlight* new terms and important words when we introduce them.
- We show filenames, URLs, and code within the text like so: `persistence.properties`.
- We present code in the following way:

```
We use a monofont type with no highlighting for most code examples.
```

SOURCE CODE

As you work through the examples in this book, you may choose either to type in all the code manually, or to use the source code files that accompany the book. Most of the source code used in this book is available for download at www.wrox.com. When at the site, simply locate the book's title (use the Search box or one of the title lists) and click the Download Code link on the book's detail page to obtain the source code for the book. Code that is included on the website is highlighted by the following icon:

Available for download on Wrox.com

Listings include a description and in some cases the filename in the title. If it is just a code snippet, you'll find the filename in a code note such as this:

Code snippet filename

> *Because many books have similar titles, you may find it easiest to search by ISBN; this book's ISBN is 978-0-470-87727-2.*

Once you download the code, just decompress it with your favorite compression tool. Alternatively, you can go to the main Wrox code download page at www.wrox.com/dynamic/books/download .aspx to see the code available for this book and all other Wrox books.

ERRATA

We make every effort to ensure that there are no errors in the text or in the code. However, no one is perfect, and mistakes do occur. If you find an error in one of our books, like a spelling mistake or faulty piece of code, we would be very grateful for your feedback. By sending in errata, you may save another reader hours of frustration, and at the same time, you will be helping us provide even higher quality information.

To find the errata page for this book, go to www.wrox.com and locate the title using the Search box or one of the title lists. Then, on the book details page, click the Book Errata link. On this page, you can view all errata that has been submitted for this book and posted by Wrox editors. A complete book list, including links to each book's errata, is also available at www.wrox.com/misc-pages/ booklist.shtml.

If you don't spot "your" error on the Book Errata page, go to www.wrox.com/contact/ techsupport.shtml and complete the form there to send us the error you have found. We'll check the information and, if appropriate, post a message to the book's errata page and fix the problem in subsequent editions of the book.

P2P.WROX.COM

For author and peer discussion, join the P2P forums at p2p.wrox.com. The forums are a Web-based system for you to post messages relating to Wrox books and related technologies and interact with other readers and technology users. The forums offer a subscription feature to e-mail you topics of interest of your choosing when new posts are made to the forums. Wrox authors, editors, other industry experts, and your fellow readers are present on these forums.

At p2p.wrox.com, you will find a number of different forums that will help you, not only as you read this book, but also as you develop your own applications. To join the forums, just follow these steps:

1. Go to p2p.wrox.com and click the Register link.
2. Read the terms of use and click Agree.
3. Complete the required information to join, as well as any optional information you wish to provide, and click Submit.
4. You will receive an e-mail with information describing how to verify your account and complete the joining process.

 You can read messages in the forums without joining P2P, but in order to post your own messages, you must join.

Once you join, you can post new messages and respond to messages other users post. You can read messages at any time on the Web. If you would like to have new messages from a particular forum e-mailed to you, click the Subscribe to this Forum icon by the forum name in the forum listing.

For more information about how to use the Wrox P2P, be sure to read the P2P FAQs for answers to questions about how the forum software works, as well as many common questions specific to P2P and Wrox books. To read the FAQs, click the FAQ link on any P2P page.

PART I
Foundations and Overview

1

SharePoint Overview

WHAT'S IN THIS CHAPTER?

➤ Introducing key solution scenarios for SharePoint 2010 and how these address an organization's business needs

➤ Understanding the core concepts of the SharePoint 2010 platform

➤ Articulating the different SharePoint software titles and editions available

SharePoint is an enormous product that touches many different aspects of business functionality and IT. It relies on and integrates with a variety of systems, and its functionality and capabilities overlap with many other products. So where does one begin when considering whether or not to deploy SharePoint?

SharePoint has the potential to deliver tremendous value to an organization if it is rigorously planned, successfully deployed, and widely adopted. All of these actions are possible by understanding what SharePoint has to offer.

This chapter introduces you to what SharePoint 2010 is, how it can be utilized and deployed, and why users, administrators, and developers will be excited about the latest version of this popular tool.

INTRODUCING SHAREPOINT

Microsoft SharePoint 2010 is the fourth major version of a web server product and platform that is one of the fastest-growing server products in Microsoft's history. Microsoft's marketing tagline describes SharePoint 2010 as the "Business Collaboration Platform for the Enterprise and the Web" and explains that it will:

➤ Connect and empower people

➤ Cut costs with a unified infrastructure

➤ Rapidly respond to business needs

SharePoint is Microsoft's web platform. Out of the box it provides a tremendous amount of functionality, but it can also be readily expanded by integrating with client applications or external servers as well as be extended with customizations. The number of ways SharePoint can be implemented and used is endless. This section walks you through some of the more common uses to give you an idea of what it can do for you or your organization.

SharePoint is an enabling technology. Merely deploying SharePoint isn't a silver bullet that will transform your organization. But consciously building a SharePoint environment and training end users how to use the tool appropriately can and will propel an organization to a higher level of productivity.

SharePoint as a Web Platform

At its core, SharePoint is a web application — a really large and full-featured web application, but still a web application. Because of its broad feature set and flexible implementation options, it can and should be considered to fulfill several roles in a consolidated web strategy for any organization. Different entry points for SharePoint exist depending on the specific needs of an organization, but common ones include intranet, extranet, and Internet solutions. SharePoint is well-suited to fill any or all of these roles.

As a web application, SharePoint uses common web concepts to deliver its features. You learn more details of the core concepts later in this chapter, but "sites" are used by SharePoint as containers for "lists" and "libraries," which in turn contain data and documents. Security can be assigned at various levels to enable both sharing and securing of the content to the appropriate audience. All of this is delivered primarily through the web browser, but also increasingly through additional web, client, and mobile devices.

Initially, users may wonder how the storage of documents and files in SharePoint is any different than what users get out of a file share today. The differences are in the features built on top of the site, list, and library concepts and increased availability of content being stored on a web server over a file server. Some features are highlighted in Table 1-1.

TABLE 1-1: SharePoint Capabilities Beyond the File Share

FEATURE	DESCRIPTION
Alerts	Users can have e-mail notifications sent to them based on changes and additions made to specific documents or entire libraries or lists.
Versioning	Documents can be locked while in use and older versions retained as documents are worked on by multiple users. This helps get past the "last person who saved wins" issue on the file share where previously saved documents are lost when they are saved over.
Metadata	With file shares, users are generally limited to the filename, last modified date, and last modified by properties. This limitation can sometimes lead to complicated file-nesting strategies as well as obnoxious file-naming conventions. SharePoint allows for additional properties, or "metadata" to be captured and managed.

FEATURE	DESCRIPTION
Security	Though file shares do allow for a variety of security settings, they are usually managed by an administrator of the server. SharePoint improves on this model by allowing for the delegation of security management to more administrative users. SharePoint also allows management of security to be done within the web-user interface, making it more accessible.
Workflow	Business processes can be automated by out-of-the-box or custom workflows. You can find more information on this in Chapter 15, "Workflow Introduction and Background."

Managing content in a web-server application like SharePoint broadens the accessibility of content beyond the capabilities of typical file share by making it available to other platforms like mobile devices, other applications via web services, and client applications. Although applications can and have been built to surface information from file shares, SharePoint enables these extensibility features in a simple and user-friendly way.

For users, this means there is a server somewhere with SharePoint installed on it and they will be accessing it primarily with a web browser.

For administrators, SharePoint relies on Microsoft Windows Server 2008 and IIS (Internet Information Services) as well as other core technologies on the server. This means administrators will need to understand concepts of the server OS, of web-based applications, and of basic networking, as well as how SharePoint uses the database and more. This is covered in more detail in the next chapter.

Developers and designers need to know that SharePoint is an ASP.NET application that conforms to many of the web standards in use today.

Microsoft's Web Platform

SharePoint is a platform not only for its own family of products, but for many other Microsoft and partner products as well. Within the SharePoint family of products, SharePoint Foundation is the core platform for all the other SharePoint, Search Server, and FAST server products that are covered later in this chapter.

Microsoft also has other server products that have been moved to or integrated with the SharePoint platform, sometimes overtly, sometimes behind the scenes. For example, Project Server 2010 is built on top of SharePoint Server 2010, which enables collaboration features within the context of projects. Microsoft Dynamics CRM 5 is tightly integrated with SharePoint, again using the collaboration features and also acting as the document repository as needed.

Another option for integration is creating Web Parts to tie applications together. SQL Server Reporting Services (SSRS) and Outlook Web Access (OWA) are both examples of Microsoft products that use SharePoint as another way to surface information.

Finally, in addition to the Microsoft-specific products, third-party vendors and partners also offer products based on the platform or that extend functionality via Web Parts. This model includes not only smaller solutions such as utility applications, but also enterprise-wide solutions such as document and records management vendors.

A term commonly heard is the "better together" solution. Though Microsoft SharePoint isn't intended to be the best of breed in all areas, it is intended to work with those best-of-breed products out in the market, with the products enhancing each other. Being based on a web platform enables these integrations to work well together.

Branding

Being a web platform means that SharePoint can be branded for specific look-and-feel scenarios using common industry standards. Details of branding SharePoint are covered in Chapters 4–6.

SharePoint as the Collaboration Platform

SharePoint's history is rooted in collaboration, from the initial versions of SharePoint to the latest 2010 platform. Collaboration features enable users to share information and work together on documents, files, and other content. These core features and the ease with which they can be used are among the reasons SharePoint is so popular with users and has grown so quickly.

Collaboration means "to work together" — a simple concept but one that can be done in many different ways. The features offered by SharePoint 2010 and its companion applications can be used for groups as small as two people and as large as thousands. Some of the same concepts can even be used by a single person striving to work more effectively.

Collaboration scenarios can vary widely, from two people co-authoring a document to a project team, a company department or division, a committee, a lab study group, and beyond.

Team Collaboration

One of the most common examples of collaboration with SharePoint is the team site. A *team site* is a SharePoint website used by a group of people, sometimes a department that is aligned with the hierarchy in an organization. Sometimes a team is an ad-hoc collection of users or a cross-departmental group put together for a specific purpose. In any case the team needs a place to organize itself and its content.

When users create a team site, they have a number of tools available, including group announcements, a team calendar, useful links, and containers for documents and files. These are just a few examples of what might be done on a site, but they are common starting points.

Announcements could be information tidbits shared within the team or shared information from the team. For example: "A new team member is starting today," "There is a new policy in place," or "There are donuts in the break room." These messages were previously distributed by e-mail. Managing them in SharePoint brings a number of advantages. First, using site-based announcements may eliminate one source of e-mail because many organizations are already overburdened with e-mail. Second, it provides an archive of announcements that wouldn't otherwise be available to folks that weren't on the team when an e-mail was originally sent out. Finally, users can also sign up for e-mail notification of new announcements or a summary message once a day or once a week if they don't want to receive notice for every announcement immediately.

Team calendars are useful resources even with enterprise-level tools like Exchange in the same environment. In fact, they actually strengthen each other. Still, teams find interesting ways of tracking, managing, or publishing team events. Some folks keep calendars in a Word or Excel document; others still rely on public folders — a technology that Microsoft has been trying to shut down for some time now. SharePoint 2010 allows users to maintain a central list of events that multiple people can manage at the same time and that can be displayed on the team site, on a mobile device, or in Outlook — even overlaying an individual's personal calendar. SharePoint calendars can also be used as a sort of host for the meeting collaboration tools that are discussed a little later.

Managing links is a relatively simple idea and has been around since browsers were introduced. A number of tools are already available for managing links both online and locally. SharePoint provides yet another option for managing links that fits right into a site, while also offering advantages of sorting, filtering, and notifications that are part of the core platform. Because SharePoint is a web application, links are also vital to its use, since every site, list, item, and document can be accessed via a link.

Finally, almost every team needs to do some sort of document management. These capabilities are covered in greater detail in the next section.

Document Collaboration

SharePoint 2010 is an excellent platform for document collaboration. From two people working on a document together to teams of people working with libraries of documentation, SharePoint has a wonderful and intuitive toolset for working on documents and files.

The first topics to consider when discussing collaboration are the availability of and access to the document or file that is being worked on. SharePoint sites provide a common repository to access and manage documents so that users no longer need to use e-mail as a method of version control and storage by sending documents back and forth to each other. This takes a load off mail servers while at the same time establishing a de facto location for content. When users access a document from a SharePoint site, they can be confident that it's the latest and greatest version of that document.

Access to documents by the correct set of users is also paramount to collaboration. Permissions can be thought of as either allowing access or denying access, but in SharePoint administrators of a list or site will primarily be controlling which users have access to content and what level of access they have. The administrators will set different users to different levels of access; some will have read-only access, whereas others will be contributors. SharePoint has the flexibility to implement a wide variety of security models and schemes, even down to the individual item if needed.

Coming back to versions, SharePoint has the capability to track document versions, both major and minor. Libraries can be configured to require users to check documents in and out when making changes to content in order to enforce versioning and manage changes cleanly. The Ribbon interface in 2010 enables users to easily manage a number of documents being checked in or out at one time. These features allow collaborative users to more comfortably edit and save documents because they no longer need to worry about "the last person who saves wins" issue where multiple people are saving versions of a document. In that scenario (typical when dealing with network file shares) when one person saves a change one minute and another person saves a change a minute later, the last person who saves retains his or her changes and the first person's changes are lost. With version control, *both* saved versions are captured. If both people made changes, they can then still access either version and merge the content together.

Although it's not specifically a SharePoint 2010 feature, Office 2010 has a new capability to co-author a document or file. This takes collaboration to a whole new level. Using a combination of tools, multiple users can have the same document open, use instant messenger or Office Communications Server (OCS) to talk, or text message each other while they are working on the same document at the same time. As a user makes changes, the application alerts other users that changes have been made, where they've been made, and who made them. This notification scheme also allows for immediate access to profile information and tools for connecting with each or any user who is editing the document.

Allowing authors to edit the same document at the same time is an example of a "parallel" operation. Some collaboration use cases are "serial," where one operation happens after another. In a simple case, e-mail notifications can be sent communicating when new documents have been added or changed. In a more robust solution, a workflow can be employed to assist with the automation of a business process by assigning users to tasks and sending status updates to users along the way. Some of the workflows are out of the box, whereas others can easily be created using SharePoint Designer for more granular control. You can find more information about workflows in Part VI, "SharePoint Workflow."

Document Workspaces

One specialized use case for document collaboration is a *document workspace*. This is a specific type of site where a single document is the center of attention. Though this might not be used for run-of-the-mill documents, a document workspace might be used when a number of users are working on a larger, more complex document over a span of time. Some examples might include a technical or operations manual or an employee handbook.

Using the employee handbook example, a whole committee of Human Resources staff may be creating, editing, and verifying content in an organization's annual employee handbook. If the handbook effort is over the course of weeks or months, the team may want to have a calendar to track milestones. They may want to track issues or tasks to coordinate efforts. They may want to use a forum to track decisions and how those decisions were arrived at. Having a site to manage all this information while at the same time restricting access from users who shouldn't see a document until it's been fully created and approved is very relevant.

Meeting Collaboration

Somewhat similar in concept to a document workspace is a *meeting workspace*. Meeting workspaces are sites that can be used to coordinate and communicate meeting details. Rather than have a single person create an agenda, assemble any documentation, and print and distribute all the materials for a meeting, a meeting organizer can create a workspace for the team to do this together.

A workspace can be created from and linked to meetings originating from a SharePoint-based calendar or an Exchange/Outlook calendar. These "mini" sites become a container for the preparation materials and content as well as any artifacts that come out of a meeting.

When a meeting is created, the list of attendees is determined at the same time. Invited attendees are automatically granted access to the site, with a link that allows them to view, add, and edit content. This link is also tracked in the meeting entity itself so that users can go to their calendars to access the meeting site. Users are all granted access to add agenda items or upload documents and materials that will be used at the meeting. Some users may request that they be notified as items are added to the agenda. If users have mobile devices or laptops they may access the site and items directly during the meeting rather than having to print off an agenda or support material. Someone taking meeting minutes or notes during the meeting could do so directly in the site, so that meeting minutes don't need to be separately created and distributed. When the meeting is over, tasks have already been assigned and notes have been taken that are available for future reference.

Taking the concept of a meeting to the next step, organizations may even identify specific types of meetings and create site templates for them, making the process even more effective. They may have a certain way to track agenda items. They may have document templates that should be made available for each meeting — whatever suits their needs.

 Windows Server 2008 R2 offers a new feature called the File Classification Infrastructure that starts to extend the file share beyond its traditional capabilities. The term "features" also has specific meaning in the SharePoint context and is described in detail in Chapter 7.

SharePoint as a Search Provider

Search is all about the "findability" of content. When looking for either content or people, users need to find what they want, when they want it, using the terms that make sense to them. Many platforms provide keyword searches — which is great — but that's not always going to return the results users want. If they are looking for content, they also want to be able to search on the words or tags that make sense to them. If users are looking for people, they want to be able to search on skills and other user properties. At the end of the day, if users can't find what they're looking for, they likely can't meet their responsibilities effectively. That might translate into bad decisions because someone didn't have the latest information. Work may also be duplicated if someone can't find a document and so creates it again. Even the best information in the world is useless if no one can find it.

Microsoft respects the importance of search in today's world. All one has to do is look at the effort that's been put behind Bing and the relationship with Yahoo!. Although getting slightly less press, before the 2010 release of SharePoint, Microsoft also acquired another search market player — FAST — and has now integrated the product and technology into SharePoint 2010. In addition to FAST, the SharePoint product line also includes two Search Server offerings. Finally, within SharePoint 2010 itself are some pretty innovative tools and technologies to help deliver the search capabilities that are expected of a robust search provider, as well as to take search to the next level.

The first thing worth mentioning isn't necessarily a specific feature but rather an approach. Search in SharePoint 2010 is everywhere. SharePoint puts search front and center throughout the platform — actually near the top on the right side, by default (Figure 1-1). On portals and collaboration sites alike, there is a search control at the top of the page almost all the time. The scope of the information being searched may change depending on where you navigate, but for the most part search is available throughout the environment.

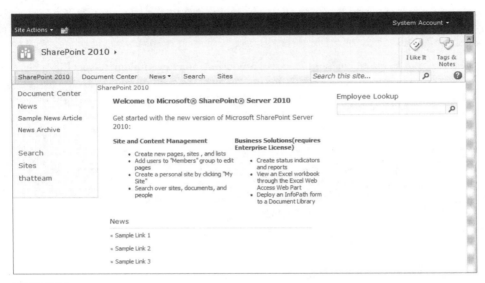

FIGURE 1-1

The next area is search relevance. SharePoint's search tool has historically done a good job of finding and returning results based on keyword searching and relevance ranking. As the product continues to evolve, the search relevance engine has gotten better thanks to new technologies, allowing for more accurate search results. It shouldn't be forgotten that SharePoint 2010 also includes wildcard searching, a long-overdue addition to the platform.

Some of the contributing factors to search result relevance in SharePoint are the additional properties, metadata, tagging, and rating information that is also tracked. This takes search results to the next level. Not only are the results scored by where a search term occurs (in the content, in the title, or both), but items that have been ranked by users as useful or not will also directly affect results. As content is ranked higher by users, that content will bubble up higher in search results.

Starting with SharePoint Server Standard, the platform includes user profile information and a People Search scope to provide search results for this content. The People Search scope is essentially an out-of-the-box company directory. For organizations without any form of searchable employee directory, this is a hands-down winner. For organizations with a solution of some sort, the comparisons usually lean toward the SharePoint solution for a number of reasons: the content may be easier to manage, the search results or functionality may be better, or the configurable and customizable potential may be better. People Search also has a phonetic search feature. This phonetic capability is SharePoint's way of interpreting your People Search term to other potential spellings of a name. An example is shown in Figure 1-2. Searching for "michael" will return results for "Michael" and "Mike." It works for more complicated names as well.

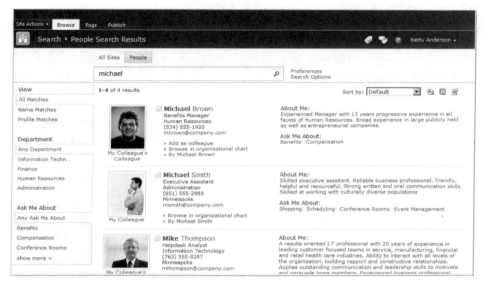

FIGURE 1-2

For all versions of SharePoint 2010 beyond Foundation, the flexibility of search, specifically the search results page, is extremely powerful. Search flexibility is also somewhat of a gray area between configuration and customization. Configuration is something a user can do without other tools. Customization is something done using SharePoint Designer, Visual Studio, or another tool. Search results can be modified in all kinds of ways and some of the configuration can be done right in the browser using XSLT manipulation. A number of Web Parts and other ways to tweak the results to fit an organization's needs also exist. Again, many more details are available in the search-specific chapters of this book.

A few specific examples of flexibility are adding, removing, or changing the fields that are displayed in the search results; being able to further refine search results; and returning search results from additional sources — either internal or external. The previously mentioned XSLT manipulation can be used to configure the fields displayed and how they are displayed. Search "refiners," or facets, are used to further narrow search results, much as is done on popular shopping websites when doing product searches by brand, size, color, and so on. Finally, Federated Search allows SharePoint to talk to other search engines and request their search results for submitted search terms.

Federated Search allows users to search remote data sources without having to index the remote sources themselves. For example, SharePoint doesn't need to index all the content Bing indexes, but it can submit a search term request to Bing, receive Bing's search results, and then display the results within SharePoint's interface, alongside results from other providers or SharePoint's own content. The SharePoint platform can act as both a Federated Search consumer or provider.

When most users think about SharePoint search, they usually think of the search box available on almost every page and keyword search results returned from a wide scope. These searches operate similar to a Bing or Google search. What users usually don't consider is that the same search components can also be used to configure focused searches with smaller scopes and very specific search results. People Search is one example that SharePoint provides by default. Many other scenarios could also be built involving products, knowledge bases, support documentation, legal documents, records, and other topics.

By default, SharePoint indexes all the content it can find inside SharePoint that it has access to and can read. It makes the results of this search available to users who use a keyword search to query the content. This, all by itself without any further configuration, customization, or tweaking, is usually a large step forward for most organizations. That's a good place to start, but there is much more.

With regards to the content that SharePoint can index, the search crawler reads everything in SharePoint by default but can also be set to read data external to SharePoint. This includes other SharePoint portals, websites, and databases. If the external location is a Federated Search provider, SharePoint doesn't even need to index the content on its own — it can request the information from the other search indexer and then display it in special areas on the results page.

Regarding security concerns and SharePoint, the search can read information from wherever it's coming inside or outside SharePoint only if it has the permissions to read the content. Part of the search process also checks who has access to what information so that the search results can also be security trimmed — meaning that if the user making the query doesn't have access to content, it won't be displayed in the search results, even if SharePoint can read the content.

Finally, SharePoint can only read files it can understand. By default this means any Microsoft-based document or generic document types. Adobe PDFs and other file types are not supported by default. Additional tools or "IFilters" can be installed to give SharePoint the ability to read the additional content. One last note regarding the reading of content: SharePoint does not have OCR capabilities at this time. If it reads a PDF image file as opposed to a PDF text-based document, it will not be able to read the image.

You can find more content and details about search in the search chapters starting with Chapter 18. You can find more information about Business Connectivity Services (BCS) in Chapters 10 and 11, and more information about tagging and ratings in Chapter 13.

SharePoint as a Presentation Layer

Anyone who works with data knows that a key principle is to have a single source of data rather than attempting to maintain multiple sources of the same information. SharePoint 2010 has a number of tools, services, and methods that allow data owners to maintain their existing data sources outside SharePoint, enable users to create new shareable data sources inside SharePoint, and facilitate data synchronization when multiple copies of data must be created.

Jumping between systems and web pages can make for a confusing user experience, which may ultimately affect efficiency. This challenge sometimes leads organizations to use SharePoint as a one-stop shop for data from disparate locations, regardless of where data is being surfaced from, but all within a consistently styled environment. Administrators and organizational stakeholders also want the platform to take on the organizational brand, rather than the out-of-the-box SharePoint look.

SharePoint branding is covered in detail in Chapters 4–6.

External Data

Where organizations have existing data, SharePoint has a number of integration points for accessing data outside the platform. This can be particularly useful in the workplace when users need information from an application that they are not familiar with or which only a limited number of people may be licensed to use. The Business Data Catalog (BDC) can create connections to external data, for both reading and writing as necessary. External Lists can be used to display data directly from tables outside SharePoint as if they were lists *in* SharePoint. Finally, SharePoint Designer and Visual Studio can be used to create controls and other SharePoint components that surface data from other sources.

The BDC can create connections that may be used as fields in lists or libraries. This enables users to create views of data that include SharePoint-sourced data alongside externally sourced data in the same display table or chart.

For example, an organization may have a document library for product support documentation in which documents are grouped by product name. Rather than create a list of products in SharePoint when a list likely already exists somewhere else, SharePoint can connect directly to the existing list. When a new document is added to the library, the user assigns a product name to the document. As new products are added and removed or names are changed, the field in SharePoint is automatically updated and the source list can be maintained in the current location without needing to update additional lists. This goes a long way toward maintaining data consistency and integrity throughout the organization. It's also easier for users when they don't see different information in different places.

BDC connections can be used in a number of ways, which are covered in greater detail starting in Chapter 10.

External Lists are another way for users to interact with existing data (stored outside of SharePoint) within the SharePoint context. SharePoint can configure a connection to a database table and view or edit the data as if it were stored in a SharePoint list — using the existing new item, edit item, and view item pages they are familiar with. This allows users who are comfortable with the SharePoint user interface to create new views of the data without needing IT resources or developers to get involved.

Finally, when specific functionality or more specialized views are required, SharePoint Designer or Visual Studio can be used. Both SharePoint Designer 2010 and Visual Studio 2010 may use the BDC to connect to data or may use more traditional direct-access methods such as ODBC, web services, and so on. More details on this topic are reviewed in the next section, "SharePoint as a Development Platform," as well as in Chapter 7.

Internal Data

SharePoint can store a great deal of information within its own lists and libraries. Users have two main approaches to choose from when accessing this data: accessing the data that already exists in SharePoint directly or making SharePoint-specific information available *outside* SharePoint.

The presentation of data that exists inside SharePoint is primarily done using list views and other Web Parts, which are covered in more detail later in this chapter in the "Core SharePoint" section. In short, SharePoint itself can contain large volumes of information using lists and libraries and the content stored within documents and files in the libraries. List views of this content can be configured to display specific items by filtering, sorting, and grouping, all within the web interface. A third-party market for data presentation Web Parts is available when specific requirements need to be fulfilled and/or developers are not available to create them.

Making data inside SharePoint available for systems outside SharePoint is made possible with SharePoint services. Three separate services available with the 2010 platform allow Excel, Visio, and Access data to be accessible as a data source both inside and outside SharePoint. For example, with Excel Services, selected data in a spreadsheet can be made available as a data source that can be consumed by other SharePoint controls or even external systems. This is different from merely uploading an Excel file into a library. Although uploading the file to a single location and sending out links to the document is a great step forward over the traditional e-mail file distribution method, using Excel Services allows users who don't have Excel on their PC to view content as well. Additional details on these services are outside of the scope of this book.

Solutions

Business Intelligence (BI) can mean a lot of different things to different people, but generally it includes the display of business information in meaningful ways. SharePoint 2010 can fill this bill by simply using some of the tools just mentioned — views, Web Parts, BDC, and so on. It can also be as complex as using PerformancePoint components to integrate with data cubes and other systems. At the end of the day, BI is about making large volumes of information more easily accessible to a group of users.

In the past, business users would take long printouts of data and work through them line by line looking for the information that was relevant to their specific needs. BI tools like connectible controls and *key performance indicators* (KPIs) make interpreting large amounts of data much more efficient. With data surfaced in SharePoint, data sets can be filtered, sorted, and searched easily. KPIs can be put in place to make data discovery easier. For example, when looking at something like a table of sales figures by product, visual cues can be configured to highlight sales numbers: $100,000 of sales for a product per month might be a favorable figure and be displayed as green; $80,000 to $99,999 might be at the warning level and be displayed as yellow; below $80,000 might be cause for concern and be displayed as red.

These visual cues allow people reviewing the data to glean much more quickly the information they need from the data rather than having to mentally process each individual row of data and reach a conclusion. Taking this to the next step, the data could also be sorted by the color values so that all the "reds" are displayed at the top of a list. And yet one more step: users no longer need to wait for the daily, weekly, or monthly reports to be created, because live or nearly real-time data can be made available. Being able to act on such data more quickly may be critical to an organization's success.

PerformancePoint is a BI-specific toolset in SharePoint 2010 that is available at the enterprise level. PerformancePoint tools can provide single Web Parts or components, or they can build more complex scorecard solutions similar to the KPI example discussed earlier.

Whether or not you use PerformancePoint, creating pages that display data from one or more sources in one or more page components may be referred to in a variety of terms. Commonly used terms are scorecards, dashboards, mash-ups, and composite solutions. In general, all these terms mean the same thing.

Tagging

Tagging is a new feature in SharePoint 2010 and allows users to add tags to content throughout the environment. You can find more details about tagging in Chapter 13. The reason this is worth mentioning as part of the presentation layer topic is that the tagging mechanism allows users to affect how data is surfaced. Tagging a document may allow it to show up in a search result for that tag or a Web Part that is aggregating content based on a specific tag. Tagging holds a lot of potential, though at the time this book was written best practices and tips had yet to be established.

User Profiles

SharePoint Server 2010 provides a My Profile page as part of the My Site experience. Profile information is displayed on individual profile pages and may also be surfaced in People Search results. This information initially comes from Active Directory (AD) and/or other employee management systems like PeopleSoft. The information is then presented in a consistent framework that administrators can control and users can contribute to.

SharePoint's user profile information is a good example of how SharePoint can surface information from other systems, as well as an example of an exception to the single-source-of-data practice. By default, SharePoint imports data from AD and stores it in its own database rather than accessing AD every time the information is displayed in SharePoint. Though this is an exception, SharePoint also manages the synchronization so that after initial configuration it does not require an additional effort to maintain similar examples of having multiple copies of data. Having the additional copy of data also provides additional performance and capabilities, so we can forgive an exception this time.

As an additional note, system administrators may use BDC or other connectivity solutions to import profile information from systems other than, or in addition to, AD. Administrators may also enable users to update their own information in SharePoint, which may in turn be updated in the connected external systems.

You can find more information on My Site and User Profile information in Chapter 14.

SharePoint as a Development Platform

"I need a solution that . . ." is where it all starts. Before .NET, Java, Microsoft Access, or SharePoint, someone made a request for functionality to solve a business problem. SharePoint 2010 can handle a wide variety of these requests with its out-of-the-box capabilities. Some requests are just outside its native abilities. Some requests may be *way* outside of what SharePoint was intended for. This section gives you a high-level overview of how these scenarios fit into using SharePoint as a development platform for an organization.

There is a progression to which tools are used to meet requirements within the context of SharePoint. This leveled approach starts with out-of-the-box capabilities. It advances to using SharePoint Designer and then, finally, Visual Studio. Third-party components and products fall somewhere in this range as well, but they won't be covered in this book. One last topic worth mentioning is the "better together" approach pitched by both Microsoft and its partner organizations when describing integration points between SharePoint and other partners — partners that may represent best-of-breed solutions in specific areas. This range of capabilities, utilities, and solutions represents the tools we have available in our toolbox as we develop solutions using SharePoint.

Out-of-the-box solutions are developed with no code, site, and list templates and sometimes with a little ingenuity. In many cases, list and library functionality meets users' needs. Many simple CRUD (create, read, update, and delete) solutions can be built without any code at all. As discussed in a little more detail in the "Core SharePoint" section of this chapter, options for extending lists with configuration options are available right in the user interface. Finally, pages can be created by combining multiple lists and Web Parts in a single solution, sometimes even connecting the controls together.

When requirements seem just beyond what can be done with out-of-the-box capabilities, SharePoint Designer (SPD) or "Designer" extends the functionality further. SharePoint Designer takes users from the limited number of packaged workflows to power-user designed workflows using a plethora of conditions and actions. Forms used by SharePoint lists can be edited or new forms added. More advanced display options can be used to make lists and tables more user-friendly as well as to include data from other sources. SharePoint Designer's full set of capabilities are numerous. Some are visited in this book, others are not. There is easily enough content on SharePoint Designer 2010 to fill other books on the subject.

Finally, when the standard features don't cut it and SharePoint Designer's capabilities still aren't enough, Visual Studio 2010 is available to fill the gap. Developers are able to extend SharePoint directly with .NET and SharePoint-specific application programming interfaces (APIs). Features and solutions can be created and installed. PowerShell and console applications can be created to act on the SharePoint environment. Additional SharePoint Designer actions can also be created to extend what users can do in Designer. This book covers much more on this topic, with branding starting in Chapter 4, development starting in Chapter 7, and workflows starting in Chapter 15.

With so many options available, what may be the biggest challenge in using SharePoint 2010 as a development platform is determining the right direction to take with each request for functionality. Usually there's more than one way to get to a solution. The *right* way for the organization may be determined by IT strategies that are in place, the experience of the staff and the resources that are available, or any number of other variables. SharePoint allows for a lot of flexibility as a development platform.

SharePoint for Social Networking

Social Networking is a broad and somewhat undefined topic because it can be interpreted in so many ways. This section doesn't try to define it precisely, but does talk about some of the features and scenarios that can be built within this topic.

First of all, why is "social" such a big deal — especially in the business world? Many organizations still fear social features as a waste of time and productivity. They also have concerns over the sharing of confidential information or doing harm with inappropriate posts. Although these are genuine concerns, they aren't insurmountable and they shouldn't be used as excuses to ignore all the potential benefits of social features.

Used and planned appropriately, social features can actually enhance productivity and bring additional value to the organization. They can be used to record and share intellectual property within the organization. Users can find each other and communicate more easily, and enabling users to contribute can be a strong motivator. Finally, users entering the workforce these days *expect* social tools to be available. They've been using them for years, are proficient with them, and are more efficient while working with them.

Users have been able to collect and share information using documents for a long time. These practices will continue and are enhanced by SharePoint's previously mentioned collaboration tools. Newer concepts in the workplace are blogs and wikis. Though these tools are widely used elsewhere, some very useful scenarios exist for them when it comes to capturing experience and knowledge and sharing it within the workplace. Internal blogs, for example, can be a way for employees to document their experiences and findings and share them with other employees. Wikis are a great way for more than one person to capture and share knowledge about a topic on which more than one person is working, or which is being worked on over a longer period of time. Content in both blogs and wikis is also indexed and made available via search results.

Finding and connecting with the people you need when you need them contributes directly to productivity. If you already know whom you want to contact, SharePoint's integration with Office Communication Server (OCS) shows availability and contact information wherever that person's name is displayed in SharePoint. If they're online, they can be contacted via OCS instant messenger or by calling them right in the SharePoint interface. (A new version of OCS, called Lync, was released as this was being written.)

When you need to find a resource, SharePoint provides a People Search scope to search a profile database of users. More detailed user information is also surfaced in the My Site or profile page. Administrators can configure what profile information is displayed and which fields users can maintain on their own.

New to the SharePoint platform in 2010 is the ability for users to tag, rate, and comment on content. Not only is it extremely practical for users with specific knowledge to provide feedback and validation on content, it's also a strong motivator for users who feel they have a way to provide value to the organization. Again, the content provided also shows up in search results and can directly influence relevance. The higher content is rated by users, the higher up on search results the content can be.

These are just a few examples of what's available and what can be done; you can find more information throughout this book. Chapter 12 covers details of social networking and SharePoint 2010 and there is additional information on tagging and ratings in Chapter 13. My Site is covered in Chapter 14.

CORE SHAREPOINT

SharePoint 2010 has a very comprehensive feature set, most of which is based on a relatively small group of core concepts. This section briefly defines and describes these concepts to set the stage for the greater detail used throughout the rest of the book.

Sites and Webs

Users commonly use the term "website" to refer to containers or groups of content on the Web — either intranets or the Internet. In SharePoint we have a few terms along those same lines. The highest level object of this type is called a *site collection* (Figure 1-3). Sub-areas of a site collection are referred to as sub-webs.

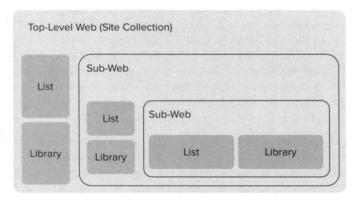

FIGURE 1-3

Site collections are themselves a web, but also contain other webs, lists, libraries, and additional content. They also have constraints that help to isolate content, security, and functionality.

Security within SharePoint can be very granular, but it defaults to being set at the site-collection level and is inherited down through webs, lists, and items. As administrators desire, security inheritance can be broken, and each list, library, and item can be secured with its own unique setting.

Webs are very similar to site collections, but are a little less robust. Security groups set up at a web level are visible and accessible throughout the parent site collection and other sibling webs. Features can be managed at both the site-collection and the web level.

Site templates are available to create sites and webs based on previously configured lists, libraries, and settings. The templates available out of the box vary with the level of product and will use a variety of list types to get things kick-started. A few templates are available with SharePoint Foundation; more are available with SharePoint Server. Other templates are also available from Microsoft and other vendors. Custom templates are commonly distributed with other products.

Administrators should also take note that site collections are assigned to content databases. A site collection belongs to one and only one content database. This will be important when planning the data and site architecture. You can find more information on this in Chapter 2.

Lists and Libraries

Lists are the heavy lifters of SharePoint. They contain all sorts of content and data and are the structure on top of which many of the features and functionality of SharePoint are built.

In many ways analogous to spreadsheets or database tables, lists contain "items" where Excel and databases have "rows." SharePoint libraries are specialized lists where the item is a file that has been uploaded to SharePoint. Lists and libraries both use columns in much the same way as spreadsheets and tables do, though you will also hear terms like "metadata," "properties," and "fields." Properties are covered in more detail in the next section.

Much of the value of SharePoint lists is that they can be created, customized, and managed without needing to rely on IT resources. If desired, they can contain millions of items with dozens of different fields.

Countless examples of lists are available, but let's take a look at some of the most common ones. As mentioned in the collaboration scenario earlier, many organizations use SharePoint as a team resource — a common place to store and manage content and to communicate to each other. A document library is created to manage common documents. I've intentionally said "manage" and not "store." Although you may have stored documents and files on the file share for years, you can now manage your documents and content more effectively using a library. You can save multiple versions of a document as it is being developed, keeping notes on what has changed or what needs to change and not having to save over previous versions or change the filename to track versions.

A new feature in SharePoint and Office 2010 gives users the ability to co-author documents, adding and changing things at the same time. The status of a document can be tracked as it moves from a draft to a final state, thus allowing users to create views to find documents more easily. Users may use a view that filters out non-final versions of documents if they're only looking for final products. Managers may use a view that shows non-final versions of documents so they can see who is working on what documents at any given time. Workflows can also be used to manually or automatically facilitate business processes. When a final approver signs off on a document, the status can be changed to "final" so that the document shows up in the correct view.

Templates

SharePoint comes with a variety of out-of-the-box default list templates (Table 1-2), but users with the appropriate permissions can also create new lists from scratch or customize the default lists to meet their needs. New list configurations can also be saved and re-used.

TABLE 1-2: SharePoint List Templates

TEMPLATE NAME	DESCRIPTION
Document Library	One of the most common library types used in SharePoint, the Document Library is used to store and manage documents and files, similar to what might be stored on a file share.
Form Library	The Form Library is used to manage digital forms like those created using Microsoft InfoPath.
Wiki Page Library	This library manages the web pages that are created as a part of a wiki solution.
Picture Library	A library used to manage graphic image files, this automatically creates thumbnail pictures and has a slide-show view.
Data Connection Library	This library contains data connection files used by InfoPath, PerformancePoint, and other tools.
Asset Library	This library is used to store media assets such as audio and video files. The libraries created are then sources for Web Parts that display these audio files to users.
Report Library	This library stores report files as well as pages used to display reporting.
Slide Library	This library stores PowerPoint slides individually and shows thumbnail images. It allows users to assemble presentations.
Announcements	This list is used to share quick news items.
Contacts	This list shows people with their contact information.
Discussion Board	This is a list for managing a newsgroup or forum type of discussion.
Links	This list is for managing URLs.
Calendar	This is a list for managing events and calendars. These can also be surfaced in Outlook and have special calendar-like views.
Tasks	This list is for tracking individual or team task lists.
Project Tasks	This extension of the Tasks list also makes a Gantt chart available and allows integration with Microsoft Project.

TEMPLATE NAME	DESCRIPTION
Issue Tracking	This list for managing issues is similar to content a help desk might use to capture specific issue details and resolutions.
Survey	This is a list of questions and possible answers for surveying users. It allows for graphical summary reports.
Custom List	This list template has a clean slate. Fields and functionality can be added to create solution-specific lists.
External List	This creates a shell list that can be used to display data from an external data source.
Status List	This is a Key Performance Indicator (KPI) type of list that shows a list of values and how close these values are to set target values.
Import Spreadsheet	This creates a list based on the structure and content of an existing Excel-like spreadsheet.

Views

Views are another powerful feature of lists. Views define what information from the list is displayed, which columns are displayed and in what order, what items are displayed and in what order, and how a list of items is sorted, filtered, or grouped together. Too many options and business scenarios exist to cover them in great detail here.

Views are important and powerful because of what they offer the user. When looking at a document library, users may prefer to see a listing of documents by name in alphabetical order. They may also prefer to see a listing that shows the most recently updated documents first. Or they may prefer to look only at documents that they themselves have created or edited. All of these options and more are available and easy to navigate.

Default views are available for all lists, but users with the appropriate security level are also able to customize existing views or create new views as needed. As with changes to the list, views can be changed through the web user interface, which is a very powerful option for power users and administrators. Additional tweaking can also be done using SharePoint Designer.

Many of the options for defining a view are based on what properties, columns, or metadata are available, because these are the bits of information by which the list is filtered and sorted. These are covered in more detail in the "Properties and Metadata" section later in this chapter.

The Ribbon

The Ribbon that Microsoft introduced as part of the user interface in some of the Office 2007 products is now a key part of the SharePoint 2010 experience. Because lists and libraries play such a central part in the user experience with SharePoint, it's useful to take a quick look at what is available on the Ribbon for lists. It's important to note that different options are available for the list itself versus the item or items in a list, as shown in Figures 1-4 and 1-5.

FIGURE 1-4

FIGURE 1-5

What you can't immediately see in Figures 1-4 and 1-5 are that options in the Ribbon become active and disabled based on the context — what the users are doing at any given moment as well as by what their security settings allow them to do.

You'll notice that most of the features covered for lists are directly accessible via the Ribbons. This is what makes the Ribbon so valuable.

Properties and Metadata

Lists and items are the core objects managed inside SharePoint. Much of the value in these lists is in the additional properties that capture more data about the item, allow the lists to be sorted and filtered, and enable the item to be discovered via searches. The terms used when discussing this topic can be a little confusing because a number of interchangeable words are used: columns, fields, properties, and metadata are the most prevalent examples.

When using a file share, users are accustomed to having a few basic fields, including filename, date modified, and the last user who modified the file. With SharePoint 2010 the core fields are filename, created by (user), created date, modified by (user), and modified date. Users with the appropriate permissions can add more columns as needed. Additional columns may tell the user if a file is a draft or a final version. A Category field might be added to more easily organize links or documents. A Review Date might be added to documents in a library. Although this concept has great potential, use caution when designing and implementing list properties so that these data structures don't get overwhelming for users and become more of a hindrance than a benefit.

In the simplest cases, columns can be added directly to the list and are only used by that particular list. Columns can also be configured at the site level and used by more than one list. In this way, changes to the custom column can be initiated in one location and propagated to any list using the columns. Many of the list and library templates listed earlier come preconfigured with additional columns.

This concept of a single source of data for columns can be taken to the next step as well by using *content types*. Content types are a collection of fields and functionality that allows users to build and manage groups of columns so they can be implemented consistently as a group of columns.

In addition to content type columns, content types can also be containers for policies and workflows. For example, a list being used to track books and other materials might have a content type for books. The content type may include a title, author, publisher, format (hardcover or softcover), ISBN number, and Dewey decimal number — fields that would ideally be used for cataloging library books in any list. On top of the data fields, administrators might also want all physical books to be checked for damage every other month. Implementing this would require both a policy and a workflow. The policy defines an action that takes place every 60 days. The action is a workflow that is started. The workflow notifies a user that a book is in stock and assigns that user a task for checking the book. The policies and workflows might not be used in every list for which they are implemented, but they are available, and when used they are consistently applied.

Content types can be added to lists and libraries throughout a web or site collection very easily. New with SharePoint 2010, site columns and content types can be syndicated — copied across multiple site collections or even wider scopes.

Properties can be surfaced in a number of ways. They can be seen when navigating to the SharePoint library through a view. They can be seen when looking at the specific item details.

Web Parts

Web Parts are the building blocks of SharePoint pages. They can be as simple as an image Web Part, or as complex as any custom application. Within SharePoint, among the most common examples are list-view Web Parts. These are exactly what they sound like — views of SharePoint lists. As soon as a list is created, a list-view Web Part is available to place on a page and configure to meet the user's needs.

Dozens of Web Parts are available out of the box with the various editions of SharePoint 2010. More Web Parts are available when integrating with other Microsoft products such as Microsoft Project and SQL Server Reporting Services, as well as third-party providers like Documentum and SAP. There is also an established community of third-party commercial and open-source Web Part authors providing a wide variety of additional functionality.

When business requirements call for functionality that isn't available with other Web Parts, this functionality can be developed. An introduction to creating custom Web Parts is included in Chapter 8.

SHAREPOINT 2010 EDITIONS

The name "SharePoint" actually refers to a whole line of products and editions. This book is specifically about the 2010 product line and focuses on that line.

SharePoint Foundation 2010

SharePoint Foundation (SPF) is the entry point product for SharePoint and is available to licensed users of Windows Server 2008 at no additional charge. It is the successor to Windows SharePoint Services (WSS) v3 and v2 and Team Services before that.

Foundation contains the core functionality that is used in all SharePoint products, including sites, lists and libraries, granular security, metadata, and alerts. It is the same codebase but doesn't have a lot of the more robust features offered by the SharePoint Server products. Anything created in Foundation can be upgraded or imported to SharePoint Server 2010 and is compatible with the other 2010 versions of SharePoint. Because of this, many organizations have used Foundation as a starting point with SharePoint, building robust solutions on it and upgrading when higher level features are required.

Basic search functionality is also part of SharePoint Foundation. That means that every word in every document that SharePoint can read will be indexed and made available for search query results. (You can find more detail on this in Chapters 18-20.) Typically this is a step or two beyond what users have been used to with file share and local search utilities. This is exciting, but still only a fraction of the functionality that is available with the other search products. The widest search scope available with Foundation is limited to a single site collection.

It should also be noted that SharePoint Foundation offers some very robust functionality that was not available in previous versions of WSS — specifically the BCS or Business Connectivity Services and external-list functionality. These features are explored in greater detail throughout this book. External lists are new with 2010, but the BCS replaces functionality that was previously available only with Microsoft Office SharePoint Server–Enterprise.

SharePoint Server 2010: Intranet

When organizations need more advanced features for their internal portal or collaboration environment, the next step after SharePoint Foundation is SharePoint Server 2010. The server product for the intranet — internal to organizations — comes in two flavors: Standard and Enterprise. The difference between Standard and Enterprise is the cost of the licensing as well as the features that are summarized in this section.

Licensing costs are outside the scope of this book, so details aren't covered here. What's important to note is that intranet licensing is based on both server licensing and CALs (Client Access Licenses). This translates into the number of servers the software is installed on as well as the number of users who are accessing the software. The best resource for specific licensing details for an organization is a Microsoft sales representative or licensing partner.

Standard

The features made available in the Standard SharePoint Server package are too numerous to cover in an overview. The following are a few highlights:

➤ **Enterprise Content Management (ECM):** The content management features provide an industry standard framework for separation of content from branding and the underlying infrastructure. This allows content managers to provide content in the areas they are supposed to, while keeping them from working in areas they shouldn't, all without having to worry about styles and formatting. The managers just provide the content. Designers are able to provide custom layouts and branding separate from data and content. When all is said and done, SharePoint is a platform that is capable of delivering Internet-friendly sites and professionally designed portals for employees, partners, and clients.

➤ **Managed metadata:** SharePoint Server 2010 introduces a centrally managed metadata store and framework that can deploy consistent taxonomy across the farm.

➤ **Tags, notes, and ratings:** In addition to the organization-defined taxonomy, SharePoint also introduces tags, notes, and ratings that allow for user-defined "folksonomy" tags and terminology as well as the ability to collect and act on feedback from users.

➤ **Profiles and My Site:** SharePoint enables organizations to build user profiles that can drive personalization features as well as user directory content. These profiles can be based on existing profile information from Active Directory (AD) or other systems and can also capture any new properties defined in the SharePoint profile. My Site personal SharePoint sites can go beyond traditional personal file shares, but in SharePoint 2010 they also surface all the aggregate information generated by tagging and rating content throughout the environment.

➤ **Search:** Search capabilities take a big step forward from the basic capabilities of SharePoint Foundation, allowing for configuration and customization of the search results as well as surfacing people results based on user profile information. Long overdue and highly anticipated wildcard search and phonetic search functionality are also introduced. The search scope is also wider, allowing searches across site collections.

A lot of other features and capabilities are available with SharePoint Server 2010, and many of these are discussed throughout this book.

Enterprise

The most notable features that the enterprise level provides are these additional service offerings:

➤ **InfoPath Services:** These allow digital forms to be created and served up via the server rather than having to load a client application.

➤ **Excel Services and PowerPivot:** These publish and manipulate Excel data and make data available as a source for other applications.

➤ **PerformancePoint:** This service provides professional business intelligence capabilities, Web Parts, scorecards, and dashboards.

➤ **Access Services:** These import and publish Access databases in the SharePoint farm, bringing data into a centrally managed and supportable environment.

➤ **Visio Services:** These allow users to view, edit, and embed Visio content in other SharePoint applications.

➤ **FAST search:** The additional capabilities of FAST search include thumbnails, previews, and configurable relevance. See Chapter 20 for more information.

SharePoint Server 2010: Internet/Extranet

External-facing solutions built on the SharePoint platform can be built with SharePoint Foundation as some minimalistic blog and collaboration sites are. Professional Internet and extranet solutions, however, require the more robust web-content management capabilities offered by SharePoint

Server 2010 with licensing for the Internet and extranet. The differences between the Standard and Enterprise levels are consistent with the intranet licensing models, with a few external-facing feature differences listed later in this section.

Licensing for external-facing solutions is also different than internal-facing solutions because users can be anonymous; there are no Client Access Licenses. What is also important to understand is that external-facing licenses cannot be used for employees. Again, refer to the appropriate licensing expert to identify the organization's specific needs.

Standard

SharePoint Server 2010 Standard for the Internet/extranet has the same capabilities as the Standard CAL for the intranet. Specifically for the external-facing farm, the Standard license supports only a single domain (for example, www.something.com) and related sub-domains (for example, http://my.something.com).

Enterprise

SharePoint Server 2010 Enterprise for the Internet/extranet has the same capabilities as the Enterprise CAL for the intranet.

Search Server 2010

Search Server and Search Server Express bridge part of the gap between the basic search capabilities offered by SharePoint Foundation and some of the richer search features of SharePoint Server. Where SharePoint Foundation allows searching within a site collection, Search Server Express allows users to search across an entire farm and to configure the search results page using both search Web Parts and XSLT.

The only differences between Search Server 2010 and Search Server Express 2010 are the licensing model and scaling limitations.

Microsoft Search Server 2010 Express

The Search Server Express license is free but allows for only a single server, with no redundancy or scaling capabilities, and it is limited in the content it can crawl:

➤ When using SQL Server Express, search will crawl approximately 300,000 items.

➤ When using SQL Server, search will crawl approximately 10 million items.

Microsoft Search Server 2010

Moving beyond the free version of Search Server 2010 allows for a more robust and enterprise-capable search option. The crawling limitation is raised to approximately 100 million items and multiple servers can be deployed for both scaling and redundancy. The crawling and query roles can also be separated to different servers, allowing crawling activities to continue without affecting the performance of users' search queries.

FAST Search

FAST Search Server 2010 adds new elements and depth to the SharePoint search capabilities. Where SharePoint Search returns search results based on keyword searches, FAST does additional processing on the content and allows for more context-sensitive content. From an end-user perspective, one of the most obvious and exciting features of FAST is the search results preview feature that displays the actual document or file right in the search results page.

You can find more information in Chapter 20, "FAST Search."

FAST Search Server for SharePoint (Intranet)

FAST for SharePoint intranet sites is a service within the server farm and expands the functionality just described, adding contextual search as well as search result preview functionality for starters. The service also provides a framework for search-based customizations and functionality.

FAST Search Server for SharePoint Internet Sites (FSIS)

Similar to the intranet functionality, FSIS is licensed for public-facing solutions based on the SharePoint platform.

SharePoint Online

SharePoint can be deployed on-premises via a hosted offering, or in the "cloud." As part of the ever-growing cloud offerings in the market, SharePoint Online is available from Microsoft as a part of the Office 365 suite of communications and collaboration products. Though the feature had yet to be finalized when this was written, the 2010 online version of SharePoint is expected to be much more consistent with the on-premises feature set. The most notable difference will likely be with the online version's not supporting BCS or other data integration features, PerformancePoint, or FAST.

At the time this book was written, BPOS had not yet reached RTM status.

Other Related Products

SharePoint as a whole continues to find its way into more and more products either as integration points or as the core framework for functionality. The full breadth of SharePoint's integration is outside the scope of this book, but some examples include:

- ➤ **Microsoft Office products:** The deepest integration is with the 2010 version of Office, but previous versions also have integration points. Commonly referred to as the "Good, Better, Best" document, a Microsoft white paper titled "Business Productivity at Its Best" details some of the integration with older versions of Microsoft Office.

- ➤ **InfoPath 2010:** Yes, this is part of Office, but is worth mentioning specifically because of InfoPath's role in creating and editing digital forms.

- ➤ **PowerPivot for SharePoint:** This provides enhanced BI capabilities for working with large data sets.

➤ **Microsoft Excel, Visio, and Access:** All have SharePoint Server services associated with them, providing server-side management of content.

➤ **Project Server 2010:** Built on SharePoint Server 2010.

Many examples are available. A few specifics are highlighted in the following sections.

SharePoint Designer 2010

SharePoint Designer 2010 (SPD) is a client application tool used to edit, configure, and extend SharePoint solutions without having to write code. When looking at the full landscape of options available for configuring and customizing SharePoint, SharePoint Designer falls somewhere in the middle. It allows for more customization than the user interface of SharePoint alone, but doesn't offer as many capabilities as Visual Studio. Likely users of SPD will include power users, designers (branding), and developers.

With SharePoint Designer 2010, a number of significant improvements and enhancements have been introduced:

➤ Improved workflow design

    ➤ Reusable workflows that can be used with different lists

    ➤ Integration of workflows with Visio 2010 process diagrams

    ➤ Ability to export a workflow from SPD into Visual Studio for further customization

➤ Dramatically improved ability to add and edit list forms

➤ Kick-start development efforts that can be further extended in Visual Studio

➤ Integrate external data and lists into SharePoint

SPD 2010 is the latest in a line of products that includes Microsoft Office SharePoint Designer 2007 and FrontPage. It is important to note that SPD 2010 will work only with the SharePoint 2010 platform. SPD 2010 will not work with earlier versions of SharePoint. Similarly, earlier versions of SharePoint Designer will not work with the 2010 platform. If users need to install both versions of SPD, these will need to be the 32-bit version of both because Microsoft does not support 64-bit and 32-bit versions of Office products on the same system.

More specific examples and guidelines for SharePoint Designer are noted throughout this book.

A number of books are available for specific topics related to SharePoint Designer 2010.

SharePoint Workspace 2010

SharePoint Workspace is the latest iteration of the product formerly known as Microsoft Office Groove. Workspace is both a client and peer-to-peer application that allows users to take SharePoint site content offline, make changes while offline, and then synchronize with the SharePoint server at a later time. Workspace also allows for sharing of content between Workspace clients. Workspace has a number of interesting features, but these are outside the scope of this book.

SUMMARY

This chapter has painted a broad picture of how SharePoint 2010 can impact an organization and why users should be excited about how it can change their day-to-day activities for the better.

Core concepts were introduced, first through the business perspective and then with SharePoint-specific terminology, setting the stage for deeper topics to come later in this book. Understanding how lists, libraries, and sites work is required before digging into all the configuration and customization options that are available.

Finally, the different versions of SharePoint 2010 were introduced, with some familiar concepts from previous versions, but with Foundation and Server taking over from WSS and MOSS. Also added are new Search editions and cloud capabilities. With so many options available, there surely will be a solid choice for every organization.

The next chapter introduces planning and preparation topics for implementing SharePoint both technically and in the business. With all the capabilities and options available, it's even more important to start from a strong foundation.

Planning for SharePoint

WHAT'S IN THIS CHAPTER?

➤ Introducing topics that should be considered before and during a SharePoint implementation

➤ Discussion of some implications of decisions made during the planning phase

➤ Suggested strategies and methods to prepare for deployment and mitigate challenges

Effectively planning for a SharePoint platform in an organization is critical to the platform's success in the long term. Similar to the importance of requirement-gathering and design before custom development, SharePoint deployment requires forethought and diligence before rolling out an implementation. And as with development efforts, you can either put the effort in beforehand, or you'll be forced to do more work catching up later.

Many organizations have experienced SharePoint's tendency to grow "organically" in an environment when given the chance. Because SharePoint works well with existing client tools and because it enables people to work better together, once users start experiencing the benefits they usually want to use the tool for all kinds of purposes.

The term "governance" has been used and abused over the past few years as an all-encompassing term for planning and operations preparation for SharePoint. Unfortunately, it's been overused to the point where the word itself has lost value. But whatever name you put on it, planning is required for successful implementation.

Also bear in mind that not all organizations will need answers for every planning topic, but at a minimum the list of topics should be reviewed to find what *does* need to be addressed in your scenario. This chapter tries to address enough of the preparation topics needed to plan for a SharePoint platform but does not cover everything — that would require a far larger volume. The chapter also does not cover planning topics for specific solutions built on top of SharePoint.

BUSINESS PLANNING

Identifying a business stakeholder or sponsor of a SharePoint project is essential to provide the necessary clarity, direction, funding, and sometimes clout for the project. Without a sponsor high enough in the organization, projects may stall while waiting for the necessary buy-in from different departments, staffing for the platform and supporting technologies, funding for hardware or software, and training for staff and users. Projects driven solely by an IT leader or specific business unit may have challenges in bringing these resources together, and the projects may end in frustration because they overlap with functionality already provided by other systems, they encounter different corporate strategies already in place, or their strategies just aren't defined enough.

In smaller organizations, defining SharePoint's role in an organization may be a simple process involving a single IT resource or even a managing service provider. In that case the scenario might be as straightforward as a sponsor's deciding to use SharePoint and giving the "make it happen" order.

The beneficiaries of the technology solutions also need to be informed and educated. The more users understand both the organization's intentions as well as how the platform will meet their needs, the happier they will be to assist in the process. The more users understand the capabilities, the more they will be able not only to meet their original requirements, but also to find new ways of using the tool to benefit the organization.

Regardless of the size of the organization, having a vision for the capabilities that SharePoint brings is essential to its success. Sometimes this vision is what drives a SharePoint project. Other times generic organizational needs fit with the technology solution SharePoint brings. In many cases an envisioning session for key business decision-makers that covers both general technology solutions and the specific capabilities of SharePoint goes a long way toward getting a business sponsor interested, or even excited, about the prospects. Many of the items discussed in Chapter 1 could provide content for the vision conversation. Additional decision points for vision and strategy areas that may be covered in an envisioning session are discussed in the next few sections.

Finally, because SharePoint Server 2010 integrates with so many technologies, business stakeholders need to understand at least at a product-to-product level what integration points exist between systems, so that they can effectively make strategy-level decisions. Managers of these areas also need to be involved in the planning. Topics for these areas are discussed later in this chapter.

Web Strategy

At one time web strategy was as simple as deciding what platform would be used for intranet, extranet, and Internet-facing solutions. Now the market has evolved and matured to the point where many products offer web-enabled functionality and access. The SharePoint platform itself offers functionality that extends into numerous other areas where strategy needs to be defined, further complicating matters. Defining a plan with or without SharePoint now requires a bit more diligence to make sure all bases are covered.

SharePoint is a web application. Therefore any organization considering deploying SharePoint needs to define what SharePoint will and will not be used for, and how it will integrate with other web-based solutions. In many cases, the functionality that SharePoint brings crosses paths with other solutions that are already in place. Sometimes SharePoint is brought in explicitly to replace old or more expensive platforms. In cases where solutions don't have a web component, SharePoint can be used to provide access to content and functionality not otherwise available to users. In other circumstances SharePoint needs to be evaluated alongside other technologies to determine the best technology fit.

As was pointed out in Chapter 1, SharePoint *has* the capability to be the core solution for many use-cases including the intranet, extranet, and Internet solutions. In fact, one of the benefits of SharePoint is that it can be used for all three scenarios, as well as others. Having a consolidated platform allows for some efficiencies when it comes to skill sets to manage more than one farm, provide custom development across the platform, and even license the environments.

Although functionality is generally the primary decision point (defining whether or not a list of requirements is met), each organization will have its own specific decision points when figuring out where SharePoint fits in the organization. Other frequently used decision points might include:

➤ Whether or not skilled staff is available for both administration and customization tasks. More details are covered later in this chapter.

➤ Licensing costs of existing or potential solutions.

➤ Supportability of platforms. It's not uncommon to have a solution in place so long that it is no longer supported.

Part of the web strategy now includes where solutions are deployed: whether they are deployed on premise or hosted off-site; whether they are installed on physical hardware or virtualized environments; and whether in-house staff or managed services are managing the infrastructure. These aren't necessarily SharePoint-specific questions, but they certainly play a part in defining the solution and the requirements needed to support it.

A growing number of hosted SharePoint providers are available with varying levels of support and functionality. Some providers are hosting simple site collections on shared environments; others are building dedicated SharePoint environments that clients still manage, relying only on the hardware and OS to be hosted. Finding an appropriate solution depends on the needs of your organization, but there are obvious benefits in not needing SharePoint IT professional (IT pro) resources in-house and being able to offload some of the infrastructure management.

Cloud-computing solutions using shared infrastructure resources are another option, with Microsoft offering its SharePoint Online solution as part of Office 365. At the time of writing, the 2010 version of SharePoint Online and Office 365 was not yet available but was expected to be closer to on-premises functionality than the 2007 product, though still with a few significant exceptions. These include external data integration and no ability to host publicly accessible sites. Only Internet-facing environments will be able to be hosted. As with the more generic hosted solutions, customers are off-loading the infrastructure management and relying on a remotely managed service.

Other Strategies

Although web strategy is the underlying topic and delivery mechanism, other organizational strategies probably need to be reviewed when determining which pieces of functionality will be delivered via SharePoint.

Collaboration

Collaboration is a sweet spot for SharePoint and can be one of the easier decisions when deciding whether or not SharePoint is the platform of choice. In many cases no other products or solutions are in place, or solutions that are in place are not enterprise-ready, or a smattering of solutions are being used by different teams and departments with no unified strategy.

SharePoint for collaboration can also be an easy sell because so many organizations use Microsoft products for their office productivity tools (MS Word, Excel, Access, and others) and the tight integration between the client and server products provides a good user experience.

When no clear collaboration strategies are identified, users are left using file shares and e-mail. Using file shares has been the default method for organizations for years, but has a number of limitations. File shares don't allow for check-in/check-out control and are apt to allow one user to overwrite another's work. No versions are tracked and access must be controlled by IT.

E-mail is certainly part of the collaboration experience, but can be abused when a real collaboration tool isn't available. Rather than using e-mail only as a communication tool, users lean on MS Outlook or Exchange to *store* documents and versions. This can lead to higher traffic and storage levels and may also conflict with enterprise retention practices that regularly delete old e-mail.

Document Management

Document and records management strategies are common for organizations of all sizes. Where no specific system is already in place, SharePoint is a capable solution for many organizations; however, its out-of-the-box capabilities may fall short for organizations that have more demanding requirements. If another product is already being used, management may choose to reevaluate the existing document management systems side-by-side with SharePoint. Because of the typically high licensing and support costs for dedicated document management systems, some organizations lean toward SharePoint because of the cost savings alone. When SharePoint features are compared with these products, SharePoint often comes out ahead because of its wider set of functionality and better user interface. Where it is determined that two systems are to coexist, many mainstream document management tools have Web Parts available to work *with* SharePoint. Users can work in the SharePoint web interface while seamlessly accessing and managing documents in the other systems.

Finally, SharePoint's ability to extend its capabilities with customizations is also an option because specific features may be requested and can be created for less cost than buying a separate dedicated document system.

Business Process/Workflow

Organizations interested in business process management or workflows should consider SharePoint for its out-of-the-box capabilities, its ability to extend those capabilities, and its ability to integrate with a number of robust third-party workflow platforms. You can find more on this capability in Chapter 15.

Business Intelligence

Business Intelligence (BI) is an area where SharePoint brings a wide range of solutions, from simple lists, views, and graphing to more robust dashboards and KPI (Key Performance Indicator) controls.

It's also able to interact with a diverse set of data from data stored inside SharePoint, to Excel content, to external data, and all the way to fully generated existing cubes.

In organizations where no BI solution is in place, SharePoint brings new capabilities. Where BI solutions do exist, SharePoint is often used as an additional way to surface data stored in BI-specific systems. This can be a cost-efficient way to expose additional users to data typically reserved for a small set of users, a limitation often imposed by the licensing costs for the BI platforms.

Search

Search strategies for organizations today still tend to be hit or miss. Some organizations have specific search tools in place for specific data like company directories, but not as a holistic company approach for all content. Other companies have wider-range search solutions or hardware but still may or may not reach all the content and users they'd like to reach or return the kinds of results users need. Because SharePoint's search capabilities are so robust, they can be used as little or as much as an organization determines the need to be. SharePoint commonly is introduced as a portal or collaboration tool that initially enables search for its own environment but then quickly adds scopes and Search Result pages for more and more content as users get accustomed to its powerful search engine. As with other functional overlaps, administrators will need to determine if SharePoint's search functionality infringes on any existing search solutions, and if so how they will interact. The Federated Search capabilities described in Chapter 1 allow for an effective coexistence between new and existing third-party search solutions.

SharePoint Road Map

SharePoint 2010 is a platform with lots of capabilities and many moving parts. The key to success with SharePoint is to think big and act small. In other words, put some thought into where SharePoint fits in a larger, organizational strategy and then implement that strategy in smaller, more manageable projects. Coordinating those smaller projects into a longer-term plan is your SharePoint road map. It's not rocket science, nor is the approach unique to SharePoint, but it is still a valid concept that needs to be applied to SharePoint projects and deployment.

Ideally, defining a road map requires stepping back from a technology solution and focusing on business needs. You need to understand what the organization is doing, how work is being done, and who is doing the work. You should also understand what's working and what the pain points are. You must identify end-user priorities and understand any business improvement initiatives that might be under way. You should ask your end users for this input rather than getting only management's perspective. The two views are often very different and getting both perspectives is important.

Once gathered, use all this information, along with how these needs align with the SharePoint platform, to determine what to implement and when — where along the road map different features or solutions will be tackled. Aligning the technology solution to the business need will require someone with a solid understanding of the platform capabilities so that the appropriate solutions can be identified and an effort made to deploy those solutions. Working with the IT organization is also critical in aligning their skills and efforts with business needs.

Controlling the scope of a SharePoint project can be so challenging that it becomes a risk to both individual projects and the platform itself. Trying to do too much too quickly has been the downfall of many IT projects, SharePoint included. Fortunately, it's also true in that many projects have been successful when kept in small enough pieces to control the execution as well as its place in the larger road map.

Typical starting points for SharePoint in an organization are as an intranet or portal solution or as a collaboration tool. Deeper data integration or more robust workflow and business process automation are usually introduced a little later in the process so users can get used to the platform before investing in these more costly solutions.

When some of the more robust features are the reason for deploying SharePoint, they can certainly still be deployed, but in a balanced manner. For example, rather than deploying a whole suite of workflows, a few smaller processes should be identified and deployed first as a proof of concept (POC) before tackling larger or more detailed processes. In this way, users can become accustomed to how the system works and what its capabilities are. Administrators can make sure the environment can handle the workload and any data needs. Developers can ease their way into what is likely a new genre of development. Once these POC examples are successful, the momentum can be carried to the more challenging solutions.

Budgeting

Initial considerations for budgeting of SharePoint usually lean toward SharePoint-specific hardware and licensing costs. Though these are obvious and traditional, broader subjects should also be considered. Each organization is different, so remember to review the particular scenario for your organization so as to not underestimate what's required. Business stakeholders should work with the IT organization and development staff when appropriate. Some general examples that are detailed later in this chapter include:

➤ **Test/stage/development environments:** In addition to the production environment, other SharePoint environments may be necessary to conform to development standards or other standards in the environment.

➤ **Additional staffing:** New staff may need to be added to manage the SharePoint environment.

➤ **Multiple locations:** If an organization has more than one location, additional architecture, hardware, or software may be necessary to fulfill business needs.

➤ **Disk space:** If SharePoint is being used for a storage-intensive solution like document management, records management, or other storage-heavy solutions, be sure that adequate disk space and room for growth are considered.

➤ **Third-party tools:** Licensing costs for additional software.

➤ **Contractor costs:** If everything can't be done in-house, be sure to plan for service or consulting costs to round out your internal resources.

➤ **Training, communication, and internal marketing:** Just deploying SharePoint isn't the end of the project. Rolling out a solution to users and empowering them to be successful with the new tool are critical to the success of the project.

When aligning with functionality and specific solutions, the budgeting approach for SharePoint is going to go along with the road map that decision-makers establish. For example, some features, like People Search, are relatively easy to deploy and deploy early for little additional cost. More robust features like advanced process automation or Business Intelligence solutions will likely involve more time and cost and often will be scheduled further down the road.

Staffing

Staffing a SharePoint platform or project requires a range of roles and expertise over the course of the project and product lifecycle. Organizations may choose to use internal resources when available or external resources and services when needed. Depending on the size of the organization, one or more dedicated SharePoint resources may be required to manage SharePoint-specific functionality and support. In diversified IT organizations additional resources from supporting technology teams, such as the database, server, network, and Active Directory teams, may be needed. These teams will need to commit some part of their resources to supporting SharePoint-related activities.

Of the supporting services and technologies, the database team will likely demand the most commitment due to SharePoint's dependence on SQL as its back end. The server team will need familiarity with the Windows Server 2008 platform, IIS, and any other supporting software used in the environment, such as server management solutions and virus-checking software. This team should also be aware that server OS patches may have unintended consequences for the SharePoint platform.

SharePoint-specific roles don't necessarily need to be full-time responsibilities of internal or external resources, but they will certainly be the main focus of their attention. The roles of various players in the process are shown in Table 2-1.

TABLE 2-1: SharePoint Project and Platform Roles

ROLE	DESCRIPTION
Architect	A seasoned veteran of SharePoint implementations big and small with both development and IT professional skills and experience. The architect will oversee the big picture of how SharePoint is used in the business, and how it fits into the larger IT services environment. Architects don't necessarily need to be the best at everything, but do need to know enough about most topics to understand why one decision is better than another.
Developer	SharePoint developers are specialized .NET application developers. They understand ASP.NET applications, solutions and features, Web Parts, and the underlying SharePoint object model. They understand when to use SharePoint Designer vs. Visual Studio for building solutions.
IT pro	IT pros are the server administrators for SharePoint and understand how to install and configure SharePoint on top of a core Windows Server 2008 and IIS server. They understand how to best design server architectures based on the use-case and business needs.

continues

TABLE 2-1 *(continued)*

ROLE	DESCRIPTION
Creative designer	Creative and design staffers understand both core HTML and web-design concepts and technologies, and know how to apply these branding concepts in the SharePoint platform. Frequently these individuals work with marketing and communications teams or outside design firms to both design a suitable brand as well as apply it effectively to the SharePoint platform.
Project manager	A SharePoint-specific project manager may seem somewhat odd to many people, but there is a lot of benefit to having someone who understands the deployment and customization process and can coordinate initial deployments as well as ongoing customization work.
Analyst	Business analysts with SharePoint experience are essential for understanding the business and its needs and identifying solutions that are appropriate for the SharePoint platform. It is important for the analyst to have a solid understanding of SharePoint's feature set and the pros and cons of different approaches in order to translate business needs into the correct technical solution.

Other roles at an organization may have SharePoint-specific requirements, but only as part-time focuses. These should not be overlooked, however, because the success of the platform depends heavily on the services that holders of these provide (Table 2-2).

TABLE 2-2: Others with SharePoint Responsibilities

ROLE	DESCRIPTION
Server team	The server team is responsible for the health and stability of the Windows Server 2008 servers on which SharePoint and SQL are installed. The team members understand IIS (web server) configuration as well as how other server tools like server backups and virus-checking solutions will impact SharePoint.
Database team	The database administrators (DBAs) are responsible for the health, stability, and performance of the database servers and databases. DBAs may also work closely with a SAN (storage area network) team to manage data capacity, duplication, backup, and restoration of data.
Network team	The network team coordinates where SharePoint servers are deployed within the network, and/or how they are connected to the outside word and users while maintaining high performance and security.

ROLE	DESCRIPTION
Security and Active Directory team	The domain and information security teams work with the SharePoint team to create and manage service accounts as well as define the approach used for security groups.
Trainers	If a training department is available, members will need to add SharePoint content to their curricula and skill sets.

IT PROFESSIONAL PLANNING

Just as a business sponsor is important to delivering the business requirements for SharePoint, a platform sponsor is necessary to consolidate the various technical requirements needed to deploy and maintain SharePoint. This often requires bringing together resources from various teams to ensure the SharePoint platform is built and managed to organizational standards and defined service levels.

Many organizations make the mistake of considering SharePoint as just another application installed on a server rather than as the platform it really is. IT organizations need to understand where SharePoint fits as a part of the larger strategies in an organization to effectively plan for its use. The platform owner coordinates and communicates these strategies and resources.

Server Standards and Builds

SharePoint is a web application that requires Microsoft Windows Server 2008. So before any of the SharePoint-specific tasks are even started there needs to be a server that will host it. Many organizations will have an image or standard for an application server build that should be considered first to see if it will meet all the requirements of SharePoint. The more these standards can be kept in place, the easier it is for the organization to manage the infrastructure across the board. Typically the changes that need to be made can be applied after the core image is installed.

Many organizations may not have 64-bit Windows Server 2008 as a standard yet, which may create additional work to come up to speed before installation of SharePoint. This particular challenge will likely wane as more organizations naturally mature and adopt the server standards required for SharePoint.

Other standard considerations for servers also need attention. Although Microsoft has made general minimum recommendations for RAM and drive sizes, organizations need to ensure that their standards mesh with Microsoft's recommendations while keeping in mind any additional drive space required for other standard organizational software such as virus-checkers or management agents.

Backup solutions for the underlying infrastructure as well as the SharePoint software itself need to be considered as part of the disaster recovery, business continuity, and backup and restore plans. In many cases organizations are already using a vendor to meet some or all of the required backup options for application servers and database servers. If the vendor also has SharePoint-specific capabilities, it may be a very easy transition to add the remaining modules or agents to attain the coverage desired.

Finally, once the core OS has been built to organizational norms and standards and properly patched up, SharePoint service accounts need to be added to the system. Where other applications may request one or two accounts, SharePoint tends to be on the other end of the spectrum. The final number is defined by which services will be activated, but will typically be more than four or five.

Architecture Considerations

Planning for SharePoint begins with understanding both the initial intended use as well as what it might be used for in the foreseeable future. With this information in hand, architectures can be designed to meet immediate needs while also being as flexible as possible to keep future re-architecting to a minimum. Luckily, SharePoint 2010 is the most flexible version ever of such software, due primarily to its service-based architecture.

So what is SharePoint being used for? Is it going to be an internal-facing solution like a portal or collaboration environment? Is it going to be external-facing as a publicly accessible Internet site or a restricted client and partner extranet? Do both scenarios need to be supported? What requirements are there for uptime and availability? Does the database need to be clustered or mirrored? Locally or remotely?

Deploying SharePoint as an internal solution generally allows it to fit into an existing networking model, so few network changes are needed to accommodate its servers. SharePoint servers will need to be a part of a domain, have a number of domain service accounts, and be able to talk to the domain server and SQL Server.

Deploying SharePoint as an external solution is a bit more complex. Internet-facing solutions require different licensing than internal-facing solutions. Architecture is dependent on how robust an external-facing environment the organization has and what policies and procedures are already in place. Does the organization have a perimeter network? What belongs in the perimeter network and what doesn't? What standards are there for configuration across the firewall, and so on? A variety of architectures are available, but SharePoint servers still need to talk to a domain and SQL.

External environments may also involve additional authentication methods that allow non-employees to access the environment without needing to be added to an Active Directory domain (which would require additional licensing costs). Forms-Based Authentication (FBA) is a common replacement when using a model other than the AD model. FBA may use a SQL database that stores credentials; it may leverage Windows Live accounts or may even use AD as a data store. SharePoint 2010 allows for multiple authentication models while still using the same URL — an improvement over previous versions.

Along similar lines as the FBA vs. AD discussion, administrators need to identify whether the system needs to be able to handle Claims or Kerberos authentication. These may be necessary when SharePoint is connected with external systems and they require individualization rather than a single generic connection.

If SharePoint is being used as a search solution for content outside SharePoint, are service accounts created for SharePoint to access the external data? Do any network changes need to be made to allow the SharePoint system to access the other data?

Capacity planning and the use of SAN and hierarchical storage management (HSM) storage should also be considered from a number of angles. In many organizations SAN space needs to be requested with a longer lead time than other resources and should be considered as part of deployment planning and scheduling. The intended use of the platform may influence the capacity plan; if specific document or records management solutions are being planned, they will require more drive space. It ultimately requires more disk space to store a file in SharePoint than on the file server due to the way it is stored, usually in a SQL table itself.

Assuming that a cloud or hosted environment is not being used, it should also be decided whether virtualized or physical servers will be used. SharePoint supports virtualization, so the decision is typically left to the organizational strategy recommendations. In many cases the SQL server is the last server to be virtualized, though performance of the latest generation of software and hardware seem to make a virtualized SQL environment acceptable. It all comes down to whether or not performance standards can be met.

Regardless of the use-case, there will be a test or stage environment that as accurately as possible reflects the production environment. Administrators may want to test anything that can affect the platform's functionality and stability — anything from DNS settings, load balancers, and IIS settings to software patches, security settings, and custom solutions. The stage environment may be on the same domain or a different one, depending on the types of changes that need to be tested or how strict corporate policies are for isolating production data.

PowerShell

PowerShell is a scripting language built on and tightly integrated with the .NET platform. Microsoft has positioned PowerShell as the primary method for managing SharePoint, as it has for other platforms such as SQL Server and Exchange, by producing a large number of *cmdlets* (or *command-lets*) for administrators to use. The basics of PowerShell are a must-have skill set for SharePoint administrators and developers, starting with the 2010 platform.

You can find a detailed list of SharePoint cmdlets by using the following command in the SharePoint 2010 Management Shell:

```
Get-Command -PSSnapin "Microsoft.SharePoint.PowerShell" | select name, definition |
format-list > C:\SP2010_PoSh_Cmdlets.txt
```

PowerShell can be used for any number of activities, which can include, but are certainly not limited to:

➤ **Installing and configuring a SharePoint farm:** Scripting a production installation allows for a predictable and reproducible environment that can be useful for building consistent environment between stage and production, or be used as part of a disaster recovery process to rebuild servers. It can also be used to rebuild development environments quickly when you need to produce clean environments for testing.

➤ **Installing and deploying solutions and features:** Any custom solution should be deployed using a script for consistency and predictability.

➤ **Deploying updates**

➤ **Changing service accounts and/or passwords**

➤ **Moving, importing, or exporting data**

DEVELOPER PLANNING

One of the great features of SharePoint 2010 is its capability to be customized and extended. Although the broad feature set allows for a great deal of functionality out of the box, most every organization eventually wants to extend the platform to meet a requirement that just doesn't quite work the way the organization would like it to. This section covers some of the topics that should be considered before introducing customizations into the environment.

First of all, there are a lot of ways to customize SharePoint. As best they can, organizations need to provide guidance to their users and development staffs regarding what can and should be customized and how customizations are designed, developed, and deployed in the environment. The "what can and can't" part is used to set expectations with users so they understand why some things can't be done.

As discussed in a bit more detail later in this chapter, training for developers is very important. Developers may choose to utilize classroom courses or self-study resources. Many will rely on books (like this one), blogs, and other online resources.

Platform owners from both the business and technical sides need to determine whether they will build internal SharePoint resources or hire partners to do some of the work for them. Bringing in external help also usually means opportunities for the in-house folks to ramp up and use mentoring and knowledge transfer to bring your folks up to speed faster than they could manage by themselves. Whether or not there is local talent available to hire should also be a consideration.

Development Standards

It's important for developers to define and follow consistent methods of development on the SharePoint platform, just as it is on other platforms. Ideally, project templates and code samples will be created that can be reused as much as possible. Similarly, the packaging of solutions and features should be consistent so that all developers can support each others' work. Finally, every organization should have a method of source control, in which any SharePoint customizations should also be managed.

Development should be done on an environment other than the production farm. Ideally, there should be separate development machines or environments for each developer. If more than one developer is working on the same effort, they'll need an environment where they can combine their efforts before promoting it further. There should be an environment where code can be deployed as a test run to production — some call it "test," while others refer to it as "stage." Finally, the same process used to deploy the customization to the test environment should then be used to deploy to production. Some organizations like to have a waiting period between when code is deployed to test and when it is rolled out to production, to further safeguard the production environment.

Specific standards get to be a bit trickier to nail down because so many kinds of customizations can be done. For example, aside from being deployed both by a solution and feature, a branding customization is going be very different from a BDC connection to a database customization. Additional examples are highlighted throughout the rest of this chapter.

Tools

The primary tools developers use with SharePoint are SharePoint Designer (SPD), Visual Studio 2010, and possibly a text editor. Each tool has its niche in the development process, with the line between SPD and Visual Studio moving back and forth depending on whom you are talking to. Some developers have found a good balance between the tools, whereas others have biases one way or the other, usually based on their individual skill set and comfort levels with each of the tools. Outside the standard tools, a range of utility applications is available as well, and some developers use these to enhance their workspace.

Other tools fall into something of a gray area for developers — areas where code can certainly be used, but doesn't need to be. Applications like InfoPath fall into this category where simple digital forms can be created by end users dragging and dropping controls, but more complicated functionality requires development behind the scenes that quickly turns into efforts too complex to justify when better technologies or approaches are also available.

Finally, the reference material and sample code available online is extensive. Even Microsoft has already (early in the SharePoint product cycle) produced more content in MSDN and TechNet than it has in past versions of the product.

INSTALLATION, CONFIGURATION, AND MIGRATION

Many organizations have existing pre-2010 SharePoint installations they want to migrate to the 2010 platform. A number of upgrade paths are available, each with its own pros and cons. This book won't go into detail on the migration steps, but does review some of the topics that organizations should consider before proceeding with a migration effort.

Migration Options

Two primary methods exist for migrating from SharePoint 2007 to SharePoint 2010: in-place and database-attach migrations. These are the approaches recognized and documented by Microsoft. Other variations and more manual and granular data migrations are possible, but are used in so few cases and in such specialized scenarios that they are not considered relevant methods.

The first step in preparing for an upgrade is choosing the appropriate migration approach. In some cases either approach may work just fine, in others there may be factors that eliminate one method or the other. If considering an in-place upgrade, is the hardware up to the requirements for 2010? In many scenarios this is not the case, which makes the decision easier for some.

Taxonomy, architecture, and farm use-cases are also things that need to be considered when migrating. If a single environment is being migrated to a new single environment, there aren't too many factors to worry about, but it might be a good opportunity to consider a re-organization of data at the same time.

Where the process gets a little more complicated is when the migration is also part of a consolidation of multiple environments — even more so if they have divergent purposes or core architectures, as an intranet and extranet may have. Even consolidating multiple intranet environments can be dicey because sites and site collections must be determined to have unique URLs, duplicate content may be purged, and site collections may need to conform to a new or altered information architecture and site map.

Finally, it should also be noted that no options exist for direct migration from versions of SharePoint previous to 2007. Data must be migrated from 2003 to 2007, then on to 2010 using the content database-attach method.

Planning and Design

Once an approach has been determined, all the users and providers will need to prepare for the migration. Much like an initial configuration, the communication, support, and training plans discussed later in this chapter are critical to the success of the migration. For existing users, the importance is even higher because these users and the organization have a vested interest in their data coming across successfully.

Everyone will have responsibilities in a migration. Users, power users, and site administrators need to identify and catalog the content and functionality that they have in a current site so that it can all be validated after migration. Farm administrators obviously have very specific tasks ahead of them in determining the method and steps for the whole process. The farm admin or IT pro are generally the ones coordinating the details of the whole migration, sometimes alongside a project manager for larger efforts. Developers need to be informed of any existing customizations in the current environment so they can be reviewed for whether or not they'll work and can be successfully deployed in the new environment.

OPERATIONS AND ADMINISTRATION

The ongoing operation of the SharePoint platform is just as important as all the effort that is put into preparation for deployment. After deployment, it's all about execution. If plans have been made, but not followed through with, users will lose confidence in the platform and any solutions built on it. So it's important not only to plan, but to execute the communication, training support, and maintenance plans while continuing to keep users informed regarding the status of the platform.

Most concepts described here aren't necessarily specific to SharePoint, but can be applied to a number of platforms and solutions.

Communication Planning

Regardless of what your SharePoint environment has been built for, it has users and it will require maintenance. To meet or exceed user expectations, there should be a communication plan in place to both communicate effectively to users as well as collect feedback from them. At its core, the communication needs to identify:

➤ Who needs to be communicated to

➤ What needs to be communicated

➤ When the communications need to go out

➤ Who will generate the communication

Ideally, the initial parts of the communication plan will be implemented before deployment of the platform or new solutions to let the user community know what solutions are in development. If the core platform is already in place, there may be an ongoing list of planned improvements and projects. Strategically, this allows users to plan for the new solutions while also preventing any duplication of effort to solve the same issues.

If the SharePoint solution is being brought in as a replacement to an existing system, or if it will in any way be a significant change in how users do business, the communication plan may also take on some aspects of a marketing campaign designed to win over the users to the new way of doing business.

One of the easier perspectives of a communication plan is that in most organizations the methods and media for communication with the users are already established. Tapping these existing methods is both efficient and comfortable for the users. There may be a portal in place where announcements are distributed. There may be RSS feeds that users follow to stay informed, and there likely are e-mail distribution channels that users are accustomed to using. If these aren't already in place, the deployment of SharePoint may introduce some of them with its implementation.

Plenty of options are available for how to communicate with users. Whoever is creating the communications plan should understand that a variety of methods should be used to meet the needs of a larger percentage of the users. It should also be recognized that regardless of how well communication is done, it will not meet every user's needs.

Examples of what and when to communicate:

➤ When the project is first starting, communicate what the goals of the project are and who is on the team.

➤ As soon as milestone dates have been established these should be displayed somewhere.

➤ As deployments are getting close, users and implementers should be informed of their roles and expected outcomes.

Training Planning

Education and empowering of the user base is critical to the success of SharePoint projects as it is with any tool or system that users are expected to use and rely on. It's important to meet the needs of the different user roles and to accommodate the different ways users learn. It's also important to continue training beyond the initial phase that leads up to deployment because new employees will continue to come on board, and people who went through training will need refresher information from time to time. Table 2-3 describes who should be trained and the curriculum for each.

TABLE 2-3: Roles Targeted in Training

GROUP	CURRICULUM
Business users and management	These people need to understand the capabilities and business value as delivered by using an overview and examples, preferably specific to the organization. Generally these are delivered by an external resource, unless the organization is large and has developed internal resources with the breadth of experience needed.
Developers	Development training generally takes .NET developers and introduces them to the SharePoint object model, types of customization projects, and best practices regarding tools and processes like deployment. Usually delivered via classroom or knowledge transfer sessions.
IT pros/farm administrators	Information needed to build and manage a SharePoint environment. Usually delivered via classroom training and if possible bolstered with mentoring.
Site administrators	Site administrators have mastered end-user training and have a deep understanding of the SharePoint site-security model, so that they can properly manage security of the site.
Power users	Power users have mastered end-user training and extend their capabilities by understanding more about SharePoint features, Web Parts, and creating and customizing lists. They may also be introduced to SharePoint Designer.
End users	There are usually too many end users to send everyone to external classroom training within a budget. Organizations generally rely on internal training and "train the trainer" approaches to get this basic day-to-day operational content to everyone.

Staffers responsible for User Interface (UI) and creative design don't typically attend classes or formal SharePoint branding training because the majority of their workloads deal with non-SharePoint specific tasks. They can apply much of their knowledge and experience to the SharePoint platform because of the way content management has been implemented in SharePoint. Many of the same CSS and layout concepts are the same. There is value, however, in acquiring knowledge on methods and best practices for how to apply designs to the SharePoint platform as there are some challenges. Finally, in many cases the design team is needed only early in the process or for a specific migration rather than for ongoing branding work. This one-time use doesn't generally justify the cost of training for the creative staff members.

Training Content

Training for SharePoint development usually assumes that developers are at least experienced with .NET. Training curriculums are pretty consistent at covering the different types of customization projects that are available to SharePoint developers and telling when to choose one method over another. They also cover toolsets and best practices.

IT pro training is similar to developer training in that it is usually a very consistent curriculum, walking through the installation and configuration and then onto all the details in the Configuration Manager. PowerShell will likely be covered during the session as well.

Most, if not all, of the training content discussed up until this point has been for out-of-the-box functionality. In many SharePoint implementations, organizations create custom solutions. Users need to be trained on these as well, and due to the nature of the content the training generally needs to be driven from in-house resources because it is so specific and sometimes confidential.

Training Approach

Several training methods were suggested earlier, starting with traditional classroom instruction and mentoring. Any number of methods can and should be used as long as the user needs are being met effectively. One key challenge that you should mitigate is that different people learn differently; you have to offer up a variety of tools and methods to assist your clients, partners, and co-workers.

The first thing to consider in training is the timing. Training needs to happen before many of the people will need it because administrators/IT pros need to design and build a platform. Developers likely need to build a few customizations even for initial launch iteration, so their training should start early. User training can also begin before a launch, but it would be hampered somewhat by not having an environment to see and touch.

The typical tripping point for an organization is that training and resources should continue to be available *after* the launch of the platform. Not only will new employees come on board and need to be trained, but existing users will get smarter and more experienced and want new materials to allow them to use the SharePoint platform fully.

A variety of options are available for delivering the training materials. Some companies may choose to use training partners who come with their own classroom, trainers, and curriculums. Other organizations may send a select group of people to training and then use those people to train the next batch of users, repeating the process internally until all users have been trained. A few of the trainers then offer the course work from time to time to new employees.

Training Resources

A full range of materials should also be made available to users to support the coursework, what was learned, and what users will continue to learn as they use the tool. Some examples:

➤ **Center of excellence sites:** Not just for the SharePoint platform but also for other platforms in the environment, center of excellence sites can be used as one-stop shopping for users to find information about a particular tool. Administrators and management can use the site as a communication center for the tools. Tools, resources, and other information can also be made available — anything that can make the user experience better.

➤ **Brown bag sessions and internal user groups:** These are good ways to meet periodically with users and share new or interesting information with them about or for the platform, such as new third-party tools that have been installed and solutions that have been built by other teams.

➤ **Handouts and desk drops:** A number of products are available such as SharePoint quick guides or cheat sheets. These make great desk drops for everyone, giving them core information they might need about getting started with SharePoint.

➤ **Online resources:** The center of excellence site should include a list of links to online resources within and beyond the organization. New articles, videos, and how-to resources are being added every day.

➤ **Productivity hub:** Microsoft has a free site collection that can be used to store educational materials, track who is using them, and provide a platform for adding additional material as needed. It doesn't have to be a SharePoint-only set of data. It's more about being a framework to build on.

Finally, as specific solutions are built on the SharePoint platform, be sure to set aside time to train the users and administrators of these new systems as well as time to create reference materials for them.

Support Planning

Support planning is an activity in which the IT department defines how it will run the platform on a day-to-day basis as well as how it will meet any service-level agreements (SLAs) that have been negotiated with the business owners. Defining the plan and delivering on it consistently is necessary to build confidence with the users and in the platform.

SLAs act as the requirements document for a support plan. They should define roles and responsibilities so that users know whom to call for questions. They should define how the support team is reached and for what services. Support plans should clearly identify when the system should be up and running and when service windows will be. The support team should be able to effectively communicate when those service windows are being used, what is being done, and how it may affect users.

Backup and restore options are another area that falls under support planning. Though restores have taken a bit of a back seat with the introduction of the SharePoint recycle bin, instances still exist where content needs to be restored. The recycle bin allows users and site administrators to restore most content. When circumstances require additional support, administrators will need to rely on third-party solutions or restoring from backup.

From the IT side of things, defined processes are needed for rolling out service packs and other deployable changes. Ideally, this will include deploying changes in a stage or test environment with sufficient time for testing and validation before using a repeatable process to deploy the same change to production, followed by the same validation and testing scripts. Third-party tools are available to assist with deployment activities as well.

The more traditional support topic of disaster recovery also needs to be addressed and can vary from simple to complex. Organizations with high availability demands may have a second instance of a production farm with database mirroring in place, whereas a simpler environment may have expected downtime with tools or scripts in place to restore or rebuild from backup.

Support plans should also work in concert with the communication plan to effectively communicate expectations and schedules with users and the rest of the IT organization.

SUMMARY

This chapter covered a lot of the potential topics that should be reviewed as part of readying an organization for SharePoint. Even though the market is starting to see more commoditization of both developer and IT pro resources, stakeholders need to understand enough of the general concepts to coordinate internal and external resources effectively. So many roles and responsibilities can be confusing, but everyone has a part to play in a successful SharePoint implementation.

Stakeholders from the business side need to work with the technical implementers to prioritize their needs based on a strategic vision and road map. Administrators need to plan for and build a stable platform for the organization as well as execute a successful support and maintenance plan. Developers need not only to deliver quality solutions but to identify standard development practices for both internal and external resources. Everyone needs to be trained and empowered to do his or her part effectively.

Although there is a lot to do, no one part is overwhelming. When each phase is complete, all the contributors can be confident that added value has been brought to the organization.

3

Getting Started with SharePoint

WHAT'S IN THIS CHAPTER?

➤ Justifying investment in the SharePoint platform and measuring success

➤ Defining platform strategy and prioritizing phased implementations

➤ Aligning business needs with the SharePoint platform capabilities

Chapter 1 introduced SharePoint's features, capabilities, and product line. Chapter 2 broached the subject of who needs to be involved with planning for a SharePoint deployment and what topics may need to be discussed. This chapter reviews the business approach, justification, and values that SharePoint delivers and how to make the most of the platform.

Implementing SharePoint successfully is about more than just the technical preparations. Successful SharePoint platforms owe their success to thinking big and acting small: taking on the right-sized projects and solutions. Taking on too large or complicated an effort will increase the risk of project failure.

Because SharePoint has so many features and capabilities, it's easy for business stakeholders and project managers to get pulled into a long list of deliverables. Resist the urge.

BUSINESS JUSTIFICATION AND ROI

A quantifiable business value for SharePoint is regularly sought after by both business stakeholders and technical platform owners. They may be justifying the expenses of an initial implementation or of the small or large projects and solutions that are eventually built upon it. Fortunately, a variety of options are available for both how to measure and what to measure when calculating the return on investment (ROI) of a SharePoint project.

Before defining a solution, the business requirement needs to be defined. There shouldn't be a solution without first defining a problem. Otherwise, how would you tell whether or not you've been successful in meeting the need?

Return on investment should be straightforward to define, but it isn't always as easy as that. Even SharePoint Foundation 2010 and Search Server Express 2010, as the "free" versions of SharePoint, cost something. From the hardware, software, and SAN disk space allocated, to the man-hours spent on the simplest of implemented architectures, costs can be measured. What may be considerably more challenging is measuring the value that solutions deliver.

On the other hand, organizations that own SharePoint Server through Enterprise License Agreements (ELAs) and aren't using the platform at all are wasting resources.

Some values are easier to measure than others. When SharePoint is used to replace existing systems in which legacy licensing fees and resources are expensive, cost benefit is easy to see and measure. Many benefits of SharePoint, however, are more intangible or "soft" benefits. These take a bit more effort to measure or acknowledge. Reviewing some of SharePoint's specific feature areas and examples might also prove useful.

Finally, for any of the scenarios involved, doing deliberate surveys of the users before and after a change should allow administrators to show value and success. As you go forward, users should have a conduit within the portal or tool to provide feedback and new user requests.

Measuring Value

Measuring and demonstrating value in SharePoint is as varied as the ways it can be used. The following are a few examples and suggestions to investigate in your environment. There are certainly many more, some unique to each organization and others common to similar business types or across the platform in general.

Business Processes

Business processes or workflow involve both the collection of information and the automation of processes. Both provide business value, but both can also be overdesigned, outweighing or reducing the return. Digital forms are used to collect information in a consistent and structured way, in the hope of reducing erroneous data and errors created when people need to re-enter the same data more than once. Forms can be created using a variety of methods, including out-of-the-box SharePoint forms, custom web forms, or InfoPath. Each method has its own pros and cons as well as its own tipping point, where complexity eventually makes the effort more of an investment than a time saver. Measuring the value of digital forms means understanding the cost of correcting errors and measuring how many errors were occurring before and how many are occurring after a new process is introduced.

Business processes and the tools used to automate them are similar to digital forms in that some processes fit well into SharePoint and workflow tools whereas others would take considerable effort to make fit. Finding the sweet spot involves understanding both the business process and SharePoint's capabilities. Once the solution has been deployed, success can be measured in terms of the number of processes that are completed in a specific amount of time. Both digital forms and processes may also be measured for the value of being able to track and report on the information collected and processed.

Search

Search is all about findability — anywhere from the general keyword search solutions like Bing or Google, to more specific search scopes and scenarios. If users can find the documents or information they're looking for faster than they could before, that is success. Measuring the value of that success could be as easy as measuring the time saved and the hourly value of workers' time. If a controlled environment is available, testers can measure the number of clicks or the time it takes to find content with a new SharePoint search compared to older searches or via navigation methods.

Search value can also be measured and calculated by looking at the additional work that can be done by employees because they're more effective at finding information or the resources they're looking for.

Administrators can look at the number of searches being made and the search terms being used. Just seeing a volume of searches going up may be a valuable result. Other search tools also show which search results are selected. If users are able to find what they're looking for in the first page of results, that may show value as well.

Collaboration

Collaboration is one of the more challenging topics to measure. Smaller pieces here and there can be measured, but these are usually the pieces with less impact. Ultimately, collaboration is about making individuals, teams, and projects more effective. Collaboration solutions save time, reduce duplicated work, and lessen the burden on the messaging system. It's easy to monitor e-mail systems and watch for volumes to drop and disk space to go down. This will translate into some savings. More value is likely to be gained by improving communication among the team members and improving the consistency of project processes.

One way to show value with collaboration, however, may be simply in the use of sites. Assuming that the request for and creation of sites is easy enough for users, just seeing the number of sites created and the content being added to the sites over time may be a validation of success for collaboration.

Intranets and Portals

Intranet and portal success is usually measured in how many users visit the site, using traditional web page hits and statistics. This is the first and most obvious example. More detailed site usage figures that are available with third-party site measuring would also show additional value in how long the user stayed on the site, how many pages were visited, and how the visitor moved through the site.

Portals can also demonstrate their usefulness both in a measurable decrease in mail volume, much as the collaboration solution does, and also in the harder-to-measure value of capturing historical information. Traditional content sent via e-mail is available only to the receivers of the e-mail. Newer participants to the conversation or thread do not get to see the history. In a SharePoint list, participants are able to go back and see the various threads and messages they didn't have access to via e-mail.

Identifying Business Needs

The challenge of identifying business needs isn't a SharePoint-specific effort. Plenty of well-known and practiced methods exist for requirements gathering, business improvement planning, and strategy development. With many software tools, the feature set is fairly well concentrated in one area and aligns well with one business need or another. With SharePoint's broad feature set, aligning the business needs with the platform isn't necessarily more difficult, but it does require a little more effort. This section covers some approaches to this process for a SharePoint project.

Before starting a SharePoint project, the business should first understand what additional capability is desired or what problems exist and need to be resolved. In most organizations, there are usually obvious lists of employee requests for changes and improvements as well as known functionality gaps. There may also be specific business initiatives that management or departments are looking to implement. Any or all of these are solid places to start.

If time and budget allow, spending a little extra effort on investigation and preparation may also yield valuable results. Lots of established strategies exist for gathering information from your organization and users. The following method is one that seems to work well with SharePoint-centric projects:

1. Introduce the participants to the SharePoint platform enough for them to understand the possibilities. This usually involves presentations and examples.

2. Meet and discuss the business process and activities with relatively small break-out groups, usually aligned by department or groups of people who do the same type of work. Company culture may determine whether having management part of the discussion is beneficial or not.

   a. Remember that talking about SharePoint is *not* the focus during these meetings.

   b. Conversations during the breakouts typically start with things like: "We can't find anything on the intranet," "The portal hasn't been updated in months/years," or "I don't know who in the company has what skills."

The process sounds simple, but it does require a SharePoint subject matter expert to deliver the sessions, guide the break-out discussions, and then analyze and deliver the results. The analysis takes into consideration what is known about the business and the SharePoint platform and aligns the organization's needs with the platform's capabilities to suggest a possible starting point and road map for SharePoint use in the organization.

Regardless of the process used, the more information that can be gathered, the better. Even if the initial goal is fairly general, gathering information from users may identify some easy wins that can be included if only as an effort to build some momentum for the SharePoint platform and add some excited users to the mix.

Prioritization

Countless ways exist to implement SharePoint in an organization. The challenge for most organizations is determining where to focus their efforts. These prioritization decisions are based on both the importance of company initiatives and how easy or difficult it is to implement the solution in SharePoint — which will be determined in part by the knowledge and experience of the analyst processing the information. Similarly, as more people gain experience and understand SharePoint's capabilities, more ideas will be brought up about how to use them.

Ultimately, the prioritization assessment will evaluate commonly used starting points and determine a strategy for SharePoint for the organization. Both of these topics are covered in more detail later in this chapter.

What shouldn't be a priority is jumping to custom solutions before they are justified. While customizations are certainly part of SharePoint implementations, making the leap to custom enhancements before understanding the platform and its capabilities can be costly. It's often better to wait until an informed decision can be made, ultimately ending up with fewer but more effective custom projects or saving your effort for more worthwhile choices as the platform matures in your environment.

Measuring Success

Measuring success relies on showing the differences between how people and processes worked before deploying a solution and how things are done after the solution is in place. Many organizations don't explicitly spend time on finding and using measures, but still look at results that can be measured using one method or another. Formalizing measures gives platform owners and business sponsors more real justification for the expense.

Plenty of tools are available to organizations for measuring value and success. Some measures are simple and intuitive, whereas others are more complex. Microsoft provides tools and services for measuring value, through the Business Value Planning Services (BVPS) offered via an Enterprise License Agreement (ELA). Many times BVPS engagements are used early in SharePoint initiatives, as organizations are investigating SharePoint and the broader Microsoft Office and Information Worker solutions. Some organizations have Six Sigma practices and strategies that can be applied to the SharePoint platform or solutions built on it.

Measures may be as simple as looking at traditional web statistics — how many people are hitting a page. This may be a measure of success for any of the broader solution types. For Internet sites, there is a long history and established value in measuring both page hits and user activity. Page hit count can also be used as an initial success measure for both extranet and intranet solutions, though other measures may eventually demonstrate more business value.

Search statistics represent a slight variation from page hit counts but also demonstrate the growing importance of search in any web-based solution. For some initiatives, merely seeing an increase in search *usage* may be a goal. This is especially important when striving to change user culture from not having or not using search to integrating search in daily usage. Separate from tracking search volume is evaluating what users are searching *for*: reviewing the terms that users are entering into the search box and what results they are finding. SharePoint addresses both of these needs by tracking both the number of searches made as well as what is being searched for.

Document management measures will depend on the goals of the initiative. Volume goals are relatively easy to measure, either by looking at the number of documents or storage volume moved off of a file share or by looking at the number of documents moved into document libraries. In some cases, value can be measured by the savings in physical storage requirements when converting physical documents to scanned/digital documents. In this case it's also important to weigh the physical costs against the digital storage costs; larger implementations can make disk requirements much larger than initially anticipated.

More often, goals for document management solutions are challenging to measure. Increasing the quality of documents or increasing the findability of documentation are more difficult scenarios to quantify, though some measures can be created.

Business process management or workflows have all kinds of opportunities for measurement. In many cases, just getting a process *into* SharePoint adds more scalability as well as the ability to track the volume of requests and capture requests in a more standardized method than physical processes allow. Many simple workflows implemented in SharePoint replace legacy processes that originate with e-mail requests, aren't scalable because one person is managing them via that person's inbox, and aren't structured data because they are using e-mail messages only.

Digital forms can reduce errors in the entry of data into the system as well as speed up the delivery of form content to other users and systems. Paper forms have to be entered a minimum of one time, but are typically passed around during the process, with multiple users entering part or all of the same information. Entering the data once reduces the chance of mistakes during this process and allows data to be made available more easily to the systems and people who need it.

If the user community is used to sending copies of documents to one another (especially forms and Microsoft Excel documents), there may be some gains to be had and measured on the MS Exchange side. This approach would require some forethought and before-and-after snapshots to see what, if any, difference they make in mail volume.

Business Intelligence (BI) is another category with two initial measures. The first is very specific — measuring when license fees for access to BI tools can be bypassed by using SharePoint to directly access reports, raw data, and other content. The second measure is of the time saving for users over the time they previously spent running around from system to system getting the information they need and then manipulating the same data on a single dashboard.

One of the benefits of measuring success is in identifying areas for improvement. Search statistics, for example, show what terms users are searching for, allowing administrators to add Best Bets to the search results page to make users more effective.

CHOOSING AN ENTRY POINT

SharePoint has found a lot of success with what people are referring to as "organic adoption." Someone in an organization has installed SharePoint somewhere — maybe even on a server under someone's desk. Before IT gets a whiff of it, several teams have built solutions they deem as business-critical. Although monitoring tools are making this scenario less likely, and the example is extreme, it's not that big a stretch. In many organizations IT departments are asked to spin up a SharePoint environment before they have the skills or governance in place to properly manage that environment — and they quickly find themselves needing to patch, fix, and update it. Obviously it's much better to plan an entry point and at least consider the larger strategy for SharePoint in an environment before moving forward and doing it the right way.

The process used when planning can work in various ways. An organization may have a very specific idea of how it wants to start using SharePoint and can then build a strategy around that. Or it may want to take a more holistic approach, look at all of its needs, define a strategy, and pick an entry point based on that strategy.

Traditional Entry Points

Because SharePoint 2010 is such a feature-rich platform, there is a wide range of entry-point options, though a few have bubbled to the top as more traditional solutions. It's open for debate whether the following examples have become popular because they are so general, because there is a high-demand for better solutions in these areas, or because they align well with SharePoint's strong points. In any event, the following sections describe a few areas that should be considered as solid and proven entry points for implementing SharePoint in an organization.

Collaboration

If the only reason an organization is implementing SharePoint is to leverage its collaboration capabilities — while not using any of the other long list of features — collaboration alone is still a very compelling case for using SharePoint 2010. When comparing usage and volume statistics to other common entry points, collaboration tends to be larger and more popular than many alternative solutions, because it becomes the daily dashboard for users. After Outlook, team sites are the first thing users open in the morning.

Starting with collaboration sites also generally leads to wider SharePoint adoption because it gives a lot of folks hands-on experience. As users grasp the core concepts of SharePoint, many take solutions to the next step and start to envision other solutions and use cases.

Intranet

With SharePoint's strong content management capabilities, it is commonly considered for new or replacement intranet and portal efforts. In many circumstances, SharePoint is already being considered for several use cases, with the replacement of an existing intranet solution typically freeing up licensing costs or freeing the organization from aged legacy systems that were previously used as the portal or web content management solution.

Starting with intranet solutions is good for IT professionals because it allows end users to ease into SharePoint use, while giving administrators time to grasp the operational complexities of SharePoint. Moving from intranet sites to more collaborative and solution-oriented sites increases end-user participation and the general effort needed to support them as well.

Document Management

Though SharePoint by itself isn't generally pitched as a best-of-breed document management solution, it does offer plenty of capabilities for the job. If the requirements identified by the organization fit within SharePoint's features, it can be a cost-effective and user-friendly alternative to many of the other document management systems on the market.

Document management may also include document scanning and other solutions that help with the importing of both daily and archived documents. This may also be an entry point to additional document management capabilities such as policies and workflows.

Extranet

Extranets may also be a starting point for organizations if they are looking for a collaborative environment between their employees and their partners, clients, vendors, and others. Plenty of examples are available:

➤ Product-producing companies may need to share information with distributors.

➤ Services companies may want to share project information with clients and to have a convenient place for document transfer.

➤ Students and teachers may want to communicate and transfer assignments back and forth.

As with anything in SharePoint, activities can be as simple or complex as needed to meet the organization's requirements. It should also be noted, however, that external-facing solutions like the extranet and Internet require additional network and farm configuration to ensure a stable and secure environment.

Internet

Internet solutions on SharePoint aren't usually taken on because they are a simple solution, but because they are a deliberate solution. Although the solutions don't need to be technically difficult, they generally require additional time and effort to properly plan and implement design and branding for the site.

Product Integration

Many organizations initiate SharePoint use because they're using another tool or solution that was built on the SharePoint platform. Having SharePoint is a mere afterthought in this case, until they realize what they've got and find they want to expand its usage within the organization. Microsoft Project 2010 and Team Foundation Server (TFS) are two products that use SharePoint to expand their capabilities.

Creating a Road Map

Choosing an entry point for organizations to get into the SharePoint platform resolves an immediate concern; however, it can and should lead directly to a road map — a plan for implementing broader solutions over a longer time. This road map should be an illustration of what SharePoint will be used for in an organization, giving administrators a better idea of how to plan the environment and giving business users an idea of when various features and solutions will be available. It will help organizers accommodate a longer list of business needs without having to solve all the challenges in one fell swoop by organizing features into multiple phases. Prioritization will help identify which solutions should be addressed first. It also identifies what will not be delivered in the first phase, while showing that there is indeed a plan and a timeline — something that generally goes a long way to keep users happy. The SharePoint road map was first mentioned in Chapter 2. This chapter digs a little deeper into several examples used by organizations.

One model revolves around more specific business solutions, whereas the other focuses on getting the operational capabilities of SharePoint online.

The more common model starts with a list of business requirements. This list is translated into prospective SharePoint-specific solutions and prioritized into phases of implementation. The process frequently starts with getting the SharePoint platform up and running in the organization with at least a minimum amount of governance to ensure stability and scalability. While the platform is being built and configured, the planning phase is generally worked on for the first set of deliverables. Depending on budget and resource availability, while the first phase of deliverables moves into development, planning on the next phase can begin. This cycle continues through the list of requirements, a list that will probably continue to grow.

A second model revolves around creating a somewhat general SharePoint environment, a framework that could apply to either extranet or intranet solutions. This environment has a tighter governance model that has additional policies, processes, and templates available. Site requests go through a well-defined process and site administrators are required to go through a training program before getting access to their new sites. If consulting or services are needed, packaged solutions may be offered to give departments or users a jump start on functionality. This type of model becomes more self-service as sites are requested by users, then reviewed, approved, created and configured automatically or with very little administrative oversight, so that turn-around time is minimized. In this model, the management of the site is now delegated to the site administrator, leaving the farm administrators to manage the general farm health instead of all the lower-level details of daily site management.

Regardless of how formal a road map process is implemented, someone needs to understand the larger picture when it comes to implementing SharePoint 2010 in an environment and be able to guide others appropriately.

TACKLING BUSINESS NEEDS WITH SHAREPOINT BASIC CONCEPTS

SharePoint 2010's capabilities offer solutions to common business challenges that can be applied very quickly for rapid results. Many of these concepts can be extended further with more time and effort, but gaining immediate value is important to both administrators and users. Because of the relative ease with which these scenarios can be implemented, they also typically play a part in the entry point options covered earlier in the chapter.

The following scenarios are some commonly available solutions. Each typically has "good, better, or best" options for deploying more complicated and valuable solutions, but each can also offer significant value to users by initially delivering the "good" option while not compromising the ability to eventually deliver the "better" and "best" options later.

User Directories and People Search

If SharePoint Server 2010 is being implemented, users will be able to use People Search and Profile pages with relatively little configuration of its out-of-the-box capabilities, and thus deliver a quick and effective company directory. This functionality is generally well-received by employees looking for a better way to find up-to-date information.

Delivering this solution requires a few components to be in place. The search service needs to be configured and running in order to return People Search results. The Profile Synchronization Service needs to be configured to import the information from Active Directory (AD). And finally, Active Directory needs to have current and accurate information.

SharePoint provides the mechanics of an employee directory with a People Search scope, people-specific search results, and a Profile page. The content of the directory is provided by Active Directory. Therefore, having up-to-date information in AD is very important. One of the fields important to SharePoint functionality but commonly *not* ready for prime time is the Manager field. This field enables the organizational hierarchy to be displayed and navigated via a couple of Web Parts on the Profile page.

With these components in place, SharePoint provides a solid People Search capability that most organizations don't have available. Taking the solution further into the "better" and "best" solutions may include a number of options and upgrades:

➤ Adding additional profile properties or details to the import from AD

➤ Adding additional properties to the profile in SharePoint

➤ Allowing employees to add and update selected fields

➤ Importing data from additional systems, usually by either connecting to other systems with the BCS or by pushing additional information into AD to be pulled in via the synchronization

➤ Custom-configuring the search results

General Search

Search in SharePoint offers very powerful functionality straight out of the box. It indexes everything stored inside SharePoint by default and offers several search scopes and configurable Web Parts. Administrators can fairly easily extend these capabilities with additional configuration, delivering lots of user value, as shown in the following:

➤ **Custom search results:** The search results pages can be configured to add, remove, or customize the fields displayed in the search results.

➤ **Additional search refiners:** These can be configured to allow users more options when narrowing down search results using methods similar to common commercial websites.

➤ **Additional properties:** These can be configured for indexing. As additional properties are added to list and library items, they are indexed and available for searching as well as being configured in the search results.

➤ **Best Bets:** These can and should be configured based on what users are searching for, as shown in search reports that administrators have access to.

➤ **Additional content sources and scopes:** These can be added. Content sources outside SharePoint can also be indexed and searched.

Search is one of SharePoint's strong suits and has plenty of capabilities that offer great value to the user, with a variety of effort levels. You can find more information about what can be configured and how it is configured in the search section of this book, Chapters 18, 19, and 20.

Document and File Storage

Documents and files are easily stored in SharePoint as an alternative solution to storing them on a file share or public folder. Document storage in SharePoint 2010 can be as ad hoc as a collaboration or team site and be as structured and controlled as a document or records management system. The difference in effort will vary just as widely, with collaboration sites being created within minutes and records management systems requiring considerable design and planning to create the right way. In either case, the following benefits are notable in the features they offer.

One should also note that the more time spent thoughtfully and deliberately configuring libraries and lists for each specific instance, the more value will be returned to users. It is a classic "good, better, best" example, where the out-of-the-box capabilities meet a broad set of requirements (the "good"), but further activating and configuring the features of the library will deliver the "better" and "best" user experiences.

➤ **Check-out/check-in:** The check-out capabilities allow users to lock files so they are not overwritten by other users.

➤ **Version control:** Turning on version control frees users from worry about the "last person who saves wins" scenario. It also provides more substantive benefits in tracking multiple versions of files.

➤ **Recycle bin:** SharePoint's recycle bin gives users a few levels of comfort that if a document, list item, or entire list are deleted they can be undeleted using a self-service tool within the web user interface.

➤ **Metadata:** Additional properties can be added to items that describe them further and allow for more access via searches, sorting, and filtering.

➤ **Workflows:** Once items are stored in SharePoint, they can be acted upon with automated business processes.

BUILD OR BUY, ON-PREMISE OR HOSTED

SharePoint is more often than not installed on a corporate network. Today that's not the only option available, and a growing number of alternative solutions are available for where a SharePoint implementation may fit organizational requirements. The decision on where to host SharePoint's web platform now becomes part of a wider strategy as well as part of the SharePoint strategy for the organization.

Aside from the selection of where to host, but still part of the larger strategy, decision makers need to determine if they are going to implement multi-tenancy or use a charge-back model in their architecture, because these may affect the server architecture and method of implementation.

On-Site Server Farms

Installing servers in your own environment is the traditional way of implementing SharePoint — using physical or virtualized servers in a local domain and server farm. In the past, on-site installations were slam-dunk solutions and made sense in most situations. Now organizations have some legitimate alternatives with hosted and online offerings.

Within a corporate network are even a few variations. Will all information and scenarios be run off the same SharePoint farm, or will there need to be more than one farm to accommodate all the uses? Many organizations will separate farms based on security needs; a prime factor will be which servers need to have external access enabled.

Decision makers also need to consider whether on-premise servers will be the only model allowed, or if these will be just one of several approaches used in the overall strategy. Some companies will maintain an on-premise intranet site while setting up an external extranet for internal and external users to collaborate on.

Hosted Options

If your organization doesn't want to build and maintain its own server hardware to host SharePoint or manage the software itself, it can choose from a growing number of services to fill the gap.

Hosted options allow your organization to have access to a stable platform without needing to invest in server administrator training, staffing, or maintenance. Users are able to move past the effort to implement the platform and focus on how to best utilize the tool. This option also transfers a significant number of governance issues and topics from the user organization to the hosting company.

Some risks are involved with hosting SharePoint solutions outside the organization. Specifically, company information will be stored on systems outside of the company infrastructure. Though the hosted solution should be a secure system, being outside the network and managed by staff other than internal employees does pose some level of risk that should at least be discussed, understood, and agreed upon by all parties.

Because hosted solutions are generally set up outside the organization's home network, the organization will need to consider integration points with any internal systems that may be required for business or operational reasons. Some limitations may ultimately limit functionality or force a change in existing approaches. Many scenarios can be worked around, but some factors will need to be accounted for.

Hosted Servers

A number of Internet service providers (ISPs) offer SharePoint hosting options. Their services range anywhere from single-site collections to full server farms. These services may be offered on either dedicated or shared servers and on physical or virtualized hardware. The variety of options meets a wide range of needs.

In any case, hosted offerings are aimed at taking hardware, OS, and software platform management off the organization's plate so that it can focus on its business rather than the stability of a platform.

SharePoint Online (Office 365)

Microsoft also has online hosted offerings, though at the time of writing only the SharePoint 2007 version was available. The 2010 version of SharePoint Online was expected shortly. Microsoft SharePoint Online is offered as a part of Office 365, previously known as Business Productivity Online Suite (BPOS). Though similar to on-premise installed products, the SharePoint Online products and SharePoint Server products *are* different. There are two general variations of the online products: Standard and Dedicated. In either case, Microsoft manages the SharePoint server environment so that your organization doesn't need to.

Having Microsoft manage your server has obvious benefits in that it will maintain the patching and other server maintenance. The drawback to the SharePoint Online products is that they don't have full product parity; the features available with a locally installed SharePoint Server aren't the same as the features available with SharePoint Online. Although many of the collaboration and portal features are available, extending SharePoint's reach beyond the software boundaries with features like Business Connectivity Services (BCS) isn't expected to happen.

The differences in features between SharePoint Online and SharePoint Server again stress the importance of knowing during envisioning and planning phases what the organization intends to do with the product. Because SharePoint Online has different capabilities, you need to know what is and isn't required in order to determine if using it is even a possibility.

BEYOND OUT-OF-THE-BOX

Although SharePoint is an enormous product that offers a wide range of features and functionality, users will inevitably reach the limits of its capabilities. Depending on the complexity of your requirements, these boundaries are sometimes reached sooner rather than later. In these circumstances two primary types of solutions are available — using third-party tools and add-ons, or creating your own customizations. Custom development topics are discussed throughout the rest of this book.

Users often want to jump right in with customizations and add-ons to the core SharePoint product. Though this is a great way to explore its capabilities, best practices suggest that organizations new to SharePoint wait a bit before investing time and money on customizations. This waiting period can be used to become comfortable with the platform and better understand when and how custom configurations should be handled, if they are necessary at all.

SharePoint Designer 2010

As described in Chapter 1, SharePoint Designer 2010 (SPD) is a free tool from Microsoft that allows users (usually power users or site administrators) to manage SharePoint sites, pages, and lists. SharePoint Designer has enough capabilities to fill books of its own, but some of the highlights include:

> ➤ **Views:** When out-of-the-box view options can't deliver the view or functionality required, custom views can be created in SPD. SPD views might include conditional formatting, more complex sorting and filtering, or other display options.

➤ **Forms:** The forms created and used by SharePoint lists can be readily extended, edited, and added to by using SPD. Users can create alternate new item forms that display only certain fields to the submitter — a significant enhancement over earlier versions of SharePoint and SPD.

➤ **Workflows:** One of the primary areas of functionality for SharePoint is business process automation or workflows. Though SharePoint makes a handful of workflows available out of the box, users often want more functionality. SPD allows users to create simple workflows based on "for this condition, do this action" that are not available elsewhere.

Third-Party Add-Ons

As with many popular and established platforms, there is a healthy and expanding market for product add-ons. The unofficial message from Microsoft to partners and the marketplace is that where the product has functionality limitations, it expects partners to fill the gap as consumers identify their needs.

The easy and logical area for partners is custom Web Parts — the building blocks of pages. A number of companies offer a general collection of single or bundled Web Part packages that cover a wide variety of uses. Some "better together" products that integrate their solutions with SharePoint commonly offer Web Parts specific to their products.

Workflow is an area with only a few major players. The products offered by these companies fill the gap between what SharePoint Designer offers for workflow capabilities and what you can create with a fully customized solution. They offer more user-friendly interfaces for power users and business analysts to create workflows, while also offering additional conditions and actions to build more complicated processes.

For the IT professional group, a variety of tools and add-ons can be used to better manage the SharePoint environment. Many of these tools are offered by companies with a history for operational software that has expanded their product lines into the SharePoint space. Some functional examples are shown in Table 3-1.

TABLE 3-1: Third-Party Software for SharePoint IT Professionals

CATEGORY	BRIEF DESCRIPTION
Monitoring tools	Where tools in the past have allowed for network, database, and server monitoring, new tools offer SharePoint-specific information such as web application, site collection, and search information.
Backup and recovery	A number of solutions have been on the market for a while that offer server- and database-specific functionality. SharePoint-specific tools have been added to most vendor products for some time, adding SharePoint-specific database actions and site, list, and item capabilities for backup and restore capabilities.

CATEGORY	BRIEF DESCRIPTION
Security management	With the potential complexity of permissions in SharePoint, several companies have produced solutions to view and manage user permissions in a consolidated interface rather than leaving users to dig through the environment manually. These companies also offer tools for adding, removing, and replicating users, which can be handy.
PowerShell cmdlets	PowerShell has become a much more important tool to manage and manipulate the SharePoint 2010 platform. Though there haven't been many commercial offerings, a wide range of cmdlets are available for download, configuration, and use.

Finally, some companies offer additional site and list templates for getting started quickly when building specific solutions. Many of these templates are aligned with specific vertical market types and targeted to specific roles.

SUMMARY

Plenty of good reasons exist to use SharePoint 2010 as a way to enhance how organizations function and do business day to day. This chapter has offered information on *why* your organization might adopt it, and *how* SharePoint would take your way of doing business to the next level. The chapter has also covered ways to measure success in your organization by implementing SharePoint 2010 in the most effective way possible.

With the tools, methods, and approaches described here, you should be able to start matching SharePoint 2010's capabilities with appropriate solutions in your organization. You should be able to understand these prospective SharePoint 2010 solutions and how they come together to shape a consolidated platform strategy. Finally, you should have a variety of methods that can be used to measure the improvements and successes delivered with SharePoint 2010 in your environment.

Now you're prepared to read the remaining chapters of this book to see in much greater detail how the tools Microsoft SharePoint 2010 offers can be used in your organization to make your business and your employees more productive.

PART II
Branding with SharePoint 2010

4

Master Pages

WHAT'S IN THIS CHAPTER?

➤ Why you should brand SharePoint 2010

➤ Defining SharePoint master pages

➤ How working with master pages has changed

➤ What to consider in designing a master page for SharePoint

➤ What is the Ribbon and how do I deal with it?

➤ What tool do I use for branding?

Branding, design, and look and feel are all terms commonly used to describe the way a website appears in a visual format. These terms are often used interchangeably and mean much the same thing. With SharePoint Server 2010, master pages are used to facilitate changes to the visual representation of your sites. But before you get to this chapter's main topic of master pages, it's essential that you understand branding and that we agree on just what it is. Then you can go ahead with determining which method of branding will work best for your SharePoint Server 2010 sites, and finally proceed with the discussion of master pages.

WHAT IS BRANDING?

Whether you call it branding or design, it is all about perception. The design of a site is often developed from a company's brand. Branding is a noun defined as "the promoting of a product or service by identifying it with a particular brand," according to Webster's Dictionary online.

Creating a brand is a method of creating a unique image that is identifiable by the public with a particular company or organization. This brand can be created through many avenues, including the Internet. A brand is composed of images, colors, logos, and fonts that make the viewer recognize the particular company or organization.

Branding is much more than just pretty colors and pictures, it is all about making sure that the total end-user experience from start to finish is exceptional. Branding involves a plan for colors, images, content, navigation, and functionality of your site whether it is an intranet, extranet, or public-facing site.

A good branding design will help you connect to your target prospects emotionally. This emotional response will help either increase or decrease your end-user adoption rates. Responses come from the first and last impressions of a SharePoint site; it all boils down to whether it looks nice and helps users achieve their goals.

Branding can also help you motivate the user and cement user loyalty. The end goal of branding is to help promote the company brand while also solving business problems for the company.

If you can achieve each of these branding goals, you will have worked to design and create sites that people will continue to use, thus increasing your end-user adoption.

Why Do You Need to Brand SharePoint?

You may be asking why you need to create branding for SharePoint. Just as with traditional branding, you should look to brand SharePoint to create a positive impression on your end users. Branding should have a positive effect on the entire experience so that users will continue to use the site.

The branding of SharePoint can be either simple or complex depending on your needs. You can take a brand design for SharePoint in many directions — you can change the logo and colors of the site or you can do a complete branding redesign. You use the same methods to make all these changes to the design of SharePoint. There are many methods to brand SharePoint, the first and most powerful of which is branding SharePoint using the master page.

Why Brand Using SharePoint Master Pages?

Using master pages in your branding design offers many advantages. Master pages provide designers and developers with a single platform to control many common elements like headers, footers, search, and navigation. Having these elements controlled on one page lets you cut down on the development and design overhead when a change is needed.

When working with SharePoint Server 2010, you'll use master pages to make significant layout changes to the core elements of the SharePoint site. The master page in SharePoint is the basic building block for all the main elements of your site. SharePoint master pages enable you to make changes to the navigation elements and many other out-of-the-box elements as well as add custom design components to your site.

The SharePoint master page combined with the page layout are the two main components for how a page is displayed. The master page controls the components that are standard on all pages, and the page layouts control the placement of the information on the page that is edited at a page level.

SharePoint master pages are similar to ASP.NET master pages, but with a few differences. For example, the biggest difference between a SharePoint master page and an ASP.NET master page is that you cannot nest SharePoint master pages.

However, SharePoint master pages do contain content placeholders that are used to control the placement of additional elements throughout your site. This functionality is similar to a standard .NET master page. When you customize SharePoint master pages you should be careful not to remove any of the standard content placeholders, because these may be needed for some of the SharePoint 2010 functionality.

WHAT'S NEW WITH SHAREPOINT SERVER 2010 MASTER PAGES?

In the 2007 version of Microsoft Office SharePoint Server, the master pages were often used to change the branding of a site. This has not changed in the 2010 version; you still use master pages to change the design of sites. However, there have been many changes to the master pages between the two versions. This section describes in detail the highlights of the changes to master pages and how these will affect your design.

Tables Are Out and Dynamic Positioning Is In

One of the biggest changes SharePoint Server 2010 has made to the functionality in its master pages is the move from table-based layouts to dynamic positioning.

Dynamic positioning is the ability to use CSS to position elements on the site instead of the absolute positioning used with HTML table-based layout designs.

What makes dynamic positioning so special? When working as a designer or developer with a website, whether it is an intranet or a public-facing one, you will need to be concerned with cross-browser compatibility. This is one place where working with dynamic positioning can be helpful. Having your elements positioned on a page based on a dynamic grid allows you the freedom of worry-free positioning in the Microsoft-supported browsers for SharePoint 2010.

What the Changes Mean for Your Branding Plans

With the addition of the Ribbon control in SharePoint 2010, you now have to keep some additional considerations in mind when it comes to your branding designs for sites. One item you'll need to think about is what elements will be hidden by the Ribbon control. You also need to consider how you want the Ribbon to appear on the page, either in a fixed position or with a scroll bar.

Another change in SharePoint 2010 is the addition of modal windows to the functionality of sites. The modal window functionality was put in place to replace the post-back functions in the previous sites. You no longer have to navigate away from a page to make changes or additions to it. These modal windows are created and controlled using JavaScript. Figure 4-1 shows the dialog boxes/modal windows as they function out of the box with SharePoint 2010.

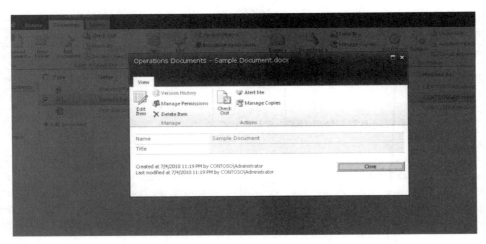

FIGURE 4-1

These pop-up dialog boxes or modal windows will display your full master-page branding. So in your branding plans you must make a decision as to whether you want this behavior to occur or if you need to make a change so that dialog boxes do not display the full master-page customizations.

One of the most frequent questions about SharePoint when working with large groups of people involves compliance. SharePoint Server 2010 addresses these issues. It now has more added features for compliance, and the change to DIV-based/CSS-based formatting of the master page in SharePoint 2010 is the biggest advantage for compliance.

Another consideration for working with SharePoint 2010 is the browsers supported for your sites. In the past these were supported only for Internet Explorer, which affected how you dealt with the document types (doctypes) in the header of the master page. With the out-of-the-box master pages in SharePoint 2010, you're now given a cross-browser–compliant doctype to work with right away.

In SharePoint Server 2010 you can also set and use one master page for all your pages throughout your sites. You no longer have to edit or find multiple master pages to enforce consistent branding throughout the application. This is a giant change from past versions of SharePoint.

How to Apply Them: Central Administration and Site Settings

How you apply master pages in SharePoint 2010 has not changed much from previous versions of SharePoint. The most often used method of changing a master page is using the Site Settings menu. You can see this method for applying master pages in Figure 4-2.

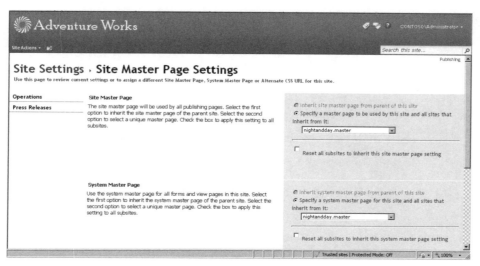

FIGURE 4-2

For those who need a more stringent master page change, the best option is to create a custom-coded feature that will programmatically change the master page called at run time for the page. This feature will need to be coded and installed in Central Administration. Once this feature has been installed it can be activated or deactivated to change the master page in the SharePoint 2010 site.

SIMPLE.MASTER

In the latest version of SharePoint, the base master page used for many pages is the simplev4.master page file. Seven pages in SharePoint 2010 including SharePoint Foundation use this master page.

Using the Simple.Master Page

This simplev4.master page file is used by SharePoint 2010 to render some specific pages. Certain pages within SharePoint need to have a failover method of display if the customizations on the pages have gotten corrupted. The following seven pages utilize the simple.master page for rendering without customizations or if the customizations cause errors during run time. You can see a sample of one of these pages in Figure 4-3.

➤ Login.aspx

➤ SignOut.aspx

➤ Error.aspx

➤ ReqAcc.aspx

➤ Confirmation.aspx

➤ WebDeleted.aspx

➤ AccessDenied.aspx

FIGURE 4-3

How to Make Changes to the Simple.Master

The simplev4.master page can be customized for each of the seven pages listed earlier. To customize a page you will need to make a replacement page that will be stored in the _layouts directory on the server. This customized page or even customized pages should be stored on the server in your own custom folder under the _layouts directory.

You can customize these pages by creating a feature that calls the UpdateMappedPage (SPWebApplication.SPCustomPage, String) function that was added to the SPWebApplication object to map the original simple page and the replacement page.

This customized SPWebApplication.SPCustomPage object will define the page that should be replaced by the custom page. You can determine the mapping by calling the SPWebApplication .GetMappedPage function in the SharePoint 2010 object model. You can also use a null setting to remove an alternate mapping by calling the same function.

DYNAMIC MASTER PAGES

Within SharePoint 2010 the document library that houses all page layouts and master pages is called the Master Page and Page Layout gallery. This gallery is a special document library created and located at the top level site for a site collection. This library supports versioning and workflows and allows you to use these features when it comes to any custom master pages or page layouts that you create and customize for your SharePoint 2010 implementation. The Master Page and Page Layout gallery is shown in Figure 4-4.

FIGURE 4-4

The exception to this master-page location is the simplev4.master page discussed in the previous section.

What Are the Out-of-the-Box Dynamic Master Pages?

SharePoint Server 2010 is delivered with two out-of-the-box dynamic/publishing master pages. The difference in the master pages comes in the design of the pages. The form is different in the two, but the function is the same.

In a publishing site, you can select your master page using the Site Actions menu. In the Site Settings menu you will find a Look and Feel section where you can change the master page of your site.

You can see an example site with the Night and Day master page applied to it in Figure 4-5.

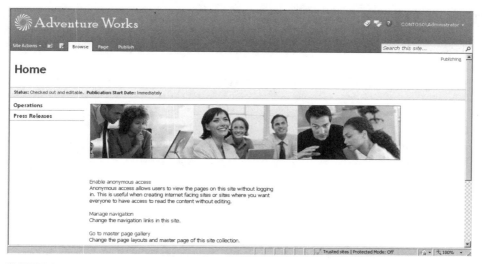

FIGURE 4-5

This Night and Day master page, as applied to a basic publishing site, illustrates a few things that are different from what you're used to from SharePoint 2007 and even the other master pages in SharePoint 2010. When you are using the Night and Day master page file in your site you'll notice that there's no top navigation bar on this type of page. The navigation on this page type has moved to the location where the quick launch is typically located.

You can see an example of the v4.master page as applied to a SharePoint Server 2010 site displayed in Figure 4-6.

FIGURE 4-6

The v4.master page file is the closest to the default.master page you're used to from Microsoft Office SharePoint 2007. This master page file, though different to accommodate the addition of the Ribbon, recalls features from past versions of SharePoint with the top navigation bar firmly at the top of the page.

Working with Dynamic Master Pages to Change the Look of SharePoint

 The following walk-through and sections assume that the SharePoint Server 2010 site you are using is a publishing site.

In SharePoint Server 2010, you will often want to move things around on the page to change the positioning of the native SharePoint controls. To do this in the new version of SharePoint master pages, you need to be aware of the `<div>` tags and how these work to create a structure for the controls.

A `<div>` tag is an element that defines a division or section in an HTML document. It is also most often used with CSS to lay out a web page. So what does this mean for SharePoint master pages? It means that you now have more flexibility to move items around and make more changes to the structure of your sites.

One of the items that a lot of people will be looking to modify in SharePoint is the appearance of all the controls inside the Ribbon. You can also use this method on any of the controls on the SharePoint master pages. An example of this would be moving around the search control. The code for this control is:

```
<div class="s4-notdlg" style="float: right;">
<asp:ContentPlaceHolder
 id="PlaceHolderSearchArea" runat="server">
<SharePoint:DelegateControl runat="server"
 ControlId="SmallSearchInputBox"
 Version="4"/>
     </asp:ContentPlaceHolder>
</div>
```

Once you have identified this `<div>`, you can now begin to dissect it and move it around on the page with the assurance that this control will stay intact. In examining the code for this particular control you will notice that it has the `s4-notdlg` class assigned to it. This class is covered in the CSS chapter that follows in this section. You will also notice that there is a Content Placeholder and a Delegate control that makes this Search control work.

By keeping these items together you can add in additional classes to style the control as well as move it around on the master page to position it exactly where you want it. Don't be afraid to create your own `<div>` tags in the master page document to contain custom components that you would like to include in your sites.

One of the most common items that's changed when branding SharePoint using a master page is the addition of a reference to a custom CSS file. In the past, when rendering a SharePoint site, you could not control the order in which your custom CSS file was called by the object model. Now when you add in a call to a custom style sheet in the head tag of your master page you can specify the order in which to call this CSS file. You will notice the addition of an `After` tag in our reference. The following code is set up to call after the last out-of-the-box CSS file.

To reference your custom CSS style sheet you should use the following:

```
<SharePoint:CssRegistration name="/SiteAssets/yourfilename.css"
After="corev4.css" runat="server"/>
```

For additional information on master pages and how they are structured, you can check out the following links that will give you more insight into how the out-of-the-box pages are structured. They will also give you a great start to customizing your own master-page files.

http://startermasterpages.codeplex.com/

http://code.msdn.microsoft.com/odcSP14StarterMaster/Release/ProjectReleases
.aspx?ReleaseId=3861

APPLICATION.MASTER PAGE

In previous versions of SharePoint it was not easy to change the appearance of the _layouts pages for your sites. These pages in SharePoint Server 2007 use the application.master page file. This file is the same page that is used to control Central Administration and also how it looks. It's easier to change this now than it was in the past.

The way master pages interact with application pages has changed in SharePoint Server 2010. This change now allows the setting of a customized site master page by modifying the `DynamicMasterPageFile` attribute. This feature is also available in the SharePoint 2010 Foundation space.

Changing the Application.Master Page

You will want to change the application.master page so you can keep a consistent master-page scheme throughout your sites.

By altering the `DynamicMasterPageFile` attribute you can reference any custom master page other than the default application.master page. When you create a change feature for your SharePoint Server 2010 branding, you will need to make sure you are applying your custom master page to both the site master pages and the system master pages. You now have the ability to apply the same master page to both by changing a setting at the web-application level. In Figure 4-7 you can see the Web Application Setting in Central Administration to allow you to let pages in the _layouts folder reference the site master page instead of the system master page.

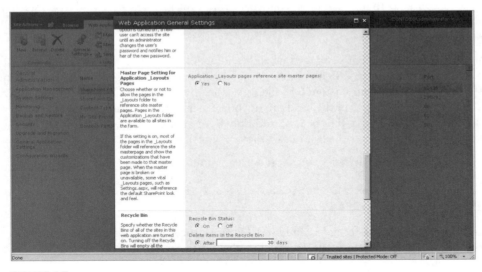

FIGURE 4-7

Changes to the Application.Master Page

With the ability to change what master page the application pages use also comes the possibility of having corrupt files that could cause an application page to fail to load. If this were to occur it would open administrators to limited functionality.

SharePoint Foundation 2010 has added safeguards in an attempt to prevent a loss of functionality on these pages due to errors in the custom master-page files. If an error occurs when loading an application page using the custom dynamic application master-page file, a control is triggered that loads the pages using a safe master page in the _layouts folder of the server instead. The following list shows the application pages that use this particular safeguard control. Figure 4-8 shows the Recycle Bin page, which is one of the pages that will default to the safe master page.

- ➤ AccessDenied.aspx

- ➤ MngSiteAdmin.aspx

- ➤ People.aspx

- ➤ RecycleBin.aspx

- ➤ ReGhost.aspx

- ➤ ReqAcc.aspx

- ➤ Settings.aspx

- ➤ UserDisp.aspx

- ➤ ViewLsts.aspx

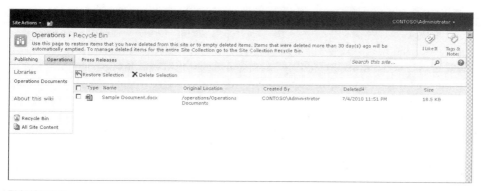

FIGURE 4-8

DESIGNING WITH THE SHAREPOINT RIBBON

With the addition of the Ribbon to the interface of SharePoint Server 2010, you have additional considerations when it comes to your branding designs. The Ribbon takes up some real estate on the page, making planning your interface even more important. These considerations should also include any customizations to the items inside the Ribbon. Understanding the Ribbon and just how far you can take it past the out-of-the-box Ribbon behavior and appearance will help make your planning easier.

Planning Your Branding Customizations for the Ribbon

Although SharePoint Server 2010 now includes the Ribbon to give users additional functionality, there is one drawback to the addition of the theme when it comes to branding SharePoint 2010. You now have a menu that takes up additional space on the page.

You will need to plan for this usage of space by the Ribbon menu when planning to change the look of SharePoint. The Ribbon expands and contracts on the page as needed, so it will not always exist in its fully expanded state on your page. You can see in Figure 4-9 how the Ribbon appears when fully expanded in a document library within the browser.

FIGURE 4-9

The out-of-the-box master pages also are set so that the page will scroll below the Ribbon. You can modify this functionality when working with the SharePoint master pages in 2010.

Another consideration when it comes to the Ribbon in SharePoint 2010 is what elements of the Ribbon you might want to customize by adding custom elements and options or hiding/disabling elements and options. Making edits to the elements and options that are displayed in the Ribbon requires a feature package consisting of your custom developed code. The custom code will involve making edits to the elements.xml file of your solution to add in your feature. However, you can take this customization as far as you like, even adding in your own tabs and controls on those tabs.

Customizing the Ribbon with Branding

Now that you understand how the Ribbon is set to work when you install SharePoint Server 2010 and create your web application, let's examine different methods and options for customizing the look and feel of the Ribbon in the master page.

The first option that you need to explore is how to move the Ribbon. The Ribbon is controlled by a series of <div> tags, so you'll need to select all the controls on the master page in order to move this feature to another location on the master page. In the following long code snippet, you see a portion of the <div> that contains the Ribbon controls.

```
<div id="s4-ribbonrow" class="s4-pr s4-ribbonrowhidetitle">
        <div id="s4-ribboncont">
                <SharePoint:SPRibbon
                        runat="server"
                        PlaceholderElementId="RibbonContainer"
                        CssFile="">
                <SharePoint:SPRibbonPeripheralContent runat="server"
                        Location="TabRowLeft"                      CssClass="ms-
siteactionscontainer s4-notdlg">
        <span class="ms-siteactionsmenu" id="siteactiontd">
                <SharePoint:SiteActions runat="server"
                 accesskey="<%$Resources:wss,tb_SiteActions_AK%>"
                 id="SiteActionsMenuMain"PrefixHtml=""
                 SuffixHtml=""
                 MenuNotVisibleHtml=" ">
                <CustomTemplate>
                    <SharePoint:FeatureMenuTemplate runat="server"
                        FeatureScope="Site"
                        Location="Microsoft.SharePoint.StandardMenu"
                        GroupId="SiteActions"
                        UseShortId="true">
                    <SharePoint:MenuItemTemplate runat="server"
                        id="MenuItem_EditPage"
                        Text="<%$Resources:wss,siteactions_editpage%>"

Description="<%$Resources:wss,siteactions_editpagedescriptionv4%>"
                        ImageUrl="/_layouts/images/ActionsEditPage.png"
                        MenuGroupId="100"
                        Sequence="110"

ClientOnClickNavigateUrl="javascript:ChangeLayoutMode(false);" />
                    <SharePoint:MenuItemTemplate runat="server"
                        id="MenuItem_TakeOffline"
                        Text="<%$Resources:wss,siteactions_takeoffline%>"

Description="<%$Resources:wss,siteactions_takeofflinedescription%>"
                        ImageUrl="/_layouts/images/connecttospworkspace32.png"
                        MenuGroupId="100"
                        Sequence="120"/>
                    <SharePoint:MenuItemTemplate runat="server"
                        id="MenuItem_CreatePage"
                        Text="<%$Resources:wss,siteactions_createpage%>"

Description="<%$Resources:wss,siteactions_createpagedesc%>"
                        ImageUrl="/_layouts/images/NewContentPageHH.png"
                        MenuGroupId="200"
                        Sequence="210"
                        UseShortId="true"
                        ClientOnClickScriptContainingPrefixedUrl="if
                        (LaunchCreateHandler('Page')) {

OpenCreateWebPageDialog('~site/_layouts/createwebpage.aspx') }"
                        PermissionsString="AddListItems, EditListItems"
                        PermissionMode="All" />
```

```
                    <SharePoint:MenuItemTemplate runat="server"
                        id="MenuItem_CreateDocLib"
                        Text="<%$Resources:wss,siteactions_createdoclib%>"

    Description="<%$Resources:wss,siteactions_createdoclibdesc%>"
                        ImageUrl="/_layouts/images/NewDocLibHH.png"
                        MenuGroupId="200"
                        Sequence="220"
                        UseShortId="true"
                        ClientOnClickScriptContainingPrefixedUrl="if
                        (LaunchCreateHandler('DocLib')) {
                        GoToPage('~site/_layouts/new.aspx?FeatureId={00bfea71-
                            e717-4e80-
                        aa17-d0c71b360101}&amp;ListTemplate=101') }"
                        PermissionsString="ManageLists"
                        PermissionMode="Any"
                        VisibilityFeatureId="00BFEA71-E717-4E80-AA17-
                            D0C71B360101" />
                    <SharePoint:MenuItemTemplate runat="server"
                        id="MenuItem_CreateSite"
                        Text="<%$Resources:wss,siteactions_createsite%>"

    Description="<%$Resources:wss,siteactions_createsitedesc%>"
                        ImageUrl="/_layouts/images/newweb32.png"
                        MenuGroupId="200"
                        Sequence="230"
                        UseShortId="true"
                        ClientOnClickScriptContainingPrefixedUrl="if
                        (LaunchCreateHandler('Site')) {
                        STSNavigate('~site/_layouts/newsbweb.aspx') }"
                        PermissionsString="ManageSubwebs,ViewFormPages"
                        PermissionMode="All" />
                    <SharePoint:MenuItemTemplate runat="server"
                        id="MenuItem_Create"
                        Text="<%$Resources:wss,siteactions_create%>"
                        Description="<%$Resources:wss,siteactions_createdesc%>"
                        MenuGroupId="200"
                        Sequence="240"
                        UseShortId="true"
                        ClientOnClickScriptContainingPrefixedUrl="if
                        (LaunchCreateHandler('All')) {
                        STSNavigate('~site/_layouts/create.aspx') }"
                        PermissionsString="ManageLists, ManageSubwebs"
                        PermissionMode="Any" />
                    <SharePoint:MenuItemTemplate runat="server"
                        id="MenuItem_ViewAllSiteContents"
                        Text="<%$Resources:wss,quiklnch_allcontent%>"

    Description="<%$Resources:wss,siteactions_allcontentdescription%>"
                        ImageUrl="/_layouts/images/allcontent32.png"
                        MenuGroupId="300"
                        Sequence="302"
                        UseShortId="true"
                        ClientOnClickNavigateUrl="~site/_layouts/viewlsts.aspx"
                        PermissionsString="ViewFormPages"
                        PermissionMode="Any" />
```

```
            <SharePoint:MenuItemTemplate runat="server"
                id="MenuItem_EditSite"
                Text="<%$Resources:wss,siteactions_editsite%>"

Description="<%$Resources:wss,siteactions_editsitedescription%>"
                ImageUrl="/_layouts/images/SharePointDesigner32.png"
                MenuGroupId="300"
                Sequence="304"
                UseShortId="true"

ClientOnClickScriptContainingPrefixedUrl="EditInSPD('~site/',true);"
                PermissionsString="AddAndCustomizePages"
                PermissionMode="Any"/>
            <SharePoint:MenuItemTemplate runat="server"
                id="MenuItem_SitePermissions"
                Text="<%$Resources:wss,people_sitepermissions%>"
                Description="<%$Resources:wss,siteactions_
                sitepermissiondescriptionv4%>"
                ImageUrl="/_layouts/images/Permissions32.png"
                MenuGroupId="300"
                Sequence="310"
                UseShortId="true"
                ClientOnClickNavigateUrl="~site/_layouts/user.aspx"
                PermissionsString="EnumeratePermissions"
                PermissionMode="Any" />
            <SharePoint:MenuItemTemplate runat="server"
                id="MenuItem_Settings"
                Text="<%$Resources:wss,settings_pagetitle%>"
                Description="<%$Resources:wss,siteactions_
                sitesettingsdescriptionv4%>"
                ImageUrl="/_layouts/images/settingsIcon.png"
                MenuGroupId="300"
                Sequence="320"
                UseShortId="true"
                ClientOnClickNavigateUrl="~site/_layouts/settings.aspx"

PermissionsString="EnumeratePermissions,ManageWeb,ManageSubwebs,
                AddAndCustomizePages,ApplyThemeAndBorder,ManageAlerts,
                ManageLists,ViewUsageData"
                PermissionMode="Any" />
            <SharePoint:MenuItemTemplate runat="server"
                id="MenuItem_CommitNewUI"
                Text="<%$Resources:wss,siteactions_commitnewui%>"

Description="<%$Resources:wss,siteactions_commitnewuidescription%>"
                ImageUrl="/_layouts/images/visualupgradehh.png"
                MenuGroupId="300"
                Sequence="330"
                UseShortId="true"
                ClientOnClickScriptContainingPrefixedUrl="GoToPage
                ('~site/_layouts/prjsetng.aspx')"
                PermissionsString="ManageWeb"
                PermissionMode="Any"
                ShowOnlyIfUIVersionConfigurationEnabled="true" />
            </SharePoint:FeatureMenuTemplate>
          </CustomTemplate>
      </SharePoint:SiteActions></span>
```

```
<!-- global navigation dhtml popout menu -->
<asp:ContentPlaceHolder id="PlaceHolderGlobalNavigation" runat="server">
    <SharePoint:PopoutMenu runat="server" ID="GlobalBreadCrumbNavPopout"
        IconUrl="/_layouts/images/fgimg.png"
        IconAlt="<%$Resources:wss,master_breadcrumbIconAlt%>"
        IconOffsetX=0
        IconOffsetY=112
        IconWidth=16
        IconHeight=16
        AnchorCss="s4-breadcrumb-anchor"
        AnchorOpenCss="s4-breadcrumb-anchor-open"
        MenuCss="s4-breadcrumb-menu">
    <div class="s4-breadcrumb-top">
        <asp:Label runat="server" CssClass="s4-breadcrumb-header"
            Text="<%$Resources:wss,master_breadcrumbHeader%>" />
    </div>
        <asp:ContentPlaceHolder id="PlaceHolderTitleBreadcrumb" runat="server">
            <SharePoint:ListSiteMapPath runat="server"
                SiteMapProviders="SPSiteMapProvider,SPContentMapProvider"
                RenderCurrentNodeAsLink="false"
                PathSeparator=""
                CssClass="s4-breadcrumb"
                NodeStyle-CssClass="s4-breadcrumbNode"
                CurrentNodeStyle-CssClass="s4-breadcrumbCurrentNode"
                RootNodeStyle-CssClass="s4-breadcrumbRootNode"
                NodeImageOffsetX=0
                NodeImageOffsetY=353
                NodeImageWidth=16
                NodeImageHeight=16
                NodeImageUrl="/_layouts/images/fgimg.png"
                RTLNodeImageOffsetX=0
                RTLNodeImageOffsetY=376
                RTLNodeImageWidth=16
                RTLNodeImageHeight=16
                RTLNodeImageUrl="/_layouts/images/fgimg.png"
                HideInteriorRootNodes="true"
                SkipLinkText="" />
        </asp:ContentPlaceHolder>
        </SharePoint:PopoutMenu>
        </asp:ContentPlaceHolder>
    <SharePoint:PageStateActionButton id="PageStateActionButton" runat="server"\
        Visible="false" /></SharePoint:SPRibbonPeripheralContent>
    <SharePoint:SPRibbonPeripheralContent
        runat="server"
        Location="TabRowRight"
        ID="RibbonTabRowRight"
        CssClass="s4-trc-container s4-notdlg">
    <SharePoint:DelegateControl runat="server" ID="GlobalDelegate0"
        ControlId="GlobalSiteLink0" />
            <div class="s4-trc-container-menu">
                <div>
                    <wssuc:Welcome id="IdWelcome" runat="server"
                        EnableViewState="false">
                    </wssuc:Welcome>
                    <wssuc:MUISelector ID="IdMuiSelector" runat="server"/>
                </div>
            </div>
```

```
<SharePoint:DelegateControl ControlId="GlobalSiteLink2" ID="GlobalDelegate2"
    Scope="Farm" runat="server" />
<span>
    <span class="s4-devdashboard">
        <Sharepoint:DeveloperDashboardLauncher
            ID="DeveloperDashboardLauncher"
            NavigateUrl="javascript:ToggleDeveloperDashboard()"
            runat="server"
            ImageUrl="/_layouts/images/fgimg.png"
            Text="<%$Resources:wss,multipages_launchdevdashalt_text%>"
            OffsetX=0
            OffsetY=222
            Height=16
            Width=16 />
    </span>
</span>
</SharePoint:SPRibbonPeripheralContent>
</SharePoint:SPRibbon>
</div>
```

You can make many changes to the Ribbon to enable additional functionality for your users. The main thing you might want to change with the Ribbon is its position on the page. In the out-of-the-box master pages, the Ribbon is pinned to the top of the browser window and does not move when you scroll the content. You can make changes by breaking apart the individual controls of the Ribbon code and determining how you want those to appear and function.

TOOLS FOR WORKING WITH SHAREPOINT MASTER PAGES

You can work with SharePoint Server 2010 master pages in many ways, and you should use the tool that you're most comfortable with. The preferred software programs for working with SharePoint to customize your master pages are SharePoint Designer or Visual Studio. Which one you choose is up to you. This section examines the major differences in working with the two tools on your master pages for SharePoint 2010, and how you can work with both of them to deploy your solutions.

SharePoint Designer

SharePoint Designer 2010 is the program that many people use to work with the master page to make customizations. Using this software you will gain the added features for working with SharePoint Server 2010. These features allow you to choose a method of working that best suits your level of knowledge and comfort.

In this software you have the options of working with SharePoint master pages using a What You See Is What You Get (WYSIWYG) method. The visual editing of a SharePoint master page allows people who are unfamiliar with .NET master-page code construction to perform successful edits to their site.

As in many web-editing software programs, with SharePoint Designer 2010 you are also able to select from three different view options: Code, Design, or Split View. These options allow you to customize your SharePoint 2010 editing experience. In Figure 4-10 you can see the master page opened in Split View edit mode in SharePoint Designer 2010.

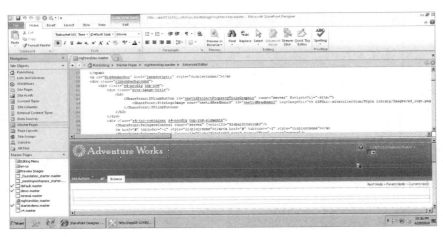

FIGURE 4-10

Other built-in enhancements are available in the interface for using SharePoint Designer 2010 to edit the SharePoint Server 2010 master page. You can work more easily with content placeholders that are native to SharePoint Server 2010. The toolbars and dialog boxes in SharePoint Designer 2010 are set up to provide you with an easy-to-use environment for customizing master pages. In Figure 4-11 you can see the master-page edit Ribbon for working with master pages in SharePoint Designer 2010.

FIGURE 4-11

SharePoint Designer 2010 has added enhanced information panels for working with SharePoint 2010 files. Some of these panels are shown in Figure 4-12, including the version history of your page and the permissions for the page; both will make managing changes easier.

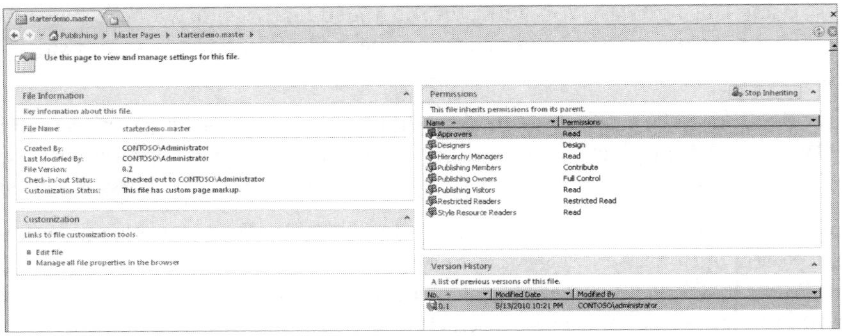

FIGURE 4-12

From this window you can get a quick view of the file properties as well as versions of any of your master-page files. From this page/panel you are able to edit the file, go back to a previous version, and even view the people who have permissions on the file.

Another modification to the SharePoint Designer 2010 experience is the change in the file structure window. In the past you saw only the file structure in the _layouts directory; now you have a list broken down by category, although you can still use the traditional file structure that you're used to. This new category structure makes it easy for you to find the type of file you're looking for. It also introduces the new Site Assets category of file type. This category provides an easy library structure to store and manage image files as well as custom CSS files that are created for your site.

The master pages are also clearly identified and are now separated from the other .aspx files that were in the previous views in SharePoint 2007. This allows you to get a quick and easy view of what modifications and customizations have occurred with a SharePoint 2010 site. You can see the new file structure layout in SharePoint Designer 2010 in Figure 4-13.

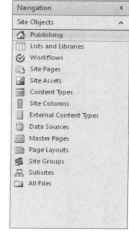

FIGURE 4-13

Visual Studio

The second option for working with master pages is Visual Studio 2010. This is not the tool most people prefer for working with master pages; it has some challenges in handling the SharePoint-specific controls. The way that Visual Studio performs when working with SharePoint master page files is a code-only view. In order to use Visual Studio to perform edits to the master page file, you will need to work in code view and open the file in the Master Page Editor (Default) mode to gain the ability to expand and collapse the code into sections.

Despite the addition of IntelliSense for writing and making code modifications to SharePoint 2010 master pages, you do not have the ability to view the master page in Design or Split View. This makes seeing your changes as you make them more difficult.

Despite its drawbacks for working with SharePoint 2010 master pages in Visual Studio for the non-developers, it is still the preferred tool for creating the appropriate solution packages to deploy your branding to your sites.

Solution Packages

When deploying your customizations to a SharePoint site, you should use a solution package as the method of implementation and deployment. A solution package is a group of files that are deployed as a feature to the SharePoint server.

The advantages to using a solution package come mostly in the administration and management of customizations. Deploying your customizations as a feature allows this code to be treated as managed code. In the past with other versions of SharePoint, you had to use Visual Studio combined with a CodePlex project to build your solution packages. And as a designer you were often taking your code from SharePoint Designer and moving it into Visual Studio or passing it off to a developer to take into Visual Studio to package.

With SharePoint Designer 2010 and Visual Studio 2010, the ability to easily create solution packages is now built in. You can also build a solution package in SharePoint Designer 2010 and move it into Visual Studio 2010 to add additional functionality.

Creating a solution in SharePoint Designer begins with creating your custom branding elements in SharePoint Designer 2010 in a development environment. Select the site and then use the Save as Template option, as highlighted in Figure 4-14.

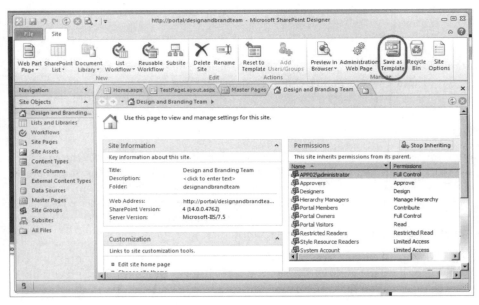

FIGURE 4-14

Once you have performed this action you'll be prompted to create a template name and description. By saving the site as a template, you will be creating a solution package. This solution package or .wsp file will get saved into the Solution gallery for your site. Once the solution has been placed into the gallery as shown in Figure 4-15, you will need to deactivate the solution and save the .wsp file to a location that you can access from Visual Studio 2010.

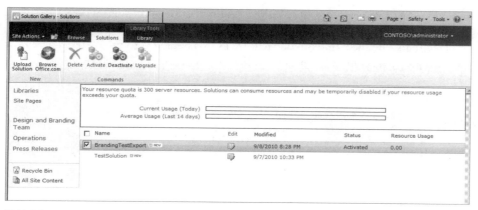

FIGURE 4-15

By saving the .wsp file from the SharePoint 2010 Solution gallery for your site, you will be able to take this branding feature into Visual Studio 2010 and perform any additional changes to the solution before you deploy this solution to your SharePoint Server 2010 implementation. To perform these actions you will first need to import the solution as created by SharePoint Designer 2010 into Visual Studio 2010. Start Visual Studio 2010 and create a new project by selecting New Project as shown in Figure 4-16.

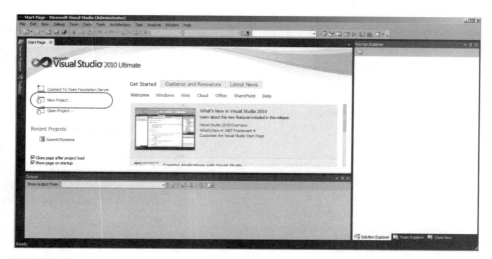

FIGURE 4-16

Next, select SharePoint 2010 from the list of Installed Templates. Once the SharePoint 2010 templates have loaded, select the Import Solution Package option and give the Visual Studio solution a name. This name will also be the name of your feature as it is deployed to your sites. You can see the options for creating a SharePoint 2010 project in Figure 4-17.

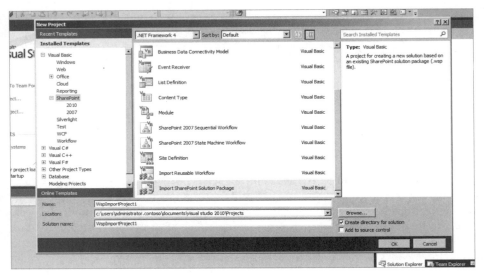

FIGURE 4-17

Once the solution has been imported into Visual Studio, you will be able to see the components and modules of the solution. You will then need to determine whether you want to keep the structure that SharePoint Designer 2010 created for the solution or take it a couple steps further and create a new solution using these files. You can see the file structure, as the solution was created in SharePoint Designer 2010 for the solution package, in Figure 4-18.

The best practice for deploying branding customizations, including your master pages, to SharePoint Server 2010 is to do this as a solution package. Determining what options and what level (web application, site collection, or site) you would like this feature to activate will be determined by the solution and the elements.xml file. Another added bonus for deploying branding in a solution is that it makes troubleshooting issues easier and reduces human error in updating different sites/servers.

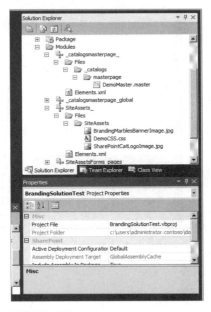

FIGURE 4-18

UPGRADE CONSIDERATIONS FOR 2007 MASTER PAGES

Although this chapter covered a lot of changes to the branding functions of SharePoint 2010 master pages, you may be wondering what you would do to upgrade any customizations that you created for branding in a Microsoft SharePoint Server 2007 site. The 2010 sites include an option for using a `Visual Upgrade` method. This will allow you to have an upgraded backend of SharePoint 2010 while still using the branding from 2007.

You can use the options at site level once the visual upgrade option has been selected by your administrator at the migration and configuration period. After the visual upgrade has been selected, you can modify which sites are using the 2007 User Interface (UI) or the 2010 UI in Site Settings. When you are ready to upgrade you can apply the 2010 UI easily through the Visual Upgrade screen in the Site Settings menu, as shown in Figure 4-19.

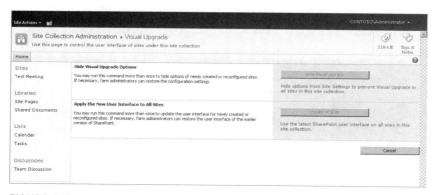

FIGURE 4-19

SUMMARY

Working with a master-page file to make customizations to your SharePoint Server 2010 site is now more of a necessity than a choice. There are more items to consider for your branding of SharePoint Server 2010. We now have to decide how to include and customize the Ribbon.

Now that it is easier to apply our custom master pages we must plan accordingly for all the controls and also how we will deploy these customizations to our SharePoint Server 2010 implementations. This can be achieved by deploying these customizations in solution packages.

You will also want to choose the tool for working with SharePoint 2010 master pages that suits your skill level the best. If you are used to working with code only, Visual Studio could be the tool for you. If you need a little more guidance and assistance for creating your customizations SharePoint Designer 2010 might be the tool you choose to work with.

There are also other methods for changing the look of SharePoint Server 2010 that will be covered in the following two chapters. This will include the modification of the SharePoint theme and how to make changes to your CSS files and get them to be included in your site using a master page.

5

SharePoint Themes

WHAT'S IN THIS CHAPTER?

➤ Themes are not what they used to be

➤ Creating themes using Office applications

➤ Where do themes get stored?

➤ Exactly what gets changed with a theme?

What exactly are SharePoint themes, and what can they do for your branding and design schema? SharePoint themes are a basic method of changing the colors and fonts of your SharePoint sites without knowing any code at all. This method will not change or affect any of the positioning of items on your site; it will only change the colors and fonts used within the site.

In the past, SharePoint themes required the creator to know how to work with CSS and where to store the theme files in the web server properly in order for them to work. In SharePoint Server 2010 the way themes work has completely changed. Now there is a new theme engine, and the functionality of themes has been transformed.

SHAREPOINT THEMES AND BRANDING

How do themes apply to branding? They are now a method that end users can employ to develop their own branding for their sites. The theme engine has changed to become more familiar to users if they have used previous versions of PowerPoint. These new themes are easier to create but not as powerful as a custom CSS file or custom master page when it comes to branding and design for SharePoint Server 2010. It is a basic method for simply changing the color scheme of your site.

Changes to SharePoint Themes

The way themes worked in the past made it more difficult to use them for different sites to differentiate different items. With the changes to the Theme engine and the power to create and modify themes, more people can now create their own themes for use in sites.

Nevertheless, you still need to make informed decisions about when to create custom themes and how they are applied across sites. Allowing free-for-all theme creation will be a great asset in places like My Site, but for your corporate intranet it may make your sites difficult for your main user base to navigate and understand. Still, there are times when a custom theme may be the best option out there for branding your SharePoint Server 2010 sites.

When to Use a Theme

You should take many things into consideration when planning your branding and design needs for SharePoint 2010. You need to consider the desired end result of your design for the user interface.

If you simply want to change the colors and fonts of your SharePoint 2010 site, a theme may be the best option for you. The biggest limitation with a SharePoint theme is that it will simply change the colors and fonts; it won't change the position of any items on the page.

A theme can be used in conjunction with a custom master page and even with a custom CSS file. There are times when this may be used to advantage by allowing end users to take control of their own sites. This ownership can help to improve end-user adoption by allowing users to feel more in control than ever when it comes to creating a site.

For large corporations some people want to show division among markets or departments. This would be a great place to use one of the new SharePoint Server 2010 themes. You can work in conjunction with a custom master page to create a strong design that is "themable" and then allow the individual groups to create themes to set themselves apart.

Where Can Themes Be Created?

In SharePoint Server 2010, you have several options for how to create themes for your sites. The new theme engine uses the same .thmx files that can be created in the Microsoft Office Suite. This means that you can create themes for SharePoint in your favorite Office programs. You can even use themes from previous versions of the Office Suite. This is one of the biggest advantages in the revamp of themes in SharePoint Server 2010.

One of your options is to create or use an existing theme from PowerPoint. To create a theme file in PowerPoint, you simply create a new slide design. You can also use any of the existing PowerPoint themes for branding your SharePoint 2010 sites. If you want to customize a theme, create a new theme, or use a theme that already exists in PowerPoint, you can go to the Design tab in the Ribbon to perform this action as shown in Figure 5-1.

FIGURE 5-1

The Design tab of PowerPoint enables you to create your own theme color palette, select your fonts, and even add images to be used in your PowerPoint theme. When adding images into this theme, you need to take into consideration that not all the images will translate over to your SharePoint 2010 site.

When you create your own theme or customize an existing one, you can make use of the color palette selection panel. This panel is very similar to what you encounter in the SharePoint 2010 browser experience of creating a custom theme. Once you've made your selections, name your theme and click Save to use it in your SharePoint 2010 sites like in Figure 5-2.

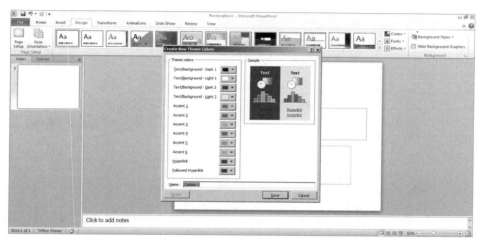

FIGURE 5-2

You can also use these theme files in any of the Office Suite applications. If you're creating a theme from Word, you use the Page Layout tab in the Ribbon as shown in Figure 5-3 to access the theme and its associated components.

FIGURE 5-3

The method for selecting your theme colors in Word is also very similar to how these theme colors are created and selected in the browser experience using SharePoint 2010. You can see this in Figure 5-4 with the color selection panel in Word; open this panel by selecting to create new theme colors under the Colors option. Once you have made your selections, name your theme and click Save.

You may be wondering why I have shown you how to create themes in both Microsoft Office Word and PowerPoint. This is because many companies have already done this work, so you may already have a theme created that can be used in your SharePoint 2010 sites. Also, if you are looking to use a theme in any type of SharePoint 2010 site other than publishing, you'll need to create your themes in an Office application and then upload and apply them to your sites.

Creating themes in the browser for publishing sites is similar to creating them in Office applications. The difference between the

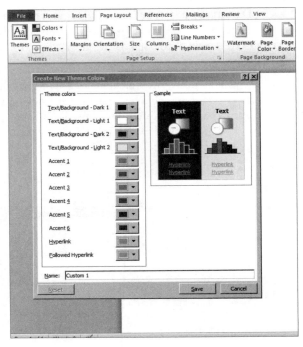

FIGURE 5-4

browser experience and the in-application theme creation experience is minimal, but the display of a theme is much different, as you can see in Figure 5-5.

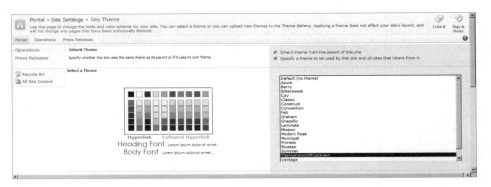

FIGURE 5-5

In a later section of this chapter you learn how to create a theme using the in-browser experience of SharePoint Server 2010.

Goals of Themes

When working with themes you need to make sure that you have a clear goal. Having an expected outcome in mind will help you as you create the theme and influence changes to your sites. SharePoint 2010 themes work with a selection of 10 main colors and then variations of these colors are generated by the product and these colors will then be used to create the design of your site. You should also have a firm goal in mind when it comes to the fonts that you would like to use in your site and how those will come across to every one of your end users.

What Will It Change?

SharePoint themes can be used to change colors and fonts for all pages of your SharePoint site, including the site settings and the modal windows, depending on how you elect to apply and inherit a theme. You can see a custom theme applied to a publishing site in Figure 5-6.

FIGURE 5-6

Out-of-the-Box Themes vs. Custom Themes

The decision to use an out-of-the-box theme versus a custom theme is all about how far you want to take the customization. Table 5-1 lists the 21 different themes you can use on a SharePoint 2010 site. When you start moving into custom themes you will have more options for the types of colors and color combinations you can use.

TABLE 5-1: Out-of-the-Box Themes

THEME NAME	DESCRIPTION OF THEME
Default	Prominent Colors: Blue and Gray Font Used: Calibri
Azure	Prominent Color: Aqua Font Used: Verdana
Berry	Prominent Colors: Burgundy and mustard Font Used: Trebuchet MS

continues

TABLE 5-1 *(continued)*

THEME NAME	DESCRIPTION OF THEME
Bittersweet	Prominent Colors: Pumpkin and sage Font Used: Georgia
Cay	Prominent Colors: Light gray and purple Font Used: Verdana
Classic	Prominent Colors: Two shades of blue Font Used: Verdana
Construct	Prominent Color: Blue-gray Font Used: Trebuchet MS
Convention	Prominent Colors: Dark aqua and gray Font Used: Verdana
Felt	Prominent Colors: Olive and gray Font Used: Verdana
Graham	Prominent Colors: Brown and cream Font Used: Georgia
Grapello	Prominent Colors: Gray and purple Fonts Used: Arial, Trebuchet MS
Laminate	Prominent Colors: Taupe and purple Font Used: Verdana
Mission	Prominent Colors: Tan and brown Font Used: Verdana
Modern Rose	Prominent Colors: Pink and gray Font Used: Verdana
Municipal	Prominent Colors: Red and gray Font Used: Verdana
Pinnate	Prominent Colors: Black, gray, and green Fonts Used: Arial, Trebuchet MS
Riccaso	Prominent Color: Gray Fonts Used: Arial, Trebuchet MS
Summer	Prominent Color: Green-gray Font Used: Calibri
Vantage	Prominent Colors: Blue and orange Font Used: Verdana

THEME NAME	DESCRIPTION OF THEME
Viewpoint	Prominent Colors: Purple and light sage Font Used: Verdana
Yoshi	Prominent Colors: Black, white, and orange Font Used: Verdana

If you are looking to create a theme that will match your company or personal style and design, you'll more than likely embark on the custom theme route. When you create custom themes you can specify web-safe colors for use in your site.

If you choose a custom theme for your SharePoint 2010 site you should consider the amount of control you would like on your sites. Some of the things that you might want to have control over with a theme is which themes people can choose from and at what level they can choose a theme at. Themes are now easier to create, which will also translate into the need for more control for site collection administrators.

Themes Infrastructure

Simply understanding how to create themes and what they will change is not enough. You must also understand how the themes work and how they're applied and stored. This will give you a better sense of how you can reuse themes throughout your sites and the best method for creating and applying them as you work on your SharePoint implementation.

How Are Themes Stored?

In SharePoint Server 2010, themes are stored in the Theme gallery, which is a specialized document library. You can access this library by navigating to Site Actions ⇨ Site Settings ⇨ Galleries ⇨ Themes.

You can upload your own .thmx files using the Add New Item link at the bottom of the gallery in Figure 5-7.

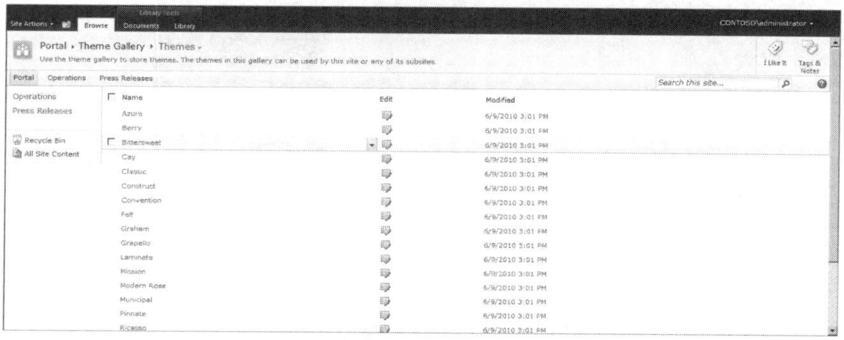

FIGURE 5-7

When you select the Add New Item option in the Theme gallery you are presented with the Upload Document modal window, which is the same window you get for any document library. This modal window is shown in Figure 5-8.

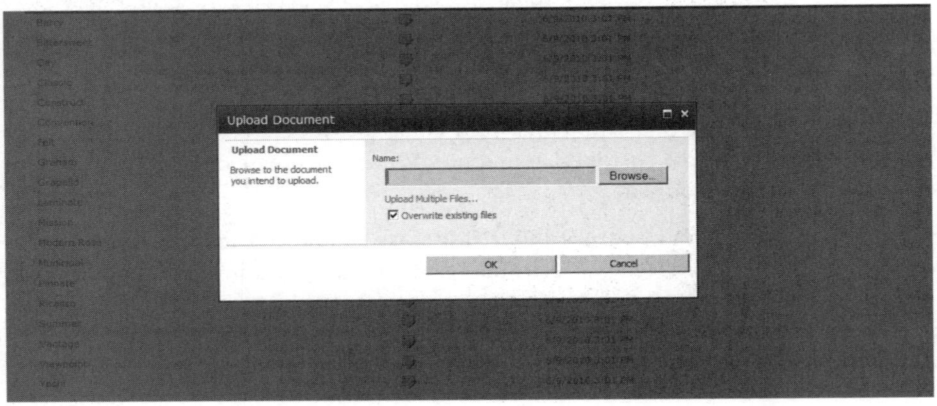

FIGURE 5-8

Once you browse to and select the .thmx file that you want to upload to the Theme gallery, you are prompted to name your theme and give it a description. The name that is given here is the one that will be displayed in the theme selection menu of your site. The description is purely saved with the theme file in the library, but not displayed anywhere so it is not necessary. The dialog box where you are prompted is shown in Figure 5-9. Because this name is the one that will be displayed as your theme name, you want to make sure that it's a clear name that accurately describes the theme to your users.

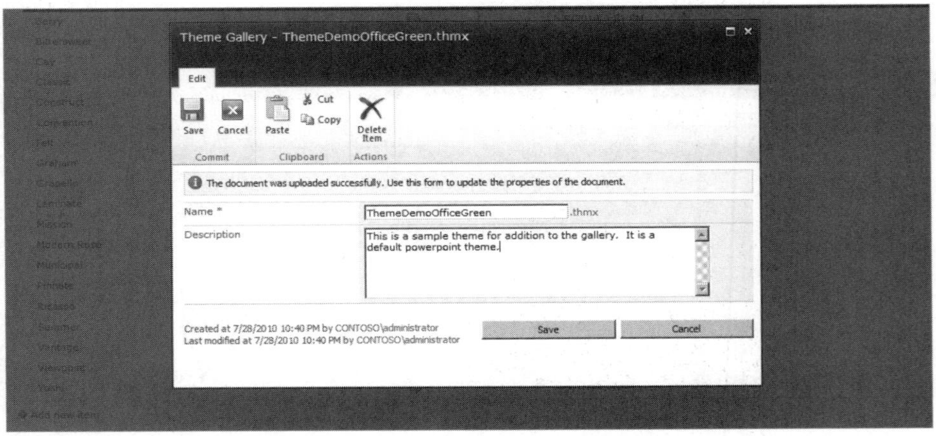

FIGURE 5-9

You can also add themes to the server. You can locate the theme files on the server by using the following file path: C:\Program Files\Common Files\Microsoft Shared\Web Server Extensions\14\Template\Global\Lists\Themes.

CSS Calls with Themes

The order in which style sheets are applied to a SharePoint site is important to designers. In the previous versions of SharePoint a theme that was applied to the site was called in the CSS order near the end of the server load. In SharePoint 2010, the theme is called first, when the site is loaded. Other out-of-the-box style sheets are applied after the theme.

How a Theme Affects the CSS File

With the drastic changes to the way themes are created in this version of SharePoint, there has also been a change in how the CSS that controls SharePoint works for themes. In previous versions a theme was created by customizing a CSS file and the classes to fit your needs. A theme in the current SharePoint 2010 theme engine does not create a CSS file, only a .thmx file.

To determine how a theme is applied and how this affects the CSS for your site you can look at the files in SharePoint Designer 2010. You will notice that themes in the _themes folder are displayed as their .thmx file. If you open this file to edit it from the SharePoint Designer menu, it will open the theme file in PowerPoint. You can see this file structure in Figure 5-10.

When you apply a theme to a SharePoint Server 2010 site, the theme is translated by the server and a series of corresponding CSS and image files are created at run time. You can examine these files in SharePoint Designer 2010 as shown in Figure 5-11.

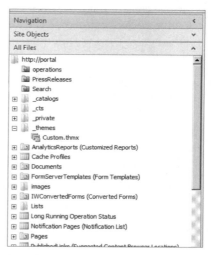

FIGURE 5-10

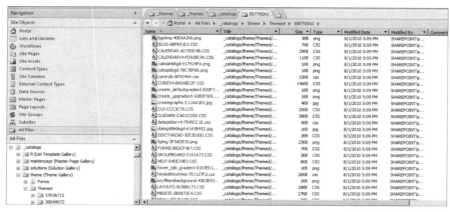

FIGURE 5-11

These files are used to generate the SharePoint site on the server. You will notice that, much like the Microsoft Office SharePoint Server 2007 theme files, each theme file is amended with a random number, and themes that have been applied to the site are stored in the _themes folder. If you would like to take the theme further and progress to custom CSS, you can use this set of CSS files and images as a starting point for further customizations.

You can also view out-of-the-box CSS files in SharePoint Designer 2010. When you view these files you will see the CSS files that are applied to your site at run time and that are stored in the content database. You might also need to examine some of the CSS files stored on the web server. You can see the CSS files applied to a default non-customized publishing site in Figure 5-12.

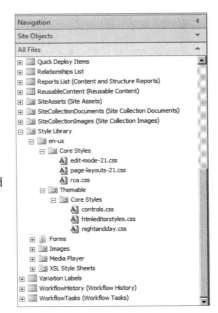

FIGURE 5-12

When you examine the out-of-the-box style sheets in SharePoint Designer 2010, you'll notice that the classes that will change with the application of a theme have been commented out so you can tell what theme element will affect the class. This is a bonus because you can now start to translate and examine what color options will change as you apply them in a theme format. You can see these commented classes in the following code sample:

```
.nightandday h1
{
    margin: 0;
        /* [ReplaceFont(themeFont: "MajorFont")] */
        font-family: "Trebuchet MS","Times New Roman", Times, serif;
        font-size: 22pt;
        font-weight: bold;
        /* [ReplaceColor(themeColor:"Accent1")] */
        color: #12386b;
        text-align: left;
}
.nightanday-menu ul.root ul.static ul.dynamic li:hover a{
        /* [ReplaceColor(themeColor: "Light1")] */
        color: #ffffff;
        /* [ReplaceColor(themeColor: "Accent1")] */ background-color: #05ACC3;
}
.nightanday-menu a.selected.static.menu-item,
.nightanday-menu a.selected.static.menu-item-text
{
        /* [ReplaceColor(themeColor: "Accent2-Lightest")] */
        background-color: #E6F1FA;

}
```

These commented styles in the out-of-the-box CSS will be a great aid in working with themes to create a more custom look. If you would like more control over the styles and how they can be customized using a SharePoint theme, you can create a custom CSS sheet that blocks the customization of a particular class by the theme file.

Using Themes across Products

The unification of theme files that can be used across the Microsoft product stack is an added bonus with this version of SharePoint Server 2010. This also allows many who have already invested in creating custom themes for Office products to use them in their SharePoint sites for a more custom look than they would get using out-of-the-box features.

CREATING THEMES

Previous sections of this chapter described how you can edit an Office theme from one of the Office applications and add these customized theme files to your SharePoint sites. The other option for creating a custom theme is to use the in-browser experience of a SharePoint Server 2010 publishing site. You can do this by navigating to Site Actions ➪ Site Settings ➪ Look and Feel ➪ Site Theme.

Customizing Colors and Fonts in Your Site

When you start out in a publishing site of SharePoint Server 2010, you can create your own custom theme files. Simply navigate to the theme section in Site Actions ➪ Site Settings ➪ Look and Feel ➪ Site Theme and start selecting your custom colors for the site.

Pick a theme name and then start making your customizations. Next to each color there is a link to Select a Color. When you click this link, it will load a modal window of the color selector as shown in Figure 5-13. In this modal window you can either select a color using the standard colors or you can add your own custom hexadecimal color number and apply that. You will have more color options if you use custom hexadecimal color numbers instead of the colors shown in the hexagon of colors displayed in the modal window.

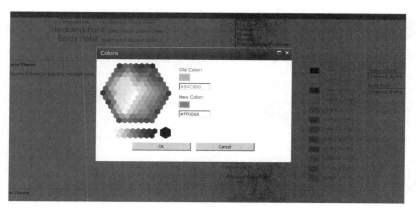

FIGURE 5-13

Also in the top section with the color selections you have the option to change the fonts used in the site. You should note a couple of things in this font selection section. The fonts that are displayed as options in this section are any fonts installed on your web server. The implications of this are that not all fonts are web-safe fonts, and they may not display properly for all users. You can see the font selection options in Figure 5-14.

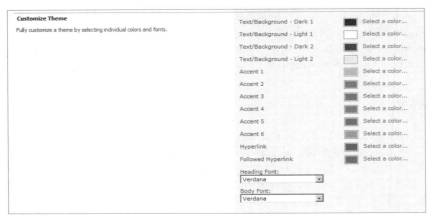

FIGURE 5-14

Now that you have customized the colors for your theme and also the fonts in your theme, you will need to examine how this theme looks when applied to your SharePoint 2010 sites. In previous versions you would have had to apply the theme and then navigate to the site to see how the theme affected the pages. With the new version of SharePoint you have the option to preview the theme while still in the Site Settings page.

By simply selecting the Preview button on the Site Theme page, you will see a modal window display that gives you an accurate view of how your custom theme will appear. This modal window is shown in Figure 5-15.

FIGURE 5-15

Now that you have seen how your theme will appear in the browser as applied to your SharePoint site, you can either make further changes or you can choose to apply your theme to your sites. You have two options for how these themes are applied. You can choose to apply only the selected theme to this site or apply the selected theme to this site and reset all subsites to inherit this setting. You also have the ability to inherit themes from this menu. The Apply Theme settings are shown in Figure 5-16.

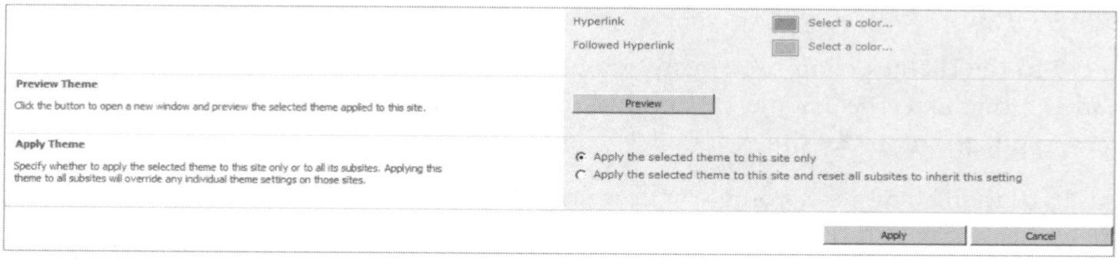

FIGURE 5-16

Design Separation

When you create custom themes for SharePoint Server 2010 you must keep in mind that this is a method for changing the colors of your site, but not a method for changing the design elements of the site. This means that you can change the colors and fonts, but not the placement of many of the default elements that are contained on the pages. Some of these default elements are the navigation, search, and footer components.

Themes are separated from the design layer of SharePoint sites. The design of SharePoint 2010 sites is created from the master page and also the page layouts applied to a SharePoint site. In Figure 5-17 you will notice that having a customized theme applied to an out-of-the-box publishing site using the v4.master page changes only the colors of the items on the page. (The screenshot is in black and white here, but the change will be obvious on your screen.)

FIGURE 5-17

SUMMARY

With all the changes to the theme engine in SharePoint Server 2010 it's important to understand what each of these changes means. Being able to use the same theme files across the Office platform and SharePoint will allow you to bring consistency to your entire user experience.

However, the new theme engine has few limiting factors. If you customize your themes in the browser, these themes are not stored in the Theme library so they are not reusable like themes that have been uploaded to the Theme gallery.

One improvement to the themes from previous versions is the way in which themes are applied. If you have uploaded a theme to the Theme gallery and make an edit to that theme, the theme will be changed in every application on the site.

The SharePoint 2010 theme engine is going to allow your site owners to have a stronger feeling of control over their sites. This will translate from My Site all the way up to publishing and team sites. When creating custom themes you'll need to check the functionality of all types of pages and sites to make sure your theme design will work appropriately in all these locations.

Themes are not simply a stand-alone part of the branding puzzle either. You can use themes with a custom master page and even custom CSS as well. They can also be published in a solution file as a feature. This allows a greater breadth of changes to be made in your branding and design plan while maintaining the customizations as managed code.

Cascading Style Sheets and SharePoint

WHAT'S IN THIS CHAPTER?

➤ What are cascading style sheets?

➤ Where SharePoint CSS lives

➤ How are cascading style sheets applied?

➤ Tools for editing SharePoint CSS

In previous chapters you learned about ways of branding SharePoint. This chapter discusses using cascading style sheets to change the way SharePoint looks. With the changes discussed in the section on master pages and with the material on themes for SharePoint Server 2010, it is now more important than ever that you understand exactly how CSS works.

CASCADING STYLE SHEETS: USING THEM FOR BRANDING SHAREPOINT

Cascading style sheets, or CSS, are used by web designers to add style to SharePoint. This standard of styling is translated into reality by a list of browser guidelines for HTML. There is a specific language for creating CSS syntax.

A style sheet is a set of one of more rules that should be applied to a website. A rule is a statement about how to apply a style to an element. The basic components of a rule come down to two parts. The first is a *selector*, which is the link between the element and the style. After the *selector* in the rule comes the *declaration*. The *declaration* is the part that determines exactly what will be changed and what it will be changed to. The selector and the declaration should be separated by a colon. In Figure 6-1 you can see the breakdown for the selector and declaration.

FIGURE 6-1

Once you understand the basic makeup of a CSS rule, you need to understand exactly how you can work with CSS to form more complicated rules. You can group selectors together if they all will have the same declaration. This would appear as follows: `H1, H2, H3 {color: red}`.

You can also assign more than one declaration to a selector. Grouping multiple declarations together will help to reduce the size of your style sheets. An example of grouping multiple declarations together with one selector follows: `CustomTopNav {background-color: red; height: 25px; color: #ffffff;}`.

This would set the element associated with the CustomTopNav style to have a background color of red, be 25 pixels high and the text in this area is white. The key to grouping declarations is that declarations must be separated by semicolons for them to be recognized.

The next component in understanding CSS is how you tie your styles into the site. The most common method used by SharePoint 2010 is to associate a single rule with an element. You would perform this action by adding in a style attribute to an individual element. This would appear like the Top Header style in Figure 6-2.

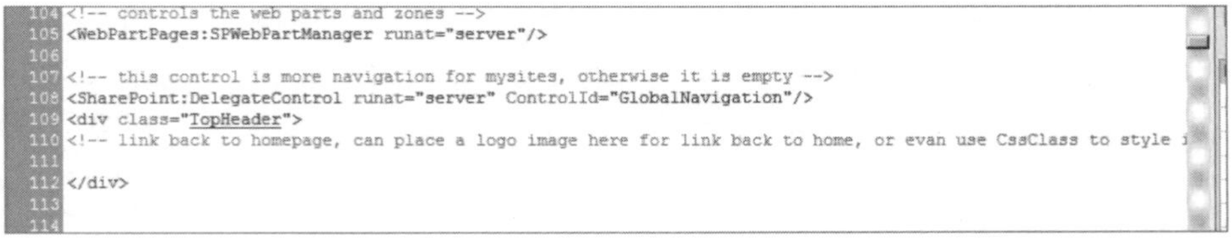

```
104 <!-- controls the web parts and zones -->
105 <WebPartPages:SPWebPartManager runat="server"/>
106
107 <!-- this control is more navigation for mysites, otherwise it is empty -->
108 <SharePoint:DelegateControl runat="server" ControlId="GlobalNavigation"/>
109 <div class="TopHeader">
110 <!-- link back to homepage, can place a logo image here for link back to home, or evan use CssClass to style
111
112 </div>
113
114
```

FIGURE 6-2

CSS is a standard method for creating style changes and can be combined with elements to create either complex or simple design changes to items in a browser. This allows you to further separate your information from how these items should appear on the page. The use of these style sheets enables you to manage only a single or a few files to control the appearance of your site instead of each page. This cuts down on the amount of overhead in both time and resources needed to maintain and change sites.

How Does CSS Drive the Branding of SharePoint?

In SharePoint Server 2010, CSS plays a major role in determining not only how each element is styled, but now also how it is placed on the page. With the change in SharePoint Server 2010 master pages to be `<div>`-based instead of HTML table-based, you now have greater ability to use CSS to control the placement of elements on the page in the browser.

SharePoint sites are run by CSS. Almost every element on the pages as displayed in the browser can be customized through an application of custom CSS. This makes CSS a very powerful tool when creating custom branding solutions for SharePoint 2010 sites.

Locations of CSS Files

You need to know where SharePoint Server 2010 stores its CSS files and where you should store them in order to create customized branding solutions. Advantages to learning where SharePoint stores its files include speeding up how long it will take you to make your own customizations and where you should store your own files when applying SharePoint custom branding.

In SharePoint Server 2010 the out-of-the-box CSS files are stored in several different locations throughout the SharePoint root folders. You can see one of the folders housing SharePoint CSS styles in Figure 6-3.

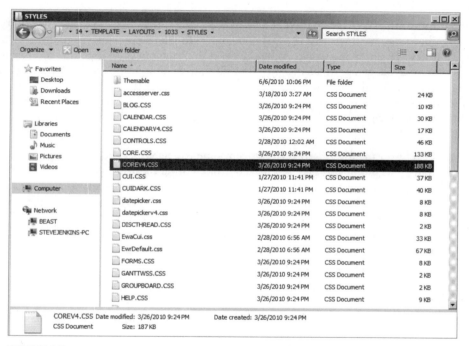

FIGURE 6-3

These files are stored in the file server, which gives you a good indication of where SharePoint starts to look for CSS files. However, you can also store your custom CSS files in the content database as exposed through the SharePoint Designer 2010 interface. You also need to plan out exactly what you're going to customize and how you're going to customize the files.

The best practices method for storing your custom SharePoint Server 2010 CSS files is still to deploy these as part of a solution package to the file server in the SharePoint root. This gives you the most flexibility on how to access and manage your customized files in a traditional managed code methodology.

What's New in SharePoint 2010 CSS?

Some changes have been made to SharePoint 2010 CSS and to what exactly is being utilized and displayed via CSS. The biggest of these changes is the ability to position items using CSS. The advantages of using CSS to position items in a website are many, but the most advantages for SharePoint Server 2010 sites will come in increasing the accessibility of sites. By separating the visual layer from the content of your sites to a greater degree, you're removing the inline styles from the page that would be viewable by page readers. You also have the added feature of more universal cross-browser style declarations that pertain to site accessibility. These declarations allow you to do things like resizing the text on the page from a selection. You also have the ability to use multiple style sheets for different types of browsers and screen readers. Making sites accessible is a huge advantage and something that was problematic and time-consuming in SharePoint Server 2007 and earlier.

Another advantage and feature new to SharePoint Server 2010 CSS is that you now have the ability to use CSS Sprites. This concept allows you to create one image to which you can add multiple items and then use CSS to position and display only the portion of the image that you would like to show. This allows you to avoid the performance hit of needing to load multiple images for a page or site. The thing to keep in mind when working with CSS Sprites is that these will work only for non-repeating images. So if you are looking to create a background gradient graphic that will repeat across an area like the top navigation, this must continue to be treated like a traditional image in your file structure and CSS.

But how exactly do CSS Sprites work? They're a relatively simple concept to understand but a little more difficult to actually put into place. The best method for creating these is to create an image that is as wide as the largest image you would like to display, and then simply stack all your images into this one image file down the left side separated by a predetermined pixel height. Most people use one pixel as their separator. You will need to remember this height because it will affect your positioning of items in CSS. As you then create your CSS for your items, you will begin by setting the background image to be your entire image file. Then you will select and style the background for the individual items and include positioning on these items.

Modifying CSS Files

As you plan your SharePoint Server 2010 branding customizations, you will inevitably be planning for some customized CSS to change the appearance of your site. You should keep a few things in mind as you begin to make your own custom CSS files.

The biggest thing to remember is that you should never edit the out-of-the-box CSS files directly, for many reasons. The main one is that editing the out-of-the-box files will render any support contract with Microsoft null and void and you will no longer be able to use this support as a method of help. The supporting reason for this logic is also that some service packs and cumulative updates may contain changes to the out-of-the-box files and will overwrite your customizations.

The method that you should undertake when creating customized CSS files for your SharePoint Server 2010 sites is to create your own new CSS file. Once you have created this file you will then put all your customizations to the out-of-the-box classes as well as any completely customized classes in this sheet. You are not restricted to one CSS sheet in working with SharePoint Server 2010. You can create separate style sheets as you see fit. These can include specialized print CSS files or even cross-browser substitution CSS files.

Applying Custom CSS

When you have created your own style sheets for use with your SharePoint Server 2010 sites, you also need to be aware of how you can actually apply these sheets to your sites to customize the look and feel. Two methods exist for adding these sheets to your sites and having them called for display.

The first of these is to use the publishing site features to apply your custom CSS through the user interface of SharePoint. You can do this by navigating to Site Actions ⇨ Site Settings ⇨ Modify All ⇨ Look and Feel ⇨ Master Pages. Once in this menu you can scroll to the bottom and apply a custom style sheet that has been added to a document library through the alternate CSS link method as shown in Figure 6-4.

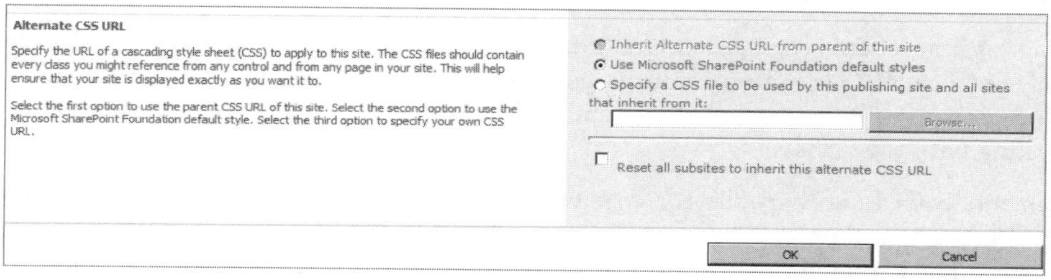

FIGURE 6-4

It's important to keep in mind that in using this method of application you must have Publishing features for your site. Also, you can apply only one style sheet at a time.

The other option for applying your custom CSS to your SharePoint Server 2010 sites is to do so through the use of a custom master page. To do this you will need to add a CSS registration link in the head tag of your custom master page. In Figure 6-5 you see a sample custom CSS sheet applied to a master page and you will notice the `after` call is for after the corev4.css file.

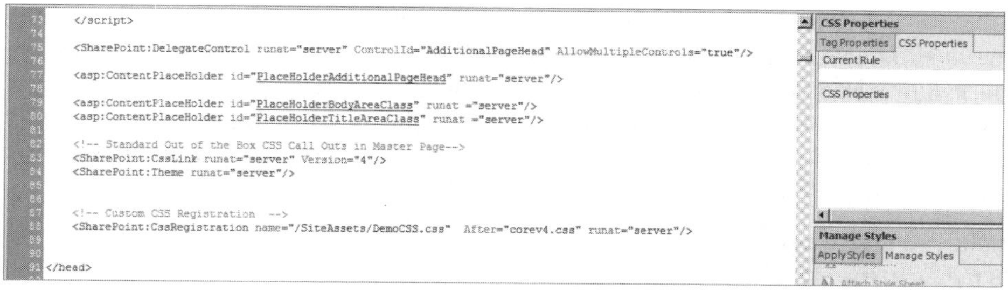

FIGURE 6-5

The added advantage of using this method is that it allows you more control over the inheritance of your CSS which determines when it is called at run time. It also gives you the flexibility to add multiple style sheets to your site whereas the in-browser option allows you to select and apply only one custom CSS sheet to your site. By applying your style sheets in this manner as well, you can also include them as part of you solution package.

Inheritance of Styles

How does SharePoint Server 2010 apply the CSS classes and style sheets at run time to make the sites display properly? This has always been a bit of a mystery in the logic of the product. In previous versions of SharePoint Server, the only method for trying to control the call of CSS files was to place those in the <head> tag of a custom master page at the very bottom.

In SharePoint Server 2010 sites you now have the ability to instruct SharePoint on when to apply the style sheets at server run time. You can do this in your custom master page files by using the after call in your CSS reference in the <head> tag.

Creating Themable CSS

With the changes to the Theme engine in SharePoint Server 2010 you now have the ability to create custom CSS files and styles that can take advantage of the Theme engine. This means you can create custom controls and items as well as customize the existing items with the Theme engine simply by working with the CSS.

In the CSS elements you can now specify that you would like a particular class to be themed by the new engine. To do this you simply add the correctly commented CSS declaration to the area where the rules are listed. Then you tell this rule how to choose a color and what shade of that color to apply. You can see an example in the following code:

```
.CustomCSSStyle {
/* [ReplaceColor(themeColor:"Light5-Lightest")] */ border:solid 1px #333333;
/* [ReplaceColor(themeColor:"Light2")] */ background-color:#f5f6f7;
}
```

In the corev4.css file you will notice that there are themable declarations in many of the out-of-the-box classes and elements. You can also remove the ability for an item to be re-colored by the Theme engine by simply removing this rule from the class.

You can also do this for custom items that you develop like a Web Part. You have a few extra considerations for working with items like the Visual Web Part in Visual Studio 2010. The most important thing in adding your custom CSS that is themable to any custom item is knowing where you need to place your CSS styles. In the SharePoint root you will notice that there is a normal Styles folder and then within that folder there is a Themable folder. You will need to place your custom style sheet into both of these locations. This will allow the part to display appropriately without a custom theme applied and also to perform appropriately when a theme is applied to the site.

The last thing that you will need to do when developing custom items is apply the EnableCSSThemeing attribute. You will want to set this attribute to True if you would like it to be themed or False if you would like to exclude this item from being themed. This attribute is added into the <SharePoint:CssRegistration> tag.

CSS and Page Layouts

Page layouts are the method used to control how the content is placed on the page and displayed to the end user. The master page in SharePoint Server 2010 sites controls the common elements on a site, and the page layouts control the other elements. Page layouts can contain Web Parts, Web Part zones, custom controls, and even content that is applied and saved directly to the layout file.

The creation of custom page layouts is another great method for customizing your SharePoint sites into the branded masterpieces that you desired and designed. When creating custom page layout files, which are simply .aspx pages, you can add your own customized CSS classes to the elements and then style and control the elements using that class.

When working to modify the out-of-the-box page layout files, you will want to examine which core out-of-the-box styles have been applied to the elements and then make your own versions of those styles in your custom CSS style sheet.

CSS AND WEB PARTS

Just like the rest of the elements of SharePoint Server 2010, the Web Parts are also branded and controlled by CSS styles. You will need to make modifications to the styles that control these elements if you want to change the way these items appear in the browser.

Customizing Out-of-the-Box Web Part Design Using CSS

To customize the out-of-the-box Web Parts, you will first have to determine which styles are being applied to a Web Part and what exactly you can change. You can use tools like the Internet Explorer Developer tools to find the classes that are applied to a site in the browser.

The CSS that is working to style many of the out-of-the-box Web Parts is the same for each Web Part. This has not changed since the 2007 version of SharePoint. You will need to consider this as you create your branding design. Though most components of a Web Part can be changed to suit your needs or desires, it will often affect each Web Part unless you are working with custom parts.

Using CSS to Style Custom-Developed Web Parts and Controls

When you are working with either third-party or custom-developed Web Parts, you will want to change the way that these items appear in your branding schema. In working with these items you will need to determine first if they can be styled by CSS and then what classes are applied to the elements of the Web Part so that you can add them to your custom CSS sheets.

As developers are creating custom Web Parts, you will need to get the proper class names from them for each component so that you can create a custom style list for these parts in your style sheet. If you are working with a third-party Web Part, most of these will have the ability to either be styled or skinned to match your needs.

TOOLS FOR WORKING WITH CSS

In understanding that you will need to customize CSS to make SharePoint Server 2010 branding customizations, you know you'll also need to pick a tool for making these customizations. So what should you be looking for in the tool for working with CSS and SharePoint?

The biggest consideration is to pick a tool that you are comfortable with. This will make working with all the CSS easier. Various factors need to be considered for each of the Microsoft-recommended tools to change CSS for SharePoint Server 2010.

SharePoint Designer

The first tool to examine is SharePoint Designer 2010. This tool, much as we determined with SharePoint master pages in Chapter 4, has some additional built-in functionality for working with SharePoint sites.

SharePoint Designer 2010 has a new built-in Site Assets library in the file structure of site objects where you can store your custom CSS files as you are developing and testing them in your development environment. The asset library is a new function in SharePoint Server 2010 that is associated with the digital asset management process.

You can add a custom asset library to any site collection or site and use this library to manage media and graphics files for your sites. Within a graphics asset library you can give some more management responsibilities for the files and also provide some files for use by end users on their sites.

In Figure 6-6 you can see the Site Assets library opened to display the customized files for working with this site in its beginning stages, including a custom DemoCSS.css file.

FIGURE 6-6

Because CSS files are code files, you may not feel comfortable in working with them in their native format. SharePoint Designer 2010 also has several customizable toolbars and task panes that can provide visual guidance and help as you are working with CSS files. This allows you to choose exactly how much help or how little help you need when working with CSS. These additional toolbars and task panes will provide you the extra support in a visual or text format to help you make modifications or customizations as needed to CSS styles.

The first out-of-the-box SharePoint Designer 2010 feature for working with CSS files is the Style tab in the Ribbon menu of the program itself. When you open a CSS file in SharePoint Designer you will be given the option of using the Style tab in the Ribbon. This tab has many built-in options that can guide you in working with CSS and SharePoint Server 2010. In Figure 6-7 you can see the expanded Style tab in the Ribbon and some of the tools it provides.

FIGURE 6-7

The Style tab in the SharePoint Designer 2010 Ribbon is not the only built-in functionality for working with CSS files. There is also a CSS Properties Task Pane that you can use to understand and create styles. In Figure 6-8 you see an expanded CSS Properties Task Pane on the right side. In this task pane you can see the options for declarations that you can add to selectors.

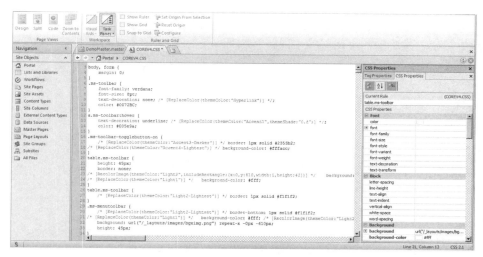

FIGURE 6-8

The CSS Properties Task Pane can be used to have a much more visual method of creating CSS. The only catch to this task pane is that you must create the selector name in the file as code before you can use the more visual method to create styles.

The Manage Styles Task Pane is a quick and easy way to see all the styles currently being used in a page. It also provides a preview of the style with all the declarations applied to some sample text. You can see this task pane in Figure 6-9.

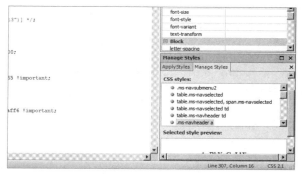

FIGURE 6-9

Another option in the Manage Styles Task Pane is the Apply Styles tab. This tab allows you to select and apply styles to elements through a visual list of the styles available.

SharePoint Designer 2010 also enables you to run a CSS report. This report will examine the CSS being used on an open site in SharePoint Designer. In Figure 6-10 you can see the options for running a report on CSS errors in the site.

Once the report has run, you will get a report window at the bottom of the SharePoint Designer 2010 interface. You can see this report in Figure 6-11.

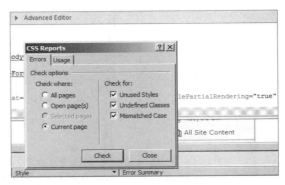

FIGURE 6-10

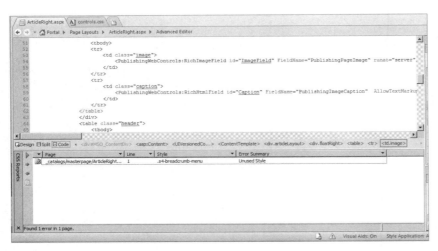

FIGURE 6-11

The second type of CSS report that you can run in SharePoint Designer 2010 is a CSS usage report. With this report you can find out what styles are being applied to your selections. You can see the options for the usage reports in Figure 6-12.

SharePoint Designer 2010 has many options for working with cascading style sheets that make it most people's preferred tool. Other options are available for working with CSS in your SharePoint sites.

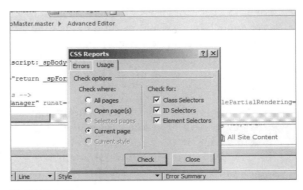

FIGURE 6-12

Visual Studio

Another tool for working with cascading style sheets for your SharePoint Server 2010 sites is Visual Studio 2010. The tools provided out of the box for working with CSS in Visual Studio are not quite as advanced as many graphics programs or web programs like SharePoint Designer. This is a tool you might use if you are more accustomed to working with code.

If you are not comfortable creating new styles in the code view of Visual Studio, you can make use of some of the more visual menus for working with CSS in this software. In Figure 6-13 you can see the menu for creating a new style rule.

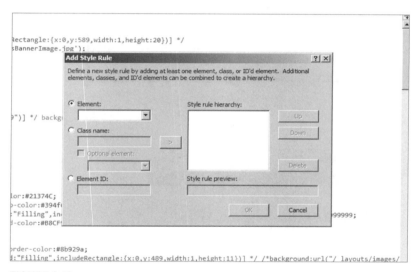

FIGURE 6-13

There is a menu structure for creating or modifying styles in Visual Studio 2010. You can use the Modify or Build Style menu to get a more visual method of creation. This menu is displayed in Figure 6-14.

Visual Studio displays CSS in a code-view format. One item that can be helpful when working with larger CSS files, like the one you may run across in creating custom CSS for SharePoint Server 2010 sites, is the CSS Outline view. This task pane allows you to view all the items involved in your CSS file from either an element or a class perspective. By using this menu to drill down into the CSS, you are able to quickly get to the item you need without knowing code line numbers. You can see this menu structure in Figure 6-15.

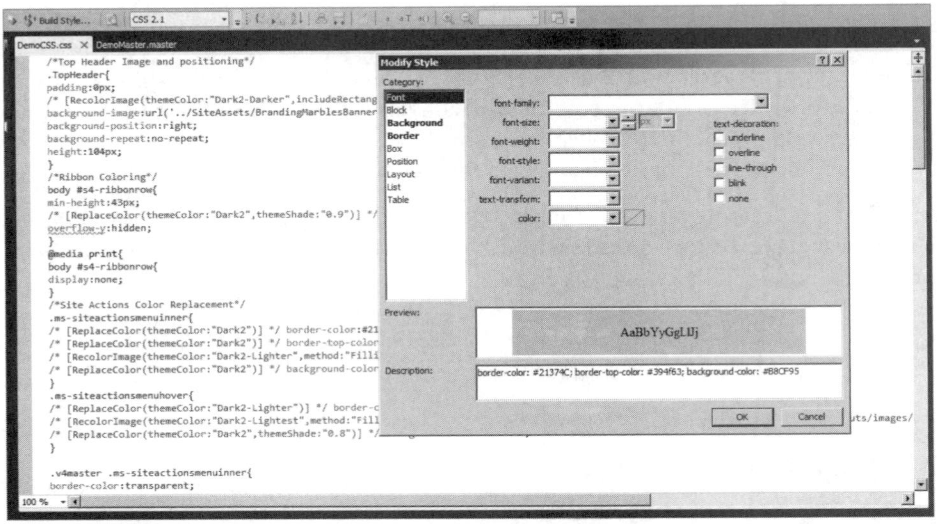

FIGURE 6-14

FIGURE 6-15

Visual Studio 2010 is a tool most often used by developers and then by designers after moving their files from another program.

Other Tools

You can use many other tools to work with your CSS files. The tool you choose should be one that you are comfortable working with. This could be anything from Dreamweaver to Notepad.

A few browser-specific tools can be used to identify the CSS being used in your sites at run time. Among these are the developer tools built into Internet Explorer 8 and later. With these tools, you can use the cursor to select an item and then explore the CSS and HTML of that item in the Tools window. You can make modifications to the CSS in this window and see them applied to your site. You can see this in action in Figure 6-16.

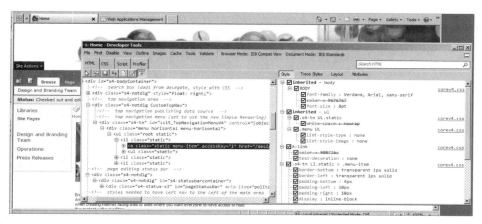

FIGURE 6-16

Internet Explorer is not the only browser with a helpful tool that you can use to examine the CSS applied to a site. FireFox also has a tool that you can use in a similar way. The FireFox FireBug tool functions similarly.

If cross-browser compatibility is a concern, a number of tools are available that you can use online or purchase to view your site in multiple screen resolutions or multiple browsers without the hassle of creating multiple virtual machines.

SUMMARY

Working with cascading style sheets in SharePoint Server 2010 is now more important than ever. With the sheer number of lines of CSS that are now employed by the product to control how the sites appear, you need to be comfortable with the concepts. Once you understand the concepts of basic CSS you can apply them to a custom style sheet to expand your site to fit your branding needs. Branding for SharePoint Server 2010 may be a confusing process, but if you continue to break apart the items you're trying to change, you can find the common elements for them. Once you have started to find the common elements you can take the sites as far as you like.

A couple of final things to remember when working with your custom CSS will make your life easier as you continue down the branding path. You should try to put all your styles into one style sheet or at most a couple. Also make sure that you comment out your CSS in a manner that describes the items in a way that makes sense to you. This could be in the form of color descriptions or item descriptions.

PART III
Development with SharePoint

7

Features and Solutions

Have you ever been in a discussion with colleagues about new software you were developing when someone requested a particular "feature" to be included? Or have you ever referred to the software you were writing as a software "solution"? Although the terms *feature* and *solution* are often used when describing software solutions, these words have very specific meanings in SharePoint 2010.

The purpose of this chapter is to help you understand how functionality in SharePoint is packaged, deployed, and utilized, using SharePoint features and solutions. In addition, this chapter shows you how you can use Visual Studio 2010 to build your own features and solutions.

UNDERSTANDING FEATURES

The Merriam-Webster dictionary defines the word *feature* as "a prominent part or characteristic" and Roget's thesaurus gives us synonyms like *unit*, *item*, *constituent*, and *element*. In its most basic sense, a SharePoint feature is a constituent unit or element of functionality within a SharePoint farm, web application, site collection, or site. Features provide a way for developers to turn on custom functionality within a SharePoint server farm. Features can do things like:

➤ Add a site column, content type, or list definition to a site collection

➤ Add an instance of a list or library to a site

➤ Add an item to a list

➤ Attach an event receiver to a list or library

➤ Start a timer job

➤ Add and activate a custom workflow

➤ Add a Web Part to a page

➤ Add a Web Part to the Web Part gallery in a site collection

➤ Activate a master page

This is by no means an exhaustive list, but it should give you an idea of the kinds of things a feature can do. Nearly every piece of custom functionality in SharePoint can be packaged into a feature and deployed to a SharePoint farm.

Features are created by deploying one or more files to the filesystem on the server. One of these files, an XML file called the *feature manifest*, instructs SharePoint as to how to use the files, whether that means executing code or adding content to a SharePoint site. (You can find a detailed explanation of the feature manifest file later in this chapter, in the section titled "Configuring a Feature.") When a feature is activated, SharePoint carries out the instructions specified in the feature manifest file.

SharePoint 2010 itself depends on features for providing functionality. For instance, the Three-State Workflow feature makes it possible for users to instantiate a three-state workflow on list items. Until that feature has been activated for a given site, users cannot create instances of that particular kind of workflow.

To see the kinds of features that SharePoint uses for its own operation, navigate to the directory on your server where your core SharePoint files are installed. Open up the folder called TEMPLATE and then open up the folder called FEATURES. By viewing the names of the folders, you can get an idea of what some of the features do, whether it's "provisioning" (making available) a library definition, configuring a site, or enabling a workflow.

Many of these features also appear in a list of available features, which can be accessed from your browser. For instance, to see the features that are available in a particular site collection, navigate to that site collection using your browser, then open up the Site Settings page and click the Site Collection Features link under the Site Collection Administration heading. This will take you to the Site Collection Features page, as shown in Figure 7-1. On this page, you can see a list of some of the features that are available for activation in a site collection on a SharePoint Server 2010 farm.

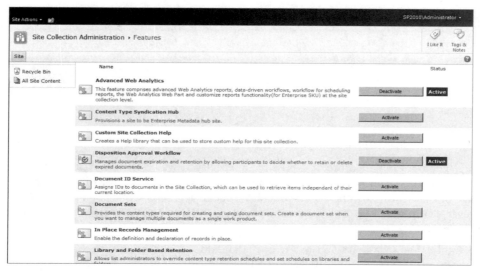

FIGURE 7-1

Here's a list of some of the features that come installed with SharePoint Server 2010:

➤ **Document Sets:** Provides the content types required for creating and using document sets, and allows you to create a document set when you want to manage multiple documents as a single work product

➤ **Search Server Web Parts:** Makes all the search Web Parts used by the Search Center site definitions available in the Web Part gallery

➤ **SharePoint Server Publishing:** Creates a library for storing web pages as well as supporting libraries (such as image and style-sheet libraries) to create and publish pages based on page layouts

➤ **Team Collaboration Lists:** Provides team collaboration capabilities for a site by making standard lists, such as document libraries and issues, available

As you can see, a feature can do more than one thing, but the collective set of actions taken by a feature creates a unit of functionality, such as making it possible to publish web pages, create document sets, or use Web Parts. Features can be used in combination with one another to create a blend of functionality. For instance, enabling the Document Sets feature and the SharePoint Server Publishing feature means that you'll have a site collection in which you can both publish web pages and create document sets.

The place where your SharePoint files are installed on your server is called the SharePoint root. You might hear some developers refer to this as the 14 *hive. If you didn't modify the installation path when you installed SharePoint, you can find this folder at* C:\Program Files\Common Files\Microsoft Shared\Web Server Extensions\14 *on your server.*

You can leverage several characteristics of features:

➤ **Scope:** When building a feature, it is possible to specify at which level the feature can be activated, whether at the server farm, web application, site collection, or site. Only one instance of that feature can be activated at a particular level or "scope" at a given time. (However, features can be deactivated and then reactivated, again performing the actions specified in the feature.)

For example, if you wanted to write a feature that added a master page to the Master Page gallery, you would set your feature's scope to the site-collection level because that action needs to happen just once in a particular site collection (as opposed to needing to happen in many sites within the site collection). However, if you wanted to create a feature that added an instance of a given list to a particular site within your site collection, you could decrease the scope to the site level, which means you could activate that feature in any number of sites in your site collection, adding that list instance to each site where the feature was activated.

Certain assets can only be deployed at certain scopes or levels. For instance, although it's possible to create a site column for a subsite within a site collection using the browser, when deploying a site column using a feature the feature's scope must be set to the site-collection level. Content type and workflow features must also be scoped to the site-collection level.

➤ **Reusability:** Features can be used in more than one instance of the specified scope, as previously mentioned. In addition, although certain functionality can be added to a site using the browser or a tool like SharePoint Designer, adding functionality manually is time-consuming and prone to human error. Using a feature to add functionality ensures that the exact same action will happen every time in the same way.

➤ **Activation dependency:** A feature can require that you activate one or more other features before you activate it. For instance, if a feature called My Content Types is dependent on a feature called My Site Columns, then My Site Columns must be activated before My Content Types is activated. If My Site Columns is not activated, users activating My Content Types will receive a message notifying them that they must first activate My Site Columns before they can activate My Content Types.

A feature can only be dependent on other features at its own scope or greater. In other words, a feature scoped at the web application level can be dependent on a feature scoped at the farm level, but not the other way around, or a feature scoped at the site-collection level can be dependent on a feature also scoped at the site-collection level, but not on a feature scoped at the site level.

HIDDEN FEATURES AND ACTIVATION DEPENDENCIES

A feature can be *hidden*, which means the feature will not appear in the list of features that the user sees in the browser. If a feature is not visible, it means a user cannot explicitly activate the feature using the browser.

A hidden feature can be automatically activated by a visible feature when the visible feature is activated, so long as that visible feature has a dependency on the hidden feature.

For example, say you have two features: one called List Definition, which provisions (or makes available) a custom list definition in a site collection, and another called List Instance, which provisions an instance of that custom list in the top-level site of the site collection. You can't create a custom list instance without the definition, so you would make the List Instance dependent on the List Definition. If you hide List Definition, the user sees only List Instance in the browser. If the user activates List Instance, List Definition automatically activates (if it isn't already activated — if a hidden feature is already activated, no action will be taken on it).

Please note that a hidden feature cannot activate another hidden feature. That means you cannot create a chain of feature activations, where visible Feature A activates hidden Feature B automatically, which then automatically activates hidden Feature C as well. In cases where you would like three or more features to be activated in a particular order, you simply need to ensure that the features are listed in the correct order when listing the visible feature's activation dependencies. As an example, say you have three features: your List Definition and List Instance features, and an additional feature called Lookup Column that provisions a Lookup site column based on the list that was provisioned when List Instance was activated. You need them to be activated in the following order: List Definition, List Instance, Lookup Column. To have these execute in the proper order, you would make Lookup Column visible. You would then have List Definition as the first activation dependency, and List Instance as the second activation dependency. (See the feature.xml code snippet a little later in the chapter to find out how this looks in a feature manifest file.) When List Definition is activated, List Instance will be activated first, then Lookup Column.

By hiding features and letting them be activated automatically by other features, you reduce the number of features a user must scroll through when choosing a feature to activate. Furthermore, it prevents the risk of users trying to activate features in the wrong order, if a particular order of activation is needed.

Installing, Activating, Deactivating, and Uninstalling Features

Five events can take place in the lifecycle of a feature:

➤ **Installation:** This takes place when SharePoint becomes aware that a feature is available for use. This usually takes place after the feature's constituent folder and files are deployed to the server. A feature can include files such as assemblies, images, XML files, ASPX pages, JavaScript files, CSS files, and so on. For instance, if you installed a feature containing a list definition, installing the feature would mean that the file containing the schema that defined the list definition had been deployed to the web server inside the FEATURES folder in the SharePoint root. A feature can be installed by using a PowerShell command or the STSADM tool.

➤ **Activation or enabling:** This happens when the functionality contained in the feature is turned on for the given scope. You can activate a feature in the browser by using a PowerShell command or by using the STSADM tool. If you activated a feature that provisioned a list instance, your site would contain the list that was defined in the feature.

➤ **Deactivation or disabling:** This happens when the functionality contained in the feature is turned off. A feature can be deactivated in the browser by using a PowerShell command or by using the STSADM tool.

➤ **Uninstallation:** This takes place when SharePoint is no longer aware of the feature's availability for use. This action usually coincides with the removal of the feature's constituent folder and files from the file system. You can uninstall a feature by using a PowerShell command or the STSADM tool.

➤ **Upgrading:** A developer can attach a set of actions that should take place when a feature is upgraded to a newer version. The upgrading event executes the specified upgrade actions. (To learn more about upgrading features, read the section in this chapter titled "Upgrading a Feature.") The upgrade event happens automatically when a newer version of a feature is installed using a solution. (Solutions are discussed later in this chapter.)

This next section will help you understand how you can activate and deactivate features using the browser and how you can execute any of the five events using PowerShell. In addition, this section introduces you to topics such as handling feature events, upgrading features, and localizing features.

FEATURE DEACTIVATION

Although activating a feature can add new content to a site (like site columns, content types, lists, or list items), deactivating a feature doesn't necessarily remove content or artifacts from a site. For instance, if activating a feature adds a new list to a site, deactivating that same feature won't always delete that list from the site. This functionality prevents users from accidentally removing existing content from the site by deactivating a feature. However, it's possible to explicitly write code that will tell SharePoint to remove content from a site when a feature is deactivated.

Activating and Deactivating Features Using the Browser

Once a feature has been installed, if it's not hidden, it's possible for users with proper permissions to activate or deactivate it using the browser. (For example, farm administrators can activate features scoped to the farm and web application, and site-collection administrators can activate features scoped to the site collection and site.) Table 7-1 provides instructions for how to find the Feature Management page in each scope.

TABLE 7-1: Feature Management Pages

FEATURE SCOPE	INSTRUCTIONS
Farm	Log in to Central Administration. Click the link to System Settings in the navigation on the left side of the page. Click the Manage Farm Features link in the Farm Management section.
Web application	Log in to Central Administration. Click the Application Management link in the navigation on the left side of the page. Click the Manage Web Applications link in the Web Applications section. Select the web application you would like to manage from the list of web applications. Once the web application is highlighted, click the Manage Features button found in the Manage section of the Web Applications tab in the Ribbon.
Site collection	Browse to the site collection you would like to manage. Click Site Actions ➪ Site Settings. Find the Site Collection Administration section on the Site Settings page. Click the Site Collection Features link.
Site	Browse to the site collection you would like to manage. Click the Site Actions menu and select Site Settings. Find the Site Actions section on the Site Settings page. Click the Manage Site Features link.

SharePoint Feature PowerShell Commands

SharePoint enables you to manage features using PowerShell commands. Table 7-2 shows these commands and some of their commonly used parameters. For a complete list of parameters, open the SharePoint PowerShell command prompt and type `get-help` followed by the name of the command and the `-detailed` parameter, like this: `get-help Enable-SPFeature -detailed`

TABLE 7-2: PowerShell Commands for Features

COMMAND	PARAMETERS	DESCRIPTION
Install-SPFeature	-Path: The name of the Feature folder in the ~/14/TEMPLATE/FEATURES directory on the server	Installs a feature using its feature.xml file
Enable-SPFeature	-Identity: Either the name of the Feature folder or the feature's GUID -Url: The URL of the web application, site collection, or site in which the feature is being activated	Activates a feature
Disable-SPFeature	-Identity: Either the name of the Feature folder or the feature's GUID -Url: The URL of the web application, site collection, or site in which the feature is being deactivated	Deactivates a feature
Uninstall-SPFeature	-Identity: Either the name of the Feature folder or the feature's GUID	Uninstalls a feature
Get-SPFeature	-Identity: Either the name of the Feature folder or the feature's GUID -Farm: Indicates that only enabled farm features should be returned -WebApplication: The name of the web application from which to get enabled features -Site: The URL of the site collection from which to get enabled features -Web: The URL or the GUID of the website from which to get enabled features	Retrieves either a single enabled feature or a list of enabled features, at a given scope

Listing 7-1 shows several examples of the preceding PowerShell commands in action.

LISTING 7-1: Features.ps1

```
Install-SPFeature -Path MyFeature
Enable-SPFeature -Identity MyFeature -Url http://sitename
Disable-SPFeature -Identity MyFeature -Url http://sitename
Uninstall-SPFeature -Path MyFeature
Get-SPFeature -Identity MyFeature -Site http://sitename
```

SharePoint Feature STSADM Commands

Although SharePoint 2010 now utilizes PowerShell to administer the SharePoint environment, it's still possible to use the STSADM tool (an executable file called STSADM.exe located in the bin folder inside the SharePoint root) to carry out certain commands. This provides continuity with the way older SharePoint sites were administered. Table 7-3 lists the STSADM commands that can be used to manipulate features. As with the PowerShell commands, the parameters listed are partial. You can view a complete list of parameters by adding `-?` after each command, like this: `STSADM.EXE -o installfeature -?`

TABLE 7-3: STSADM Commands for Features

COMMAND	PARAMETERS	DESCRIPTION
`-o installfeature`	`-name`: The name of the Feature folder `-id`: The feature's GUID; can be used instead of the folder name	Installs a feature
`-o activatefeature`	`-name`: The name of the Feature folder `-id`: The feature's GUID; can be used instead of the folder name `-url`: The URL of the location where the feature should be activated	Activates a feature
`-o deactivatefeature`	`-name`: The name of the Feature folder `-id`: The feature's GUID; can be used instead of the folder name `-url`: The URL of the location where the feature should be deactivated	Deactivates a feature
`-o uninstallfeature`	`-name`: The name of the Feature folder `-id`: The feature's GUID; can be used instead of the folder name	Uninstalls a feature

Listing 7-2 shows an example batch file that calls the STSADM tool.

LISTING 7-2: Features.bat

```
cd "C:\Program Files\Common Files\Microsoft Shared\Web Server Extensions\14\BIN"
stsadm -o installfeature -name MyFeature
stsadm -o activatefeature -name MyFeature -url http://sitename
stsadm -o deactivatefeature -name MyFeature -url http://sitename
stsadm -o uninstallfeature -name MyFeature
```

Feature Events and Event Receivers

It is possible to execute code when any of the feature events are fired (installed, activated, deactivating, uninstalling, and upgrading) using an event handler. The class that handles each of these events is called a *feature event receiver* and inherits from the `Microsoft.SharePoint` `.SPFeatureReceiver` class.

Notice the verb tense associated with each event receiver: installed, activated, deactivating, uninstalling, and upgrading. The `FeatureInstalled` and `FeatureActivated` event receivers execute after the event has taken place, whereas the `FeatureDeactivating`, `FeatureUninstalling`, and `FeatureUpgrading` event receivers execute before the event has taken place. This is important to note, because it can make a difference as to the kinds of actions you will want to perform in your event receiver. If the event has already taken place, it means your files are in place and your items have been provisioned, so you're most likely adding to those items or making modifications. If the event has not taken place yet, it means you can do things like check certain conditions to see if the event should indeed fire, and cancel the event from executing, if necessary.

Suppose you had a feature that provisioned a new list instance. However, only certain groups of people should have permission to view the list. You can't apply security to the list until the list has already been provisioned, so you provision the list in your feature, and then add a feature event receiver and attach it to the `FeatureActivated` event. When the feature is activated and the list is provisioned, your code executes, making changes to the default permissions on the list.

Using a similar scenario, if you created a feature event receiver and added code to its `FeatureActivated` method, which would assign custom permissions to a list instance in the current site, you could also add code to the `FeatureDeactivating` method, which would remove the custom permissions from the list so the list inherited permissions from its parent when a user deactivated the feature.

Upgrading a Feature

In the previous version of SharePoint, it could be difficult to make changes to existing features. In some cases, to make updates and changes to an existing feature, your best option was to create a whole new feature that had to be activated after the first feature was activated. For example, if you had a feature scoped to the site-collection level that provisioned several site columns and a content type, and then you decided you wanted an additional column in your content type, you might end up creating an additional feature that simply added that single column to the existing content type. This could be problematic because someone might forget to activate the second feature if a new site collection was provisioned, meaning you might not have consistency across your farm. In addition, you could conceivably end up with multiple updates to a single feature, creating a maintenance headache.

With this version of SharePoint, it's possible to upgrade an existing feature, telling SharePoint what modifications it should make to older, already activated features to make them compatible with a newer version of the feature. This means that, after the upgrade process takes place, you should have consistency across your farm because older versions of the feature have been brought into sync with the functionality of the newest version of the feature. It also means that if a user activates the feature in a new location (such as a new site collection), he or she will be activating the newest (and most complete) version of the feature.

Imagine that the first version of your feature is scoped to the site-collection level and provisions a content type with four site columns when the feature is activated. You then create a second version of your feature, but this new version now has an additional site column, so when the feature is activated for the first time, a content type with five columns is provisioned. You can tell SharePoint that, when the new feature is installed, SharePoint should at the same time go look at every site collection, find where that older version of the feature has already been activated, and add only the one new additional column to the existing content type in that site collection. This means that all the existing site collections will have a content type with five columns, and any new site collections where the feature is activated for the first time will also have a content type with the same five columns.

When an older feature is upgraded, SharePoint will fire the `FeatureUpgrading` event on the older feature. If you want to execute certain actions when the feature is upgraded, you can add custom code to the `FeatureUpgrading` event handler in your feature event receiver class. The upgrade event fires when a solution containing the new feature is deployed or upgraded. (Solutions are discussed later in this chapter.)

 Any changes made during the feature upgrade process will be executed using the farm administrator's credentials.

Feature Localization

Features can use resource files to display text in various languages. This includes text such as the name of the feature and the description of the feature. Typically, the resource files for a feature are stored in a folder called Resources inside the Feature folder. However, it's also possible to deploy your resource file to a common location used to store resource files for the SharePoint product in general.

SharePoint 2010 enables you to create multi-lingual sites, including localized web pages, Web Parts, web controls, and so on. A detailed explanation of creating multi-lingual sites, however, is outside the scope of this current chapter.

Configuring a Feature

Each feature has its own folder in the ~/14/TEMPLATE/FEATURES directory. That folder must contain a file called feature.xml. Feature.xml is a configuration file that tells SharePoint information about the feature, such as its name and scope, as well as which files are included in the feature and where those items are located. This is sometimes called the *feature manifest*.

The root element of the XML file is an element called `Feature`. Table 7-4 outlines commonly used attributes that can be added to a feature element.

 Table 7-4 is not a complete list. Read the MSDN documentation for the complete list of attributes, which you can find at http://msdn.microsoft.com/en-us/library/ms436075(office.14).aspx.

TABLE 7-4: Feature Element Attributes

ATTRIBUTE NAME	REQUIRED	ATTRIBUTE DESCRIPTION
ID	Yes	The globally unique identifier (GUID) for the feature.
Scope	Yes	Specifies the scope of the feature. Possible values are `Farm` (farm), `WebApplication` (web application), `Site` (site collection), or `Web` (website).
Title	No	The name of the feature. This value will appear in the browser if the feature is visible. Although this value is not required by SharePoint, it's recommended that you use a title so that your feature is easily identified.
DefaultResourceFile	No	If this value is not set, SharePoint looks for all its resource files inside a folder called Resources inside the Feature folder. Furthermore, SharePoint assumes that the name of each language's resource file follows the pattern of Resources.*culture*.resx, where *culture* is the abbreviation for the resource file's culture.* For example, the Austrian German resource file would be called Resources.de-AT.resx.
		If a value is given for the `DefaultResourceFile`, SharePoint will look for a file starting with the given value in the ~/14/Resources folder. For example, if the attribute is given a value of `MyFeature`, SharePoint will look for an Austrian German SharePoint resource file at ~/14/Resources/MyFeature.de-AT.resx.
Description	No	A description of the feature. This value will also appear in the browser if the feature is visible.
Hidden	No	A Boolean value indicating whether or not the feature is visible in the browser.
ImageUrl	No	The URL for the icon that appears next to a feature in the browser, relative to the ~/14/TEMPLATE/IMAGES folder. For example, if you deployed a new directory inside the IMAGES directory called MyCustomImages and added your image MyImage.gif to that directory, the `ImageUrl` property would be `MyCustomImages/MyImage.gif`.
ImageUrlAltText	No	The alternate text associated with the feature icon.
ReceiverAssembly	No	If a feature event receiver class has been created in order to handle events associated with the feature, this value contains the fully qualified assembly name of the assembly containing the class.

ATTRIBUTE NAME	REQUIRED	ATTRIBUTE DESCRIPTION
ReceiverClass	No	If a feature event receiver class has been created in order to handle events associated with the feature, this value contains the name of the class (including its namespace).
RequireResources	No	This is a Boolean value which, when set to true, tells SharePoint to hide the feature from the list of available features in the browser if a resource file is not present for the active language.**
Version	No	The version number of your feature. This has to be a valid version number with up to four parts, such as 1.0.0.0.

* For a complete list of culture names, visit http://msdn.microsoft.com/en-us/goglobal/bb896001.aspx.

** There are some conditions in which setting this to true will not prevent a feature's activation. For a comprehensive explanation of the RequireResources attribute, visit http://msdn.microsoft.com/en-us/library/ms436075(office.14).aspx.

The next code snippet is a sample feature element. This feature, titled My Visual Web Part, has a description, a scope set to the site-collection level, a custom icon that appears beside it in the browser, and a custom feature event receiver.

Available for download on Wrox.com

```
<Feature Id="1c82a5a3-0609-40a6-b6a9-6de9bceddb66"
    Scope="Site"
    Title="My Visual Web Part Feature"
    Description="This Feature deploys a Web Part to the Web Part Gallery."
    Hidden="FALSE"
    ImageUrl="MyVisualWebPartFeature.gif"
    ImageUrlAltText="My Visual Web Part Feature"
    ReceiverAssembly="MyVisualWPSolution, Culture=neutral,
        PublicKeyToken=a5d015c7d5a0b012, Version=1.0.0.0"
    ReceiverClass="MyVisualWPSolution.MyVisualWPFeatureReceiver" />
```

code snippet Feature.xml

The Feature XML element can also contain several additional elements:

➤ ActivationDependencies: Contains a list of the additional features that must be activated before the current feature can be activated. A feature is referred to by its unique identifier, not its title. However, for readability, it's recommended that the name of the feature be added as a comment next to each ActivationDependency element.

➤ ElementManifests: This element instructs SharePoint where to look for the various assets on the filesystem that are necessary components of the feature. Two types of files can be referenced inside the ElementManifests element.

➤ The first kind of file is referenced using an `ElementManifest` element. An element manifest file tells SharePoint which items to add to a site collection or site, such as site columns, content types, list definitions, list instances, list items, custom menu items, and so on. For example, an element manifest file could instruct SharePoint to create a new site column or provision a new list definition. The `Location` attribute of the element tells SharePoint where it can find the manifest file relative to the Feature folder.

➤ The second kind of file is referenced using an `ElementFile` element. This kind of file is simply a supporting file, such as an image or a Web Part configuration file. As with an `ElementManifest` element, the `Location` attribute of the element tells SharePoint where it can find the file relative to the Feature folder.

The next code snippet is an example feature, but with some modifications. The feature can no longer be activated until another feature that provisions several custom site columns is activated first. The feature's folder has another folder inside of it called MyVisualWP. That folder contains two files: an element manifest called elements.xml, and a file used by the feature, called MyVisualWP.webpart.

```
<Feature Id="1c82a5a3-0609-40a6-b6a9-6de9bceddb66"
        Scope="Site"
        Title="My Visual Web Part Feature"
        Description="This Feature deploys a Web Part to the Web Part Gallery."
        Hidden="FALSE"
        ImageUrl="MyVisualWebPartFeature.gif"
        ImageUrlAltText="My Visual Web Part Feature"
        ReceiverAssembly="MyVisualWPSolution, Culture=neutral,
        PublicKeyToken=a5d015c7d5a0b012, Version=1.0.0.0"
        ReceiverClass="MyVisualWPSolution.MyVisualWPFeatureReceiver">
    <ActivationDependencies>
        <!-- Custom Site Columns Feature -->
        <ActivationDependency FeatureId="836eaf63-0cbd-4c24-90f2-06f74374f529" />
        <!-- Custom List Instance Feature -->
        <ActivationDependency FeatureId="dacd31aa-8a5f-434d-a53f-084aae7e6e41" />
    </ActivationDependencies>
    <ElementManifests>
        <ElementManifest Location="MyVisualWP\Elements.xml" />
        <ElementFile Location="MyVisualWP\MyVisualWP.webpart" />
    </ElementManifests>
</Feature>
```

code snippet Feature.xml

Using the UpgradeActions Element

To tell SharePoint that certain actions need to take place when upgrading a feature, you need to add an `UpgradeAction` element to your feature element in your feature.xml file. The `UpgradeAction` element has two elements: `ReceiverAssembly` and `ReceiverClass`. These values are used just as they are in the feature elements. `ReceiverAssembly` specifies the long assembly name of the assembly containing the feature event receiver class, and `ReceiverClass` contains the name (including namespace) of the feature event receiver class. By passing in values for these attributes, you are telling SharePoint to look for an event receiver class implementing the `FeatureUpgrading` method.

The `UpgradeAction` element has several child elements, listed in Table 7-5.

TABLE 7-5: Table UpgradeAction Elements

ELEMENT NAME	ELEMENT DESCRIPTION
AddContentTypeField	This element allows you to add a new field to an existing content type. The element has three values: `ContentTypeId` is the unique identifier of the content type you want to add a field to; `FieldId` is the unique identifier of the column you want to add to the content type; and `PushDown` is a Boolean value indicating whether the changes to the content type should be pushed down to all the content types inheriting from this one.
ApplyElementManifests	If additional files or assets need to be deployed during the upgrade process, this element allows you to specify the element manifest and element files to use. These are the same kind of element manifest and element files used when deploying a feature, except these files are utilized only during the upgrade process. You can specify one or more element manifests to include by adding one or more `ElementManifest` elements. You can specify one or more element files to use by adding one or more child `ElementFile` elements.
CustomUpgradeAction	This contains values that get passed to the `UpgradingFeature` method in your feature event receiver class. This element contains an attribute called `Name`. You need to specify a name only if you have more than one `CustomUpgradeAction` element. This element can contain a child element called `Parameters`, which can contain one or more `Parameter` elements. As with the `Name` attribute, the `Parameter` element values will be passed to the event receiver method.
MapFile	This element is used for changing the path to a specific file on the server. The element contains two attributes: `FromPath` and `ToPath`. If you want to simply rename a file used in your feature, you can just put different filenames in the path, like `FromPath="oldfile.gif" ToPath="newfile.jpg"`. If you want to change the path of a physical file on the server (relative to the Feature folder), you can do that too. For instance, this example changes the path of a file from being in a folder called WebPages in the Feature folder, to being in a folder called PublishingPages in the Feature folder: `FromPath="WebPages/MyPage.aspx" ToPath="PublishingPages/MyPage.aspx"`.

continues

TABLE 7-5 *(continued)*

ELEMENT NAME	ELEMENT DESCRIPTION
VersionRange	This element tells SharePoint what actions it should perform on a specific range of versions of a feature. The `BeginVersion` attribute specifies the lower range of the version numbers that SharePoint is looking for, and the `EndVersion` attribute specifies the upper range of the version numbers SharePoint is looking for. For example, `<VersionRange BeginVersion="1.0.0.0" EndVersion="3.0.0.0"></VersionRange>` means that SharePoint will find the older versions of the current feature, between version 1.0.0.0 and 3.0.0.0, and will execute the upgrade actions specified. The `VersionRange` element can contain `AddContentTypeField`, `ApplyElementManifests`, `CustomUpgradeAction`, and `MapFile` elements.

The `FeatureUpgrading` feature event receiver method has the following signature:

```
FeatureUpgrading(SPFeatureReceiverProperties, String,
    IDictionary<(Of <(String, String>)>))
```

If this method were implemented in conjunction with the code example in next code snippet, the second parameter passed in would be the value contained in the `Name` attribute of the `CustomUpgradeAction` element, which is `AddListInstance`. The parameter with a name of `ListName` and a value of `Sample Documents` would be passed in through the last parameter of the `FeatureUpgrading` method as a key/value pair.

The example in this next code snippet tells SharePoint to execute the `FeatureUpgrading` method of the `MyNamespace.CustomFeatureEventReceiver` class stored in the assembly called CustomFeatureReceiver, passing in the custom action name and parameter list. It also tells SharePoint to follow the instructions listed in the element manifest file called columns.xml and to use the file called NewPage.aspx located in the Pages folder inside the feature's folder. The `MapPath` element tells SharePoint that any reference to MyImage.gif in the older feature(s) should now refer to MyImage.jpg instead. Finally, it specifies that for any older features having a version number between 1.0.0.0 and 3.0.0.0, the given content type should have an additional field added to its definition, and that field should be pushed down to any other sites or lists that currently reference that content type.

```
<UpgradeActions
  ReceiverAssembly="CustomFeatureEventReceiver, Version=1.0.0.0,
    Culture=neutral,
    PublicKeyToken= b77a3c59194set29"
    ReceiverClass="MyNamespace.CustomFeatureEventReceiver">
  <CustomUpgradeAction Name="AddListInstance">
    <Parameters>
      <Parameter Name="ListName">Sample Documents</Parameter>
    </Parameters>
```

```
      </CustomUpgradeAction>
      <ApplyElementManifests>
        <ElementManifest Location="Columns.xml" />
        <ElementFile Location="Pages/NewPage.aspx" />
      </ApplyElementManifests>
      <MapPath
        FromPath="MyImage.gif"
        ToPath="MyImage.jpg" />
      <VersionRange
        BeginVersion="1.0.0.0"
        EndVersion="3.0.0.0">
        <AddContentTypeField
          ContentTypeId = "0x010100F7F810E0559211DF98790800200C9A66"
          FieldId = "{1808d630559311df98790800200c9a66}"
          PushDown = "TRUE" />
      </VersionRange>
    </UpgradeActions>
```

code snippet Feature.xml

The new feature upgrading functionality included with SharePoint 2010 provides a helpful way of gracefully enhancing your existing features.

UNDERSTANDING SOLUTIONS

Designing and building a feature is just the first step. It has to be deployed in order for it to be useful. You can do this using SharePoint solutions.

One of the strengths of the SharePoint platform is its ability to scale well. If a single front-end web server is nearing capacity, another front-end web server can be easily attached to the farm. When this happens, SharePoint attempts to make the new server behave exactly like the first server by deploying the same files to the new server as it has deployed to the other server(s). The SharePoint solution framework makes this possible.

A SharePoint solution, in reality, is nothing more than a cabinet file whose file extension has been changed from .cab to .wsp. However, a solution contains special instructions telling SharePoint what to do with the various files contained in the solution file, as well as indicate certain changes that need to be made to a web application's web.config file. These instructions might tell SharePoint to place files in a particular location on the server, deploy an assembly to the Global Assembly Cache, or mark an assembly as "safe" in the web.config. Because SharePoint has a record of where items need to be deployed to on the server, SharePoint can simply extract the solution contents and follow the instructions to deploy the files to their proper locations when a new server is attached to the farm. In the same way, if the deployed files need to be removed from their respective locations, it's important that the files are removed from all the load-balanced servers in the same way so as to enforce uniformity among the servers. Because the solution contains these instructions, SharePoint can carry out the process of removing files in an identical way.

Understanding the Solution Lifecycle

Several steps are involved with getting a solution ready for operation. The first step is to make SharePoint aware of the new solution. If the solution is a farm solution, you can do this by adding it to the list of available solutions called the *solution store*. If the solution is a sandboxed solution, you can do this by adding it to the Solution gallery in a given site collection. (The difference between a farm and sandboxed solution is discussed in the next section.)

As mentioned previously, the contents of a solution file need to be deployed to multiple servers if those servers are load balanced. When dealing with farm solutions, in some cases the contents of the file will be placed in locations that are commonly available to all the SharePoint web applications in the farm. When this happens, the solution will be considered *globally* deployed. In other cases, files must be deployed to a particular web application. For example, an assembly might need to be deployed to the bin directory of a web application rather than to the GAC. In those cases, a farm administrator must specify which web application(s) the solution is being deployed to.

The solution must be retracted to remove its contents from one or more servers. If a solution was deployed globally, it will be retracted globally. If it was deployed to individual web applications, it can be retracted from one web application at a time.

Finally, removing the solution from the farm means SharePoint is no longer aware of its presence.

Sandboxed Solutions

Although SharePoint enables end users to customize their SharePoint sites to a certain degree, some customizations can only be made by deploying custom code and custom assets to the server via a solution. However, only a farm administrator has the ability to deploy a solution to the farm. In some cases, farm administrators don't have the available time to deploy solutions in a timely manner, leaving end users frustrated that their solutions are not being deployed as quickly as they would like. Furthermore, if a solution is deployed globally, particular features could become available to all site collections across the farm. This could be undesirable, especially in environments with hundreds or thousands of site collections, and especially in hosted environments in which one site-collection owner should be unaware of any activity in any other site collection on the server.

What Are Sandboxed Solutions?

SharePoint 2010 has introduced the concept of sandboxed solutions. A sandboxed solution is one that can be uploaded to a specific site collection by a site-collection administrator using a browser. By providing this functionality, site administrators are no longer required to wait for their farm administrator to deploy their solution because they can do it themselves. In addition, sandboxed solutions are applied only to the site collection to which they have been uploaded. No other site collection has any knowledge of the solution's existence, just as another site collection would not be aware that a document had been uploaded to a document library in another site collection.

As great an idea as this might seem, because solutions deployed this way are not required to go through a thorough vetting process this approach could cause havoc in a farm for several reasons:

➤ A single solution deployed to a single site collection could potentially consume so many server resources that it bogs down the entire server. Because the farm administrator isn't necessarily aware of the sandboxed solution's existence (it was uploaded without his knowledge), he would not immediately know why his server was performing slowly. It could potentially take some time to figure out the source of the problem.

➤ A malicious or clumsy programmer could write code inside a solution that accesses objects in the farm, such as other site collections or even web applications. A sandboxed solution deployed without a farm administrator's consent could potentially delete web applications and otherwise bring down the farm.

Microsoft has provided a solution to each of these problems:

➤ Farm administrators can specify a threshold of server resources (a combined value that takes into account things like CPU and memory usage) that a site collection's sandbox can use. Once that threshold has been met in a particular site collection, all the sandboxed solutions in that site will be turned off for the rest of day. (Clearly, this is a stop-gap measure to protect the server. The goal is for your solutions to not consume so many resources that they exceed that quota in a day.)

➤ Sandboxed solutions do not run with full trust in the web application; instead, they run with a custom code access policy that grants them minimal permissions. A limited API is available to sandboxed solutions, eliminating the ability for sandboxed solutions to access anything in the object model above the site collection (such as the web application or farm objects), or allowing code in sandboxed solutions to run with elevated privileges. Sandboxed solutions cannot deploy any files to the SharePoint root folder, and they cannot deploy objects such as site definitions and workflows.

 It is possible to get around some of the limitations of a sandboxed solution by writing a custom full trust proxy, then consuming that proxy using the SPUtility.ExecuteRegisteredProxyOperation *method.*

When a sandboxed solution is deployed, any features associated with it are automatically activated.

Table 7-6 compares the characteristics of farm and sandboxed solutions.

TABLE 7-6: A Comparison of Farm and Sandboxed Solutions

FARM	SANDBOXED
Assemblies are placed in the GAC or in the bin directory of a SharePoint web application. Assemblies placed in the GAC are fully trusted, whereas assemblies placed in the bin directory of a web application can be partially trusted. Assembly execution takes place in the web server process (w3wp.exe).	Any assemblies associated with a solution are extracted, kept in memory, and executed within a special worker process called SPUCWorkerProcess.exe. This isolates the execution of sandboxed solutions from the operations of the underlying web process.
Solutions must be installed and deployed by a farm administrator.	Solutions can be installed and deployed by a site administrator.
There are no limitations on which SharePoint classes and objects can be used in farm solution assemblies.	Developers must leverage a subset of the SharePoint API when developing sandboxed solutions.
Solutions will use however many server resources are necessary.	Farm administrators have the ability to throttle the server resources used by a given solution.

Sandboxed solutions are deployed to the Solution gallery in a given site collection. You can view the Solution gallery by navigating to the Site Settings page in the root site of the site collection, then clicking the Solutions link under the Galleries heading.

Sandboxed Solution PowerShell Commands

SharePoint has several PowerShell commands that can be used for solution installation, deployment, retraction, removal, and upgrade. Table 7-7 reviews these commands and some of their commonly used parameters. For a complete list of parameters, open the SharePoint PowerShell command prompt and type `get-help` followed by the name of the command and the `-detailed` parameter, like this: `get-help Add-SPUserSolution -detailed`

TABLE 7-7: PowerShell Commands for Sandboxed Solutions

COMMAND	PARAMETERS	DESCRIPTION
Add-SPUserSolution	`-LiteralPath`: The path to the solution file; can be a path to a drive (such as C:\Solutions\MySolution.wsp) or to a UNC path (such as \\servername\MySolution.wsp). `-Site`: The URL, GUID, or SPSite object of the site collection to which this sandboxed solution will be added.	Uploads a new solution to the Solution gallery in a site collection.

COMMAND	PARAMETERS	DESCRIPTION
Install-SPUserSolution	-Identity: The name of the sandboxed solution or a sandboxed solution object. -Site: The URL, GUID, or SPSite object of the site collection in which this sandboxed solution will be activated.	Activates a sandboxed solution in a site collection.
Uninstall-SPUserSolution	-Identity: The name of the sandboxed solution or a sandboxed solution object. -Site: The URL, GUID, or SPSite object of the site collection in which this sandboxed solution will be deactivated.	Deactivates a sandboxed solution in a site collection.
Remove-SPUserSolution	-Identity: The name of the sandboxed solution or a sandboxed solution object. -Site: The URL, GUID, or SPSite object of the site collection from which this sandboxed solution will be removed.	Completely removes a solution from the Solution gallery in a site gallery; solution must be uninstalled before it can be removed.
Update-SPUserSolution	-Identity: The name of the sandboxed solution or a sandboxed solution object. -Site: The URL, GUID, or SPSite object of the site collection where the sandboxed solution lives. -ToSolution: The name of the solution file with which you want to replace the old solution file.	Upgrades a sandboxed solution that has already been activated.
Get-SPUserSolution	-Identity: The name of the sandboxed solution or a sandboxed solution object. -Site: The URL, GUID, or SPSite object of the site collection in which the sandboxed solution lives.	Gets one or more solutions.

Listing 7-3 lists examples of various PowerShell commands you can execute from the SharePoint PowerShell command prompt to add, install, uninstall, and remove sandboxed solutions.

LISTING 7-3: SandboxedSolutions.ps1

```
Add-SPUserSolution -LiteralPath C:\Solutions\MySolution.wsp
    -Site http://sitename
Install-SPUserSolution -Identity MySolution.wsp
    -Site http://sitename
Uninstall-SPUserSolution -Identity MySolution.wsp
    -Site http://sitename
Remove-SPUserSolution -Identity MySolution.wsp
    -Site http://sitename
Update-SPUserSolution -Identity MySolution.wsp
    -Site http://sitename -ToSolution MySolutionV2.wsp
Get-SPUserSolution -Identity MySolution.wsp -Site http://sitename
```

Farm Solutions

Farm solutions cannot be installed using a browser the way that sandboxed solutions can be. Instead, PowerShell is needed. To install a farm solution, use the `Install-SPSolution` PowerShell command. This will add the solution to the solution store in Central Administration.

To find the solution store, navigate to the Central Administration website and click the System Settings link in the navigation on the left side of the page. Under the heading Farm Management, click the link that says Manage Farm Solutions. This will take you to the Solution Management page.

Clicking a solution in the list brings up a page for managing the solution properties. This page shows when and where the solution was deployed (if at all). In addition, the toolbar has buttons for deploying or retracting the solution. If the solution deploys globally, no configuration is required beyond simply deploying the solution. Otherwise, the Deploy To? section will have a drop-down list containing the web applications in the farm. By selecting an item from the list, a user can select the web application to which the solution will be deployed. In the same way, the user can choose the web application from which the solution should be retracted, when applicable. Once a solution has been completely retracted from every location in the farm, it can be removed by clicking the Remove Solution button in the toolbar.

As with sandboxed solutions, PowerShell can be used to add, deploy, retract, remove, and upgrade solutions. Table 7-8 shows the PowerShell commands you can use for farm solutions.

TABLE 7-8: PowerShell Commands for Farm Solutions

COMMAND	PARAMETERS	DESCRIPTION
Add-SPSolution	`-LiteralPath`: The path to the solution file to be added; can be a path to a drive (such as `C:\ Solutions \MySolution.wsp`) or to a UNC path (such as `\\servername\MySolution.wsp`).	Adds a solution to the farm.
Install-SPSolution	`-Identity`: The name or SolutionId of the solution to be deployed. `-GACDeployment`: Specifies that the assembly can be deployed to the GAC. `-AllWebApplications`: If this solution is to be deployed to web applications (as opposed to globally), this specifies that it should be deployed to all the web applications in the farm. `-WebApplication`: A specific web application to which to deploy the solution; must be a valid web application GUID, name, or `SPWebApplication` object.	Deploys a solution, either globally or to a specific web application.

COMMAND	PARAMETERS	DESCRIPTION
Uninstall-SPSolution	`-Identity`: The name or SolutionId of the solution to be retracted; if the solution was deployed globally, this is all that needs to be passed in. `-AllWebApplications`: If this solution has been deployed to one or more web applications (as opposed to globally), this specifies that it should be retracted from all the web applications in the farm. `-WebApplication`: The specific web application from which the solution must be retracted; must be a valid web application GUID, name, or `SPWebApplication` object.	Retracts a solution, either globally or from a specific web application.
Remove-SPSolution	`-Identity`: The name or SolutionId of the solution to be removed.	Removes a solution from the farm.
Get-SPSolution	`-Identity`: The SolutionId of the solution you're trying to retrieve; if no identity parameter is passed, the command will return all the solutions installed in the farm.	Gets one or more solutions.
Update-SPsolution	`-Identity`: The name or SolutionId of the solution to be upgraded. `-LiteralPath`: The path to the solution file to be added; can be a path to a drive (such as `C:\Solutions \MySolution.wsp`) or to a UNC path (such as `\\servername\MySolution.wsp`). `-GACDeployment`: Specifies that the assembly can be deployed to the GAC. `-Time`: The time when the upgrade should take place; if no time is specified, the solution is upgraded immediately.	Upgrades an existing solution.

Listing 7-4 lists examples of various PowerShell commands you can execute from the SharePoint PowerShell command prompt to add, install, uninstall, remove, upgrade, and retrieve solutions.

LISTING 7-4: FarmSolutions.ps1

```
Add-SPSolution -LiteralPath C:\Solutions\MySolution.wsp
Install-SPSolution -Identity MySolution.wsp -GACDeployment
Install-SPSolution -Identity MySolution.wsp
    -WebApplication IntranetSite
Uninstall-SPSolution -Identity MySolution.wsp
```

```
Uninstall-SPSolution -Identity MySolution.wsp
    -AllWebApplications
Remove-SPSolution -Identity MySolution.wsp
Update-SPSolution -Identity MySolution.wsp
    -LitearlPath C:\Solutions\MySolutionV2.wsp -GACDeployment
Get-SPSolution -Identity MySolution.wsp
    -Identity MySolution.wsp -Site http://sitename
```

As with features, it's possible to work with solutions using the STSADM command tool. Table 7-9 enumerates the STSADM commands you can use to work with them. Because the STSADM command is a legacy tool, it doesn't include commands for sandboxed solutions.

TABLE 7-9: STSADM Commands for Solutions

COMMAND	PARAMETERS	DESCRIPTION
-o addsolution	−filename: The absolute path to the solution on the server, such as C:\Solutions\MySolution.wsp.	Adds a solution to the farm.
-o deploysolution	−name: The name of the solution being deployed. −url: If the solution is being deployed to a single web application, the URL of the web application. −immediate: A parameter with no value; if you pass the parameter, SharePoint will deploy the solution immediately. −allowGacDeployment: A necessary parameter if your solution is deploying an assembly to the Global Assembly Cache.	Deploys a solution, either globally or to a specific web application.
-o retractsolution	−name: The name of the solution being retracted. −url: If the solution is deployed to a single web application, the URL of the web application from which the solution should be retracted. −immediate: A parameter with no value; if you pass the parameter, SharePoint will retract the solution immediately.	Retracts a solution, either globally or from a specific web application.
-o deletesolution	−name: The name of the solution to be deleted.	Removes a solution from the farm.

COMMAND	PARAMETERS	DESCRIPTION
`-o upgradesolution`	`-name`: The name of the solution being upgraded. `-url`: If the solution is being deployed to a single web application, the URL of the web application. `-immediate`: A parameter with no value; if you pass the parameter, SharePoint will deploy the upgraded solution immediately. `-allowGacDeployment`: A necessary parameter of your new solution is deploying an assembly to the Global Assembly Cache.	Upgrades an existing solution with a newer version.

Listing 7-5 shows some sample STSADM commands for working with a farm solution.

LISTING 7-5: FarmSolutions.bat

```
cd "C:\Program Files\Common Files\Microsoft Shared\Web Server Extensions\14\BIN"
stsadm -o addsolution -filename C:\Solutions\MySolution.wsp
stsadm -o deploysolution -name MySolution.wsp
    -url http://sitename -immediate -allowGacDeployment
stsadm -o retractsolution -name MySolution.wsp
    -url http://sitename -immediate
stsadm -o deletefeature -name MyFeature.wsp
stsadm -o upgradesolution -filename C:\Solutions\MySolution.wsp
    -name MySolution.wsp -immediate -allowGacDeployment
```

Configuring a Solution

The file which contains the instructions that SharePoint uses to deploy or retract the files in a solution is called a *solution manifest* file. The file itself must be called manifest.xml. Similar to the feature manifest file, the solution manifest file is an XML file containing configuration information.

The root element of the XML found in a solution manifest file is an element called `Solution`. Each solution must have a GUID associated with it, added to an attribute of the `Solution` element called `SolutionId`.

The `Solution` element has an optional attribute called `ResetWebServer`, which takes a Boolean value indicating whether IIS should be restarted when the solution is deployed. In some cases, items from SharePoint get cached in IIS. For this reason, it's often necessary to recycle a website's application pool in order for changes to be picked up. However, if the solution is going to be deployed to the web server during peak business hours, it can make sense to set this value to `FALSE` and schedule an IIS reset for a later time. If the `ResetWebServer` attribute is not specified, SharePoint will assume a value of `FALSE`.

SharePoint 2010 introduces a new optional attribute to the `Solution` element: `ResetWebServerModeOnUpgrade`. This attribute tells SharePoint what it should do when the solution itself is being upgraded on the server. The possible values are `Recycle` (which tells SharePoint to simply recycle the IIS worker process) or `StartStop` (which tells SharePoint to reboot the IIS server).

Another optional attribute, called `SharePointProductVersion`, is for informational purposes only. It simply contains the version of SharePoint that the solution is targeted for, whether that value is `12.0` (for Windows SharePoint Services 3.0) or `14.0` (for SharePoint Foundation 2010).

Finally, the `Solution` element can have an additional attribute called `DeploymentServerType`. In general, this value will be set to `WebFrontEnd` to indicate that the files will be deployed to a front-end web server. Alternatively, the solution could be deployed to a SharePoint application server, in which case the attribute value would be `ApplicationServer`. If this attribute is not used, SharePoint will use a default value of `WebFrontEnd`.

SAFE CONTROLS

One of the benefits of SharePoint's framework is its usability; users can easily upload files, including ASPX files. Because ASPX files can contain code that could conceivably execute within the SharePoint environment, this presents a security risk. To reduce that risk, it's necessary to explicitly tell SharePoint which controls on a page have permission to execute (preventing end users from adding malicious or unhelpful code to an ASPX page they add to a site). You do this by marking a control as "safe" in the SharePoint web application's web.config file. Because presumably only farm administrators would have permission to access the IIS server's file system to get access to the web.config file to make the change, this prevents end users from embedding and executing unauthorized code on pages they add to a SharePoint site. In practice, what this means is that, if you want to deploy an assembly containing one or more Web Part classes, you must mark the Web Part assembly and types as safe.

The following code snippet demonstrates a sample `Solution` element:

```
<Solution SolutionId="6f0f0225-21f4-40a3-9871-91e71be08a24"
    ResetWebServer="TRUE"
    DeploymentServerType="WebFrontEnd"/>
```

code snippet Manifest.xml

The `Solution` element can contain a number of child elements, listed in the following sections. (Note that these are presented in a long bulleted list, interspersed with code snippets and other material.)

➤ `Assemblies`: This element can contain one or more `Assembly` elements and is used to define where assemblies are located and installed. The element uses the following attributes:

    ➤ `DeploymentTarget`: Possible values are `GlobalAssemblyCache` and `WebApplication`. This attribute indicates where an assembly contained in your solution will be deployed. If this value is set to `WebApplication`, the assembly will be deployed to the bin directory of the IIS web application folder containing the SharePoint site.

    ➤ `Location`: This is the location of the assembly in the solution relative to the root of the cabinet file (*not* the location where it will be deployed on the server). In other words, passing in a value such as `Assembly\MyAssembly.dll` means SharePoint will look for a directory in the solution file called Assembly, containing an assembly called MyAssembly.dll.

➤ `Assembly`: The `Assembly` element can contain two other child elements: `SafeControls` and `ClassResources`.

    ➤ `SafeControls`: This element contains one or more `SafeControl` element. When a solution is deployed, SharePoint will automatically add the `SafeControl` element(s) defined in the solution manifest file to the web application's web.config file. The `SafeControl` element can have the following attributes:

        ➤ `Assembly`: The fully qualified assembly name.

        ➤ `Namespace`: The namespace associated with the assembly.

        ➤ `Safe`: A Boolean value, which will be set to `TRUE` if the purpose is to authorize the assembly for use. Setting the value to `FALSE` would indicate that the assembly is not safe for SharePoint to use.

        ➤ `TypeName`: The assembly type name associated with the control to be used. If you pass in an asterisk (*), this will indicate to SharePoint that all the types available in the given assembly and namespace are safe (or not safe, depending on the value specified in the `Safe` attribute).

➤ `ClassResources`: Contains one or more `ClassResource` elements. The word *resource* can mean different things in SharePoint. In this case, it is not referring exclusively to resource files containing textual translations stored in a file with a .resx extension. In this case, a "resource" is simply any file that is needed for a given control or Web Part to function properly, such as an image embedded in a Web Part. The `ClassResources` element has the following two attributes:

    ➤ `FileName`: The name of the resource file associated with the assembly.

    ➤ `Location`: The path of the resource file relative to the root of the folder into which the class resource files are placed. For instance, image resources might be grouped into a folder called Images, so the value of the `Location` attribute would be `Images\MyImage.gif`.

Where the resources are placed depends on the destination of the assembly. If the assembly is being deployed to a web application, the class resources will be deployed relative to a folder called wpresources inside the web application's IIS directory. If the assembly is being deployed to the GAC, the class resources are placed in the `C:\Program Files\Common Files\ Microsoft Shared\Web Server Extensions\wpresources` folder on your web server, which is mapped as a virtual directory called _wpresources inside your IIS web application.

The example in the next code snippet shows a solution that contains an assembly called MyVisualWebPartSolution.dll, which is stored in the root of the solution, and will be deployed to the GAC. This solution manifest is instructing SharePoint to add a `SafeControl` entry to the web application's web.config file, so that it knows that it's safe to execute code in any class in the MyFirstFeature.MyFirstWebPart namespace in the MyVisualWebPartSolution assembly. This assembly has a class resource file called template.xsl that will be deployed to the global wpresources folder on the server.

Available for
download on
Wrox.com

```xml
<Assemblies>
  <Assembly
    Location="MyVisualWebPartSolution.dll"
    DeploymentTarget="GlobalAssemblyCache">
    <SafeControls>
        <SafeControl
            Assembly="MyVisualWebPartSolution, Version=1.0.0.0, Culture=neutral,
            PublicKeyToken=f7cdad460df595d5"
            Namespace="MyFirstFeature.MyFirstWebPart" TypeName="*" />
    </SafeControls>
    <ClassResources>
        <ClassResource Location="Template.xsl" />
    </ClassResources>
  </Assembly>
</Assemblies>
```

code snippet Manifest.xml

The following bullet items and subitems continue the list started earlier in the chapter:

➤ FeatureManifests: The `FeatureManifests` element contains one or more `FeatureManifest` elements. Each `FeatureManifest` element has one attribute: `Location`. This is the location of the feature.xml file for each feature that is being deployed with the solution, relative to the cabinet file. For instance, if the solution contains a feature whose folder is called MyFeature, the `Location` attribute value would be `MyFeature\Feature.xml`. It's not necessary to specify each asset associated with each feature in the solution manifest file because that information is stored in each feature's manifest file. Each feature in the solution will be deployed to the ~/14/ TEMPLATE/FEATURES directory on the server.

The following example shows how to reference the feature manifest file inside the MyFeature folder.

Available for
download on
Wrox.com

```xml
<FeatureManifests>
    <FeatureManifest Location="MyFeature\Feature.xml" />
</FeatureManifests>
```

code snippet Manifest.xml

➤ RootFiles: This element contains one or more RootFile elements. Each RootFile element has one attribute: Location. This attribute indicates where the file will be copied to on the server, relative to the SharePoint root folder on the file system. For example, to deploy a configuration file to the ~/14/CONFIG directory on the server, the Location attribute value would be set to CONFIG\MyConfigFile.config. Note that your file must exist in the same location relative to the root of the solution as well as to the ~/14/ directory. That means that, to deploy a configuration file to the ~/14/CONFIG directory on the web server, the solution must also contain a folder called CONFIG in the root of the solution, and the custom configuration file must be placed in that folder.

The following snippet is an example of a RootFiles element telling SharePoint to deploy a file called MyConfigFile.config to the ~/14/CONFIG folder on the web server.

```
<RootFiles>
    <RootFile Location="CONFIG\MyConfigFile.config" />
</RootFiles>
```

code snippet Manifest.xml

➤ TemplateFiles: This element contains one or more TemplateFile elements. Each TemplateFile element functions just like a RootFile element, except that template files get deployed relative to the ~/14/TEMPLATE folder instead of the ~/14 folder. As with root files, a template file must exist in the same location within the solutions as the location to which the file will be deployed on the server.

The following snippet is an example of a TemplateFiles element telling SharePoint to deploy a file called MyUserControl.aspx to the ~/14/TEMPLATE/CONTROLTEMPLATES folder on the web server.

```
<TemplateFile
    Location="CONTROLTEMPLATES\MyUserControl.ascx" />
</TemplateFiles>
```

code snippet Manifest.xml

➤ SiteDefinitionManifests: This element contains one or more SiteDefinitionManifest elements and is used for deploying site definitions to the server. The SiteDefinitionManifest element has the same Location attribute as the RootFile and TemplateFile elements. This Location value points to the location of the custom site definition to be deployed, relative to the root of the solution. When the solution is deployed, it will copy the folder into the ~/14/TEMPLATE/SiteTemplates directory on the server.

For a site definition to be available for use, it must have an XML configuration file, and this file must be deployed to a culture-specific directory in the ~/14/TEMPLATE directory on the server. The culture-specific folder must be named according to the culture's locale identification number. For example, the American English version of a site definition configuration file would need to be deployed to the ~/14/TEMPLATE/1033/XML directory.

It's possible to instruct SharePoint where to place the configuration file by using an element called `WebTempFile`, which is a child element of the `SiteDefinitionManifest` element, and contains a `Location` attribute specifying the relative location of the file within the solution.

Creating a custom site definition is beyond the scope of the current chapter.

 For a complete list of Locale IDs, visit `http://msdn.microsoft.com/en-us/ goglobal/bb964664.aspx`.

➤ `DWPFiles`: Web Part configuration files are deployed using the `DWPFiles` element. The `DWPFiles` element can contain one or more `DWPFile` elements, corresponding to each Web Part configuration file. (These configuration files have either a .dwp or a .webpart extension.) DWP files are deployed to a directory called wpcatalog, which sits inside the IIS web application folder on the file system. The `DWPFile` element has an attribute called `FileName`, which is used to pass in the name of the configuration file. Using the `FileName` attribute drops the file right in the root of the wpcatalog directory. The element now has an additional element called `Location`, which you can use to pass a path to the file. The path is relative to the wpcatalog directory.

The following code snippet would place the Web Part file in a directory called MyVisualWebPart inside the wpcatalog directory.

```
<DwpFiles>
    <DwpFile Location="MyVisualWebPart\MyVisualWebPart.webpart" />
</DwpFiles>
```

code snippet Manifest.xml

➤ `ApplicationResourceFiles`: Resource files are XML that contain localized translations of text that appears in SharePoint and are deployed using the `ApplicationResourceFiles` element, which can in turn have one or more `ApplicationResourceFile` child elements. The `Location` attribute specifies the location of the resource file relative to the solution root. This file will be copied to the ~/14/TEMPLATE/Resources directory on the server.

➤ `CodeAccessSecurity`: The `CodeAccessSecurity` element is used for passing in a custom Code Access Security (CAS) policy. Creating custom CAS policies is an advanced topic that is outside of the scope of the current chapter.

FEATURES AND SOLUTIONS IN VISUAL STUDIO 2010

In previous versions of SharePoint, one of the great barriers to developing custom SharePoint solutions was the lack of available development tools. The user community released development tools for SharePoint that plugged into Visual Studio 2008 and eventually Microsoft released the Visual Studio Extensions for Windows SharePoint Services (VSeWSS). VSeWSS provided several templates for developing SharePoint items such as list definitions and Web Parts. Although these tools provided good starting points for developing assets to be used in SharePoint, they were all created as afterthoughts to the release of the SharePoint product itself.

That has changed with the release of Visual Studio 2010 and SharePoint Foundation 2010. For the first time, the Visual Studio product team has developed full-fledged SharePoint development tools and templates that are fully integrated with the Visual Studio 2010 development environment.

For the SharePoint tools to be available in Visual Studio 2010, you must make sure you install the SharePoint tools when you install the Visual Studio product. You can do this by choosing to do a Full install, or by choosing a Custom installation and selecting the Microsoft SharePoint Development Tools checkbox. Figure 7-2 shows the option you need to select during the Visual Studio installation process in order to have the SharePoint 2010 templates available to you.

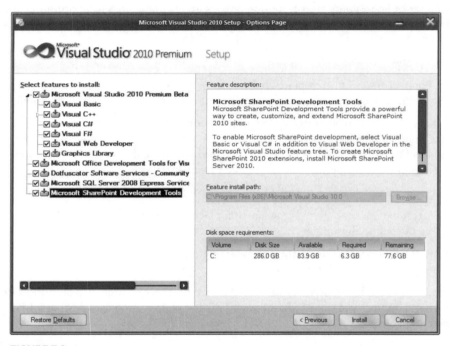

FIGURE 7-2

For a production environment, SharePoint 2010 requires Windows Server 2008 or Windows Server 2008 R2. Many developers use virtualization technologies to create virtual development environments. This permits them to install Windows Server 2008 or Windows Server 2008 R2, providing a development environment that is similar to their production environment, yet still allows them to run an operating system with a friendlier desktop user experience like Windows 7 on their host machine. However, for people who would rather develop without a virtualization layer, it's possible to run a stand-alone installation of SharePoint 2010 on Windows 7 as a development environment.

To take advantage of the SharePoint development tools in Visual Studio 2010, you must have SharePoint installed on the same machine as Visual Studio.

 For detailed, step-by-step instructions for setting up a development environment, read the article on MSDN titled "Setting Up the Development Environment for SharePoint 2010 on Windows Vista, Windows 7, and Windows Server 200" at `http://msdn.microsoft.com/en-us/library/ee554869(office.14).aspx`.

SharePoint 2010 Visual Studio Project Item Templates

A *project item template* is a preconfigured item that can be used to create or add an item to a Visual Studio project. A number of SharePoint project item templates are available in Visual Studio 2010. Some of these SharePoint project item templates are available for use when first creating a project. Others are available when choosing to add a new item to an existing project.

These project item templates include:

➤ **Empty SharePoint Project:** This template creates a new Visual Studio project configured to work with SharePoint Foundation, and contains no other SharePoint project item templates.

➤ **Visual Web Part:** Traditional Web Parts are compiled controls, meaning items in the user interface must be added to the control via code. A Visual Web Part allows Web Part designers to develop the Web Part in the same way they would develop an ASP.NET user control, by dragging and dropping controls onto a design surface.

➤ **Web Part:** This template creates a compiled Web Part control.

➤ **Sequential Workflow:** This template is the starting place for creating a new sequential workflow to be hosted in SharePoint.

➤ **State Machine Workflow:** This template is the starting place for creating a new state machine workflow to be hosted in SharePoint.

➤ **Business Data Connectivity Model:** A Business Data Connectivity Model is a definition for getting external data into and out of SharePoint. This template is used for creating a BDC model using compiled code.

➤ **Application Page:** This template is used for creating a new SharePoint application page with code-behind.

➤ **Event Receiver:** This template creates an event receiver that can be attached to an artifact in SharePoint such as a site, list, or list item.

➤ **List Definition:** This template facilitates the creation of a new, custom list definition.

➤ **List Definition from Content Type:** This template creates a new list definition that uses the same columns as an existing content type. In addition, the content type is the default content type for the custom list definition.

➤ **List Instance:** This template is used for creating a new list instance based on an existing list definition.

➤ **Content Type:** This template is used for provisioning a new custom content type.

➤ **Module:** Modules are used to deploy items to lists, libraries, and galleries in SharePoint. This template creates an empty SharePoint module.

➤ **Empty Element:** Element files are used for provisioning things like site columns, content types, event receivers, and list instances. This template creates an empty element file that serves as a starting point for a developer wanting to create a new element "from scratch."

➤ **User Control:** Provisions an ASP.NET user control that can be embedded in a SharePoint page.

➤ **Import Reusable Workflow:** This template is used for importing a reusable workflow, which was created in SharePoint Designer 2010, into Visual Studio 2010.

➤ **Import SharePoint Solution Package:** This template provides the ability to import the contents of an existing SharePoint solution file into Visual Studio 2010.

After you have installed the SharePoint Development Tools, you will see a list of new templates available for you to use when creating a new Visual Studio project, as shown in Figure 7-3.

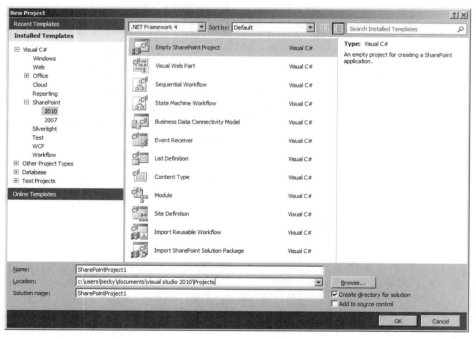

FIGURE 7-3

Creating a SharePoint 2010 Project in Visual Studio 2010

When a developer uses Visual Studio to write code or configuration files for SharePoint, the ultimate goal is to create a solution that will deploy those assets to a SharePoint farm. Every SharePoint project in Visual Studio contains a single solution.

When developers are writing code and creating provisioning files in their Visual Studio project, it's important that they have the ability to see what their changes will look like when deployed to a SharePoint environment. In addition, it's important that they are able to debug their code in an environment that is running their code.

Because of these reasons, when a new project is created, Visual Studio requires that the URL of an existing SharePoint site be specified. This is the URL of a live SharePoint site that can be used to test the Visual Studio project.

 Because it's often necessary to recycle an application pool to successfully deploy a solution, it's not recommended to use a production SharePoint site when developing SharePoint projects in Visual Studio, because this could cause frequent disruptions of service to users browsing a live site. Also, if your development site is utilizing Alternate Access Mappings (AAM), be sure the URL you specify belongs to the AAM default zone.

When creating a new SharePoint project, it's also necessary to specify whether the solution being generated will be used as a farm solution or a sandboxed solution. If you specify that your solution is a farm solution, when you deploy your solution from within Visual Studio, it will deploy it to the farm. If you specify that you're creating a sandboxed solution, Visual Studio will deploy your solution to the Solution gallery of the site collection you specified. (Once you have created your project, you can change this setting at any time by modifying the Sandboxed Solution property on the Visual Studio project, found in the project Properties window.)

 Sandboxed solutions do not have permission to access certain objects in the SharePoint object model. However, if you use one of these invalid objects in your code, Visual Studio will not let you know that you're using these invalid objects when it compiles your assembly. The Visual Studio team has released a product called Visual Studio 2010 SharePoint Power Tools that corrects this behavior. You can download the Power Tools by visiting `http://visualstudiogallery` `.msdn.microsoft.com/en-us/8e602a8c-6714-4549-9e95-f3700344b0d9.`

Every SharePoint project has several common items:

➤ **Features folder:** Any feature that is added to the project will be contained in this folder.

➤ **Package folder:** This contains the solution file for the project.

➤ **Key file:** This is a key used for digitally signing the project's assembly.

SharePoint projects also have an additional tab on the project Properties page called SharePoint. This tab is discussed later in the chapter.

Adding and Configuring a Feature in Visual Studio 2010

To add a new feature to a project, right-click the Features folder and select Add Feature. This will generate three items:

➤ **Feature folder:** This represents the folder that will be created for the feature inside the ~/14/TEMPLATE/FEATURES directory on the file system of the server where the feature will be deployed.

➤ **Feature Designer file:** This is a file with an extension of .feature, which sits inside the Feature folder. It is a configuration file generated by the *Feature Designer* in Visual Studio. The Feature Designer is a visual tool for displaying the properties and contents of a feature.

➤ **Feature manifest template file:** A file with an extension of .template.xml, this file contains XML configuration information for the feature. The feature manifest file that gets included in the solution is a combination of the information stored in the Feature Designer file and the information stored in the feature manifest template file.

Double-clicking a Feature folder in the Solution Explorer brings up the Feature Designer, as shown in Figure 7-4.

This brings up the *Design* view of the Feature Designer. This view allows a developer to set properties of the feature such as the feature title and description. The designer surface allows developers to browse through the assets that are part of the Visual Studio project and to select those particular items that should be included in the feature.

Developers can also add activation dependencies for their feature from the design surface. They can choose to add a dependency on another feature that is part of the current Visual Studio project, or they can enter the GUID of a feature upon which this feature is dependent.

FIGURE 7-4

Clicking the Manifest button at the bottom of the design surface displays a preview of the final feature manifest file. If developers would like to manually add additional configuration information to the feature manifest file, they can click the Edit Options link on the design surface and edit the contents of the feature manifest template file.

Various other configuration properties for a feature are visible and editable in the Properties window in Visual Studio when the Feature Designer window is active for a given feature, as you can see in Figure 7-5.

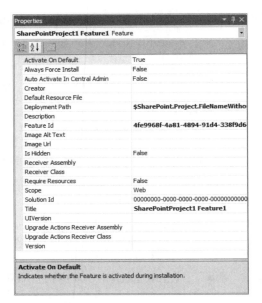

Creating a Feature Event Receiver

To add a feature event receiver to a Visual Studio project that is utilizing a SharePoint project item template, right-click the feature and select Add Event Receiver from the menu. This will automatically add a new class file to your feature. The file will be a sibling of the feature manifest template file and will have an extension of .EventReceiver.cs or .EventReceiver.vb (depending on the language you are programming in).

FIGURE 7-5

The class that is created for you will contain five methods that have been commented out for you. To use a method, simply uncomment the method you would like to implement. Here are the methods you'll find in the event receiver class:

- ➤ `FeatureActivated`: Occurs after the feature has been activated
- ➤ `FeatureDeactivating`: Occurs before the feature has been deactivated
- ➤ `FeatureInstalled`: Occurs after the feature has been installed
- ➤ `FeatureUninstalling`: Occurs before the feature has been uninstalled
- ➤ `FeatureUpgrading`: Occurs before the feature has been upgraded

There is no `Cancel` property or method that can be used to terminate the execution of the event receiver and the event itself. However, if an error is thrown, the rest of the event receiver method will not execute. In addition, if an error is thrown during the execution the `FeatureActivated` event handler method, the feature will not be marked as activated.

Adding a Feature Resource File

To add a language resource file to your feature, you can right-click the feature and select Add Feature Resource from the context menu. This will pop open a window, from which you can select the language and culture for which you want to create a resource file.

Configuring a Solution in Visual Studio 2010

A Visual Studio project can contain one and only one solution file. The Package folder in the project contains two files:

➤ **Package Designer file:** This file has an extension of .package and contains the configuration information generated by the *Package Designer* tool, a Visual Studio tool similar to the Feature Designer.

➤ **Solution manifest template file:** A file with an extension of .template.xml; this file contains XML configuration information for the solution. The solution manifest file that will be included with the solution file is a combination of the information stored in the Solution Designer file and the information stored in the solution manifest template file.

The Package Designer, as shown in Figure 7-6, allows a developer to give the solution a title and to specify whether the IIS server process should be recycled when the solution is deployed. The design surface provides a list of all the features that are included in the Visual Studio project and allows a developer to select which ones should be included in the solution.

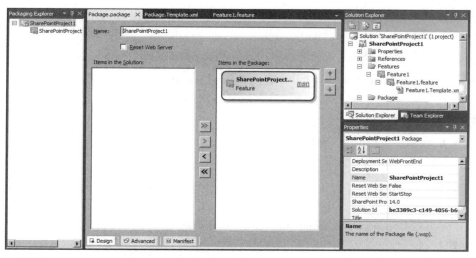

FIGURE 7-6

Each Visual Studio project generates a single assembly. If developers are creating multiple features and want each feature to use a unique assembly, they might choose to create a new project for each feature. If this is the case, the Package Designer will display all the features available in the Visual Studio solution and allow the developers to select which features they would like to include in the solution. This enables multiple features from multiple Visual Studio projects to be included in a single solution.

Developers can also choose to include additional assemblies in the solution, whether the assemblies are part of the Visual Studio solution, or exist on the file system.

Finally, developers can choose to modify the package template file in much the same way that they can modify a feature template file. The changes made to the package template file are merged with the Package Designer to create the final solution manifest file that is included with the solution.

When viewing a Package Designer file, it's possible to view additional properties of the solution by examining the Properties window for the solution, as shown in Figure 7-7.

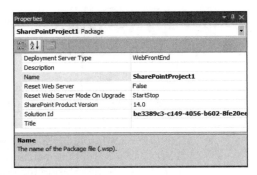

FIGURE 7-7

Visual Studio also provides a tool called the *Packaging Explorer.* This tool provides a visual tree-view of the contents of a solution, much the way the Visual Studio Solution Explorer provides a tree-view containing the contents of a Visual Studio project. The following tasks can be carried out with the Packaging Explorer:

➤ Opening SharePoint project items and files

➤ Dragging and dropping SharePoint project items from one feature to another

➤ Dragging and dropping SharePoint project items and features from one package to another

➤ Adding a new feature to a package

➤ Opening a feature in Feature Designer

➤ Validating features and packages

You can find this list on MSDN at `http://msdn.microsoft.com/en-us/library/ ee231544.aspx`.

In many cases it becomes necessary to deploy files (such as site definitions, resource files, configuration files, application pages, and so on) to various locations within the ~/14 directory on the server. As you learned earlier in this chapter, it's possible to indicate where a file should be deployed on the server, by adding `TemplateFile` or `RootFile` elements to the solution manifest. However, it can be cumbersome to add these instructions manually to the solution manifest. Instead, Visual Studio enables you to add a mapped folder to your project, allowing you to manually browse the SharePoint root and select which folder you want to deploy one or more files to. When the SharePoint solution is being compiled, Visual Studio will find your mapped folders and convert their contents into the appropriate elements in the solution manifest.

For instance, if you wanted to deploy your feature icon to the IMAGES directory on the server, you could simply add a mapped folder to your Visual Studio project that points to the IMAGES directory in the SharePoint root, then add your feature icon file to that mapped folder. When the solution gets compiled, a `TemplateFile` node will automatically be added to the solution manifest, telling SharePoint to deploy your feature icon file to the IMAGES directory on the server.

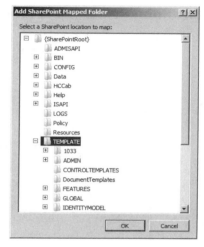

A mapped folder can be added to a project by right-clicking the project and selecting Add and then selecting SharePoint Mapped Folder from the fly-out menu. Selecting this item produces a pop-up window displaying the contents of the ~/14 directory in a tree view. Selecting a folder from the tree view (as shown in Figure 7-8) and clicking the OK button adds that mapped folder to the project.

FIGURE 7-8

Deploying, Retracting, and Debugging Solutions in Visual Studio 2010

The Visual Studio product team has enabled developers to carry out various activities regarding solutions and features directly from the Visual Studio IDE. These activities include deploying and retracting solutions, activating and deactivating features, and debugging code running in the context of a SharePoint site's IIS worker process.

The Build Menu

When working with a SharePoint project, the Build menu in the Visual Studio toolbar includes additional commands for working with solutions. Figure 7-9 shows the Build menu for SharePoint projects.

FIGURE 7-9

Although some commands are familiar to Visual Studio users, some new commands are available only for SharePoint projects:

➤ **Deploy:** Executes another set of commands, which usually includes deploying the solution to the server URL that was specified when the project was configured. The set of commands to execute are configured on the SharePoint tab on the project Properties page.

➤ **Package:** Builds a new solution file based on the contents of the project.

➤ **Retract:** Similar to the Deploy command, this also carries out a specific set of actions that have been defined in the SharePoint tab on the project Properties page. The actions usually revolve around removing a solution from the server.

The SharePoint Project Property Page

Right-clicking a Visual Studio project brings up the project properties. SharePoint projects have an additional tab, labeled appropriately SharePoint. The SharePoint tab is shown in Figure 7-10.

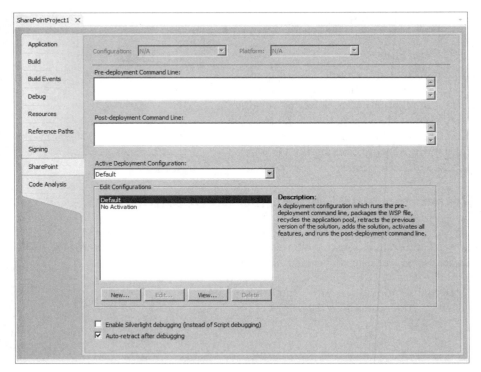

FIGURE 7-10

The configuration and platform settings do not impact the SharePoint settings that can be configured on this page, so their menus are inactive.

At the top of the page are two textboxes, labeled Pre-Deployment Command Line and Post-Deployment Command Line, respectively. Each textbox is used for entering a command line argument, in case a developer would like an action to be completed before or after deployment, such as executing a batch file.

At the bottom of the page are two checkboxes. The first says Enable Silverlight Debugging (instead of Script Debugging). If a project includes Silverlight functionality, selecting this box facilitates the debugging of the Silverlight code. The second checkbox says Auto-Retract after Debugging. When debugging starts, the solution that's being tested is typically deployed to the server. Checking this checkbox ensures that when the debugging process has been terminated, the solution will be automatically retracted from the server or site that it was deployed to.

A drop-down menu can be found in the middle of the page. It can be used to select an *Active Deployment Configuration*. This menu is populated with items from the list box below it, titled Edit Configurations. A developer can choose to create a new configuration, or to view, modify, or delete an existing configuration (with the exception of the Default and No Activation configurations, which cannot be modified or deleted) by clicking the appropriate button below the list box.

The purpose for various configurations is to allow developers to choose which actions should take place when the "deploy" and "retract" commands are issued, and in which order. Out of the box, Visual Studio comes with a set of six commands that can be issued:

➤ Run Pre-Deployment Command

➤ Run Post-Deployment Command

➤ Recycle IIS Application Pool

➤ Retract Solution

➤ Add Solution

➤ Activate Features

When creating a new configuration or editing an existing one, a pop-up window appears, which provides an interface where a developer can choose which of these actions should happen when the Deploy command is issued, and in which order. The developer can also go through the same selection process for determining what should take place when the Retract command is issued. For example, the Default configuration is set up so that the following actions happen in the following order when the Deploy command is issued:

➤ Run Pre-Deployment Command

➤ Recycle IIS Application Pool

➤ Retract Solution

➤ Add Solution

➤ Activate Features

➤ Run Post-Deployment Command

When the Retract command is issued, the following two actions are executed:

➤ Recycle IIS Application Pool

➤ Retract Solution

Example: Creating a Feature and Solution Using Visual Studio 2010

Now that you've gotten an overview of features and solutions in SharePoint Foundation 2010, it's time to try building a feature and solution yourself. This section takes you step by step through the process of creating a Visual Web Part, creating and activating a SharePoint feature, and creating and deploying a solution. You will need a SharePoint Foundation development site for this exercise.

The following example can be downloaded from Wrox.com under MyVisualWPSolution.

1. Open Visual Studio 2010 and select New ⇨ Project from the File menu.

2. On the left side of the New Project window, find the heading titled Installed Templates. Under the heading, expand the item titled Visual C#, then expand the item titled SharePoint. Select the 2010 item to see the available SharePoint 2010 project templates.

3. Choose the project template titled Empty SharePoint Project from the list of project templates.

4. In the Name textbox at the bottom of the window, type "MyVisualWPSolution." This should populate the Solution Name textbox with the text MyVisualWPSolution as well. Click the OK button.

5. When the SharePoint Customization Wizard window appears, pass in the URL of a SharePoint Foundation 2010 website that you can use for development. Select the radio button next to Deploy as a Farm Solution. Click the Finish button.

6. Right-click the project and select Add ⇨ New Item.

7. Select Visual Web Part from the list of items. Give the Web Part a name of MyVisualWP. Click the Add button.

8. `MyVisualWebPartUserControl.ascx` should open up in Visual Studio. (If not, right-click the file and select View Markup to edit it.) Below the last line of text, type "Hello, World!" Save your change.

9. Find the folder called Features in the root of your Visual Studio project. In this folder, look for an item called Feature1. Right-click Feature1 and select Rename from the menu. Rename the feature MyVisualWPFeature. This should rename the feature, the Feature Designer file, and the manifest template file.

10. Double-click the feature to open up the Feature Designer. In the Title textbox at the top of the page, type "My Visual Web Part Feature." In the Description textbox, type "This feature deploys a Web Part to the Web Part gallery." Save your changes. The Scope drop-down menu should be set to Site.

11. Click the Build menu in the Visual Studio toolbar, and select Deploy MyVisualWPSolution.

12. Open up a browser window and navigate to the website to which you deployed your solution.

13. Click the Edit icon in the Ribbon to edit the site homepage.

14. Find a Web Part zone and click it. A tab, called Insert, should appear in the Ribbon. Click the tab, then click the Web Part button in the Web Parts section of the Insert Ribbon.

15. You should see a section at the top of the page for managing Web Parts. On the left side of the page, you should see a column titled Categories, followed by folders with names. Click the folder called Custom.

16. After clicking the Custom folder, MyVisualWP should appear in the list of Web Parts in the column titled Web Parts, which sits to the right of the Categories column. Select MyVisualWP and click the Add button. You should now see a Web Part that says "Hello, World!" in your page.

17. If you navigate to the Web Part gallery of your site collection, you should see MyVisualWP.webpart listed. If you navigate to the list of site-collection features for your site collection, you should see the My Visual Web Part feature listed.

SUMMARY

In this chapter, you learned that a SharePoint feature is a unit of functionality that can be reused at its given scope. Features can be installed, activated, deactivated, uninstalled, and upgraded. Each of these events can be handled using a feature event receiver. Features can be configured by modifying their manifest file, which is an XML file defining the properties of the feature. When older features are upgraded, it's possible to execute certain actions to bring them into a consistent state with the newer version being deployed.

You also learned that solution files are cabinet files with a .wsp extension used by SharePoint to deploy assets to a single server or load balanced servers in a SharePoint farm. A solution contains a solution manifest file, which is an XML file providing SharePoint with information about where to place files on the file system as well as which assembly types should be marked as safe in the web .config. Solutions must first be added to the solution store before they can be deployed. Solutions can be deployed globally, which means the solution is available to the whole farm, or they can be deployed to a particular web application.

Finally, you learned how to install the Microsoft SharePoint Development Tools in Visual Studio 2010 and create a Visual Studio project using a SharePoint project item template. You learned how to use the Feature Designer and Solution Package Explorer to create a feature, `Feature` event receiver, and solution. You learned how to configure deployment using the SharePoint project Property page, how to package and deploy a solution using the Build menu, and how to debug a SharePoint solution from Visual Studio.

Introduction to SharePoint Development

WHAT'S IN THIS CHAPTER?

- ➤ How to use the server-side object model
- ➤ How to use Collaborative Application Markup Language (CAML) to provision items and retrieve information
- ➤ How to use LINQ to SharePoint
- ➤ What a Web Part is and how to build one
- ➤ Understanding the REST interface
- ➤ How to use the client-side object model
- ➤ How to use the SharePoint web services

It is true to say that SharePoint is a product, in the sense that you can order, buy, and install it, as you would other software products. However, SharePoint is so flexible and extensible, it's also reasonable to use talk about SharePoint as a *platform* or a *framework*. SharePoint's breadth of functionality can be the platform upon which you build other applications, and SharePoint's functionality can provide the supporting structure for your custom applications.

For example, imagine that you work for a company that has offices abroad. Before you can travel to another country, you must fill out an online form requesting permission to go. If your manager approves the trip, you must add an entry to the company calendar. Upon return, you must fill out an expense report, detailing expenses for the trip. Your manager must approve the expense request, at which point someone from the accounting department is notified of the expense report and reimburses you.

To build the functionality described in this scenario using SharePoint, you would probably take advantage of some of the fundamental components found in SharePoint, like InfoPath forms, workflows, and lists. However, the end result of combining these features would be the creation of a true *application* — that is, software that helps users execute a specific set of tasks.

Many times, the available functionality in SharePoint is not enough to achieve the kind of application you want; it may be necessary to create a custom form, define a custom workflow, or create a custom list definition. Luckily, a number of ways exist to interact with SharePoint programmatically, whether that means extending the core functionality of the product itself, or accessing and manipulating the data stored within SharePoint.

This chapter gives you an overview of how you can use the server object model and Collaborative Application Markup Language (CAML) to access and manipulate data stored in SharePoint. You learn how to simplify the process of accessing information in SharePoint using LINQ to SharePoint. This chapter introduces you to compiled and visual Web Parts, which you can use to create a custom user experience. In addition, this chapter helps you understand how you can access data stored in SharePoint from an external location using the client-side object model, SharePoint's REST interface, and SharePoint web services.

Developers can modify and extend the SharePoint environment in myriad ways. This chapter is by no means exhaustive, but is meant to give you a brief overview of some of the kinds of SharePoint 2010 development you can do. To dive deeper into developing SharePoint 2010 solutions, consider reading Wrox's other books, *Beginning SharePoint 2010 Development* and *Professional SharePoint 2010 Development*.

> ### CUSTOMIZATION VS. DEVELOPMENT
>
> In the SharePoint world, *customization* often refers to changes that are made to a SharePoint environment using the browser interface or a tool like SharePoint Designer. Customizations are changes that get stored in a SharePoint content database and have no relationship to a file on the filesystem. *Development* usually refers to the creation of solution packages and features that deploy assemblies and/ or other files to the SharePoint server(s) in your farm. These files might add content to a content database, but they originate as files on the filesystem. Development is often done using a tool like Visual Studio.

AN INTRODUCTION TO THE SHAREPOINT SERVER-SIDE OBJECT MODEL

There are many times when the code you write to manipulate SharePoint will run directly on your SharePoint server. In these cases, your custom code will interact with the assemblies, which were installed as a part of the SharePoint product. In this kind of scenario, your code is interacting with the SharePoint *server-side object model*. This is in contrast to code you write, which could be executed on a different server or run within the context of a client application, and which will be discussed later in the chapter.

The SharePoint server-side object model is contained in several assemblies that are added to your server when SharePoint is installed. Most of these assemblies reside in the ISAPI folder in the SharePoint root. Each assembly contains one or more primary namespaces, such as `Microsoft.SharePoint`, `Microsoft.SharePoint.PowerShell`, or `Microsoft.BusinessData.MetadataModel`. (For a list of the namespaces used in SharePoint Foundation 2010, including a mapping of namespaces to assemblies, visit `http://msdn.microsoft.com/en-us/library/ms453225.aspx`.)

SHAREPOINT 2010 DEVELOPMENT AND WINDOWS 7

If you are writing code that will be compiled into an assembly, and your assembly references a SharePoint assembly, the SharePoint assembly must be installed on a functioning SharePoint server. Because SharePoint must be installed on a server running Windows Server 2008 when deployed in a production environment, developers often develop their solutions as well on a computer running Windows Server 2008 (whether the OS is installed on a physical drive or in a virtual environment). However, it is possible to install SharePoint on a development machine running Windows Vista or Windows 7 OS, provided additional changes are manually applied. With that said, Windows Vista or Windows 7 machines should *never* be used as production environments for SharePoint.

Luckily, the object model is fairly intuitive for people who are familiar with SharePoint. If you know what a list, list item, or folder is in SharePoint, it's not hard to figure out what an `SPList`, `SPListItem`, or `SPFolder` object is. Table 8-1 gives you an overview of some of the most commonly used classes.

TABLE 8-1: Commonly Used Classes in the SharePoint Foundation Object Model

CLASS NAME	DESCRIPTION
SPFarm	The very top-level object, providing access to configuration information for the entire SharePoint farm
SPWebApplication	A load-balanced IIS web application that is part of the SharePoint farm

continues

TABLE 8-1 *(continued)*

CLASS NAME	DESCRIPTION
SPSite	A site collection inside a web application
SPWeb	An individual site within a site collection
SPList	A list within a particular site
SPListItem	An item in a SharePoint list
SPFolder	A folder within a SharePoint site
SPFile	A document stored in a SharePoint list
SPGroup	A SharePoint group
SPUser	A SharePoint user
SPContentType	A content type
SPField	A column (either a site column or a list column, depending on its location)
SPView	The view on a particular list

 Note that an SPSite *object represents a site collection, not a site.*

The object model is fairly hierarchical in nature, reflecting the hierarchical nature of SharePoint itself. Just as a site contains lists, so an SPWeb object contains SPList objects. Following this convention, nearly every object is a member of a larger collection of similar objects. This facilitates the ability to iterate through multiple items at once. For instance, SPWeb.Lists returns an SPListCollection object. An SPListCollection object contains a collection of SPList objects. Figure 8-1 gives you an idea of the object hierarchy.

It's possible to move both up and down the object hierarchy. For instance, to find the parent site to which a list belongs, you can easily access the ParentWeb property of the SPList object with which you're working. In the same way, accessing the Site property of an SPWeb object returns the site collection to which the current site belongs. The SPSite.WebApplication property returns the web application of which the site collection is a part, and so on. Figure 8-2 shows you how you can traverse the object model up the hierarchy.

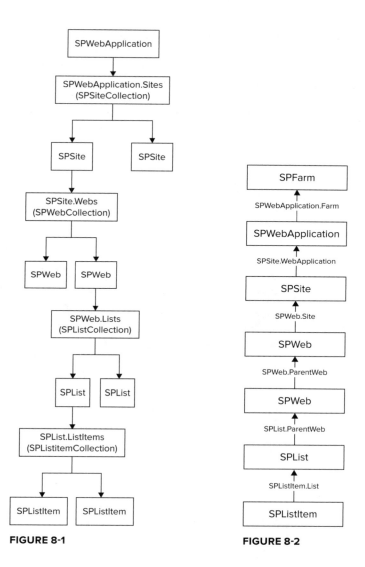

FIGURE 8-1   **FIGURE 8-2**

Because SharePoint utilizes a hierarchy of sites with a site collection, one of the most common things you'll need to do is get a reference to a site collection or a particular site within the site collection as a starting point. You have two ways to access an SPSite or SPWeb object within SharePoint:

➤ **Using the current context:** If your code is running within a SharePoint site that is being accessed via a browser, it's possible to access the context in which the code is running using the Current property of the SPContext object. This allows your code to behave dynamically based on the location in which your code is executed. For instance, if you created a Web Part that displayed the title of the current site, you could retrieve that value by accessing SPContext.Current.Web.Title.

➤ **Creating a new object using a constructor:** If your code is executing in a console or Windows application, a user is not browsing a SharePoint site, so there is no way to access any sort of context. Instead, it's necessary to create a new site collection object. You can use various constructors; some allow you to pass in the URL or GUID of the site collection you want to open, and others allow you to also pass in the credentials of the account with which you want to access SharePoint. For example, if you wanted to access the title of the site at the URL `http://intranet/sites/hr/health`, you could do so using the following code:

```
using (SPSite hrSite = new SPSite("http://intranet/sites/hr"))
{
    SPWeb healthWeb = hrSite.OpenWeb("health");
    string title = healthWeb.Title;
}
```

OBJECT DISPOSAL

It's often necessary to explicitly dispose of SharePoint objects like `SPSite` and `SPWeb` to prevent them from remaining active and taking up an increasing amount of server memory. It's possible to dispose of objects either by nesting your code in a `using` block or by using a `try`/`catch` block and explicitly disposing of your object in a `finally` block.

For a complete explanation of when you should dispose of objects see the SDK article titled "Disposing Objects" at `http://msdn.microsoft.com/en-us/library/ee557362.aspx`. In addition, the Microsoft team has released the SharePoint Dispose Checker Tool, which you can download at `http://code.msdn.microsoft.com/SPDisposeCheck`.

Working with Site Collections, Webs, Lists, and List Items

One of the most common tasks you will probably encounter is to retrieve information stored in a SharePoint site collection.

Each site collection has a single top-level site (called the root site or the root web), which can be accessed by retrieving the `SPWeb` object at `SPSite.RootWeb`. Once you have the top-level site's `SPWeb` object, you can iterate through each of the child sites by accessing the `SPWebCollection` object at `SPWeb.Webs`. It's possible to retrieve a particular site in the `SPWebCollection` by using an indexer, which can be either the index number of the site within the site collection, the display name of the site, or the GUID of the `SPWeb` object. The four listings that follow are included in the SitesAndWebs.cs section of the code download at `Wrox.com`. Listing 8-1 shows how you can retrieve a site titled Subsite A, where Subsite A is a direct child of the top-level site.

LISTING 8-1: Getting an SPSite Object (SitesAndWebs.cs)

```
SPSite siteCollection = SPContext.Current.Site;
SPWeb topLevelSite = siteCollection.RootWeb;
SPWebCollection webs = topLevelSite.Webs;
SPWeb subsiteA = webs["Subsite A"];
```

Whereas accessing the Webs property of an SPWeb object will return the direct child sites of a given site, the AllWebs property of the SPSite object will return a collection of all the sites in a site collection, regardless of how deep they lie in the site collection hierarchy. Figure 8-3 shows which sites are returned in a Webs collection and in an AllWebs collection.

Listing 8-2 shows you how you can iterate through all the sites in a site collection using the SPSite.AllWebs property.

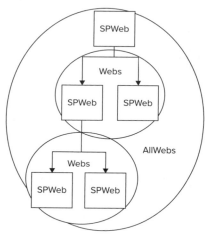

FIGURE 8-3

LISTING 8-2: Creating a New SPSite Object (SitesAndWebs.cs)

```
using (SPSite intranetSiteCollection = new SPSite("http://intranet/"))
{
    SPWebCollection websCollection = siteCollection.AllWebs;

    foreach (SPWeb web in websCollection)
    {
        Console.WriteLine(web.Title);
        web.Dispose();
    }

    Console.Read();
}
```

Note that when retrieving SPSite or SPWeb objects directly from the SPContext.Current object, you should not explicitly dispose of the objects, which is why you don't see a "using" block or Dispose() method in Listing 8-1. Since the SPContext object is continually used, disposing of this object will produce significant errors. However, when creating a new SPSite object "from scratch," you do need to explicitly dispose of it when finished. In Listing 8-2, the SPSite object will be disposed of properly because of the "using" block it is a part of. Each SPWeb object that's retrieved from the AllWebs property is also being disposed of explicitly, this time using the Dispose() method.

Once you have a site collection object, you can also retrieve a particular site in the site collection, even if it's more than one level deep, by using the SPSite.OpenWeb() method. This method allows you to retrieve a particular site within the collection by passing in the GUID or the URL of the site (or retrieve the top-level site by passing in no parameters). Listing 8-3 demonstrates how you can get the top-level site of a site collection (http://intranet), as well as retrieve the SPWeb object for a site that's a grandchild of the top-level site.

LISTING 8-3: Using OpenWeb() (SitesAndWebs.cs)

Available for
download on
Wrox.com

```
using (SPSite sc = new SPSite("http://intranet/");
{
    SPWeb rootWeb = sc.OpenWeb();
    rootWeb.Dispose();

    SPWeb web = sc.OpenWeb("subsite1/subsite2");
    web.Dispose();
}
```

Once you have retrieved an object representing the site whose data you want to use, you can start retrieving information about the lists, list items, folders, and files within that site.

To access a list object for a particular list in your site, you simply need to pass in the display name or GUID of the list to the SPListCollection indexer of the parent SPWeb.Lists property, like this:

```
SPListCollection lists = subsiteA.Lists;
SPList myList = lists["My List"];
```

You can retrieve a specific item from a list in much the same way. You can pass in the value of the Title column of a particular list item in order to retrieve it, like this:

```
SPListItem myListItem = myList["My List Item"];
```

You can also use the SPListItemCollection.GetItemById() method to retrieve a particular list item by its ID number. (This is the SPListItem.ID property, not the SPListItem.UniqueIdentifier property. See side note.)

> SPListItem *objects have two identifiers: the* ID *property is an integer that uniquely identifies the list item. It's possible to display a list item's* ID *when creating a new view of a specific list or library. The* UniqueIdentifier *property is a GUID used to identify the list item. This value is rarely, if ever, visible to end users.*

Although it's possible to retrieve information from SharePoint, it's also possible to make changes to these objects and persist your changes to the content database. To do this, it's usually necessary to call the Update() method of the object you're working with, which commits the changes you have made in your code to the database. The following code snippet demonstrates how you can update the URL of the master page for a given site:

```
SPWeb currentWeb = SPContext.Current.Web;
currentWeb.MasterUrl = "/_catalogs/masterpage/Custom.master";
currentWeb.Update();
```

In much the same way as you would retrieve an item from a collection, you can often add an item to a collection using an Add() method, whether it's SPWebCollection.Add(), SPListCollection.Add(), or SPListItemCollection.Add(). Each object has its own set of overloaded Add() methods. For instance, you can easily add a new child site to an existing site by simply passing in the URL of the new site, and you can create a new list by passing in the name and description of the new list and the type of list that you want to create, as demonstrated in the next code snippet. To add a new list item to a list, you need to first add the item, set its properties, then call the SPListItem.Update() method to commit the item to the database.

```
SPWeb newWeb = SPContext.Current.Web.Webs.Add("MyNewSubsite");
SPList newList = newWeb.Lists.Add("New List", "Another list",
    SPListTemplateType.GenericList);
SPListItem newListItem = newList.Items.Add();
newListItem["Title"] = "New List Item";
newListItem.Update();
```

Not only can you add items to a collection or update an existing item in a collection, but you can also delete an item from a collection. This is usually done using the Delete() method for an object, such as SPSite.Delete(), SPWeb.Delete(), SPList.Delete(), and SPListItem.Delete(). The next example demonstrates how you can delete a site collection, site, list, and list item:

```
//Deletes a site collection used for testing
using (SPSite siteCollection = new Site("http://intranet/sites/test"))
{
    siteCollection.Delete();
}

//Deletes a site in the current site collection
using (SPWeb testSite = SPContext.Current.Site.OpenWeb("test"))
{
    testSite.Delete();
}

//Deletes a list called "Invoices" in the current site
SPContext.Current.Web.Lists["Invoices"].Delete();

//Deletes a list item with a title of "My List Item"
SPList myList = SPContext.Current.Web.Lists["My List"];
myList["My List Item"].Delete();
```

It's possible to execute code during particular events such as websites, lists, or list items being added or deleted. To learn more about event receivers, read the section titled "Example: Taking Advantage of Event Receivers" in Chapter 17.

Example: Creating a SharePoint Console Application

The goal of this example is to walk you through the process of writing a console application, which will access SharePoint using the server-side object model, using the kind of code you have reviewed so far in the chapter. It will walk you through the creation of a console application that you can use to return the titles of all the sites within a site collection. This example can be downloaded from the `Wrox.com` site. The project is called SP2010ObjectModel.

There are two things to note when creating a new console application that will access SharePoint 2010:

> ➤ At the time of the printing of this book, SharePoint 2010 does not utilize the .NET Framework 4.0. You will need to target your Visual Studio project to .NET Framework 3.5.

> ➤ By default, your project might target a 32-bit processor. Because SharePoint targets a 64-bit processor, it's necessary to set your Visual Studio project deployment target to x64.

Here are the steps in the process:

1. Open Visual Studio 2010 and select New ⇨ Project from the File menu.

2. On the left side of the New Project window, find the heading titled Installed Templates. Under the heading, click the item titled Visual C#. Select the Console Application project template. In the drop-down menu above the center column, select .NET Framework 3.5 as the framework that your project will target. In the Name textbox at the bottom of the window, type "SP2010ObjectModel." Click OK.

3. Right-click the project and select Properties. Click the Build tab and select x64 from the Platform target drop-down menu. Save your changes.

4. Right-click the References folder and select Add Reference. Navigate to the SharePoint root folder. Open up the ISAPI folder and select Microsoft.SharePoint.dll, then select OK.

5. Open up Program.cs and add the following "using" statement to the top of the class: `using Microsoft.SharePoint;`

6. Add the code from Listing 8-2 to your `Main()` method, substituting `http://intranet` with the URL of your site collection.

7. Save your file and run your application using the account of a user who has access to the site collection that you are querying. A command window should pop up and display the names of all the sites within the site collection whose URL you supplied.

Working with Folders and Files

Folders are used in SharePoint to denote a logical collection of items, in much the same way you might use a folder on your computer to store documents. As with your desktop folders, a folder can contain other folders. Folders can serve several purposes in SharePoint:

> ➤ Each list can contain folders for organizing list items within that list. These kinds of folders are visible to end users who are browsing the list, as shown in Figure 8-4. For SharePoint, a folder in a list is actually a list item in and of itself, and as such has an associated content

type as well. Folders in document libraries can contain files. You can see in Figure 8-5 how the December folder in the Documents library contains a Word document called MyDocument.doc.

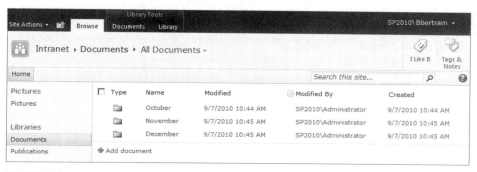

FIGURE 8-4

➤ Folders can be a container for holding files. However, they are not necessarily visible to users in the browser. You can see some of these folders when you open up a site in SharePoint Designer. For example, master pages are stored in a folder called _catalogs in the top-level site of your site collection, as shown in Figure 8-5.

➤ Every list is also a folder, with that folder having the same name as the URL of the list. For instance, a document library called Documents also is a folder. If a list is a library, it usually contains a child folder called "Forms" that is used for storing files like the "new," "edit," and "display" forms for that list, as well as content-type document templates. The Forms folder is not visible to users in the browser. You can see the Forms folder in Figure 8-5, as seen in SharePoint Designer. The list folder also contains any folders that have been created in the browser and are visible to end users, as mentioned in the first bullet point.

FIGURE 8-5

Understanding Folder and File Objects

A folder in SharePoint is represented by the `SPFolder` object. It's possible to retrieve a collection of all a folder's child folders by accessing the `SPFolder.SubFolders` property, which returns an object of type `SPFolderCollection`. If the folder is contained inside another folder, it's possible to retrieve the parent folder by accessing the `SPFolder.ParentFolder` property.

Listing 8-4 shows how you can retrieve the name of each folder in the top-level site of a site collection, as well as the number of subfolders that each folder contains.

LISTING 8-4: SPFolder.cs

```csharp
using System;
using System.Text;
using Microsoft.SharePoint;

namespace Wrox.SixInOne
{
  class Program
  {
    static void Main(string[] args)
    {
      StringBuilder folderName = new StringBuilder();

      using (SPSite site = new SPSite("http://intranet/"))
      {
        using (SPWeb web = site.RootWeb)
        {
          foreach (SPFolder folder in web.Folders)
          {
            folderName.Append(folder.Name);
            folderName.Append(" ");
            folderName.Append(folder.SubFolders.Count);
            folderName.Append("<br>");
          }
        }
      }
    }
  }
}
```

Folders in SharePoint can contain one or more files. A file can be any kind of file, such as an ASPX page, an image, or a document. A list item in a list is not a file in and of itself. However, if the SharePoint list is actually a library (such as a document library, image library, and so on), each item in that library also has an accompanying file. Additionally, if a list item allows attachments, any file attached to the list item would also be considered a file.

Files are represented by the SPFile object, and as you can probably guess by now, the collection of files belonging to a folder can be returned by accessing the SPFolder.Files property, which is of type SPFileCollection. You can also find out which folder a file belongs to by accessing the SPFile.ParentFolder property.

Deleting a file or a folder is pretty straightforward; you can simply call SPFolder.Delete() or SPFile.Delete(). However, in some cases you might prefer to send the folder or file to the recycle bin, rather than delete it permanently from the system. You can do that by calling SPFolder.Recycle() or SPFile.Recycle().

Adding a new folder programmatically to an existing folder is as simple as using an `Add()` method that passes in the name of the folder, like this:

```
SPContext.Current.Web.Folders.Add("NewFolder");
```

Adding a new file to a folder is quite a bit more difficult, because it involves uploading a binary object (such as an Excel document) to the SharePoint database. The `SPFileCollection.Add()` method has a number of overloaded methods, but most of them involve uploading a byte array or a data stream.

Listing 8-5 is an example of a console application that adds a new file to a list, then updates the new list item by adding a title to it.

LISTING 8-5: AddFile.cs

```csharp
using System;
using System.IO;
using Microsoft.SharePoint;

namespace Wiley.SixInOne
{
    class Program
    {
        static void Main(string[] args)
        {
            //Instantiate a new site collection object
            using (SPSite site = new SPSite("http://intranet/"))
            {
                //Get the list object inside the subsite
                SPWeb web = site.OpenWeb("sites/HR");
                SPFolder listFolder = web.Lists["Documents"].RootFolder;

                string folderUrl = web.ServerRelativeUrl + listFolder.Url;
                string fileUrl = folderUrl + "/Application.docx";

                FileStream stream = System.IO.File.Open(@"C:\Application.docx",
                    FileMode.Open);
                byte[] contents = new byte[stream.Length];
                stream.Read(contents, 0, (int)stream.Length);
                stream.Close();

                SPFile file = web.Files.Add(fileUrl, contents);

                SPListItem listItem = file.Item;
                listItem["Title"] = "Job Application";
                listItem.Update();

                web.Dispose();
            }
        }
    }
}
```

As you can see, the first step is to get a reference to the site collection that will be used, then get a reference to the subsite that will be used, and finally retrieve the list to which the file will be uploaded. To upload a file to SharePoint, you need to tell SharePoint where you want the file to go (that is, into which site, list, folder, and so forth it will be placed). You can do this by passing in the URL of the new document, which maps to the location of the file within the site. In the following example, you'll tell SharePoint that you want the new file to be placed in the Documents document library in the HR subsite, and you want the document to have a name of Application.docx. That means that the final URL of the new document should be `http://intranet/sites/HR/Documents/Application.docx`.

Once you've determined where you want your new document to go and what you want the document to be called, you'll serialize the document you want to upload into a byte array, then tell SharePoint to take that byte array and create a new file within SharePoint at the location you specified. Simply uploading a file to a document library automatically creates a new list item, but if that's all you do, your new list item won't have any metadata (that is, no custom column values) assigned. To add metadata, you'll get a reference to the new list item that was just created and add metadata, such as a document title, then update the new list item with your changes. In this example, the new list item will be given a title of "Job Application."

The Relationship between Folders and Lists and between Files and List items

Imagine, for a moment, a blue truck. How could you categorize it? You could say that the vehicle is a truck, whereas other vehicles on the road are cars and motorcycles. You could also say that the truck is blue, whereas other vehicles are white or red. The point is that the vehicle is more than one thing at once. The same goes with lists, list items, folders, and files. Because there is an overlap, the relationship with them can be confusing. A couple guidelines may help you out.

First, every list is a folder, but not every folder is a list. If you had a list called Events, then your site would have a folder called Lists, and that folder would contain a folder called Events. The folder called Lists is not a list itself, but is simply a folder in the organizational sense of the word. However, the folder called Events also corresponds to the list called Events. It would not be possible to have a list called Events without that list also being a folder called Events. You can see the Lists folder and the Events list/folder in Figure 8-6.

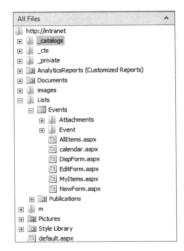

FIGURE 8-6

If you are working with the SPList object for a given list, you can access the list's folder object by calling the SPList.RootFolder property. This will return an SPFolder object that you can work with. If you are working with an SPFolder object, it might be that the folder is inside a list, but it's also equally possible that the folder is not inside a list. To find out, you can access the ParentListId property on the SPFolder object. If the GUID that is returned is all zeros, then the folder is not inside a list; otherwise, the GUID of the list is returned.

Because every folder must belong to some site, accessing the `SPFolder.ParentWeb` will always return an `SPWeb` object representing the site that contains the folder.

There is a similar overlap when dealing with files and list items. A file can be associated with a list item, but not necessarily. A list item might have a file, but not necessarily. For instance, a list might have an ASPX page that contains the form for creating new list items. That file is associated with a list, but not a list item per se. A list item might actually be a document (because the list is actually a type of library), or it might have an attachment file. However, if a list is not a document library so the list item has no accompanying document, and the list item has no attachment, there would be no file associated with the list item.

The `SPFile.Item` property returns the list item associated with a file if there is one. So if your file is actually a document in a document library, the `SPFile.Item` property would return the `SPListItem` object that your file is a part of. However, if your file is not associated with a list item (as in the example of the input form), the property value would be `null`. If you were accessing an `SPListItem` object and the list item was a document, accessing `SPListItem.File` would return an `SPFile` object representing the document. If the `SPListItem` had no document, this value would be `null`. If you wanted to access any attachment files associated with the list item, you could access the `SPListItem.Attachments` property, which would return a collection of `SPFile` objects that are attached to the list item.

AN INTRODUCTION TO COLLABORATIVE APPLICATION MARKUP LANGUAGE (CAML)

Collaborative Application Markup Language, or CAML, is an XML language that is used for defining certain assets within SharePoint, such as site columns, content types, site definitions, list definitions, list views, and list instances.

According to the dictionary, the noun "imperative" means "a command." Executing code that you have written using the SharePoint object model is often referred to as *imperative* programming, because you are executing commands at a point in time. For instance, you can use the SharePoint object model to create a new instance of a list in a site, but the new list will not be created until your code is executed.

In contrast, CAML is considered *declarative* programming, because it "makes known" or "explains" how various objects are to be configured within SharePoint, once they are created. An object such as a field or a list that has been described using CAML still needs to be created at some point in time in order to be useful, but the CAML file itself can serve as a succinct way of telling SharePoint how that object should be configured when it's first created. Or it can serve as an ongoing configuration definition that SharePoint can refer back to over the course of an object's life within SharePoint.

Many of the activities in SharePoint can be carried out either imperatively (using code) or declaratively (using CAML), and in many cases the end result is exactly the same. Many people want to know whether one method is the "right" way to do things, but in most cases both roads get you to the same destination.

For example, you could use the SharePoint server object model to create a new Yes/No column, like this:

```
using (SPSite siteCollection = new SPSite("http://intranet/"))
{
    SPWeb rootWeb = siteCollection.RootWeb;
    rootWeb.Fields.Add("New Field", SPFieldType.Boolean, true);
}
```

You could create a new feature and add this code to the `FeatureActivated` method in the feature event receiver. When the feature is activated, it will execute the code and add a new Boolean field with a display name of New Field to the site collection. (For an explanation of what a feature is and how to use one, please see Chapter 7: Features and Solutions.)

You could alternatively create a new feature that included an element manifest file. Inside the element node in the element manifest file, you could add the following CAML:

```
<Field ID="{6E43255B-14CF-49c5-9331-A8BC65921140}"
Name="NewField"
DisplayName="New Field"
Type="Boolean"/>
```

When this feature is activated, SharePoint will execute a command to create a new field, but it will use the CAML file to configure the new field, giving the field the ID, internal name, display name, and type, defined in the `Field` element in the CAML.

An important difference between imperative and declarative programming that you need to keep in mind, is that when you program imperatively the same code could be executed multiple times. If the code adds a new field to your site collection, you could get an error if that field already exists, or you could end up with duplicate fields. You need to make sure your code has proper validation and error handling before performing an operation like adding or modifying an item. In contrast, SharePoint determines when and how CAML will be used. If you create a feature that uses CAML to define a new field, the first time you activate the feature, the new field will be created. However, if you activate the feature again, if that field already existed in the site, SharePoint won't provision a duplicate version of that field or throw an error saying that the field already exists.

CAML is also used to determine the configuration of list views. An important part of defining a view on a list is the ability to filter and sort data in that list. You can do this by defining "where," "group by," and "order by" statements, just as you might do when querying a database using T-SQL. As an extension of this kind of functionality, it's possible to execute a *CAML query* independent of a list or a list view. A CAML query allows you to retrieve specific list items directly from the SharePoint database, by passing in the filtering, ordering, and grouping criteria of your query.

Working with Fields, Content Types, List Definitions, and List Instances Using CAML

One of the most common ways you might use CAML is to provision something new within SharePoint, whether this is creating a new column, adding a new list or file to a site, or making a new list definition available. You'll probably use a feature to provision your item, which means you need to create a new feature that contains your CAML markup. (About the only time you won't use a feature to use your CAML markup is when you create a site definition. Site definition CAML is used when a new site is created using a custom site definition.) Because lists usually include content types, and content types usually include columns, it's important to understand how columns, content types, and lists can build upon one another using CAML.

The first step you need to take after creating your new feature is to create an element manifest file, which you will reference in your feature. When your feature is activated, SharePoint will automatically read the CAML defined in your element manifest file(s) and provision the items defined there. All your CAML markup will be contained within the `<Element>` node of the element manifest. (For more information about what features are and how to configure them, see Chapter 7.)

Because CAML can be used to configure numerous kinds of SharePoint objects and each of those objects' properties, the volume of nodes, child nodes, and attributes that can be used within CAML is extensive and can in no way be described in its totality in this chapter. For a complete explanation of CAML, read the SDK documentation of CAML at `http://msdn.microsoft.com/en-us/library/ms462365.aspx`.

The next section walks you through a few of the most commonly used CAML elements.

Field Element

The `Field` element defines a column. If the `Field` element has been added directly to an element manifest file, the site column gets directly added to the site collection where the feature is activated. If the `Field` element is used in a list definition, the column will be provisioned as part of that list. Each `Field` element must have an ID, whose value is a globally unique identifier, as well as a `Type` property, which identifies what kind of column will be created.

 When a site column that has been added to a site collection is added to a list within that site collection, SharePoint actually creates a copy of that column and adds it to the list. The column will have the same ID as the site column, but is actually a copy of, not a reference to, the site column. If you update a site column in the site collection, you have a choice about whether you want to push your changes to all the lists that have a copy of the column. If you choose to propagate the changes, SharePoint will find every copy of that column with the same ID in the site collection and update it with the changes. If you don't propagate the changes, SharePoint simply leaves the copied columns with the same ID alone. After you've made changes to your site column, each time that column is added to a list, the list will use the modified column. In this way, it's possible for new lists to use the new column configuration, while allowing existing lists to remain as is.

Every column has at least two name values: an *internal name* and a *display name*. Although this could potentially cause confusion, it can be helpful in certain scenarios. Imagine you want to create a column called Day of Week, which is a column of type Text. You want to use the column to store the name of a weekday, such as Tuesday, in a list. However, imagine that you have a list within the site where you also want a column called Day of Week, but in this case, you want to store a numerical value from 1 to 7, which represents which day of the week something takes place. You want to deploy both columns to your site collection; however, you can't have two columns with the same name but different types. In such a scenario, it's possible to create one column with an internal name of DayOfWeekText and another with an internal name of DayOfWeekNumber, while giving both of them a display name of Day of Week.

If you create a column with an internal name that includes spaces, such as Column Name, SharePoint will automatically convert those spaces to hexadecimal format, which means a non-breaking space will be converted to the text _x0020_. Once this happens, you will always need to refer to your column using the hexadecimal notation, which means you would need to refer to your column title Column Name with an internal name of Column_x0020_Name. To avoid this scenario, simply create your column with an internal name that doesn't include spaces, and give your column a display name that includes spaces. When creating columns via the browser, you can do the same thing by creating your column the first time without spaces, (which generates an internal name without spaces), and modifying the column name to include spaces (which will modify the display name of the column).

Listing 8-6 shows an example of several `Field` elements.

LISTING 8-6: Fields.xml

```xml
<Elements xmlns="http://schemas.microsoft.com/sharepoint/">
    <Field ID="{C65F47C9-4358-48ae-BB03-79E8F5EEC0FA}"
        Name="PublicationHeadline"
        DisplayName="Publication Headline"
        Group="My Custom Columns"
        Type="Text"/>
        <Default>Quarterly News</Default>
    </Field>
    <Field ID="{F792E8FA-1464-4cec-BA66-75DC784DC132}"
        Name="DisplayOnHomepage"
        DisplayName="Display on Homepage"
        Group="My Custom Columns"
        Type="Boolean"/>
    <Field ID="{4BEC2FC9-51D0-4f11-B99F-2D01359FAE9C}"
        Name="PubicationNumber"
        DisplayName="Publication Number"
        Group="My Custom Columns"
        Type="Number"
        Min="0"
        Decimals="0"/>
```

```
<Field ID="{071B0E41-900C-47e3-ACB3-F9A03ED45023}"
    Name="PublicationDate"
    DisplayName="Publication Date"
    Group="My Custom Columns"
    Type="DateTime"
    Format="DateOnly"/>
<Field ID="{0DFD4BB2-DBC8-461b-8A2E-E7E5D077F679}"
    Name="FiscalQuarter"
    DisplayName="Fiscal Quarter"
    Group="My Custom Columns"
    Type="Choice">
    <CHOICES>
        <CHOICE>Q1</CHOICE>
        <CHOICE>Q2</CHOICE>
        <CHOICE>Q3</CHOICE>
        <CHOICE>Q4</CHOICE>
    </CHOICES>
</Field>
</Elements>
```

Notice that the `Group` attribute used with each `Field` element tells SharePoint the group heading under which the column will appear on the Site Columns administration page. Notice also that each different field type has its own attributes such as `Min` and `Decimals` for Number columns, `Format` for DateTime columns, and so on. Read the `Field` element SDK article at `http://msdn.microsoft.com/en-us/library/aa979575.aspx` for detailed information regarding type-specific attributes for specific field types.

Visual Studio 2010 does not provide any sort of import functionality for defining a site column in CAML the way it provides functionality for importing content types (as you will read about in the next section). In order to define your site columns, you'll need to add a new element file to your SharePoint solution and manually add your `Field` elements to it.

Content Type Element

The `ContentType` element defines a content type. Like a column, this will add a content type to the top-level site of a site collection unless it has been defined within a list definition instead.

Unlike fields, content types can inherit from one another. For instance, a calendar event content type is actually a type of list item content type, whereas a picture in a picture library is a type of document content type. SharePoint content type IDs reflect their inheritance structure. To start with, every single item contained in any list in SharePoint has a content type ID that beings with 0x01. A document is a kind of list item, so its content type ID begins with the list item's ID, but then it adds its own additional ID numbers, like this: 0x0101. An XML document is a kind of document, so it uses the content type ID of the document content type, but then adds its own numbers onto the end, too: 0x010101. (If you want to see some of the out-of-the-box content type IDs, view the file found in your SharePoint root at ~/14/TEMPLATE/FEATURES/ctypes/ctypeswss.xml.) When you want to add a new content type that inherits from a parent content type (which all content types must), simply append two zeros ("00") to the end of the content type ID that you want to inherit from, and then add a new GUID to the end of it, removing the dashes and curly brackets from the

GUID. For instance, to create a new content type that inherits from the document content type, you would follow this formula:

0x0101 + 00 +

{7F4D3961-97EA-4D68-AA90-F23EC36D0A1F} -

{----} =

0x0101007F4D396197EA4D68AA90F23EC36D0A1F

To prevent a content type ID from getting too long, it's possible, after having created the initial inherited ID as seen in the preceding formula, to start adding just two additional numbers to the end of that content type ID, to indicate inheritance. For instance, if you want to create a parent content type that every document in your site will inherit from, you can give it the content type ID defined in the previously mentioned formula. Then you could create a new Policy content type that inherits from your custom content type, by giving the Policy content type an ID of 0x0101007F4D 396197EA4D68AA90F23EC36D0A1F01. If you create a Procedure content type that also inherits from your custom document content type, the Procedure content type ID can be 0x0101007F4D396 197EA4D68AA90F23EC36D0A1F02, and so on.

One of the primary reasons for using content types is so you can create collections of columns that can be used together. For instance, an Event content type uses columns such as Start Time, End Time, Location, and so on. To include columns in your `ContentType` element, you will add child `FieldRef` elements, which reference site columns that have already been provisioned.

Listing 8-7 shows an example of a `ContentType` element that uses the columns defined in Listing 8-6.

LISTING 8-7: ContentType.xml

```xml
<Elements xmlns="http://schemas.microsoft.com/sharepoint/">
    <!-- Parent ContentType: Document (0x0101) -->
    <ContentType
        ID="0x01010025f589d93b3b41ac93c3e91064b18358"
        Name="Publication"
        Group="My Content Types"
        Description="Quarterly publication document">
        <FieldRefs>
            <FieldRef Name="PublicationHeadline"
                ID="{C65F47C9-4358-48ae-BB03-79E8F5EEC0FA}"/>
            <FieldRef Name="DisplayOnHomepage"
                ID="{F792E8FA-1464-4cec-BA66-75DC784DC132}"/>
            <FieldRef Name="PublicationNumber"
                ID="{4BEC2FC9-51D0-4f11-B99F-2D01359FAE9C}"/>
            <FieldRef Name="PublicationDate"
                ID="{071B0E41-900C-47e3-ACB3-F9A03ED45023}"/>
            <FieldRef Name="FiscalQuarter"
                ID="{0DFD4BB2-DBC8-461b-8A2E-E7E5D077F679}"/>
        </FieldRefs>
    </ContentType>
</Elements>
```

Content types do not have internal and display names the way columns do. Notice that you can assign a group name to your content type, so that your content type will appear under that group name on the Content Type administration page, just as you would add a group name to your column.

It's fairly easy to create a new content type element in Visual Studio. First, create a new Visual Studio project and point that project to your development SharePoint site. Add a new item to your project, using the SharePoint 2010 Content Type project item template. When you do so, SharePoint will contact the development site and will show you all the content types that are installed in that particular site collection. Choose the content type that you want your new custom content type to inherit from, and SharePoint will automatically generate the content type CAML for you. Keep in mind that if you want to add columns to the content type that are not already installed in the site collection, you must be sure to add the custom columns to your solution (as described in the previous section) and then reference them in your new content type.

List, List Template, and List Instance Elements

A list schema defines the structure of a kind of list. One or more definitions can be created from that schema, and one or more instances of a list can be generated from that definition. For example, if you want to create a new document library in your site, you might select the Documents list template. However, you might create two instances using that template: one called Company Documents and another called Departmental Documents. They both use the same definition, but they are two different libraries.

Figure 8-7 demonstrates the one-to-many relationship between list schemas, definitions, and instances.

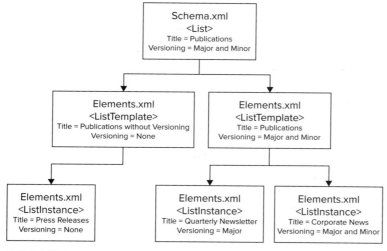

FIGURE 8-7

A list's schema must always be contained in a file called Schema.xml. If the file is not named Schema.xml, SharePoint will not be able to find it, and will throw an error if you try to provision or use the list. The Schema.xml file contains a single `List` element. That list element can be used to define properties on the list that would be created from it, such as:

➤ Is versioning enabled?

➤ Are attachments allowed?

➤ Can users create folders in the list?

➤ What content types are a part of this list?

➤ Which columns are included in this list?

➤ Which views are available on this list, which columns are part of these views, and how are the views grouped, sorted, filtered, or paged?

Listing 8-8 shows a very basic list schema.

LISTING 8-8: Schema.xml

```xml
<?xml version="1.0" encoding="utf-8"?>
<List xmlns:ows="Microsoft SharePoint" Title="CustomList"
  FolderCreation="FALSE"
  BaseType="0"
  xmlns="http://schemas.microsoft.com/sharepoint/">
  <MetaData>
    <ContentTypes>
      <ContentTypeRef ID="0x01">
        <Folder TargetName="Item" />
      </ContentTypeRef>
      <ContentTypeRef ID="0x0120" />
    </ContentTypes>
    <Fields></Fields>
    <Views>
      <View BaseViewID="0" Type="HTML"
        MobileView="TRUE" TabularView="FALSE"
        DisplayName="All Items" Url="AllItems.aspx"
        DefaultView="TRUE">
        <Toolbar Type="Standard" />
        <XslLink Default="TRUE">main.xsl</XslLink>
        <RowLimit Paged="TRUE">30</RowLimit>
        <ViewFields>
          <FieldRef Name="LinkTitleNoMenu"></FieldRef>
        </ViewFields>
        <Query>
          <OrderBy>
           <FieldRef Name="Modified" Ascending="FALSE"/>
          </OrderBy>
        </Query>
```

```
      </View>
    </Views>
    <Forms>
      <Form Type="DisplayForm" Url="DispForm.aspx"
        SetupPath="pages\form.aspx" WebPartZoneID="Main" />
      <Form Type="EditForm" Url="EditForm.aspx"
        SetupPath="pages\form.aspx" WebPartZoneID="Main" />
      <Form Type="NewForm" Url="NewForm.aspx"
        SetupPath="pages\form.aspx" WebPartZoneID="Main" />
    </Forms>
  </MetaData>
</List>
```

Each list definition must also have an element manifest containing a `ListTemplate` element that tells SharePoint where to find the list definition file. The `ListTemplate` element gives the list definition an ID (which will be used when instantiating instances of the list), and gives SharePoint additional information about properties of the list definition. Listing 8-9 shows a sample `ListTemplate` element.

LISTING 8-9: ListTemplate.xml

```
<Elements xmlns="http://schemas.microsoft.com/sharepoint/">
  <ListTemplate
    Name="PublicationsListDefinition"
    Type="10000"
    BaseType="1"
    OnQuickLaunch="TRUE"
    SecurityBits="11"
    Sequence="110"
    DisplayName="Publications"
    Description="My List Definition"
    Image="/_layouts/images/itdl.png"
    DocumentTemplate="121"/>
</Elements>
```

Some of the properties assigned to the `ListTemplate` element might have already been defined in the Schema.xml file, but the `ListTemplate` element overrides those values. The idea is that you could create more than one list definition based on the same schema. For instance, you could have a list definition called Publications defined in a Schema.xml file. You could create one `ListTemplate` element that has versioning enabled and another that doesn't. When users try to create a new list, they would see one list template called Publications with Versioning and another called Publications without Versioning. Both of these list templates reference the same underlying schema and include the same columns, content types, views, and so on, but they are configured slightly differently. To sum up, the `List` element provides a base list definition, and the `ListTemplate` element tells SharePoint which definitions should appear in the browser when a user tries to create a new list or library (as shown in Figure 8-8).

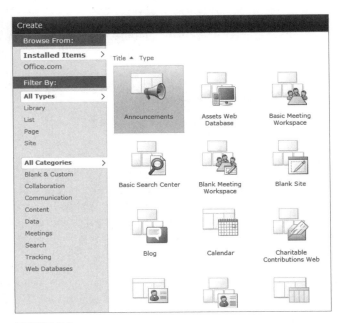

FIGURE 8-8

List definitions can be incredibly difficult to define manually. Luckily, you rarely have to. To create a custom list definition in Visual Studio, you can use one of two SharePoint 2010 project item templates. The List Definition project item template will ask you which kind of list you would like to create (such as document library or announcement list), then will generate a list definition schema for you, which you can modify as necessary. If you would like your list to be preconfigured to contain a particular content type and that content type's columns, you can select the List Definition from Content Type project item template. This template will show you all the content types that are currently installed on your development SharePoint site, and will ask you to select a content type to base your list definition on.

To generate an instance of a list, you will use the `ListInstance` element. This element tells SharePoint which list template to use, as well as information such as the display name, description, and URL of the new list. Listing 8-10 shows a sample `ListInstance` element.

LISTING 8-10: ListInstance.xml

```xml
<ListInstance Title="Publications"
    OnQuickLaunch="TRUE"
    TemplateType="10000"
    Url="Lists/Publications"
    Description="List of publications">
</ListInstance>
```

You have two simple ways to generate a list instance in Visual Studio. If you create a list definition in Visual Studio using one of the aforementioned project item templates, you can instruct Visual Studio to include a list instance in the Visual Studio project at that time. You can also add a list instance to your project by using the List Instance Visual Studio SharePoint 2010 project item.

When creating list templates and list instances, remember that they will most likely be deployed using a feature, and that this feature will have a scope assigned. List definitions must be deployed to a site collection. If you include a list instance in the same feature where you deploy your list definition, it means that when you activate that feature in your site collection, it will also provision an instance of that list in the root of your site collection. Furthermore, because the feature has already been activated, it will not be possible to activate that feature in any other site in the site collection. For that reason, it's sometimes helpful to create one feature with a scope of `Site`, which deploys your list definition, and to create another feature with a scope of `Web`, which provisions an instance of that list. When your features are constructed in such a way, your list definition only needs to be provisioned once in your site collection, but you can create a new instance of your list in any site within the collection by activating the feature scoped for just that site.

> *When you are creating a new list definition from scratch, it's not unusual to include an element manifest that provisions your site columns, another element manifest that provisions your content types based on the site columns defined in the first element manifest, and finally to create a list definition based on the content type you defined. Remember that a feature will process its constituent element manifests in the order in which they are listed in the feature. Make sure your element manifests, list definitions, and list instances are listed in the proper order in your feature. Furthermore, if you have separate features for your list definition and list instance, make sure your list instance feature has an activation dependency on the list definition feature.*

Module Element

The `Module` element allows you to add files to a SharePoint library. Modules are often used for adding files like master pages to the Master Page gallery, or cascading style sheets to the Style library. Listing 8-11 shows a sample `Module` element that is adding a master page to a Master Page gallery.

LISTING 8-11: Module.xml

```
<Module Name="Masterpage" Url="_catalogs/masterpage">
    <File Path="masterpage\Custom.master"
        Url="Custom.master" Type="GhostableInLibrary">
        <Property Name="Title" Value="AECI Intranet Master Page" />
```

continues

LISTING 8-11 *(continued)*

```
        <Property Name="MasterPageDescription"
            Value="Custom intranet master page." />
        <Property Name="ContentType" Value="Master Page" />
    </File>
</Module>
```

The `Module` element allows you to specify the path to the file on the server (in your Feature folder) where the files you want to add to SharePoint live, and the URL of the location in SharePoint to which you want to add the file. `Module` elements contain one or more child `File` elements. The `File` element tells SharePoint which specific file should be added to SharePoint, along with any properties the file might have.

Files where the `Type` property is set to `Ghostable` or `GhostableInLibrary` are considered un-customized (also known as "ghosted"); that is, until the file is modified using a tool like SharePoint Designer, whenever a user views that file in the browser, SharePoint will actually utilize the file in the Feature folder on the web server rather than a file stored in the content database to show that file to the user. If you are deploying a file that is to be a part of a list whose list definition is a kind of document library, then you will set this property to `GhostableInLibrary`; otherwise, you can set this property to `Ghostable`.

You can download a Visual Studio project on Wrox.com that deploys the Publication site columns, content type, list definition, list template, and list instance to your site collection. The project is called Wrox.SixInOne.CAML.

CAML Queries

Iterating through list data utilizing the server-side object model requires a certain amount of server resources. For each list item that SharePoint retrieves, it must create an `SPListItem` object and populate that object with all the column values for that list item. If you wanted to retrieve a batch of items from a list or even a whole site collection, it could be very resource-intensive to loop through every single item to find just those particular items you're looking for. SharePoint provides a more efficient way of querying the content database, requiring lower overhead. This is done using CAML queries. Basically, a CAML query is like a typical T-SQL or LINQ statement, in the sense that you can use keywords such as "select," "where," "order by," and "group by." In SharePoint 2010, it's now possible even to create a query that uses a *join* statement to join more than one list in a query, just as you might use a join statement in a T-SQL query.

CAML queries are actually used to define the views available on lists as well as a means for you, the developer, to perform queries against data stored in SharePoint. The next section will focus on the latter topic.

Understanding the CAML Query Syntax

If you are using CAML to return only certain items from a list, to be used in a particular view that you're defining in a list definition, your query must start with `<Query/>` tags. If you are using the CAML in a query object, you will omit this tag.

You'll want to define three basic things:

➤ The criteria of the list items you want returned in your query, defined in your `Where` tags

➤ How you want your results sorted, defined in your `OrderBy` tags

➤ How you want your results grouped, defined in your `GroupBy` tags

The following snippet shows a simple CAML query that returns all the documents whose content type is Policy Document:

```
<Where>
    <Eq>
        <FieldRef Name='Content Type'/>
        <Value Type='Text'>Policy Document</Value>
    </Eq>
</Where>
```

Inside your `Where` clause, you can specify multiple criteria that can be met. If all the criteria must be met, you will use the `And` operator. If either of the criteria must be met, you will use the `Or` operator.

Your query usually revolves around finding list items that have a particular field value, or a set of column values. You can compare these column values by passing in operators such as "equals," "greater than," "less than," "is null," "is not null," "begins with," "contains," and the like. These are represented by tags such as `<Eq/>`, `<Gt/>`, `<Lt/>`, `<IsNull/>`, `<IsNotNull/>`, `<BeginsWith/>`, `<Contains/>`, and so on.

Finally, your comparison operators will be comparing field values and some other value. Field values are represented by the `<FieldRef/>` tag, similar to what you use when referencing columns in content types.

CAML queries can be nested, which can make them confusing to read. The following example demonstrates the CAML representation of a statement such as "Select all the list items in the site collection where the content type is equal to 'Policy Document' and the Created date is more than one year old. Sort the results so the oldest document is first and group the results by the policy number."

```
<Where>
    <And>
        <Eq>
            <FieldRef Name='Content Type'/>
            <Value Type='Text'>Policy Document</Value>
        </Eq>
        <Gt>
            <FieldRef Name='Created'/>
            <Value Type='DateTime'>
                <Today OffsetDays='-365' />
            </Value>
        </Gt>
    </And>
</Where>
```

```
<OrderBy>
    <FieldRef Name='Created' Ascending='TRUE'/>
</OrderBy>
<GroupBy>
    <FieldRef Name='PolicyNumber'/>
</GroupBy>
```

Because a query such as this can be difficult to both write and read, it can be advantageous at times to utilize LINQ to SharePoint, which will be covered later in this chapter.

For another example of a CAML query in use, see the section titled "Example: Building the GetItems Web Part" later in this chapter.

Using the SPQuery and SPSiteDataQuery Objects

Sharepoint provides two query objects that use CAML queries. These are SPQuery and SPSiteDataQuery. SPQuery can query only a single list whereas SPSiteDataQuery can be used to query data throughout a site collection. Both objects have a Query property that accepts CAML query text as a string value.

You can create an SPQuery object and pass it in as a parameter to the SPList.GetItems() method to retrieve all the items (sorted and grouped as you've specified) that meet the appropriate criteria in the list. The following example shows a query that returns all the list items from a list where the Title column value starts with the word "Policy."

```
string camlQueryText =
    "<Where><BeginsWith><FieldRef Name='Title'/>" +
    "<Value Type='Text'>Policy</Value></BeginsWith></Where>";
SPQuery camlQuery = new SPQuery();
camlQuery.Query = camlQueryText;
SPListItemCollection items = list.GetItems(camlQuery);
```

The SPSiteDataQuery object works in a similar way, except you can use it to retrieve list items from multiple lists. You can choose either to retrieve items from just one site, or to retrieve items from that site and any child sites.

Both query objects also provide you with the ability to specify which fields you would like returned as well as a limit to the number of items you want returned.

AN INTRODUCTION TO LINQ TO SHAREPOINT

Language Integrated Query (LINQ) is a way of accessing external data sources using a SQL-like syntax, and has been integrated with C# 3.0 and Visual Basic 2008. To use LINQ in your code, you need a LINQ provider to provide a bridge between your code and whatever data source you are accessing. SharePoint Foundation 2010 comes with its own LINQ to SharePoint provider, contained in the Microsoft.SharePont.Linq.dll assembly. This allows us to query SharePoint lists and libraries using LINQ syntax.

One of the most compelling reasons for using LINQ to SharePoint instead of CAML is that LINQ provides strongly typed classes, whereas CAML is written as a string of text that will be executed only at runtime. Visual Studio's IntelliSense will help you program against your lists and their columns in an easy manner, and will alert you at compile time if you are referencing a list or column incorrectly. In addition to being easier to write, LINQ provides a more readable syntax than CAML.

Using SPMetal.exe

For your lists to be strongly typed, each list must have its own representation in code. You do this by using the command line tool *SPMetal.exe*, which generates a class file that contains your column, content type, and list information represented in code. You can find the SPMetal tool in the bin folder in the SharePoint root folder on the server. The SPMetal tool takes a number of parameters, as outlined in Table 8-2.

TABLE 8-2: SPMetal Parameters

PARAMETER	DESCRIPTION	EXAMPLE
/web	The absolute URL of the site you want to use.	/web: http://intranet/sites/hr
/code	The path (relative or absolute), including the name, of the file that will be generated.	/code:HumanResources.cs /code:C:\HumanResources.cs
/language	The programming language that the output file uses. C# is the default, otherwise you can specify VB. If the file you specified in the /code parameter has an extension of cs or vb, SPMetal can figure out which language you want to use, in which case this parameter is not needed.	/language:csharp /language:vb
/namespace	The namespace used for your entity classes. If none is specified, no namespace will be used, in which case the entity classes will pick up the namespace of the Visual Studio project to which the class is added.	/namespace:Wrox.SixInone .Linq
/useremoteapi	This parameter has no value, but indicates that the site being used is not on the same server as SPMetal. This can be helpful if you want to create a solution package that will be uploaded to a remote server as a sandboxed solution.	/useremoteapi

continues

TABLE 8-2 *(continued)*

PARAMETER	DESCRIPTION	EXAMPLE
/user	If you want SPMetal to execute as some other user, pass in the domain name and username of the user in whose context you want SPMetal to execute.	/user:wrox\bbertram
/password	The password for the username you passed in using the /user parameter.	/password:J9&*!sp
/serialization	If you want your objects to be serializable, specify a value of unidirectional. The default value is none.	/serialization: unidirectional /serialization:none
/parameters	Path to an XML file containing additional configuration of SPMetal.	/parameters:HRSiteConfig .xml

For a complete explanation of the SPMetal parameters, visit `http://msdn.microsoft.com/en-us/ library/ee538255.aspx`.

Using these parameters, you could generate a C# file in the current location called HRSite.cs with a namespace of `Wrox.SixInOne.Linq` by executing the batch file in Listing 8-12.

LISTING 8-12: SPMetal.bat

Available for
download on
Wrox.com

```
CD "C:\Program Files\Common Files\
    Microsoft Shared\Web Server Extensions\14\BIN"
SPMetal /web:http://intranet/sites/hr
    /code:HRSite.cs /namespace:Wrox.SixInOne.Linq
```

In general, if you execute the SPMetal tool against a particular site, SP Metal will create entity classes for each list or library in the site and one `DataContext` class. The entity classes are created at the time the SPMetal tool is executed, so the classes will reflect the state of the lists at that time only; the entity classes will not reflect changes made afterward to the site. One of the powerful features of SharePoint is the ease with which people can make changes to things like lists, columns, and content types, so it makes sense that you would want to use LINQ only to access content types and lists whose composition (content types or columns) don't change on a regular basis. Otherwise, your entity classes will not reflect the true makeup of the site, and you'll encounter errors when you try to execute your LINQ queries.

It's possible to create a configuration file for SPMetal that tells it exactly which lists, content types, and columns you want included or excluded in the entity class that gets created. For instance, to include a list called Contacts, but to exclude all other lists in the site, you could add the following to your SPMetal configuration file:

```
<List Name="Contacts">
    <ContentType Name="Item" Class="Contact" />
</List>
<ExcludeOtherLists/>
```

You can learn how to write this configuration file by visiting http://msdn.microsoft.com/en-us/library/ee535056.aspx.

Example: Creating Entity Classes

Once you have created your entity classes file, you can reference that file in your custom code solution. This example walks you through the steps you'll need to create this file for the first time.

Follow these steps:

1. Find a SharePoint site that you can use and create a new Customers list, using the Custom List template.

2. Create a new C# project in Visual Studio using the Empty SharePoint Project template.

3. Right-click your project and select Add Reference from the context menu.

4. Browse to the SharePoint root folder (usually located at C:\Program Files\Common Files\ Microsoft Shared\Web Server Extensions\14), then open up the ISAPI directory. Select the Microsoft.SharePoint.Linq.dll assembly and add it to your project.

5. Create a new folder in your project, called LINQ.

6. Right-click the folder and select Add ⇨ New Item from the context menu. Select an item template of type Text File and give it a name of SPMetal.bat.

7. Type the following text on the first line of the text file, replacing http://siteurl with the URL of the SharePoint site you will be using:

```
"C:\Program Files\Common Files\Microsoft Shared\Web Server
Extensions\14\BIN\SPMetal.exe"
    /web:http://siteurl /code:Site.cs /parameters:config.xml
```

8. Click the File menu, then select Save LINQ\SPMetal.bat As. . . . In the menu that appears, click the arrow next to the Save button, and select Save with Encoding (Figure 8-9).

9. Select "Unicode (UTF-8 without signature) – codepage 65001" encoding.

10. Right-click your project and select Properties from the context menu.

11. Click the Build Events tab.

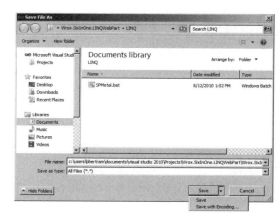

FIGURE 8-9

12. In the Pre-Build Event Command Line box, type the following:

```
cd $(ProjectDir)/LINQ
SPMetal.bat
```

13. Save your changes.

14. Right-click the folder and select Add ➪ New Item from the context menu. Select an item template of type XML File and give it a name of Config.xml.

15. Add the following XML to the file:

```
<?xml version="1.0" encoding="utf-8" ?>
<Web xmlns="http://schemas.microsoft.com/SharePoint/2009/spmetal">
<List Name="Customers">
      <ContentType Name="Item" Class="Customer" />
</List>
      <ExcludeOtherLists/>
</Web>
```

16. Build your project. You should see a new file in the LINQ folder called Site.cs. (If you can't see the file, make sure the Show All Files button is selected in your Solution Explorer, and refresh your view of the project.) This file contains the classes generated by SPMetal from your lists. If you open up the file, you should see a class called Customers.

Using LINQ to Access Site Data

Now that you have created your entity classes, it's time to use them in your code. The first thing you need to do is to create a new `DataContext` class. This class is part of the `Microsoft.SharePoint.Linq` namespace and it serves as the entry point for accessing or updating data in a SharePoint site. To use the `DataContext` class, you pass in the URL of the site whose data you would like to access, as in these examples:

```
DataContext dc = new DataContext("http://intranet/sites/finance");
DataContext dc = new DataContext(SPContext.Current.Web.Url);
```

You can then use your `DataContext` object to get a list object, by passing in the list's entity type (which is defined in the class file you generated using SPMetal) as well as the name of the list. The list object that's returned has a type of `EntityList<T>`, with the `<T>` being the type of objects in the list. In the example you just walked through, you specified in your Config.xml file that the class name (that is, the type) of an item in the Customers list is called Customer.

```
<ContentType Name="Item" Class="Customer" />
```

If you had a list called Customers in your site, you would retrieve the Customers list from the `DataContext` object like this:

```
EntityList<Customer> customers = dc.GetList<Customer>("Customers");
```

Once you have retrieved your `EntityList<T>` object, you can create a LINQ query using the list. LINQ queries are similar to T-SQL or CAML queries, in that they allow you to select items using keywords such as "select," "from," "orderby," "group by," and "where." Unlike SQL queries, however, the select statement comes at the end of the statement. A very basic query, such as the one shown here, retrieves all the items from the Customers list:

```
var customerDataSource = from customer in customers
                         select customer;
```

The variable `customers` refers to the entity list that was retrieved from the `DataContext` object. SharePoint knows that the entity list is a collection of objects of a given type, so you can make up whatever variable name you would like to denote a single object from the entity list. In the previous snippet, the variable `customer` denotes a single object of type `Customer` in the `customers` entity list. The "select" statement simply returns the entire list item for each SharePoint list item in the list.

If you would like to return a particular field from the list you selected, and that field has been included in your entity class, you can use IntelliSense to reference it in your code. For example, to return just the Title column from the Customers list, you can execute the following LINQ query:

```
var customerDataSource = from customer in customers
                         select customer.Title;
```

In some cases, if you query a list that has a Lookup column to another list, IntelliSense will even allow you to select the column names from the joined list in your query. Say you have another list in your SharePoint site called Contacts, and this list has a column called First Name. If you created a Lookup column on your Customers list in SharePoint that pointed to the Contacts list (calling that Contact list content type PrimaryContact), you could actually return columns from both lists in a single LINQ query, like this:

```
var customerDataSource = from customer in customers
                         select new { customer.Title,
                             customer.PrimaryContact.FirstName };
```

Because you are selecting more than one field, it's necessary to create a new array of selected fields by using the `new` keyword.

One of the many ways you might use data you retrieve from your LINQ query is to bind the results of your query directly to a web control that will be rendered in a browser, such as an ASP.NET GridView control. For an example of LINQ to SharePoint used in this way, see the following section of this chapter, "Example: Using LINQ to Query Lists."

A custom `DataContext` object is created for you when you use SPMetal to create your entity classes, and you can use it to retrieve strongly typed list objects, instead of retrieving an entity list with a defined type. This presents an alternative way of executing the query you just walked through. When executing a query using your custom `DataContext` object, you can use an anonymous variable (for which you want to use the "using" keyword to prevent memory leaks) to create your object. If you called your entity class file Site.cs, your custom `DataContext` object would be called `SiteDataContext`. (If you're not sure what your class name is, open up your automatically generated file and view the class name used at the very top, which inherits from `Microsoft.SharePont.Linq.DataContext`.) You would use your custom object like this:

```
using (var dc = new SiteDataContext(SPContext.Current.Web.Url))
{
}
```

You could then use your custom object directly to access the list you wanted to query, without needing to retrieve an entity list object first, as shown in this code snippet:

```
using (var dc = new SiteDataContext(SPContext.Current.Web.Url))
{
    var customerDataSource = from customer in dc.Customers
                             select customer;
}
```

The `SiteDataContext` object is already aware of the fact that there is a list called Customers.

 Sometimes it's possible to view the underlying CAML query that got executed when you executed a LINQ query. You can do this by accessing the `DataContext.Log` *property. To read more about how to use this property, visit the online SDK article "How to: View CAML Generated by LINQ to SharePoint" at* `http://msdn.microsoft.com/en-us/library/ff798464.aspx`*.*

Example: Using LINQ to Query Lists

This example walks you through the process of retrieving information from linked lists in SharePoint using LINQ to SharePoint. You will bind the results of your query to an ASP.NET GridView control, which you will deploy inside a Visual Web Part. You can download this project from `Wrox.com`. The project is titled Wrox.SixInOne.LINQWebPart.

Follow these steps:

1. Open the SharePoint site you used in the previous example. Create a new list called Contacts, based on the Custom List template.

2. Add a new Text column to the list, called First Name.

3. Add several new items to your new Contacts list.

4. Go to the Customers list you created in the previous example. Add a new Lookup column to the Contacts list called Primary Contact. Make the column required. In the Get Information From drop-down menu, select Contacts. In the In This Column drop-down menu, select Last Name. Click OK.

5. Add several new items to your Customers list.

6. Open up the Visual Studio project you created in the previous example.

7. Open up your Config.xml file. Add a new `<List>` node under the first one, which will reference the new Contacts list you created. Your new node should look like this:

```
<List Name="Contacts">
        <ContentType Name="Item" Class="Contact" />
</List>
```

8. Right-click your project and select Add ⇨ New Item from the context menu.

9. Select the Visual Web Part item template from the SharePoint 2010 node. Name your new Web Part Customers.

10. Open up the user control CustomersUserControl.ascx. Open up the Visual Studio Toolbox and drop a GridView control on the user control. Give the GridView control an ID of CustomerGridView.

11. Open up the code behind for the user control, CustomersUserControl.ascx.cs.

12. Add the following "using" statements to the top of the page:

```
using System.Linq;
using Microsoft.SharePoint;
using Microsoft.SharePoint.Linq;
```

13. In the `Page_Load` method, add the following code:

```
DataContext dc = new DataContext(SPContext.Current.Web.Url);

var customers = dc.GetList<Customer>("Customers");

var customerDataSource = from customer in customers
                    select new {CustomerName = customer.Title,
                        ContactLastName = customer.PrimaryContact.Title,
                        ContactFirstName = customer.PrimaryContact.
                        FirstName};

CustomerGridView.DataSource = customerDataSource;
CustomerGridView.DataBind();
```

14. Go to the Build menu in Visual Studio and deploy your project. This should automatically compile your solution package and activate the feature in the SharePoint site to which you deployed your project.

15. Open up your site and add your new Web Part to a page. You should now see a grid that contains three columns of data (Figure 8-10).

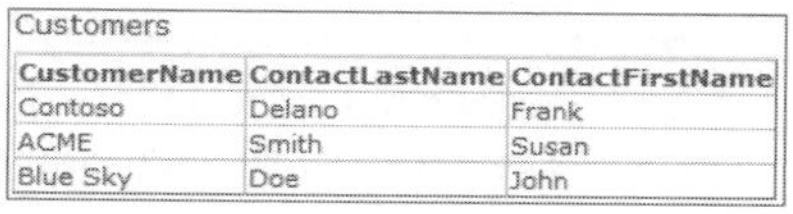

Customers

CustomerName	ContactLastName	ContactFirstName
Contoso	Delano	Frank
ACME	Smith	Susan
Blue Sky	Doe	John

FIGURE 8-10

AN INTRODUCTION TO WEB PARTS

This section will help you understand what a Web Part is and the difference between a Web Part server control and a Visual Web Part. It also walks you through the creation of a Web Part server control.

What Is a Web Part?

A Web Part is a self-contained unit of functionality that can be hosted on a web page and whose settings can be configured using a browser-based user interface called a *tool pane*. (Figure 8-11 shows the tool pane for the Tag Cloud Web Part.) The SharePoint Web Part framework is based on the ASP.NET Web Part framework; in fact, a Web Part is actually a compiled ASP.NET server control. As such, you can build a Web Part to have just about any kind of functionality you could build into a traditional web application.

FIGURE 8-11

Instances of a Web Part can be used again and again by being placed multiple times on a single page, or placed on multiple pages in a SharePoint site. Because Web Parts can be configured, it's possible for the same Web Part to look very different when configured in different ways. Some Web Parts display information that is tied to some unique data source, so it's possible for the same Web Part to return very different information, depending on which data source it has been connected to. For instance, a List View Web Part might show documents from your Shared Documents library or it might show files from your Style library, but the underlying Web Part was coded one time and simply configured two different ways.

A Web Part must be able to function completely by itself (that is, it should not be dependent on any other Web Part on the page for its functionality), but can interact with other Web Parts hosted on the same page, by either supplying or consuming data from those other Web Parts. For instance, you might have one List View Web Part that displays a list of the names of images from a picture library in your SharePoint site. If you placed that Web Part on a page, the Web Part would function properly, returning a list of pictures. However, it would be possible to place an Image Viewer Web Part on the same page, then instruct the List View Web Part to connect to the Image Viewer Web Part, so that each time a user selected an image from the picture library, that image would be rendered in the Image Viewer Web Part. When Web Parts work with each other on a page, they are considered *connected*. Figure 8-12 shows a List View Web Part that is displaying

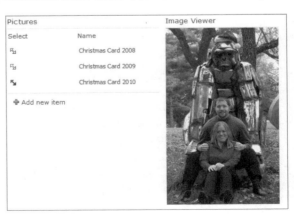

FIGURE 8-12

a list of documents in a library called Pictures. The Web Part is connected to an Image Viewer Web Part. When the user selects a picture from the Pictures list, a preview of the image shows up in the Image Viewer Web Part.

Although a Web Part can be configured so that every person who visits that Web Page sees the same configuration of the Web Part, it's also possible for each user to configure a Web Part individually. And SharePoint can save the user's personal configuration, so that on the next visit to the page hosting that Web Part, the user will see the version of the Web Part that he or she configured and not the configuration of the Web Part that was configured for all users. This is called Web Part *personalization*.

Personalization can reduce performance because SharePoint is required to save a separate version of a given Web Part for each individual who has personalized a Web Part. In addition, users who are not well trained in using Web Parts can accidentally delete or misconfigure Web Parts. For these reasons, it's important to weigh the risks and benefits of enabling Web Part personalization for your end users. It's possible to eliminate the ability for users to personalize Web Parts by modifying the underlying permission set(s) that users have been assigned to. To do so, unselect the Add/Remove Personal Web Parts and Update Personal Web Parts checkboxes on the Edit Permission Level administration page. You can also remove the ability for users to personalize a particular Web Part by unchecking the Allow Editing in Personal View checkbox in the Advanced section of a Web Part's tool pane.

It's possible to both close and delete a Web Part; if you close a Web Part, the Web Part is no longer displayed when you load the page, but the configuration of the Web Part is still stored with the page. You could add the Web Part back to the page at any time. In contrast, if you delete a Web Part, the Web Part is forever gone from the page.

If a Web Part is closed but not deleted, every time the page is retrieved, SharePoint must retrieve the information for that closed Web Part as well, reducing performance. If you believe you might need a Web Part added back to the page in the future, you might find it helpful to close the Web Part instead of deleting it, because the Web Part will still be available to you. However, if you don't think you'll need that Web Part again, it's better to delete it than to close it, so that your page will render more quickly.

Building a Web Part

Building a new Web Part server control is easy with Visual Studio 2010. Once you have a SharePoint 2010 Visual Studio project, you can create a new Web Part by choosing the Web Part project item template. This will automatically add a new class to your project, which inherits from the class `System.Web.UI.WebControls.WebParts.WebPart`. When your class first gets created, it will look like this:

```
namespace Wrox.SixInOne.WebParts.WebPart1
{
    [ToolboxItemAttribute(false)]
    public class WebPart1 : WebPart
    {
        protected override void CreateChildControls()
        {
        }
    }
}
```

The first thing to note is the attribute `ToolboxItemAttribute`, which decorates your class. This attribute would be set to `true` if you were going to make this control available in the Visual Studio toolbox. However, because that's not necessary for creating a SharePoint Web Part, this value can remain `false`.

A Web Part is essentially a container for other web controls. As such, you can create additional web controls and add them to the collection of controls in the Web Part you are building. You will do this in the `CreateChildControls()` method. For instance, if you wanted your Web Part to display the text "Hello, World!" you could add this code to your `CreateChildControls()` method:

```
Literal helloWorld = new Literal();
helloWorld.Text = "Hello, World!";
this.Controls.Add(helloWorld);
```

One of the things that makes Web Parts so versatile is the ability for end users to modify the properties of the Web Part in their browsers. It's possible to create public properties on your class and then add attributes to those properties that will make those properties visible in the tool pane the user sees when configuring the Web Part. Table 8-3 shows some of the attributes you can use.

TABLE 8-3: Web Part Public Property Attributes

ATTRIBUTE	DESCRIPTION	EXAMPLE
`WebBrowsable()`	A value of `true` indicates that this property will be editable in the Web Part tool pane.	`WebBrowsable(true)`
`WebDisplayName()`	The name of the field in the tool pane.	`WebDisplayName("Days")`

ATTRIBUTE	DESCRIPTION	EXAMPLE
WebDescription()	The description of the field, which will be displayed as a tooltip when the user mouses over the name of the field in the tool pane.	WebDescription("Number of days")
Personalizable()	Indicates whether the property, when saved, will be available to every user who visits the page, or just the person who set the property. Possible values are PersonalizationScope.Shared or PersonalizationScope.User.	Personalizable (PersonalizationScope .Shared)

To allow a user to set a public property in your Web Part class, you could add the following code to that class:

```
private int days = 3;

[WebBrowsable(true),
WebDisplayName("Days"),
WebDescription("Number of days"),
Personalizable(PersonalizationScope.Shared)]
public int Days
{
    get { return days; }
    set { days = value; }
}
```

This property would generate a field called "Days" with a description of "Number of days" in the Web Part tool pane. Figure 8-13 shows what this would look like.

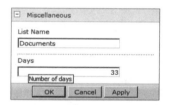

FIGURE 8-13

Deploying Your Web Part to SharePoint

Now that you have your underlying Web Part class written, you need to get the Web Part deployed to your site collection. Each Web Part must have a configuration file. This file will have an extension of .webpart. (In older versions of SharePoint, this file had a .dwp extension, which you might still find in legacy SharePoint applications.) The configuration file tells SharePoint basic information such as the name and the description of the Web Part. It also tells SharePoint that this Web Part references the underlying class that you just created. It does this by giving the assembly and type name of the Web Part class. The configuration file can also be used to set initial property values for the Web Part.

Listing 8-13 shows a sample configuration file. Notice that it is telling SharePoint that the name of the Web Part is "Web Part 1" and the description of the Web Part is "My Web Part." It's also telling

SharePoint that this Web Part utilizes the type Wrox.SixInOne.WebParts.WebPart1.WebPart1 in the assembly Wrox.SixInOne.WebParts.

LISTING 8-13: WebPart1.webpart

```xml
<?xml version="1.0" encoding="utf-8"?>
<webParts>
  <webPart xmlns="http://schemas.microsoft.com/WebPart/v3">
    <metaData>
      <type name="Wrox.SixInOne.WebParts.WebPart1.WebPart1,
        Wrox.SixInOne.WebParts.GetItems.GetItems,
        Wrox.SixInOne.WebParts, Version=1.0.0.0,
        Culture=neutral, PublicKeyToken=531c676be3760df2" />
          <importErrorMessage>Cannot be imported.</importErrorMessage>
    </metaData>
    <data>
      <properties>
        <property name="Title" type="string">Web Part 1</property>
        <property name="Description" type="string">My WebPart</property>
      </properties>
    </data>
  </webPart>
</webParts>
```

Once the configuration file is in place, you need to create a `Module` element to deploy this configuration file to your site collection Web Part gallery. The URL of the Web Part gallery in any site collection is `/_catalogs/wp`. Your `Module` element might look like this:

```xml
<?xml version="1.0" encoding="utf-8"?>
<Elements xmlns="http://schemas.microsoft.com/sharepoint/" >
  <Module Name="WebPart1" Url="_catalogs/wp">
    <File Path="WebPart1\WebPart1.webpart" Url="WebPart1.webpart"
Type="GhostableInLibrary">
      <Property Name="Group" Value="My Custom Web Parts" />
    </File>
  </Module>
</Elements>
```

This is telling SharePoint that you want to deploy your Web Part configuration file to the Web Part gallery, and your Web Part should be placed into a group called "My Custom Web Parts." The group name becomes important when users want to add Web Parts to their pages. Web Parts with the same group name will appear in a folder under the Categories heading when a user wants to add a Web Part to a page. Figure 8-14 shows that the Web Parts Content Editor, Image Viewer, and so on all fall under the group name Media and Content.

FIGURE 8-14

Luckily, when you create a new Web Part using the Visual Studio project item template, Visual Studio will automatically generate your Web Part configuration file and your `Module` element for you. However, it's important to know how to manually configure each of the files because you will most likely want to be able to configure the Web Part's name, description, and group before you deploy it to your server. Figure 8-15 shows you the three files that Visual Studio creates for you when you create a Web Part using the Web Part project item template: the class (.cs) file that defines the Web Part; the Web Part configuration (.webpart) file; and the element manifest (.xml) that deploys it to the Web Part gallery.

FIGURE 8-15

Example: Building the GetItems Web Part

Follow these steps (you can find all the code snippets in the example on the Wrox website, identified as Wrox.SixInOne.WebParts):

1. Create a new Project in Visual Studio 2010.

2. Select the Visual C# Empty SharePoint Project template. Give your project a name of Wrox .SixInOne.WebParts and click the OK button.

3. On the SharePoint Customization Wizard dialog box, enter the URL of the website you would like to use for debugging, select the Deploy as a Farm Solution radio button, and click the Finish button.

4. Right-click your project and select Add ➪ New Item from the Context menu. Select the Visual C# ➪ SharePoint ➪ 2010 node from the Installed Templates pane, then select the Web Part item template. Give your Web Part a name of GetItems.

5. Open the GetItems.cs file.

6. Add the following "using" statements to the top of the page:

```
using System;
using System.ComponentModel;
using System.Data;
using System.Web.UI.WebControls;
using System.Web.UI.WebControls.WebParts;
using Microsoft.SharePoint;
```

7. Add the following two private variables:

```
private string listName = "Documents";
private int days = 3;
```

8. Add the following two public properties, with their accompanying attributes:

```
[WebBrowsable(true),
WebDescription("Select the name of the list you would like to query."),
WebDisplayName("List Name"),
Personalizable(PersonalizationScope.Shared)]
public string ListName
```

```
    {
        get { return listName; }
        set { listName = value; }
    }

    [WebBrowsable(true),
    WebDescription("Number of days"),
    WebDisplayName("Days"),
    Personalizable(PersonalizationScope.Shared)]
    public int Days
    {
        get { return days; }
        set { days = value; }
    }
```

9.   Add the following code to the `CreateChildControls()` method:

```
SPWeb web = SPContext.Current.Web;
SPList list = null;
try
{
    //Get the list specified in the tool pane
    list = web.Lists[listName];
}
catch
{
    Literal errorMessage = new Literal();
    errorMessage.Text =
        String.Format("A list with name {0} does not exist in this site.",
        listName);
    this.Controls.Add(errorMessage);
}

//Get all the items which are newer than the number of days old
//specified in the tool pane
string camlQueryText =
    String.Format("<Where><Geq><FieldRef Name='Modified' />" +
    "<Value Type='DateTime'>" +
    "<Today OffsetDays='-{0}' /></Value></Geq></Where>",
    days);
SPQuery camlQuery = new SPQuery();
camlQuery.Query = camlQueryText;
SPListItemCollection items = list.GetItems(camlQuery);
DataTable data = items.GetDataTable();

//If the query returns list items, bind them to a DataGrid control
if (data != null)
{
    DataGrid dg = new DataGrid();
    dg.AutoGenerateColumns = false;

    BoundColumn bc = new BoundColumn();
    bc.HeaderText = "Title";
    bc.DataField = "Title";
    dg.Columns.Add(bc);
```

```
              BoundColumn bc2 = new BoundColumn();
              bc2.HeaderText = "Modified";
              bc2.DataField = "Modified";
              dg.Columns.Add(bc2);

              this.Controls.Add(dg);
              dg.DataSource = data;
              dg.DataBind();
          }
          else
          {
              Literal errorMessage = new Literal();
              errorMessage.Text = "No items returned.";
              this.Controls.Add(errorMessage);
          }
```

10. Press the F5 button to debug your solution.

11. Browse to your site and add your new Web Part to a page.

12. Modify the Web Part to open up the tool pane. Expand the section titled Miscellaneous. You should see two fields that reflect the List Name and Days public properties on your class (as shown in Figure 8-13). Modify the properties and see if your Web Part returns additional or fewer items.

Understanding Visual Web Parts

It can be difficult to build Web Part server controls because you are programmatically adding child web controls, and you lack any sort of visual indication of what your Web Part will look like when rendered on a web page. An alternative to building your Web Parts using server controls is to create something called a Visual Web Part. A Visual Web Part is essentially a Web Part that contains a single child control, and this child control is an ASP.NET user control. By leveraging a user control, you have the ability to use the Visual Studio designer to drag and drop other controls onto your design surface. This provides a much more user-friendly way of designing Web Parts.

To create a Visual Web Part, simply add a new Visual Web Part to your existing Visual Studio SharePoint 2010 project using the Visual Web Part project item template. This will automatically create the Web Part class, configuration file, and `Module` element, but it will also create the user control and user control code-behind page, which you can use to design your Web Part.

User controls must be deployed to the ~/14/TEMPLATE/CONTROLTEMPLATES folder on the filesystem to be considered "safe" by SharePoint. This is a location shared among all web applications in the server farm. As such, it is not possible to deploy Visual Web Parts in a sandboxed solution. However, Microsoft has released a Visual Studio add-on called Visual Studio 2010 SharePoint Power Tools, which allows you to deploy Visual Web Parts in a sandboxed solution. To download the add-on, visit http://visualstudiogallery.msdn.microsoft .com/en-us/8e602a8c-6714-4549-9e95-f3700344b0d9.

To build your own Visual Web Part, follow the steps laid out in the section "Example: Creating a Feature and Solution Using Visual Studio 2010" in Chapter 7.

AN INTRODUCTION TO THE REST INTERFACE

Up until now, you've learned about how to access SharePoint information using code that executes on the SharePoint server itself. The rest of this chapter focuses on methods of accessing SharePoint data from remote locations, whether that means accessing SharePoint using HTTP, a client application such as Silverlight, or web service.

SharePoint 2010 provides a way of accessing list data using a Representational State Transfer (REST) interface. (Interfaces utilizing the REST interface are referred to as *RESTful*.) The RESTful interface provides a simple way for external applications to access and modify SharePoint data. It makes it possible to retrieve an XML representation of list data by simply supplying a URL. It's possible to carry out basic CRUD (create, read, update, and delete) operations using the REST interface, by using the HTTP operations of POST, GET, PUT, and DELETE. By passing in various parameters with your URLs, it's possible to filter and sort the data that you get back.

 For your RESTful service to work, you must have installed the ADO.NET Data Services Update for .NET Framework 3.5 SP1.

 You can supply ADO.NET Data Services with a SharePoint data source by passing it a RESTful URL from SharePoint. To learn more about this, read the article "Query SharePoint Foundation with ADO.NET Data Services" at `http://msdn.microsoft.com/en-us/library/ee535480.aspx`.

To access the RESTful service, you'll need to reference the following URL: `/_vti_bin/ListData.svc`.

This URL should be appended to whichever site you are querying. For instance, if you want to retrieve list data from the accounting department's site in your intranet, you would use a URL of `http://intranet/sites/accounting/_vti_bin/ListData.svc`.

 You can see what kinds of results get returned by browsing to the list data service URL of the SharePoint site in your browser. If the results conform to an RSS standard, your browser may interpret the results as an RSS feed for you to subscribe to, which means it won't display straight XML. When querying a particular list item, your browser might not be able to interpret the results as a feed and might give you an error.

You can get every list item out of a particular list in the site by appending the name of the list to the end of the URL. For example, to get all the documents from the Documents library in your accounting site, you would use a URL of:

```
http://intranet/sites/accounting/_vti_bin/ListData.svc/Documents
```

You can retrieve one particular list item from a list by passing in the ID of that list item after the list name, like this:

```
http://intranet/sites/accounting/_vti_bin/ListData.svc/Documents(2)
```

You can also find out the column value for one particular list item by passing the column name after the item number like this:

```
http://intranet/sites/accounting/_vti_bin/ListData.svc/Documents(2)/Title
```

You can sort your results by using the parameter `$orderby` and passing in the name of the column you would like to sort your results by. For instance, if you want to sort your documents by title, you would use a URL of:

```
http://intranet/sites/accounting/_vti_bin/ListData.svc/Documents?$orderby=Title
```

You can even execute a CAML query on your list by passing in a `$filter` parameter. For instance, if you wanted to retrieve a document whose title was My Document, you could use a URL like:

```
http://intranet/sites/accounting/_vti_bin/ListData.svc/Documents?$filter=Title eq
'My Document'
```

Although it's unconventional to have spaces in your URL, it's permitted when using the RESTful service.

To read more about the RESTful service, visit the SDK article online:

```
http://msdn.microsoft.com/en-us/library/ff521587.aspx
```

AN INTRODUCTION TO THE CLIENT OBJECT MODEL

At times it becomes helpful to contact your SharePoint server from a client application, whether that client is a Windows or web application. You might want to be able to retrieve and update information from SharePoint from a Web Part that lives on one of your SharePoint pages, without needing to post the entire page back to the server, causing the whole page to reload. That Web Part could be created using managed .NET code, or it could even be a Silverlight control. SharePoint 2010 provides developers with a new tool that makes it easy to contact the SharePoint server in a lightweight manner. It's called the *client-side object model* (CSOM).

The CSOM includes a set of objects that mirrors the server-side object model, allowing you to interact with objects such as site collections, sites, lists, and list items. However, the object model itself is pared down, providing a subset of functionality that focuses on the most heavily used operations. This means that smaller class libraries need to be downloaded to the client when the CSOM is being utilized by Silverlight or ECMAScript.

 ECMAScript is a scripting language standard that adheres to a specification set out by an organization called Ecma International. In SharePoint, ECMAScript is usually written using JavaScript or Jscript.

SharePoint 2010 contains three subsets of the client object model:

➤ Client-side API for code running in a .NET 3.5 or higher managed code application

➤ Silverlight API

➤ ECMAScript API

The client object models are implemented as a Windows Communication Foundation (WCF) service. Each of these object models uses a proxy that serializes commands and sends them asynchronously as XML to the server in a single HTTP request. When the request reaches the server, the server-side object model takes over to access the server. A response is sent back to the client using JavaScript Object Notation (JSON). The proxy then takes that information and associates it with the appropriate client objects.

Understanding the Client Objects

The .NET and Silverlight client object models use the namespace `Microsoft.SharePoint.Client`, whereas the ECMAScript client object model uses a namespace of `SP`. For instance, to reference the `WebParts` class using the .NET or Silverlight client object models, you would use the namespace `Microsoft.SharePoint.Client.WebParts`, whereas using ECMAScript you would use `SP.WebParts`. The names of the objects are similar to the server object names, but with the absence of the "SP" prefix. For instance, using the server-side object model, to access a site collection you would reference an `SPSite` object. Using the client object model, you would reference a `Site` object. In the same way, using the CSOM you would access sites, lists, and list items using `Web`, `List`, and `ListItem` objects.

One of the advantages of the CSOM is that queries and updates to the server are performed in batches, reducing network traffic. That means you can create a set of commands that tell SharePoint what you want to do, then send them off to the server all at once, rather than having to send multiple commands to the server one at a time, consuming network resources. SharePoint does this by keeping track of an object on the client side, both before and after the object has been retrieved from the server.

The first step to utilizing the CSOM is to create an object that will manage the connection with the server. This object is the `ClientContext` object. This object is used to retrieve information from the server that can be assigned to a client object. As when creating a new SPContext object using the server object model, using the CSOM you must also create a new context object by passing in the URL of the SharePoint site you wish to use. For instance, Listing 8-14 creates a new context object that is connected to the marketing department's site on the intranet. (This and the following three listings can be downloaded from Wrox.com, where they are identified as part of the CSOM.cs code block.) The listing creates a Web object, but that object will remain empty unless a request is made to the server to populate it with information about the site. This can be done using the Load() method of the ClientContext object. Although the code is telling SharePoint that it wants information about the marketing site assigned to the marketingSubsite object, the object will not actually be populated until the ExecuteQuery() method of the context object is executed, at which point a call to the server is made. When the proxy class receives a response from the server, it will populate the marketingSubsite object with property information, such as the name of the site.

LISTING 8-14: Creating the ClientContext (CSOM.cs)

```
ClientContext ctxt = new ClientContext("http://intranet/sites/marketing");
Web marketingSubsite = ctxt.Web;
ctxt.Load(marketingSubsite );
ctxt.ExecuteQuery();
string siteTitle = marketingSubsite.Title;
```

Keep in mind, however, that only the specific information requested will be populated when the query is executed. For instance, trying to access the collection lists that are inside the marketing site will return an error unless that collection has been retrieved from the server as well, as in Listing 8-15.

LISTING 8-15: Getting List Data (CSOM.cs)

```
ListCollection lists = marketingSubsite.Lists;
ctxt.Load(lists);
ctxt.ExecuteQuery();
```

To update objects, you must call the Update() method on them, much as you would when using the server object model. However, as with retrieving information, the update will not actually take place on the server until the ExecuteQuery() method is executed. For instance, Listing 8-16 demonstrates how you can update the title of a site.

LISTING 8-16: Updating Site Data (CSOM.cs)

```
marketingSubsite.Title = "New Title";
marketingSubsite.Update();
ctxt.ExecuteQuery();
string newTitle = marketingSubsite.Title;
```

To delete an object, you'll call the `DeleteObject()` method on the object. (This is slightly different than the server object model, where you use a method simply called `Delete()`.) As always, you must call the `ExecuteQuery()` method to communicate the deletion to the server.

Because code is executing on the client side, the less code that can be retrieved from the server the better, because it means less processing on the client. It's possible to use complex queries, LINQ, and Lambda expressions to create detailed queries that return just the information needed to perform an action. To learn more about these kinds of queries, read the Managed Client Object Model SDK documentation online at http://msdn.microsoft.com/en-us/library/ee537247.aspx.

Example: Creating a CSOM Console Application

This section walks you through the steps of creating a console application that uses the client-side .NET managed object model to access your SharePoint site. (You can find all the code snippets in the example on the Wrox website, identified as Wrox.SixInOne.CSOM.)

1. Create a new project in Visual Studio 2010 using the C# Console Application project template. Make sure your project is targeted to the .NET Framework 3.5 or the .NET Framework 4.5. Give your project a name of Wrox.SixInOne.CSOM.

2. Add a reference to the following two assemblies, located in the ISAPI folder in your SharePoint root folder: Microsoft.SharePoint.Client.dll and Microsoft.SharePoint.Client .Runtime.dll. (Verify that your project is still targeted to the framework you initially set when creating the project. Visual Studio might reset your project to be targeted to the .NET Framework 3.5 or 4.0 Client Profile once you include the client assemblies. If it has changed your targeted framework, you will need to change it back to your initial setting.)

3. Copy the code from Listings 8-14, 8-15, and 8-16, and place it inside the `Main()` method of your Program class, replacing the URL of the site with the URL of a site on your development SharePoint server.

4. Add the following line of code after the code you just added:

```
Console.WriteLine(lists.Count.ToString());
Console.WriteLine(newTitle);
```

5. Run your project. You should see the console write out the number of lists that are in your site. You should also notice that the name of your site has now changed to "New Title."

AN INTRODUCTION TO THE SHAREPOINT WEB SERVICES

You have now learned how to access SharePoint using the server object model, LINQ to SharePoint, REST, and the client object model. Another way to access your SharePoint server is to use the traditional ASP.NET web services that are included as part of your SharePoint server.

Separate web services exist for interacting with objects on the server such as site collections, sites, lists, permissions, people, alerts, meetings, and versions of list items. You can find each of these web services in the _vti_bin virtual directory of your IIS web application.

In the last version of SharePoint, SharePoint web services were the primary means of communicating with SharePoint from an external location. However, with the advent of the CSOM in SharePoint 2010, Microsoft is encouraging developers to utilize the CSOM technologies instead of the SharePoint web services. As a result, not all web service methods may function as smoothly in SharePoint 2010 as they did in SharePoint 2007.

When accessing information from SharePoint using a web service, it's important to let SharePoint know where you want to get information from. To add a reference to the web service in your Visual Studio project, pass in the URL of the site you want to access, followed by the web service URL in the _vti_bin folder. For example, if you wanted to access list information in the marketing site, you would add a web reference in Visual Studio to the Lists.asmx web service using this URL:

```
http://intranet/sites/marketing/_vti_bin/Lists.asmx
```

One of the first things you will need to establish when connecting to the server is the credentials with which you are authenticated against SharePoint. Just as when logging into SharePoint via a web browser, a web service will be able to retrieve or update only those objects on the server that a user has permission to access or update. To connect to your SharePoint server using the credentials of the user running the web service, set the `Credentials` property of the object you created from the web service to `System.Net.CredentialCache.DefaultCredentials`, like this:

```
Web_Reference.Lists listsService = new Web_Reference.Lists();
listsService.Credentials = System.Net.CredentialCache.DefaultCredentials;
```

Each web method for each web service is different. In some cases you will need to create XML nodes that contain information you want to send with your web service request. For instance, if you want to retrieve list items from a given list, you can tell SharePoint information about the items you want to get back from your call to the web service. You can do this by telling SharePoint to execute a specific CAML query, or telling SharePoint to retrieve items from a particular view set up on the list. You can also tell SharePoint to retrieve items from a particular folder within the list.

The following code snippet creates a new XML node called `Query`, which contains a CAML query telling SharePoint to retrieve the items where the column Season has a value of Spring:

```
XmlDocument xmlDoc = new XmlDocument();
XmlElement query = xmlDoc.CreateElement("Query");
query.InnerXml = "<Where><Eq><FieldRef Name=\"Season\"/>" +
    "<Value Type=\"Text\">Spring</Value></Eq></Where>";
```

When retrieving items from a particular list, you will also create a node called `ViewFields`, which tells SharePoint which fields you want returned with your query and in which order, as well as a

QueryOptions node, which will tell SharePoint information such as whether the items retrieved should come from a particular folder in the list.

The following snippet shows an example of a web service call that returns the title of all the items from a list called Products in the intranet site where the Season column is set to Spring.

```
//SharePointWebService is the namespace of the Web Service that was registered
//with the project.
SharePointWebService.Lists listSvc = new SharePointWebService.Lists();

listSvc.Credentials = System.Net.CredentialCache.DefaultCredentials;

listSvc.Url = "http://intranet/_vti_bin/Lists.asmx";

System.Xml.XmlDocument xmlDoc = new System.Xml.XmlDocument();
System.Xml.XmlElement query = xmlDoc.CreateElement("Query");
System.Xml.XmlElement viewFields = xmlDoc.CreateElement("ViewFields");
System.Xml.XmlElement queryOptions = xmlDoc.CreateElement("QueryOptions");

XmlElement query = xmlDoc.CreateElement("Query");
query.InnerXml = "<Where><Eq><FieldRef Name=\"Season\"/>" +
    "<Value Type=\"Text\">Spring</Value></Eq></Where>";
viewFields.InnerXml = "<FieldRef Name=\"Title\" />";
queryOptions.InnerXml = "";

System.Xml.XmlNode nodeListItems =
    listSvc.GetListItems("Products", null, query, viewFields, null, queryOptions,
null);
```

SUMMARY

In this chapter you learned about various ways to interact with SharePoint programmatically and declaratively. You learned how to work with site collections, sites, lists, list items, and folders, using the server-side object model. You learned how to provision new items in SharePoint using CAML and how to use CAML to retrieve information from the SharePoint database. This chapter showed you how you can use LINQ to SharePoint to access SharePoint content in a strongly typed and readable way. This chapter gave you an introduction to what a Web Part is, and how to build a Web Part server control as well as a Visual Web Part. You learned about accessing information in SharePoint using the REST model and the client object model. Finally, you learned about the availability of the SharePoint web services.

Publishing in SharePoint Server 2010

WHAT'S IN THIS CHAPTER?

➤ What is a publishing site?

➤ How to create and edit publishing pages

➤ Understanding page versioning and approval

➤ How to configure publishing sites

➤ Understanding anonymous access, content deployment, and variations

➤ How to create a page layout using SharePoint Designer

➤ How to create a page layout using Visual Studio 2010

Some websites you visit regularly because they allow you to perform a task, whether this is checking your e-mail, connecting with a friend on a social media site, checking in for a flight, or checking the balance of your bank account. However, you might visit other websites because they provide information you're seeking, such as the latest bestseller paperback books or the available shades of paint at your local hardware store.

Web Content Management (WCM) refers to the process of storing and managing web content that is primarily textual and graphical in nature. (This is in contrast to sites that are collaborative or transactional in nature.) Web Content Management software products have several common characteristics:

➤ Non-technical users have the ability to publish content (text, images, and documents) to a website without the need for intervention from any IT staff.

➤ Content is standardized across a website through the use of page templates.

➤ Content can go through an approval process before it appears "live" on a website.

➤ Content can be scheduled to appear or disappear from a website at a given point in time.

➤ Content is often stored in a database rather than in files on a filesystem.

Many WCM solutions are available for free on the Web. Many of the free blogging sites available online provide a WCM solution for their users. Blogger.com, for instance, allows non-technical users to post content, including text and graphics, to their own websites. Blogger.com users can decide how they want their sites to look by choosing from available templates. Blog authors can choose to save draft versions of their postings, preventing that content from appearing on the site until they choose to explicitly "publish" the content. Additionally, many of the social media sites (like MySpace and Facebook), though not traditional WCM solutions, do allow non-technical users to upload their own content, content that is stored in a back-end database rather than on files on a filesystem. The wide adoption of WCM solutions on the Internet in recent years is an indication of its usefulness in both private and public spheres.

SharePoint Server 2010 provides WCM capabilities that can help small, medium, and large businesses and organizations publish content on their own websites. This chapter reviews the basic functionality provided in SharePoint Server 2010, and reviews how you can create your own page templates using Visual Studio 2010 and SharePoint Designer 2010.

UNDERSTANDING THE PUBLISHING PROCESS

This section helps you understand the process of getting content into SharePoint and making that content available on a website for other users to view.

Planning

Before you start the process of creating and managing your content, it's important to do a little leg work. This section walks you through some basics of SharePoint WCM sites, answering some of your questions such as, "What is a publishing site?" and explaining which lists and libraries are included in a publishing site.

What Is a Publishing Site?

Sites that use SharePoint's WCM features utilize a publishing process, so they are frequently referred to as *publishing sites* (a term that is used for the remainder of the chapter).

As you have probably discovered by now, SharePoint has a broad range of capabilities, such as allowing users to collaborate with each other, network with one another, or interact with external data. As was mentioned at the beginning of this chapter, the WCM features of SharePoint focus primarily on the ability to create attractive web pages, filled with textual content and images, which can be maintained easily by a non-technical staff of content authors.

SharePoint is a web-based application, so end users interact with SharePoint almost exclusively by using their web browsers. That being the case, *every* page in SharePoint that a user interacts with via the browser is a web page, whether the user is using a publishing site or not. So what differentiates a publishing site from any other SharePoint site, and what makes a publishing page different from any other page?

In a collaborative site, users frequently make use of lists and libraries to store and retrieve content such as documents and other data. Users might click a link that takes them to the View All Site Content page, where they can view all the lists and libraries that are a part of the given site. If they want to add an item to a list, they might navigate to a view of that list and enter data into that list using an input form. In a publishing site, it's not intended that users interact in any way with underlying list data in the site's list format. In fact, users should not even be aware they are browsing a SharePoint site. Every page they encounter should have a unique look and feel that does not reflect the "out-of-the-box" SharePoint look and feel.

Publishing sites provide the ability to create and use page templates, called *page layouts*, which are in turn used to create new web pages on the site that will be used to communicate textual and graphical content to end users. These pages stand in contrast to *administrative pages* (such as the Site Settings page, or any page whose URL includes "_layouts") or pages used in collaborative sites such as *Web Part pages* or *wiki pages*. We call these pages — which are created using page layouts — *publishing pages*.

SHAREPOINT PUBLISHING INTRANET SITES

The WCM features of SharePoint are meant primarily for public-facing Internet sites. This means that the publishing features of SharePoint are meant to hide the underlying list and library data from end users, so they are aware only that they are browsing a uniquely branded website, and not that they are browsing a SharePoint-powered site in particular.

However, it's not uncommon for companies to implement the publishing features of SharePoint on their corporate intranet site(s). Doing so provides the ability to deliver relevant content to users, such as the latest news stories or announcements, yet in a uniquely branded way that avoids the typical SharePoint look and feel.

Please keep in mind that choosing to implement SharePoint's WCM features in a site collection that will also be used for collaboration requires additional design effort. The reason for this is that a publishing site is geared toward sites that are based on a site hierarchy and publishing pages, where end users don't see or even know about the existence of lists and libraries. Collaboration sites, however, require users to interact with lists and libraries on a regular basis. It's possible for users to do so in a publishing-enabled intranet site; it just means extra time must be put into designing a user interface that explicitly enables users to interact with a site's underlying lists and libraries in a user-friendly way.

Publishing Lists and Libraries

Several libraries are included in every publishing site collection and every publishing site. Because you might have multiple people authoring content on your site, it's important that you have an organizational plan for where you will store particular assets such as images and documents. This will prevent people from uploading the same document or image multiple times in different locations throughout your site collections.

Site Collection Lists and Libraries

There is only one instance of each of the following libraries or lists in a given site collection, and that instance is located in the top-level site of the site collection:

- ➤ **Site Collection Images:** The Site Collection Images library is used for storing images that could be used across the site collection, such as logos.

- ➤ **Site Collection Documents:** The Site Collection Documents library is used for storing documents that might be referenced across the site collection. For example, if you include a link to your site's privacy policy in the footer of every page in your site collection, you could place a downloadable copy of the privacy policy in the Site Collection Documents library.

- ➤ **Reusable Content:** The Reusable Content list is used for storing text or HTML content that can be used on multiple pages in the site collection. The power of reusable content is that it can be updated once in a central location, and all the pages that reference that item will also be updated. For example, you could place a banner ad on each page of your site that references an ad you have stored in your Reusable Content list. If you then update the ad in the Reusable Content list, every page that references that item will now display the new ad. You can read more about the Reusable Content list later in this chapter, in the section titled "Making Use of Reusable Content."

- ➤ **Style library:** This library is used for storing cascading style sheets (CSS) and XSL style sheets that can be referenced from anywhere in the site collection.

Site Lists and Libraries

An instance of each of the following libraries exists once per publishing site:

- ➤ **Pages:** Every publishing site has a Pages library. Each new publishing page you create in a particular site will be stored in that single library. A site cannot have more than one Pages library.

- ➤ **Images:** This library is like the Site Collection Images library, except each publishing site has its own Images library. The Images library is used to store images that are local to the particular site the library is a part of. For instance, if you were building a public-facing Internet site for a company that sells products, you might have a different subsite for each product group. If you had one subsite for carpeting products and another subsite for tiling products, you would put the carpeting images in the Images library in the carpeting subsite and the tiling images in the Images library in the tiling subsite.

- ➤ **Documents:** Each publishing site has its own library called Documents. This library is for storing documents that are local to the particular site to which the library belongs.

Things to Consider when Planning Content

Before you start creating a web page in SharePoint, it's important to think about the content that's going to be on the page. You need to ask yourself such questions as:

➤ Which page template am I going to be using? What pieces of content need to be added to the kind of page layout I've chosen?

➤ Are there images on this page? If so, are the images I need already stored in SharePoint? If not, where should I add my new image(s) in SharePoint; should my image be uploaded to the local Images library or to the Site Collection Images library?

➤ Does this page link to documents, such as PDF files, which the user can download? If so, do these documents already exist in SharePoint? If not, where should I add my referenced document(s) in SharePoint; should I upload them to the local Documents library, or should I upload them to the Site Collection Documents library?

➤ Is there content on this page that's being used on other pages and that could be a candidate for content stored in the Reusable Content list?

Creating and Editing

This section walks you through the process of creating a publishing page and editing the content of that page.

Creating Your Page and Choosing a Page Layout

A publishing site collection is made up of a hierarchy of sites, and each site can contain publishing pages. The URL associated with each site is based on the site's location in the hierarchy. For instance, if you had a top-level site located at `http://www.wrox.com/`, you could create a site inside that top-level site called "Books," and give that subsite a URL of "Books." In that case, the URL of your Books subsite would be `http://www.wrox .com/Books`. If you wanted to create a new publishing page for a new book, you would have to first navigate to the Books subsite. If you created a new page with a URL of Six-in-One.aspx, the new page would be placed in the Pages library of the Books subsite, and would have a URL of `http:// www.wrox.com/Books/Pages/Six-in-One.aspx`. If you were to navigate to the Authors subsite instead of the Books subsite, and you created your new publishing page there, your new page would end up with a URL of `http://www.wrox.com/Authors/Pages/Six-in-One.aspx`. As you can see, choosing the location in which you create your new page will affect the URL, and thus the logical organization of the content on your site.

FIGURE 9-1

With that said, if you have navigated to any page within a site and choose to create a new page, it will be added to the given site's Pages library. You can do so by clicking the Site Actions menu and selecting New Page, as illustrated in Figure 9-1.

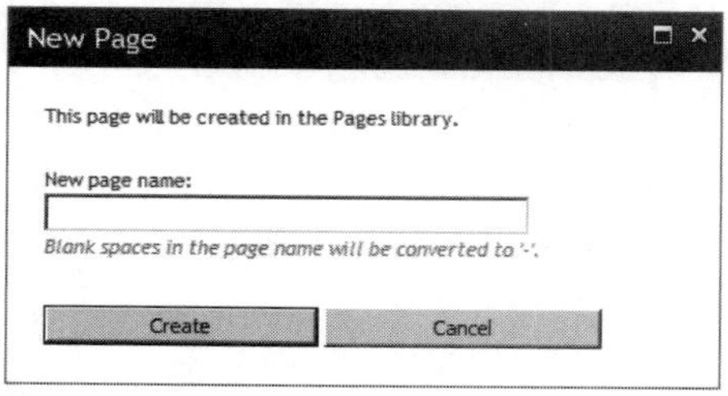

Doing so brings up the New Page dialog, as shown in Figure 9-2.

When you give your new page a name, keep in mind that this name will be used for the URL of your new

FIGURE 9-2

page. URLs have "reserved" characters, such as ampersands, parentheses, percentage signs, and so on, which have special meanings in a URL. In light of this, it's not possible to use these kinds of characters in your page name because they would interfere with the URL of the page. Additionally, if you provide a name that includes spaces, these spaces will be converted to dashes (–) in your URL.

> *Although it's common practice to remove spaces from words to generate a URL, (such as giving a page called "Bolts and Nuts" a URL of BoltsAndNuts .aspx), most external search engines don't have the ability to parse page URLs without spaces. What this means is that if you did a search for the word "Bolts" using an external search engine, the search engine wouldn't know that the page BoltsAndNuts.aspx had anything to do with bolts. However, many external search engines do understand that a dash represents a non-breaking space in a URL. If your page has a URL of Bolts-and-Nuts.aspx, an external search is more likely to return that web page when a user does a search for the term "bolts," because it recognizes the word "bolts" in the URL.*

When you are satisfied with the name of your new page, click the Create button.

Each site has a default page layout that has been assigned with it. Each new page that gets created will use that page layout by default. However, you can change which page layout your new page uses by clicking the Page tab in the Ribbon and then selecting the Page Layout button in the Page Actions section of the tab. This will present you with a number of page layouts that you can use, as shown in Figure 9-3.

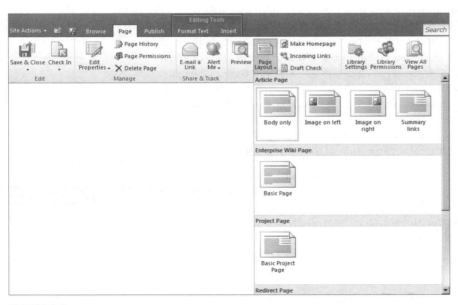

FIGURE 9-3

Each heading in the Page Layout selector reflects the kind of page (that is, content type) you want to use, and each kind of page can have multiple visual representations. For instance, an article page is a page used for communicating news article information. A news article has an article title, an article date, and a byline. However, it's possible to have more than one visual representation of an article. Your article could have an image floating to the right or the left of the page, or it could have no image at all. You can select a new page layout for your page by clicking a page layout from the list of available layouts in the fly-out menu. (As you can see in Figure 9-3, the currently selected page layout, "Body only," is outlined.)

Using the Publishing Placeholder Controls

A *placeholder control* is a region on a publishing page where you as an author can place content while editing the page. Three kinds of placeholder controls are unique to publishing sites: the image placeholder control, the rich link placeholder control, and the rich text placeholder control. This section walks you through each of these controls.

Image Placeholder Control

The *image placeholder* control allows you to place an image on the page. The image must already be stored somewhere within the site collection. When you click an empty image placeholder control, a window pops up that allows you to apply the properties of the image, such as the URL of the image, how the image is aligned, the size of the image, and so on. Figure 9-4 shows this window.

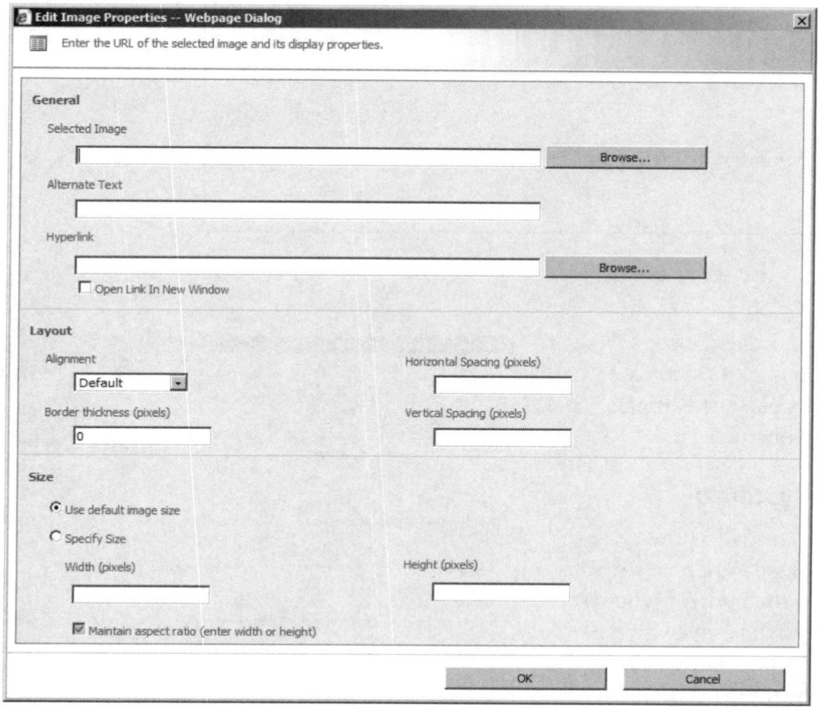

FIGURE 9-4

To choose an image from SharePoint, you can click the Browse button next to the Selected Image textbox. This will open another window that displays the tree structure of the site collection hierarchy. This will allow you to browse the site for an image to insert into the page. Typically, that image is stored in the Images library of the current site, or in the Site Collection Images in the top-level site. Figure 9-5 shows this window.

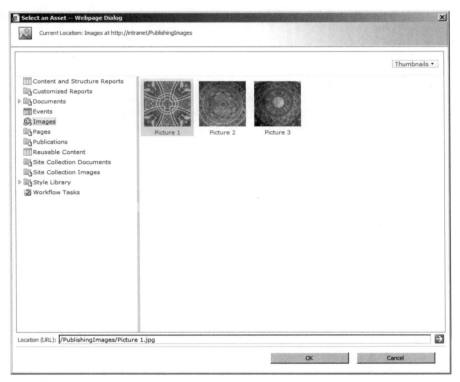

FIGURE 9-5

When you have selected an image, click OK to close this window, then click OK to close the first window. This will place the image in the image placeholder control.

Rich Link Placeholder Control

The rich link placeholder control allows you to add a hyperlink to your page. When you want to add a new hyperlink to the control, you can click the text in the control that says Click to Add a New Hyperlink. Doing so opens up a new window (as shown in Figure 9-6) that allows the user to specify the link's URL and the text of

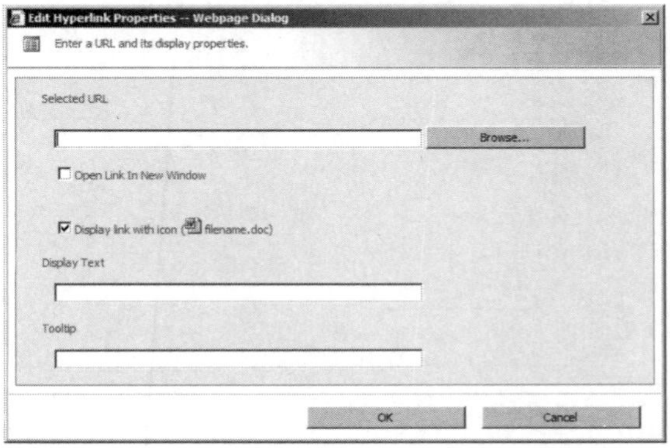

FIGURE 9-6

the hyperlink. In addition, the user can also specify whether the link should open in a new window, whether the link should have a tooltip, and whether an icon should appear next to the link if the item being linked to is a Microsoft Office document. (For instance, if the link were to a Microsoft Word 2010 document, the user would see a Word 2010 icon next to the hyperlink.)

Clicking the OK button adds the link to the rich link placeholder control on the page.

Rich Text Placeholder Control

The rich text placeholder control provides maximum flexibility for authors. This placeholder allows them to insert text, images, links, videos, tables, or Web Parts into their pages. You can add text to the page with the benefit of a Ribbon similar to that seen in Word 2007 or Word 2010. An Editing Tools tab becomes available when you click inside the rich text placeholder control. This Ribbon enables you to select fonts, colors, and sizes, as well as to add bullets to the text, or format the text by making it bold, italic, or underlined. You can also apply unique styles (such as highlighting text) or adding markup styles to the page (such as adding a header using the Heading 1 style.) The Format Tools ribbon used for editing the textual content of the page is shown in Figure 9-7. (Please note that page layout designers can disable various editing features of the rich text placeholder as necessary.)

FIGURE 9-7

As mentioned, you can add a number of non-textual items to the rich text placeholder control. Images and hyperlinks are added to the rich text placeholder control in the same way they are added to the image placeholder control or the rich link placeholder control. Items can be added to the page using the Insert tab on the Ribbon, which becomes available when a user clicks inside a rich text placeholder control on a page. Users can also add tables, videos, reusable content, and even Web Parts to their rich text placeholder control by using the Insert Ribbon (as shown in Figure 9-8.)

FIGURE 9-8

Making Use of Reusable Content

Sometimes you have content that you want to appear on multiple pages in your site. However, you don't want to have to re-create the same item multiple times on multiple pages. In addition, at times you want to be able to update content easily, from a central location, without having to manually edit, update, and save multiple publishing pages in your site. Luckily, the Reusable Content list helps you do just that. This kind of functionality is perfect for content such as banner ads that you want to place on multiple pages in your site. First, just add a reference to a banner that's stored in your Reusable Content list to each publishing page on your site where you want the banner to appear. When it's time to begin a new ad campaign, simply swap out the old image in your Reusable Content list with a new image, and the publishing pages that are referencing the banner in the Reusable Content list will now automatically display the new image instead.

The Reusable Content list lives in the top-level site of your publishing site collection. Because the Reusable Content list is just like any other list in SharePoint, you can add a new item to the list the way you would normally add an item to a list; you navigate to the list, and click the New Item button on the Items tab in the Ribbon. You can choose to add either a string of text or full-blown HTML to your Reusable Content list. (Text would be appropriate for content such as a disclaimer that you might want to appear in the body of multiple pages. HTML allows you to use images, hyperlinks, and so on). If you choose to add reusable HTML, you will see a dialog like that in Figure 9-9.

FIGURE 9-9

You will notice a checkbox in this dialog called Automatic Update. A thorough explanation of the option appears below the checkbox, which reads as follows:

> *If this option is selected, the content of this list item will be inserted into web pages as a read-only reference. New versions of this item will automatically appear in the web pages. If the option is not selected, the content of this list item will be inserted into web pages as a copy that page authors can then modify. New versions of this item will not appear in the web pages. Any change to this setting will not affect existing web pages that are using this item.*

Another option available for this Reusable Content list item is for this item to be available for easy access when editing a page. You can do this by checking Show in the drop-down menu. Doing so adds your item to a drop-down menu in the editing Ribbon when a user is editing rich content on a publishing page.

You might also notice that the Reusable HTML field functions much like the rich text placeholder field used in publishing pages. You have the ability to add formatted text, images, hyperlinks, tables, or video. If you are carrying out an ad campaign, you might even want to link your image to a page in your site. For instance, the banner ad displayed in Figure 9-9 advertises registration for the fall semester. If users click the banner, you might want them to be taken to a registration page. You can add clickable images to the Reusable Content list.

Now that you've added an item to your Reusable Content list, it's time to use it in a publishing page. To do so, edit your page, place your cursor inside the rich text placeholder control, and click the Insert tab in the Ribbon. You will notice a button called Reusable Content. Clicking this button displays a list of available items in the Reusable Content list, as shown in Figure 9-10.

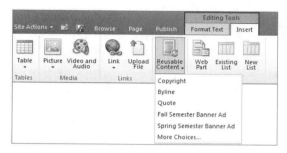

FIGURE 9-10

When you add a reusable content item to a rich text placeholder control, you will notice that the item appears slightly grayed out, and has a border surrounding it. This is to notify you, when you are editing the page, that the item is reusable content and needs to be edited centrally from the Reusable Content list, and not from the current placeholder on the page.

Once an item has been added to the Reusable Content list (with the Automatic Update checkbox selected), you can add it to your page and continue editing. If you update the item in the Reusable Content library, that change will be reflected in the Reusable Content list.

Saving Your Changes: Understanding Check-In/Check-Out, Versioning, and Approval

If the Pages library you are working with has check-in/check-out enabled, it means that when you check out a page no one else can work on that page at the same time as you. (If check-in/check-out is not enabled on the library, it's possible that users could edit the page at the same time and inadvertently overwrite each other's changes. This scenario is not likely, however, if there is only one content author responsible for the content in a particular site.) Depending on how the Page library is configured, editing a page can automatically check the page out for you.

If check-in/check-out has been enabled, it's possible to simply save your changes while leaving the page checked out. You can do this by clicking the Save and Close button on the Page tab of the Ribbon. When you do this, you can safely close your browser and return to the page at a later time. However, remember that if you do so, other users will not be able to work on the page until it is checked in.

Luckily, you never need to wonder about the status of your page. A notification bar appears below the Ribbon, indicating the status of the page, as shown in Figure 9-11.

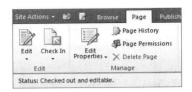

In some cases, SharePoint can have two versions of a page available at once. A draft version is available only to content owners, whereas published versions are available to anyone with Read permission. It's important that you understand how versioning

FIGURE 9-11

and the approval process have been configured in your Pages library, so you will know when and how your page will be versioned and published. The following list reviews the various scenarios you might encounter and how a publishing page behaves in each scenario.

> ➤ **Versioning and approval disabled:** If versioning and approval are not enabled on a Pages library, every page that gets edited and saved becomes immediately live on the website and available for visitors to view.

> ➤ **Versioning disabled and approval enabled:** If versioning has been disabled, it's possible for a content author to save the page. The page will not have a version number, but it will not be live on the site until it has gone through an approval process.

> ➤ **Major versioning enabled and approval disabled:** Each time a content author makes changes to the page and saves it, a new whole number (1.0, 2.0, and so on) version of the page gets generated, and the page is immediately live on the site.

> ➤ **Major versioning enabled and approval enabled:** Each time a page gets saved, a whole number version of the page gets saved, but the page is still not live on the site until it has gone through the approval process.

> ➤ **Major and minor versioning enabled and approval disabled:** Each time a page is saved, a draft version of the page is saved. This draft version has an incremental number (such as 1.1 or 1.2). The draft version of the page will be visible to content owners, but will not be visible to general users of the site. However, if a previous version of the page has been published, the published version will still be available on the site for visitors (while the draft version is visible to content owners). For the draft version of the page to be visible on the site, a content author must explicitly click the Publish button on the Publish tab. Once that happens, the incremental version of the page gets converted to a whole number (that is, 1.2 becomes version 2.0) and the new version of the page becomes live.

> ➤ **Major and minor versioning enabled and approval enabled:** Each time a page is saved, a draft version of the page is saved. This draft version has an incremental number (such as 1.1 or 1.2). The page will be visible to content owners, but will not be visible to general users of the site. However, if a previous version of the page has been published, it will still be available on the site for general users. A content owner will submit the draft version of page for approval. Once the page goes through the approval process, the draft number is converted to a whole number, and the new version of the page becomes live.

Scheduling Your Page

Sometimes you want to create a new page, but you don't necessarily want to publish the page right away. For example, you might have a new promotion on your site and want the promotional page available on Jan. 1, but you want it already built and ready to go ahead of time. SharePoint allows you to do this. It also allows you to specify if the page should be taken down from the site at a particular time. (By default, pages are published immediately and will stay up on the site indefinitely, unless otherwise specified.)

To set the scheduling for a page, navigate to the Publishing tab and click the Schedule button. This will bring up the Schedule Page dialog, as shown in Figure 9-12.

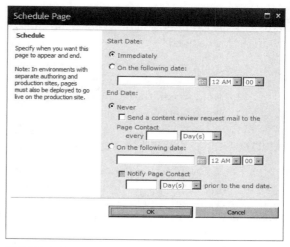

FIGURE 9-12

You can see that, by default, the page is set to be published immediately. However, you can specify a date and time when you want the page to go live.

Oftentimes you want to ensure that content does not become stale. Each publishing page has the possibility of having a user assigned to the Page Contact field. If a user has been assigned to this field, the Schedule Page dialog gives you the option of notifying that person on a regular basis, via e-mail, that the page needs to be reviewed. You can specify whether this user should be notified at a specific interval of days, months, or years. By doing this, the user is reminded of the page and can choose to update the content, leave the content alone, or delete the page.

You might also want to specify that a page should expire on a specific date. If you do so, you have the option of notifying the Page Contact user a specified length of time in advance. At that point, the user has the option of deferring the expiration date of the page or removing the expiration date of the page altogether.

If a user without contributor permissions tries to navigate to a page that has been scheduled but is not yet live, or to a page that has already expired, this user will get a 404 error, also known as a "Page not found" error, in his or her browser. To unauthorized users, the page does not exist. If authorized users were to view the Pages library, they would be able to view that publishing page. The Page list item still exists in the Pages library.

If a page has gone through the approval process, but the publication date has not arrived yet, authorized viewers looking at the page will see a message in the status bar saying something like "Status: Approved and scheduled for publication on 3/18/2011 12:00 AM. Publication Start Date: 3/18/2011 12:00 AM." This clearly indicates that the page has gone through the approval process but is not yet live on the site. In the same way, if a page has expired, a user will see a similar message indicating that to be the case.

You should note several things about page scheduling:

➤ Both major and minor versioning, as well as content approval, must be enabled on a Pages library in order for publishing pages within that library to have the option to be scheduled.

➤ You cannot schedule an *edit* of a page to go live at a particular time. Doing so will take the currently published version of the page off the site until the specified date has arrived. If you want to edit the contents of the page, the changes must be published or approved at the time when you want the updated content to go live.

Approving Your Page

If a Pages library has been configured to require content approval, it's necessary to initiate the approval process on a publishing page when you are ready for the page to go live. You can do this by clicking the Publish tab of the Ribbon. If the page is not already in an approved state, you have the option of initiating the approval workflow by clicking the Submit button on the Publish tab.

This will bring up a form that you will need to fill out. If the approval process or approval form has not been modified, you will have the following fields to fill out:

➤ **Request:** This is where you can add a personalized note to the person or people approving your page. This message will appear in the e-mail notification each approver receives.

➤ **Due Date for All Tasks:** This indicates the date by which the entire approval process should be completed. This is especially important if multiple people are involved in the approval process. This notifies approvers that even if one or more of them takes more than the allocated time to approve the page, the entire process should be completed by the date you specify here.

➤ **Duration per Task:** This is a number indicating the amount of time each approver has to complete his or her particular approval task.

➤ **Duration Units:** This indicates what unit of time you used in your Duration per Task field, whether that's days, weeks, or months.

➤ **CC:** Each approver will receive an e-mail when assigned a new task. This field allows you to send a carbon copy of that e-mail to a particular user.

Once the approval process has been kicked off, a task will be added to the Workflow Tasks list that belongs to the same site to which the publishing page belongs. Additionally, approver(s) will receive e-mail notifications that a new page is awaiting approval.

How do approvers know that pages are waiting for approval? There are several ways:

➤ They will receive an e-mail notifying them that a page is awaiting approval. The e-mail will contain a link to the page.

➤ They can navigate directly to the Workflow Tasks library for that site. If users have been specifically assigned tasks, they can navigate to the My Tasks view of the task list and see all the tasks assigned to them. If a user is a member of a group that has been assigned the tasks (such as the Approvers group), this user can navigate to the By My Groups view to see all the tasks that have been assigned to any groups of which the user is a member.

➤ Approvers can click the Site Actions menu and click the Manage Content and Structure link. This will show them a tree view of the site collection. To the right, they will see a toolbar with a button that says View. When users click that button, they can select the My Tasks view from the drop-down menu. This view will not only show the users any tasks assigned to them in the current site, but it will also show them any tasks assigned to them in any subsite of the currently selected site.

If approvers want to approve or reject the publishing page, they must do so by modifying the tasks list item stored in the Workflow Tasks list. They can do this in two ways:

➤ They can navigate to the publishing page itself and click the Approve or Reject buttons on the Publishing tab of the Ribbon. This will take them to the task form.

➤ They can navigate directly to the Workflow Tasks list and view the task form.

If approvers want to leave comments regarding why they took the action they took, they have that option in the workflow task form. They also, by default, have several other options available to them:

➤ **Approve:** This approves the item. If the approval process is tied to the publishing process, this will make the page live on the site.

➤ **Reject:** This does not allow the page to advance through the approval process.

➤ **Cancel:** This allows the user to close the task form.

➤ **Request Change:** This keeps the workflow going, but notifies the author that a change is required before the page can be approved.

➤ **Reassign Tasks:** This allows the approver to assign this task to some other user.

Once the approval process has been completed, a message will be placed in the Workflow History list saying that the workflow completed properly. You can view the workflow history for a given page by clicking the Status button of the Workflows section on the Publish tab.

PUBLISHING SITE CONFIGURATION

Now that you have walked through the basic process of creating, editing, scheduling, and approving a publishing page, it's time to talk about how you can configure a publishing site collection, a publishing site, and a Pages library.

Creating a Publishing Site

Before any SharePoint site can be created, a site collection must be in place. The easiest way to get a publishing-enabled site is to create a new site collection using the Publishing Portal template, as shown in Figure 9-13. A farm administrator can do this from Central Administration.

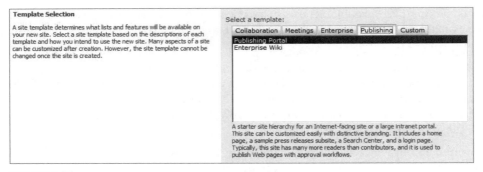

FIGURE 9-13

This site collection template will automatically create a top-level publishing site, activate the proper features, and create a sample subsite called Press Releases, as well as a Search Center site for searching.

Each publishing site collection must have, at a minimum, the SharePoint Publishing Infrastructure Site Collection feature enabled. This feature, among other things, ensures that the site collection lists and libraries (mentioned previously in the "Publishing Lists and Libraries" section of this chapter) are created.

Once you have your top-level site, you can start creating child sites. You have two choices when creating a publishing site (as shown in Figure 9-14): you can create a site using the Publishing with Workflow site template or you can create a site using the Publishing Site site template.

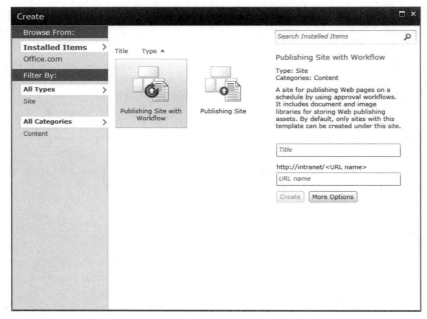

FIGURE 9-14

The Publishing Site with Workflow template will create a new publishing site. In that site, any publishing page that gets created in the Pages library will automatically be routed through an approval workflow. It's possible to modify that workflow, as discussed later in this chapter, as well as to disable or remove it.

The Publishing Site template creates a publishing site without any sort of approval workflow attached to the Pages library. It's possible to create an approval workflow and attach it to the Pages library after the fact, if this template is chosen; this simply means that the process of attaching the workflow is manual, instead of the workflow's being automatically wired up, as it is in the site created with the Publishing Site with Workflow site template.

For a site to have publishing enabled, it must have a site-scoped feature, SharePoint Server Publishing feature, enabled. As mentioned previously, each publishing site (as opposed to site collection) has the following three libraries automatically added: Pages, Documents, and Images. The SharePoint Server Publishing feature ensures that these libraries are available in the site.

Setting the Site Homepage

Because a SharePoint site's URL is tied to its site structure, it's possible that a user might try to browse to a site by typing in a URL that ends with a slash ("/"), such as `http://www.wrox.com/ Books/`. However, it's not possible to browse a site; users can only browse pages. Because that's the case, every site needs to have its own homepage, also known as a *welcome page*. The purpose of the welcome page is to give users a page that they can be redirected to when they navigate to a subsite. Imagine that a page called Homepage.aspx has been set up as the welcome page for the Books subsite. Anyone browsing to `http://www.wrox.com/Books` will be automatically redirected to the publishing page with a URL of `http://www.wrox.com/Books/Pages/Homepage.aspx`.

You can set the welcome page for a site in two ways using the browser. The first is to navigate to the page that you want to serve as the site's homepage and display the Ribbon on the page. You can click the Make Homepage button on the Page tab of the Ribbon to make that page the site homepage. (Remember, this is the homepage for the particular subsite you are browsing, not for the entire site collection.)

Another way to modify the welcome page for a site is to navigate to the Site Settings page, then click the Welcome Page link under the Look and Feel heading. This will take you to a page that lets you browse to the page that you want to serve as your welcome page.

Modifying the Site Master Page and Style Sheet

Because publishing sites are often used for public-facing websites, site owners frequently want their sites to have a custom look and feel that doesn't make users feel as if they're navigating a typical SharePoint site. The easiest way to customize the look and feel of a site is to create a custom master page and custom style sheet for your site. Once you have done so, a site administrator has the option to easily select and apply a master page and/or a style sheet to a particular site or site hierarchy.

As with many other properties of a SharePoint site, the master page or style sheet selection can inherit its setting from its parent site. Additionally, a user has the option to reset the settings of all subsites below the current site to use the same settings as the current site.

To change the master page and style sheet that a site uses, navigate to the Site Settings page for your site and click the Master Page link under the Look and Feel section. This will take you to the Site Master Page Settings page, as shown in Figure 9-15.

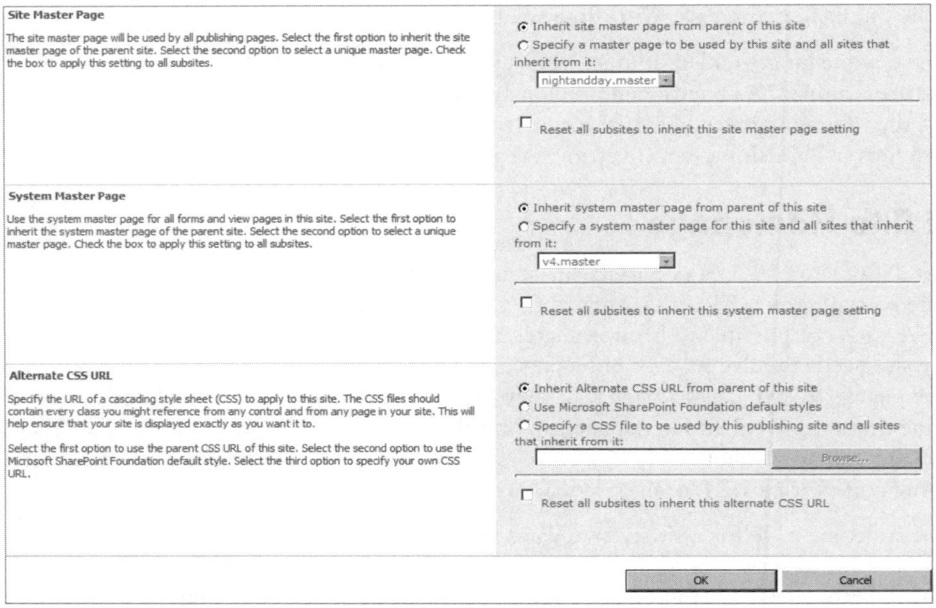

FIGURE 9-15

In the first section, called Site Master Page, you can choose for this site to use the same master page as its parent site by selecting the radio button titled Inherit Site Master Page from Parent of This Site, or you can specify your own master page by selecting the radio button titled Specify a Master Page to be Used by This Site and All Sites that Inherit from It. A drop-down menu will allow you to select a master page from any of the approved master pages in the site collection's Master Page gallery. Regardless of which radio button you choose, you can check the checkbox labeled Reset All Subsites to Inherit This Site Master Page Setting. This will propagate your setting to all child sites.

In SharePoint, the master page used for administrative pages, such as the Site Settings page or the View All Site Content page, is different than the master page used for publishing pages. In the System Master Page section, you have the ability to specify which master page your system pages will use. The settings for this section are identical to the settings for the previous section.

At the bottom of the page, in a section titled Alternate CSS URL, you have the option to specify a style sheet that will be used with your site. You have three options:

➤ Inherit Alternate CSS URL from parent of this site.

➤ Use Microsoft SharePoint Foundation default styles.

➤ Specify a CSS file to be used by this publishing site and all sites that inherit from it. After this third option, you can browse the site to find the CSS file you would like to choose. Typically, CSS files are stored in the Style library in the root of your site collection.

As with the master pages, you can choose to select a checkbox to indicate that you want to reset the CSS settings for all this site's subsites.

WHEN WOULD YOU USE SEPARATE MASTER PAGES OR CSS FILES WITHIN A SITE COLLECTION?

In many publishing sites, the entire site collection will use a single master page and style sheet, so as to implement a unified look and feel across the site. However, it can be advantageous at times to use separate ones. This can be the case if you have multiple subsites that should intentionally have a different look and feel. For instance, a corporation might have a single site collection, and each product line might have its subsite and child sites. Each product line might need its own custom look and feel for its site hierarchy.

When it comes to style sheets, the style sheet used by a particular master page is often referenced directly in the master page itself, so it's not necessary to explicitly set the style sheet using the Site Master Page Settings page. However, at times you can leverage the "cascading" functionality of cascading style sheets.

For instance, you might have a "base" style sheet, referenced inside your master page, which helps position elements on the page and set default font colors and sizes. However, for each subsite you might want to specify a separate font header style, so each subsite's page titles appear in a different color from the others. You could easily create a small style sheet for each subsite, adding a class that overrides the header style. Then you could tell each subsite to use its own custom style sheet, using the Site Master Page Settings page. When SharePoint outputs the styles to the browser, the base style sheet's reference will be added to the page, and the custom style sheet reference will be added afterward, ensuring that the secondary styles override the primary ones for that particular subsite.

Modifying Available Page Layouts and Site Templates

Sometimes you, as a site administrator, will want to limit the kinds of pages or sites available to users when they want to create something new. For instance, if you have a subsite called Press Releases, you might want to ensure that users can only create pages with a page layout of Article with Image on Left, so that users won't be tempted to create a page using a page layout that wouldn't be appropriate in that location, such as an About Us page layout. In the same way, you might create a subsite where people are allowed to create new blogs. However, as in the previous example, you might want to prevent users from creating a blog subsite inside the Press Releases subsite.

To specify which page layouts and site templates people can use when creating new pages or sites, browse to the Site Settings page for your publishing site, and click the Page Layouts and Site Templates link under Look and Feel. This will take you to the Page Layout and Site Template Settings page.

When setting which site templates users can use, you have three options:

➤ Inherit settings from the parent site.

➤ Allow users to use any site template which is installed in the site collection.

➤ Manually specify which particular site templates users can use. If this option is chosen, you can add or remove site templates from the list of available site templates.

You have the option of checking a checkbox to indicate that you want your choice propagated to all sites below the current one.

The same three options are available for page layouts. In the same way, you can manually specify which page layouts people can use, and reset all the current site's subsites to use the current setting.

When a user creates a new page in a site, the user doesn't have the ability to choose a page layout right away; a page is created using a predetermined page layout, and the user has the option of changing it. The last setting on this management page allows you to specify which page layout will be used by default when a user first creates a page in this subsite.

Modifying Site Navigation

Navigation in publishing sites is slightly different than navigation in other kinds of SharePoint sites. The navigation is not driven by a Quick Links list. Rather, the navigation is driven by the site hierarchy of your site collection, and the publishing pages that are a part of each site within that hierarchy.

Each subsite can have its own navigation settings. As with many other settings in SharePoint, child sites can inherit the properties of their parent sites, or they can have their own settings.

To modify the navigation of a particular site in your site collection, navigate to the Site Settings page for that site, and click the Navigation link under the Look and Feel heading. This will bring up the Navigation Settings page, shown in Figure 9-16.

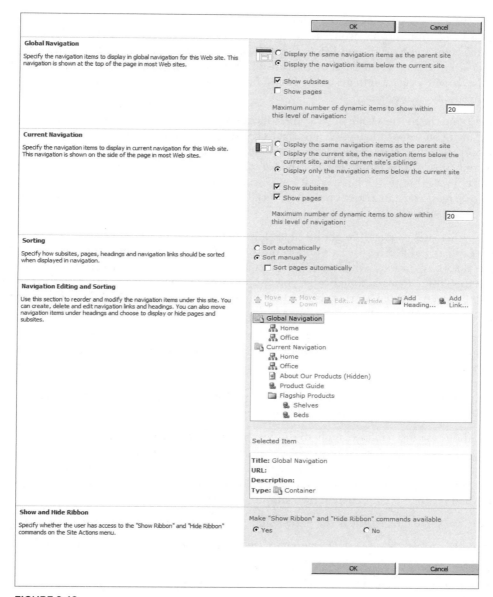

FIGURE 9-16

Global navigation is the term given to the navigation that usually sits at the top of a page. *Current navigation* is the term given to the navigation that usually sits on the side of the page. In many sites, the top navigational elements remain static throughout the site collection, no matter where a user is within the site hierarchy. In the same way, the current navigation is often contextual, meaning the navigation will change based on where the user is within the site collection.

When you are modifying a site's global navigation, you have one major decision: do you want to inherit the same navigation settings from the parent site or do you want to configure the settings especially for this site (and for any sites below this site that inherit this site's settings)? To inherit the global navigation settings from the site's parent site, you can simply select the radio button that says Display the Same Navigation Items as the Parent Site. Once you have done that, all your other options are grayed out or disappear.

If you are modifying the top-level site of your site collection (and have no other site to inherit settings from), or if you want unique global navigation settings for your site, you can choose the second radio button in the Global Navigation section, which reads Display the Navigation Items below the Current Site. At this point, you can choose for SharePoint to automatically display either sites, pages, or both, within the global navigation. If you choose for SharePoint to automatically show subsites or pages, you can also set a threshold value as to the maximum number of dynamic items for SharePoint to show.

Because items (either sites or pages) might be added automatically by SharePoint to the navigation without being explicitly added by you, it's important to specify how those items are to be sorted. You have several sorting options, which can be set in the Sorting section of the page. If you choose for SharePoint to sort the items automatically, you can specify that the items be sorted by their titles, the date they were created, or their last modified date. Furthermore, each of those values can be sorted in either ascending or descending order.

SharePoint also provides a helpful hybrid approach; you can choose to manually sort the subsites within your navigation, but still have SharePoint automatically sort any new pages that get added to your site. In many publishing site collections, subsites are set up when the website is first created, and it's important to the site owner that the subsites are listed in a particular order. However, as the site grows and content authors create new pages, those new pages can be automatically added to the navigation in a sorted order when this option is selected.

Choices made about sorting will also apply to the current navigation, whose settings can be modified in the Current Navigation section of the page. When configuring the site's current navigation, you have the same options as with the global navigation, in terms of choosing to automatically display any subsites or pages automatically. You have three fundamental options to choose from when setting up your current navigation:

➤ Display the same navigation as the parent site.

➤ Display the current site, the navigation items below the current site, and the current site's siblings.

➤ Display only the navigation items below the current site.

Learning how this works is best understood with examples.

Figure 9-17 shows a sample site hierarchy that includes both sites and pages.

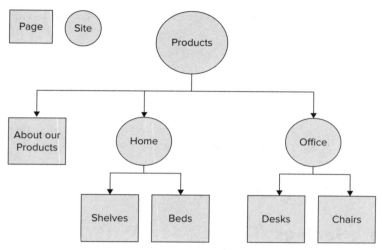

FIGURE 9-17

If you are browsing in the Home subsite, and you select Display the Same Navigation Items as the Parent Site, you might see current navigation that looks like Figure 9-18.

If you are browsing the Home subsite, and you select Display the Current Site, the Navigation Items below the Current Site, and Current Site's Siblings, you might see something like Figure 9-19.

Notice that in Figure 9-19, you don't see the pages inside the Office subsite. That's because this navigation option shows only the sibling sites to the Home subsite, but doesn't display everything inside those sites.

Finally, if you select Display Only the Navigation Items below the Current Site, you would see something like Figure 9-20.

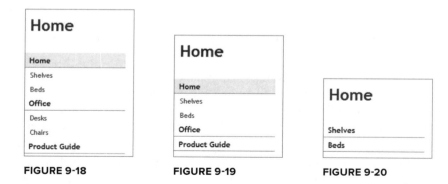

FIGURE 9-18   **FIGURE 9-19**   **FIGURE 9-20**

Once you have set up the automatic configuration of your global and current navigational elements, you have the option to manipulate the settings further. Using the Navigation Editing and Sorting section of the Navigation Settings page, you can do the following:

➤ **Hide an item so it doesn't show up in the navigation.** This is helpful for subsites such as Search. If your search box appears on the master page of your site, it's therefore on most of your site pages, so you might not want it to appear in the global navigation, even if you told SharePoint to automatically display subsites.

➤ **Move an item up or down.** This option is available only if you chose Sort Manually in the Sorting section.

➤ **Manually add a link.** This is helpful if you want to include a link to a page located within a different subsite in SharePoint, or if you want to link to an external web page.

➤ **Manually add a heading.** If you want to add links manually, you can also manually add a heading. When this is done, a heading with links looks to the end user just like a subsite with pages.

The last navigation setting on this page allows you to specify whether the Show Ribbon and Hide Ribbon commands should be available from the Site Actions menu for that site.

Modifying Pages Library Settings

This section reviews some of the Pages library settings that are relevant to a publishing site. All these settings are accessible from the Document Library Settings page for each Pages library.

Several administrative pages are quite straightforward. If you click the Audience Targeting Settings link, you are taken to a page where you have a checkbox indicating whether the Pages library should utilize audience targeting. All Pages libraries utilize audience targeting, so it's not necessary to modify this value. If you click the Manage Item Scheduling link, you are taken to a page with a checkbox that indicates whether or not you want page authors to utilize page scheduling.

Versioning and Approval

The importance of versioning and approval in the publishing process has already been described previously in this chapter. To configure the versioning and approval settings, click the Versioning Settings link under the General Settings section on the Document Library Settings page. (You can get to the Document Library Settings page of the Pages library by navigating to the Pages library, then selecting the Library tab and clicking the Library Settings button in the Settings section of the tab.)

It is here that you can specify whether or not publishing pages require content approval, by selecting a radio button response of Yes or No to the question, Require Content Approval for Submitted Items? Configuring the actual approval workflow can be done from a different configuration page, as described in the section in this chapter titled "Modifying the Approval Workflow," which you can find later in this chapter.

The next part of the page allows you to specify whether you want versioning enabled at all in the library, and if you do want it enabled, whether you want major and minor versions of pages to be created or just major versions.

Because additional versions of pages can take up database space, as well as make for a "cluttered" user experience when viewing past versions of a page, it's possible to limit the number of major and minor versions of a page that SharePoint will retain.

The next section on the Versioning Settings page, Draft Item Security, allows you to configure security for those items that have been saved but have not gone through any approval or publishing process; they are still considered in a draft state. You have three options:

➤ Allow anyone who has read access to the site to see a draft version of the page.

➤ Allow any user who has permission to edit the page to see a draft version of the page.

➤ Allow only the author of a page and whoever is supposed to approve the page to be able to see the draft version of the page.

Typically, in a publishing site, you don't want end users to be able to see draft versions of content, so the first option would not be optimal. By default, the second option is selected.

Understanding Content Types and Columns in the Pages Library

Each publishing page in SharePoint is associated with a particular content type. If a page is added to your Pages library, and its particular content type has not yet been used in the site, that content type will be added automatically to the list of available content types in the library the first time that page is created. Each time a new content type is added to the Pages library, any columns belonging to that content type, and which have not yet been added to the Pages library's list of available columns, will be added.

This is important for several reasons. First, remember that only certain users have permission to modify library settings. Often, users with contributor rights do not have permission to add content types or columns to any list, including the Pages library. What this means is that if a user with only contributor rights tries to add a page with a new content type to a Pages library, this user might encounter an error, or SharePoint might prevent the user from saving the page using the content type desired.

It's also important to understand about content types and site columns in a publishing site because future updates to content types and site columns are affected by it. When a new content type is added to the Pages library, in actuality a *copy* of that content type is being added to the library. In the same way, a *copy* of any site column is being added to that library. Why is this important? If you update the parent content type or site column, from which the Pages library content type or site column has been copied, the change will not automatically be updated in every Pages library. You must ensure that changes made at the site collection or site level are pushed down to all libraries (including Pages libraries) that use them. This is especially important if you add a new site column to a content type. Because a content type's columns were added to the Pages library when that content type was first used, SharePoint might not know that it needs to update the Pages library with a new site column when you add a new site column to a content type at the site collection level.

Modifying the Approval Workflow

By default, when a site is created using the Publishing with Workflow site template, the Pages library is automatically associated with a default Approval workflow. This workflow assumes that pages must be approved by any user who has been assigned to the SharePoint group for Approvers. Luckily, it's possible to modify the approval workflow settings for each individual Pages library.

To do so, click the Workflow Settings link under the Permissions and Management section on the Document Library Settings page of your Pages library. You should see a workflow entitled Page Approval. Click that workflow name to modify it.

The first settings on this page are quite similar to the workflow settings you would see for nearly any out-of-the-box workflow for SharePoint. The key thing you want to note on this first page is the checkbox that says Start this Workflow to Approve Publishing a Major Version of an Item. If you want your workflow to be tied to the publishing process of a page, it's important that you leave this checkbox checked.

If you click the Next button at the bottom of the first administration page, you will be taken to another page, which looks like the page shown in Figure 9-21.

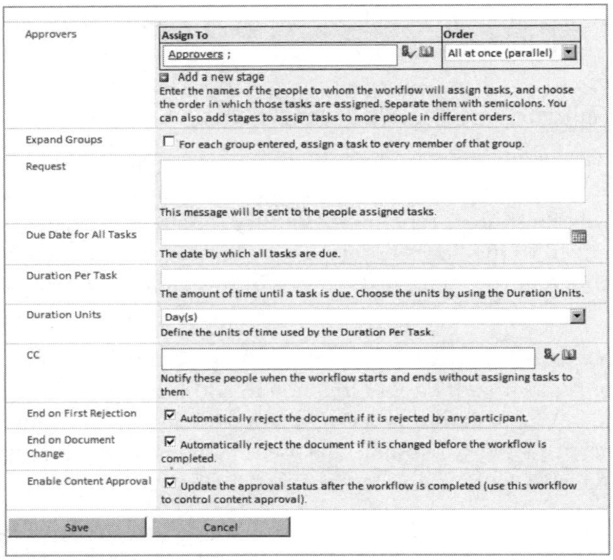

FIGURE 9-21

One of the first things you must decide is how many *stages* you want in your approval process: that is, how many times does the item need to pass approval?

The next thing you need to understand is the difference between *serial* and *parallel* approval. Serial approval means that *first* Person A approves the item, and *then* Person B approves the item. If Person A rejects the item, Person B will never even know the item was waiting for approval. Parallel approval means *both* Person A and Person B must approve the item, but the order in which they approve it doesn't matter. If they both approve the item, it advances to the next stage. (You can read examples of serial and parallel approval in "The Association Process" section of Chapter 16.)

The first section of the workflow configuration form allows you to create different stages in the approval process. For each stage, you can specify who is a part of that process, and whether the people or groups listed must approve their tasks in serial or parallel order.

The next checkbox on the page allows you to tell SharePoint whether it should assign a separate task for everyone who is a member of a group that has been added to one of the stages specified in the previous section. Say you have a group called Approvers, and Approvers contains two users:

User Y and User Z. If the Approvers group has been assigned to a stage in the workflow and the Expand Groups checkbox is unchecked, it doesn't matter whether User Y or User Z approves the page; as long as one person in that group approves the page, that stage has passed approval. However, if the Expand Groups checkbox is checked, both Users Y and Z would receive a task, and they both would need to approve the item before it could pass that stage of approval.

> *It's generally best practice to assign a group, rather than individual users, to an approval process. This ensures that if a person becomes unavailable for a time, some other user can be added to the group and carry out the approval workflow in the first person's absence.*
>
> *If no users have been added to a specific group that was assigned to the workflow, it will automatically progress to the next stage of approval.*

The next section allows you to set a due date for all tasks. Because you're not actually configuring a particular workflow instance right now, but you're modifying the workflow template for all the publishing approval workflow instances that take place in this library, it usually doesn't make sense to populate this field with a date.

If you wanted to set a default duration for each individual task, you could do it here, by modifying the Duration per Task and Duration Unit fields.

As with the Due Date for All Tasks, it doesn't usually make sense to specify a user to copy an e-mail to, unless you want that person to be notified about every single approval workflow that gets executed for every page in the site.

At the end of the workflow configuration page, you have three checkboxes available:

➤ Automatically reject the document if it is rejected by any participant.

➤ Automatically reject the document if it is changed before the workflow is completed.

➤ Update the approval status after the workflow is completed (use this workflow to control content approval).

It's advisable that the last checkbox always remain checked for publishing sites if you want this approval process to tag into the publishing process.

SITE ORGANIZATION, HIDDEN FIELDS, AND THE CONTENT QUERY WEB PART

When the World Wide Web was new, every web page was static, and the power of the Web lay in the ability to hyperlink to different pages. What this meant was that if you created a new page called Page A, and you wanted to create a link to Page B, you had to edit Page A and hard code a link to Page B on that page. Figure 9-22 gives you an idea of what this looks like.

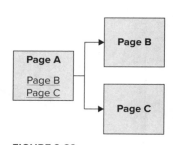

FIGURE 9-22

In contrast, think about object-oriented programming. You might have an object whose type is "Car." That Car type has properties for Number of Doors, Paint Color, and Miles per Gallon. You could create an instance of that car object and assign each of those properties a value: 4 doors, red paint, 28 MPG. You could actually create 20 different instances of your Car object. What if you needed to find out what's in your fleet of cars? You would loop through each of your objects and retrieve each object's property values. This looks more like what's shown in Figure 9-23.

Publishing sites are meant to work much the same way. Each publishing page is an item in a list, and works like an object, and each field that you fill in on a page is like setting a property for that page. Each time you add content to a content placeholder on your page, you're actually adding content to a column in the page's underlying list item. In fact, you can easily find out what column values have been populated for your page by clicking the View Properties button of the Ribbon when looking at a publishing page. Figure 9-23 showed you an example of what the properties of a publishing page might look like.

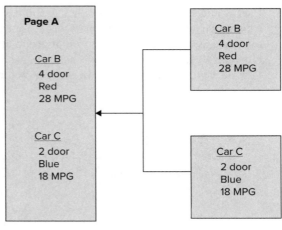

FIGURE 9-23

In Figure 9-24, the Page Image field contains an image that was added to the page using a rich image placeholder control. On the Properties page, it's easy to see that the image is simply a value assigned to the Page Image column.

FIGURE 9-24

In the same way that you looped through your Car objects to retrieve their property values so you could display those values on Page A, you could loop through publishing pages to retrieve their column values in order to display those column values from other pages on Page A, as represented in Figure 9-25.

This is important to know because a key feature of SharePoint is the ability to categorize and display information in a variety of ways. More importantly, once this categorization has been implemented,

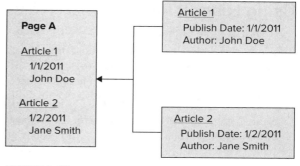

FIGURE 9-25

SharePoint can automatically handle the display of new or updated content. You no longer have to "hard code" links to other pages; SharePoint will do the linking for you.

This can work its way out in a variety of scenarios. Imagine that you have a SharePoint site for a company that has multiple subsidiaries. Each subsidiary has its own press releases that it displays on the site. Each time a new press release is written, it gets added as a publishing page in the subsidiary's Pages library. In this scenario, you might want to have a "rollup" page that displays a list of all the press releases that have been released for a given subsidiary in the last year. At the corporate level, however, you might also want to display a list of all the press releases that have been released in the last year across all subsidiaries. Imagine how much work it would be to have to update multiple pages each time a new press release got added to a subsidiary's site. Instead, SharePoint allows you to give it instructions telling it which content to retrieve and display. When a user clicks a link to a publishing page, that link goes to a specific destination in a specific subsite; however, links to that page can show up throughout the site collection, providing multiple avenues to get to that same information.

Here's another scenario in which this functionality could be helpful. Say you had a site that displays product information. Each product is made up of several parts. When users view a product, they should be able to click a link for each constituent part, with that link taking them to detailed information about that part.

How could this second scenario happen? Imagine that each time users created a new page using the Parts page layout, they had the option to select one or more products in which the part is included, from a checkbox list. (This checkbox list is actually a site column of the multi-choice type, and all the available products have been preconfigured as choices in this column.) When someone visits a product page, SharePoint simply retrieves all the Parts pages in the site, then looks to see which products have been selected in the Products column of each Parts page. If the current product has been checked in the Parts page, SharePoint displays a link to that Parts page on the product page, as shown in Figure 9-26.

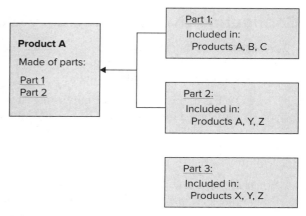

FIGURE 9-26

Using Hidden Fields

Although it would be possible to have users edit column values for a publishing page using the Edit Properties dialog, that's not the most user-friendly experience. One of the key benefits of using page layouts is that authors get to edit the contents of a page within a page that looks very similar to what the page will look like when it's published. Because each field that a user edits is also visible to end users, how can you assign these "behind the scenes" column values?

SharePoint provides a special control that a page layout designer can put on the page. This control shows up only when an author is editing the page. In this way, authors can enter content into the page that will not be displayed on the page itself when the page is in display mode, but that can be used when that page is retrieved from another place in the site to display its data. To view this in action, try editing a page layout that uses the out-of-the-box Article content type. At the bottom of the page you'll see a special area (as shown in Figure 9-27) where a user can add a thumbnail image to the page. The thumbnail image will be added to the Rollup Image column for this particular page.

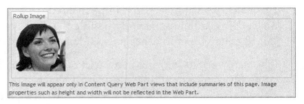

FIGURE 9-27

Although the rollup image that has been added to the page in Figure 9-27 will not be visible to end users who visit the page itself, that thumbnail image can still be used elsewhere in the site. Figure 9-28 shows a Content Query Web Part that has been added to the site's News homepage and has retrieved several news articles from the current News subsite. You can see that it has retrieved and displayed this thumbnail picture from the news article it retrieved. (If users click the name of the article "New Product Released!" they will be taken to the page itself, but they won't see the thumbnail picture on that page.)

FIGURE 9-28

Configuring the Content Query Web Part

Now that you have entered content into your page — content that you can retrieve from other locations within your site collection — you have the opportunity to leverage the Content Query Web Part (CQWP) to do the heavy lifting.

The CQWP is a powerful tool for publishing sites. Its power lies in its flexibility. The CQWP allows you to configure a query that can be executed directly against the content database with which you're working. The results are returned as a string of XML, which can be styled using an XSL style sheet. To sum up, the CQWP can return almost any list item in the site collection and give you the flexibility to render that list item's properties in the browser just about however you'd like.

When adding a new Web Part to your page, and to select the CQWP in particular, click the Content Rollup category, then select Content Query from the list of available Web Parts, as shown in Figure 9-29.

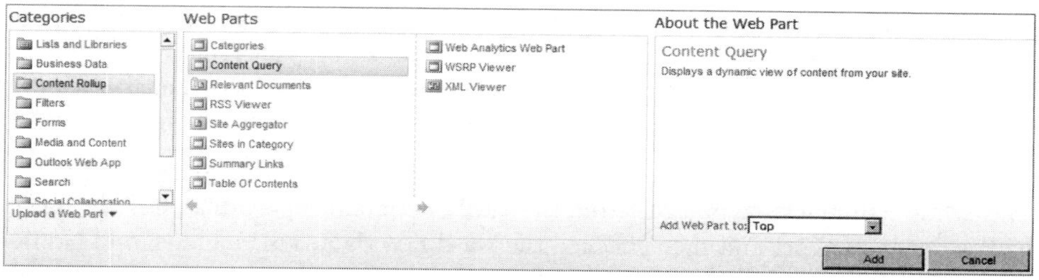

FIGURE 9-29

Once you have added the Web Part to your page, you can modify its properties.

The first section you'll come across in the CQWP tool pane is titled Query, as shown in Figure 9-30.

The first choice you'll have to make is where your list items will come from. You have three choices:

➤ **Show items from all sites in this site collection:** Items can come from anywhere in the site collection, regardless of which site or subsite they might be in.

➤ **Show items from the following site and all subsites:** Items must come from a particular site within the site collection. Additionally, items will be returned from any subsite that is in the hierarchy of the chosen site. This option allows you to browse the site collection to find the site you would like to select.

➤ **Show items from the following list:** Items will be retrieved only from a particular list. Just as with the previous choice, this choice allows you to browse the site collection to find the list you want to query.

The next choice you'll need to make is the type of list from which you want to pull your items. If you chose to retrieve items from a particular list while setting the Source property, this drop-down menu will be grayed out, because it's clear which kind of library you're querying. Otherwise, you will see different kinds of lists or libraries, such as Pages library, Document library, and so forth.

FIGURE 9-30

The section in Figure 9-30 below List Type, called Content Type, allows you to specify if you only want items returned when they have a particular content type. The kind of library you choose in the List Type section is important because your choice of list will dictate the kind of content types you have available to choose from. For instance, if you want to retrieve items from any list that was generated from the Custom List definition, those lists won't contain documents. As a result, you won't have the choice of retrieving items that have a content type of Document. If you say you want to retrieve items from a Pages library, then most likely you are trying to retrieve publishing pages. If that's the case, you can specify that you only want to retrieve publishing pages that have a particular content type, such as Article Page. You also have the option of telling SharePoint that you want to retrieve any list item that's returned from the kind of list you chose, regardless of its content type.

If you have chosen a particular content type, you also have the option of telling SharePoint to retrieve any items whose content type inherits from the kind of content type you chose. For instance, if you chose the Page content type, and then checked the checkbox that says Include Child Content Types, your query will return any publishing page, whether the content type was Article Page or Welcome Page, because both those content types inherit from the Page content type.

The nearby section called Audience Targeting tells you about enabling audience targeting on the Web Part. Audience targeting works differently for the CQWP than it sometimes works for other types of Web Parts. Typically, if a Web Part has had audience targeting enabled, it means that the entire Web Part will appear on the page only if a user belongs to an audience to which the Web Part has been assigned. In the CQWP's case, the Web Part will show up for everyone, regardless of their audience membership. However, the results will be trimmed according to the user's audience. It's possible that some pages won't have any audience assigned to them. If that's the case, you have the choice of determining whether those kinds of pages should be displayed or not displayed, by default.

AUDIENCE TARGETING

Just as with other values that have been assigned to a page, leveraging audience targeting in your publishing site depends on authors assigning the appropriate audience or audiences to each publishing page they author. For example, an author could create a page and assign it to an audience called Vendors.

If audience targeting has been enabled on the CQWP, the Web Part will find out who is currently logged in to the site and looking at the Web Part. It will then determine which audiences the current user is a member of. If the current user (John Doe) is a member of the Vendors audience, he will see the page that was authored and assigned to the Vendors audience. If the page has been targeted to an audience of which John is not a member, he won't see the page in the list of pages displayed in the CQWP. Keep in mind that other pages may or may not show up in the CQWP. Each page that's pulled into the Web Part is being evaluated in the same manner.

Audience targeting is not the same as security. If John were to navigate to the page itself, he would have permission to view it, even if he wasn't in the page's target audience. The target audience setting simply tells Web Parts such as the CQWP whether the content is *relevant* for the current user.

One more thing to note: a user can only be a member of an audience if the user has logged in. You cannot effectively use audience targeting in a site where users are "anonymous," or not logged in.

The final choice you have in the Query section of the CQWP tool pane is how you want to filter your results, if indeed you want to filter them. For each filter, you can specify a field to filter by (such as Article Date), an operator (such as "greater than or equal to"), and a value (such as "1/1/2011" or "[Today]"). If you have told SharePoint that you want to query items from a particular list or a particular content type, the list of available fields to filter by will be determined by your choice.

The next major section of the CQWP tool pane is called Presentation. This section allows you to group and sort items, as well as determine other aspects of the pages' presentation in the Web Part. You can see this section of the tool pane in Figure 9-31.

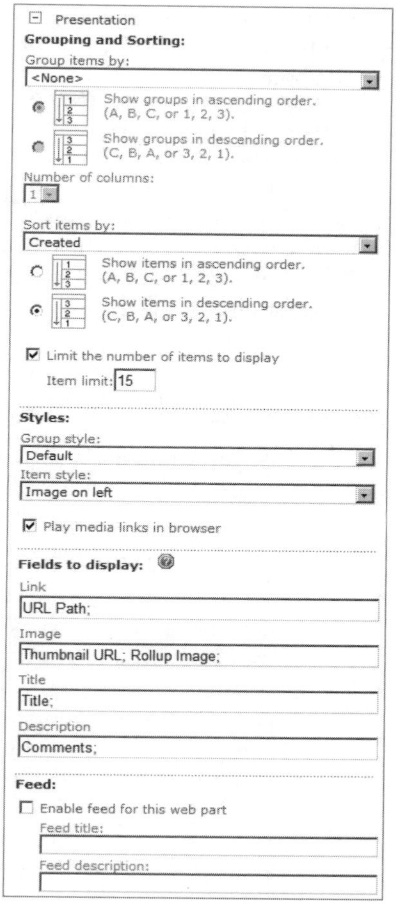

Under the Grouping and Sorting heading, you have the choice of grouping items by a particular column, in either ascending or descending order. You can also specify the number of columns that you want your results to be displayed within. In addition, you can specify if you want your items sorted, in either ascending or descending order, by a particular column. You can also decide whether there is a limit to the number of items to be returned. (This is often critical when retrieving items. If you don't limit the number of items returned, your Web Part could show increasingly more items, because the CQWP does not implement any paging mechanism.)

The next section of the Web Part allows you to choose from various predetermined styles. If your items are appearing in groups, you can choose how your group will look (by selecting an item from the Group Style drop-down menu). Each item will be rendered according to the choice you select from the Item Style drop-down menu. (For instance, Figure 9-28 is using the item style titled Image on Left.)

FIGURE 9-31

Each of these styles is chosen from several XSL style sheets stored in the Style library in the root of your site. It's possible to modify your available styling options by modifying these style sheets, or by modifying the CQWP properties to point to a new style sheet of your choosing. (You can learn more about how to customize the CQWP by reading the online documentation at http://msdn .microsoft.com/en-us/library/ee558385.aspx.)

Each XSL style sheet that renders the list items provides tokens that essentially tell SharePoint something along the lines of "the title of the page goes here" and "the image of the page goes here." The CQWP will look at the item style that you chose, and find out which pieces of information the style sheet needs for that item style. You can then map each of these "placeholders" to a column. For instance, if you look again at Figure 9-31, you can see that the XSL style sheet needs a description. In this case, the contents of each page's Comments column will be displayed when the XSL style sheet is looking for a description. Looking back at Figure 9-28, the Comments column of the first page read, "Please welcome Jim Wesson, our new Customer Service department manager, to our team." The second page's Comments column read, "Our latest product was released this week. Read all about it!"

The last section of the Presentation section of the CQWP tool pane concerns Really Simply Syndication (RSS). It's possible to turn on an RSS feed for your particular CQWP. One reason people like RSS is that it allows them to read new information when it's published. Because your CQWP will dynamically display new publishing pages when they become available, this can be a simple way for users to be notified of new content on your site. By checking the Enable Feed for This Web Part checkbox, you are turning on an RSS feed for this CQWP. You can specify a title and description for this feed.

CONTENT TYPE AND COLUMN PLANNING

As you can see, the CQWP enables you to retrieve list items, including publishing pages, from all over your site collection. However, much of this functionality is dependent on filtering your result sets by content type or site column. Because of this, it's critical that you plan your content types and site columns ahead of time to accommodate list items being retrieved by the CQWP.

For instance, if you have two different kinds of pages and want both to show up in the same CQWP, maybe you need to create a parent content type with two child content types that inherit from that parent content. In that case, you could set your CQWP to retrieve any pages that use that parent content and any inherited contents. For example, if you wanted to display both appetizer and dessert food items in a CQWP, you could create a Food content type, and then create Appetizer and Dessert content types that each inherit from the Food content type. You could then set up your CQWP to display any pages that use the Food content type, or any content types that inherit from the Food content type.

In the same way, if you want to display only pages that describe classes available this semester, you need to ensure that your Class Publishing Page content type has a column called Semester, where a content author can specify which semester the class is for.

Careful planning is key, because it's much more difficult to edit existing content with new values after the content has been created. It's much better to plan your content types and columns ahead of time.

ADVANCED TOPICS

This section briefly mentions some of the more advanced topics regarding Web Content Management in SharePoint 2010. If you want to learn more about each of these topics, please read Andrew Connell's book, *Professional SharePoint 2007 Web Content Management Development* published by Wrox. Although the book was written for SharePoint 2007 and not SharePoint 2010, many of the core concepts have not changed between versions of SharePoint.

Anonymous Access

Many publishing sites are used for public-facing websites. Often these websites should be available for general users to access information. This means that users should not have to log in to the site to access the publishing pages on the site, and these users are therefore considered *anonymous*.

Anonymous access must be granted in two places in order for anonymous users to have access to your site: at the web application level (that is, in IIS) and in any site collection within the web application that anonymous users will be accessing.

To modify a web application's settings, log in to Central Administration and click the Application Management link, then click the Manage Web Applications link. Select the particular web application whose settings you want to modify from the list of web applications. Each web application can have multiple *zones*. (Zones allow users to access the same site content using different authentication mechanisms.) The first thing you need to do is to tell SharePoint which zone you want to set up for anonymous access. To do so, click the Authentication Providers button on the Web Applications tab. This will bring up a dialog that displays which zones have been configured for the web application. Choose a zone to modify by clicking its name. This will bring up the Edit Authentication dialog, as shown in Figure 9-32.

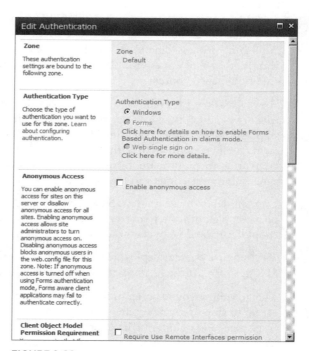

FIGURE 9-32

Check the checkbox that says Enable Anonymous Access and save your changes.

Now that you have granted anonymous access to your web application, you can give your site collection anonymous access as well. You can do this by navigating to your site collection's Site Permissions page. You will see a button in the Ribbon called Anonymous Access. This will pop open a dialog that allows you to grant three types of access for anonymous users:

➤ Access to the entire website.

➤ Access just to lists and libraries.

➤ Access to nothing.

Typically, in a public-facing website, you want anonymous users to have access to the first setting, the entire website. However, you don't want users to be able to navigate to administrative pages, such as the Pages library list view. You can lock down your site collection so that anonymous users have permission to view only publishing pages on your site, and that's it. You can do this by activating the ViewFormPagesLockDown feature on your site collection.

Content Deployment

In the majority of SharePoint environments, it's permissible to allow anonymous users to access a public-facing website using a particular URL, and then allow content authors to access the same site collection content using a different URL. Content authors can be authenticated and begin the publishing process. There's no need to move content from one server to another, because SharePoint handles things like versioning and approval (as discussed earlier in the chapter) so end users don't see unpublished content.

However, some sites require tighter security. In some cases, there needs to be no way for content authors to edit content outside their corporate firewall. If this is the case, it's possible to actually ship approved content from one SharePoint server farm to another. When this happens, the external farm can have no form of authentication enabled, so external users can have no way of editing content on the public site. Instead, content is authored within the firewall, and once published, a timer job moves content to the external content database.

Content deployment is advisable in scenarios only where extremely tight security is required. It can be a complex process to correctly configure and execute content deployment between servers and should only be done when necessary.

To configure content deployment, log in to Central Administration and click the General Application Settings link. At the bottom of the page, you will see a section titled Content Deployment.

The first thing you're going to do is to tell SharePoint whether the server farm you're working with is set up to ship or receive content or both. Additionally, content that gets moved between servers needs to be placed in an intermediate location that's accessible to both the source and destination servers. You need to tell SharePoint where the intermediate location is. You can configure these settings by clicking the Configure Content Deployment link on the General Application Settings page.

The next thing you need to do is to set up a path, which is a mapping between servers and site collections. You have to have both a source and a destination site collection. The next thing you need to do is set up a job, which dictates how often content is moved along its path. You can set up both paths and jobs by clicking the Configure Content Deployment Paths and Jobs link in the Content Deployment section of the General Application Settings page. Once a job has been scheduled, it's possible to check the status of that particular job.

Finally, if you want to check whether a particular piece of content was shipped between servers, you can click the Check Deployment of Specific Content link on the General Application Settings page. This page allows you to type in the URL of the page whose status you want to check. SharePoint will provide you with details about both the source and destination list item, so you can compare them to see if they're the same.

For more information about content deployment, read the online documentation at http://technet.microsoft.com/en-us/library/ee721058.aspx.

Site Variations

SharePoint Server provides a mechanism for handling multiple publishing sites with similar content in multiple languages, and this mechanism is called *site variations*. The idea behind site variations is that you have a publishing site where the site content is written in the original language, then multiple other "variation" sites for other languages. After content has been authored in the original language, content owners can execute a workflow that copies that page and that page's content into the variation sites. At that point, content owners for those other languages are made aware that a new page has been added to their sites and needs to be translated.

Variation sites try to balance the need for each language's site to have a certain degree of autonomy as well as the need to have similar content appearing in multiple languages. Because each variation site is an independent site, content owners for that variation have the ability to create their own content at the variation level. However, the workflow process provides a means for content to be pushed out across languages.

Constructing a multi-lingual site is a complex process and cannot be explained in totality in this chapter. However, you can read about constructing multi-lingual sites using site variations in the online documentation at: `http://msdn.microsoft.com/en-us/library/ms493894.aspx`.

DEVELOPING PUBLISHING SOLUTIONS

This section gives you an overview of how page layouts are constructed, and how you can build your own page layouts using SharePoint Designer or Visual Studio.

Understanding the Publishing Site Columns and Content Types

A content type, at its simplest, is a container for a collection of columns. Every single list or library in SharePoint ultimately inherits from the Item content type, which has just one column: Title. When you add a content type to a list, you can edit the columns that make up that content type by viewing the edit form for that list item.

Say you create a new content type called Biography, and you give it two columns: Biography Image (of type Publishing Image) and Biographical Data (of type Publishing HTML). You could assign this content type to any list and edit the list data in an edit form, such as the one shown in Figure 9-33.

A content type assigned to a Pages library is really no different than a content type

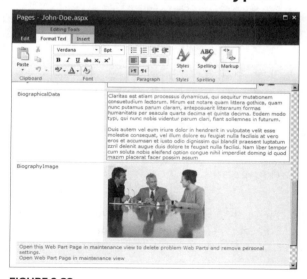

FIGURE 9-33

assigned to any other kind of library. The problem is that the visual representation of the data is not nearly
as attractive for a publishing site when it's in list format as when it's displayed using a page layout.

As you've already learned in this chapter, page layouts provide a way of displaying and editing content from a particular content type. Just as a page is really a document in a document library with an assigned content type, so a page layout is simply a document that has been added to a document library (called the Master Page gallery) with an assigned content type.

Publishing pages must inherit from the Page content type, and page layout documents must inherit from the Page Layout content type. One of the columns associated with the Page Layout content type is called Associated Content type. This means that each time you create a new page layout, you must associate that page layout with a content type.

This association means that it's possible to have multiple renderings of the same underlying content. If you create an item in a Pages library called John-Doe.aspx and assign it a content type of Biography, you can assign the Biographical Data column a value of "John Doe was born in 1976" and add a picture of him to the Biography Image column. You could create one page layout that has the person's picture on the left side of the page, another page layout with the picture on the right side of the page, and another page layout that doesn't show any picture at all. Regardless of which page layout is used to display the information from the list item, the underlying data in the list item remains the same and will still be associated with the Biography content type.

Figure 9-34 illustrates the Page content type and the Page Layout content type.

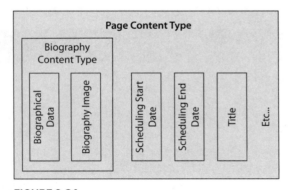
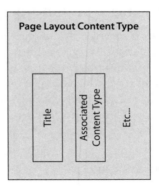

FIGURE 9-34

Figure 9-35 shows each of the content types that have been added to a Pages library. Each of the content types listed inherits from the Page content type.

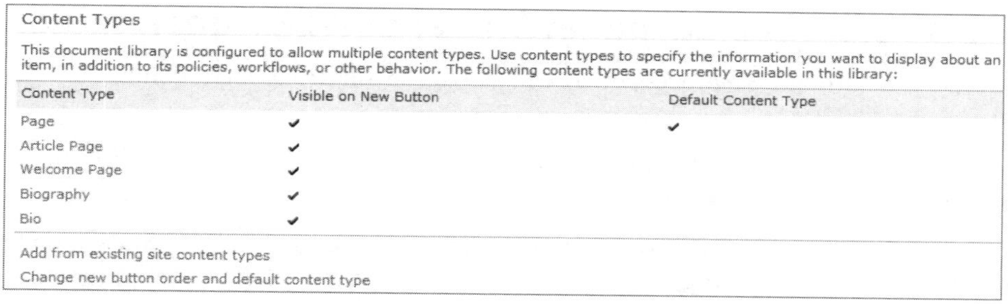

Content Types

This document library is configured to allow multiple content types. Use content types to specify the information you want to display about an item, in addition to its policies, workflows, or other behavior. The following content types are currently available in this library:

Content Type	Visible on New Button	Default Content Type
Page	✔	✔
Article Page	✔	
Welcome Page	✔	
Biography	✔	
Bio	✔	

Add from existing site content types

Change new button order and default content type

FIGURE 9-35

Figure 9-36 shows you the contents of a typical Master Page gallery. Notice that multiple page layouts display content for the Article content type.

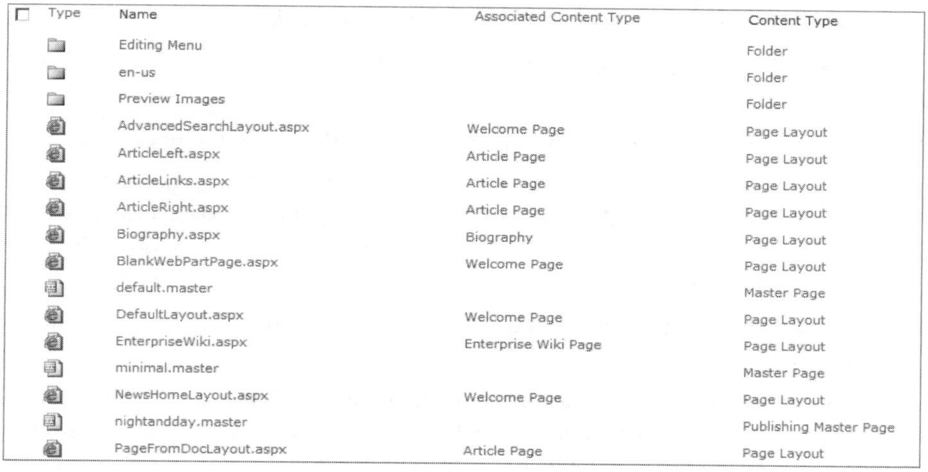

Type	Name	Associated Content Type	Content Type
	Editing Menu		Folder
	en-us		Folder
	Preview Images		Folder
	AdvancedSearchLayout.aspx	Welcome Page	Page Layout
	ArticleLeft.aspx	Article Page	Page Layout
	ArticleLinks.aspx	Article Page	Page Layout
	ArticleRight.aspx	Article Page	Page Layout
	Biography.aspx	Biography	Page Layout
	BlankWebPartPage.aspx	Welcome Page	Page Layout
	default.master		Master Page
	DefaultLayout.aspx	Welcome Page	Page Layout
	EnterpriseWiki.aspx	Enterprise Wiki Page	Page Layout
	minimal.master		Master Page
	NewsHomeLayout.aspx	Welcome Page	Page Layout
	nightandday.master		Publishing Master Page
	PageFromDocLayout.aspx	Article Page	Page Layout

FIGURE 9-36

Each page layout corresponds to an item in the Page Layouts fly-out menu that you can see in Figure 9-3, back near the beginning of this chapter. As you can see in Figure 9-3, each page layout is listed below its associated content type.

The next two sections of this chapter walk you through the process of creating your own site columns, content types, and page layout. The first example demonstrates the process of creating a page layout using SharePoint Designer, and the second example demonstrates the process of creating a page layout that can be deployed using a solution package and added to your site collection by activating a feature.

Example: Creating a Page Layout in SharePoint Designer

This example walks you through the process of creating a page layout using SharePoint Designer 2010.

1. Open up your browser and browse to the top-level site of the publishing site collection to which you would like to add a page layout.

2. Click the Site Actions menu and navigate to the Site Settings page. Click the Site Columns link under the Galleries heading on the Site Settings page.

3. Click the Create button at the top of the page to create a new site column.

4. Give your new column the name Biography Picture. Give it a type of Image with Formatting and Constraints for Publishing. Put the site column into a new group called Wrox Columns. Click OK.

5. Create a new column again, this time naming it Biographical Data and giving it a type of Full HTML Content with Formatting and Constraints for Publishing. Add the column to the Wrox Columns group you created in the preceding step. Click OK.

6. Navigate back to the Site Settings page. Click the link that says Site Content Types under the Galleries heading.

7. Create a new content type by clicking the Create button at the top of the page.

8. Give your new content type the name Biography. In the first drop-down menu, titled Select Parent Content Type From, select Publishing Content Types. Make sure that the second drop-down menu, titled Parent Content Type, is set to Page. Create a new content type group called Wrox Content Types. Click OK.

9. On the content type management page, under the Columns section, click the link that says Add from Existing Site Columns.

10. Select Wrox Columns from the drop-down menu. Add both the Biographical Data and the Biography Image columns to the Columns to Add group. When you see a warning prompt, click the OK button to close it. Click OK to save your changes.

11. Start SharePoint Designer. Open up the top-level site of the publishing site collection to which you would like to add a page layout.

12. Click the Page Layouts icon under the Site Objects heading on the left side.

13. In the Ribbon, you should see a tab called Page Layouts. Click the button that says New Page Layout in the Ribbon. This will pop open a window titled New.

14. Select Wrox Content Types from the first drop-down menu, titled Content Type Group. The second drop-down menu should have Biography selected. Give your new page layout a URL Name of Biography.aspx, and a title of Biography.

15. You should now see the HTML markup for your new Biography page layout in the SharePoint Designer main window.

16. Put your cursor inside the content placeholder called PlaceHolderMain, which you will find in the middle of your page layout. Click the Insert tab in your Ribbon, and click the Table button. Add a one-row, two-column table to your page.

17. If you do not see your Toolbox on the right side of your screen, click the View tab in your Ribbon, then click the Task Panes button and select Toolbox from the menu.

18. Expand your Toolbox (which should be on the right side of SharePoint Designer) and select the SharePoint Controls node. Inside this node, you will see another node titled Page Fields. This displays all the fields that are a part of the Biography content type's parent content type, which is the Page content type.

19. Select the field called Title, under the Page Fields heading inside the SharePoint Controls section of your Toolbox, and drag and drop it into the right column of the table, which you added to your page layout.

20. Expand the HTML node of the Toolbox and select the Break item you find inside the Tags section. Drag and drop that Break item under the Title field you just added to the page layout.

21. Return to the SharePoint Controls node in the Toolbox, but this time, expand the Content Fields section. Drag and drop the Biographical Data field below the line break you just added to the page layout in the preceding step.

22. Drag and drop the Biography Image field into the first column in your table.

23. Save your changes to the page layout by clicking the disk icon at the top of SharePoint Designer, or press Ctrl+S.

24. In the breadcrumb that appears above the page layout, you should see the name of your site followed by Master Pages, followed by Biography.aspx, followed by the words Advanced Editor. Click Biography.aspx in the breadcrumb.

25. Your page layout is currently checked out and cannot be used until it is checked back in. Click the Check In button on the Page tab of the Ribbon. Select the Publish a Major Version radio button under the question "What type of version do you want to check in?" Add any comments you might have and click OK. Although your page layout is checked in, by default, items in the Master Page gallery require content approval. You will now approve your new page layout.

26. Return to your browser and navigate to the Site Settings page in the top-level site of your site collection. Click the Master Pages and Page Layouts link under the Galleries heading.

27. Ensure that the account that you are currently using has been granted approval rights in the site. (You can easily do this by adding that user to the SharePoint Approvers group.)

28. Find Biography.aspx. Hover over the item and select Approve/Reject from its context menu. This will bring up a dialog called Approve/Reject.

29. Select the Approved radio button and click OK.

30. Now it's time to try out your new page layout. Click the Site Actions menu and select New Page. Give your new page the name John Doe.

31. Click the Page tab in the Ribbon. Click the Page Layout button in the Page Actions section of the Ribbon. You should now see a section called Biography with a page layout called Biography. Select the Biography page layout. You should now see a publishing page that uses your new Biography page layout.

Example: Creating a Page Layout in Visual Studio 2010

This section builds on the work you did in the preceding example. It will help you re-create the Biography page layout, but this time you will use Visual Studio 2010 to create a page layout that will be deployed with a solution package and become available once a feature has been activated. You can download the final Visual Studio project from the Wrox site; it's called Wrox.SixInOne .PageLayouts.

1. Open Visual Studio 2010 and create a new project.

2. Select the Visual C# ➪ SharePoint ➪ 2010 ➪ Module project template. Give your project a name of Wrox.SixInOne.PageLayouts. Click OK.

3. On the SharePoint Customization Wizard's first screen, type in the name of your SharePoint development website that you'll be using to test your solution. Select the Deploy as a Farm Solution radio button. Click the Finish button.

4. Right-click the project in your Solution Explorer and select Add ➪ New Item. Select Empty Element from the list and call it Fields. Click the Add button.

5. If the Elements.xml file is not already open, double-click the Elements.xml file inside the newly created Fields element. Add the following XML inside the `<Elements></Elements>` nodes:

```
<Field ID="{CC20765D-FA68-42a8-8E10-FEB763207AA2}"
    Name="BioImage"
    DisplayName="Bio Image"
    Group="Wrox Columns"
    Type="Image"
    RichText="TRUE"
    RichTextMode="FullHtml"/>
<Field ID="{BA4F50F9-0046-449f-BA81-B70903C8EEAD}"
    Name="BioData"
    DisplayName="Bio Data"
    Group="Wrox Columns"
    Type="HTML"
    RichText="TRUE"
    RichTextMode="FullHtml"/>
```

6. Right-click the project in your Solution Explorer and select Add ➪ New Item. Select Content Type from the list and call it Biography. Click the Add button.

7. Select Page from the drop-down list of available content types. (If you don't see Page listed, ensure that the site you're connecting to is a publishing site.) Click Finish.

8. If the Elements.xml file is not already open, double-click the Elements.xml file inside the newly created Biography element. Change the `ContentType` element's `Name` attribute's property value from `Wrox.SixInOne.PageLayouts - Biography` to `Bio`. Find the `<FieldRefs></FieldRefs>` nodes inside the file, and add references to the fields you created in your Fields element, by adding the following child elements to the `FieldRefs` element:

```
<FieldRef Name="BioImage" ID="{CC20765D-FA68-42a8-8E10-FEB763207AA2}"/>
<FieldRef Name="BioData" ID="{BA4F50F9-0046-449f-BA81-B70903C8EEAD}"/>
```

9. Select the module called Module1 in your Solution Explorer, and rename in Page Layouts. Delete the file inside the module called Sample.txt.

10. Open up the Elements.xml inside the module. You should see a module element that says `<Module Name="Page Layouts">`. Add the following attribute to the module, telling SharePoint that the files in this module are to be deployed to the Master Page gallery (which has a URL of `/_catalogs/masterpage`): `Url="_catalogs/masterpage"`. Your new module element should now look like this: `<Module Name="Page Layouts" Url="_catalogs/masterpage">`.

11. Right-click the project in your Solution Explorer and select Add ➪ New Item. Add a new Text File, (under the C# ➪ General section), but give it a name of Bio.aspx. (If you tried to add an ASPX page using the default project item template, Visual Studio would also add a code-behind file, which in this case you do not need.)

12. Open up SharePoint Designer. Open up the Biography.aspx page layout you created in the previous example, and edit it in Advanced Mode. Copy the entire page markup, and paste it into the Bio.aspx page you just created in Visual Studio.

13. Look at the Page directive of your Bio.aspx page in Visual Studio. (This is the first line of code, that starts with `<%@ Page`.) Scroll toward the end of the line. If you find the following text, delete it: `meta:progid="SharePoint.WebPartPage.Document" meta:webpartpage expansion="full"`. (If you don't remove these tags, SharePoint will think that your page has been customized from its original version, even though it has not.)

14. Now look at the markup in your new page. Find the control that starts with `<PublishingWebControls:RichImageField`. Notice that the `FieldName` property of the control is actually a GUID. To make the field more readable, it's possible to replace this value with the field's internal name. In our Visual Studio solution, our field has an internal name of BioImage. Replace the GUID you find in the `FieldName` attribute with the word BioImage, so your control now looks like this: `<PublishingWebControls: RichImageField FieldName="BioImage" runat="server" id="RichImageField1"> </PublishingWebControls:RichImageField>`.

15. Repeat the same process with the `<SharePointWebControls:TextField />` control, replacing the `FieldName` property value with the word Title.

16. Repeat the same process, this time replacing the `<PublishingWebControls: RichHtmlField />` control's `FieldName` property value with the Bio Data field's internal name, BioData.

17. Next, open with the Elements.xml file inside your Page Layouts module. Notice that your new Bio.aspx file has been added to the parent Module element that you edited in a previous step.

18. The `File` element has a `Url` property value of `Page Layouts/Bio.aspx` by default. Remove `Page Layouts/` from the URL, so the new property looks like this: `Url="Bio.aspx"`. (If you don't make this change, SharePoint will try to deploy your page layout to a folder called Page Layouts inside the Master Page gallery.)

19. Add the following property to the `File` element: `Type="GhostableInLibrary"`. (Without this, the page layout will not be visible to you when choosing a layout.) Your new `File`

element should now look like this: `<File Path="Page Layouts\Bio.aspx" Url="Bio`
`.aspx" Type="GhostableInLibrary" />`.

20. All this will do so far is provision a list item in the Master Page gallery. The next thing you need to do is assign properties to the page layout file. These properties will tell SharePoint things such as the name of the page layout, the page layout's preview image, and the page layout's associated content type. Add the following elements inside the `File` element:

```
<Property Name="Title" Value="Biography Page Layout" />
<Property Name="ContentType" Value="$Resources:cmscore,contenttype_pagelayout_
name;" />
<Property Name="PublishingPreviewImage"
Value="~SiteCollection/_catalogs/masterpage/Preview Images/Bio.jpg,
~SiteCollection/_catalogs/masterpage/Preview Images/Bio.jpg" />
<Property Name="PublishingAssociatedContentType" Value=";#Bio;#;#"/>
```

21. Open up the Elements.xml file inside your Biography content type. Copy the `ContentType` element's `ID` property.

22. Return to the Elements.xml file you were just modifying inside the Page Layouts module. Find the property with a name of `PublishingAssociatedContentType`. Insert the content type ID you copied in the previous step into the `PublishingAssociatedContentType` property value string, between `";#Bio;#"` and the final `";#"` of the string. Your new property value might look like this: `<Property Name="PublishingAssociatedContentType" Value=";#Bio;#0` `x010100C568DB52D9D0A14D9B2FDCC96666E9F2007948130EC3DB064584E219954237AF39003` `263756b51a44d9098ce3c00bf1186e3;#"/>`.

23. Notice that one of the properties you added to the `File` element was called `PublishingPreviewImage`. The property specified that the page layout had a preview image called Bio.png stored inside a folder called Preview Images, inside the Master Page gallery. You need to create this new folder and add your preview image to your solution package. To do so, right-click the Page Layouts module in your Solution Explorer and select Add ⇨ New Folder. Give your folder the name Preview Images.

24. Create a thumbnail picture of your new page and call it Bio.jpg. Add your new image to the Preview Images folder.

25. Open up the Elements.xml inside your Page Layouts module. Notice that Visual Studio added a reference to this new image for you. However, you need to make some modifications. First, modify the `Url` property value of the new `File` element, deleting `Page Layouts/` from the property value, so the new property looks like this: `Url="Preview Images/Bio.jpg"`. Also, add the `Type="GhostableInLibrary"` attribute to the `File` element.

26. Now that you've created your site columns, content type, and page layout, you can modify your feature that you'll be using. Rename your feature folder from Feature1 to Wrox.SixInOne.PageLayouts.

27. Open up the Feature designer and remove the word Feature1 from the title. Give the feature a description of "Deploys the Biography site columns, content type, and page layout to the site collection." Set the Scope to Site. Ensure that the items in the feature are listed in the following order: Fields, Biography, Page Layouts. (If they're not listed in the correct order, SharePoint will throw an error when the feature is activated, if it tries to provision the page layout before the content type and site column are in place.) Save your changes to the feature.

28. Build your project and deploy it to your server. You should now be able to create a new page using the Bio content type and the page layout called Bio Page Layout. You should see your preview image when you try to select your new layout from the available page layouts. Notice that, unlike creating a page layout in SharePoint Designer, your page layout is already checked in and approved and ready for use.

SUMMARY

This chapter walked you through the process of creating, editing, approving, and publishing new pages in a SharePoint publishing site. It also walked you through some of the configuration settings of a publishing site, such as configuring versioning and approval on a Pages library. You learned how to retrieve content from other locations in your site collection by using the Content Query Web Part. You learned about some of the advanced features in SharePoint such as anonymous access configuration, content deployment, and variation sites. Finally, you learned about how you can create your page layouts using SharePoint Designer or Visual Studio 2010.

PART IV
Business Connectivity Services

10

Introducing Business Connectivity Services

WHAT'S IN THIS CHAPTER?

➤ Introducing the various components of Business Connectivity Services (BCS) and its part in SharePoint's Composites capabilities

➤ Understanding the various solution types available when building a BCS solution and what tools are used to build the solutions

➤ Identifying what components you have available based on your edition of SharePoint 2010

Organizations generally have data stored in several systems with SharePoint being only one of those systems. The Business Connectivity Services component of Microsoft SharePoint 2010 is a tool for bringing data from external systems into SharePoint and Office. The external data can come from a variety of sources and can be leveraged in your SharePoint environment in a number of ways.

This chapter introduces you to the various components that make up Business Connectivity Services, how it works behind the scenes, what kinds of solutions you can build, and what tools you'll need to get started.

WHAT IS BCS?

The Business Connectivity Services (BCS) component of Microsoft SharePoint 2010 allows you to define external systems, create models that represent the data in those systems, and then surface that data for use in both SharePoint and Office. An overview of BCS is shown in Figure 10-1.

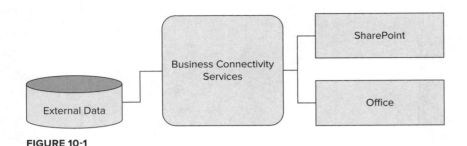

FIGURE 10-1

The external data being presented by BCS can be accessed using one of the built-in connectors. There is a connector for SQL server databases, which are accessed by ADO.NET, one for connecting to web services, and one for connecting to custom-coded .NET assemblies. Regardless of the source, once the data is accessible to BCS it can then be used in SharePoint and Office in a predictable way.

The idea of integrating external data with SharePoint is not new to the release of Microsoft SharePoint 2010. BCS is the evolution of the Business Data Catalog that shipped with Microsoft Office SharePoint Server 2007. BCS includes a number of improvements over its predecessor, including the ability to both read from and write back to external data sources. Another key improvement with BCS is increased tool support for working with BCS in the form of Microsoft SharePoint Designer 2010 and Microsoft Visual Studio 2010.

By leveraging BCS, power users and site designers in SharePoint (sometimes called information workers) can connect to external systems without knowing the system-specific connection details. Using common building blocks, these information workers can create interactive solutions that incorporate external data.

It is important to note that a BCS solution is not necessarily built to solve one specific business problem, as a custom Web Part might be. BCS is a framework that makes external data available to users of a SharePoint site, so they can quickly build solutions using the external data. This concept is known as Composites.

BCS and Composites

The feature areas of SharePoint 2010 are sometimes broken up into capabilities, one of which is Composites. Composites allow you to quickly build solutions using reusable components.

One way to look at Composites is to think of building blocks. In Composites, building blocks are first developed and then are assembled by users to build solutions. The building blocks can come from a variety of different sources; for instance, an architect in your organization could build a Web Part that connects to your organization's HR database. A third party could also offer building blocks such as a web service that presents information relevant to your business. SharePoint itself is made up of building blocks such as Web Parts and lists.

Once these building blocks are available, users can construct solutions with them. A solution could be a dashboard that shows user-specific information from your organization's HR database side-by-side with data from a third-party web service. The solution could show relevant SharePoint list and library content alongside data from these other sources. The possibilities are nearly as endless as the possible problems a user might need to solve. That flexibility, along with the speed of solution development is the key to the power of Composites.

BCS makes a number of building blocks available for users to consume and it also facilitates connecting those building blocks to external systems. The administration of BCS was built with awareness of the Composites strategy. Users don't necessarily know the connection details for how to get to the organization's HR database — they just know they need the data and need to know how to use the related building blocks. Similarly, BCS administrators don't need to be concerned with how users will lay out their Web Parts on the page or connect them; they simply need to make the data available.

External Content Types in Depth

Core to any BCS solution, External Content Types (ECT) are a representation of an entity that exists in an external data source. Though an ECT does not define the connection details for an external system, it does have a property that tells the ECT which external system it should be associated with. This allows solution designers to switch what system an ECT is connected to without having to re-create the ECT from scratch, providing a great deal of flexibility during development.

The external system definition and the ECT together make up a BCS model. If you worked with the Business Data Catalog in SharePoint 2007, you may be painfully familiar with how the BCS model works. Behind the scenes a BCS model is a large XML file that contains metadata about your entities. When building BDC solutions in 2007, you likely had to edit the XML file, which was commonly hundreds or even thousands of lines long. Thankfully, the tool support in 2010 makes manual updates to the BCS model largely unnecessary. Tool support is discussed in detail later in this chapter.

An example of an ECT could be a Customer entity. The Customer entity could be connected to an external system which is configured to talk to a CRM database. Next we'll discuss some of the other properties of an ECT, using Customer as an example.

Fields

Each ECT contains a list of fields from the external data source that should be made available and their data type. The data types available are similar to what you would find in a database or even a SharePoint list. Some possible fields could include:

- ➤ Customer Name field of type String
- ➤ Order Count field of type Integer
- ➤ Last Order Date field of type Datetime

You do not have to include every field from your external data source. The selection of what fields to display and in what order are actually defined in operations, which are discussed later.

Associations

Just like entities in external data sources, External Content Types frequently have related entities. BCS supports related entities through the use of associations. An ECT contains the definition of any associations, which define how two ECTs are related. In our Customer example, there could be a related Order entity for which we could define an association. The complexity of your associations can be a factor when choosing how to design your BCS solution. Simple one-to-many associations can be handled in SharePoint Designer, whereas more complex many-to-many associations must be created by editing the BCS model file, probably using Visual Studio.

Operations

External Content Types typically contain multiple operations, which are sometimes also referred to as methods or MethodInstances. Many different types of operations can be created, although the types available differ depending on the tool you are using. SharePoint Designer supports the common operations listed in Table 10-1. At a minimum your ECT should include the Read Item and Read List operations, because they are required to support read-only scenarios.

TABLE 10-1: SharePoint Designer Operations

OPERATION NAME	METHOD INSTANCE TYPE	DESCRIPTION
Read Item	SpecificFinder	Returns information about a single item
Read List	Finder	Returns a list of items
Create	Creator	Creates a new item
Update	Updater	Updates an item
Delete	Deleter	Deletes an item

A number of more advanced operations are available including StreamAccessor, which allows you to retrieve a binary stream from an external data source. In our Customer example, a StreamAccessor method could retrieve a company logo that is stored in the CRM database. These more advanced operations cannot be leveraged if you are creating your BCS solution with SharePoint Designer.

Permissions

ECTs can be configured so that only specific users or groups can access them. Administrators can define who has access to execute operations defined on the ECT, who can make changes to the ECT, and even who can set the permissions on the ECT. It's important to note that this is not the same as defining how BCS should connect to the external data. The next chapter walks through the details of defining connections and permissions.

Now that you better understand the details of what makes up an External Content Type, you can explore how to use an ECT for leveraging the out-of-the-box building blocks that come with SharePoint.

BCS BUILDING BLOCKS

SharePoint 2010 ships with a number of building blocks that can be used to construct a BCS solution. This section highlights the available building blocks and how they are used when building a BCS solution. Note that not all these building blocks are available in all versions of SharePoint 2010. Later in this chapter you can find details on the feature differences by product.

External Lists

An external list presents an ECT in the form of a SharePoint list, giving users the ability to work with external data using a familiar interface. Most of the features available to a SharePoint list are also available on external lists with a few notable exceptions. One exception is that it's not possible to extend the schema of an external list by adding a new column as you would on a traditional SharePoint list. Another notable exception is that workflows cannot be attached to an external list. Still, external lists provide you with the new, edit, and display forms that allow you to work with your data as if it were a SharePoint list. Users on your site will see the data being displayed in a familiar format with the same paging, grouping, sorting, and filtering options you would expect from a SharePoint list. In fact, the only major difference users are likely to see is a loading animation that's displayed by default while the data is being loaded from the external system.

Workflow

As discussed, workflows cannot be attached to external lists. That doesn't mean that you can't use SharePoint workflows to work with external data. SharePoint Designer 2010 contains several conditions and actions that can access and work with external data. Some examples include:

➤ Using a workflow condition to check the value of an item in an external list

➤ Actions that support creating, updating, or deleting an item in an external list

External Data Columns

In some cases it's not necessary to present an entire list as can be done using an external list. Instead, a traditional SharePoint list or library may be extended using external data columns. An example might be adding a customer or order number to a document in a document library. This is similar to adding a choice or lookup field to a list except that the data is actually coming from your external data source. This is a great way to add powerful metadata associations to your documents or list items.

Business Data Web Parts

A number of Web Parts can be used to present data from external systems. These Web Parts can be used on any Web Part page and also to support Web Part connections for advanced scenarios. Using these Web Parts, it becomes possible to create extremely powerful dashboards and data visualizations.

Business Data List

The Business Data List Web Part returns a list of items for a BCS entity (Figure 10-2). It's similar to creating an external list, but it can be used to display a list of items on a simple dashboard page when that is all that is required. Similar to a List View Web Part that displays a SharePoint list, the Business Data List Web Part allows you to customize the view by selecting which fields are displayed and in what order, setting sort and filter criteria, as well as setting the paging and grouping behavior. The Business Data List Web Part also supports Web Part connections, allowing you to send a selected item to another Web Part or receive filter or query values.

Employees List

Actions ▾   1 - 20 ▸

EmployeeID	Title	FirstName	MiddleName	LastName	JobTitle	Phone	City	StateProvinceName	PostalCode
1		Guy	R	Gilbert	Production Technician - WC60	320-555-0195	Monroe	Washington	98272
2		Kevin	F	Brown	Marketing Assistant	150-555-0189	Everett	Washington	98201
3		Roberto		Tamburello	Engineering Manager	212-555-0187	Redmond	Washington	98052
4		Rob		Walters	Senior Tool Designer	612-555-0100	Minneapolis	Minnesota	55402
5		Thierry	B	D'Hers	Tool Designer	168-555-0183	Bothell	Washington	98011
6		David	M	Bradley	Marketing Manager	913-555-0172	Redmond	Washington	98052
7		JoLynn	M	Dobney	Production Supervisor - WC60	903-555-0145	Seattle	Washington	98104
8		Ruth	Ann	Ellerbrock	Production Technician - WC10	145-555-0130	Everett	Washington	98201
9	Ms.	Gail	A	Erickson	Design Engineer	849-555-0139	Bellevue	Washington	98004
10		Barry	K	Johnson	Production Technician - WC10	206-555-0180	Snohomish	Washington	98296
11	Mr.	Jossef	H	Goldberg	Design Engineer	122-555-0189	Renton	Washington	98055
12		Terri	Lee	Duffy	Vice President of Engineering	819-555-0175	Renton	Washington	98055
13		Sidney	M	Higa	Production Technician - WC10	424-555-0189	Edmonds	Washington	98020
14		Taylor	R	Maxwell	Production Supervisor - WC50	508-555-0165	Edmonds	Washington	98020

FIGURE 10-2

Business Data Item

The Business Data Item Web Part displays a single item from a BCS entity (Figure 10-3). It can be used with or without Web Part connections. If you are not using Web Part connections, you must select a specific item to display. With Web Part connections, you can receive a selected item from another Web Part (a Business Data List Web Part, for example). The Web Part can be configured to display only the fields you select and in the order you want. The Web Part can also be highly customized by a developer using XSLT (you see an example of customizing XSLT in Chapter 11). You can also configure which BCS actions (which are discussed later) should be made available.

FIGURE 10-3

Business Data Item Builder

The Business Data Item Builder Web Part is meant for use on BCS Profile pages only and does not display on the page unless it is in edit mode. It reads identifiers in a page request URL, constructs the appropriate business data item, and then makes it available via Web Part connections. Don't expect to use this Web Part on your own dashboard pages.

Business Data Related List

The Business Data Related List Web Part displays a related list of BCS entities using Web Part connections. When an association has been defined between two ECTs, this Web Part can be used to display any related items. This Web Part allows users to create powerful dashboards that enable end users to browse related data without knowing the details of the data sources (Figure 10-4).

FIGURE 10-4

Business Data Connectivity Filter

The Business Data Connectivity Filter Web Part allows you to send a specific column from an ECT to a connected Web Part. Figure 10-5 shows the Web Part connection dialog box being used to configure a connection between a connectivity filter and a Business Data List Web Part. This Web Part can also be used to send filter values to non-Business Data Web Parts for use in filters.

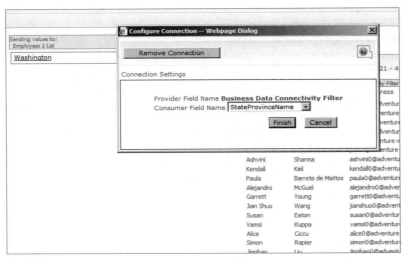

FIGURE 10-5

Business Data Actions

The Business Data Actions Web Part displays links to actions defined for the current Entity. BCS actions are covered in detail later but for now think of them as dynamic URLs. Figure 10-6 shows two actions that are available for the selected entity. This Web Part can be configured to point to a specific business data item, or it can use

FIGURE 10-6

Web Part connections to select a single item from a Business Data List Web Part. This Web Part also has options to configure which actions display as well as their style or format.

Profile Pages

As discussed before, BCS Web Parts can be used on any Web Part page within SharePoint. One special Web Part page is called the Profile page. Profile pages are created by an administrator during the configuration of a BCS entity. Only one Profile page is created per entity definition. These pages take a parameter that is the unique key needed to display a single business data item. By default, the Profile page contains a Business Data Item Builder Web Part as well as a connected Business Data Item Web Part (Figure 10-7). It's important to note that these pages are Web Part pages and can be fully customized;

Business Data Item Builder
This web part builds a business data item from identifiers in the URL and sends i... mode.

Employees 2

Map Location	Display Email

Receiving Item from Business Data Item Builder	
EmployeeID:	1
Title:	
FirstName:	Guy
MiddleName:	R
LastName:	Gilbert
Suffix:	
JobTitle:	Production Technician - WC60
Phone:	320-555-0195
EmailAddress:	guy1@adventure-works.com
EmailPromotion:	0
AddressLine1:	7726 Driftwood Drive

FIGURE 10-7

however, the Profile pages also play a key role in search, so care should be taken when customizing the pages. One other item of note is that when you create a Profile page, a new BCS action is created for the ECT called View Profile, which links to the Profile page.

Search

One of the most powerful features of the BCS is the ability to surface line-of-business data in enterprise search results. Administrators can create content sources that will index external data as shown in Figure 10-8. Once a crawl has run, the items in your external system will be visible in search results pages.

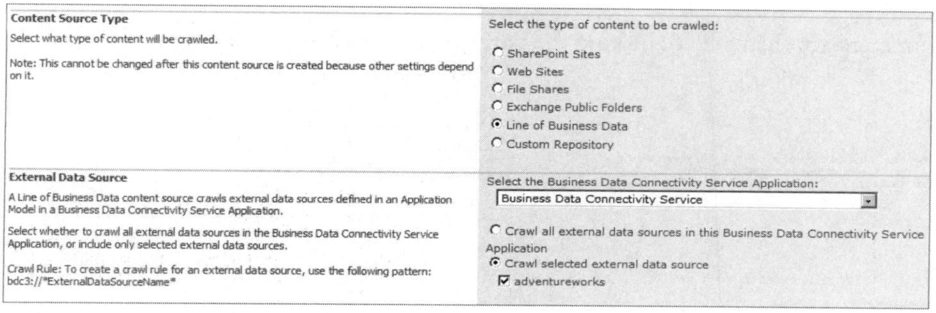

FIGURE 10-8

Figure 10-9 shows a sample of search results for business data items. The links for items returned in the search results point to the Profile page that was created for the entity. Both the Profile page and the Search Results page can be customized to provide a richer user experience; however, the out-of-the-box experience surfaces your external data in search results with very little effort and is often an easy win for SharePoint deployments.

FIGURE 10-9

BCS Actions

BCS actions allow you to interact with your external data. BCS actions are parameterized URLs that are dynamically populated with business data before the links are displayed to end users. Each entity can have multiple actions defined as well as a default action, which is typically a link to view the Profile page for the item.

An example of a URL that can be parameterized is a link to Bing Maps:

```
http://www.bing.com/maps/?v=2&where1=Seattle,WA
```

The URL can be broken up into several parts:

SERVER BEING ACCESSED	APPLICATION ADDRESS	SETTINGS	PARAMETERS
http://www.bing.com	/maps/	?v=2	&where1=Seattle,WA

The administration screen for creating BCS actions requests a URL and explains how to configure parameters. This example creates a Map Location action which has two parameters, one for city and one for state:

```
http://www.bing.com/maps/?v=2&where1={0},{1}
```

Two URL parameters are then added, linking the parameter properties as shown in Figure 10-10.

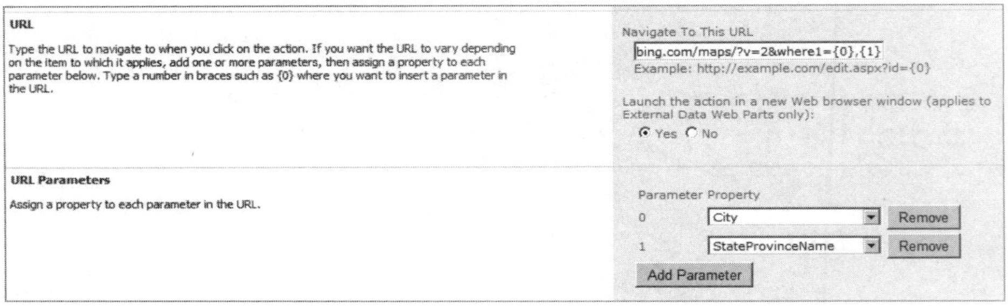

FIGURE 10-10

The Map Location action allows end users to click an action link wherever it is displayed and have it open a new browser window that displays a map for the current business data item.

BCS SOLUTION TYPES AND TARGETS

BCS solutions are sometimes grouped into three types: simple, intermediate, and advanced. Each of these types has a set of tools and target audiences in mind, and each type can be used to create a different kind of solution.

Simple Solutions

These solutions are typically built by users. External Content Types for simple solutions either already exist or are created by an Information worker with SharePoint Designer. Once the ECT exists, the user assembles a solution using external lists, external columns, and/or the many BCS Web Parts discussed earlier. These simple solutions are the "killer apps" of BCS because they can be built quickly by non-developers to respond to business needs.

Intermediate Solutions

These solutions are typically built by Information workers and developers. Intermediate solutions build upon simple solutions and add additional functionality, such as SharePoint Designer workflows and custom forms designed with InfoPath. One unique solution type in this category is called a Declarative Outlook solution. These declarative solutions don't require any development per se, but usually do require someone familiar with development techniques. They are created by assembling a collection of assets including XML files and other supporting files. Once assembled and customized, the assets are packaged and deployed to Outlook. The resulting solution allows you to view and interact with BCS entities via customized task panes within Outlook.

Advanced Solutions

These solutions are typically built by enterprise developers. Advanced solutions focus on creating reusable components that can be used in simple and intermediate solutions. The reusable components could be advanced BCS models developed in Visual Studio, custom workflow activities, custom Web Parts, or any other reusable component. Types of solutions are shown in Table 10-2.

TABLE 10-2: Solution Types

	SIMPLE	INTERMEDIATE	ADVANCED
Creator	User	Information Worker/Developer	Enterprise Developer
Tools	SharePoint Designer	SharePoint SDK	Visual Studio
Types of Solutions	Out-the-box with configuration	Customization	Development

Solution Targets

BCS solutions are usually deployed and surfaced within SharePoint but that does not have to be the case. SharePoint 2010 supports BCS solutions that can be hosted in the Office client as well as in custom applications, as follows:

➤ **SharePoint:** The building blocks discussed earlier can all be used to create solutions within SharePoint. Those solutions can be search solutions or dashboards with Business Data Web Parts or even just a normal SharePoint list or library that contains a business data column to provide meaningful metadata. Because of SharePoint's role in many organizations as a portal, SharePoint is a natural target for surfacing BCS solutions.

➤ **Office client:** BCS solutions can also be surfaced within two products in the Office Suite: Outlook 2010 and Word 2010. Outlook has the deepest integration, allowing you to browse external data as Outlook items, including appointments, tasks, or contacts. We also talked about creating intermediate declarative solutions for Outlook. Word includes support for a

BCS Entity Picker control, which can be surfaced using Quick Parts, allowing end users to specify metadata within the document's content. You see examples of BCS solutions created for Office in Chapter 11.

➤ **Custom client:** BCS solutions aren't limited to SharePoint and the Office Suite. Because of SharePoint's support for web services and the new Client Object model, external lists can be remotely accessed and used in custom applications. This means you can leverage your BCS framework in custom Silverlight applications or desktop applications, allowing you to manage the details of your external connections in SharePoint while still allowing developers access to line-of-business data.

TOOLS FOR BCS SOLUTIONS

One of the major pain points of the Business Data Catalog included in Microsoft Office SharePoint Server 2007 was the lack of tool support for building solutions with the Business Data Catalog. With Microsoft SharePoint 2010, the tool support for building BCS solutions has been dramatically improved.

Microsoft has provided two main tools for use in building BCS solutions: SharePoint Designer 2010 and Visual Studio 2010. Although both tools allow you to build BCS solutions, each has a specific audience in mind — SharePoint Designer targets users and information workers whereas Visual Studio targets enterprise developers.

Introducing SharePoint Designer 2010 for BCS

SharePoint Designer is a powerful tool for building SharePoint applications including BCS solutions. The 2010 release includes some major user experience enhancements including the Ribbon and an all-new navigation scheme. In addition to the updated user experience, SharePoint Designer 2010 also now supports building and managing External Content Types.

FIGURE 10-11

Although including the Ribbon is new with 2010, most users familiar with the 2007 release of Office will be comfortable with it almost immediately. The bigger user experience change, if you were familiar with the 2007 release of SharePoint Designer, is the new navigation scheme. In 2007 (and earlier with FrontPage) the navigation came in the form of a file and directory structure. With SharePoint Designer 2010, the navigation is based instead on site objects as shown in Figure 10-11.

Most of your BCS solution configuration will take place in the External Content Types navigation element. From there you can view all your ECTs that have been defined as well as create new External Content Types. Clicking an existing ECT brings up the summary view for the External Content Type as shown in Figure 10-12. The summary view provides a great overview of all the properties related to the ECT.

As Figure 10-13 shows, the Operations Design View (available on the Ribbon) is a screen that gives the ability to edit existing operations and add additional ones. This view is also where you can create new connections to an external data source. Chapter 11 walks through creating a simple solution using SharePoint Designer 2010 where you can see how each of these components is created.

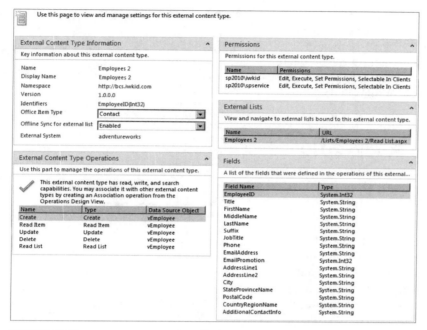

FIGURE 10-12

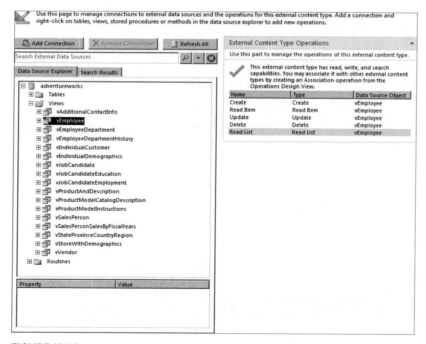

FIGURE 10-13

The External Content Types navigation element also presents options in the Ribbon to manage advanced connection properties as shown in Figure 10-14. The Ribbon also gives the option to create Profile pages and external lists. Again, you walk through each of these options in detail in Chapter 11.

Introducing Visual Studio 2010 for BCS

Visual Studio 2010 has also been greatly improved from the prior release. As it relates to BCS, the biggest improvement is the inclusion of a project template called the Business Data Connectivity model (Figure 10-15). This template provides a visual designer for your BCS model and a fully functional sample entity. Though you can still edit your XML model file by hand, the visual designer is powerful enough that this is rarely necessary.

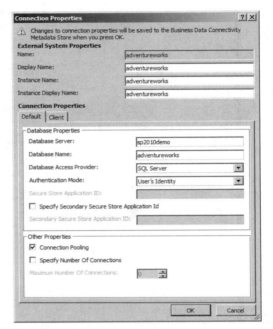

FIGURE 10-14

FIGURE 10-15

Another improvement in Visual Studio 2010 is support for building sandboxed solutions, the details of which were discussed in Chapter 7. When you create a new SharePoint 2010 Visual Studio project, you are prompted to choose your deployment method. BCS solutions cannot be deployed as sandboxed solutions, so when you are prompted (Figure 10-16) you will have the ability to deploy only as a farm solution.

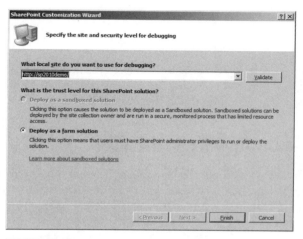

FIGURE 10-16

Additional Tools

Microsoft provides some additional tools, including the BCS Solution Packaging tool, which allows you to package and deploy declarative solutions. The BCS Artifact Generator is also available. Both tools are referenced in the Microsoft SharePoint Server 2010 Software Development Kit (SDK). The SDK itself is an invaluable tool and contains a wealth of documentation, sample code, and examples.

BEHIND-THE-SCENES COMPONENTS OF BCS

An architect needs to understand a number of components to plan and create a successful BCS solution. Although a deep dive into each of these topics is outside the scope of this chapter, a brief explanation of each follows:

➤ **Business Data Connectivity Service:** Although the previous version of the BCS was called the Business Data Catalog (BDC), this specific feature set within BCS is also referred to as BDC, though the acronym has a different meaning. This service is the framework for building BCS solutions. The BDC facilitates connectivity between the data source and the various building blocks that consume business data (including Web Parts, external lists, search, and so on).

➤ **Metadata Store:** The Metadata Store is a database provisioned by the service application to store metadata regarding the various BCS entities that are defined. It does not store any external data or cached data from line-of-business systems.

➤ **BDC connectors:** These are the components that actually talk to line-of-business data sources. Out-of-the-box SharePoint 2010 ships with connectors for talking to databases, WCF web services, and .NET assemblies. Third-party vendors can also build and distribute additional connectors for their systems.

➤ **BCS client run time:** Whenever external data is being accessed on the client through Office applications, the line-of-business data is not actually traveling through SharePoint;

rather the data is being accessed directly from the client's machine through a client run time. This client run time also can be configured to leverage a client cache to improve performance.

➤ **Secure Store Service:** This is the successor to SharePoint 2007's Single Sign On feature. The Secure Store allows you to map individuals or groups to a single set of credentials, simplifying the login process to external data sources.

BCS ADMINISTRATION

Several tools are available to help administrators configure and maintain BCS. The first two you learn about are familiar to farm administrators and the third option speaks to the flexibility of BCS from a development perspective.

SharePoint Central Administration

In SharePoint 2007, the Business Data Catalog was managed as part of SharePoint's Shared Services model. A Shared Service Provider management web application was provisioned, and from there administrators could manage shared services like the BDC and search. With the release of SharePoint 2010, the Shared Services model has changed to a Service Application model. A number of service applications can be created and mapped to web applications, allowing for a more scalable configuration. All the service applications are managed from the Central Administration website.

One of the service applications is the Business Data Connectivity Service, which is accessible from the Application Management section of the Central Administration website (Figure 10-17). Using the management screens, administrators can configure components of BCS including permissions for ECTs, creating Profile pages, and managing BCS actions.

FIGURE 10-17

One of the first things an administrator will want to do is to configure the permissions for the Metadata Store, which can be found on the Ribbon of the Service Application Information screen (Figure 10-18). External Content Types created in SharePoint Designer will inherit the permission settings on the Metadata Store, so it's important that these settings are configured before creating your first ECT.

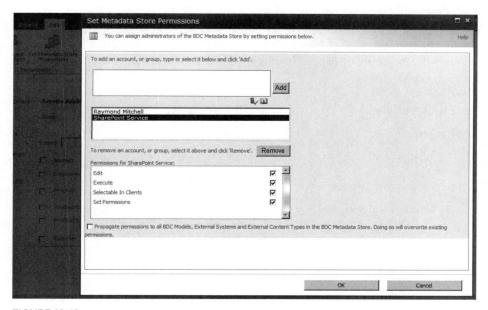

FIGURE 10-18

One of the other powerful options surfaced in Central Administration is the ability to export and import BCS model files. In simple applications your BCS model is created for you in SharePoint Designer and remains behind the scenes unless you go looking for it. If you have a multi-region environment, your process might be:

1. Create your BCS model using SharePoint Designer in your development region.

2. Export the BCS model file (which is XML but has a .bdcm file extension).

3. Edit the contents of the file and make any region-specific configuration changes to the external system.

4. Import the BCS model file into your test/stage/production region.

By using this approach you can ensure the consistent creation of your BCS models from one region to another. Another benefit of this approach is the ability to store your BCS models in source control in between Steps 2 and 3 in the foregoing list.

PowerShell and STSADM

Two command line administration tools are available in SharePoint 2010:

➤ **STSADM:** This is a deprecated tool that was the core command line tool available in earlier versions of SharePoint.

➤ **SharePoint 2010 Management Shell:** This is a customized Windows PowerShell console that includes SharePoint-related snap-ins.

Because the STSADM tool has been deprecated, administrators should use the SharePoint 2010 Management Shell whenever possible. A number of cmdlets (Table 10-3) are available for working with BCS, but they will likely only be needed in advanced scenarios when automation is required.

TABLE 10-3: Example BCS cmdlets

COMMAND	DESCRIPTION
Disable-SPBusinessDataCatalogEntity	Disables an External Content Type
Import-SPBusinessDataCatalogModel	Imports a BCS model file
Grant-SPBusinessDataCatalogMetadataObject	Gives permissions to an object in the Metadata Store
Set-SPBusinessDataCatalogMetadataObject	Sets a property for an object in the Metadata Store

BCS Administration Object Model

Another resource that is available for advanced scenarios is a rich Administration Object model that is made available for developers. The model exists in the form of a DLL that can be referenced in custom-developed .NET applications. The namespace Microsoft.SharePoint.BusinessData .Administration contains a number of classes that allow developers to interact with the Metadata Store programmatically.

FEATURE DIFFERENCES BY PRODUCT

In SharePoint 2007, the Business Data Catalog was only available with the enterprise license. With the 2010 release, the core Business Connectivity Services are available with all editions of SharePoint (Foundation, Server, and Server Enterprise). Details follow on what is supported with each edition:

➤ **SharePoint Foundation 2010:** The core framework for the BCS is included with SharePoint Foundation. This framework supports the creation of models, entities, and External Content Types. Using SharePoint Foundation you also have access to create external lists and external data columns.

➤ **SharePoint Server 2010 Standard Edition:** In addition to the functionality available in Foundation, SharePoint Server Standard also supports the creation of Profile pages and the ability to search your external data sources. The Secure Store Service is also available with this edition.

➤ **SharePoint Server 2010 Enterprise Edition:** In addition to the functionality available in SharePoint Server Standard, the Enterprise edition also supports the Business Data Web Parts and deeper integration with Office clients.

SUMMARY

This chapter introduced Business Connectivity Services and the various components that can make up a BCS solution. It discussed how the BCS fits with the Composites strategy and what some of the potential solution types are that can be built with BCS.

Armed with the understanding of what the various components of BCS are and in general how they are used, Chapter 11 walks through scenarios that show how to use the key components in various BCS solution types.

11

Building Solutions Using Business Connectivity Services

WHAT'S IN THIS CHAPTER?

- ➤ Learn how to assemble out-of-the-box BCS building blocks into solutions
- ➤ Review steps to build External Content Types (ECT) using SharePoint Designer 2010 and Visual Studio 2010
- ➤ Understand how to extend Office using external data and BCS

In Chapter 10 you were introduced to Business Connectivity Services (BCS) and the types of solutions that can be built using BCS. This chapter walks you through several scenarios to show how you can build solutions using BCS. A detailed walk-through of each solution is beyond the scope of this book; however, this chapter should provide you with the guidance you need to decide which methods might be appropriate for your business needs.

BCS BUILDING BLOCKS: DEEP DIVE

The first solutions explored here leverage some of the out-of-the-box building blocks discussed in the previous chapter. For simplicity the walk-throughs in this section assume any entities used already exist in the environment — you explore creating entities later in this chapter.

Walk-Through: Using External Lists

Once an External Content Type exists, one of the most common next steps is to create an external list using the ECT. You have several ways to create an external list, but this walk-through uses only the browser. To get started, browse to a site where you have designer or full-control permissions. From the Site Actions menu, select More Options to bring up the Create dialog. To make it easier to find, you may want to select the List option to filter by, as shown in Figure 11-1. Select External List from the installed items window and click Create.

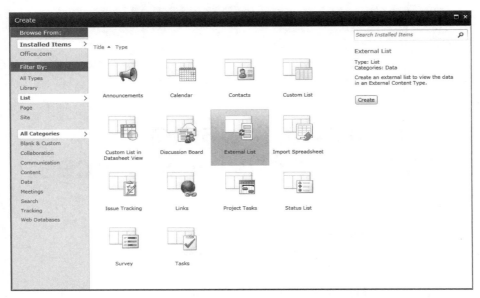

FIGURE 11-1

The next screen allows you to configure your external list. Figure 11-2 shows the sample configuration values. In addition to Name and Description (common fields when creating a traditional list), you also can specify a data source (an External Content Type). The External Content Type Picker control allows you to view a list of all installed ECTs and choose the appropriate data source.

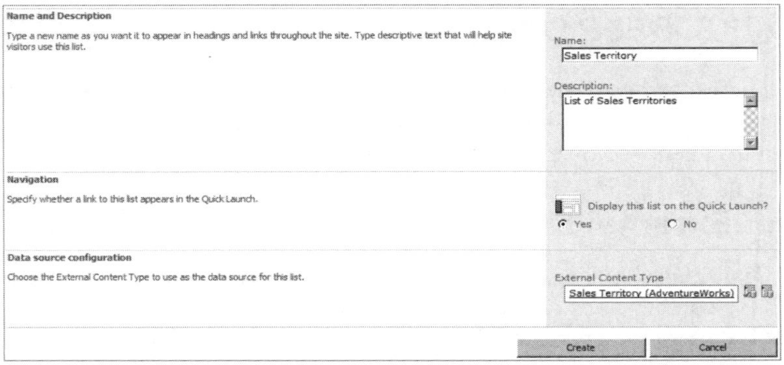

FIGURE 11-2

After clicking Create, your external list is created and displayed using the default view as shown in Figure 11-3. A few clicks will show you that the external list acts very much like a traditional list. You can sort by each of the columns, apply filters, and navigate to individual items just as you would with a traditional list.

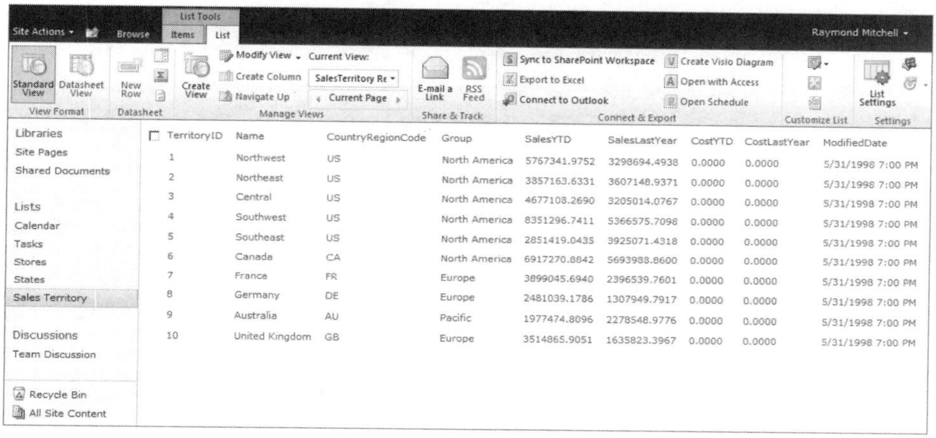

FIGURE 11-3

One piece of functionality you might expect to have is the ability to change column names and their order. In a traditional list this would be configurable on the List Settings screen. Note that for an external list the column names, types, and order appear fixed as shown in Figure 11-4. To change any of those options you need to modify the related External Content Type (specifically the Read List and Read Item operations). Creating operations is discussed in detail later in this chapter.

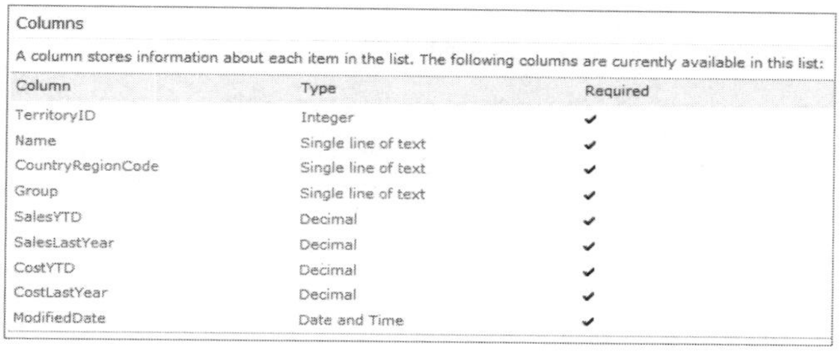

FIGURE 11-4

One important piece of functionality you do get with an external list is the ability to define new views. On the List Tools section and List tab of the Ribbon, select Create View. Just as with a traditional list, you can select a view format or choose to start from an existing view. For this example, choose to start with the SalesTerritory Read List view. You will need to give your view a name (United States in this example), and then you'll have the ability to select columns and their order. Uncheck CountryRegionCode and Group as shown in Figure 11-5.

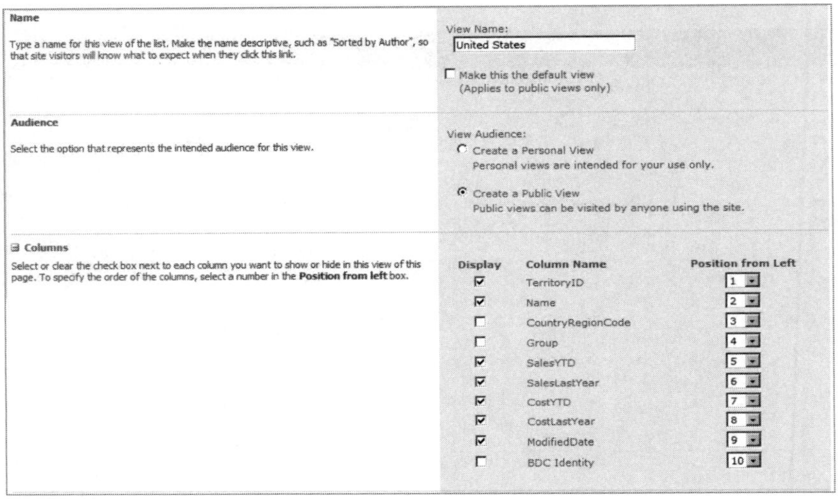

FIGURE 11-5

Next you can define a filter to ensure that only sales territories from the United States appear. To do this, select CountryRegionCode, select "is equal to," and type the value "US" as shown in Figure 11-6.

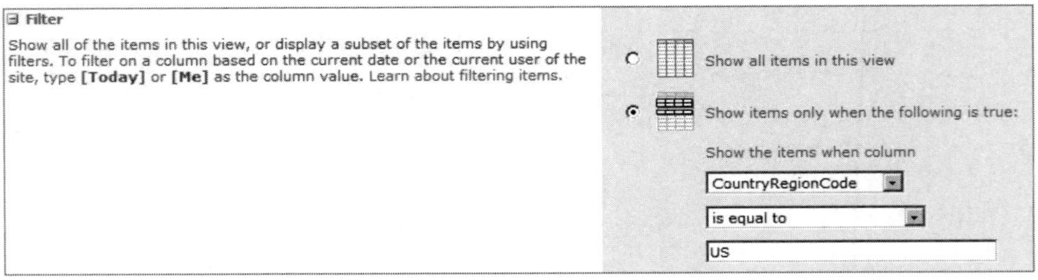

FIGURE 11-6

Click OK to save your view and your new, filtered view will be displayed. Views are an easy way to create powerful data visualizations through filtering, sorting, and grouping.

Walk-Through: Using BCS Data Columns

Another very useful feature of External Content Types is the ability to add a field from an ECT to a traditional list or library. In this example, you add a sales territory to a standard document library. Browse to the Shared Documents library, and when you are on the default view for the document library, select Library Settings from the Library tab in the Library Tools section of the Ribbon. This will bring up the Library Settings screen. Scroll down to the Columns section (shown in Figure 11-7) and select Create Column.

Columns

A column stores information about each document in the document library. The following columns are currently available in this document library:

Column (click to edit)	Type	Required
Title	Single line of text	
Created By	Person or Group	
Modified By	Person or Group	
Checked Out To	Person or Group	

Create column
Add from existing site columns
Column ordering
Indexed columns

FIGURE 11-7

On the Create Column screen you can choose what kind of column you want to create. To add a BCS data column, select External Data for the type. Once you have selected External Data, a new configuration section will display with an External Content Type picker. Once you have selected the Sales Territory ECT, the list of fields to be shown will be populated. From this, Name should be selected as shown in Figure 11-8.

SharePoint 2010 supports a new feature when using External Data or Lookup fields; this is the ability to display additional fields alongside lookup values. In this scenario, CountryRegionCode and Group are also selected, so those fields will also show up in your views alongside the BCS data column. Click OK to save the change to the document library, and then browse back to the Shared Documents library. Your fields will already display, but any existing content will not have a value to display. Click a sample document and choose to edit the properties. On the edit form your new column will be displayed as an External Data Picker control. Select

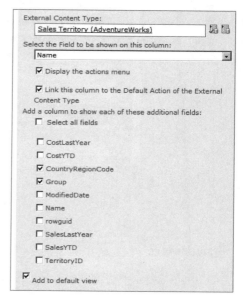

FIGURE 11-8

a sales territory and save your changes. When you return to the default view, you should see data displayed in the three new columns shown in Figure 11-9.

FIGURE 11-9

You can now add powerful metadata from external systems to your SharePoint lists and libraries. Later in this chapter you'll explore how to surface BCS data columns inside your document content as updatable External Data Picker controls.

Walk-Through: Using BCS Web Parts

Next you explore how to use the out-of-the-box Business Data Web Parts to create an interactive dashboard page. The first thing you need to do is create your dashboard page. To create the page, select Create Page from the Site Actions menu and then enter a page name (we'll use "Dashboard") when prompted. Before creating any content it's a good idea to determine the layout of the page you want to use. For this example, select Two Columns from the Text Layout drop-down on the Format Text Ribbon as shown in Figure 11-10.

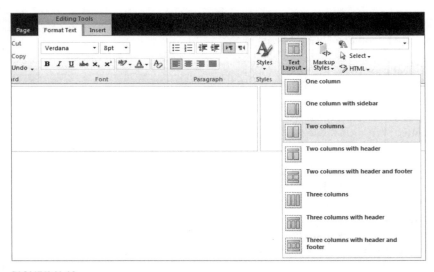

FIGURE 11-10

Now that your dashboard page exists, you can add Business Data Web Parts to it. Click the table cell on the left and select the Insert tab from the Editing Tools section of the Ribbon. Choose Web Part and then browse to the Business Data category. Choose to add a Business Data list and click Add.

Now that the Web Part has been added, you are given a link to open the tool pane and configure the Web Part. Click the link and open the tool pane. From the Business Data List tool pane, configure the Web Part to display the Sales.

Note that Display Animation While Loading is *not* checked in this example. The option to display a loading animation is useful when your data may take a long time to load (relative to the loading of a web page). In this instance the data should load within a second or two, so you may choose not to display the loading animation that some users may find distracting.

The Sales Territory Web Part is now displaying the default view as defined by its default Read List operation. Because you're going to have multiple Web Parts on the page, you should reduce the number of fields that are being displayed. From the Web Part's drop-down menu choose Edit Web Part to enter edit mode. Once in this mode, the Edit View link is displayed, and when clicked you are taken to an Edit View screen. From the Edit View screen, make the changes shown in Figure 11-12 to display fewer fields and also to pick a title field. You can also take this opportunity to define any sorting or filtering you want to do.

FIGURE 11-11

Now that your Sales Territory Web Part has been added and configured, add another Web Part that can show what states are in each territory. You may have to enter edit mode again by selecting Edit Page from the Site Actions menu. Click the table cell on the right and select the Insert tab from the Editing Tools section of the Ribbon. Choose Web Part and then browse to the Business Data category. Choose to add a Business Data Related list and click Add. As with the Business Data List Web Part, you must now configure your Related List Web Part. Click the link to open the tool pane and configure the Web Part to use the StateProvince ECT and the default association shown in Figure 11-13.

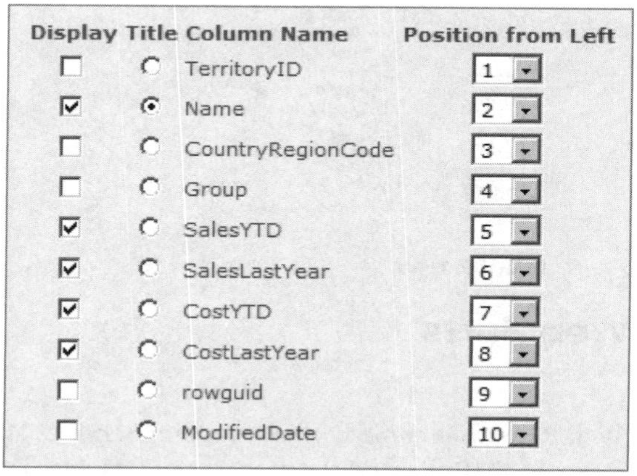

FIGURE 11-12

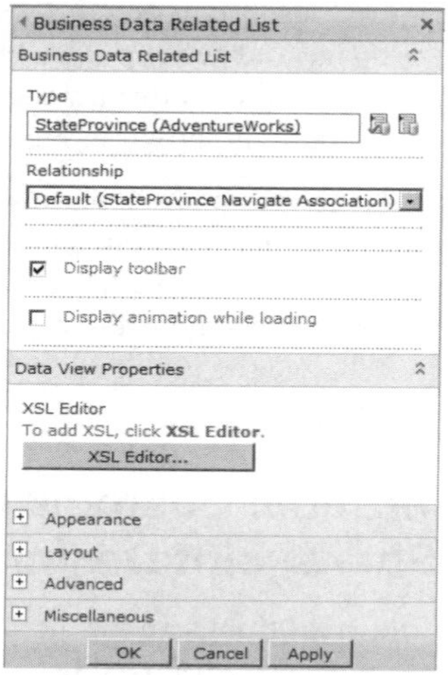

FIGURE 11-13

Again you will want to limit the columns that are being displayed. Select the Edit Web Part from the Web Parts menu and once in edit mode, select Edit View. Modify the columns as shown in Figure 11-14.

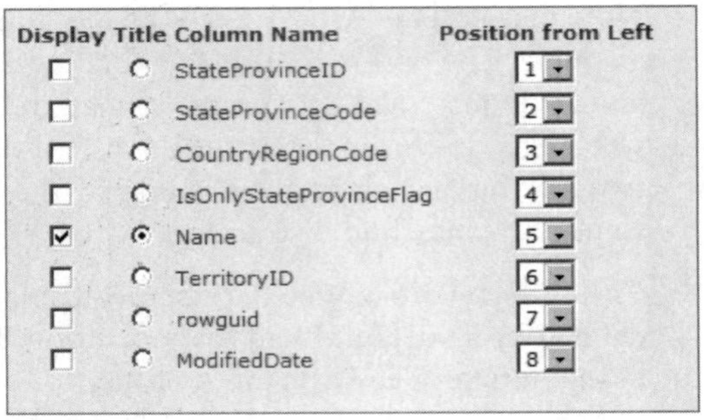

Display Title	Column Name	Position from Left
☐ ○	StateProvinceID	1 ▾
☐ ○	StateProvinceCode	2 ▾
☐ ○	CountryRegionCode	3 ▾
☐ ○	IsOnlyStateProvinceFlag	4 ▾
☑ ●	Name	5 ▾
☐ ○	TerritoryID	6 ▾
☐ ○	rowguid	7 ▾
☐ ○	ModifiedDate	8 ▾

FIGURE 11-14

Now that the view has been configured, you must connect the two related Web Parts. Again, enter edit mode by selecting Edit Page from the Site Actions menu. Choose Edit Web Part from the Sales Territory list. Next, configure part-to-part connections by selecting Connections ➪ Send Selected Item To ➪ StateProvince List as shown in Figure 11-15. Select Save and exit edit mode from the Ribbon to display the page in browse mode.

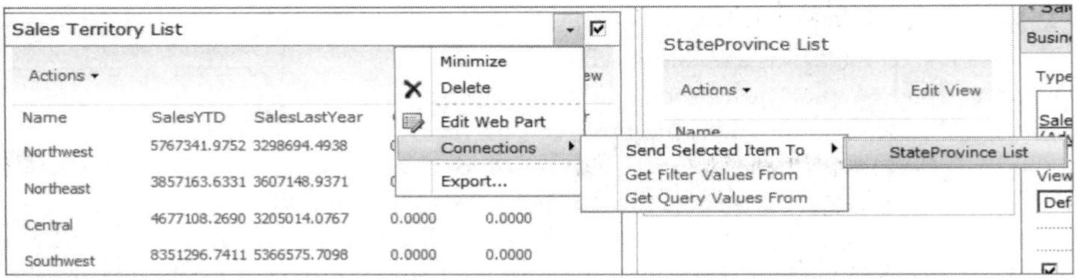

FIGURE 11-15

As configured, users can now browse to this dashboard page and select a sales territory from the left, which will then display the related states on the right as shown in Figure 11-16.

Creating dashboard pages like these are a key piece of the Composites strategy discussed in Chapter 10. You can also add non-business-data Web Parts to the dashboard to add additional content or change the look and feel of the dashboard page.

FIGURE 11-16

Walk-Through: Customizing BCS Web Parts Using SharePoint Designer

One of the great things about the Business Data Web Parts that come with SharePoint Server 2010 is their ability to be customized using SharePoint Designer 2010. Behind the scenes, the Business Data Web Parts rely on XSLT to control how the Web Part should be rendered. SharePoint Designer is a great tool for customizing XSLT, and in many cases it can customize the XSLT in its design view. In other words, SharePoint Designer lets you customize the XSLT without requiring you to know the details of how the XSLT itself is being changed.

This example walks through how to customize the way individual fields are being rendered in a Business Data List Web Part. To get started, browse to the dashboard page created in the previous section. Once on the page, choose Edit in SharePoint Designer from the Site Actions menu. This will open SharePoint Designer but will not open the dashboard page you created. From the Site Objects navigation, select Site Pages and then click the Dashboard.aspx page. Under Customization, select Edit File to open the page in design mode.

Once in edit mode, you'll make two changes. The first is to update the format of the SalesYTD, SalesLastYear, CostYTD, and CostLastYear fields. Right now those fields are being displayed simply as text. To improve the display you should choose to format them as currency instead. Click one of the values in the SalesYTD column (XSLT is a template language, so by modifying any of the rows you will actually be configuring all of the rows). Now right-click the value (which should select the value) and choose Format Item As ➪ Currency as shown in Figure 11-17. Keep the default values and click OK. Make the same change to the other three columns (SalesLastYear, CostYTD, and CostLastYear).

FIGURE 11-17

The second change you'll make is to apply conditional formatting to the SalesYTD field. Conditional formatting allows you to specify a condition based on values in your data set. If the condition(s) is met, formatting can be applied such as highlighting, changing text size/decoration, or showing/hiding content. To configure conditional formatting, place your cursor inside one of the SalesYTD cells, and from the Ribbon click the Conditional Formatting dropdown and select Format Column. This opens the Condition Criteria dialog box where you'll specify your condition. In this scenario, your condition should be specified as shown in Figure 11-18, which evaluates as true if the SalesYTDfield is greater than 4,000,000.

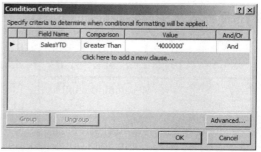

FIGURE 11-18

To define a style, click the Set Style button. The Modify Style dialog allows you to specify a number of possible style characteristics. For this example, select Background as the category and choose a nice shade of green, then click OK to save your change. Next, walk through the same steps to add an additional conditional formatting rule such that if the SalesYTD field is less than 2,000,000 a less-nice shade of red is displayed. Click

Save to commit your changes, then browse back to your dashboard page to see the changes. (Note that because this book does not have color, screenshots display only in black and white.) In Figure 11-19 you can see that the conditional formatting has been applied.

As you can see, SharePoint Designer and specifically conditional formatting allows you to create very rich data visualizations. As you can see in Figure 11-20, the changes you made visually in SharePoint Designer were actually translated into the appropriate XSLT. This means that developers with XSLT experience can make even more advanced data visualizations.

Sales Territory List

Actions ▾

Name	SalesYTD	SalesLastYear	CostYTD	CostLastYear
Northwest	$5,767,341.98	$3,298,694.49	$0.00	$0.00
Northeast	$3,857,163.63	$3,607,148.94	$0.00	$0.00
Central	$4,677,108.27	$3,205,014.08	$0.00	$0.00
Southwest	$8,351,296.74	$5,366,575.71	$0.00	$0.00
Southeast	$2,851,419.04	$3,925,071.43	$0.00	$0.00
Canada	$6,917,270.88	$5,693,988.86	$0.00	$0.00
France	$3,899,045.69	$2,396,539.76	$0.00	$0.00
Germany	$2,481,039.18	$1,307,949.79	$0.00	$0.00
Australia	$1,977,474.81	$2,278,548.98	$0.00	$0.00
United Kingdom	$3,514,865.91	$1,635,823.40	$0.00	$0.00

FIGURE 11-19

```
<td class="ms-vb">
  <xsl:attribute name="style">
    <xsl:choose>
      <xsl:when test="$dvt_1_form_selectkey = @*[name()=$ColumnKey]">color:blue;</xsl:when>
      <xsl:otherwise />
    </xsl:choose>
      <xsl:if test="@SalesYTD &gt; '4000000'">background-color: #89DF5F;</xsl:if>

      <xsl:if test="@SalesYTD &lt; '2000000'">background-color: #FF0000;</xsl:if>

      </xsl:attribute>
  <xsl:value-of select="format-number(@SalesYTD, &quot;$#,##0.00;-$#,##0.00&quot;)" />
</td>
```

FIGURE 11-20

BUILDING ENTITIES

This section looks at how to create BCS entities using both SharePoint Designer 2010 and Visual Studio 2010. The examples connect to data in a Microsoft SQL Server database. To give you the option to try these walk-throughs on your own, the scenarios reference the Adventure Works database.

This database is freely available as part of the Microsoft SQL Server Community Projects and Samples Portal, which you can access here: `http://sqlserversamples.codeplex.com`. You can download the sample database from here: `http://msftdbprodsamples.codeplex.com`. Releases are available for multiple versions of Microsoft SQL Server, including 2005, 2008, and 2008 R2 at the time of this writing.

Configuring Permissions

Before you attempt to use the sample data, you should first ensure that you will have the appropriate access to the sample database. This of course assumes you have both the access to and the knowledge of how to configure permissions in Microsoft SQL Server. In many environments you will instead need to work with your database administrator to configure the appropriate level of access. Do the following:

➤ Make sure the consuming users have read-and-write access to the sample database.

➤ To enable searching later, ensure that the default content access account has read access to the sample database. You'll review this later when you look at configuring search.

In addition to database permissions, you also need to configure permission to the BCS Metadata Store. This was briefly discussed in Chapter 10 under the section "SharePoint Central Administration." Again, both the consuming users and the default content access account will need permissions defined; in this case both will need Execute permissions as shown in Figure 11-21.

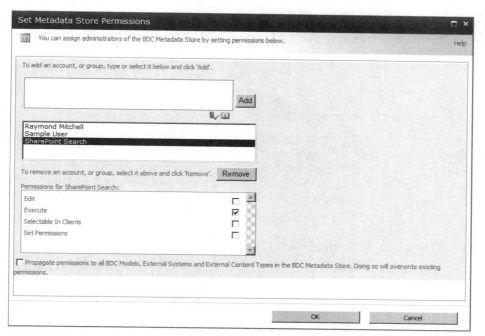

FIGURE 11-21

You will need access to at least one SharePoint site that you can open in SharePoint Designer. This means you need to be at least a contributor on the site, though this scenario will assume design or full control, which allows you to create additional pages, lists, and libraries. Later, when you're building solutions with Visual Studio 2010, your account will need access to deploy farm-level solutions to your local SharePoint server.

Building BCS Solutions with SharePoint Designer 2010

SharePoint Designer is the ideal tool for quickly building External Content Types. This walk-through shows how to expose the Sales.SalesTerritory table (shown in Figure 11-22) as an External Content Type. Then it goes on to add a States ECT that reads from the Person.StateProvince table. Finally, an association will be created between the two ECTs.

	TerritoryID	Name	CountryRegionCode	Group	SalesYTD	SalesLastYear
1	1	Northwest	US	North America	5767341.9752	3298694.4938
2	2	Northeast	US	North America	3857163.6331	3607148.9371
3	3	Central	US	North America	4677108.269	3205014.0767
4	4	Southwest	US	North America	8351296.7411	5366575.7098
5	5	Southeast	US	North America	2851419.0435	3925071.4318
6	6	Canada	CA	North America	6917270.8842	5693988.86
7	7	France	FR	Europe	3899045.694	2396539.7601
8	8	Germany	DE	Europe	2481039.1786	1307949.7917
9	9	Australia	AU	Pacific	1977474.8096	2278548.9776
10	10	United Kingdom	GB	Europe	3514865.9051	1635823.3967

FIGURE 11-22

Open a Site in SharePoint Designer 2010

Before you can work with External Content Types in SharePoint Designer, you must first open a site. When External Content Types are created, they are available to all web applications that are associated with the same BCS service application. Because many environments will have only a single BCS service application (the default configuration), which site you open will be up to you. As a general rule you should open the site where you want to consume the External Content Type that you are creating. To open a site, choose Open Site and enter the URL of the site you want to open.

Configure External System in SharePoint Designer

Although an external system must exist before you can build an External Content Type, you must choose to create an External Content Type in SharePoint Designer before you can be presented with the screen for creating and managing external systems.

To manage ECTs, select External Content Types from the Site Objects navigation pane. As discussed in Chapter 10, this brings up the summary view for a new ECT (Figure 11-23).

Before defining any operations, you must define an external system. Switch to the Operations Design view by using the navigation option in the Views section of the Ribbon. Now choose Add

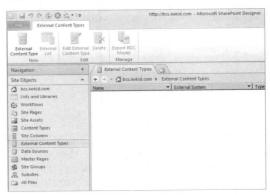

FIGURE 11-23

Connection to define an external data source. A dialog will display (shown in Figure 11-24) asking what data source type you would like to use. In this scenario, select SQL Server.

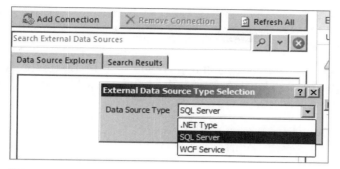

FIGURE 11-24

A SQL Server Connection dialog will then display (Figure 11-25), which allows you to configure the name of the database server and the database you want to access. You are also presented with your choice of authentication methods. For simplicity choose Connect with the User's Identity.

The other two authentication methods use the Secure Store. As discussed in Chapter 10, the Secure Store is the evolution of the Single Sign On feature available in SharePoint 2007. The Secure Store can be used to map a single user (or a group of users) to a single set of shared credentials. For example, if your organization has an Active Directory group called Finance that contains all the employees from the Finance Department, the Secure Store could be configured to recognize those employees and use a shared set of credentials to access the external system.

Now the Data Source Explorer (visible on the Operations Design view) shows the new external system as shown in Figure 11-26. From the Data Source Explorer you can browse the tables and views that you have access to in the external database.

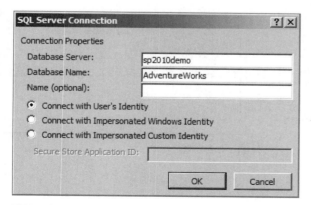

FIGURE 11-25

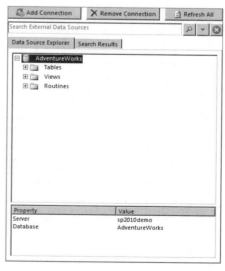

FIGURE 11-26

Create the SalesTerritory Entity

Now that an external system is configured, you can continue with creating an External Content Type. Switch back to the summary view using the Views section of the Ribbon and fill in the Name and Display Name fields as shown in Figure 11-27. The default options will work for the rest of the properties (the Office Item type is discussed more later). Note that the default value for Namespace will match the URL of the site you are currently on.

External Content Type Information		^
Key information about this external content type.		
Name	SalesTerritory	
Display Name	Sales Territory	
Namespace	http://bcs.iwkid.com	
Version	1.0.0.0	
Identifiers	There are no identifiers defined.	
Office Item Type	Generic List	▼
Offline Sync for external list	Enabled	▼
External System	Click here to discover external data s...	

FIGURE 11-27

The next step is to create operations. Switch back to the Operations Design view and expand the Tables element and find the SalesTerritory table. Right-clicking the table enables you to define different types of operations. Remember from Chapter 10 that at a minimum an ECT requires the Read List and Read Item operations if it will be used for read-only scenarios. For this scenario you want to support both read and write operations so the fastest way to do that is to select Create All Operations as shown in Figure 11-28.

This brings up an Operation Configuration Wizard that steps you through the process of configuring your operations. To keep things simple, leave the default options. Once you click Finish, your ECT will be configured with five separate operations:

➤ Create

➤ Update

➤ Delete

FIGURE 11-28

➤ Read List

➤ Read Item

The last thing you'll need to do is to save your changes by clicking the Save icon (or by using the Save button that is accessible on the File tab of the Ribbon). Saving actually publishes your ECT to the BCS Metadata Store and makes it available for use.

Create the StateProvince Entity

Creating a second External Content Type is much easier because the external system has already been defined. To create another ECT, navigate to External Content Types in the Site Objects navigation pane. Choose to create a new External Content Type from the Ribbon and enter a name of StateProvince as shown in Figure 11-29.

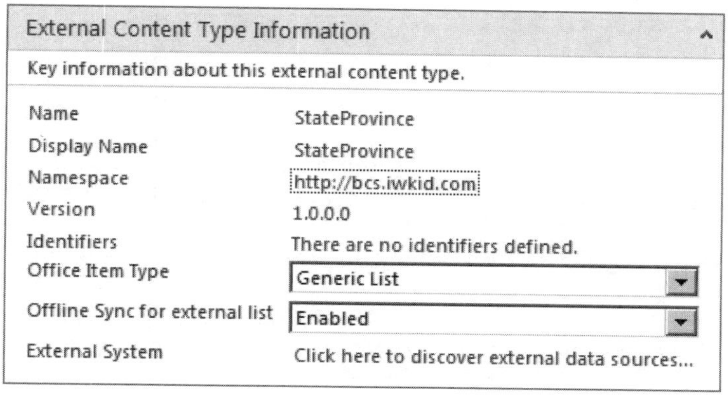

FIGURE 11-29

Just as when you created the Sales Territory ECT, the next step is to create operations. Switch back to the Operations Design view and expand the Tables element and find the StateProvince table. Right-clicking the table enables you to define different types of operations. For this ECT you want only the ability to read the data, so you need to create the required two read operations individually.

First, right-click the table and choose New Read List Operation. When the Operation Configuration Wizard pops up, choose Next to display the Filter Parameters screen as shown in Figure 11-30. Choose Add Filter Parameter to add a new parameter. Here you want to create a filter that will allow you to select only states in the United States.

From the Data Source Element drop-down, select CountryRegionCode. Next to Filter, click the Click to Add hyperlink to configure the filter. Name the filter CountryRegionCode and check the Is Default checkbox. Then click OK. For the Default Value field, enter US. The resulting parameter configuration should look similar to Figure 11-31.

Read List
Operation Properties
Filter Parameters
Return Parameter
Filter Parameters Configuration
Configure filter parameters and default values to define the default behavior of the query and enable user customizations.
Filter Parameters
Operator
Element
Filter
Properties
Add Filter Parameter
Remove Filter Parameter
Errors and Warnings
It is strongly recommended to add a filter of type 'Limit' for this operation type. Without a limit filter, this operation may result in large result sets.
To configure Return Parameter, click Next.
< Back
Next >
Finish
Cancel

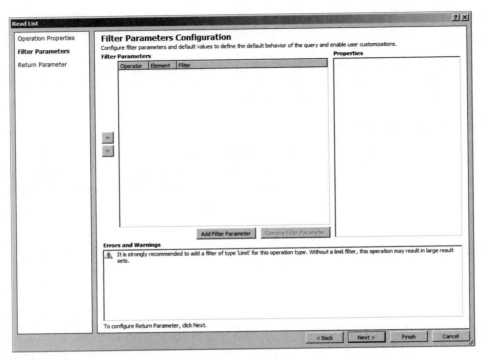

FIGURE 11-30

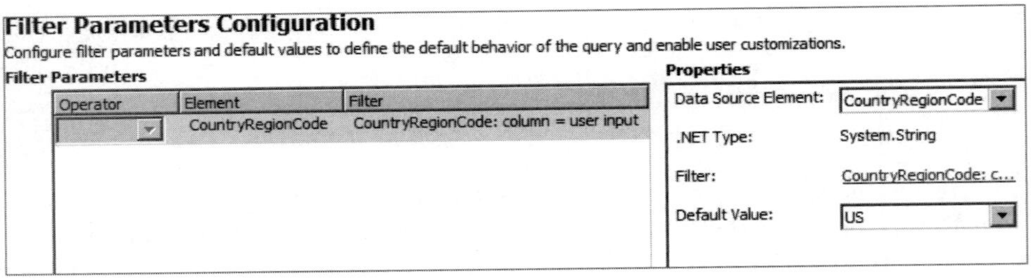

Filter Parameters Configuration
Configure filter parameters and default values to define the default behavior of the query and enable user customizations.
Filter Parameters
Operator
Element
Filter
CountryRegionCode
CountryRegionCode: column = user input
Properties
Data Source Element:
CountryRegionCode
.NET Type:
System.String
Filter:
CountryRegionCode: c...
Default Value:
US

FIGURE 11-31

Click Finish to exit the Operation Configuration Wizard and save your ECT. To make sure this ECT can be used, you need to add one more operation. Right-click the StateProvince table and choose New Read Item Operation. When the Operation Configuration Wizard pops up, you can click Finish to complete the operation with the default values. Notice in Figure 11-32 that you now have two operations defined, and you also get a notification that your ECT is ready to be used in external lists. Save your ECT.

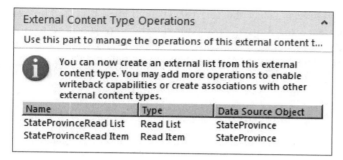

FIGURE 11-32

Create Association

Now that you have two External Content Types with a relationship (both share a TerritoryID), you can create an association between the two. Associations are created in much the same way as operations. While still configuring the StateProvince ECT, right-click the StateProvince table again and select New Association as shown in Figure 11-33.

In the Association Configuration Wizard, click Browse to select a related External Content Type. Choose SalesTerritory and notice that the related identifier is automatically populated in Figure 11-34.

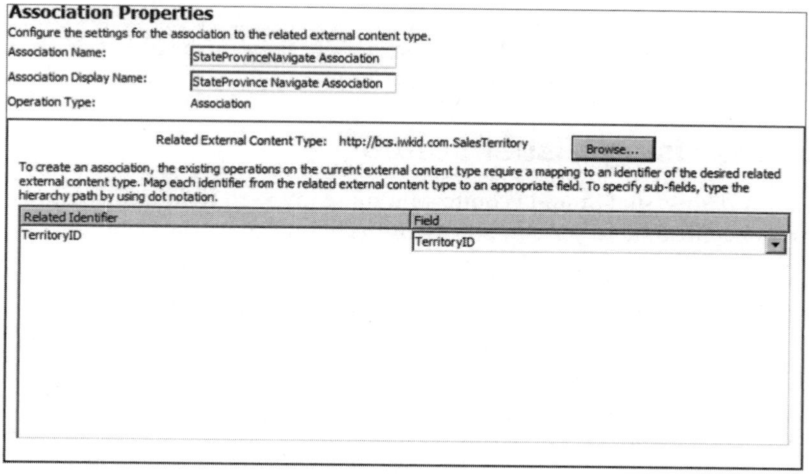

FIGURE 11-33

Association Properties

Configure the settings for the association to the related external content type.

Association Name:	StateProvinceNavigate Association
Association Display Name:	StateProvince Navigate Association
Operation Type:	Association

Related External Content Type: http://bcs.iwkid.com.SalesTerritory   Browse...

To create an association, the existing operations on the current external content type require a mapping to an identifier of the desired related external content type. Map each identifier from the related external content type to an appropriate field. To specify sub-fields, type the hierarchy path by using dot notation.

Related Identifier	Field
TerritoryID	TerritoryID

FIGURE 11-34

Click Next, and on the Input Parameters screen, select the TerritoryID field and check the box for Map to Identifier. Click Next until you reach the Return Parameter screen. Here you need to further define the relationship between the two ECTs. Select the TerritoryID field and in the Properties window click the Click to Add hyperlink after Foreign Identifier. Choose to select a foreign identifier, then select SalesTerritory as the referenced External Content Type and StateProvince as the Association External Content Type. The final configuration should look similar to Figure 11-35. Now you can click Finish and save your changes to complete the association.

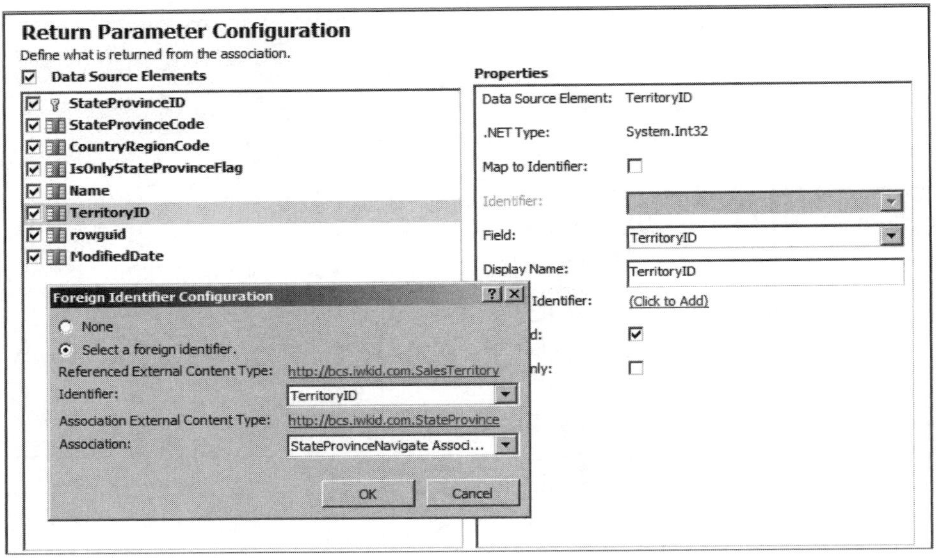

FIGURE 11-35

You have now seen how to create ECTs using SharePoint Designer 2010. In the next section, you learn how to create a very simple ECT using Visual Studio 2010.

Building BCS Solutions Using Visual Studio

The process for creating an ECT in Visual Studio is quite a bit more involved than using SharePoint Designer. A number of factors contribute to the complexity of the approach:

➤ In SharePoint Designer you are presented with the option to create external systems and External Content Types. Visual Studio allows you to create only a BCS Model. Behind the scenes SharePoint Designer is also creating a BCS Model; however, SharePoint Designer presents you with a more simplified view.

➤ There are no wizards to create all operations quickly — you must create each operation by hand.

➤ You must write code to define your operations.

Though more complex, the ability to build BCS Models using .NET code provides a great deal of power and flexibility. Consider scenarios in which you need to connect to multiple services or databases. A wizard-driven approach to connecting with these various data sources is unlikely to meet all your needs. With custom code, you have the flexibility to do whatever is required to return the necessary data in whatever format is required.

The next example is a very simplified one meant to illustrate the difference in techniques and is not meant to be an in-depth exercise, which is well beyond the scope of this book. The example will, however, create a usable BCS Model.

Create the Store Entity

To begin, open Visual Studio 2010 and select Business Data Connectivity Model from the list of installed Visual Studio project templates. Provide a name and location and then click OK to create the project as shown in Figure 11-36.

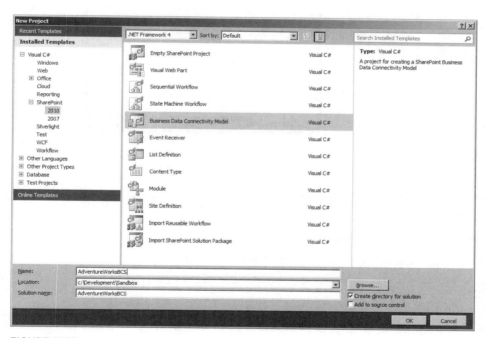

FIGURE 11-36

You will be prompted to select what type of solution should be generated, sandbox or farm. Because BDC Model Solutions apply to the entire farm you will have only the option to deploy as a farm solution. Enter the URL of a local SharePoint server and choose Validate to confirm that you have connectivity and access. Click Finish and your project will be created.

After your project has been created, you will see the BCS Model Browser in the main design window (shown on the left in Figure 11-37). You will also see the BDC Explorer window (shown on the right in Figure 11-37). Because the Business Data Connectivity Model Visual Studio project template contains sample data, you will see sample values appearing in both windows.

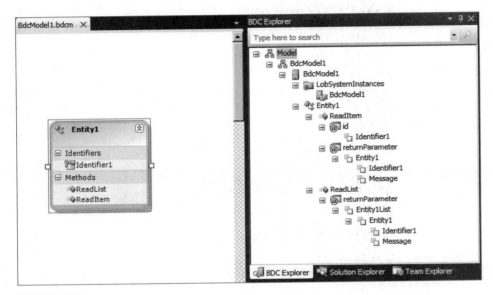

FIGURE 11-37

To configure the BCS Model you can start by renaming the existing objects. You'll make the required updates in three steps:

➤ Update the Model Browser window.

   ➤ Change the name of the entity from Entity1 to Store.

   ➤ Change the identifier name from Identifier1 to CustomerID.

➤ Update the BDC Explorer objects.

   ➤ Rename the three instances of Idenifier1 to CustomerID by selecting the objects and modifying their Name property in the Properties window.

   ➤ Rename the two instances of Message to Name.

   ➤ Rename the two instances of Entity1 to Store.

   ➤ Rename the instance of Entity1List to StoreList.

➤ Update the related code-behind files.

    ➤ Rename the Entity1.cs file to Store.cs.

    ➤ Open the Store.cs file and make the following changes:

        ➤ Rename the property Identifier1 to CustomerID. When making the change, allow Visual Studio to handle the rename action across all references as shown in Figure 11-38.

        ➤ Rename the property Message to Name.

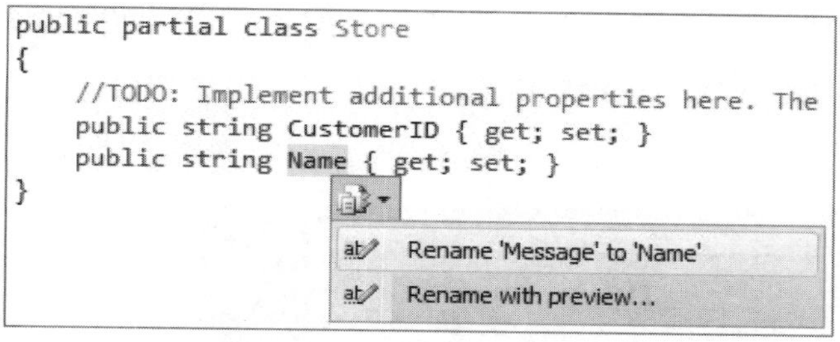

```
public partial class Store
{
    //TODO: Implement additional properties here. The
    public string CustomerID { get; set; }
    public string Name { get; set; }
}
```

ab/ Rename 'Message' to 'Name'

ab/ Rename with preview...

FIGURE 11-38

Once these changes have been made your model should look like Figure 11-39, and selecting Build Solution from the Build file menu should yield no build errors.

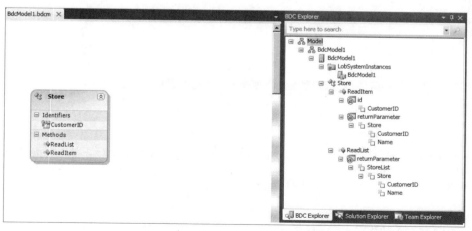

FIGURE 11-39

Next you'll look at the StoreService.cs file, which contains the sample code provided by Visual Studio. You'll notice that there is one method defined for each of the operations defined in the Model Browser window (ReadList and ReadItem). Each of these methods has been configured to return sample Store entities. Ideally, each of these methods would contain the required actions needed to open a Store from the AdventureWorks database, but for simplicity you will work with just the sample data.

To deploy your custom BCS Model, simply press F5, and Visual Studio will attempt to deploy the solution to the local farm that was mentioned in creating the project. Behind the scenes, Visual Studio has created a SharePoint Feature and Solution file that is installed and deployed to the server. If the deployment is successful, Visual Studio will launch a web browser and take you to your SharePoint site. To work with your new model, create an external list using the steps outlined earlier in this chapter. If everything was configured properly, your external list should display a single object that displays when clicked on as shown in Figure 11-40.

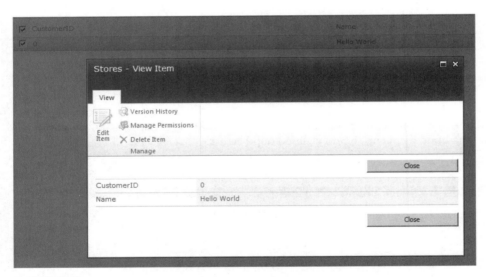

FIGURE 11-40

Though this is obviously not a fair representation of the effort required to create a BCS Model using Visual Studio 2010, it should give you some insight into how the development experience changes as you move from SharePoint Designer to Visual Studio.

BCS INTEGRATION WITH OFFICE

Now that you've seen how to create External Content Types with both SharePoint Designer and Visual Studio, as well as how to expose those ECTs inside SharePoint, you'll explore next how you can also consume your external data within Microsoft Office 2010.

Walk-Through: Integration with Word

Microsoft Word includes support for external data in the form of Quick Parts. Quick Parts allow you to insert external data fields into a Word document and support inline editing of that metadata value. An example of a document containing Quick Parts is shown in Figure 11-41.

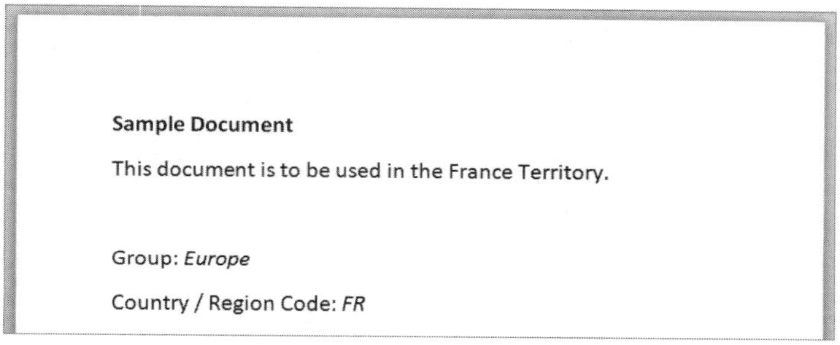

Sample Document

This document is to be used in the France Territory.

Group: *Europe*

Country / Region Code: *FR*

FIGURE 11-41

In the example, "France," which appears to be simply text, is actually an External Data Picker control connected to the Sales Territory External Content Type. As shown in Figure 11-42, content editors can modify the Sales Territory field within the content and by doing so can also update the related fields throughout the document.

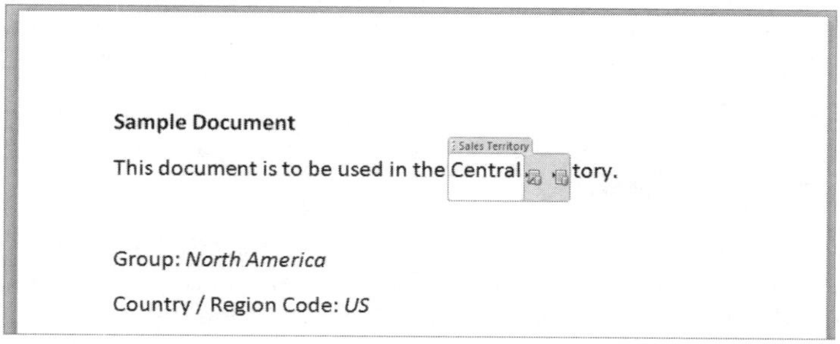

Sample Document

Sales Territory

This document is to be used in the Central   tory.

Group: *North America*

Country / Region Code: *US*

FIGURE 11-42

Adding a Quick Part is extremely easy, as shown in Figure 11-43. After opening a document from a location that contains a Business Data column, choose Quick Parts from the Insert tab of the Ribbon. From the Document Property submenu, select the field you want to display. Note that not only Business Data columns display in the list — Quick Parts are also a good way to bring any metadata into your Word documents.

FIGURE 11-43

Although this example shows some of the power of Quick Parts and BCS data columns, a more powerful use would be to create a Word template for a specific document library or content type that contains a number of Quick Parts. This ensures that, as new documents are created, valuable metadata is captured as the document is being authored.

Walk-Through: Integration with Outlook

To show the BCS integration with Outlook you must first create a new External Content Type. Two key differences in this ECT will allow Outlook integration. The first difference is configured on the ECT summary view. As shown in Figure 11-44, you can set the Office Item type to Contact, Appointment, Task, or Post. This change surfaces an additional field when configuring your operations called Office Property.

The Office Property is the second difference that allows Outlook integration. As you define the parameters in your operation, you can map each property to an Outlook property of the selected type. In Figure 11-45 you can see a mapping of the EmailAddress field to Outlook's Email1Address field.

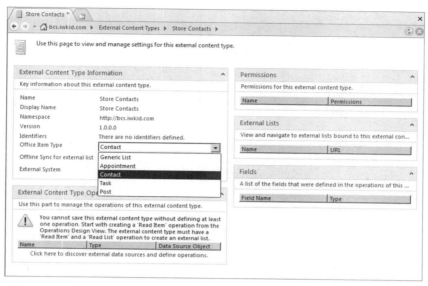

FIGURE 11-44

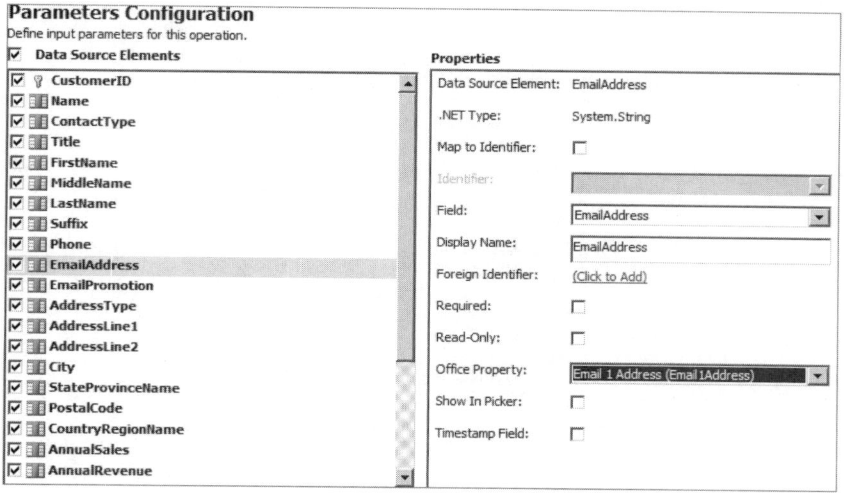

FIGURE 11-45

Once the ECT has been defined, an external list should be created using the ECT. Once you are able to navigate to the external list, you can select Connect to Outlook from the List tab on the Ribbon to create the connection to Outlook. As shown in Figure 11-46, an Office Customization Installer prompt will appear and prompt you to install the add-in that supports the connection. Click Install to finish configuring the connection.

FIGURE 11-46

Once the add-in is installed, Outlook will launch and a new data file will appear in the navigation pane called SharePoint External Lists. The connected list (in this case, Store Contacts) will be selected, and the default view will display. There will likely be some delay while all records are loaded and displayed as shown in Figure 11-47.

FIGURE 11-47

Each contact record is displayed as a business card and can be opened like any other Outlook contact record as you can see in Figure 11-48. Any fields that were mapped during the creation of the ECT will display in the contact's record. Any fields that were not defined can still be modified; they will not, however, be saved back to the external data source. If the ECT supports read/write, any mapped fields that are updated will be updated in the database as well as in the contact record.

Fields that exist in the ECT but were not mapped can still be accessed by choosing the button called [ECT Name] Details in the Ribbon. In this scenario the button is called Store Contacts Details as shown in Figure 11-49.

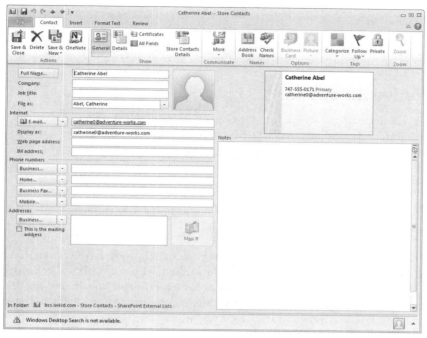

FIGURE 11-48

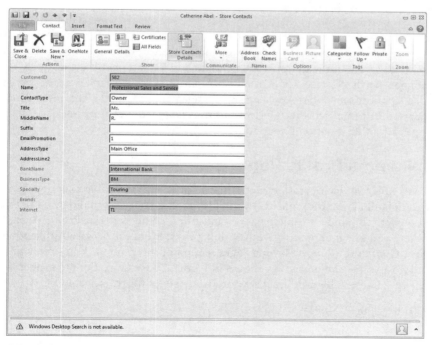

FIGURE 11-49

The ability to bring external data into Outlook is a great way to surface external data in a known application. If properly configured, the external data is also available offline and can be searched within Outlook for fast data access. Although powerful, this approach to bringing external data into Outlook is not very configurable. Next, let's revisit a more customizable approach.

Overview: Declarative Solutions

As discussed in Chapter 10, one additional solution type available for connecting external data to Outlook is a special solution type called a Declarative Outlook Solution. A declarative solution is composed of many different resource files that get packaged up and deployed. Included in the resource files are:

➤ `.bdcm`: A BDS Model file

➤ `.xml`: A subscription file that defines caching for BCS entities used in the solution

➤ `.oir`: A manifest file for the solution

A solution can consist of several other resource files including custom Outlook form regions and view definitions as well as resources to define task panes and Ribbon actions. A full walk-through of building a declarative solution is beyond the scope of this chapter; however, the SharePoint 2010 SDK provides a step-by-step guide detailing how to create a declarative solution as well as sample files that help you get started. Declarative solutions are a great way to customize and extend the "Connect to Outlook" experience.

BCS ADMINISTRATION SCREENS

This last section explores configuration options within Central Administration. The configurations mentioned in this section are likely going to be made by an administrator; however, anyone building solutions with BCS should be aware of the options. As mentioned in Chapter 10, most of the BCS-related configuration happens at the Service Application Information screen, which is accessible by selecting Manage Service Applications under Application Management in Central Administration. From the Service Application Information screen, select Business Data Connectivity Service to be taken to the Service Application Information screen for the BCS.

Walk-Through: Building a Profile Page

Building a Profile page is a fairly simple operation, but doing so provides a valuable experience. A Profile page provides a default action for your ECTs and also makes your external data available to SharePoint's search crawler. To build a Profile page you must first configure your Profile page settings to determine where you are going to host your Profile pages. From the Service Application Information screen, select Configure from the Profile Pages section of the Ribbon. You simply need to specify a site that will host your Profile pages as shown in Figure 11-50. Once the site property has been configured, clicking Create/Upgrade creates your Profile pages for the selected ECT.

You can find a sample Profile page in Chapter 10, Figure 10-7.

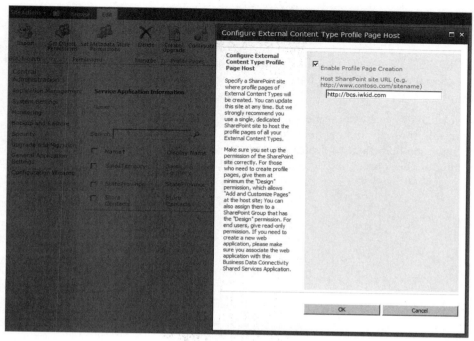

FIGURE 11-50

Walk-Through: Configuring Search

Once your Profile page has been configured, SharePoint search can be configured to index your external data sources. You can access Search configuration via the Service Applications screen as well; however, you select Search Service Application instead of Business Data Connectivity Service. For this example, a new Content Source and selected Line of Business Data were created as the content to be crawled as shown in Figure 11-51.

FIGURE 11-51

Once the external content source has been configured (assuming the default content access account has been given read permission to the external data), the SharePoint crawler will discover and index the data in your External Content Types. This allows you to find external data even if it has not been configured in an external list or Business Data column.

SUMMARY

This chapter used several walk-throughs to show how to use External Content Types as well as how to create those ECTs using both SharePoint Designer 2010 and Visual Studio 2010. It also showed how to surface external data not only in SharePoint but also by using Microsoft Office in various ways as a consumer of external data.

Chapter 10 provided an overview of Business Connectivity Services and this chapter provided several hands-on walk-throughs of how to build solutions using BCS. Using what you have learned in these chapters you should be able to determine which solution types are right for your business and locate the additional resources needed to create a solid business solution that leverages external data with BCS.

PART V
Social Networking with SharePoint 2010

12

Why Social Networking Is Important in SharePoint 2010

WHAT'S IN THIS CHAPTER?

➤ Discussion of the popularity of social networking and the psychology behind it

➤ Walk-through of the social-computing functionality inside SharePoint 2010

➤ Levels of planning necessary for a successful SharePoint 2010 My Site deployment

Microsoft has invested an enormous amount of time and effort in SharePoint to transform it into an enterprise-level social platform. My Site in MOSS 2007 was a good start toward collaboration, but it was missing one key component that all existing social media sites have: what is happening right now!

Twitter can be described as a stream of data. When you jump in, you don't care about the water behind you, just the water that currently surrounds you. At any given moment, it's possible to determine what anyone in the world is doing with a product or service. This is exactly where SharePoint 2010 is going, but it caters to internal communications. It essentially takes the best aspects of external communications (Twitter statuses, marking tweets as favorites, initiating conversations based on statuses, spotting current trends) and secures them for internal company-wide collaboration. This chapter spends some time discussing what social data is, and how it can positively affect your work life.

CURRENT STATE OF SOCIAL NETWORKING

The use of social data has been exploding for the past couple of years. In the past, each communication channel took a different amount of time to reach a 50-million user base:

- ➤ Radio: 38 years
- ➤ Television: 13 years
- ➤ Internet: 4 years
- ➤ iPod: 3 years

Facebook added 100 million users in less than nine months.

 You can find the source of the statistics for user base related to media channel in the United Nations Cyberschoolbus Document (`http://www.un.org/ cyberschoolbus/briefing/technology/tech.pdf`*).*

We're starting to see the end of e-mail as an effective mode of communication for collaboration. How can you easily share communication on an e-mail thread? How can you share the ideas in an e-mail thread so that others can search or discover these ideas on their own?

Social networking serves a purpose of expression, but if properly used it can also help assist us in our daily lives. Microsoft is using the concept of social collaboration with SharePoint 2010. This collaboration can help users find data inside the enterprise that will aid them in knowledge transfer and knowledge mining.

HOW SOCIAL NETWORKING AND PSYCHOLOGY ARE RELATED

Before jumping into the social computing aspect of SharePoint 2010 and the popularity of social networking sites such as Facebook or Twitter, it's worth seeing if anyone has tried to uncover why social networking is popular right now. After researching the work of Edward L. Bernays, a pioneer in public relations, I believe two main themes are behind the growth of social networking: crowd psychology and conformity.

The theory of crowd psychology describes why individuals act differently when part of a larger group. People want to gravitate to others who share the same ideas or thoughts. The motivation for being part of a group is the perception that ordinary people can gain direct power by acting collectively — the voice of one individual is amplified in a crowd of like-minded individuals. Because of this amplification, the group can achieve change in more dramatic and sudden ways.

Several social psychologists have developed different theories about crowd psychology, and these theories are of great importance to government and corporations, who understand that groups contribute money and purchase goods and services. Selling to one person might produce one dollar, but selling to a group of like-minded people will generate significantly more revenue. The secret of marketing is to make that group as large as possible.

Bernays used the concepts of crowd psychology to fuel marketing campaigns by manipulating public opinion. His approach to this was through the indirect use of third-party authorities. Bernays believed that if one could influence leaders, that influence would extend to the group following that leader.

The impulse to conform is also a factor behind crowd psychology. Being part of a group has several advantages: inside a group, one can learn new ideas, overcome obstacles quicker, and have a support system. However, not conforming to the group can cause social rejection.

These factors help explain why social networking is so popular right now. Some enjoy feeling they are conforming to the activities of others. Such social activity is also a way to express your inner self, or to show others your hidden qualities. Like buying trendy clothing, social networking is both a form of expression and an ideal way to sell yourself to others by portraying your better qualities to them.

The other aspect of social networking's popularity lies within the crowd. For many people, embracing social media makes it easy to follow the crowd. Why spend time reviewing each individual product, when most of your friends already have used the product and can provide instant feedback?

Historically, marketing has used conformity and leaders/experts to sway public opinion. Social networking today combines this "leader" appeal with the crowd mentality and attempts to remove bias. In 2007, 78 percent of consumers trusted peer recommendations; that number jumped to 90 percent in 2009. At the same time, consumer trust in traditional channels has hit an all-time low. Traditional marketing campaigns using radio, television, and websites are no longer as effective as they once were.

For more information regarding the shift in consumer trust, visit Nielsen Global Online Consumer Survey: Trust, Value and Engagement in Advertising, at http://www.slideshare.net/pingelizabeth/Nielsen-trust-and-advertising-global-report-july09.

We are now experiencing a shift from the opinion of one to the opinion of the crowd. In the past we were told what experts believed in and were encouraged to conform; today we can break down the communication walls and interact directly with experts more easily than before. Social media allows a more accurate portrayal of the group in relation to certain topics or products. People can now share ideas from any location at any time. Word of mouth has quickly turned into World of Mouth, and companies are more concerned about how their brand is perceived than where their products rank on Google. Social media is not a fad; it is a fundamental shift in how we communicate.

You can explore the concepts of World of Mouth and Socialnomics on the following blog post: "Statistics Show Social Media Is Bigger Than you Think" at http://socialnomics.net/2009/08/11/statistics-show-social-media-is-bigger-than-you-think/.

SOCIAL COMPUTING WITH SHAREPOINT 2010

SharePoint 2010 brings social computing to the enterprise with several new features. My Site personal sites are enhanced with a newsfeed that is similar to existing social networking sites. SharePoint encourages users to attach identifiers or keyword descriptions to SharePoint items with the concept of tagging. Users can also rank items using the SharePoint rating system. Each area of this functionality is discussed in more detail in this chapter and Chapters 13 and 14.

Tagging

Typically a document has a few properties attached to it, such as title, date modified, and author. Those properties determine how documents can be organized. Associating a custom tag to a document helps each individual organize items differently. For example, one user might tag with the word *SharePoint*, whereas another might tag using the term *Managed Metadata*. This document now has two unique tags associated with it, which makes it even easier for subsequent readers to understand what an item is without having to read it.

SharePoint 2010 gives users the ability to attach informal tags to various items. The items that can be tagged inside SharePoint are list items, documents, and SharePoint pages. In essence this means that anything with a URL can be tagged with social activity. The flexibility of tagging allows the Tag Cloud Web Part to display tags appropriately and allows users to view different artifacts based on tags.

The Tag Cloud Web Part is now native to SharePoint 2010. This Web Part is a visual depiction of user-generated tags. The font size of individual words will become larger as the frequency of that term increases on the page, and users will be able to visually inspect pages within a few seconds for popular tagged content. Clicking a tag cloud term will also filter the page content for the specified term, hiding all irrelevant items.

User-generated tags will start to grow as adoption becomes more prevalent with the user base. These tags are stored in the database like everything else inside SharePoint. Each user-generated tag will be suggested to other users in a Suggested Tags drop-down list, which is dynamically populated as the user types. So typing in the letter S will start the filter, with fewer suggestions being displayed as the user types more letters. This type of informal tagging does not replace a true taxonomy structure.

The good news is that SharePoint can handle a defined list of terms in taxonomy by using Managed Metadata. Organizations can plan their terms ahead of time using Managed Metadata, and the terms inside this taxonomy will appear along with the user-generated terms in the Suggested Tags drop-down list (Figure 12-1). Using a structured Term Set or list of tags will help provide uniform attributes. Some users might not understand a specific project acronym, whereas others might use a different acronym for a project. Specifying the official project name will cut down the confusion between segregated users.

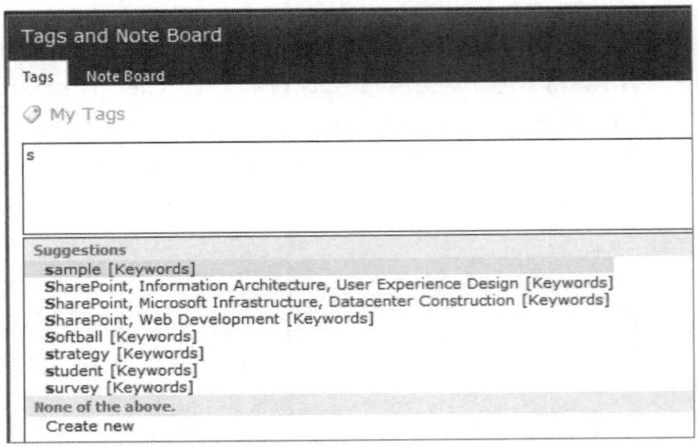

Tags and Note Board

Tags | Note Board

My Tags

s

Suggestions
sample [Keywords]
SharePoint, Information Architecture, User Experience Design [Keywords]
SharePoint, Microsoft Infrastructure, Datacenter Construction [Keywords]
SharePoint, Web Development [Keywords]
Softball [Keywords]
strategy [Keywords]
student [Keywords]
survey [Keywords]
None of the above.
Create new

FIGURE 12-1

SharePoint does a great job of providing a solution for project file management and organizing different Office documents with SharePoint lists. However, some projects have external data sources as well, and it is possible to tag external sites using SharePoint 2010. Adding the SharePoint Tags and Notes tool to your browser favorites or bookmarks toolbar will provide the functionality to tag any external site and these external tags will be visible to colleagues and teammates. Knowledge that is normally hidden inside documents is starting to be uncovered with social tagging. Combining the tags from multiple project documents will form relations between projects. Adding external social tags will enhance existing knowledge and provide a more balanced view of a subject.

Rating

Adding identifiers or terms to SharePoint items is one way of organizing content. SharePoint brings a method to organization that also answers how to find high-quality content. Similar to the five-star rating system with the Netflix movie service, users can now attach a rating to SharePoint items. Items can be rated with one click, and document libraries are flexible to enable ratings where they are needed. Rating has essentially the same purpose as tagging, which is to expose items that are normally hidden among other items. Unlike looking for a needle in a haystack, users can now find high-quality documents without having to read or inspect each document in the stack.

The Content Query Web Part (CQWP) has returned in SharePoint 2010 and is another out-of-the-box feature. This edition is enhanced with the inclusion of ratings. Typically CQWP is used to combine multiple document libraries from one site or multiple sites. This is powerful because it allows users to view items in one central view as opposed to multiple pages. Imagine telling CQWP to display only items that are rated higher than four stars. Immediately, high-quality documents are thrust into the spotlight, which in turn saves your employees from having to dig or search multiple websites for information.

Note Board

Attaching terms and ratings certainly helps individuals with organizing content, but it doesn't necessarily help readers attach notes or thoughts to items. SharePoint 2010 addresses this by providing users with a Note Board to attach individual notes to items. The Note Board functionality extends beyond SharePoint by allowing users to attach notes to external websites in a way similar to the tagging process. By writing complete thoughts, the writer allows other users to obtain more meaning than they would by reading individual tags or one-word descriptions.

Typically the Note Board will appear as a tabbed option in the Tags and Notes modal pop-up (Figure 12-2). However, there is another method to drive user adoption. A Note Board Web Part can be attached to SharePoint pages. By including this Web Part, users can quickly add notes to a SharePoint page and also cycle through and read other users' notes. The note-taking process will appear as an activity separate from tagging and will be displayed under each individual's

FIGURE 12-2

My Site and in the newsfeed. My Site and the attributes that constitute My Site, such as My Newsfeed, are reviewed in the next sections.

My Site

My Site personal sites are SharePoint sites that are dedicated to individual users. These sites are composed of three core sections: My Newsfeed, My Content, and My Profile (Figure 12-3). Each core section has its own compelling argument for enterprise-wide adoption, as shown under the next three headings.

FIGURE 12-3

My Newsfeed

My Newsfeed is related to social activity such as tagging and rating. This section is dedicated to displaying social data to others spread throughout the enterprise.

My Newsfeed contains two basic data sources: activity related to colleagues and activity related to interests. Colleagues are automatically assigned to users based on the information contained in the organization settings from Active Directory. The Colleagues designation can also be managed and altered manually from the Colleagues tab under My Profile. Activity related to interests is based on the interests specified under the individual's profile. SharePoint provides flexibility to scale back the types of activities that are followed, in order to make the newsfeed seem less overwhelming. The newsfeed settings are on an individual level; altering newsfeed settings will affect only the specified individual.

My Content

My Content is a personal place to store and share documents. This core section behaves very much like the typical SharePoint site. It can be described as a replacement for a file share or for saving documents on personal computers. Obviously, projects or departments will have dedicated SharePoint sites on which to store their individual items, but My Content fills a gap by providing a place to store items that are not necessarily project-related. Items stored here have the same features as other SharePoint sites, including version history, multiple-staged recycle bin, workflow support, and automatic backups (related to SQL storage maintenance plans).

The My Content section of My Site will look very familiar even to the novice SharePoint user. It essentially looks like a typical SharePoint site with a few pre-created document libraries. Personal Documents is a basic document library with unique permissions that allow only the current individual to have access to add/view/manage documents. (The SharePoint administrator can still view individual My Site personal sites for security and management purposes.) Shared Documents is an open document library intended for users to store documents that do not have a SharePoint home elsewhere. Both these document libraries have the typical benefits that come with SharePoint.

Looking past the pre-generated document libraries, the My Content section has all the same elements as a generic SharePoint site: breadcrumb navigation, left-hand navigation, Web Parts, and site actions. Users can create their own lists, document libraries, and even subsites. Even the landing page can be altered to include whatever Web Parts users desire, although this is limited to Web Parts that currently reside in the Web Part gallery. The dangers that might accompany such freedom in creation are limited by the site quota specified by the SharePoint administrator. The administrator can create blanket quota templates that can be applied to multiple My Site personal sites or use individual quotas to limit My Site growth. Keep in mind that My Site personal sites are essentially site collections. As you would with a line of business sites, these site collections need to be included in existing governance and capacity planning.

My Profile

My Profile is the last core section and completes the social-computing triangle. This section is similar to existing social networking sites like Facebook, but with a more professional feel and intent. For a large corporation with multiple offices or a small technology firm with consultants who are never in the office, the Profile page creates an identity based on Active Directory information and SharePoint collected artifacts.

The My Profile section of My Site provides the personal aspect of social computing that has become so popular with mainstream networking sites. Some of the fields are automatically populated by Active Directory. The user can optionally decide to add more attributes manually, such as skills, schools, birthday, and interests. Remember that the terms placed into the Interest attribute fuel one aspect of the newsfeed. The rest of the Profile page consists of six subsections: Overview, Organization, Content, Tags and Notes, Colleagues, and Memberships.

Subsections of My Profile

The Overview subsection of My Profile (Figure 12-4) contains information on the specified user's activity, suggested topics or subjects to collaborate on, people who have common interests with the user, and the organization chart. The organization chart is fueled by Active Directory and is displayed as a tree view or with Silverlight. The same Silverlight control is available as the Organization Browser Web Part, which can be added to any additional SharePoint page. The point of bringing this up is that social data and information regarding the organization, typically found in My Site, can be exposed outside the traditional Profile site. The same Organization Browser Web Part is viewable under the Organization subsection.

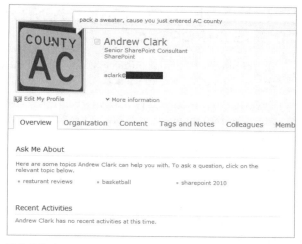

FIGURE 12-4

In a previous section we discussed the My Content core section of My Site and how this is essentially a SharePoint site where individual users can create anything they want and apply custom permissions to their SharePoint items. When visiting other My Site personal sites, the items displayed in the Content subsection of My Profile are based on those custom permissions that the owner declared. The typical SharePoint security trimming is being applied to items in this subsection as well, meaning that if you do not have rights to the item, that item will not be visible.

The Tags and Notes subsection is dedicated to social computing data for the specified user. The Tag Cloud Web Part is available and used to sort information listed in the Activities list. The Activities list can be sorted by month, tags, or tag type. Visiting users can quickly view tags or notes, which then assist in finding related activities. It is also possible to administer existing tags by marking tags as private or deleting them. (Keep in mind that this is only possible with your own tags, not with those of others.) The same Tag Cloud Web Part used in this subsection is available for other SharePoint sites and is a great tool to filter content based on tags.

The Colleagues subsection will be pre-populated by suggestions made from Active Directory integration. These suggestions can be altered manually and organized into subgroups. Users can add their own colleagues to enhance the relationships set from Active Directory. Colleague management is important because this fuels the second aspect of the newsfeed. Social activity from colleagues will appear in the individual's newsfeed even if that activity is not related to any tags that match the individual's interests.

The last subsection, Memberships, lists all sites and distribution lists to which the user belongs. These memberships are compiled automatically and can be altered later by the individual.

SharePoint 2010 collects and displays social data in order to portray or attach a personal depiction of each user. As with other networking sites, users may prefer to share more information with friends than with strangers, and it is possible to mark notes and certain social attributes as private. Because the individual's colleagues are mapped into groups, it is possible to display data in a different manner to people who share the same team.

WHY SOCIAL NETWORKING WITH SHAREPOINT 2010 IS IMPORTANT

SharePoint 2010 brings a flurry of new social media features to the public with tagging, rating, and a revamped My Site experience.

The My Site functionality has been revisited with SharePoint 2010. Individual activity is now captured into a newsfeed. Your SharePoint activity in relation to social tagging and rating is now shared. It is possible to extend your social activity with the entire company/community or simply with your teammates/colleagues. A similar type of status that many will be familiar with from Facebook and Twitter is now being used in SharePoint as well.

In relation to social computing, a status entry is best described as another channel of communication — of letting people know your "status" in terms of your life and interests. The purpose of creating a status is to convey information, feelings, or ideas to others without having to engage in conversation with each individual. When creating a status, you might not know who will read it or even who will reply to it. More importantly, the action of posting a status update might spark a conversation with others who share an idea or interest conveyed by your status update. Each individual status update may cater to a different set of friends or colleagues. Over time, the status updates of one individual will portray an accurate representation of what interests that individual has and what type of projects that individual has worked on. Either directly, through statuses, or indirectly, through the activities users are tagging, it's possible to know exactly what anyone inside your company is working on.

As tagging becomes more prevalent in your company, you will see related project items emerge from the information pile. Teammates will be able to find related documents far more easily. Outsiders will be able to jump into a project, find all the related information, and participate more quickly. SharePoint now allows you to tag *external* content also. In the past, you might have had to create a wiki site to house external links. This approach is somewhat tedious and does not scale very well. Now it's possible to tag external sites with just a click of a button. Your existing projects will have an additional dimension with the addition of external reference material.

SharePoint 2010's rating system is yet another extremely important addition to social computing. With MOSS 2007 it was possible to bookmark your favorite items or documents, but it wasn't easy to share those items with others, especially if no one asked you for them. This ratings process allows others inside your institution to readily find highly rated items. Data finds individual users by incorporating tagging into newsfeeds. People who aren't classified as friends or colleagues can still contribute by tagging items that match individual interests. The process of inefficient reading and sifting through data is slowly being eliminated. Highly rated, extremely helpful items now find *you* with SharePoint 2010.

To complement existing taxonomies, SharePoint will provide a "folksonomy" based on the practice and method of creating and managing tags in a social and collaborative environment. Folksonomy is essentially a user-generated taxonomy. As user adoption grows, the sheer number of social tags inside a folksonomy will develop into a large collection of terms. This folksonomy will provide a more accurate portrayal of how content should be organized based on the community. The Tag Cloud Web Part will become more efficient as the folksonomy grows. This in return will enable users to filter and find related content far more easily than the typical search experience.

In the past, search was the only way to find additional documents or related artifacts within the organization. SharePoint 2010 not only brings content closer to its audience but brings the author closer to the audience as well. Finding content is one aspect, but now it is easier to find colleagues who share interests with the author. The integration with Office 2010 (with Outlook or Office Communicator) makes it easy to contact segregated teams. Content-aware Web Parts with an active community make finding SharePoint items significantly easier.

PLANNING FOR SOCIAL COMPUTING

SharePoint 2010 will be no different than earlier versions of SharePoint in regard to planning — planning will dictate how successful your SharePoint installation will be within your organization. With proper planning and governance, users will flock to your farm. Without high user adoption, SharePoint will fail, especially in regard to social computing data. It should be obvious that if no one uses your platform, you will be left with no one to tag anything.

About 80 percent of your time should be devoted to planning and 20 percent to pure development. Obviously that statement doesn't touch on every aspect of the software development cycle. However, it should give you a good idea about the effort you need to make in planning for social computing and collaboration.

Governance Planning

Governance planning with SharePoint is quickly becoming one of the more confusing terms used in the community. Ask 10 different people what governance is and they will describe it in 10 different ways. One definition of governance is: "Accountability for consistent, cohesive policies, processes, and decision rights." That formal definition may seem too broad to be helpful, and it seems clear that governance will differ according to the people and projects involved. But the intent of each different governance plan is the same. A new tool is being introduced to the company; let's set up a plan so we know how the tool should be used. This section concentrates on two proposed aspects of governance: security and terms.

Security

When enabling social computing, each feature is turned on by default. However, there may be instances where this functionality should be turned on for a small subset of users. It is fairly easy to set up access for a group of individuals in pilot program participation. In most environments, the baseline of all SharePoint profiles will come from synchronization with Active Directory. There may be groups in Active Directory that do not have a client machine and do not need to have any interaction with SharePoint. SharePoint 2010 has three permission sets related to social computing:

➤ Create personal site.

➤ Use social features.

➤ Use personal features.

These permission sets address the questions regarding how many users can create personal sites, who is allowed to tag SharePoint items, and whether users can alter their profiles. For more information on this subject, visit "Plan for My Site Websites – Determine Users and User Permissions" at `http://technet.microsoft.com/en-us/library/cc262500.aspx#section3`.

Terms

SharePoint 2010 allows users to create their own tags or to pick tags from an existing Term Set. The user-generated terms will be stored in the Keyword Term Set. As this set grows, the suggestions become more robust. However, it would be helpful to create Term Sets ahead of time to assist with proper classification. Not only can these Term Sets be created, but ownership can be determined as well.

Creating terms ahead of time will cut down confusion with users. User-generated tags can include an array of different acronyms and slang for a given subject. Formal tags will provide an accurate identifier that will resonate across the enterprise. By setting up Managed Metadata administrators, keywords can be reorganized as synonyms for other terms that reside in other Term Sets. This further enhances the tagging suggestions that SharePoint provides. For more information, visit

"Plan Terms and Term Sets (SharePoint Server 2010)" at http://technet.microsoft.com/en-us/library/ee519604.aspx#section3.

Infrastructure Planning

The next aspect of planning for My Site is related to performance. If the SharePoint farm is not set up to handle the traffic related to multiple users socially collaborating, users will complain of slow performance and view SharePoint as a time waste. There is nothing worse than a slow-loading web page, which can be avoided with the proper infrastructure planning.

Performance and Capacity Planning

The first task is to determine the company's baseline. How many users are expected to have a My Site personal site? Do users currently have a personal file share on the network? If so, on average how much hard-drive space is consumed? These questions should be fairly easy; the difficult task is predicting growth and whether the existing hardware will accommodate this growth.

My Site has a site quota, just as other site collections do in SharePoint. Quotas need to be determined before My Site adoption, because this will assist in calculating SQL server hardware requirements. Site quotas can be altered for individual users or groups to provide flexibility for the power users who emerge inside the organization. For more information on managing site collection storage limits, visit http://technet.microsoft.com/en-us/library/cc263480.aspx#BKMK_Updatequotatemplateforsite.

In regard to performance, several resources can help the reliability and efficiency of your SharePoint farm. Understanding and determining hardware requirements depends on which features are being used. The following link will assist with performance planning: "Performance and Capacity Management" at http://technet.microsoft.com/en-us/library/cc262971.aspx.

Maintenance Planning

Creating a plan to maintain the current SharePoint installation is a subject beyond this book, and in fact there are books about it. The topic is included here because someone needs to plan how to handle My Site personal sites that become stale or are attached to inactive employees (that is, those no longer employed). SharePoint has a solution for use confirmation and deletion. SharePoint will detect unused sites and send e-mail notifications to the owners of the sites. The system will automatically delete the sites after sending a specified number of notices. All these settings are configured inside the Central Administration application, which is available to the SharePoint administrator. This can be a sensitive subject because automatic deletion will permanently wipe out all the My Site content.

Training

The last piece driving user adoption for a successful SharePoint My Site deployment is training. The last thing users need is to have a new software platform thrown at them without adequate training. Typically users are already busy and will view new platforms with resistance. The key with training is to portray SharePoint My Site as a method to decrease and streamline their current workload.

However, users are not the only set of employees who need training with SharePoint My Site. The people who administer SharePoint need to understand how My Site and Managed Metadata are related. Administrators need to actively search user-generated keywords either to organize them into Term Sets or delete offensive terms. Administrators can decide which fields can be pulled into My Site for display purposes. They can also set up the ability to write SharePoint My Site data back into Active Directory. Because most of these actions cannot be reversed these actions can be considered dangerous, which warrants the need for training.

SUMMARY

Corporations have used several tactics to sway public opinion regarding their purchasing habits. There are psychological factors behind not just our actions but how we view products and services. Social media has changed how we communicate with others. The reasons for the popularity of social networking could be viewed as self-serving, but such networking also helps with making informed decisions. SharePoint 2010 embraces this social activity and brings the concepts behind folksonomy inside the corporation. The concept of searching, then qualifying data is no longer efficient. SharePoint users can now search for highly rated items without needing to individually qualify each item. High-quality SharePoint items originating from many different SharePoint sites can be displayed to users in one place. The process of finding and consuming data inside SharePoint 2010 has changed dramatically with the inclusion of a folksonomy coupled with an existing taxonomy, and it will become an asset to every corporation regardless of size.

13

Tagging and Ratings

WHAT'S IN THIS CHAPTER?

➤ Uncovering how to configure tagging and ratings

➤ Learning how to expose popular artifacts to the "social enterprise"

➤ Understanding what Managed Metadata is and how it relates to tagging

Chapter 12 discussed the origins of social networking, as well as how the popularity of social media developed. The chapter also began uncovering the social features of SharePoint 2010, and why these features will help productivity in your organization. This chapter is dedicated to tagging and ratings inside SharePoint 2010.

There are no virtually no limits to what can be tagged inside SharePoint 2010. Any item that has a URL associated with it can be tagged. Among such items are:

➤ Web pages (internal/external)

➤ List items

➤ Documents

In the past, SharePoint was mainly a closed environment, which rarely reached outside the company. The ability to tag external websites makes the possibilities staggering in regard to what can be tagged. The negative aspect of this functionality is that the number of tags users create can also become problematic. This chapter also presents a solution to help organize tags and present them in a more coherent fashion.

The action of tagging a SharePoint item is essentially attaching additional information to help with categorizing or organizing items. For example, think of a scenario where a table has a pile of random books. Nobody knows what each book contains or even what the subject is of each book. You probably don't have time to read each one. Even if you did, it would take an extremely long time to get through each book. However, because you are part of a larger group, each person grabs a book and starts reading it. As each book is read, the reader attaches a category note to it. A couple of books have an ASP.NET category, others have a Java category, and some are labeled as Rick Bayless's recipes. Over a considerably shorter period of time, you can glance at the table and see which books have identical category tags and which books are related.

The preceding scenario is basic but can be applied to SharePoint as well. Let's use the same example but replace books with documents. SharePoint provides more detailed mechanisms to help categorize items. The reader can start out by attaching an ASP.NET tag to the document but can also use more than one tag, for example "web development" or "Windows Forms." It is also possible to attach notes to the document using the Note Board functionality. For example, readers might add in "great basic overview" or "technical deep dive into the ASP.NET page lifecycle." Readers can quickly give documents a positive review by clicking I Like It. SharePoint also allows users to rank items with a one- to five-star rating. By accepting this social behavior, SharePoint is not just organizing content but also uncovering documents that are related. Documents that have positive reviews are also pushed up to the top of the pile. The social computing aspect of SharePoint provides the ability to organize large amounts of data in a relatively short period of time.

TAGGING

The next sections outline what tagging means inside SharePoint. The first sections review how to tag SharePoint items and how those tags will appear to other SharePoint users. The process of how tags will be suggested to users is also discussed. Lastly, the tag cloud Web Part that resides inside SharePoint is discussed.

How to Tag Items

Tagging items in SharePoint 2010 is an extremely easy task. It boils down to interacting with the two buttons located toward the top right-hand corner of the SharePoint page: I Like It and Tags & Notes (Figure 13-1).

FIGURE 13-1

Keep in mind that everything is contextual so the Tags and Notes buttons will apply to whatever you are currently working on.

Let's review this process by tagging an item in a document library and tagging an actual SharePoint page. Go to any document library and select one item or document. Doing so will activate the Documents tab in the Ribbon; the Tags and Notes section will appear toward the right-hand side. Keep the items selected and click Tags & Notes to bring up a modal popup. This is the area where you can specify additional terms or tags to help identify or categorize this document. For instance, I can specify a project name or time period. If someone on my team has already started tagging items, SharePoint will attempt to display suggestions. The Tags section of the popup contains three areas: My Tags, Suggested Tags, and Recent Activities. The My Tags area will display the tags that you have already placed with this item. As the user begins to type, a Suggestions drop-down will appear under the text, offering terms that it's hoped are related (Figure 13-2).

The Suggestions drop-down supplements the items located in the Suggested Tags area. What other people are doing, whether it be tagging or making notes, will appear in the Recent Activity section. The Note Board tab in the same pop-up window allows users to add freestyle notes to that item. Clicking the I Like It button does not pop up another window, but it shows up as activity to others, which will, it's hoped, put a spotlight on the item.

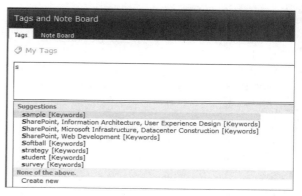

FIGURE 13-2

What Can Be Tagged; What Are Notes?

It's possible to tag any SharePoint page (even the pages in the Central Administration site) — basically anything that is housed on a page. Some examples:

➤ An entire web page

➤ SharePoint list

➤ Document library

During the tagging process, you might have noticed the ability to tag external content with a link. Right-click or drag and drop this link to your browser's favorites or bookmarks toolbar to tag external sites. Adding the tagging link to your favorites or toolbar adds a button to your browser called Tags and Note Board. Now that this link has been added to your browser toolbar, it's extremely easy to tag external items. Users just have to navigate to the external web page and click the Tags and Note Board shortcut in their browser. Doing this pulls up the same modal pop-up window with the option to add Tags or add items to the Note Board.

One reason tagging external content is important is that it adds additional knowledge to your company. For example, I found an excellent link that discusses SharePoint 2010 and wanted to share this with my teammates on the Microsoft SharePoint Team blog. All I had to do was visit the site and add some tags or notes to the item. My activity then appeared in all of my teammates' newsfeeds, which is exactly what I wanted. The activity was also displayed to anyone visiting my profile under the Tags and Notes section.

In addition to adding metadata or tags to items, it's possible to include notes on items. Unlike tagging, the interface will not display suggestions; however, SharePoint will show existing notes. These existing notes will not only be displayed on the modal pop-up (Figure 13-3) but also on the user's profile page as well as under Tags and Notes.

FIGURE 13-3

Visibility of Tags

It's possible to hide the visibility of tags on items. Tags can be marked as private, making them invisible to anyone else. During the tagging process, you'll see a checkbox labeled Private: Do Not Show My Tags on This Item to Others (Figure 13-4).

FIGURE 13-4

This will add the tags to the items and to your profile, but no one will be able to view them besides the Administrator.

You can also manage tags on your profile page. Under Your Profile, the Tags and Notes section will contain all the user's recent activity. Next to each tagging activity is a checkbox: Make Private. Either mark existing public tags as private or vice versa (Figure 13-5).

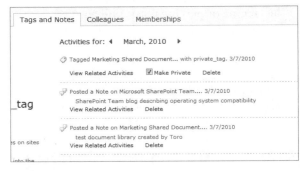

FIGURE 13-5

What Does It Mean to 'Like' an Item?

It is possible to select multiple items and click the I Like It button to tag them. Navigate to any document library or list and select multiple items. This will highlight at least a few rows inside your list. Notice that as multiple items are selected buttons begin to be grayed out in the Ribbon. One of the buttons that is not selectable is the Tags & Notes button; however, I Like It is available (Figure 13-6).

FIGURE 13-6

Liking an item is a quick and easy way to broadcast to others that a certain content or item is valuable. This information will appear in your co-workers' news feeds and on your personal page in SharePoint in the My Profile section under Tags and Notes.

Discover How Tags Will be Suggested for Future Users

Once a tag is saved into SharePoint, that item will be suggested to others when they attempt to tag items. During the tagging process, as soon as SharePoint detects a similar word a suggestions area will appear.

Saved terms will also appear in everyone's newsfeed on their personal sites. The newsfeed aggregates current activity and enables users to drill down to specific activity. This will expose the hottest terms being used at the current time. Typically it will be possible to see an influx of activity and discover new projects or uncover the active users for a given project. SharePoint 2010 is a social platform; the newsfeed will spark more communication and add more exposure to what is being worked on inside the company (all without sending out a single e-mail or phone call).

Visiting another user's personal page in SharePoint is yet another method of discovering existing tags. This allows others to uncover how one person may be tagging items.

What Is the Tag Cloud Web Part?

A tag cloud is a list of words visually depicting user-generated tags and their frequency. The concept behind the cloud is simple: as more content is added and tagged to the site, the visual size of the tag will become larger.

The tag cloud Web Part is an out-of-the-box feature. Adding this to a SharePoint page will allow users to immediately see what type of content is in the site and what content is more prevalent than others. Users can also click a term in the tag cloud to filter data. By clicking a tag, the user is redirected to a tag profile page that displays all items that have been tagged with that term along with other actions related to the term.

This Web Part can be added to any SharePoint page depending on your permission level on the site. While editing the page, Tag Cloud will appear in the Navigation category (Figure 13-7).

FIGURE 13-7

A tag cloud has the common Web Part properties that can be edited: appearance/layout/advanced. The tag cloud's configuration will allow the Web Part to show tags that were created by just the current user or every tag that exists on the site. You can change the number of terms to be displayed in the Web Part and add the count next to each term as well. The Miscellaneous properties can be altered to show terms from one month, one year, or all dates.

What Is the Tag Profile?

The Tag Profile web page is a landing area for an individual term. You get here by clicking a term or tag on the tag cloud Web Part. The Tag Profile page has four distinct areas: Title, Tagged Items, Get Connected, and Note Board (Figure 13-8).

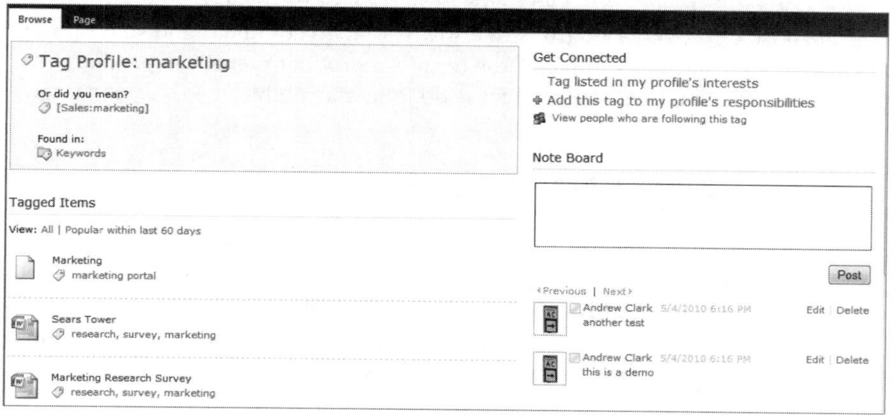

FIGURE 13-8

When first navigating to this page, the Title area will display the tag name and which Term Store the term is located in. If SharePoint detects a similar tag that exists in another Term Store, it will display the term along with the Term Store.

The Tagged Items section displays all the items that have been tagged with the term that was selected. By default, SharePoint displays only the items that have been tagged in the past 60 days. However, it is possible to retrieve a list of all items. Near the bottom of the Tagged Items list is a link that will direct the user to search based on the tag.

If you want to duplicate this behavior using SharePoint search, use the following format: socialtag:"tag"

The Get Connected section is tightly coupled to the My Site functionality of SharePoint 2010. From this page, you can add the tag to your profile responsibilities. As soon as you add the tag to your profile as a responsibility, it will appear on the My Profile page under Ask Me About. You can also add the tag to your newsfeed settings. After adding this term to your profile, it will appear in Interests under your Newsfeed Settings.

The link to view people who follow the tag is simply a link to search using the following format: Responsibilities:"tag" OR Interests:"marketing"

Keep in mind that the search functionality is dependent on when the search crawler does its job. So if you just add the term as one of your own responsibilities you will have to wait for at least an incremental crawl to pick up on the update.

The Note Board section is located under Get Connected. This section contains freehand notes or comments regarding the tag in a list view. All comments or notes will be displayed here similarly to a message board. The purpose of the Note Board is to allow people to comment and share thoughts regarding the specific topic or term. For example, if the term is a product name, the product manager could enter a note indicating that the product is no longer available.

CONFIGURATION AND ADMINISTRATION

A SharePoint installation will not have basic out-of-the-box functionality if the installation is not configured. Almost every SharePoint feature relies on a service that needs to be running and configured. These next sections walk you through the process of enabling tagging and ratings. Once the features are up and running, it is important to understand how to manage the tags or metadata that the SharePoint farm will start to collect from daily use.

Enable Tagging and Ratings

With SharePoint 2010, when you tag items or assign a rating to a document, this is then attached to your profile. That's how SharePoint organizes the information; it is tightly synchronized with your profile. The SharePoint profile is dependent on the User Profile Service application. Some of you might be familiar with profiles from MOSS (Microsoft Office SharePoint Server) 2007 and the SSP (Shared Service Provider). In 2010, the SSP was replaced with new service architecture. After configuring the User Profile Service application, a few new databases will appear in your database server:

➤ User Profile Service application_ProfileDB

➤ User Profile Service application_SocialDB

➤ User Profile Service application_SyncDB

Open up the SocialDB in SQL Server Management Studio, and you will see the following tables: dbo.SocialRatings, dbo.SocialTags, and so on. (Microsoft warns you not to query or make any changes to the database schema for any SharePoint databases. However, viewing this information certainly adds to your basic understanding of how the service application runs and what is being done behind the scenes.)

Regardless of whether your SharePoint 2010 farm is already running or whether you just finished running the configuration wizard, the easiest method to get the User Profile Service to run is with the Farm Configuration Wizard. It is also possible to start or configure services by using PowerShell.

You can start the Farm Configuration Wizard by clicking Configuration Wizards in the Central Administration application located in the left-hand menu navigation. While inside the wizard, make sure that you select the User Profile Service application.

The preceding process will create the aforementioned databases and start up the User Profile Service application. You can confirm that this service is running by looking at the Manage Service Applications link in Central Administration. In the Central Administration application, click Application Management and then click Manage Service Applications in the Service Applications section (Figure 13-9).

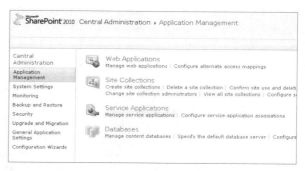

FIGURE 13-9

A complete list of all the service applications will be displayed. As you move your mouse over the services, each line will be highlighted showing context. Click the row that contains User Profile Service application so that the entire row is highlighted. Once the row is highlighted, the Ribbon (Figure 13-10) will

FIGURE 13-10

display buttons related to the service application. Typically these buttons will be New, Connect, Delete, Manage, Administrators, Properties, Publish, and Permissions.

Clicking Manage directs you to the detailed information regarding the Profile Service. From here, you can manage where and when SharePoint will load Active Directory accounts, view existing profiles, and so on (Figure 13-11).

FIGURE 13-11

The homepage has a Web Part linking to the library toward the right of the screen. Save the link for the User Profile Service Management page in the Resources link library (Figure 13-12).

FIGURE 13-12

 Several management screens inside Central Administration take a few mouse clicks to navigate to. Obviously, because this is a web application, you can save these items as browser favorites. Individual browser favorites do not help out others that might share your responsibilities. The other approach is to save the link into a link library. The Central Administration application has a link library titled Resources.

At this point you have the User Profile Management Service up and running. You can now enable ratings on your document libraries. SharePoint 2010 allows all users to rate documents/list items. I go into more detail on that later, but let's enable this feature first. Navigate to any document library or SharePoint list. In the Ribbon, select the Library tab, then click Library Settings. In the Library Settings page, under General Settings, click Rating Settings. Enabling the ratings settings simply requires selecting the Yes radio button (Figure 13-13).

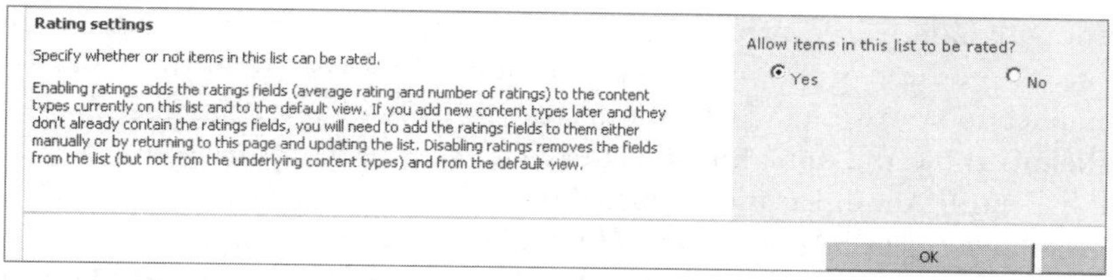

Rating settings

Specify whether or not items in this list can be rated.

Enabling ratings adds the ratings fields (average rating and number of ratings) to the content types currently on this list and to the default view. If you add new content types later and they don't already contain the ratings fields, you will need to add the ratings fields to them either manually or by returning to this page and updating the list. Disabling ratings removes the fields from the list (but not from the underlying content types) and from the default view.

Allow items in this list to be rated?

○ Yes   ○ No

OK

FIGURE 13-13

The ratings service will add a column entitled Rating (0-5) to the document library or list (Figure 13-14). When hovering over the column, the stars will turn gold; clicking the appropriate star then marks the item.

FIGURE 13-14

Managing Tags

SharePoint offers two methods for managing tags. To help understand why two methods exist, you have to fully understand how tagging works in SharePoint 2010. Once a user tags an item, that information is then attached to the item but also to the user's profile. This is why you had to ensure that the User Profile Service was running. For example, a budget spreadsheet could be tagged as 2010 Marketing Budget. The same user also can tag a PowerPoint presentation as 2010 Marketing Budget. Over time, groupings of items will start to uncover themselves through users' tagging. The key to this process is SharePoint 2010's suggesting tags to others users. Once one user tags an item, that term or description is placed into the Term Store Manager. This alleviates the potential issue that would result if one user tagged with Marketing 2010 Budget and another tagged with 2010 Marketing Budget.

One method for managing tags is to delete a tag from a user's profile, but that term will still remain in the Term Store and will be suggested to other users. The other method involves going directly to the Term Store Manager and deleting the term. Let's go down the path of managing a user who incorrectly tagged an item or doesn't want to have a tag associated with his or her profile.

Open up Central Administration and navigate to Manage Profile Service (I hope you added that link to your homepage). In My Site Settings, select Manage Tags and Notes. The next page (Figure 13-15) will allow you to search based on either tags (or notes) and username. The web page allows the option to delete any of the tags that are returned in the result set.

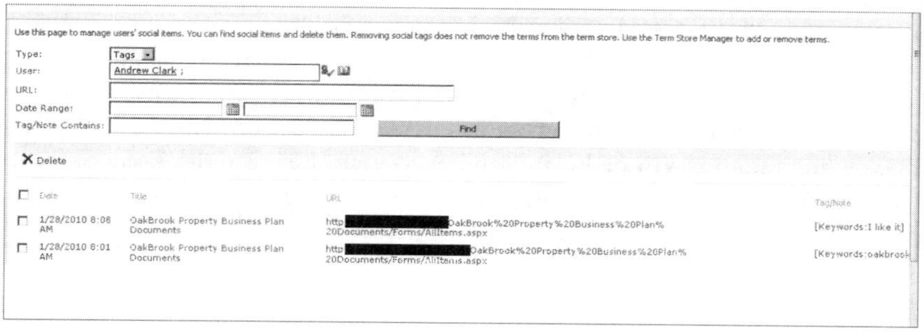

Use this page to manage users' social items. You can find social items and delete them. Removing social tags does not remove the terms from the term store. Use the Term Store Manager to add or remove terms.

Type:	Tags ▾
User:	Andrew Clark ;
URL:	
Date Range:	
Tag/Note Contains:	Find

✕ Delete

	Date	Title	URL	Tag/Note
☐	1/28/2010 8:06 AM	OakBrook Property Business Plan Documents	http▬▬▬OakBrook%20Property%20Business%20Plan%20Documents/Forms/AllItems.aspx	[Keywords:I like it]
☐	1/28/2010 8:01 AM	OakBrook Property Business Plan Documents	http▬▬▬OakBrook%20Property%20Business%20Plan%20Documents/Forms/AllItems.aspx	[Keywords:oakbrook]

FIGURE 13-15

The other tag management path handles erroneous entries or malicious entries that exist in the Term Store Manager. You can get to the Term Store Management Tool in two ways, either through the Central Administration application or through Site Administration of any SharePoint site. Because you are looking for a malicious entry and don't know what site it exists in, view the Term Store Management Tool through Central Administration. Open Application Management in Central Administration and click Manage Service Applications. Highlight the Managed Metadata Service so that the contextual Ribbon changes and gives the option to Manage. Select the Manage button in the Service Applications tab in the Ribbon.

The Term Store Management Tool is split into three sections: search, tree navigation, and properties (Figure 13-16).

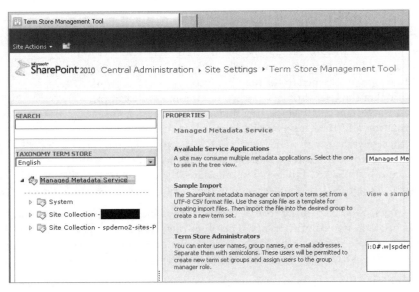

FIGURE 13-16

When navigating between terms and Term Sets with this application, keep in mind that the Properties section is related to whatever you have clicked in the tree navigation. For example, by default the first item selected is Managed Metadata Service; therefore the properties screen will display attributes for that service. If you click an individual term in the tree navigation, a completely different set of properties will appear toward the right of the screen. Terms, Term Sets, and Term Set Groups will be organized by site collection in the tree navigation. Keywords or items that are collected via users when tagging will be located under System. Because the Term Store Management Tool can administer every site collection, it might make more sense to search for the term that needs to be deleted.

When searching for terms, the same suggestions drop-down that is used while tagging will appear under your search item. By clicking the suggestion, the properties area will refresh with new attributes. In this area, the system gives the option to specify whether or not the term should be available for tagging. This option hides the term from being selected again by other users but does not delete the term. To delete a term, hover over the item in the tree navigation to bring up another contextual menu (Figure 13-17) with the options of either Move Keyword or Delete Keyword.

FIGURE 13-17

If you do not see any of these items or if the checkbox for Available for Tagging is grayed out, you have more troubleshooting to handle. In the left-hand navigation, select Managed Metadata Service. Inspect your Term Store Administrators (Figure 13-18). If this item is blank, then you've located the reason why you aren't able to delete terms.

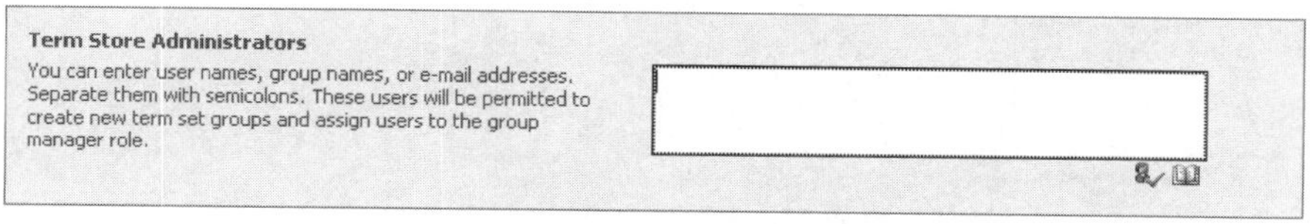

Term Store Administrators

You can enter user names, group names, or e-mail addresses. Separate them with semicolons. These users will be permitted to create new term set groups and assign users to the group manager role.

FIGURE 13-18

Term Sets have the following attributes (Figure 13-19):

➤ **Term Set name, description, and owner:** These attributes provide a short overview of the Term Set and displays who the owner is.

➤ **Stakeholders:** These are people who need to be notified before making changes to the Term Set.

➤ **Submission Policy:** This attribute opens the Term Set to contributions from users besides the metadata managers.

➤ **Available for Tagging:** With this attribute checked, it allows users to use this Term Set for tagging. If this is not checked, then users will not be able to see this Term Set in the Suggestions drop-down menu from the tagging pop-up window.

Once tags are placed into the Managed Metadata Service, it is possible to organize and move these tags or terms around. Terms inside the keywords Term Set can be only deleted or moved. Items that exist in other Term Stores have numerous other functions. Term Sets also have different functions available to them.

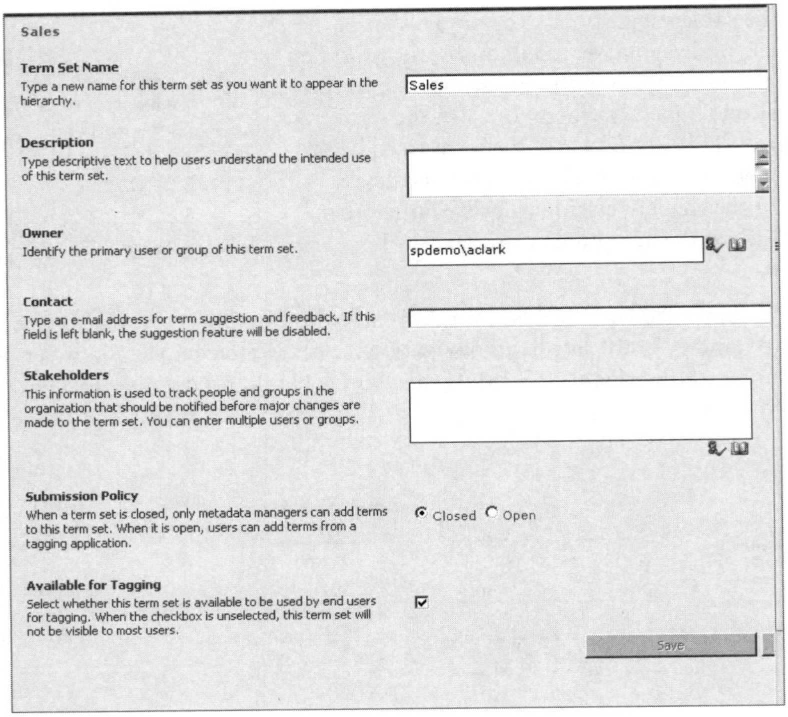

Sales
Term Set Name
Type a new name for this term set as you want it to appear in the hierarchy.
Sales
Description
Type descriptive text to help users understand the intended use of this term set.
Owner
Identify the primary user or group of this term set.
spdemo\aclark
Contact
Type an e-mail address for term suggestion and feedback. If this field is left blank, the suggestion feature will be disabled.
Stakeholders
This information is used to track people and groups in the organization that should be notified before major changes are made to the term set. You can enter multiple users or groups.
Submission Policy
When a term set is closed, only metadata managers can add terms to this term set. When it is open, users can add terms from a tagging application.
Closed
Open
Available for Tagging
Select whether this term set is available to be used by end users for tagging. When the checkbox is unselected, this term set will not be visible to most users.
Save

FIGURE 13-19

Term Sets

Term Sets have the following functionality:

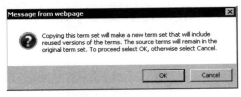

- **Copy Term Set:** When copying a Term Set, a pop-up box will appear indicating that the terms inside the Term Set will be copied over to the new Term Set (Figure 13-20).

Message from webpage
Copying this term set will make a new term set that will include reused versions of the terms. The source terms will remain in the original term set. To proceed select OK, otherwise select Cancel.
OK
Cancel

FIGURE 13-20

  SharePoint 2010 will call the term "Term Set, copy of xxx." When you click a term in the new Term Set, SharePoint will show that the term is a member of multiple Term Sets now and which set is the source.

- **Reuse Terms:** A modal pop-up (Figure 13-21) will ask the user to select a term from another Term Set. After clicking OK, SharePoint will then copy that term into the current Term Set. When viewing the properties of the term, multiple Term Sets will appear with the original Term Set being the source.

FIGURE 13-21

➤ **Move Term Set:** The Move Term Set action allows the user to move a Term Set from one group to another or change the home of the Term Set to another site collection.

➤ **Delete Term Set:** Deleting a Term Set just deletes the container that holds all the terms. SharePoint will then move these terms into a Term Set titled Orphaned Terms. It is the administrator's responsibility to then move these items to a new Term Set (Figure 13-22).

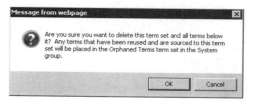

FIGURE 13-22

Terms

Items in Term Sets can be copied, reused, merged, deprecated, moved, and deleted. Selecting a term to merge to another places the originally selected term as a synonym to the second term (Figure 13-23).

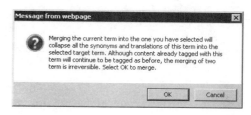

FIGURE 13-23

If a term was copied from another Term Set or is not a source term, the merge-term option will not be available.

When deprecating a term, the term will remain in the Term Store but will no longer be available for tagging.

It is also possible to import terms into SharePoint 2010 Managed Metadata by loading a comma-separated values file. Limitations to this process exist, such as requiring each file to have at least one Term Set. The import process also supports nesting up to seven levels deep. This import process is another option to get terms into Managed Metadata without allowing access into the Central Administration application. To make this process even easier, Wictor Wilén wrote a template in Excel 2010 to create Term Stores that manage the following properties:

➤ Term Set name

➤ Term Set description

➤ LCID

➤ Available for tagging

➤ Term description

For more information on the Excel 2010 template from Wictor Wilén, visit the following link: `http://www.wictorwilen.se/Post/Create-SharePoint-2010-Managed-Metadata-with-Excel-2010.aspx`.

SharePoint 2010 also provides a mechanism to support multilingual Term Sets (Figure 13-24). After installing the appropriate language packs, go inside the Managed Metadata Service to set the default language and then add the working languages.

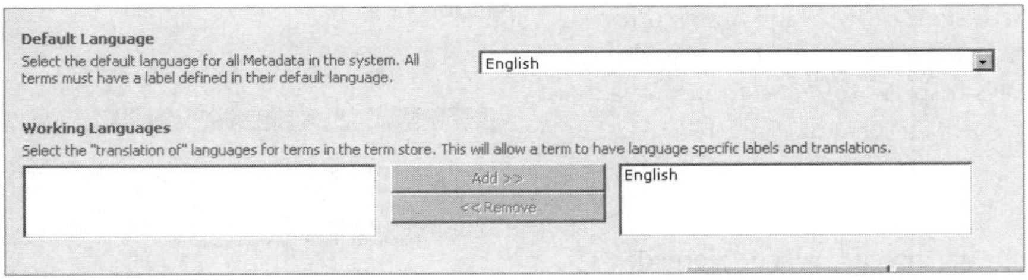

Default Language
Select the default language for all Metadata in the system. All terms must have a label defined in their default language.

English

Working Languages
Select the "translation of" languages for terms in the term store. This will allow a term to have language specific labels and translations.

Add >>
<< Remove

English

FIGURE 13-24

For more information regarding this, visit Multilingual Terms Sets (SharePoint Server 2010) at `http://technet.microsoft.com/en-us/library/ff678224.aspx`.

ADVANCED RATINGS TOPICS

While working with the beta version of SharePoint 2010, I found that the ratings service can be troublesome at times. The RTM release has proven to be extremely stable compared to previous releases. If the Ratings feature is not available as an option to be enabled in a document library, the following section walks you through the steps to enable the ratings service in a SharePoint farm. Another section reviews the concept of bubbling up content to users by looking at popular items.

Troubleshooting Ratings Service

If you don't have the Rating Settings link and have confirmed that the User Profile Service is running, I have a few troubleshooting steps that may help out. The PowerShell command is as follows:

```
enable-spfeature <insert featureid here> -url <insert url here>
```

Getting the URL is easy but the featureid will take a few more steps. Navigate to the following directory on your SharePoint server:

```
~~\Program Files\Common Files\Microsoft Shared\
      Web Server Extensions\14\template\features
```

Inside Features, find the Ratings folder, then open the feature.xml file. The feature ID is located toward the top of the xml file (Figure 13-25). The entire GUID (without the parentheses) is needed for the PowerShell command.

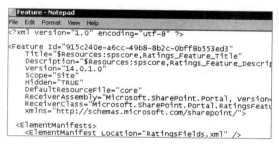

After running the PowerShell command, the Ratings Settings link should be visible for your document library.

FIGURE 13-25

Filtering Content Based on Ratings

By now I hope you have the ratings service up and running with hundreds of users' rating documents. Items that are highly rated certainly should raise awareness of their content. But unless you have a strategy of letting your users know where this content is, chances will be high that it will be disregarded. In this section you learn how to filter content based on ratings and highlight this content to your users.

When ratings are enabled on your document library or list, the ratings will appear as a column. Essentially, ratings are no different from any column that contains data. Because ratings can be viewed as columns, SharePoint 2010 gives us options for viewing, sorting, and filtering data based on ratings. For your larger document libraries or lists, it's possible to create views based on sorting the Ratings field. It is also possible to hook into the Ratings field using a Content Query Web Part.

Creating views in SharePoint 2010 is essentially the same process as in 2007. Assuming that you have permissions to create views, you should navigate to your document library and select the Library tag in the Library Tools section of the Ribbon. The Create View button will be visible toward the left-hand side of the Ribbon (Figure 13-26).

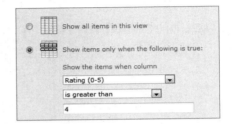

FIGURE 13-26

On the Choose A View Format splash screen, select Standard View. Give your view a new name and scroll down to the Sort section. In this area, you can sort the items in your document library by rating. In case you want to omit entries that are not highly rated, notice that the same column can be used in the Filter section (Figure 13-27).

SharePoint 2010 provides another column related to ratings called Number of Ratings. This inclusion can become quite powerful. As you create your views, filter on content that is rated higher than 4, and then sort by number of ratings. This will give your users content that is not only highly rated but also extremely popular.

FIGURE 13-27

Setting up views to expose popular, high-rated information will certainly assist your user base. However, the downside of using views is that they are limited to only one content base. Using the Content Query Web Part pulls in content from a variety of sources in your site using the same type of logic used when creating views. Navigate to any page and click the Edit Page button in the Ribbon. Depending on the page layout you're using, you will see Add a Web Part in various places on your page. Clicking that link brings up a Web Part menu directly beneath the Ribbon with three sections: Categories, Web Parts, and About the Web Part. In the Categories section (Figure 13-28), select Content Rollup, then click Content Query in the Web Parts area.

FIGURE 13-28

Pick the Web Part zone that you want the Content Query Web Part to be added to and click the Add button. The Web Part will be added to the top of the Web Part zone titled Content Query. Hover over Content Query to expose another menu displaying the options to minimize, close, delete, or edit the Web Part. By selecting Edit, another menu with the properties for the Content Query Web Part will appear on your screen. From here you can alter the title of the Web Part to something more relevant. More importantly, it's possible to edit exactly what data can be pulled into this Web Part. The first property in the Query section concerns displaying items from either all the sites, an individual site and its subsites, or a specific list. What you select will impact the next area that you have to alter, which is Additional Filters (Figure 13-29).

FIGURE 13-29

If you selected the entire site, the list of filter options will be extremely large. It is sorted by alphabetical order, and Rating (0-5) will be located toward the bottom of the list. In this example, change the value to "is greater than" and specify a numeric three. When you are done making any other changes, click OK, and the Content Query Web Part will display all the content that has been rated higher than three stars. Keep in mind that every item inside SharePoint 2010 is "security-trimmed" based on the context of the current user. This means your query will display only items that the user has access to. Adding a Content Query Web Part, along with using socially driven filters, allows administrators to "bubble up" content that would normally be hidden in either subsites or buried SharePoint lists.

How Metadata Structure Impacts Tagging

By default, everyone has permission to add tags to documents and other SharePoint items. This could become a nightmare because of the sheer number of different terms that users might create. Depending on the organization, there will be site collections where you'll want your users to be able to tag items based on a list of predefined terms. Managed Metadata is the mechanism that will provide the functionality of populating a list of terms to your users. Better yet, it's possible to have a subset of people who have the permissions to add terms, while others can only view them (and subsequently select them). Several concepts lie behind Managed Metadata. These are described in Table 13-1.

TABLE 13-1: Managed Metadata Definitions

ITEM	DEFINITION
Term	A term is identical to a tag; it is a word or phrase that is associated to content.
Term Sets	Term Sets are a collection of similar terms. For example, if you have a product called Book Production Tool and an acronym of BPT, both items would be not just terms but related terms. It would make sense to place these two items into one Term Set. Term Sets can have a couple levels of abstractions. Two types of Term Sets exist, depending on where they are created. One Term Set can contain a maximum of 30,000 terms.
Local Term Sets	Local Term Sets are not necessarily related to social data and are created inside the context of a site collection.
Global Term Sets	Global Term Sets are created in Central Administration and can be used across site collections.
Term Set Groups	Microsoft calls Term Set Groups a security boundary and these are based on who can manage or even view the Term Sets. There is a limit of 1,000 Term Sets per Term Set group.
Term Store Management Tool	Terms, Term Sets, and Term Set Groups are all managed with the Term Store Management Tool. This tool is accessed from inside the Central Administration application or from Site Actions as a site collection administrator.

Four steps are required when planning for Term Sets:

1. Identify Term Sets.

2. Identify the owner of each Term Set.

3. Determine Term Set Groups.

4. Define Term Sets.

The first step to planning for Managed Metadata is identifying potential Term Sets (with the help of Table 13-1). What might help with this process is looking for potential metadata inside each department (i.e., work group) and answering these questions:

➤ Do any of your departments have keywords that identify the progress of a project (being developed, being tested)?

➤ Do you have any ticket status or help status systems (initiated, researched, closed)?

➤ Does your institution use workflows (waiting for approval, approved)?

➤ Can you identify words or phrases that are likely to be used as tags (product names, region territories, marketing campaign names)?

➤ Do you have documents that can be filtered or sorted based on process (requirement gathering, functional documentation, technical documentation, use cases, test cases, deployment documentation)?

Setting up Term Set owners is crucial for overall maintenance and longevity of the Term Set. This user owns the Term Set and periodically reviews the terms or cleans up the terms. Organizing the Term Sets into groups adds another level of administration. A Term Set Group is a security boundary that relieves the SharePoint Administrator of administration responsibility. A contributor to the Term Set Group has the ability to manage existing Term Sets and create new Term Sets. It is common to set up Term Set Groups based on existing departments, which means that the existing owner of the SharePoint department site would also own the Term Set Group. The last step to setting up Managed Metadata is identifying and organizing the terms. While organizing terms, keep in mind that it is possible to set up synonyms. If you uncover alternate names, set the fullest or most appropriate term as primary and make the others synonyms of the first term.

To assist in usability, you can explore two scenarios within the feature of tagging:

➤ **Open tagging:** Any user can create a new tag and associate the tag everywhere.

➤ **Hybrid tagging:** Users can still add terms to the keyword Term Set, but they can also select terms from previously created Term Sets.

Open tagging is by far the easiest configuration to set up in SharePoint 2010. This approach is wide open and allows the creation of any keyword that one can imagine. By default, all authenticated users are able to create new keywords. The downside of this approach is that if SharePoint doesn't suggest a tag quickly enough or if the user disregards the suggestion, it's possible to have a ton of similar keywords. Users may also create misspelled keywords.

Hybrid tagging is another tagging approach that allows flexibility with tagging but adds a layer of preconfiguration. While working with Managed Metadata and setting up Term Sets, decide which

terms should be available for tagging by marking the
Available for Tagging checkbox (Figure 13-30). From
here, users can use select terms from the prepopulated
Term Sets when tagging items. These terms will appear to
the users as suggestions while they are typing. Users will
not be able to add terms to any Term Store unless they
have been set up as contributors to the Term Set Group. Any terms users add that do not show up as
suggestions will be tossed into the keywords Term Set by SharePoint 2010. Over time, it would be in
your best interests to review the keywords Term Set and move items over to a Term Set that can be
managed with more detail. For example, it is not possible to set up synonyms for keywords, but it
would be possible if the term resided in another Term Set Group.

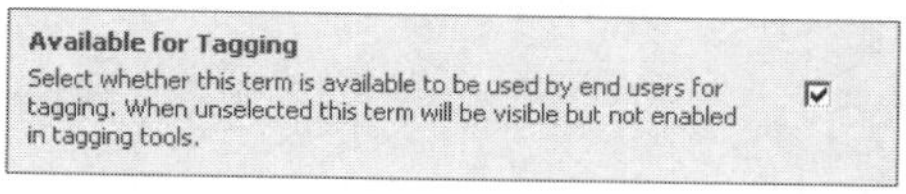

FIGURE 13-30

SUMMARY

In this chapter, you learned how tagging and ratings can be used inside SharePoint 2010 and how
metadata can be used to help assist with tagging. Social computing inside SharePoint is closely
coupled with Managed Metadata. The upfront cost of planning metadata structure will ensure a
smooth start to social computing. However, scheduled maintenance of existing terms and occasional
reorganization of metadata will keep usability high, which in return will keep social collaboration
moving forward. This process is important because with the inclusion of an active and growing
Folksonomy, SharePoint will continue to uncover relations between artifacts.

14

My Site

WHAT'S IN THIS CHAPTER?

- Introduction to the new My Site structure in SharePoint 2010
- Walkthrough of how activity data is presented to the enterprise
- Uncovering best practices for configuring My Site
- Exploration of the service applications used behind the scenes with My Site
- Learning how to administer SharePoint 2010 profiles
- Understanding what level of planning is needed for large-scale My Site deployments

The previous chapter discussed how to rate and tag items inside SharePoint 2010. This activity is great; however, it won't matter if no one can view this social data. Like a chef, you need a high-quality product but you should never neglect the final presentation. SharePoint 2010 does a great job of presenting social data with My Site. Social data is now easy to consume and use because of how the data is aggregated and presented.

SharePoint collects aspects of social data, like tagging and ratings. My Site opens the floodgates for social data related to the individual user.

In essence, the name My Site broadcasts immediately the intent of the product. This is a home for each user, a place to store information and share with others. Think of My Site as having three sections: My Newsfeed, My Content, and My Profile (Figure 14-1).

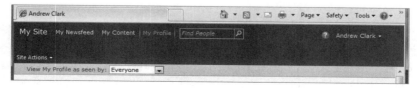

FIGURE 14-1

If you already are using My Site in MOSS 2007, you have a head start on understanding what SharePoint 2010 has to offer. My Newsfeed is a new addition that My Site didn't have in MOSS 2007. This is the section that displays what is happening around you, in a familiar newsfeed format. This is where you will view activity of your colleagues: their profile updates, tagged items, and blog entries. Depending on what your interests are, you will see activity that has been tagged with keywords that match your interests as well.

My Content is a space to place your content, whether it is meant for personal consumption or to be shared with your colleagues. Personal Documents is a private document library that can house items that only you (and administrators) can view. This location is ideal for replacing file shares or (even worse, since it's not backed up) your desktop. This immediately sounds perfect for storing OneNote files and other miscellaneous files. This location has the same capabilities as every other document library, such as versioning of files and automatic backup (to name a couple). Shared Documents is a library that can be used to save content that is then viewable by everyone who views your profile.

My Profile is essentially the landing page for a SharePoint 2010 My Site personal site. This is the gateway to viewing essentially every piece of social data regarding an individual. Profile information includes individual attributes, interests, and organizational team structure. Microsoft is taking an approach with My Site that's very similar to Facebook and other social networking sites. The intent of adding personal identifiers to your profile is to assist in helping others inside your organization find you. The ability to automatically find like-minded people who share your expertise or skills is completely new to SharePoint 2010. Earlier chapters discussed why social data is important. Imagine working in a large corporation with employees whom you might never get a chance to talk with because they are not on the same project. Now you can find people who can share expertise and experience in subject matter (such as C#), and these experiences might uncover a shortcut for your daily routines or help solve challenges.

CONFIGURATION AND ADMINISTRATION

SharePoint 2010 underwent a huge fundamental shift in regard to service architecture. Services are now managed with service applications, which can be created by three methods:

➤ Configuration wizards inside Central Administration

➤ PowerShell commands

➤ Programmatically with Visual Studio 2010

A service application consists of many individual pieces. By abstracting these pieces into applications, it is now possible to scale out services inside your SharePoint farm. Because it's not possible to discuss all the aspects of service management in this chapter, see the article from MSDN titled "Service Application and Service Management (SharePoint Server 2010)" at `http://technet` `.microsoft.com/en-us/library/ee704547%28office.14%29.aspx`.

Social data with My Site in SharePoint 2010 relies on three items: a profile sync process to bring in profiles, a process to manage tagging, and a process to search for people.

Profiles are imported into SharePoint 2010 from Active Directory (or other compatible user store) with the User Profile Service application, which relies on the User Profile Synchronization service.

Social data that consists of tags and ratings is also managed by the User Profile Service application. The tags and ratings depend on the Managed Metadata Service. The ability to search for people inside My Site is dependent on the Search Service application.

You can manage these service applications inside Central Administration under Application Management. In the Service Applications section, click the Manage Service Applications link to request a complete list of all service applications running in your farm.

You can view the services that these service applications use inside Central Administration. Navigate to the System Settings page and click the Manage Services on the Server link in the Servers section to view the status of all services running in your farm.

The following sections in this chapter outline creating these service applications. You can find additional information on creating, editing, or deleting a User Profile Service application in these articles: "Create, Edit, or Delete a User Profile Service Application (SharePoint Server 2010)" at `http://technet.microsoft.com/en-us/library/ee721052%28office.14%29.aspx`; and "Create, Update, Publish, and Delete a Managed Metadata Service Application (SharePoint Server 2010)" at `http://technet.microsoft.com/en-us/library/ee530392%28office.14%29.aspx`.

Accounts Needed for Administration

SharePoint 2010 needs a few service accounts to be created to succeed with configuration. Table 14-1 outlines what accounts are needed and what permission levels are necessary, but the table should not be a replacement for thorough planning of permissions. The information is a combination of the two TechNet articles that follow the table. It's very easy to have the SharePoint synchronization status stuck at Starting. The first two accounts can be configured ahead of time as a managed account, and Managed Metadata allows the administrator to select these accounts from a drop-down list. This chapter addresses Managed Metadata in the next section.

TABLE 14-1: Administration Accounts

LOCATION	DESCRIPTION	MANAGED ACCOUNT?
Application pool for My Site (Figure 14-9)	Domain User Account, not member of the farm administrators group	Yes
Application pool for User Profile Service application (Figure 14-16)	Domain User Account, not member of the farm administrators group	Yes
Administrator for User Profile Service application (Figure 14-28)	Domain User Account used to administer SharePoint farm	It could be a managed account, but it typically should be an individual user, since this is not for a running service.

continues

TABLE 14-1 *(continued)*

LOCATION	DESCRIPTION	MANAGED ACCOUNT?
User Profile Synchronization Service (Figure 14-18)	Local administrator, replicate Directory Changes permission inside Active Directory	Not an option
Account used in Synchronization Connections (to get to Active Directory) (Figure 14-21)		No

The following resource articles are available: "Configure Profile Synchronization (SharePoint Server 2010)" at `http://technet.microsoft.com/en-us/library/cc678863.aspx#Section3`; and "Account Permissions and Security Settings (SharePoint Server 2010)" at `http://technet.microsoft.com/en-us/library/cc678863.aspx#Section3`.

What Are Managed Accounts?

Username/password management and identities are not typically discussed when reviewing My Site. Because this chapter reviews the process of setting up services and synchronizing them with Active Directory, it is important to understand the huge improvement in how SharePoint 2010 handles service accounts.

In the past, with MOSS 2007 (or WSS 3.0), it was always a huge pain to change the passwords for the service accounts used inside SharePoint. Certainly it was possible with help from a TechNet article, but it was not a trivial task. From the management standpoint, service accounts were a security risk as well. Because the process was tedious, the service account passwords were probably never set to expire. And if consultants were hired to install the platform, they probably knew all your passwords. To be fair, the same held true for internal resources as well. Typically when people left the company, all the passwords were changed. SharePoint added another level of complexity to this change process related to turnover. To make things worse, some "create" actions inside SharePoint required the knowledge of both the service account and the password — for example, creating a web application with a unique application pool or altering the search crawler.

This process has been greatly improved with SharePoint 2010 by the inclusion of Managed Accounts. SharePoint can now manage Active Directory accounts. What this means is that an administrator or "password keeper" can create Managed Accounts ahead of time that someone else can reference by selecting from a drop-down list (Figure 14-2).

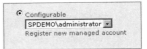

FIGURE 14-2

By using existing accounts, this eliminates the possibility of "fat-fingering" passwords or forgetting to put the domain in front of the username.

Eliminating user error is one added benefit of Managed Accounts. The other benefits involve credential management and automatic password change. It is possible to change passwords with either a generated password, user-supplied password, or existing password through Central Administration. Creating a schedule to automatically change the passwords is an option as well (Figure 14-3).

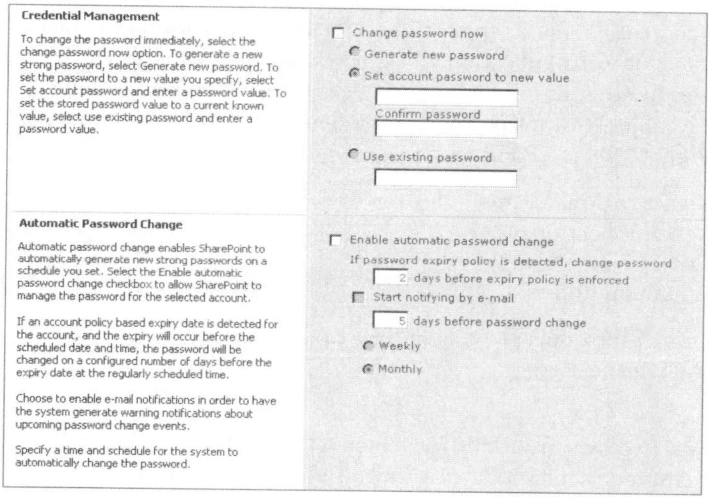

Credential Management

To change the password immediately, select the change password now option. To generate a new strong password, select Generate new password. To set the password to a new value you specify, select Set account password and enter a password value. To set the stored password value to a current known value, select use existing password and enter a password value.

☐ Change password now
  ○ Generate new password
  ◉ Set account password to new value

  Confirm password

  ○ Use existing password

Automatic Password Change

Automatic password change enables SharePoint to automatically generate new strong passwords on a schedule you set. Select the Enable automatic password change checkbox to allow SharePoint to manage the password for the selected account.

If an account policy based expiry date is detected for the account, and the expiry will occur before the scheduled date and time, the password will be changed on a configured number of days before the expiry date at the regularly scheduled time.

Choose to enable e-mail notifications in order to have the system generate warning notifications about upcoming password change events.

Specify a time and schedule for the system to automatically change the password.

☐ Enable automatic password change
  If password expiry policy is detected, change password
    [2] days before expiry policy is enforced
  ☐ Start notifying by e-mail
    [5] days before password change
  ○ Weekly
  ◉ Monthly

FIGURE 14-3

 The password that SharePoint 2010 attempts to generate is based on the complexity settings detected from network or local policy. For more information on the credential change process, bing "Plan Automatic Password Change (SharePoint Foundation)" or visit http://technet.microsoft.com/en-us/library/ee428296.aspx.

Auditing of managed accounts is available through Central Administration. Administrators can view which applications or services use a particular account and when the password was last changed.

To get a list of all managed accounts, use Get-SPManagedAccount. You can configure a managed account inside SharePoint 2010 by using Set-SPManagedAccount. For information on how to create or change a password using Set-SPManagedAccount, run Get-Help in front of the command (Figure 14-4).

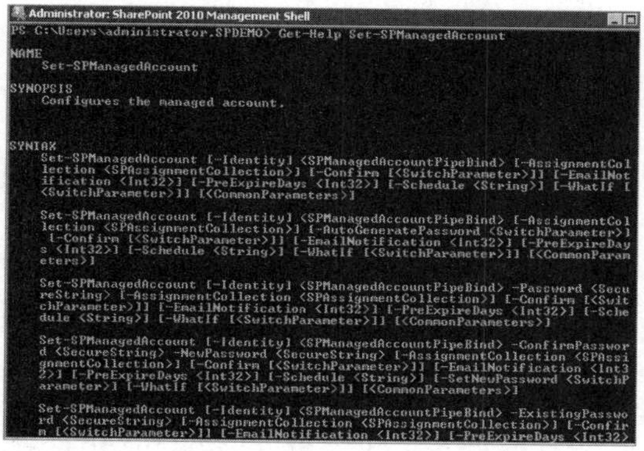

FIGURE 14-4

MY SITE WEB APPLICATION CONFIGURATION

You have two methods for configuring My Site in SharePoint 2010: automatically through the Farm Configuration Wizard or manually inside Central Administration. If the intent of the installation is for demo purposes, My Site configuration through the wizard is by far the quickest and easiest method to get started. Unfortunately, best practices are not followed when using the wizard to configure the User Profile Service/My Site. In a production environment, My Site should be configured for the user's own web application, content database, application pool, and application pool identity. Combining My Site with the main content web application will throw a configuration warning inside the SharePoint 2010 Health Analyzer. In order to follow best practices the following section walks through the creation of a dedicated My Site Host inside SharePoint. Several new features are included with creating a new web application that all SharePoint administrators should understand.

Inside Central Administration, navigate to Application Management and select Manage Web Applications. In the Ribbon toward the top left, select New to bring up the Create New Web Application modal pop-up.

In the Authentication section, Microsoft introduces a new type of authentication called Claims-Based Authentication (Figure 14-5).

FIGURE 14-5

The authentication mode that was carried over from 2007 is called Classic Mode Authentication. Classic Mode is probably the most common scenario at this time. To find out more about Claims-Based Authentication, consult the article "Plan Authentication Methods (SharePoint Server 20101)" at `http://technet.microsoft.com/en-us/library/cc262350.aspx`.

 Forms-Based Authentication (FBA) is not supported with Classic Mode Authentication. To use FBA, Claims-Based Authentication must be used.

The My Site web application should also run in a separate IIS website. This section (Figure 14-6) creates a new IIS website.

SharePoint will attempt to assign the site a random port number. Typically. web servers expect to listen to traffic on Port 80. This doesn't mean that SharePoint needs to run all the web applications on Port 80. However, in the example of setting up My Site, the port number should be changed to Port 80. When changing the port number to 80, it is imperative that a host header be used. Host

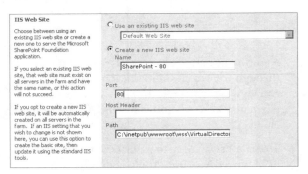

FIGURE 14-6

headers allow IIS to map multiple applications to one IP address and one port number. For example, host headers provide SharePoint the ability to set up `contoso.com` and `mysites.contoso.com` using the same IP address and port number. Typically, the default values will not be changed in the Security Configuration section (Figure 14-7).

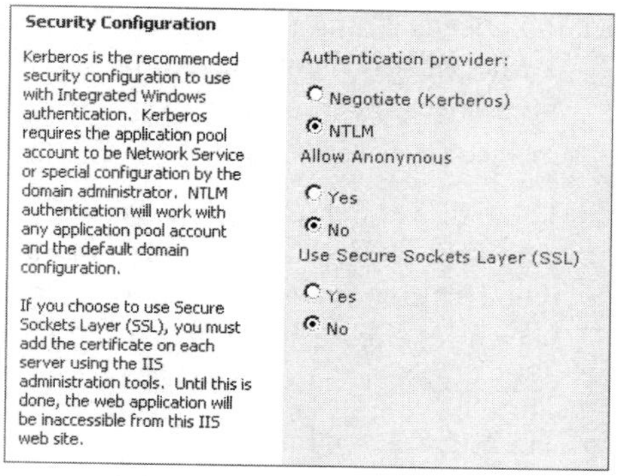

My Site personal sites are not normally open to anonymous users nor is an SSL connection used. However, these values are important when setting up an external SharePoint site. For example, if an external SharePoint site is being used with Forms-Based Authentication, SSL should be used. If SSL is being used, the port number should also be updated to Port 443.

The information in the Public URL section (Figure 14-8) will be automatically refreshed after making changes in the IIS website section. Because we are creating a new application and not extending an existing application, the Zone drop-down list is marked as Default without the option of changing it.

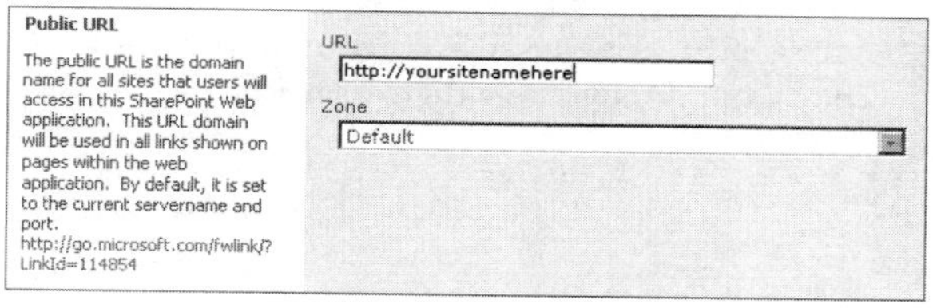

The settings located in the Application Pool section (Figure 14-9) are extremely important in regard to IIS worker process isolation. Do not share or use an existing application pool such as the application pool associated with Central Administration. Replace the generated application pool name with a more descriptive name such as SharePoint – My Site. Lastly, the security account for the application pool is basically the identity used for the newly created application pool. This security account should be unique from all the other application pools as well. This ensures that if an identity is compromised for one application pool, the other app pools will be isolated. This last attribute might look different for people who are experienced with MOSS 2007. This uses Managed Account, a concept described earlier in this chapter.

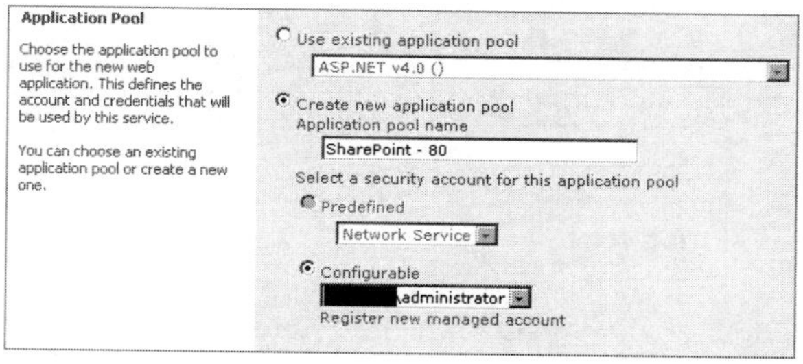

The fields in the Database Name and Authentication section (Figure 14-10) will be pre-generated as well. The database name will have a generic name of WSS_Content with a random GUID attached to it. To make maintenance and documentation easier, remove the GUID and add in *my sites* after WSS_Content_. The

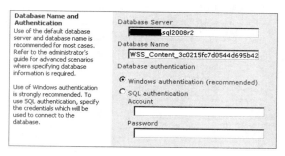

FIGURE 14-7

FIGURE 14-8

FIGURE 14-9

FIGURE 14-10

authentication mode to communicate to the database will be defaulted to Windows Authentication. It is possible to change this to SQL Authentication, but this change will not work unless the SQL instance is configured to use Mixed Mode Authentication. Microsoft recommends Windows Authentication, but to read more information on SQL Authentication and setting up SQL server for Mixed Mode, you can consult "Choosing an Authentication Mode" at `http://technet.microsoft .com/en-us/library/ms144284.aspx`.

The Failover Server option (Figure 14-11) is new to 2010. SharePoint 2010 has a more seamless approach to SQL Server Database mirroring. If mirroring is already set up in your SQL instance, then this step is self-explanatory. To explore high availability and learn what the options are, search for the TechNet article "Plan for Availability (SharePoint Server 2010)" at `http://technet .microsoft.com/en-us/library/cc748824.aspx`.

The Service Application Connections section (Figure 14-12) can be left at default for My Site. It is important to understand what this means in regard to creating other web applications. This is the area where an administrator can specify if an application should be wired up to service applications (for example, the PerformancePoint service application). Not all applications will have the need to access every single service. More importantly, if the farm has multiple segregated web applications, they should have their own User Profile Service.

FIGURE 14-11

FIGURE 14-12

After clicking OK, the new application will appear in the web applications list with the description that was specified earlier under the Name column. At this point, SharePoint has a web application that is devoid of any site collections. The next step is to create a site collection as a My Site Host. Click Application Management and then Create Site Collections in the Site Collections section. Ensure that the newly created web application is selected as the web application in context. All the fields are self-explanatory, except for Template Selection and Quota Template. For Template Selection, you must select My Site Host under the Enterprise tab (Figure 14-13).

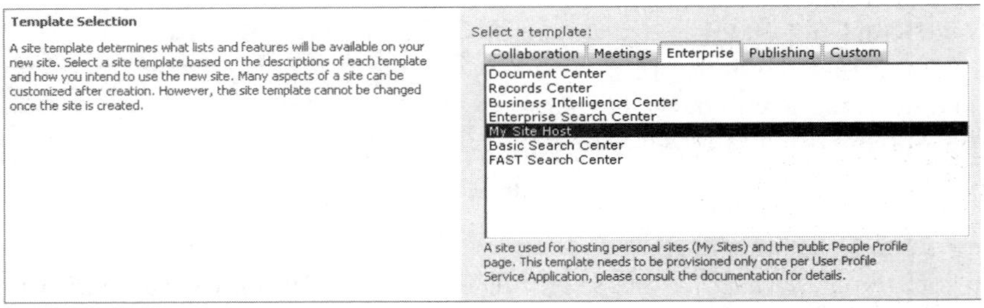

FIGURE 14-13

If the Enterprise tab is not available, confirm exactly what version of SharePoint is installed in your farm. In Central Administration, navigate to Upgrade and Migration and click Convert Farm License Type.

For Quota Template, change the drop-down list to Personal Site. This will tell SharePoint that the storage limit for each individual My Site will be 100 MB. If at any time these limits need to be changed, it's possible to increase or decrease the storage limits using Central Administration or PowerShell. See "Manage Site Collection Storage Limits (SharePoint Server 2010)" at http://technet.microsoft.com/en-us/library/cc263480.aspx for more information.

Before moving on to configuring the User Profile Service, the implications of self-creating My Site personal sites should be explored. By following the previous steps, you have isolated the main content web application from the My Site web application. This is best practice for many reasons, but one of the main concerns is related to the size and growth of the actual content database. With MOSS 2007, the recommended limit for a content database was 100 GB. This recommendation has been raised to 200 GB with SharePoint 2010. Keep in mind that if this limit is reached, the farm will not crash. The performance of the SharePoint farm will start to gradually degrade when recommended limits are exceeded.

The quota template mentioned earlier is a set limit for how large one person's My Site personal site can grow to. The default value set by SharePoint is 100 megabytes (MB). These sites are stored by SharePoint inside content databases that reside inside SQL Server. Since we know what the My Site quota template is (100MB), and we know the preferred growth limit of a content database (200GB), we can start to plan or stage the content databases ahead of time. Chances are high that the number of My Site personal sites created by employees will not fit inside one content database if your goal is to keep the size of the content database under 200GB. Table 14-2 attempts to visualize how to stage databases. The figure of 200 GB is equal to 204,800 MB, which based on the boundary that was set earlier (the default value of 100 MB) is equal to 2,048 My Site personal sites.

TABLE 14-2: Plan for My Site Limits

STORAGE LIMIT	MAX SIZE DATABASE	MAX MY SITES
50 MB	204,800 MB	4,096
100 MB	204,800 MB	2,048
200 MB	204,800 MB	1,024
800 MB	204,800 MB	256

Regardless of the number of employees at an institution, the number of My Site personal sites that should be hosted in one content database decreases dramatically as the storage limit for each site increases. Table 14-3 displays how the number of databases increases as the number of employees and the storage limit increase. Remember that My Site personal sites will not be generated or provisioned until the individual user clicks the My Site link for the first time. It is possible to calculate how many content databases are needed when looking at the number of employees and the storage limit.

TABLE 14-3: Plan for My Site Content Databases

STORAGE LIMIT	MAX MY SITES	NO. OF EMPLOYEES	NO. OF CONTENT DATABASES NEEDED
800 MB	256	2,100	9
100 MB	2,048	2,100	2

It is possible to pre-stage the content databases in the My Site web application so that when users start to trickle in, the max number of sites will never exceed the recommended limits. Inside Central Administration, navigate to Application Management, then select Manage Content Databases in the Databases section. Ensure that the appropriate web application is selected (Figure 14-14). Depending on what the determined storage limits are, change the Maximum Number of Site Collections to your calculated figure. Also remember to change the Site Collection Level Warning to a figure less than the figure entered as the max. The last step is creating the appropriate number of content databases based on the number of employees in the institution. Use the same database capacity settings that were just used, and use a logical naming convention for the database name (Figure 14-15).

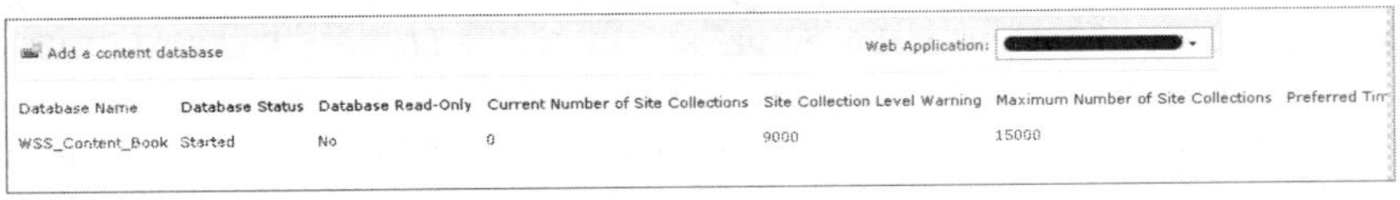

FIGURE 14-14

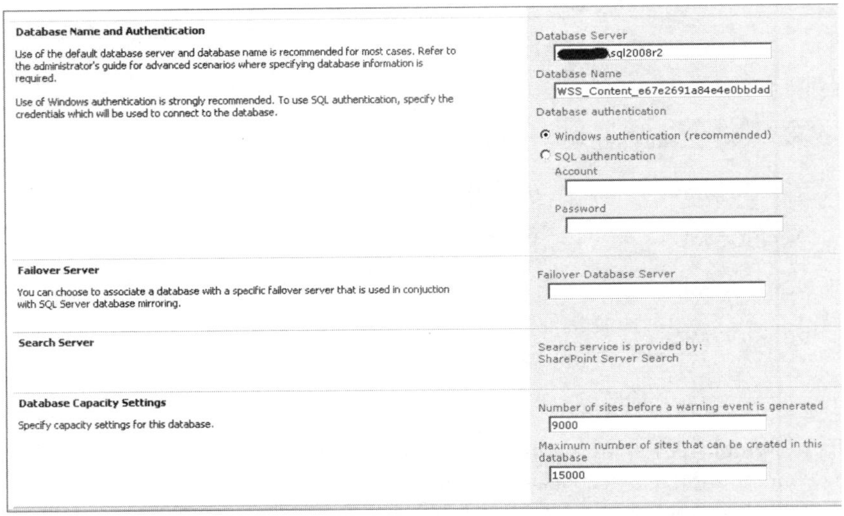

FIGURE 14-15

The one-time page-load hit that users receive when creating their My Site might seem like a long time to wait. It is possible to programmatically create a My Site personal site in SharePoint. Resist the urge to iterate through the Active Directory structure or User Profile Store to pre-generate My Site personal sites. It isn't necessary to take on the extra burden for users who might not even use the functionality. The pre-generate process also assumes that the institution's AD environment is squeaky clean. However, creating a handful of My Site personal sites ahead of time might be a good idea.

CREATING THE USER PROFILE SERVICE APPLICATION

At this point, the My Site web application is configured. With luck, the information in the previous section will start an open dialog regarding planning and user adoption. The next step is configuring the User Profile Service.

To use the My Site host that was just created, the web application has to be associated with a User Profile Service application. If this User Profile Service application has already been created, the service application will have to be deleted and then re-created. Inside Central Administration, navigate to Application Management and click Manage Service Applications in the Service Applications section. In the top-left portion of the Ribbon, click New and select User Profile Service application (Figure 14-16). Similar to creating a new web application, SharePoint will ask for application pool, profile database, and even failover database server information. To attach this application to the newly created My Site web application, enter the URL into the My Site Host URL textbox. SharePoint also provides options for how the URL will be constructed with managed paths and site-naming format. After the creation of the User Profile Service application, you will be redirected to a complete list of all service applications in the farm. Before continuing, confirm that the newly created User Profile Service is on the list and the service is started.

FIGURE 14-16

Select the newly created User Profile Service application and click Permissions in the Ribbon. Verify that the account currently used (inside Central Administration) has been granted full control of the service application. If this step is skipped, attempting to click Manage will display an expected error.

CONFIGURING THE USER PROFILE SERVICE AND THE USER PROFILE SYNC SERVICE

Profiles are synchronized between the SharePoint User Profile and Active Directory by the User Profile Synchronization Service. Getting this service to run without issues was problematic in pre-RTM releases of SharePoint. The good news is that the process to successfully start this service has become relatively easy. This service needs to be started with a specific set of steps and a little bit of patience.

Before you can start the User Profile Synchronization Service, you must create a User Profile Service application. You can do this by running the configuration wizard, by running a PowerShell script, or by using the GUI in Central Administration. You must configure a valid My Site Host as well.

Inside Central Administration, click System Settings then Manage Services on Server in the Servers section. Toward the bottom of the list (Figure 14-17), find User Profile Service and start the service (assuming the status is not at Started). Directly under that service is User Profile Synchronization Service. Click Start for the sync service and the screen shown in Figure 14-18 will appear.

User Profile Service	Started	Stop
User Profile Synchronization Service	Started	Stop

FIGURE 14-17

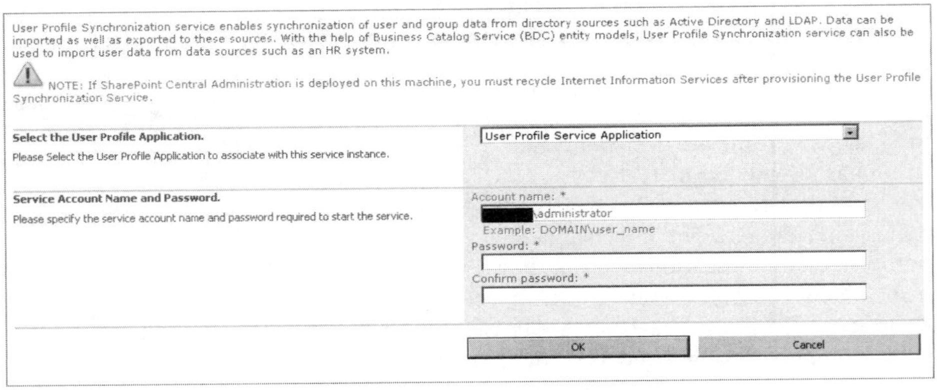

User Profile Synchronization service enables synchronization of user and group data from directory sources such as Active Directory and LDAP. Data can be imported as well as exported to these sources. With the help of Business Catalog Service (BDC) entity models, User Profile Synchronization service can also be used to import user data from data sources such as an HR system.

⚠ NOTE: If SharePoint Central Administration is deployed on this machine, you must recycle Internet Information Services after provisioning the User Profile Synchronization Service.

Select the User Profile Application.
Please Select the User Profile Application to associate with this service instance.

User Profile Service Application ▾

Service Account Name and Password.
Please specify the service account name and password required to start the service.

Account name: *
████\administrator
Example: DOMAIN\user_name

Password: *

Confirm password: *

OK   Cancel

FIGURE 14-18

For the User Profile Application drop-down list, select the User Profile Service application created in the previous steps. After entering the password for the service account, click OK to be returned to the list of services on the server.

Do not proceed any further until the User Profile Synchronization Service status has changed from Starting to Started (Figure 14-19). Some in the SharePoint community recommend an iisreset/noforce *and even a server reboot at this point (*http://www.harbar.net/articles/sp2010ups.aspx*).*

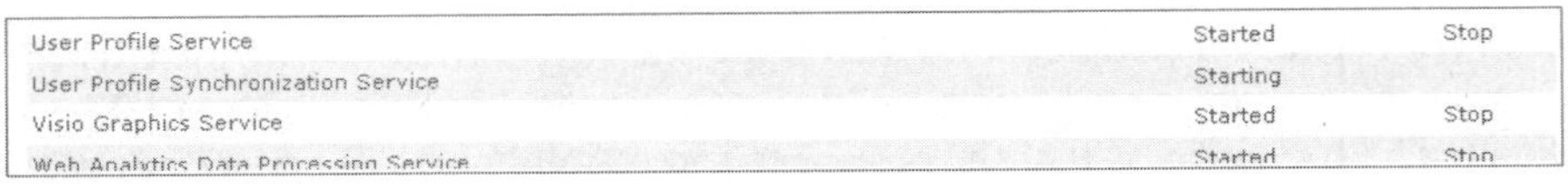

User Profile Service	Started	Stop
User Profile Synchronization Service	Starting	
Visio Graphics Service	Started	Stop
Web Analytics Data Processing Service	Started	Stop

FIGURE 14-19

Once the User Profile Synchronization Service is started, it will be time to set up a synchronization connection inside SharePoint. Go back into the administration screen for the User Profile Service.

 SharePoint 2010 has numerous navigation improvements. However, navigating to the various administration sites can become tedious. On the Central Administration homepage, add a link to the Manage Profile Service page to the Resources link library. The management screen is attached to a particular service application. Inspect the query string value for applicationid *in the URL to confirm that the management screen is unique. Keep this in mind when saving links or bookmarks in case new profile service applications are created or deleted (Figure 14-20).*

Inside the Manage Profile Service page, click Configure Synchronization Connections inside the Synchronization section. The connections page will list all current connections. Click Create New Connection to create a new connection for the User Profile Sync Service. The following screen will ask for information regarding the

FIGURE 14-20

connection source (Figure 14-21). After selecting the connection type, account name, and password click the Populate Containers button. It is not necessary to click the entire domain; just select the organizational units that are needed (Figure 14-22). After clicking OK, the connection will be saved and viewable on the connection list. Navigate back to Manage Profile Service and click Start Profile Synchronization in the Synchronization section.

Connection Settings

For the Active Directory directory service server, type in **Forest name** and **Domain controller name**.

For Active Directory connections to work, this account must have directory sync rights.

Forest name:

(•) Auto discover domain controller
(○) Specify a domain controller:
      Domain controller name:

Authentication Provider Type:
Windows Authentication
Authentication Provider Instance:

Account name: *

Example: DOMAIN\user_name
Password: *

Confirm password: *

Port:
389
☐ Use SSL-secured connection:

FIGURE 14-21

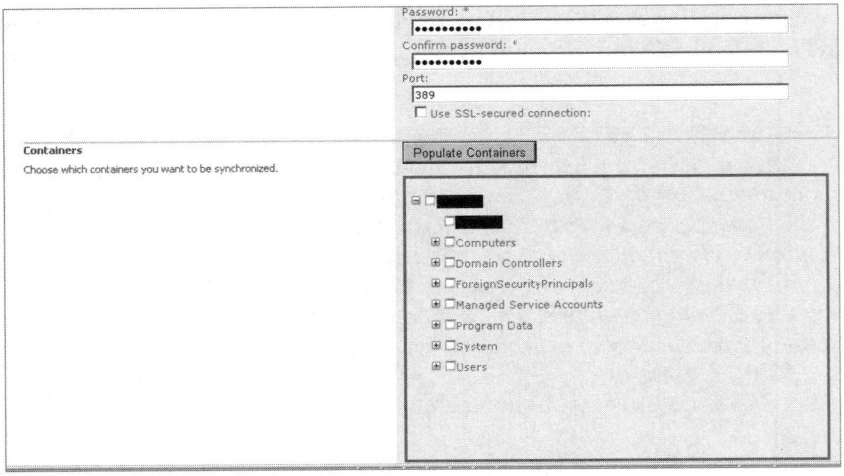

FIGURE 14-22

Do enough research on this topic with the SharePoint community, and it will be clear that the consensus regarding this process is to have a high level of patience. Luckily, you have two different ways to view the progress of synchronization. In the Profile Synchronization Settings located toward the right-hand side of the Manage Profile Service page, a Profile Synchronization Settings hyperlink will appear. Clicking the link brings up another browser window with updates regarding additions, updates, successes, and failures. This approach can be somewhat slow. The other option involves opening Forefront Identity Manager. Forefront Identity Manager is located at `C:\Program Files\Microsoft Office Servers\14.0\Synchronization Service\UIShell\ miisclient.exe`. FIM seems to be quicker in regard to displaying updates. Attempting to run FIM before having the synchronization service configured will display an error (Figure 14-23).

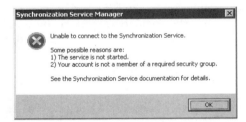

FIGURE 14-23

 For more information regarding Forefront Identity Manager and the role that it plays with the User Profile Synchronization Service, visit "Rational Guide to Implementing SharePoint Server 2010 User Profile Synchronization" by Spencer Harbar. The following link is probably the most important resource right now in regard to User Profile Synchronization: `http://www.harbar.net/articles/ sp2010ups.aspx`.

Managing Profiles

After successfully synching to Active Directory or a user profile source, statistics regarding the number of profiles and properties collected will appear in the Profiles section on the Manage

Profile Service page (Figure 14-24). To manage individual profiles, click Manage User Profiles. By default, none of the profiles will be displayed when first visiting this page. Start out by typing in the last name of a user or entering the first letter of a name; SharePoint will then display a list of matching results. On an individual basis, it's possible to edit a user's properties and My Site. By selecting Manage Personal Site, the administrator will be redirected to the user's My Site Site Settings page. As administrator, you can alter features, permissions, or content just as with any regular SharePoint site. When visiting other profile My Site personal sites as administrator, remember that the site is associated with the user but the navigation area (My Site, My Newsfeed, My Content, and My Profile) is attached to the administrator (or whatever account is currently being used). Multiple-item select is once again available on this list. However, in this example multiple select only allows the administrator to delete.

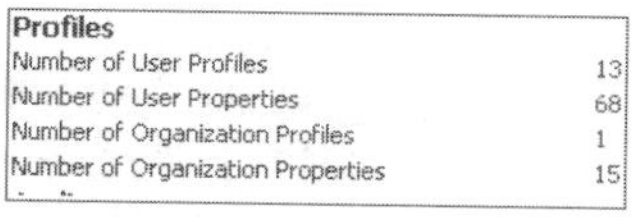

FIGURE 14-24

Because a My Site is considered a site collection, it can be configured much the same as other SharePoint sites. A My Site can also be configured for site use confirmation and deletion (Figure 14-25). SharePoint can be configured to detect unused sites so that administrators can manually alter or delete these sites. SharePoint can also automatically delete the unused sites as well. This functionality depends on configuring outgoing e-mail settings. For more information, see "Manage Unused Web Sites (SharePoint Server 2010)" at `http://technet.microsoft.com/enus/library/cc262420.aspx`.

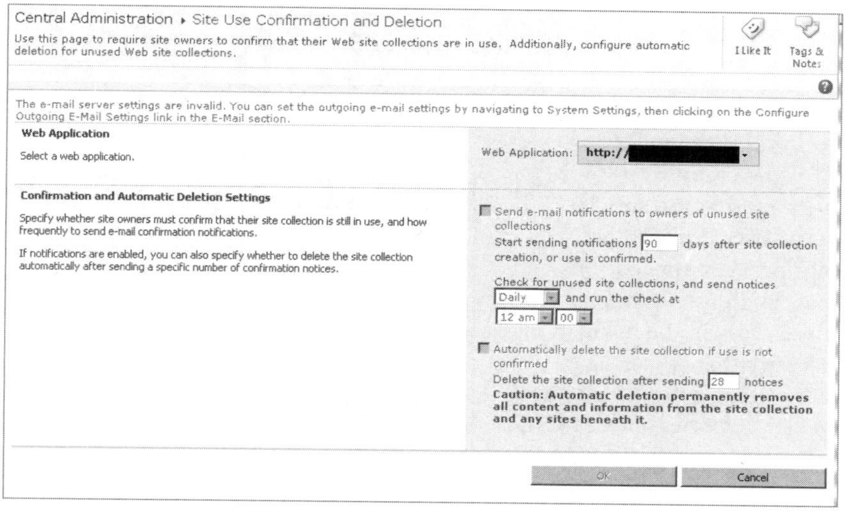

FIGURE 14-25

Configure People Search

After configuring the User Profile Service, not only will My Site personal sites be functional but so will People Search. This means that the search service (assuming it has been configured) should be able to crawl the profile store. If People Search is not working in your farm, you have two configuration items to double-check. Navigate to the Search Administration site for the Search Service application.

To visit the search administration page, navigate to Application Management inside Central Administration. In the Service Applications section, click Manage Service Applications. This should be another link to include in the Resources link library.

In the Crawling section, click Content Sources (Figure 14-26) to verify which sites are being crawled. This property page will verify that the crawler is looking at the User Profile Store. Depending on the farm, numerous content sources could be listed. In most cases, there will be one entry in this list entitled Local SharePoint sites. Click Local SharePoint sites to view which start addresses are included (Figure 14-27). Verify that `sps3://inserthostnamehere` exists as a start address. For example, if the main application is `http://contoso.com`, the entry will be `sps3://contoso`.

FIGURE 14-26

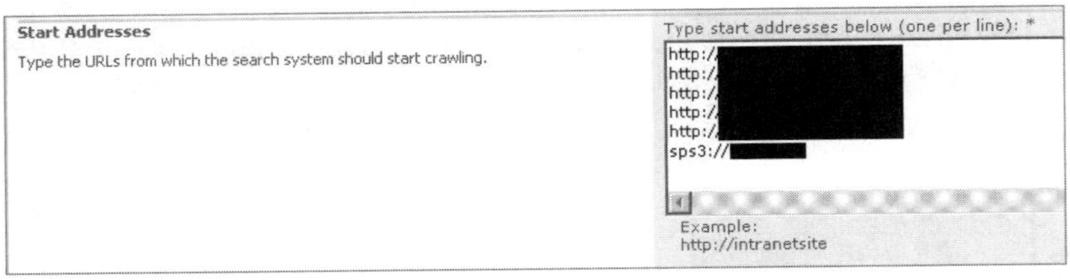

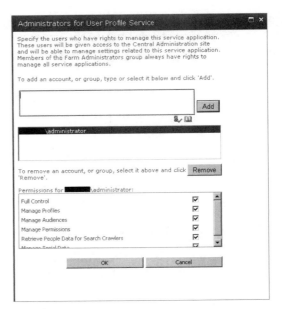

FIGURE 14-27

Once you have confirmed that the crawler has been configured to look at the User Profile Store, the next step will be verifying that the crawler has permission to enter the User Profile Store. Navigate back to Manage Service Applications on Application Management. Highlight User Profile Service and click Administrators in the navigation Ribbon (Figure 14-28). Verify that whatever account is currently being used for the crawler has access to Retrieve People Data for Search Crawlers.

Lastly, verify that a full crawl has actually been conducted in the farm. After a complete full crawl, inspect the Crawl History in the Search Administration page. Click the content source to view more details on the log. Verify the number of errors and top-level errors. Click Error Message to view the exact errors. Use the Host drop-down list to filter the errors to determine the exact root of the error. For more information, see "Post-Installation Steps for Search (SharePoint Server 2010)" at `http://technet.microsoft.com/en-us/library/ee808863.aspx`.

FIGURE 14-28

Planning for Large-Scale My Site Deployments

Earlier in this chapter, a solution regarding planning content databases — based on the number of users inside a corporation — was discussed. Managing content databases is just one aspect of planning for a large user base for My Site usage. The other side of the coin is ensuring that the SharePoint farm can handle the network load behind social computing. Discussions regarding scaling a SharePoint farm could easily fill an entire book. This section briefly describes options for planning and monitoring performance inside your SharePoint 2010 farm.

Performance is dictated by how efficiently SharePoint handles requests per second. RPS extends further than just page loads. A single page could include several requests to the server. Social computing adds even more requests to the stack:

- ➤ Users creating keyword tags, ratings, and notes

- ➤ Generating data for activity feed listviews

- ➤ User-generated profile property updates

- ➤ Storing and displaying My Site status updates

- ➤ Tagging activities that trigger security trimming

- ➤ Traffic generated by the Outlook Social Connector

- ➤ Incremental and full crawls to detect social data updates/changes

Microsoft has released a white paper that discusses social computing capacity planning for SharePoint 2010. The white paper outlines the effect of scaling a SharePoint farm to accommodate increased RPS. Microsoft lists in detail what to expect when adding multiple web front-ends or application servers to the farm. It also helps predict when and where bottlenecks might occur. For example, if a client is rolling out the Outlook Social Connector to 100,000 users, the administrator must use three front-end web servers to support the traffic. For more information, see "SharePoint Server 2010 Performance and Capacity Test Results and Recommendations" at http://www.microsoft.com/downloads/details.aspx?FamilyID=fd1eac86-ad47-4865-9378-80040d08ac55&displaylang=en.

It's possible to monitor an existing SharePoint farm with System Center Operations Manager 2007 (SCOM 2007). Installing the SharePoint 2010 Products Management pack will enable administrators to collect SharePoint-specific performance counters. As opposed to manually searching for issues, SCOM 2007 will send out e-mail alerts based on custom rules or events related to outages and performance monitoring. You can find an article on "Microsoft SharePoint 2010 Products Management Pack for System Center Operations Manager 2007" at http://www.microsoft.com/downloads/details.aspx?FamilyID=5c73415d-97ba-4bdc-8e92-2c4ea4507f91&displaylang=en.

Manage User Properties

The process of mapping Active Directory properties to the User Profile Store is generally handled automatically. However, it is possible to deviate from default behavior and present AD data differently inside SharePoint. To edit individual user properties, go to the Manage Profile Service and click Manage User Properties in the People section. Navigate to a property and select Edit. The following screen will show numerous property values. From here it is possible to hide attributes in the Policy Settings and Display Settings. Administrators can also mark properties as read-only in the Edit Settings section.

The big change with SharePoint 2010 and Active Directory is the ability to synchronize information from My Site back to Active Directory. Before the AD administrator gets angry, remember that it is possible to sync only a few fields. Very few environments are set up where users can refresh corporate information such as changed phone numbers, addresses, and images. Allowing SharePoint to handle this update process should alleviate some of the daily operational pains for the AD administrator. For more information about mapping user profile properties and what permissions are needed, see "Map User Profile Properties" in "Configure Profile Synchronization (SharePoint Server 2010)" at http://technet.microsoft.com/en-us/library/ee721049.aspx#section3.

What Are Audiences?

The use of audiences is not a new concept for SharePoint; they were around for MOSS 2007. Audiences allow SharePoint to deliver specific data to a subset of users. The SharePoint administrator has to configure audiences inside Central Administration. Audiences are extremely powerful in regard to usability. For example, a homepage can have a Content Query Web Part that looks at the current user's audience membership and delivers content that applies to just that audience. This helps cut the clutter on SharePoint pages, because the page designer doesn't have to include multiple Web Parts to display data that might not apply to each group of people. Content Query Web Part, or CQWP, is just one example that uses audience targeting. Edit the properties of most Web Parts and the Target Audience property will be available. Unlike MOSS 2007, the audience property has a People Picker–like control to assist in finding audiences.

Audiences are generated by rules set up inside Central Administration (Figure 14-29). To create audiences, navigate to the User Profile Service management page and click Manage Audiences in the People section. The rules are based on properties being returned from Active Directory (or whatever source is used for user profiles). Once rules are created, it is necessary to compile the audience to insert users into the newly created audience. It's hoped that no compilation errors will be displayed, and that the number of members will be greater than zero. Because audiences are based on rules that look at AD properties, the SharePoint administrator needs to set up a schedule to compile audiences. This will ensure that new members are added and removed from the appropriate audience.

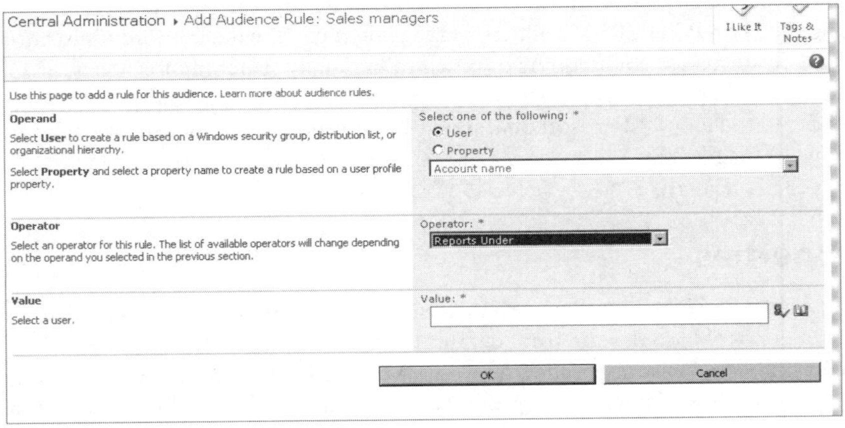

FIGURE 14-29

Personalizing Site Links

SharePoint 2010 carried over the ability to create custom links in the My Site top navigation area from SharePoint 2007. To create custom links inside the Manage Profile Service page, click Configure Personalization Site in the My Site Settings section. By adding new links here, they will appear in the top menu navigation after My Profile (Figure 14-30).

FIGURE 14-30

Now that audiences are created, it is possible to display links in this section depending on audience membership. For example, sales members will have a link displayed for them to the Sales team site inside SharePoint. Members of the development audience will have a completely different team site visible, along with an additional link to TechNet.

Managing Permissions

By default, everyone who is authenticated can participate with social networking inside SharePoint 2010. It is possible to limit the level of which groups of people can use My Site. Assuming these groups of people reside inside an Active Directory group, it's relatively easy to restrict access to groups of people by visiting the Manage Profile Service web page. Inside the People section, click Manage User Permissions to change the permission sets for either individual users or Active Directory groups.

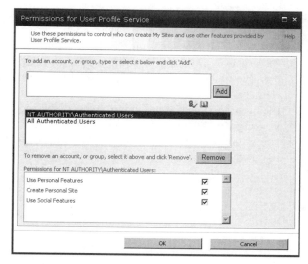

Use Personal Features allows users to alter their profiles, membership, and colleagues. Create Personal Site Permission enables users to create their My Site personal sites. Use Social Features can limit users from adding ratings and social tags to SharePoint items (Figure 14-31).

FIGURE 14-31

SHAREPOINT 2010 MY SITE WALK-THROUGH

Social data appears in a SharePoint 2010 My Site in a couple locations. The first location to concentrate on is the Recent Activity area under My Profile (Figure 14-32). As tags and notes are added to SharePoint items, these actions will be broadcast to the entire company. The Recent Activity section will display the most current actions under individual profiles but also in the Activity Feed of others.

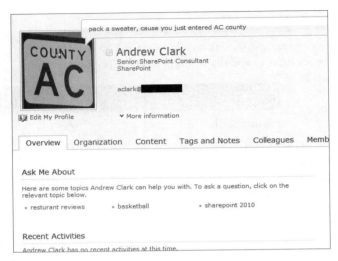

FIGURE 14-32

The Tags and Notes area under My Profile (Figure 14-33) is yet another view of your social activity. This section provides the ability to filter by All, Tags, Notes, Private, and Public. In addition, it is possible to view social data by individual months as well. In fact, the monthly view is the default refinement. It is also possible to refine the results by tags. Selecting a refinement tag will remove the month view. The individual items displayed in Activities will appear slightly different if you are viewing your own profile as opposed to someone else's profile. If you are visiting your own profile, you will have the ability to delete items or mark items as private/public. Naturally it is not possible to delete other people's items when visiting their pages.

FIGURE 14-33

Show Different Views of My Site Data

SharePoint 2010 displays My Site information differently based on a few factors. The most recognizable factor is public or private. Public and private are two refinements that are visible in the Tags and Notes section of My Profile. Data that is stored under My Content can also be protected or public. The labeling of the My Content section might be misleading because it is possible to do much more than public and private data storage. This area is just like any other SharePoint site, so it is possible to create document libraries or lists and apply security on those artifacts so that just your colleagues or teammates can view them.

Going back to My Profile, SharePoint 2010 allows the owner to see exactly how the profile will be displayed to others. The options are Everyone, My Manager, My Team, My Colleagues, and Only Me. Similar to other networking sites, SharePoint allows users to modify the security of their profiles. Facebook is a great example for this. Facebook and Picasa allow their users to display photo albums to a group of designated friends, but hide the photos from another group that contains co-workers. SharePoint 2010 follows the same idea with My Site but goes into greater detail.

To manage permissions on the individual user's properties, navigate to My Profile and click the Edit My Profile link under the photo. User properties in the Basic Information section will not be editable in regard to security, but most of the fields under Contact Information, Details, and Newsfeed Settings will be available for changes (Figure 14-34). Most of the properties will have the default setting set to Everyone. The SharePoint administrator can change the default security setting for each user property inside Central Administration by clicking Manage User Properties on the Manage Profile Service web page.

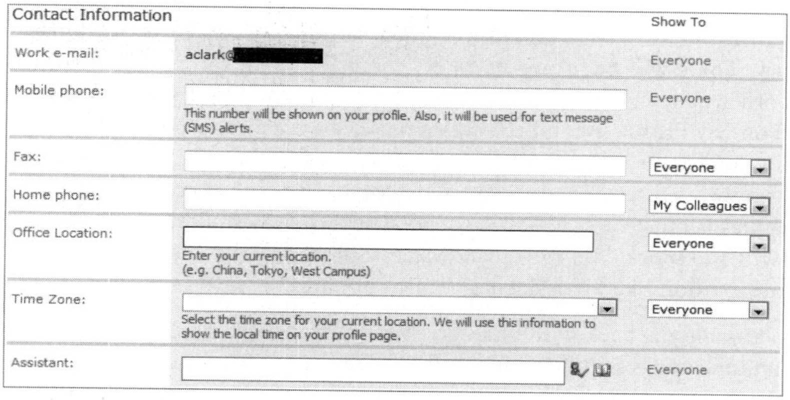

FIGURE 14-34

What Are the Organization Chart and Colleagues?

Based on Active Directory properties (or whatever data source is used to synchronize people), the My Organization Chart is populated with the current user being displayed along with co-workers and supervisors on the My Profile page. The organization browser is another way to visually see the people who comprise a team (Figure 14-35). This control is dynamic and based on Silverlight. This may sound gimmicky but according to what has been posted on the SharePoint Team blog, browsing the organization with the address book is one of the most popular features inside Outlook.

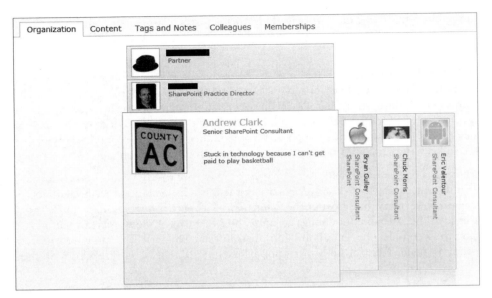

FIGURE 14-35

You now know that the organizational chart is dictated by the relationships that exist from the user store or Active Directory. There will be instances where users will want the ability to add co-workers or relationships to other people. This request is handled by the inclusion of colleagues. Clicking the Colleagues tab on My Profile lists all the colleagues who are attached to the current user. It's possible to add, edit, and remove colleagues. SharePoint also has privacy filters on these relationships as well, so that only a subset of people can view what your colleagues' relationships are. Manually adding colleagues is one example of the social aspect that SharePoint now embraces. The addition of colleagues will add more data to your newsfeed. This includes not only SharePoint activity but also personal information like birth dates or status updates.

The People Connections functionality is back with SharePoint 2010 but with an expanded role. Integration with Office Communicator is still there and will display the current status of the user. However, SharePoint now integrates with Outlook so it is easier to view contact info and to schedule a meeting. The organization chart is also visible from this People Connection menu as well. Not only did the visuals improve in SharePoint but the administration also did. Inside Central Administration, go to Application Management and click Manage Web Applications. In the next list, select the web application and click General Settings in the Ribbon. The following menu (Figure 14-36) will turn off this functionality.

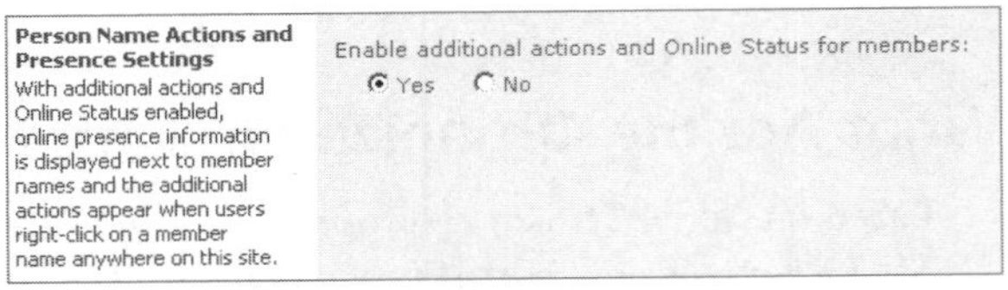

Person Name Actions and Presence Settings
With additional actions and Online Status enabled, online presence information is displayed next to member names and the additional actions appear when users right-click on a member name anywhere on this site.

Enable additional actions and Online Status for members:
⦿ Yes ○ No

FIGURE 14-36

Review the Newsfeed

The SharePoint 2010 Newsfeed is similar to most popular networking sites. This is the homepage where all the activity from your colleagues is consolidated. Expanding on this idea further is the inclusion of Interests. As items are tagged with metadata that matches any of your interests, that activity will be shown in your newsfeed. This allows you to uncover new artifacts that could become useful to your day-to-day activities. More importantly, this is where social computing separates itself from search engines. In the past users had to search for data; now it is possible for data to find you.

Each individual view of a newsfeed will look different because each user can alter what data is displayed in the newsfeed. Newsfeed settings allow users to change the activities that are followed (Figure 14-37). It is possible to create custom gatherers inside SharePoint as well. To dive into the creation of custom gatherers, see "Microsoft Office Server ActivityFeed Namespace MSDN" at `http://msdn.microsoft.com/en-us/library/ee584594.aspx`.

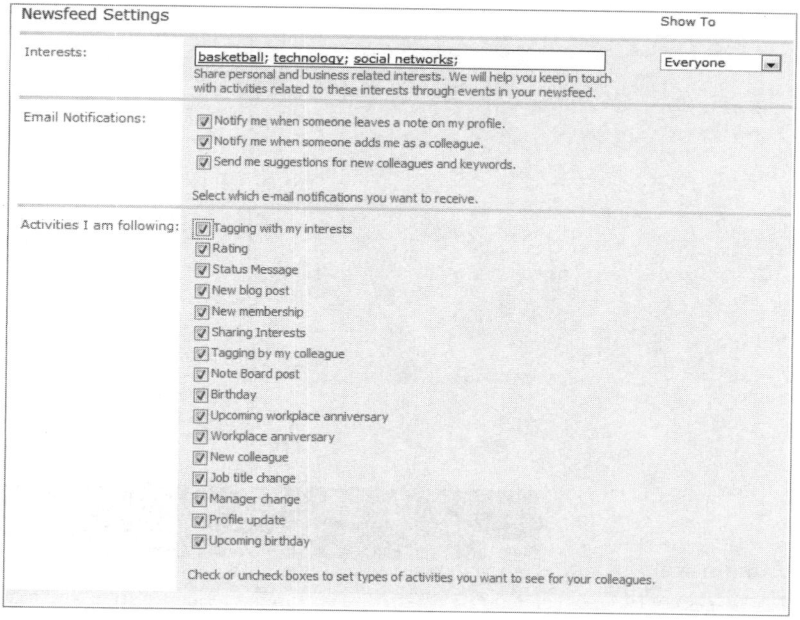

FIGURE 14-37

The Activity Feed Job is located in Central Administration under Monitoring ➪ Review Job Definitions. Verify that the status of the job is not set to disabled. Click the Activity Feed Job to set the recurring schedule for when this job runs. The default value is set to run on an hourly basis.

Colleague Mining with Outlook 2010

The integration of Outlook 2010 and SharePoint 2010 has taken another forward step with the Colleague add-in product. This is standard functionality that is available out of the box with Outlook 2010 (Figure 14-38). This add-in is an optional tool that can be configured on each individual computer. When activated, the tool scans the user's sent-items folder to uncover colleague recommendations. For more information on this tool and how to disable it using Group

Policy, consult "Enable SharePoint Server 2010 Colleague in Outlook 2010" at `http://technet.microsoft.com/en-us/library//ff384821.aspx`. Outlook supports connecting to other social networks such as Facebook, Linkedin, MySpace, and Windows Live Messenger. To view the complete list of connectable social networks, bing "Outlook Social Connector Partner Listing – Microsoft Office." Before installing any additional connectors, please test the functionality and understand the privacy concerns.

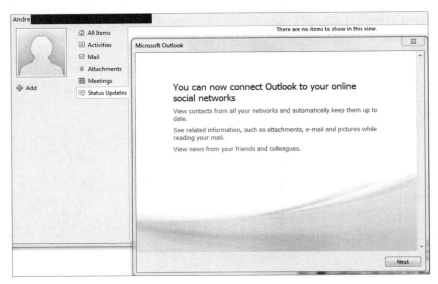

FIGURE 14-38

Troubleshooting

When visiting the Central Administration Site, the SharePoint Health Analyzer will display either a yellow bar to indicate warnings or a red bar to indicate critical issues. If the Activity Feed Job is not enabled, the Health Analyzer will report this as a warning (Figure 14-39). Some of these warnings and errors can be fixed by clicking the Repair Automatically button. It is preferable to fix items manually, especially when attempting to learn how to administer SharePoint. This error can be fixed by navigating to Monitoring ⇨ Review Job Definitions in Central Administration. Then click Activity Feed Job to enable the job.

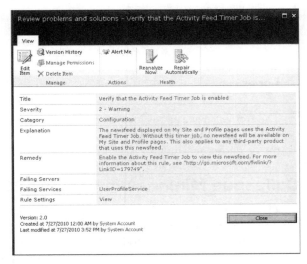

FIGURE 14-39

SharePoint administrators might field support calls when users report issues altering their My Site profiles because certain fields are reported as having a problem retrieving data (Figure 14-40). Inspect the fields more carefully, and you should start to realize that these fields are all related to Managed Metadata. The previous chapter discussed this along with the administration of Managed Metadata. When you navigate to the management screen for Managed Metadata, another error is displayed (Figure 14-41). This error message is more descriptive and informs the user that the Managed Metadata Web Service needs to be started. This can be confirmed and fixed by navigating to System Settings ➪ Manage Services on the server (Figure 14-42). Find the Managed Metadata Web Service and change the status to Started.

 If the errors are still not resolved after making these changes, either run an iisreset/noforce *or restart the machine.*

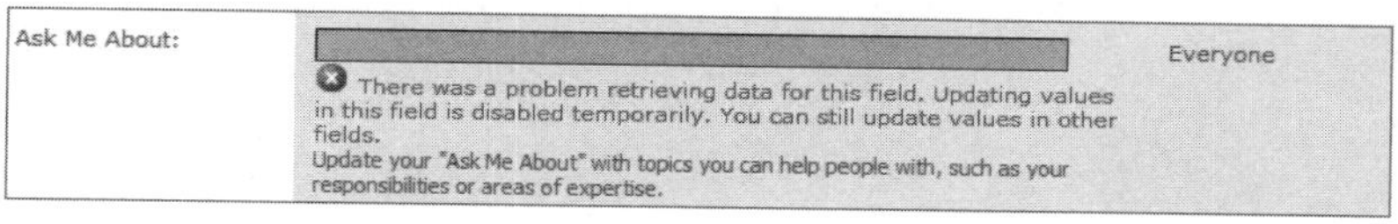

FIGURE 14-40

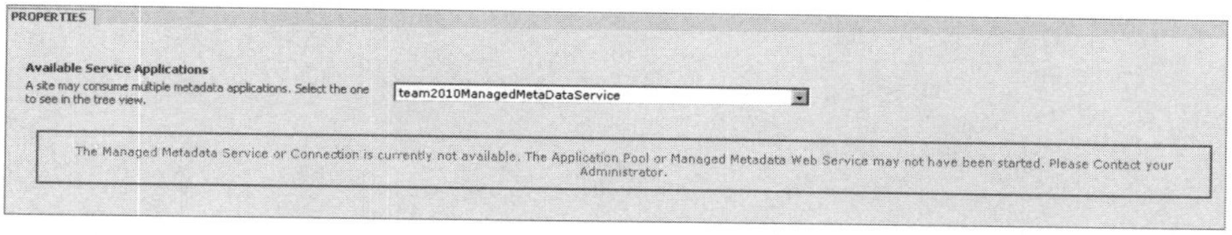

FIGURE 14-41

FIGURE 14-42

SUMMARY

In the previous chapter, the importance of an active Folksonomy was discussed. This chapter revealed how the Folksonomy activity will be exposed to SharePoint users. More importantly, you now know how to effectively leverage My Site using best practices. Yet again the recurring theme with SharePoint is planning. Every aspect of SharePoint will be impacted by the level of planning that is pursued. A poorly implemented My Site scheme will result in not only performance degradation but also low user adoption. My Site with the ability to bring content based on interests directly to the user is a fundamental shift in how we interact with data. This reason alone is why My Site and social computing should be at least considered in every corporate setting.

PART VI
SharePoint Workflow

15

Workflow Introduction and Background

The goal of this chapter is to provide you with an overview of workflow concepts and why you should care about workflow. You read about the benefits of using workflow in your organization as well as about how workflow functions in SharePoint 2010. In subsequent chapters you learn more specifics about each type of workflow and how you can leverage each piece of workflow functionality. You learn about out-of-the-box workflows, modifying these workflows with SharePoint Designer, and starting workflows with Visio as an end user. The workflow section wraps up with an introduction to the workflow developer experience.

OVERVIEW OF WORKFLOW AND JUST A TOUCH OF BPM

Ask 10 people to define workflow you will probably get at least seven different answers and explanations. Although workflow isn't new, confusion persists about just what it is. So to play it safe, take the word of the workflow people themselves, the Workflow Management Coalition (WFMC).

The WFMC defines workflow as:

> *The automation of a business process, in whole or part, during which documents, information or tasks are passed from one participant to another for action, according to a set of procedural rules.*

Keep this in mind as you read more about workflow, in this and subsequent chapters, and start to think about where workflow fits into your organization. You will find that you can't talk about workflow without at least mentioning Business Process Management (BPM). So in that respect you are going to need to know how BPM relates to workflow. Back to what our consortium says, this time about BPM:

> *Business Process Management: The practice of developing, running, performance measuring, and simulating Business Processes to effect the continued improvement of those processes. Business Process Management is concerned with the lifecycle of the Process Definition.*

You could say that BPM is an evolution of workflow. For example, you may have a generic process that you perform in your business every day, such as ordering office supplies, requesting time off, or submitting expense reports. If you automate one of these processes using some technology, such as forms, e-mail, or database entries, that could be considered a workflow. This new workflow may be of benefit and produce tangible results for you and your company. However, to truly take advantage of that automation you have to report continually on it and investigate each aspect, step, and participant to find where improvements and changes are needed. You may feel the terms workflow and BPM are overused and sometimes overlap. There may be some truth in this, but if you think of the two terms as they've been defined here you should be able to keep things clear.

WORKFLOW IN THE MARKETPLACE

With "workflow" becoming something of a buzz term, many business software products are advertising various features offering it. Workflow can be a good feature because it allows for process automation; however, keep in mind that many of these vendors are adding workflow to their product only to increase your interest. Also, if you add several such products to your environment you are likely to create confusion and interoperability issues. These other applications typically won't perform well in situations where the process needs to cross systems or manage data from multiple sources. This presents a problem because rarely is any good business process occurring in isolation.

As an example, your organization may have a finance system that is responsible for accounts payable, accounts receivable, and payroll. This system may have processes that support billing and consolidation; however, the way in which your business operates may additionally involve such items as information from Active Directory forms, and files for contracts. Each of these pieces of data is pulled from or stored in other systems. Surfacing each piece in a standard SharePoint site or page is a great use of SharePoint's portal functionality. SharePoint can provide that high-level reporting surface or the consolidation composite view (that is, a view showing data from multiple sources consolidated in one screen). What ties these pieces together nicely is workflow. Keep in mind that workflow or process automation in any form, whether in SharePoint or not, can be of great benefit to those who take advantage of it. With SharePoint, workflow, and electronic forms you can now digitize entire business processes. So now you know what workflow is. You may be asking yourself, Why should I care?

Why Is Workflow and BPM of Benefit to You?

Organizations that implement workflow do so for a variety of reasons:

➤ Better work tracking

➤ Improved work on compliance

➤ Work reduction

➤ Improved efficiency

➤ Better customer service

➤ The familiar desire to do more with less

Take a look at a very generic example of a Return on Investment (ROI) calculation for workflow.

Let's assume that an organization has calculated that the average total cost of an employee, factoring in benefits and taxes, is $50,000. The employee works 46 weeks a year after figuring in vacation, holidays, and sick days, which amounts to 230 work days per year. From there you can figure out the cost of an employee's time by week, day, hour, or even minute:

Cost Per Week	$1,086
Cost Per Day	$217
Cost Per Hour	$27.12
Cost Per Minute	$0.45

Now you can calculate the savings if you automate some processes and thus make the employee more efficient. If you make one process one minute more efficient you save $0.45 per employee participating in that process. Calculate that savings over the course of a year and you save $103.50 per employee.

This ROI assumes that you can save one minute per employee per process. You could argue that it's possible even to save one minute per step; however, for now let's start with an easy calculation and assume a saving of one minute per process. Now it's your turn to participate in this fun. Think of a process you have in your organization today. Then take your process and figure out how many employees participate in that process.

Next, multiply the number of employees by your average cost per minute. You now have, as shown in the following table, the ROI of a process that can be automated through SharePoint workflow. This ROI is only one small instance. Empowering more people to build workflows through tools such as SharePoint Designer can keep the ROI ball rolling.

Employee cost per minute	$0.45
Number of employees involved	100
Number of instances per month	45
Total savings per month	$2,025

Improving ROI is one example of how workflow can benefit your organization. This is something tangible that you can calculate. To further see the benefits of workflow, make a list of the processes you might automate and calculate the ROI for each process. SharePoint can play a huge role in workflow and not just because SharePoint offers workflow out of the box.

SharePoint: How Did We Get Here?

Microsoft realized just how powerful a tool workflow could be and integrated it into SharePoint for the 2007 release. Some of the features provided, such as the ability to customize out-of-the-box workflow and the ability to reuse workflows, left something to be desired. However, users still found that adding basic workflow to lists and libraries added value in significant ways. To this end, think of a true portal concept, which is what SharePoint is now. A portal can be thought of as a gateway to information. Portals gather information, be it files, text, or HTML, in one place. In an organization, I may use a portal to allow team sites to collaborate. The portal may include access to official corporate news, links with a stock ticker, corporate profiles, and policy updates. As a user I may have a page on my SharePoint site that pulls in a list with information on it that connects to a document library containing related files. That same site may also pull information from external sources using BCS. All these pieces of related data from different places are now presented in a unified view. Using a portal allows your users to have a one-stop shop to perform many different tasks.

You can make a logical transition to adding processes to a portal. If your users are familiar with using the SharePoint interface for collaboration, document management, announcements, and calendars, you can now logically extend their use of SharePoint by adding process automation (workflow). Incorporating workflow into SharePoint sites or pages tremendously increases the workflow adoption rate and ROI.

A well-built and integrated workflow can in a sense be considered an application. It's sometimes hard to get people to use a new application as process automation. Adoption can be slow because the new application is different and people are used to doing things the way they've always done them. You can help overcome this resistance by encouraging participation in the process. Make sure people can participate through tools they already use, like e-mail, Word, and SharePoint. Once you get your SharePoint environment set, adding processes simply adds more value, not more red tape. Keep that in mind as you plan your SharePoint processes.

THE BASIC ARCHITECTURE OF SHAREPOINT WORKFLOW

The core of workflow in SharePoint is Workflow Foundation (WF). Workflow Foundation is part of .NET Framework 3.5; it's a development framework that allows you to create workflows in your applications. At its core it is not SharePoint-specific. The SharePoint team took this framework and built in specific functionality that it could then host and offer as SharePoint-based workflow.

Workflow Foundation is actually a programming model, engine, and toolset designed for building workflow-enabled software for Windows. As a programming model, Workflow Foundation provides developers with a model-driven toolset that can take their development to a higher level and it also adds a certain graphical angle to it (see Figure 15-1).

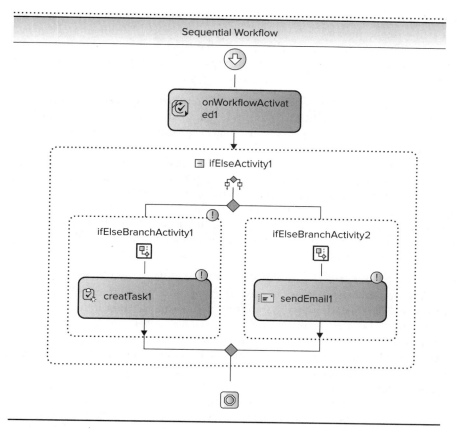

FIGURE 15-1

This graphical angle is one of the keys to success with Workflow Foundation. It allows you to be able to see the logic, or flow if you will, then be able to drill into each step and add the function (business logic) behind it. After you build a Workflow Foundation process, you are essentially left with an assembly that will need a host in order to be fully functional. This is where SharePoint comes in. Workflow Foundation does not provide management tools, executables, an installer, or the typical items that you would need to have a stand-alone application. You need a place to host this functionality — a host that is responsible for managing the functions and hydrating and dehydrating — loading from disc to memory or from memory to disc, respectively. You will also need basic task management and reporting. Thus you really need products like SharePoint to provide the plumbing. SharePoint can act as an appropriate host for workflows you build to run in or against SharePoint 2010.

Understanding WF and SharePoint as a Host

Now that you understand the relationship of Workflow Foundation to SharePoint, you should also understand the host that will execute and manage the processes you build. Within SharePoint, Microsoft provides a Workflow Foundation runtime engine that is responsible for the execution of all workflows. This runtime engine allows workflows to remain active for long periods of time, which will be required for many human-based (as opposed to system-based) workflows.

The SharePoint host enables all processes to survive resets and reboots. The runtime engine also handles the plumbing of a normal workflow service so you do not have to code it yourself. These runtime services can be such things as state management, process tracking and loading, and unloading workflows to and from memory. Loading and unloading to and from memory is especially necessary in long running workflows because you do not want every instance of every process staying resident in memory. When a process is waiting for user input, the runtime services will unload that workflow from memory and persist the data to the SharePoint database. When the workflow needs to be acted upon, the engine will load the instance into memory so that the instance can handle the event as needed. So even though your use of workflow in SharePoint may be significant, the number of actual workflows in memory at any given time will be smaller and thus actually use fewer system resources.

The SharePoint workflow host executes its workflows in one of two places. Where the execution takes place depends on what activity is being processed. If a workflow is awaiting some form of user input, the workflow will be executing on the web front end where that user input is taking place. If the workflow is in a delay state from a pause for duration or other similar context, the workflow will be executed by the SPTimer Service. With SharePoint 2010 you can specify a server where the SPTimer service will run. The flexibility in the timer service allows for more granularities in your SharePoint workflow architecture, including the dedication of a specific server to be your workflow server. In high-use environments dedicating a workflow server may be a wise use of resources. Figure 15-2 shows the settings for the workflow timer service. To get to this screen navigate to Central Administration ⇨ System Settings ⇨ Services on this server ⇨ Microsoft SharePoint Foundation Workflow Timer Service.

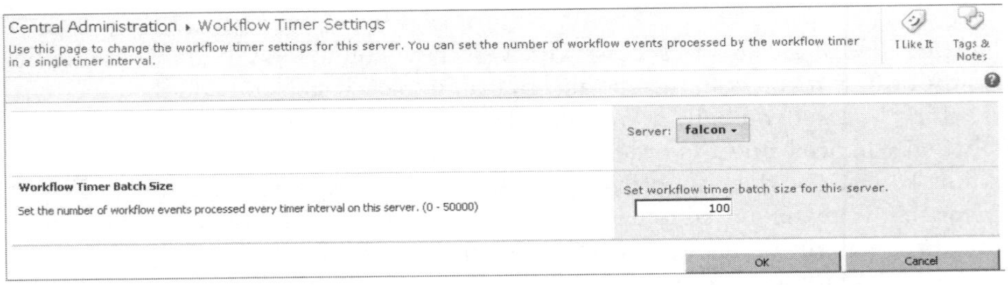

FIGURE 15-2

Understanding Workflow Types: Declarative and Compiled

Now you understand how SharePoint uses Workflow Foundation and acts as a host to workflows. Next, you need to understand the basic workflow types that SharePoint will have. SharePoint has two basic categories of workflow:

➤ Compiled

➤ Declarative

A compiled workflow is one that is typically built with Visual Studio, and is end to end a precompiled DLL that SharePoint hosts. Compiled workflows may still contain conditions and actions much as a declarative workflow does; however, compiled workflow authors can also insert custom code and calls to other systems that may be necessary to ensure proper function of their workflows. This compiled nature is an important distinction from the declarative workflow, which is deployed as an Extensible Object Markup Language (XOML) file and compiled each time an instance of the workflow is started. Similarities exist between the two types of workflows and you may not be able to tell one from the other as a regular participant in the workflow itself. Each will consist of forms, inputs, and outputs, just like other workflows.

With SharePoint 2010, the workflows are those of a new generation called declarative. Most of this chapter discusses this declarative side of SharePoint workflows. Declarative workflows may sound complicated but don't be confused. Declarative programming can be thought of as specifying the "what" without the "how." Declarative programming is about statements of the work involved to go get some document or a list item value. You don't specify which document or list item. Those values are specified at a later time. Declarative programming shows up all over the place and not just in SharePoint.

Take a basic SharePoint out-of-the-box Approval workflow (Figure 15-3). You can see that no specific details are called out; rather, parameters like Parameter: Duration Units are used. The details are specified at association or run time.

This declarative nature of workflow is one of the big benefits of SharePoint workflow. Declarative workflow makes everything reusable and significantly more configurable.

FIGURE 15-3

UNDERSTANDING CONDITIONS AND ACTIONS: THE CORE OF SHAREPOINT WORKFLOW

A typical workflow has these components:

➤ Association form

➤ Initiation form

➤ Task form

➤ Variables

➤ Conditions

➤ Actions

Not all of this will make sense right away, but by the end of this chapter you should understand. Each component is explained at some level in the next sections.

At this point you should understand the basics of the SharePoint workflow plumbing and you should understand what different components make up a workflow in SharePoint. To take the next steps you'll need to be familiar with a new set of terms and understand how they affect your workflow. In this section, you learn all about these new terms. First you need to know that workflows have many pieces but the keys that make them functional in SharePoint 2010 are *conditions* and *actions*.

You can think of SharePoint conditions and actions as "if-then statements." A conditions is your "if statement" and an action is your "then statement." Take a look at how conditions and actions are exposed to you in various workflow design surfaces (Figures 15-4 through 15-7).

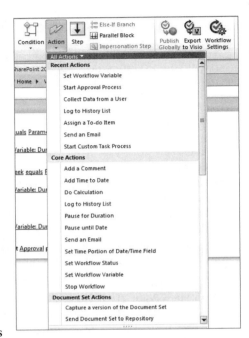

FIGURE 15-4

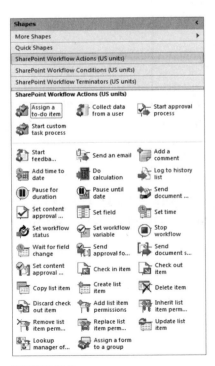

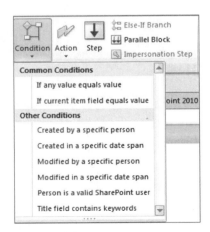

FIGURE 15-5

FIGURE 15-6

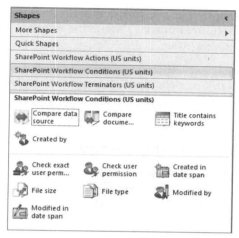

FIGURE 15-7

When you think of building these series of statements, perhaps you can liken them to another familiar surface you probably have used at one time or another, the Microsoft Outlook rules interface shown in Figure 15-8.

In Microsoft Outlook, you can set up rules for your inbox that say, in effect, "if an e-mail is received and the e-mail has me on the CC line, then move that e-mail into the CC folder."

Compare this to a condition action in SharePoint workflow in Figure 15-9.

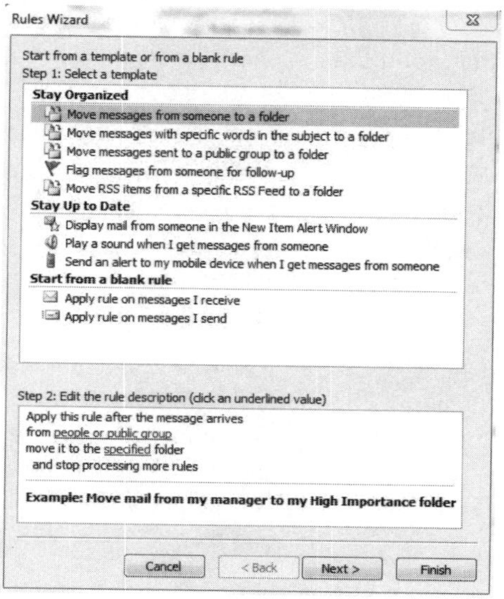

FIGURE 15-8

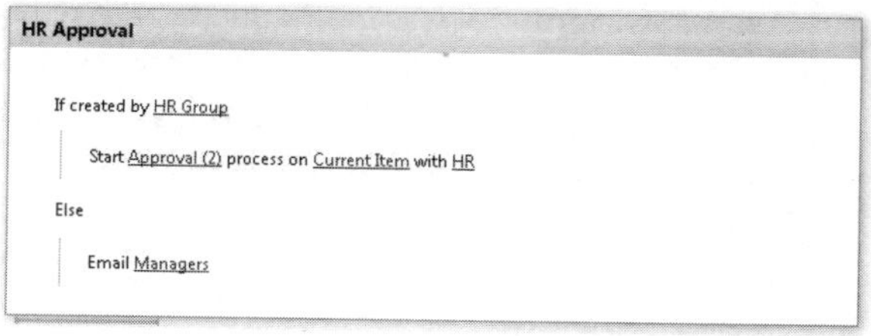

FIGURE 15-9

This basic step says when the workflow is initiated, the workflow engine checks to see if the document or list item was created by a member of the HR group. If it was, it starts the approval process. If it was not ("Else"), an e-mail is sent to the managers group.

You can see the idea here of setting up an if (condition) and next setting up a then (action). But obviously there is more to workflows than just a bunch of if/then statements. You will need to define specific details, such as variables, form parameters, and association columns; those are discussed more in a little while.

Understanding Workflow Components and Terminology

For now, let's dive into all the terms and concepts you will need to know to create a workflow. You should begin by understanding some of the universal terms. These terms are not affected by workflow type or SharePoint version in any way. Table 15-1 goes over the basic SharePoint workflow terms.

TABLE 15-1: SharePoint Workflow Terms

TERM	DEFINITION	EXAMPLE
Condition	A condition is an expression that indicates something that the workflow needs to test for a true or false result.	If this book is "AWESOME."
Action	An action is the step that needs to be taken if the "condition" is found to be true.	E-mail friends to recommend this book.
Local variables	A variable is a data storage location for use inside or in the process of a workflow. This data or variable is only viable for the use in that workflow.	Book Rating could be a variable, where you give people a drop-down list of rating options such as "Awesome," "Great," "Good."
Initiation form parameters	Initiation form parameters can be considered a second type of variable in the workflow; they are collected at the start of a workflow.	Fields on the Initiation form that are used to collect data and store them as variables.
Workflow step	A workflow step is a way of grouping items together (conditions AND actions). The items within a step will be processed together and in order as they appear.	A workflow step can be: check variable value, then e-mail users, then assign task item to group. This can be done all in one step.

TERM	DEFINITION	EXAMPLE
Serial actions	Serial actions are the default and are set up to run one after the other.	This might be sending an approval task to the HR team, and then, when that task is completed, sending the task to the legal team.
Parallel actions	Parallel actions are actions set up to run at the same time rather than in order.	An example would be sending an approval task to both the HR team and the legal team at the same time, rather than the HR team, then the legal team.

Now that you have a foundation of universal terms, Table 15-2 digs into more specifics.

TABLE 15-2: Workflow Process Terms

TERM	DEFINITION
Workflow association	Workflow association involves the process that takes place when you link a workflow with a SharePoint entity. The association process includes the use of or specification of an "association form."
Workflow instantiation	The instantiation of a workflow is the process of starting up a workflow and is accompanied by an instantiation form.
Task	The term "task" can be used in many contexts. The two important definitions for workflow are: 1. The assignment of a work item; 2. A reference to a task form, being a form that allows a user to interact with a workflow process.

Table 15-3 lists the different workflow types you need to be familiar with and will be building in your SharePoint environment.

TABLE 15-3: Workflow Types

TERM	DEFINITION	EXAMPLE
List-based workflow	A list-based workflow is a workflow type that is tied to a specific list.	The Vacation workflow is tied to (associated with) the Vacation Request list.
Site-based workflow	The site-based workflow is not tied to, or associated with, any library or list. Rather, it is associated with a site. Keep in mind that these workflows do not have an automatic trigger and must be started manually.	An example of a site-based workflow may be one that is for assigning tasks to review publishing content and ensuring that different pages are ready for archiving, updating, or deletion.
Re-usable workflow	Re-usable workflows are not tied to a specific list or library at development time; rather, they are generic and can be associated with a specific list or library at a later time.	If you create a great Approval workflow that you want to save as a template for all those within your site, you can create a re-usable workflow and make it available for others to use as is, or to modify and use.
Globally re-usable	These workflows are just like the regular re-usable workflows, but by being global they are available to all sites in the site collection.	The same great Approval workflow is made available to the entire site collection and not just your immediate site.

When building a process, you will need to be familiar with the miscellaneous terms in Table 15-4.

TABLE 15-4: Miscellaneous Workflow Terms

TERM	DEFINITION	EXAMPLE
Association columns	Association columns are columns that are specified at workflow design time and will be created at workflow association time in the list or library with which the new workflow is associated.	If this same Approval workflow has conditions to check for a value in a specific column, you could make those specific columns into association columns. The association columns would then be created in the list you associate with this workflow each time the workflow is associated with a list or library.
Impersonation step	An impersonation step is a step in a workflow that you can specify to be run as the workflow author and not the user of the workflow.	If in a step you need to modify permissions on a list, but a typical workflow initiator would not have access to make this change, you can make this part of an impersonation step.
Workflow visualization	Workflow visualization is the creation of a visual representation of a workflow through the use of Visio services.	

You learn more about how to use and implement specific actions and conditions in the next chapter as you dig into building your first workflows. Keep in mind that conditions and actions are context-sensitive, and not all conditions and or actions will be available for use in all workflows. Some actions, for example, can be used only in an impersonation step. The availability of actions is a very important aspect to keep in mind and underscores the importance of proper planning of *all* processes. Now that you have an understanding of the actions, take a look at the conditions in Table 15-5.

TABLE 15-5: SharePoint Workflow Conditions

CONDITION	DEFINITION	EXAMPLE
If current item field equals value	This condition compares some field in the workflow item to a value.	If File name = Test.txt
Created by a specific person	This condition checks whether the item was created by a specific person or group.	If current item was created by HR Group
Created in a specific date span	This condition checks the "item create" date and compares it to a specific date range.	If current item was created between 1/1/2007 and 1/1/2011
Modified by a specific person	This condition checks to see if the item was last modified by a specific person or group.	If current item was modified by HR Group
Modified in a specific date span	This condition checks the date the item was last modified and compares it to a specific date range.	If current item was modified between 1/1/2007 and 1/1/2011
Person a valid SharePoint user	This condition checks to see if a user is a valid SharePoint user as determined by your authentication provider.	Use this to validate an external user
Title field contains keywords	This condition checks the item's title against a keyword or list of keywords.	If title contains HR
File size a specific range	This condition checks the file size of an item. This condition is available only if your workflow is associated with a document content type of document library.	If file size is between 1,000 and 2,000 Kilobytes
File type a specific type	This condition checks whether the file type of the current item is of a specific type.	If file type is PPT

Now that you know your "if's" let's talk about "then's." As with conditions, some of the actions are context-sensitive. For example, in Figure 15-10 take a look at the List category actions that are available to you in a normal step.

Now take a look at the same category when you are accessing that set of List actions from within an impersonation step in Figure 15-11.

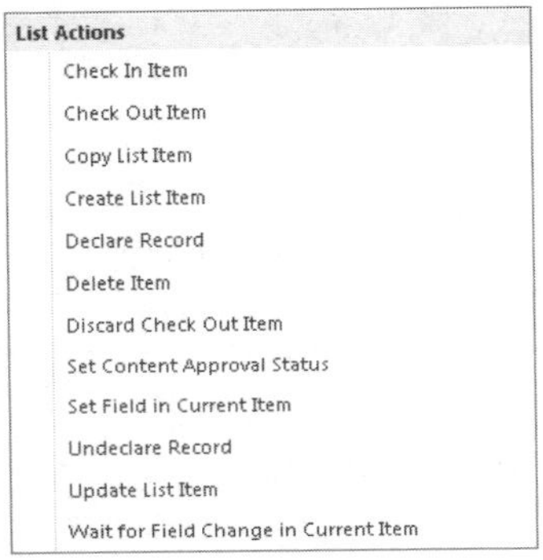

List Actions
Check In Item
Check Out Item
Copy List Item
Create List Item
Declare Record
Delete Item
Discard Check Out Item
Set Content Approval Status
Set Field in Current Item
Undeclare Record
Update List Item
Wait for Field Change in Current Item

FIGURE 15-10

List Actions
Add List Item Permissions
Check In Item
Check Out Item
Copy List Item
Create List Item
Declare Record
Delete Item
Discard Check Out Item
Inherit List Item Parent Permissions
Remove List Item Permissions
Replace List Item Permissions
Set Content Approval Status
Set Field in Current Item
Undeclare Record
Update List Item
Wait for Field Change in Current Item

FIGURE 15-11

As you can see, there is a difference in the two lists. SharePoint will not list a condition or action if it is not valid at that place in the workflow.

Table 15-6 lists the actions available in a workflow.

TABLE 15-6: SharePoint Workflow Actions

ACTION	DEFINITION	EXAMPLE
Add time to date	Adding time to date allows you to add a specified amount of time to a specified date. The result is stored in a workflow variable.	You have a workflow that has a specific service-level agreement that dictates a due date. When the workflow starts you want to calculate this to log it, and use that date in future communication as well as in the workflow history list.
Log to history list	This logs a message to the history list configured for the workflow.	Use this to log information about the progress of the workflow such as status, assignee at that step, or remaining time it's expected to run.

ACTION	DEFINITION	EXAMPLE
Send an e-mail	This sends an e-mail to specified recipients. The e-mail message can take advantage of workflow context and variables, allowing you to include extra information about the process itself.	Send an e-mail to a person or group that contains data from the workflow to give updates. This is a great action to include in all workflows.
Set workflow status	This sets the status of a workflow process to a more user-friendly status.	Set the workflow status to Awaiting Management Approval when a task item is assigned to a manager to show those interested that it is at that step.
Set workflow variable	This sets a variable in a workflow to a specific value.	Set workflow status of the running workflow to Awaiting Management Approval instead of the default "In progress."
Stop workflow	This action stops the current instance of the workflow and additionally logs a message to the workflow history list to show status.	Stop workflow and log a message, such as the fact that originator cancelled the workflow.
Copy list item	Copies one specified list item to another. Lists must contain at least one column in both the source and destination lists.	This action could be used when you have a workflow running on a larger list with lots of information and you want to copy some of the list items but leave off more sensitive columns.
Create list item	Creates a new list item in the specified list and sets specified values.	Create a new entry in the calendar list.
Update list item	Updates a value in a list item to the new specified values.	Update an entry in the calendar list if details of the event change.
Set content approval status	Used if content approval is enabled and can set the status field to a value.	Set content approval status to Approved.
Set field in current item	Sets a specified field in the current item to a value that is also specified.	Set Due Date field to Date.
Lookup	Looks up information about a user's manager, such as an e-mail address, and outputs that value to a workflow variable.	Look up the manager of the workflow initiator to send an e-mail.
Add list item perms	Grants specified permissions to specified users.	Grant edit permissions to the approvers group.

continues

TABLE 15-6 *(continued)*

ACTION	DEFINITION	EXAMPLE
Inherit list item perms	This a list item that had separate permissions to inherit the parent permissions.	Make the list inherit site permissions.
Remove list item perms	Removes permissions to a list item for specified users.	Remove edit permissions from the approvers group.
Replace list item perms	Replaces current permissions on an item with new permissions that are specified.	Overwrite all permissions with approvers group set to Full Control. All others set to None.

Absent from the previous tables are the task actions such as Start Approval Process or Start Custom Task Process. This is because they are important enough to spend some additional time on. The entire methodology for tasks in SharePoint 2010 has been re-engineered. Each task piece is itself similar to a "mini-workflow." This task process is invoked like a regular action and allows for much more customization. Understanding customization options will be important for you as you begin to plan what your processes will look like. In the next chapter you get some examples of task processes in action, but for now you should understand task basics and customization options.

Task Form Fields

Task form fields are fields that will appear on different forms in the task process. You can add task form fields depending on your needs. These fields can also be set to be required or optional. These form fields play an important role because they can be used simply to display information that helps the workflow participant make decisions, or they can be used to collect data from the participant that can be used in your conditions further down the workflow. An important step in planning your workflows is to make a good list of all the pieces of data that will be involved.

Task Outcomes

Task outcomes are more or less the options task participants have on a specific activity such as:

➤ Approve

➤ Reject

➤ Abstain

You will get into task outcomes more as you begin to build custom workflows in the next chapter. The most important concept to understand at this point is that you have options for:

➤ How a task starts

➤ How it is processed

➤ How it is completed

Task outcomes are particularly important if you need to "expire" or "escalate" tasks, or have several task outcomes such as approve, decline, re-direct, and escalate. You also have custom approval options that may fit your business (for example, when the fourth manager approves, that task process is completed, or as soon as any manager rejects, the process moves on to a "decline" step that is specified in the workflow or stops altogether. The options you have are significant.

Completion Conditions

Completion conditions are the conditions necessary for the task process to be complete. These conditions can vary based on your needs. For example, a completion condition can be as simple as "when a manager approves or rejects." A conditions can also be complex (for example, when at least 50 percent of the listed approvers approve or as soon as any approver rejects).

Additionally, some actions can be taken during the task process. The workflow can take specific actions in response to events such as:

➤ Before a task is assigned

➤ When a task is pending

➤ When a task expiries

➤ When a task is deleted

➤ When a task completes

PLANNING FOR WORKFLOW IN SHAREPOINT 2010

Now that you have learned some of the basics of SharePoint workflow, you need to begin the planning process for using SharePoint workflow in your own environment. The first step in your planning process is a big one — you need to determine whether you even want to enable workflow in your environment. Yes, enabling workflow is an option. If it is an option you choose to disable, you probably won't have much interest in reading the rest of this section on workflow. So for now, assume that you have determined you will enable this feature, at least at some level.

When you install SharePoint, user-defined workflow is enabled by default. However, you should probably know where the Off button is in case you ever want to disable workflow. The option to enable or disable user-defined workflows is in the setup for the web application scope in SharePoint Central Administration (see Figure 15-12). Enabling or disabling user-defined workflow through Central Administration affects all sites within a web application.

If you do not want to disable all user-defined workflows, you can restrict user creation of workflow in other ways. You also have

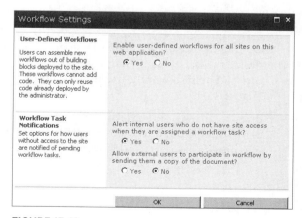

FIGURE 15-12

the option to turn off the ability to use SharePoint Designer; this setting is configurable on a site-collection basis as shown in Figure 15-13, as well as on a web application as shown in Figure 15-14.

FIGURE 15-13

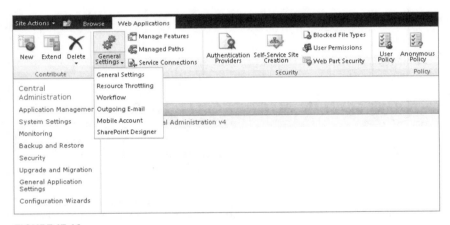

FIGURE 15-14

Disabling the use of SharePoint Designer prevents the use of SharePoint Designer to create and publish workflows, as you can see in Figure 15-15.

FIGURE 15-15

However, turning off SharePoint Designer will not disable out-of-the-box workflows. You can disable out these workflows on a site-collection basis through the deactivation of that feature as shown in Figure 15-16.

FIGURE 15-16

Additionally, a few special workflows aren't activated by default but can be activated when needed. These workflows, described in more detail in Chapter 16, are:

➤ *Three-state*

➤ *Disposition*

➤ *Publishing*

Consider each of the options for enabling workflow carefully as you design your overall site structure. Though you cannot simply deactivate workflow at the site level, you can reduce permissions in some ways that help curb its use. But more on that aspect in a little bit.

Now the question is where do you enable workflows and for whom? Once you determine that workflow is good and you want your users to take advantage of this feature, you need to determine the answers to a few basic questions. These questions will dramatically help in your implementation of workflow and what tasks may need to take place before you roll it out to your organization. The questions to consider are:

➤ Who will be creating workflows?

➤ Who will be associating workflows?

➤ Who will be participating in workflows?

Do the research and planning for each of these questions and make a list to ensure you can adequately set up permissions. Table 15-7 gets you started.

TABLE 15-7: Example Planning Worksheet

GROUP	SITE	WORKFLOW AUTHOR	WORKFLOW PARTICIPANT
HR	HumanResources	Sara	Carter, Leah-Rose, Ella

Planning for Workflow Permissions

Now that you have defined who will be doing what with regards to workflow in your SharePoint environment, you need to know what permissions they are going to need to perform those actions. Table 15-8 lays out the permissions required for each part of workflow deployment and participation.

TABLE 15-8: SharePoint Workflow Permissions

ACTIVITY	PERMISSION REQUIRED	NOTES
Deploy workflow	Manage list on the site	
Associate workflow with list	Full control of the list or library	During the association process, the owner can require additional permissions to start a workflow
Associate workflow with site	Must be a member of the site owner's group	
Associate workflow with content type	Must be a member of the site owner's group	
Initiate workflow	Edit items	
Participate in workflow	Edit items	
Terminate workflow	Full control over list or library the workflow is running on	
Remove workflow (remove association)	Full control	

Using this approach gives you a basic idea of how to establish permissions for your site structure based on the people who will be involved in workflow. You should create a chart that identifies the person and permissions, and that maps sites, lists, libraries, and content types to those who are going to be involved. You may also want to set up a special permission group to which workflow authors can be assigned. This planning helps you give just the right number of permissions to each site. However, planning is not just about rights to create or rights to participate in a workflow. Other special considerations must be made, such as the use of Task and History lists.

Planning for Custom Task and History Lists

SharePoint workflows make heavy use of both the Task and History lists in SharePoint. Each of these lists can contain a significant amount of information about the workflows running on that site. By default all users of that site have read permissions for each of these lists. You should take special care in planning the workflows that will run on each site, to ensure that any workflows containing confidential and or personal information are treated as such. An example of this may be a workflow that is responsible for maintaining an annual review for all employees. These review workflows may contain performance as well as salary information. Allowing these workflows to write information to the Task and History lists where any site member can read them may be unacceptable.

But don't fret — you still have options in regard to these special-case workflows.

The first and most obvious way of solving this problem is to restrict permissions to the Task and History lists on a site that contains one of these workflows. However, limiting permissions creates another set of problems for the users of other non-confidential workflows on that site.

You next option is to create new and more restricted Task and History lists for the confidential workflows that may run on the site. This specification can be done at workflow association time in SharePoint as shown in Figures 15-17 and 15-18.

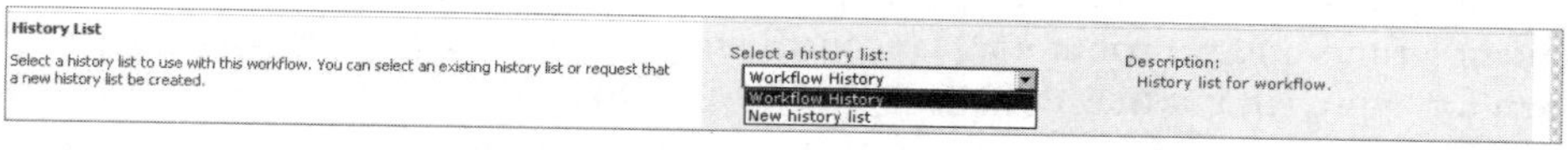

FIGURE 15-17

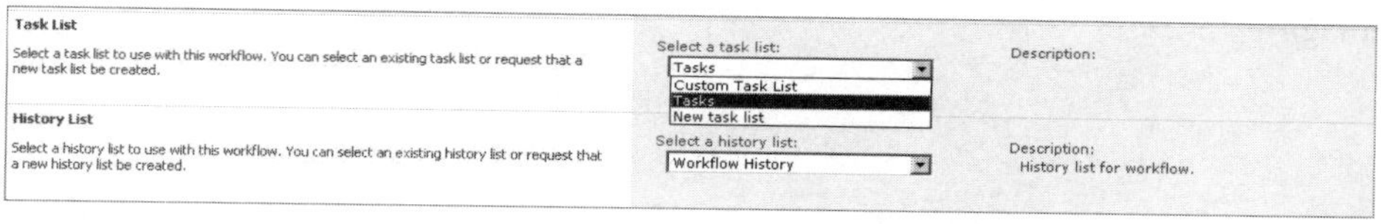

FIGURE 15-18

For cases where you are building a new list or library-based workflow in SharePoint Designer, you can also create new Task and History lists or specify existing Task or History lists when creating the workflow, as shown in Figure 15-19.

FIGURE 15-19

Let's take this concept one step further with regard to Task and History lists. Because by default all contributors can see and edit items in either of these lists, they can maliciously edit these items, which can alter a workflow's path, data, or outcome. For SharePoint-based workflows, altering the path, data, or outcome will be problematic. You should take special care to plan permissions appropriately for the Task and History lists on your sites. Additional steps to secure these lists and/or validate information may be necessary.

Another important aspect of workflow planning involves those users who will be responsible for workflow development and association. Special attention should be given to these two groups, specifically in the area of training. Not only will they need to know the steps for developing and associating workflow, but they also will need to know the ramifications. As stated before, many aspects of security, such as visibility of information, need to be understood.

An aspect of security that still needs to be discussed is security for those workflows that have impersonation steps, as shown in Figure 15-20.

FIGURE 15-20

In SharePoint 2010, workflows that are declarative (those that are out of the box or authored in SharePoint Designer) run in the security context of the workflow initiator (the one who started the workflow). A new feature in SharePoint 2010 allows the use of an impersonation step. The impersonation step switches the context in which that workflow is running for *that step* only. During the impersonation step, the workflow will run as the person who performed the workflow association.

As an example of using an impersonation step, imagine a publishing site where Sara is the owner of all the publishing pages. She is responsible for approving all content that gets published, but she has several content writers and contributors. Her contributors Carter or Leah may create new pages and submit them for approval, but they don't have permissions to actually publish them. Sara can create a publishing approval workflow in which Carter and Leah can submit content that goes to Sara for approval. If Sara approves, the content is automatically published to the site as Sara, even though the workflow was initiated by and thus is running in the context of either Carter or Leah as represented in Figure 15-21.

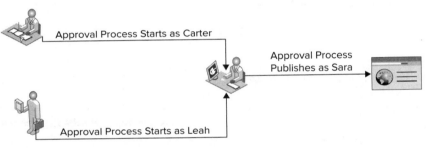

FIGURE 15-21

Some tasks that can be performed only in an impersonation step include:

➤ Set content approval status

➤ Create list item

➤ Update list item

➤ Delete list item

➤ Manage list item permissions

Because any workflow that has an impersonation step will run as the person who associated that workflow, those individuals who participate in that activity will need to fully understand what they're doing. They need to trust that tasks running as them are acceptable and are doing actions they approve of.

Keep in mind that most of the preceding information applies specifically to those processes that are considered out of the box or that are created in SharePoint Designer. Workflows that are created in Visual Studio can be dramatically different because they are not constrained to what is exposed by SharePoint. In addition, the most important aspect to consider is that workflows created inside Visual Studio and deployed to SharePoint will run as the system account and work through the identity set up as the application pool account. Running as this identity allows the process to perform actions that other users do not have the ability to perform. You must fully understand what security impact this has on your SharePoint environment.

WORKFLOW AND YOUR SKU

One last consideration to take into account about your use of workflow in SharePoint 2010 is what edition of SharePoint you are actually using. The ideas behind this are simple in terms of functionality. If you are using SharePoint Foundation server you will not get:

➤ **Out-of-the-box workflows:** With SharePoint Foundation, the only standard out-of-the-box workflow is the Three State workflow.

➤ **Forms Services:** This restricts the use of InfoPath forms in your workflow. Depending on your desire to customize the look and feel of your forms, this many not be a big deal. However, the additional option of having these forms can add tremendous value.

➤ **Visio Services:** The modeling of workflow processes in Visio, as well as the visualization of workflows in progress, can be a significant feature. Not having this feature will affect the involvement of your non-technical users in workflow design. Beyond that, as you will see in the next chapter on building workflow, you will not have the ability to visualize workflows in flight, as shown in Figure 15-22.

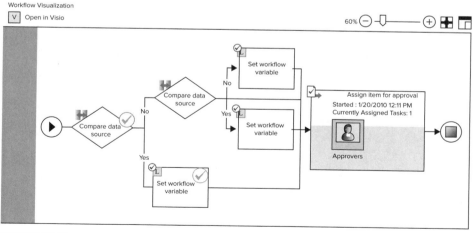

FIGURE 15-22

SUMMARY

In this chapter you learned that surfacing (that is, displaying) processes in SharePoint can be a good way of allowing users to interact with them. This process surfacing can help you achieve greater adoption rates and in turn greater ROI. You also should now have a better understanding of the host architecture in place to support workflow in SharePoint 2010 and of the relationship with Workflow Foundation. At this point you also should understand core terminology of SharePoint workflow and know that the building blocks of SharePoint workflow are based on conditions and actions.

16

Building and Using Workflow in SharePoint 2010

WHAT'S IN THIS CHAPTER?

➤ What you get with out-of-the-box workflows

➤ How to associate workflows with a list or library

➤ Taking out-of-the-box workflows and modifying them with SharePoint Designer

➤ How you can build SharePoint Designer workflows from scratch

➤ Making Microsoft Visio a part of your workflow process and strategy

At this point in your workflow adventure you understand the underlying basics of what makes SharePoint workflow tick. You also have an understanding of what to expect from a planning perspective. In this chapter you are ready to take the next step and start digging in and using workflows.

LEVERAGING OUT-OF-THE-BOX WORKFLOWS IN SHAREPOINT

As you begin your journey into SharePoint workflow, the logical step is to start with those workflows you get right out of the box — those that can be used simply by enabling them and running through an association process that ties them to a list or library for use. The different types or methodologies of SharePoint workflow are a ladder of functionality and support for complexity. At the lowest levels of functionality and support for complex workflows are out-of-the-box workflows. At the other end of the spectrum lie those workflows that can be created in Visual Studio. Depending on your workflow needs, you may need to start with the basics and grow into the more complex, or you may need to bypass lower levels and jump right into creating workflows in Visual Studio. For now you should start learning about out-of-the-box workflows and how to start using those.

 Three types of workflows exist: out of the box, SharePoint Designer, and Visual Studio 2010.

Workflow Enablement

As you learned in Chapter 15, you can enable and disable different features in creating and deploying SharePoint workflow. So before you get started with your first out-of-the-box workflows you must check whether they are enabled in your site collection. You can check on this in Site Settings ➪ Site Collection Administration ➪ Site Collection Features.

Here you'll see all the features that are enabled in your site collection. Workflows are one of those features. Within this list are several applicable workflow features to look for, starting with the Workflows feature (see Figure 16-1), the generic feature that enables all-purpose out-of-the-box workflows. This feature includes the following workflows:

➤ Approval

➤ Collect Feedback

➤ Collect Signatures

➤ Issue Tracking

FIGURE 16-1

From here you can also enable the following additional workflows:

➤ Disposition Approval

➤ Publishing Approval

➤ Three-State Workflow

➤ SharePoint 2007 Workflows

Within this site collection feature screen you can activate the workflows you plan to use, or you can activate additional workflows later.

Introduction to Out-of-the-Box Workflows

Before you get started using and associating the out-of-the-box workflows with a list or library, you should know a little bit about each workflow.

➤ **Approval:** This will route a document or list item to a person or group for approval or rejection. This workflow can contain a staged model to add different distinct stages to your workflow. Each stage can have different sets of behavior such as serial or parallel processing. A similar workflow is also used by default in the Pages library on all publishing sites. This Approval workflow can be used to manage the page approval process before publishing.

➤ **Collect Feedback:** This workflow will route a document or list item to a person or group to ask for feedback. These reviewers can provide their feedback, which is then put together and sent to the person who started the workflow.

➤ **Collect Signatures:** This routes a document that has been created in either Office 2007 or 2010 applications to a person or group in order to collect their digital signatures on the documents. In order to complete the required steps all participants must add their personal digital signatures to the document where specified. This workflow, although automatically associated with the Document Content type, will appear for a document only if that document contains Microsoft Office signature lines.

➤ **Issue Tracking:** This will route an issue to a person or group to take action and resolve the issue in question. This workflow also can have different states, such as issue opened, issue in review, or issue closed.

➤ **Disposition Approval:** This workflow operates in support of the SharePoint records management process. The process is started on potential records and allows those who participate to either keep or delete the item in question.

➤ **Publishing Approval:** This workflow will route content for approval the same way the Approval workflow does. However, the Publishing Approval workflow is designed for sites with the Publishing feature enabled and is available only on those sites. One important difference you will see from the Approval workflow is that this form hides the options to add approvers, end the workflow on first rejection, end if the document changes, and enable content approval.

➤ **Three-State:** This is designed to track the status of a document or list item through distinct states. Each state is definable based on data from columns in that list or library. A state can be things such as submitted, in review, or completed. A task or set of tasks being completed is often the trigger to move on to the next state.

➤ **SharePoint 2007 Workflows:** These are legacy, and little time will be spent on them.

Each of these workflows can be used many times with unique names in the same library. You will most likely find that the most commonly used will be the Approval and Collect Feedback workflows. Each out-of-the-box workflow can fit basic needs, but you can't go much beyond that.

The Association Process

By now you have enabled the core out-of-the-box workflows and you can begin the process of associating each workflow with a list or library as necessary. As you learned in the previous chapter, you need to take certain steps to make a workflow available for use in each list or library. This association process is virtually identical for all SharePoint declarative workflows. The first step is associating that workflow with your list or library. You can do this through the library settings and subsequently through the association form. You can access the workflow settings for a given list or library through the Ribbon as shown in Figure 16-2 or through the main Library Settings page by clicking Workflow Settings as shown in Figure 16-3.

FIGURE 16-2

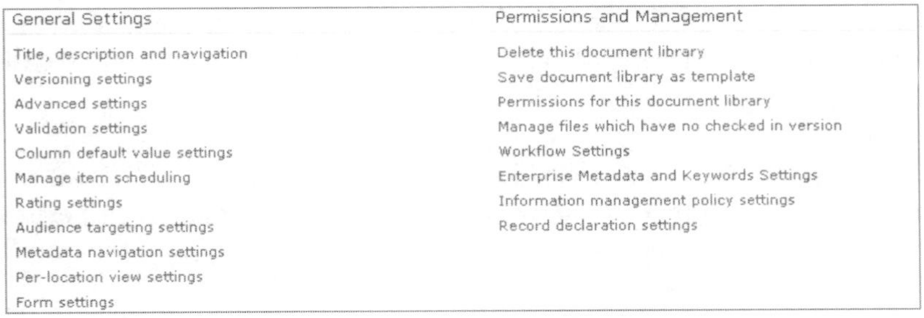

General Settings	Permissions and Management
Title, description and navigation	Delete this document library
Versioning settings	Save document library as template
Advanced settings	Permissions for this document library
Validation settings	Manage files which have no checked in version
Column default value settings	Workflow Settings
Manage item scheduling	Enterprise Metadata and Keywords Settings
Rating settings	Information management policy settings
Audience targeting settings	Record declaration settings
Metadata navigation settings	
Per-location view settings	
Form settings	

FIGURE 16-3

A user with appropriate permissions will go through the association process and assign a unique name for use only on that list or library by the workflow the user is currently associating. Doing this allows better reference for the user. For example, there may be many times when the out-of-the-box Approval workflow gets associated with a document library. Users would have difficulty in determining which workflow was which if they were all named Approval workflow. In addition to this workflow name, the workflow association can set various options such as start behavior, a default list of those participating, and the expected duration of the workflow. See Figure 16-4 for an example of how the first page of the association process appears.

The set of options you specify while performing an association is unique to that association. Each time a workflow is associated you can select different options, including a unique name. This allows you to associate each workflow multiple times with different configurations based on need. Once a workflow is enabled on your site collection it is available on each list or library to be associated as long as you have permission. You may notice that some workflows are not listed on some objects. For example, you won't see the Publishing Approval workflow listed when you are working with lists or libraries. This is because the list is trimmed for applicability of the workflow. At this point you have a basic understanding of what an association is and what you have to do when you have a list or library that you want to tie some process to. To understand these actions even better you should walk through a basic example. You can replace names of sites and lists with more appropriate names for your environment. If you need to create a new site or list, you can do this from the Site Actions menu that is available in the top left-hand corner of the page.

For this example take the owner of the listContracts. You want to add an Approval workflow to assist in the approval of different contracts that will be sent out to vendors. You know that these contracts must go through a review cycle, then be approved by Legal. You know that this can be done in stages using the Approval workflow, and that they can be done in serial or parallel, so you want to take advantage of both of these options. In your association step you'll go through and add the Approval workflow to your library and provide a basic amount of information on page one, basically just giving it a unique name for use and specifying what task and history lists to use.

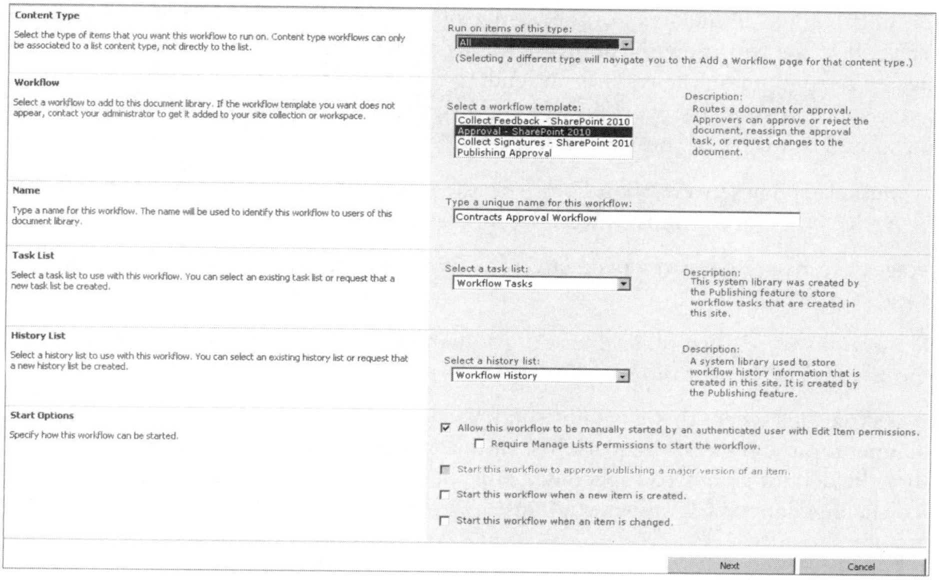

FIGURE 16-4

The next page of the workflow association form is shown in Figure 16-5. The information you provide in this step is only there to assist the person kicking off the workflow when the workflow is set to start manually. That person can change the information you are putting in at this step.

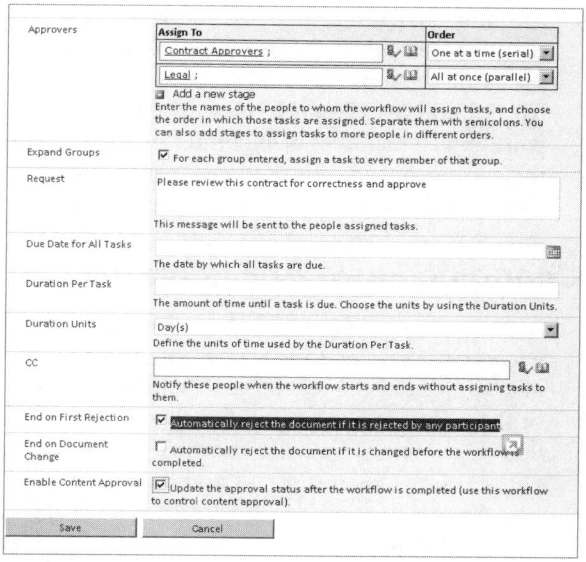

You want to make sure that you have two stages in this workflow. In Stage 1 you want the approval to go to the contract approvers group in serial. "Serial" means that if this group has three members, Sara, Carter, and Nolan, it will go to Sara first, then Carter, and finally Nolan. One very important item to note is that if any of these three rejects the contract, the workflow will stop. This is because the option is checked telling the system to "Automatically reject the document if it is rejected by any participant"

FIGURE 16-5

(Figure 16-5). Be careful with this option; if selected, it can cause problems if someone accidentally rejects or does not understand the consequences of the reject action. This can cause the workflow to terminate. If this happens you cannot recover and simply start where you left off; you must start the workflow over. Once the contract approvers group finishes, the workflow moves on to the legal group. However, in this stage all members of the legal group get the workflow task at the same time, in parallel. At the end of the workflow the approval status of the contract item in question is set to approved or rejected depending on the result, thus ending the workflow. Once you click Save you will have created/associated your first workflow in SharePoint. When looking at the workflow you just created, you should be aware of some key points:

➤ Groups were used. These were SharePoint-specific groups, but these can be Active Directory users or Active Directory groups as well.

➤ More stages can be added or removed later; this is one of the options that can be easily configured.

➤ No other options were filled in, such as duration and CC fields. These can be filled in by a user who is starting the workflow at run time.

➤ For those situations where this workflow may be automatically started by the insertion of a document to the library, the workflow initiator will not be given the opportunity to modify the default values you specified. This means that if you were expecting to be provided the due date or CC values you must have each user start the workflow manually and not automatically.

Making Changes

Workflows in many organizations are rarely static, so you should be aware of how to make some common changes to these workflows once they are associated and even after they are in use. Many changes are simple and are really just changing values you set on the initial association pages during the association process. To make a change you need to go to the Workflow Settings page in the list or library with which the workflow is associated. At that point you just click the name of the workflow, which will bring up the change-workflow screen. This screen is the same as page one of the association screens that were originally filled out. Making changes here only affects workflows that have not started yet. The changes don't affect running instances.

Changing Task- or History-List Settings

As you read in Chapter 15, there may be cases where creating special task and/or history lists becomes necessary. Creating special task and history lists for the workflow you are associating or editing takes place as part of the regular association process or through the change-workflow screen if done after association. On this first page you will see drop-downs for task and history lists. Simply use the drop-down list and select a task list that you have previously created (your best option), or you can select a new task or history list. If you choose the latter option SharePoint creates this new list for you and the list will be named the same as the workflow name. This is shown in Figures 16-6 and 16-7.

FIGURE 16-6

FIGURE 16-7

Setting Up Advanced Permissions on Your Workflow

One of the advanced-permissions items you can specify is setting the requirement to have "manage lists" permissions to start a new workflow. This can be a useful tool in reducing the number of those who can initiate your workflow. Specifying this is a simple matter of checking the box. However, the consequences can mean workflows that were supposed to be automatically started are not happening for those who are not meeting these permission requirements. Additional SharePoint permissions as they relate to your workflows will be a matter of restricting who has appropriate permissions on the lists or libraries that are involved with your workflow. Setting up these permissions properly is a core step in administering a SharePoint environment. These effects were covered in more detail in Chapter 15.

Removing Workflows

Removing workflows is an easy process that is also accessed from the Workflow Settings page, as shown in Figure 16-8.

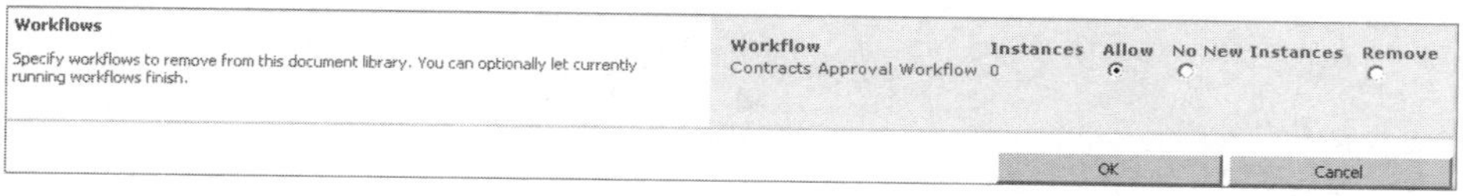

Workflows					
Specify workflows to remove from this document library. You can optionally let currently running workflows finish.	**Workflow**	**Instances**	**Allow**	**No New Instances**	**Remove**
	Contracts Approval Workflow	0	⦿	○	○
			OK		Cancel

FIGURE 16-8

Make sure you understand the ramifications of workflow removal. Removing a workflow association cancels all running instances of the workflow. To allow current instances of a workflow to complete before removing the association, select No New Instances and allow the current instances to complete. Then return to this page and select Remove to remove the workflow association.

TAKING THE NEXT STEP AND MODIFYING OUT-OF-THE-BOX WORKFLOWS

You have started learning the out-of-the-box workflows. The next step in your workflow journey is to take the workflows you were just exposed to and extend them to better suit your needs.

Extending workflows is a new ability in SharePoint 2010. SharePoint 2007 did not allow this.

One important note to keep in mind is that not all out-of-the-box workflows are available for you to modify with SharePoint Designer. The workflows you can modify when enabled are:

➤ Approval

➤ Collect Feedback

➤ Collect Signatures

➤ Publishing Approval

Before taking the next steps and modifying any of the available workflows, ensure that you are doing so with an account that has all the appropriate permissions. You can find these permissions in Chapter 15. Now that you're ready to take the next step and start using SharePoint Designer, you need to understand the tool you'll be using.

Introduction to SharePoint Designer

Opening your SharePoint site in SharePoint Designer gives you a starting dashboard that allows you to interact with different SharePoint artifacts. This is shown in Figure 16-9.

FIGURE 16-9

You can see from the top Ribbon that right from the starting page you can begin creating workflows. But for now you want to just modify an existing one, so you need to select the Workflows option from the Navigation pane on the left. From the workflow landing page/dashboard you can see the Ribbon change as shown in Figure 16-10.

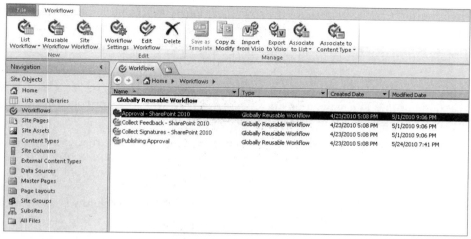

FIGURE 16-10

As with the other Office and SharePoint products, the Ribbon plays a significant role in the user experience. The Ribbon is context-sensitive, and you will see different options appear or become unavailable based on your current context. When editing a workflow you may see a Ribbon that looks as it does in Figure 16-11.

FIGURE 16-11

When not in editing mode the Ribbon look as it does in Figure 16-12.

FIGURE 16-12

The Ribbon is important for you as a workflow creator; many of the functions you need to perform are there. The Ribbon is broken into sections to increase usability. You can see them as follows:

➤ **New:** Use this section of the Ribbon, shown in the first panel of Figure 16-12, to create a new workflow.

➤ **List Workflow:** Use this button to create a new workflow that is tied to a specific list at design time. This will automatically associate the workflow for you. This button expands to display all the lists available on that site.

➤ **Reusable Workflow:** Use this to create a new reusable workflow that you can then deploy to the site for use by others.

➤ **Site Workflow:** Use this to create a new site-based workflow.

➤ **Edit:** Use this section of the Ribbon for editing workflows. When a workflow is selected you will have the Edit part of the Ribbon.

➤ **Workflow Settings:** From here you can change workflow settings.

➤ **Edit Workflow:** This brings up the selected workflow in edit mode.

➤ **Delete:** This deletes the selected workflow (Figure 16-13).

FIGURE 16-13

➤ **Manage:** This section allows you to perform various utility type functions with a selected workflow.

➤ **Copy & Modify:** This allows you to take the selected workflow and create a new workflow based on it. You will be doing this soon.

➤ **Import from Visio:** This takes a Visio file that has been exported into a Visio Workflow Interchange format (VWI) and imports that workflow into SharePoint Designer to continue the building process. More on that later.

➤ **Export to Visio:** This exports a workflow to a Visio format to allow for collaboration with a Visio workflow author.

➤ **Associate to List:** This goes through the association process for the selected workflow.

➤ **Associate to Content Type:** This goes through the association process for the selected workflow to a SharePoint content type (Figure 16-14).

FIGURE 16-14

You learn more about each of these tasks throughout this chapter.

Modification in Action

It's time for you to modify an out-of-the-box workflow. To facilitate this modification of an existing workflow, Microsoft has given you the ability to copy and modify as described earlier. Follow these steps:

1. Create a new workflow from an existing one by right-clicking the workflow you want to use and selecting Copy and Modify as shown in Figure 16-15, or by using the Copy & Modify button from the Manage section of the Ribbon.

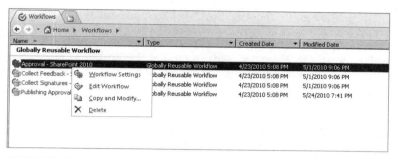

FIGURE 16-15

Selecting the Copy and Modify option creates a new workflow dialog box as shown in Figure 16-16.

2. You must provide a name and description as well if you want to associate this workflow with a content type; then click OK.

3. You are now presented with the new copy of the worklow that you are free to edit by adding new conditions and actions. For now, click on the name of the workflow located in the area above the workflow canvas.

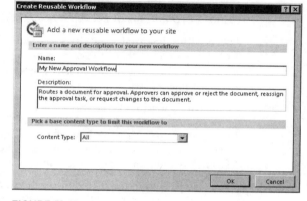

FIGURE 16-16

4. You will see the workflow dashboard here and will see that you have different settings or other options you can further customize. This dashboard is shown in Figure 16-17.

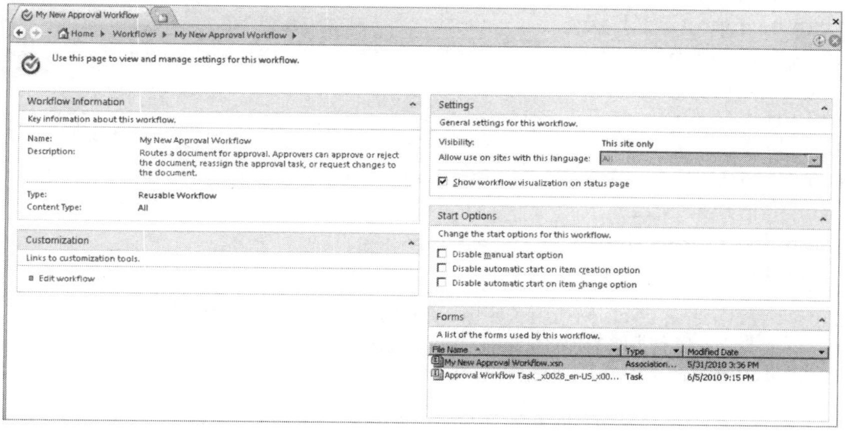

FIGURE 16-17

You can edit the basic information about the workflow, such as name and description, in the Workflow Information panel. An important option in the Settings panel is "Show workflow visualization on status page." When you select this option, SharePoint will use Visio services to visually display status. Once you are ready to modify the workflow, move on to Step 5.

5. Click the Edit Workflow link in the Customization section. This will take you to the main workflow canvas.

From here you can begin to modify your new workflow. In this example your users want to add a step to notify the site owners group after the workflow is complete.

6. Add a new step. Simply click the Step button in the Ribbon. Type in a name (in this case you can call this the Notifications step). With SharePoint Designer 2010 you have the new feature of IntelliSense. This allows you simply to start typing, with the program returning results of conditions or actions as you type.

7. Use this IntelliSense feature by starting to type "Email." Type in the first three letters, EMA; then you will see the option to click Enter to complete and add the action of sending an e-mail. This type of IntelliSense is present throughout SharePoint Designer and aids in the workflow creation process.

Define the e-mail message through the Define E-Mail Message dialog box. In this dialog you can specify principal recipients and CC as well as subject font, and take advantage of lookup fields so you don't have to know by heart all the specific values you need to insert. In this case you can add the "home owners" to specify who the e-mail is being sent to. "Home" is the name of the site you're working on; this will be different for different sites.

Then use Add Lookup at the bottom to add context from the workflow itself. In this example add the current item title along with some static content: "This is to notify you that the approval process on [Current Title] is complete."

This will grab the title of the document that went through the approval process and e-mail the document to the group specified.

8. In the next modification you need to remove the ability of workflow initiators to change who can be approvers or to change who can be CC'd in an e-mail. You can do this by modifying the Association and Initiation Form parameters. Click the Initiation Form Parameters button from the workflow Ribbon. This brings up the Association and Initiation Form Parameters dialog shown in Figure 16-18.

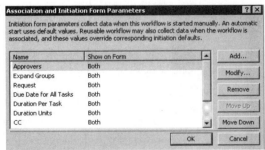

FIGURE 16-18

Highlight the Approvers item, click Modify, and select Association from the drop-down box. Do the same for the CC field. You can do this modification for all forms as well as add custom fields to either form.

9. Once you are done modifying this workflow you can publish the workflow to SharePoint as a reusable workflow or associate it directly to a list or library.

You have now taken an out-of-the-box workflow and made simple modifications. However, using SharePoint Designer to edit existing or out-of-the-box workflows is just one part of what you can do. You can also create your own workflows from scratch.

STARTING FROM SCRATCH

Before you start building your workflows from scratch you should understand some benefits of starting with the out-of-the-box workflows and doing a Copy & Modify. With these workflows a few key pieces are provided to get you started.

- ➤ Automatically generated forms
    - ➤ Initiation
    - ➤ Association
    - ➤ Task
- ➤ Automatically generated Association and Initiation Form parameters
- ➤ Automatically generated workflow variables

Performing these steps shouldn't take a significant amount of time; they allow you to create workflows faster because some of the beginning leg work is already done for you.

The first step in creating a workflow from scratch is to properly define your process, either on a whiteboard, on paper, or in Visio (more on that later). Going through this process first will pay dividends during all future steps. Some key items to note when mapping out your process include:

- ➤ Who will need to take actions in the workflow?
- ➤ Who will need to be notified at different steps in the workflow?
- ➤ Are you going to need Association forms?
- ➤ Are you going to need Initiation forms?
- ➤ Are you going to need Task forms?
- ➤ What forms technology should these be in? Can you use InfoPath?
- ➤ What data should be displayed on each of these forms?

These form decisions carry with them some other important decisions such as:

- ➤ What information do you want hard-coded and what should those associating this new workflow be able to configure?
- ➤ What should be hidden from those who are just initiating?
- ➤ Do these forms need custom branding or a particular look and feel?

As you saw when you were modifying the out-of-the-box sample, you can remove the ability to specify approvers as well as remove the ability to notify others on the CC line. Another important consideration here is what information needs to be displayed on the Task form in order for others to make informed decisions and take action as requested. By using SharePoint Designer and InfoPath you can place many different kinds of data within these forms that enable better decision-making by the workflow participants.

Once you have these data points you have the basics and are ready to start. In addition you know some of the data needed for your process. This is important to know for the creation of form parameters as well as variables. For medium to large workflows you should create each of these as a first step. This makes the creation of later steps easier, because you'll be using these fields to check values for decisions about the path taken in a workflow as well as to send out task assignments.

Building a Sample

In a business scenario, your human resources (HR) organization needs a better way to author, review, and publish corporate policies. It needs to ensure that any review and publishing process will also provide proper security. Such security is needed so that no unauthorized person can modify the policy documents during the review. Additionally, HR needs to ensure that no policy document can be written to the official published library unless placed there by an administrator after going through the process.

The solution: To address all these needs you create a process tied to a draft document library, where the HR team will store all documents while they are being authored. This draft document library will have basic permissions that give read/write access to all members of the HR team. Once authors are ready to submit the documents for official approval they will manually kick off the HR policy review workflow. Once initiated, this workflow will move the policy document to a document library reserved for all policy documents in review. In this review library, permissions will be limited to those in the HR management group.

If the new policy is approved the document will be moved to the published-policy library on the official HR SharePoint site. This HR policy document library will have broad read permissions to allow all employees to read applicable policies. Write permissions will be limited to the administrator and site owner under whom the final workflow publishing action is taken.

Although on the surface this workflow seems basic, you need to overcome some limitations when building it. With SharePoint workflows, once an item is moved the workflow loses context. You can still do such basic functions as e-mail, pause, and request information, but all functions that use the current item functionality will no longer be available. To achieve the desired solution you need to break this up into two workflows. The first workflow will be associated with the draft documents library and will serve to notify participants and move the document to the in-process library.

 There is no Move item or document command in a SharePoint workflow. Thus any move operation will involve copy and delete.

The second workflow will start automatically when the first workflow inserts the document into the in-review library. This second workflow will handle the approval steps and, if the policy document is approved, will move it to the published library while taking advantage of the *impersonation step*, which is explained later in this chapter.

You now know the business's need and have figured out how to address that need; now you need to make this workflow happen by following these steps:

1. Start off by creating a new list workflow and select your draft document library as the library to associate this with.

2. Give the first step a name by clicking the default first step, and typing a name for this step. For this example, you can call it Notify because this is the step where you will be sending out notifications to the team that this workflow has initiated.

3. Add an impersonation step to this workflow so that the moving of this document will take place with the elevated security permissions that were discussed previously. Simply place your cursor below the Notify step and select the impersonation step from the Ribbon. This will insert a new step to your canvas called Impersonation Step. Insert the Copy List Item action within this step. Once this step is inserted, click this list's hot key and select Current Item. You now need to specify where this document should be copied to. For this, select List Hot Key and from the drop-down select the document library you are using for reviews. For this example you can use Policies in Review.

4. You don't want that old draft sitting there while the document being reviewed has been placed in another library, so you need to add another action to this process to delete the document. Place your cursor underneath the copy item within the impersonation step and add a new action to this step called Delete Item. Once this is inserted select the This List hot key and select Current Item from the drop-down.

   You should now have a workflow that looks like that in Figure 16-19.

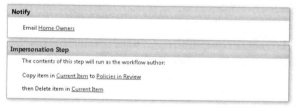

FIGURE 16-19

5. Save and optionally publish this workflow if you are ready. You now have the first part of the solution, but you still need to create the workflow that will handle the review process. This workflow will be initiated by the insertion of the copied document into the in-review library.

6. For this you need to select the List Workflow action from the SharePoint Designer Ribbon and select Policies in Review from the drop-down list. Start by renaming Step 1 under Policies in Review to Submit for Approval.

7. Within this first step add the Start Approval Process action from the list of actions. Remember that you can always just start typing and have SharePoint Designer do the work for you. Now you need to specify what users to assign this task to by selecting the Users hot key. This will bring up a standard dialog box called Select Task Process Participants. You can use the address book to find the users or just type them into the field. In this example you already have a group called HR Reviewers that you can use in this workflow. Add them in the dialog and insert any special instructions in the instructions box that you want them to see. Optionally, add parameters such as Duration per Task and/or Duration for Task Process. All these fields can use variables and different pieces of metadata. Using these can be very helpful in providing extra information to participants.

8. Now add the second step for what happens after the approval task is completed. Call this step Publish Policy. Insert a new condition of "if any value equals value." You can use this to see if the outcome of the approval process is approved or declined. In the If value you need to define a workflow lookup by selecting the hot key, then the function key (fx). For data source use "workflow variables and parameters." In Field from Source, select Variable: Is ItemApproved, and click OK. You can now select the second value hot key, which should automatically give you a drop-down of Yes and No. Select Yes.

This gives you an approval branch for what you want to happen if the new policy document meets with approval. You now want to copy this document to the published-policy library by once again using the Copy List Item action you used in the first workflow. Only now you want the destination to be the published-policy library. You also want to ensure that this document is not lying around in multiple libraries, so add the Delete item to this branch as well.

9. Next, you need to define what happens in this workflow if the document is not approved. In this case you want to copy the item back to the draft document library so that the author can modify and resubmit, then e-mail and notify the team. Once you have completed this you should see a workflow screen like that in Figure 16-20.

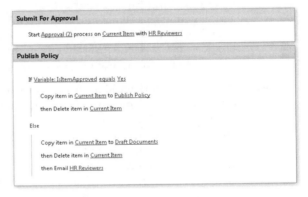

FIGURE 16-20

Now that you've seen what you can do with a workflow made from scratch, you should also learn a few situational-use cases for SharePoint workflow that may come in handy as you build other workflows.

Taking Advantage of Workflow Processes and Content Types

The more you learn about SharePoint the more you'll find that one of its best features is content types. Unfortunately this wonderful concept/feature goes largely underutilized. Covering content types in any detail is beyond the scope of this chapter. However, once you have started to take advantage of content types you should be able to see ways in which these also can help you take advantage of workflow processes. In SharePoint 2007 this was a more difficult task, because associating workflow with content types was only possible by leveraging those workflows created in Visual Studio. In SharePoint 2010 this becomes quite simple and can be a very powerful tool for you. Here's an example.

Take a simple need to have a set process for approving all contracts in your organization. Naturally, you have created a base-level content type for contracts. This content type has a series of properties associated with it that will be carried to any library in the site collection you associate it with. You also want to make sure that all contracts go through a legal review regardless of what site or library they get stored in. One way to accomplish this is to associate an Approval workflow with the Contracts content type.

Assume that you have built a custom approval process for contracts in SharePoint Designer, and that you already have created a Contracts content type. Rather than going through the typical step of associating with a list or library, you can now associate this workflow with the Contracts content type you have already created. You do this through the SharePoint Designer Ribbon by selecting the button for Associate to Content Type. This displays a drop-down menu (Figure 16-21) where you can select the content type with which you want to associate the workflow.

Once you select the content type, you are redirected to the Site Content Type settings in the SharePoint site where you fill out the typical association form — with one big difference. Pay special attention to the last option, which is "Add this workflow to all content types that inherit from this content type."

If you are familiar with content types and how they can take advantage of inheritance, this should make perfect sense. Make sure you understand this before you choose Yes or No, because this will have further consequences. If you are going to have additional content types that build off this Contract Content type (such as vendor, employee, or service contracts) and you want all contract types to use this same workflow, you should choose Yes. If you want to begin to modify this workflow for each different sub-content type, choose No.

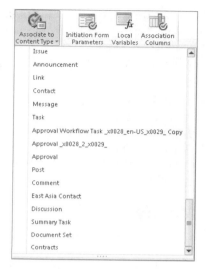

FIGURE 16-21

Modifying Workflow Outcomes

Workflow outcomes can be a powerful tool as you get deeper into customizing your workflows. Essentially these outcomes are the result of a task process. By adding a new outcome, SharePoint will place a new task action button on your forms. This will give the recipient of these tasks an additional action to take. You can then use this as an input into the workflow itself. You can see more of this in just a bit. You will probably create many workflows that go beyond the typical approve/reject outcomes. Adding an additional outcome to a workflow is fairly easy. You simply click the Approval Workflow Task, and click New in the Task Outcomes box as shown in Figure 16-22.

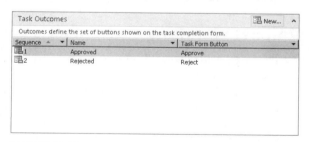

FIGURE 16-22

In this case you add an additional option to the typical approve/reject choice to allow participants to abstain from choosing. Click on the New button and add a new outcome called Abstain. Adding this new outcome automatically places the option on the Task form, but until you do a little more work on the workflow your process won't be able to take advantage of this.

To go further you need to select the Approval Workflow Task which will take you to the Approval Task dashboard. From this you need to select Change the Behavior of the Overall Task Process. This will give you a fairly lengthy set of options, which actually is one big workflow. In this example you want to scroll to the section labeled When the Task Process Completes. This set of actions will run after each task is completed. Here you can set up actions to take place when a participant selects the new option you created called Abstain. In this example you can place a new Else-If branch in the approval process and select a condition for Task Process Results, as shown in Figure 16-23.

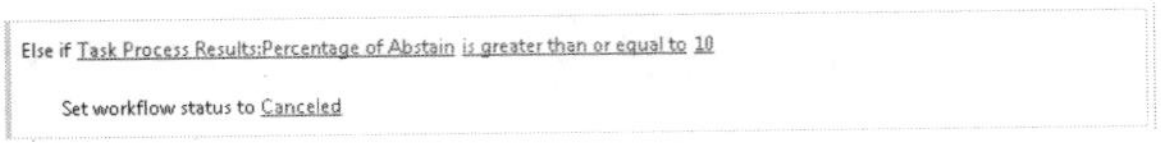

FIGURE 16-23

In this process you are setting up the workflow, so that if too many people abstain, the "vote" will be invalid and the workflow will simply cancel. Specify that if the percentage of Abstain is equal to or greater than 10, the workflow status will be set to "canceled." Your ability to modify these task processes further can be a big part of your standard workflow definitions. With this you can specify situations that allow you to complete the task after more than 50 percent of the respondents approve, or you can set up additional rules that meet your business needs.

Modifying a Form

This is a good spot to illustrate how you can modify a form associated with a workflow to provide more information or simply to "pretty up" the basics. In this example you want to make sure people understand that if they click Abstain and 10 percent or more of the respondents do so, the workflow will be canceled.

Return to the dashboard of your workflow and click the Approval Workflow Task form.

This launches the InfoPath Editor in which you can edit the form for tasks with this workflow. Be sure that you have InfoPath Designer installed so that you can edit the form. First, insert a new row below the task action buttons. Then simply type in the text you want. For this example you can use, "This workflow limits the percentage of those abstaining to 10%." Just to be sure people see and read this, you can boldface and underline the text. Now you need to save this modified form, but first you are required to save it locally. Save the modified form somewhere safe, and the form will then get published. You will also need to re-publish the workflow to have all changes take effect.

Parallel Workflow

The "parallel workflow" option on the SharePoint Designer menu may not be commonly used in your workflows, but you should understand that you have this ability and know how to use it. Simply using a parallel block is very easy. Take the previous workflow you built to support the HR policy publishing process. Go into the edit mode for that workflow after clicking Edit Workflow, place the curser just below the action that copies the policy to the published-policy library, and select the Parallel Block button in the Ribbon.

As you can see, it's easy to do, but why would you want to, and how can you take advantage of this ability? Parallel blocks are advantageous when you need certain actions not to be dependent on previous actions completing. In other cases, waiting on actions to complete would be absolutely necessary. One example is creating a new list item for e-mailing a group of people to notify them of something and including a URL. For this you would *have* to wait for the list item to be completed before e-mailing the group a link to it.

Now back to the workflow. Let's say the HR group wants to send out several different e-mails, with customized messages, notifying different groups simultaneously to ensure timely notification. For this you can simply place your cursor inside this block and add the "and Email" action shown in Figure 16-24. You can do this as many times as needed to send the custom e-mails to different groups. Figure 16-24 shows the completed workflow.

Association Columns

In SharePoint 2010, workflows have a completely new added layer of reusability. To take advantage of this new ability, Microsoft has created *association columns*. Association columns are created in a list or library during the association process. This can be a significant help in making the sharing of workflows easier. Think of a situation in which you may want to create a special Approval workflow. Within this Approval workflow you make use of special columns in the list or library to check status, values, and

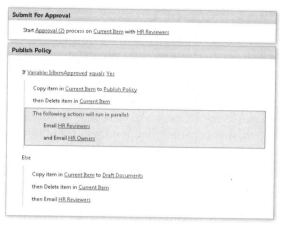

FIGURE 16-24

so on. If you shared this workflow and it was used by others in lists or libraries that did not contain these special columns, the workflow would not function. Here's where the association column comes in. When used properly, any special columns that are necessary for the workflow to function can be added at association time as part of the workflow.

STARTING WITH VISIO

Visio has long played a role for organizations in mapping the flow of a business process. Thousands of businesses have used it as a process modeling tool. Additionally, many Business Process Management and workflow vendors today leverage the power of Visio and capitalize on the level of adoption it enjoys. Going deeply into this is beyond the scope of this chapter, but for a good example take a look at Global 360 and its Analyst View product. Additionally, you can take a look at the Visio Partner Toolbox page to see a broad range of companies building on the power of Visio. The URL is http://visiotoolbox.com/2010/partner-product-trials.aspx.

In Visio and SharePoint 2010, Microsoft has taken the next step in empowering the Visio user with tools to create workflow. With these new additions, Visio can now be used at a low level to model SharePoint workflows. Notice that in this statement you did not read "to create workflows" but rather to "model" them. This is because with Visio and SharePoint you don't actually create the workflow functionality; you merely model it by using new SharePoint workflow stencils provided by Microsoft.

Why Visio?

Users today want to be more involved in workflow definition. IT organizations are looking for ways to better involve businesses in the process of building workflows. Putting a tool like Visio in the hands of your business users, a tool many of them are familiar with, enables them to participate more. Visio is a tool they're comfortable with, or if they're not, one on which they can be easily trained. For this reason, Visio is likely to gain more adoptions and have a greater level of success in organizations. This increased adoption and success helps achieve a greater return on investment. Combine this with the availability of many different Visio partners who add additional functionality, and you have a fantastic situation for adding value for your organization.

The Basics of Use

This section assumes a rudimentary understanding of Visio, so you won't find an introduction to the core use of the tool. Visio 2010 provides a new template called Microsoft SharePoint Workflow. Within this new template are new stencils that map to the new SharePoint workflow functionality you're now familiar with. Using these Visio stencils you simply lay each object onto the Visio canvas in a linear fashion. You will have a start, an end, and different steps in between. Every workflow must have a start and ensure that all paths of the workflow are terminated. Having a workflow path without a termination point will result in an error when you try to export it.

Just as with SharePoint Designer, you must lay out your different conditions and actions. These are the same as they are in SharePoint Designer. Your users will model the basic workflow steps in Visio and then will make sure that each step or action they need the workflow to take is represented in the Visio model. Once they feel the workflow is complete, they are then ready to export and share it. In this process they save a VWI file (Visio Workflow Interchange), which can then be saved in SharePoint or sent via other means to the next step. The business analysts can then do an import from the Visio operation inside SharePoint Designer. These analysts can finish up the workflow and send the file back for approval or simply publish the workflow to SharePoint.

Planning for Use

You're now familiar with the different actions and outcomes that are core to creating workflows in SharePoint Designer. These will continue to be important when you make the move to Visio. You can see that these conditions and actions now take the form of stencils in Visio. These stencils are in Chapter 15, in Figures 15-6 and 15-7. As with just about any new technology or process, before you implement you must adequately plan for how the technology will be used. If you don't do this, you can't be as effective and will experience many more problems down the road. Workflow and Visio are no exception to this; in fact, the problems can be even more acute.

The Processes

The first things you need to plan for are what role Visio will play in your workflow strategy and who will be involved in using the tool. Keep in mind that with Visio you are only performing a structure of a workflow and are adding no details to the workflow within the Visio tool. For example, when you place an action stencil of Send Email onto the Visio design canvas, you provide no data as to whom that e-mail will be sent, or what data it will contain. The business analyst must perform these functions after the workflow is imported into SharePoint Designer. Once the workflow is in SharePoint Designer the analyst will have visible placeholders that can be filled in. Each of these placeholders must be completed and the workflow published before the workflow can be available for use.

What does this mean for you as you implement SharePoint and take advantage of workflow? The question speaks to the need for effective communication between business members and IT. Visio process modeling is an important step in empowering business users to participate in creating better workflows that match their business requirements. You need to plan accordingly and remember that as business users model their workflows they need to communicate the details of each step separately from the model itself. They will also need a sharing and collaboration method in order to be most effective. One option for achieving this is the new Visio Process Repository site template that comes with SharePoint 2010. This SharePoint site will help with saving drafts of processes as well as storing basic information about each process stored. Leveraging SharePoint for this effort will help ensure that those who are looking at these Visio diagrams are looking at the most recent versions as well as having a central repository for all those diagrams in process. You'll find many other benefits for using a site like this for collaboration — which is probably why you are looking at SharePoint in the first place.

Considerations and Limitations

Before your users can be effective in leveraging Visio to model workflow, you must ensure they have all the information they need to be effective. They need to understand different modeling techniques and methods to get the results they need. Most of modeling workflow with Visio is straightforward, especially if you have used Visio in any manner before. However, you need to keep in mind several limitations when modeling SharePoint workflows. The first of these involves a common loop-back task. Within Visio and SharePoint there is no ability to loop back to previous activity. Typical business users see their workflow in very generic terms, as shown in Figure 16-25. Within this workflow a user submits a document or list item. This is then routed to a manager for approval. The manager has the options to approve, reject, or ask the submitter to perform some reworking.

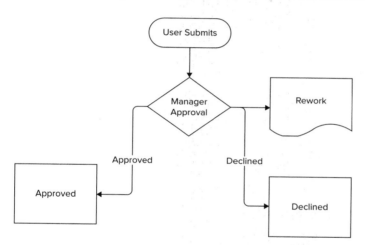

FIGURE 16-25

However, a direct loop back or "return to parent" is not possible. So you need to lay this out linearly. This means that you need to have a complete path for each outcome, and each path must root from one of two outcomes, Yes or No. This requires your building a nesting of conditions that can result in the outcome you're looking for. Each evaluation of comparable data sources for conditional evaluations is limited to two outcomes, Yes or No. Because of this limitation your users are required to put more thought and planning into each workflow modeled in Visio. The typical thought pattern that you saw in Figure 16-25 will not work in Visio. Users must be trained to think more linearly and work more closely with business analysts who will be taking these models and turning them into a usable workflow.

Another potential pitfall your users may run into is the limitation of nested conditional evaluations to 10. This means that in any one path of your workflow model you are limited to 10 conditional evaluations. For example, if I lay out my workflow model with a series of evaluation conditions, checking for Yes or No, I have to remember that no single path can have more than 10 of these evaluation conditions. This limitation won't come into play in the vast majority of your workflows, but you need to take it into account when you train your users. To help visualize the linear nature of Visio required, look at Figure 16-26. In this figure the workflow depicted in Figure 16-25 is represented as it would appear if built with Visio.

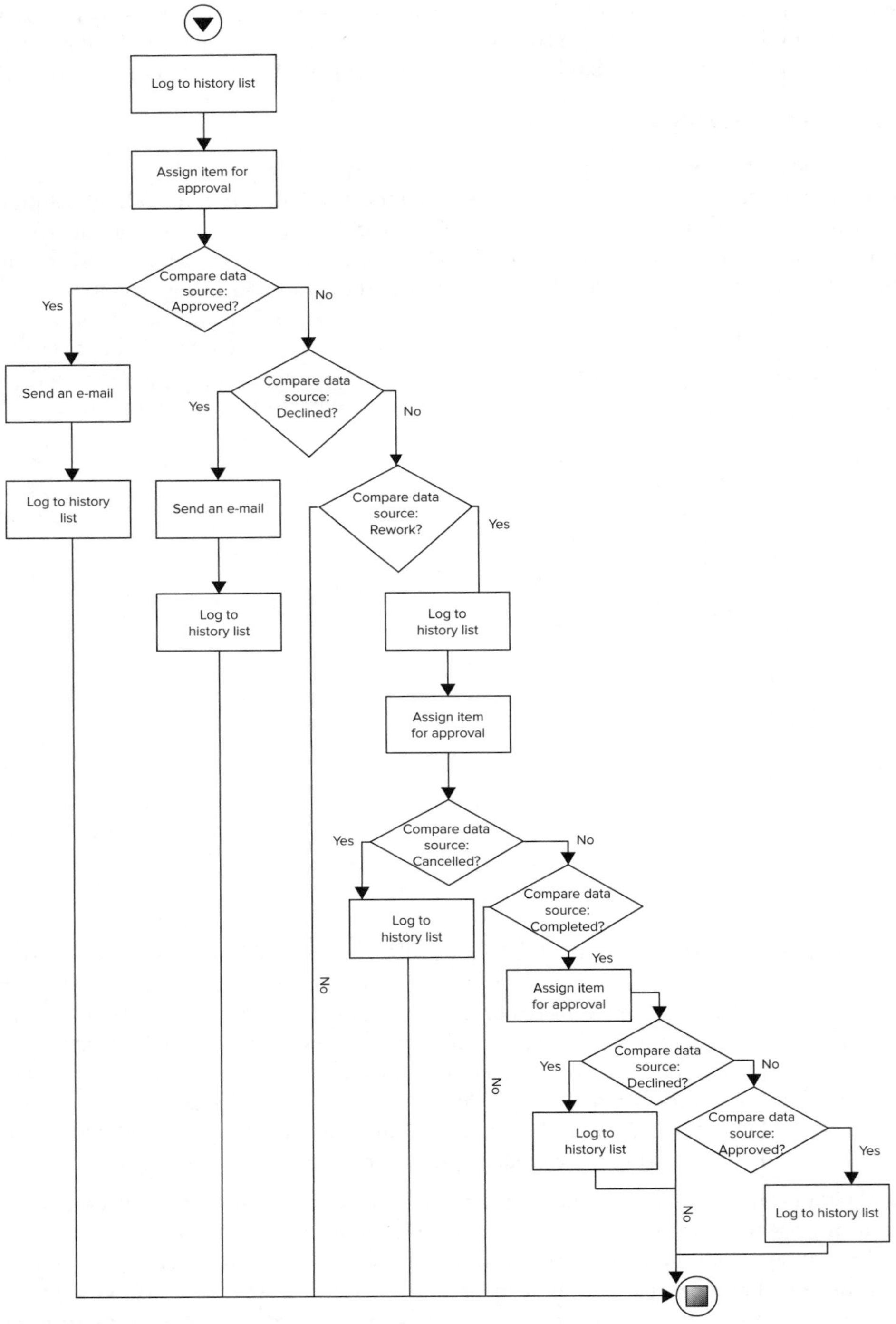

Log to history list
Assign item for approval
Compare data source: Approved?
Yes
No
Send an e-mail
Log to history list
Compare data source: Declined?
Yes
No
Send an e-mail
Log to history list
Compare data source: Rework?
Yes
No
Log to history list
Assign item for approval
Compare data source: Cancelled?
Yes
No
Log to history list
Compare data source: Completed?
Yes
No
Assign item for approval
Compare data source: Declined?
Yes
No
Log to history list
Compare data source: Approved?
Yes
No
Log to history list

FIGURE 16-26

Next Steps

Carefully plan out your workflow strategy and map the levels of functionality required for each workflow from a longer-term perspective. The leap from SharePoint Designer to Visual Studio is a big one and many times you may be better off taking a Visio map of a workflow and building this from scratch, using native Visual Studio artifacts and procedures, without going through the import process (you see more on this process in Chapter 17). Once you have imported a workflow into Visual Studio, there is no exporting again. The back and forth you enjoyed between Visio and SharePoint Designer will not be possible at this level. The real power of workflow and Visio is at the first two layers. Having a user quickly model a workflow, then having someone from IT be able to see this visually as well as import into SharePoint Designer and create a functioning workflow, is indeed a significant step in the right direction.

Now you need to know the basics of how to get a workflow diagram from Visio to SharePoint Designer and then into SharePoint. Here are the steps:

1. Model your process by dragging different shapes onto the Visio design canvas. Make sure you have a start and an end activity.

2. Once you have finished modeling the workflow and you are satisfied it's complete, you need to save and export the workflow. You can manually check for errors; however, the export process will automatically do this for you.

3. Once the workflow model is exported, you can then import the workflow into SharePoint Designer by selecting the Import from Visio button as shown earlier in Figure 16-14.

4. Provide the workflow with all the details and information on various steps that will be necessary for this workflow to function, just as you did in the sections of this chapter on modifying an existing workflow and starting from scratch. Once done with this you can optionally export the result back to Visio to allow the user to visualize any changes you've made. Keep in mind that the Visio user will not be able to see any data that was added, such as e-mail content or addresses.

5. You are now ready to publish this workflow to SharePoint. This publication will be the same as publishing those workflows that were not initially created in Visio.

Your workflow now has gone from Visio, has been imported into SharePoint Designer, and has been configured and published. You should perform several different runs of this process, each time configuring slightly different workflows and experimenting with different types of functionality.

This trip from Visio to SharePoint Designer and then perhaps to Visual Studio can be considered a ladder of functionality. With each progressive step the amounts of functionality and complexity can increase; however, taking a workflow to Visual Studio after Visio or SharePoint Designer involves some additional considerations, as you'll see in the next chapter.

SUMMARY

In this chapter you were introduced to both out-of-the-box workflows and SharePoint Designer. You also learned the basics of modifying those out-of-the-box workflows and creating new workflows from scratch. You can now take advantage of more advanced workflow features in SharePoint Designer such as parallel paths and custom workflow outcomes. You should be able to use and understand where Visio may fit into your workflow architecture. Additionally, you now have an understanding of what limitations Visio as a workflow tool introduces into your workflow design and collaboration process. Some of this will become clear in Chapter 17 as you explore workflows inside Visual Studio.

17

Visual Studio: When SharePoint Designer Is Not Enough

WHAT'S IN THIS CHAPTER?

➤ How you should be planning for taking advantage of new capabilities for building workflow in SharePoint 2010 with Visual Studio 2010

➤ How to import existing SharePoint Designer workflow into Visual Studio

➤ Creation of custom event receivers

➤ Creation of custom actions for SharePoint designer

➤ Creation of a custom SharePoint workflow in Visual Studio

The goal of this chapter is not necessarily to give you many step-by-step instructions on how to develop SharePoint workflow in Visual Studio. Rather, the goal is to dig into your options and give you some guidance as to how you should be thinking and planning for taking that next step of functionality after you have exhausted all your other options with out-of-the-box workflows as well as SharePoint Designer. With that in mind, this chapter tells you what's available in Visual Studio 2010 for SharePoint workflow. A big thank you to Ruben D'arco and Steve Thomas for helping out with the code samples provided in this chapter.

THE SHAREPOINT WORKFLOW DEVELOPER EXPERIENCE

Once you start investigating the abilities Visual Studio gives you to create workflow even outside SharePoint, you'll find that the sky is truly the limit. You can literally do anything with enough time and resources. Even after reading this book you will need to take time to understand all the different parts of workflow and leveraging the parts, all in such a way that they work well together. This is not a task for the faint of heart; you'll need to understand and account for a great many complexities.

As you probably know, the goal of any development project is typically to get the most bang for your buck. In this case that means to get the most functionality out of your workflow with the least amount of work in developing it. Most people believe in the keeping-it-simple methodology. For SharePoint workflow this can mean that you should not develop a complex workflow when all you have to do is build a basic workflow in SharePoint Designer and add in a custom action and/or an event receiver to link things together. Taking advantage of two specific pieces of SharePoint for workflow is relatively easy and doesn't usually require a long development cycle. These pieces are:

➤ Developing custom actions for use in SharePoint Designer 2010

➤ Developing event receivers for use in SharePoint

You should consider these two pieces for potential use in SharePoint workflow — they're the SharePoint workflow sweet spot.

If you have done any research or work in previous SharePoint and/or Visual Studio versions, the 2010 pairing will be a welcome change. For more information on this see Chapters 7, 8, and 9 in this book. For now you need to know what your options are in Visual Studio when it comes to SharePoint workflow.

This section should help you focus on a few important pieces before you dive in and take the next step in developing workflow for SharePoint 2010.

Within Visual Studio 2010, the project templates you'll focus on will be Import Reusable Workflow, Event Receiver, Sequential Workflow, and State Machine Workflow. These four templates, capsulized in this section, along with the Workflow Activity library in the workflow template section of Visual Studio 2010, should make up the vast majority of any SharePoint workflow development you perform. When you get started with building either State Machine or Sequential workflow, you'll find that, as with SharePoint Designer, you can target lists, libraries, and sites for any workflow you develop. You can also take advantage of all of the typical SharePoint workflow activities (actions that were in SharePoint Designer). The workflows you develop in Visual Studio can be built as Sequential workflows or alternatively as State Machine workflows. Within each template are also item templates you can use. These can be important because they will assist you in building Workflow Association and Initiation forms. The available new items are shown in Figure 17-1.

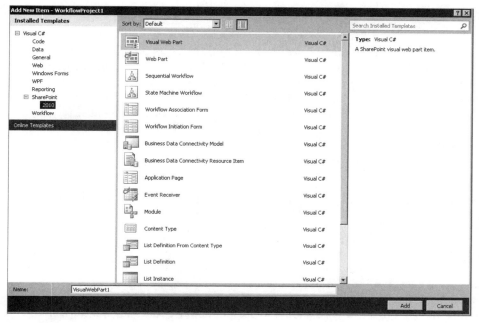

FIGURE 17-1

Importing Reusable Workflow

Your typical first step in building a new SharePoint workflow from scratch will be to start with one of these project templates. However, with SharePoint and Visual Studio 2010 you no longer *need* to start from scratch. That's because you now have the ability to import a reusable workflow. This ability is probably one of the most talked-about new abilities in the Visual Studio 2010 release specifically for SharePoint 2010. You now can import a reusable workflow that's been published via SharePoint Designer.

Importing the reusable workflow into Visual Studio converts this from a declarative workflow into a code-based workflow. Once the workflow is imported you can then add code and do any other customizations necessary. You can work through the details of this import by following examples later in this chapter.

Event Receivers

Another important ability in Visual Studio 2010 is that of building your own event receivers. As noted before, this is one of the project templates that you should become familiar with, because it could become a core pillar of your workflow strategy. For our purposes an event receiver is a programmed response to any SharePoint events that are fired. Taking advantage of these events and event receivers in SharePoint workflow can be extremely powerful.

This ability allows you to kick off workflows or even just quickly respond to the variety of different events that are available out of the box with SharePoint 2010. These events can be such simple things as adding items, moving items, deleting items, and checking in or checking out items. To drive home some of the possibilities, consider that this enables you to take action on a delete of not only a document but also a list or even a site. You could build in an event handler to prevent this or get very creative with other options. Additional events are web events such as sites being deleted, provisioned, or moved. These events and event receivers can also be leveraged to build off other workflows. Events available for this are workflows that are starting, started, postponed, or completed.

As you can see you have a great many options available when you progress up the functionality ladder into Visual Studio. At the same time this can be overwhelming. To help you better understand how these pieces work it's time to get your hands on them.

When you read about templates for Sequential and State Machine workflow the first thing you may be thinking is, what's the difference? You may be saying, "I just want workflow." The difference is fairly simple — and keep in mind that in most cases you will only use Sequential. The basic differentiation is where the decision logic for the workflow is to be housed — within the workflow itself or externally. Before moving on, you should understand more about these options.

Sequential Workflow

This is the typical workflow you're probably used to seeing and discussing. This workflow follows a predictable path much like a flow chart. When developing this type of workflow, you specify each decision point and what that decision is. Though the path of the Sequential workflow may have numerous branches and loops, the workflow still has this predefined path.

State Machine Workflow

The State Machine workflow is purely an event-driven workflow. It relies on external events to drive each step or change in state. When building the workflow you define the available states and the different transitions between states. The workflow will always be in one of these defined states. In order to move from one state to another some event has to occur. The decision-making happens outside the workflow.

By now you should have already gotten into Visual Studio as a result of reading the earlier chapters. Now you need to dig more into what you should know for taking advantage of workflow. Once you make your way into Visual Studio to build workflows, you will have many options including the use of your own custom assemblies and of web services. Those topics are beyond the scope of this chapter, but you need to know some basics of the different workflow support abilities you have in Visual Studio.

To build SharePoint workflow you'll also need to familiarize yourself with the Workflow Activity library. This project template will allow you to create custom workflow activities that can be surfaced in SharePoint Designer for use by your SharePoint Designer users. The combination of the event receiver and the custom workflow activity should be considered the sweet spot for the best ratio of functionality to amount of effort.

IMPORTING A REUSABLE WORKFLOW TO VISUAL STUDIO

There may be times when you've worked hard building a process in SharePoint Designer, as well as customizing it. Then at some point you realize you've hit the limit for what you can do using the tool. You determine that you need to move up the ladder and begin adding additional functionality that's going to be available only with Visual Studio 2010. You also determine that you don't want to lose any of the work you have already done. With SharePoint and Visual Studio 2010 you have an option to help you with this. You can import the workflow as long as it was created as a reusable workflow. You learned about these different workflow types in the previous chapter. Keep this requirement in mind as you plan the workflows you may build with SharePoint Designer. To get a reusable workflow into Visual Studio you must follow these steps:

1. Ensure you have a published workflow from SharePoint Designer.

2. In SharePoint Designer, highlight the workflow you want to import and select Save as Template. This will save the workflow as a WSP file and place it into the Site Assets library.

3. Save the resulting WSP file from the Site Assets library to somewhere local where you can open it with Visual Studio.

4. Run Visual Studio 2010 (2010 is required) and create a new project with a project type of Import Reusable Workflow.

5. You will be presented with a wizard that will walk you through the basics of different project options such as the Sharepoint Site URL as well as the path to the WSP file you should have just saved locally from the Site Assets library. Fill in these details as appropriate.

6. Select your workflow from the list of workflows to be converted, and click Finish. (If your workflow doesn't show up, make sure that the workflow you saved as a template was the correct one and was already published to SharePoint.)

At this point your workflow has been imported and you can immediately begin using it, or you can start making modifications and additions right from here. Assuming the import was successful, you should see an interface that looks like Figure 17-2.

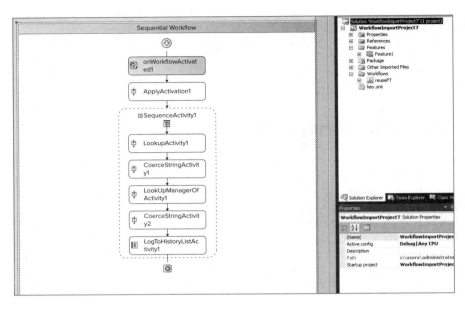

FIGURE 17-2

 Globally reusable workflows created in SharePoint Designer can't be imported. If you need to import one of these workflows, take advantage of the copy and edit functionality and then republish the workflow.

Following are some items to note when thinking of doing a reusable workflow import:

➤ It imports only one Task form.

➤ It cannot deploy a sandboxed solution.

➤ Debugging does not work for any declarative content.

Basic reusable workflows are easy to import and modify. However, as you will see if you import larger and more complex workflows (especially those that take advantage of the powerful task processes in SharePoint Designer), the resulting import can be overwhelming. You may find starting over is actually a better alternative than importing these. Note that Figure 17-2 shows a basic workflow that doesn't make use of the task processes built into SharePoint. Figure 17-3 shows that same workflow, with the only difference being that an approval process is added at the end. (The left side of Figure 17-3 is not intended to be read here, but simply to show the complexity of the workflow.)

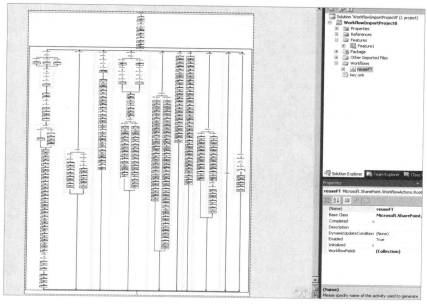

FIGURE 17-3

The overwhelming nature of the imported result is primarily because of the power and flexibility that the task and approval processes provide for your workflows. As you inspect your new workflow in Visual Studio you will notice that each of the options surfaced in SharePoint Designer is also surfaced in Visual Studio. SharePoint Designer is shown in Figure 17-4, and the corresponding functionality in Figure 17-5 shows the corresponding function in Visual Studio.

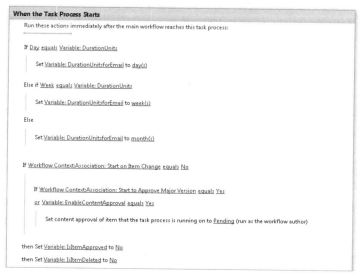

FIGURE 17-4

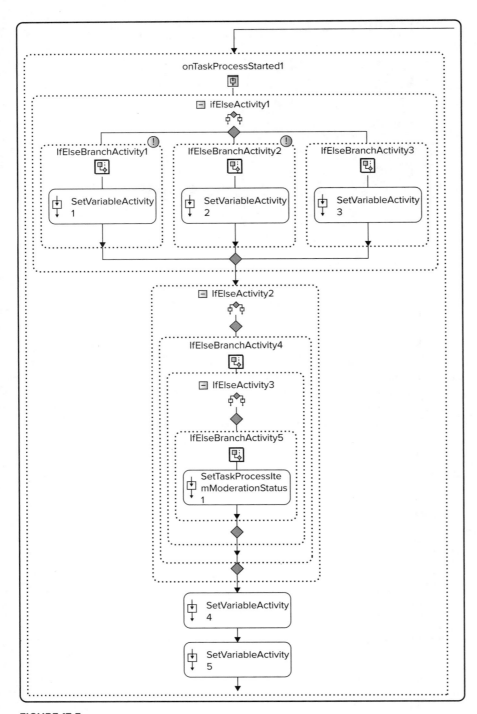

FIGURE 17-5

Being able to take full advantage of all these individual pieces will definitely take some time and research. If this is something you believe you will be using, you should take a significant amount of time to experiment broadly with the different options. Digging in and having some hands-on experience is the best way to gain a better understanding. (Obviously, you should not do this experimentation on a production system.) Now that you understand how to import a workflow from SharePoint Designer, you should understand how to make one from scratch.

EXAMPLE: TAKING ADVANTAGE OF EVENT RECEIVERS

As you previously read, event receivers and the event model for SharePoint got a huge boost in 2010. Not only has the list of events been expanded, but you now can create your own events and event receivers with ease. Table 17-1 gives you a good picture of the entire set of out-of-the-box events you can take advantage of. (Entries with asterisks are new in SharePoint 2010.)

TABLE 17-1: Out-of-the-Box Events

LIST EVENTS	LIST ITEM EVENTS
A field was added.	An item is being added.
A field is being added.	An item is being updated.
A field was removed.	An item is being deleted.
A field is being removed.	An item is being checked in.
A field was updated.	An item is being checked out.
A field is being updated.	An item is being unchecked out.
*A list is being added.	An attachment is being added to the item.
*A list is being deleted.	An attachment is being removed from the item.
*A list was added.	A file is being moved.
*A list was deleted.	An item was added.
	An item was updated.
	An item was deleted.
	An item was checked in.
	An item was checked out.
	An item was unchecked out.
	An attachment was added to the item.
	An attachment was removed from the item.

continues

TABLE 17-1 *(continued)*

LIST EVENTS	LIST ITEM EVENTS
	A file was moved.
	A file was converted.
	*The list received a context event.
List-Based Workflow Events	**Feature-Based Events**
*A workflow is starting.	A feature was activated.
*A workflow was started.	A feature is deactivating.
*A workflow was postponed.	A feature was installed.
*A workflow was completed.	A feature is being upgraded.
Web Events	**List-Based E-mail Events**
A site collection is being deleted.	*A list received an e-mail message
A site is being deleted.	
A site is being moved.	
*A site is being provisioned.	
A site collection was deleted.	
A site was deleted.	
A site was moved.	
*A site was provisioned.	

Some of the most powerful abilities provided by leveraging the events of SharePoint are those that respond to different workflow events. For now you need to understand the basics of creating an event receiver. Fortunately, Microsoft has made your life easier by baking a lot of this into Visual Studio 2010 with the Event Receiver project type shown in figure 17-6. For this example you create an event receiver that listens to the ItemChanged event and then checks a column in the list for the item status. If that item status is completed it sends an e-mail. To accomplish this, start by launching Visual Studio 2010 and creating a new project with the type of Event Receiver.

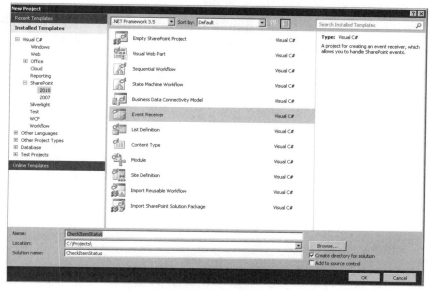

FIGURE 17-6

The name and location don't matter much, but in this case the new project is called CheckItemStatus and is saved to the local C drive in a folder called Projects. This will launch the wizard you will have become familiar with for all SharePoint-based projects in Visual Studio 2010. Ask for the URL and whether this will be sandboxed. Next you will see the selection screen where you can select the type of event receiver you want to create as well as the event source and selection of events to act on, as shown in Figure 17-7.

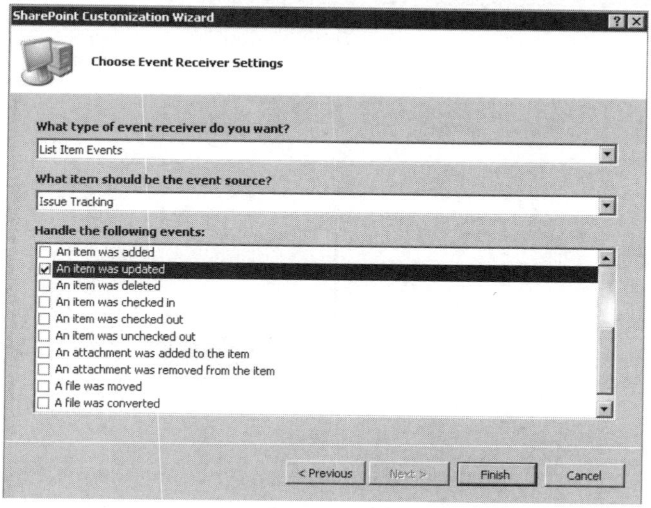

FIGURE 17-7

In this case select the Issue Tracking List type and the event to monitor when an item is updated. You can select as many events as you like, which will then create additional methods for you to add code for (and you'll have different actions for each item). The screen is shown in Figure 17-8.

```
public override void ItemAdded(SPItemEventProperties properties)
{
    base.ItemAdded(properties);
}

/// <summary>
/// An item was updated.
/// </summary>
public override void ItemUpdated(SPItemEventProperties properties)
{
    base.ItemUpdated(properties);
}

/// <summary>
/// An item was deleted.
/// </summary>
public override void ItemDeleted(SPItemEventProperties properties)
{
    base.ItemDeleted(properties);
}
```

FIGURE 17-8

For now just select ItemUpdated. After you do this, you should see a basic Visual Studio canvas like the one in Figure 17-9.

FIGURE 17-9

This is essentially a blank canvas. You can place your custom code here, and anytime the specified event occurs your code will run. However, keep in mind that you want to stay within the bounds of reason and not use event receivers for long-running items. If you need longer running ability, use workflow. On this blank canvas you now need to add some code, so take the code in Listing 17-1 and add it just underneath the `base.ItemUpdate(properties);` line.

LISTING 17-1: SharePoint Event Receiver (CodeSamples.VS2010.EventHandler.csproj)

```
try
    {
        string revisionStatus = GetFieldValue(properties.ListItem,
"CheckComplete");
        if (revisionStatus.CompareTo("Complete") == 0) SPUtility.
SendEmail(properties.Web,
                                                   false, false,
GetCurrentUserEmail(properties),
                                                   "Event Handler Email",
GetFieldValue(properties.ListItem,
                                                   "EmailBody"));
    }
    catch
    {
        //bypass exception-since this is test code;
    }
}
private string GetFieldValue(SPListItem item, string fieldDisplayName)
{
    return (item[fieldDisplayName] != null) ? item[fieldDisplayName].
ToString() : string.Empty;
}
private string GetCurrentUserEmail(SPItemEventProperties properties)
{
    string userEmail = properties.Web.CurrentUser.Email;
    return userEmail;
}

}
```

This example is pretty simple, but it gives you insight into what you need to do before taking the next step. Take this example and experiment with different options. If you wanted to take this event receiver and associate it with a specific list or library, you could do so through PowerShell as shown in Listing 17-2.

LISTING 17-2: Associating an Event Receiver with a Specific List (Associate Workflow.ps1)

```
[System.Reflection.Assembly]
::Load("Microsoft.Sharepoint, Version=14.0.0.0, Culture=neutral,PublicKeyToken=71e9b
ce111e9429c")
$url = "http://url to document library";
$spsite = new-object Microsoft.SharePoint.SPSite($url);
$spweb = $spsite.OpenWeb();
$splist = $spweb.GetListFromUrl($url);
$splist.EventReceivers.Add([Microsoft.SharePoint.SPEventReceiverType]::ItemAdded,
```

continues

LISTING 17-2 *(continued)*

```
"CodeSamples.VS2010.EventHandler, Version=1.0.0.0, Culture=neutral,
PublicKeyToken=64a56f09eb241aa2",
"CodeSamples.VS2010.EventHandler.EventReceiver1.EventReceiver1");
$spweb.Dispose();
$spsite.Dispose();
```

 One key piece of this example is the sending of an e-mail. Users must have an e-mail address specified in SharePoint for this to properly get the e-mail address it needs to send to. Keep this in mind in your SharePoint environment.

CUSTOM WORKFLOW ACTIVITIES WITH VISUAL STUDIO FOR USE IN SHAREPOINT DESIGNER

In this section you learn how to create a custom activity in Visual Studio and publish that to be consumed by a SharePoint Designer workflow.

By now you have seen the power available to you in SharePoint Designer for workflow. You also should now understand the limits imposed when using out-of-the-box as well as SharePoint Designer-based workflows. But these limits don't mean that your users cannot use SharePoint Designer to create workflows. They can, with a little help from you. You have the power to extend the functionality of SharePoint Designer by building custom actions that you can then publish to SharePoint for use by your users in SharePoint Designer. Better enabling your users with the tools they need to help themselves will go a long way toward increasing the adoption of SharePoint as well as making a happier user community.

In previous discussions about SharePoint Designer, one of the key points in its favor was that it does not let users cause significant damage to your site. There is no action for deleting a site or for running custom code that could contain a worm of some kind. This means that all the actions that are available in SharePoint Designer can be trusted. Taking this a step further, Microsoft has given you the ability to write out actions that you are comfortable with publishing and having used by your users in SharePoint Designer. This ability can help to extend the product to overcome many limitations.

The example activity in this section may not be the most conventional, but it is one that gets the point across. This activity will give you the ability to send out a tweet through Twitter as an action.

The process of building custom actions is easy once you understand the basics. What you get in return is also very appealing and rewarding. Once you publish actions they are available for all your users to take advantage of. This approach is a "code once and reuse often" proposition.

When you launch SharePoint Designer, the program queries the SharePoint Server to determine what actions should be available during your design process. This list of available actions is stored as a series of .actions files in the %SPRoot%\Template\1033\Workflow folder. Each .actions file is an XML file that will define different sets of actions that are available, as well as how each should be configured and what options are exposed for each action. Copy one of these .actions files to your desktop, open it up with Notepad or your favorite XML editor, and take a look. Once you read through one it should be self-explanatory how they work. You will see more on this shortly as you deploy your first custom activity.

You begin by creating a new project in Visual Studio. For this example you are going to use the Workflow Activity Library project type. You can use other projects such as the Empty SharePoint project. Once you create this project and give it a name and save location, you will be presented with a blank canvas. Because you will not be dragging and dropping any items from the toolbox onto the canvas at this point, you can simply switch to code view and start adding in the code you need to use.

While the code you put in there can take virtually any form and function, this example shows some important aspects to call out that may not be part of the code you would actually use.

You need two important things in this code. They are:

➤ **The DependencyProperty:** This is the information you enter into the action line of the SharePoint Designer activity.

➤ **The execution code:** This code actually performs the action you need done.

The dependency property consists of two parts:

➤ A static variable: `public static DependencyProperty TwitterUsernameProperty = DependencyProperty.Register("TwitterUsername", typeof(string), typeof(TwitterActivity));`

➤ A property that exposes the real value.

The *NAME* of the DependencyProperty variable is important. It needs to be <property>Property. That is, if you want the property to be `TwitterUserName`, the static variable needs to be `TwitterUserNameProperty`. Otherwise, it won't compile.

So in the previous line, the name is TwitterUsername. That means the static variable needs to be TwitterUsernameProperty. If this is not correct the project will not compile. The same goes for the property. It should be named TwitterUsername. As you can see from the code in Listing 17-3 it simply exposes the static variable. From the execution code, you always call this property.

The execution of this activity is done by overwriting the Execute method (`protected override ActivityExecutionStatus Execute(ActivityExecutionContext executionContext)`).

In the execute code, do what you want to do, but always use This.property, so you don't talk to the static variable directly. Using "this." will ensure you're always talking to the property, and not the public static DependencyProperty. The code for this action follows in Listing 17-3.

LISTING 17-3: SharePoint Designer Custom Activity (SP2010CustomActivities.sln)

```csharp
using System;
using System.ComponentModel;
using System.ComponentModel.Design;
using System.Collections;
using System.Linq;
using System.Workflow.ComponentModel.Compiler;
using System.Workflow.ComponentModel.Serialization;
using System.Workflow.ComponentModel;
using System.Workflow.ComponentModel.Design;
using System.Workflow.Runtime;
using System.Workflow.Activities;
using System.Workflow.Activities.Rules;
using TweetSharp.Twitter.Fluent;
using TweetSharp;
using TweetSharp.Twitter.Model;
using System.Diagnostics;
using System.Security;

namespace CustomActivities
{
    public partial class TwitterActivity : SequenceActivity
    {

        #region Private fields/constants
        private const string EventLogSource = "SP2010 Twitter Activity";
        private const string EventLogLogName = "Application";
        #endregion Private fields/constants

        #region Public Static DependencyProperty
        public static DependencyProperty TwitterMessageProperty =
DependencyProperty.Register("TwitterMessage", typeof(string), typeof(TwitterActivity));
        public static DependencyProperty TwitterUsernameProperty =
DependencyProperty.Register("TwitterUsername", typeof(string), typeof(TwitterActivity));
        public static DependencyProperty TwitterPasswordProperty =
DependencyProperty.Register("TwitterPassword", typeof(string), typeof(TwitterActivity));
        #endregion Public Static DependencyProperty

        #region Constructor(s)
        public TwitterActivity()
        {
            InitializeComponent();
        }
        #endregion Constructor(s)

        #region Public properties (for Dependency Property)
        [Category("Twitter Actions"), Browsable(true)]
        [DesignerSerializationVisibility(DesignerSerializationVisibility.Visible)]
        public string TwitterMessage
        {
            get
            {
```

```csharp
            return base.GetValue(TwitterActivity.TwitterMessageProperty) as string;
        }
        set
        {
            base.SetValue(TwitterActivity.TwitterMessageProperty, value);
        }
    }

    [Category("Twitter Actions"), Browsable(true)]
    [DesignerSerializationVisibility(DesignerSerializationVisibility.Visible)]
    public string TwitterUsername
    {
        get
        {
            return base.GetValue(TwitterActivity.TwitterUsernameProperty) as string;
        }
        set
        {
            base.SetValue(TwitterActivity.TwitterUsernameProperty, value);
        }
    }


    [Category("Twitter Actions"), Browsable(true)]
    [DesignerSerializationVisibility(DesignerSerializationVisibility.Visible)]
    public string TwitterPassword
    {
        get
        {
            return base.GetValue(TwitterActivity.TwitterPasswordProperty) as string;
        }
        set
        {
            base.SetValue(TwitterActivity.TwitterPasswordProperty, value);
        }
    }
    #endregion Public properties (for Dependency Property)

    #region Protected overridden methods
    protected override ActivityExecutionStatus Execute(ActivityExecutionContext
executionContext)
    {
        try
        {
            TwitterClientInfo info = new TwitterClientInfo() { ClientName =
"SP2010 Designer Activity", ClientVersion = "1.0.0.0" };
            IFluentTwitter iTwitter =
FluentTwitter.CreateRequest(info).AuthenticateAs(this.TwitterUsername, this.
TwitterPassword);

            ITwitterLeafNode node = iTwitter.Statuses().Update(this.
TwitterMessage).AsJson();
```

continues

LISTING 17-3 *(continued)*

```
                    TwitterResult result = node.Request();
                    if (result.IsTwitterError)
                    {
                        WriteEventLog("An error occurred when posting to twitter. {0}",
result.Exception);
                        return ActivityExecutionStatus.Faulting;
                    }
                }
            catch (Exception ex)
            {
                WriteEventLog("An exception has occurred within the Twitter
activity: {0}; {1}", ex.Message, ex.StackTrace);
                return ActivityExecutionStatus.Faulting;
            }


            return ActivityExecutionStatus.Closed;
        }
        #endregion Protected overridden methods

        #region Private helper methods
        private void WriteEventLog(string msg, params object[] args)
        {
            string text = string.Format(msg, args);
            this.WriteEventLog(text);
        }

        private void WriteEventLog(string msg)
        {
            try
            {
                if (!EventLog.SourceExists(EventLogSource))
                {
                    EventLog.CreateEventSource(EventLogSource, EventLogLogName);
                }

                EventLog.WriteEntry(EventLogSource, msg);
            }
            catch (SecurityException ex)
            {
                // I know this is a bad thing to do, but where else should we log if
we simply are not allowed to log to the event log?!
                // AKA: you're SP user needs to have access for this.
            }
        }
        #endregion Private helper methods

    }
}
```

At this point you have the code that performs your action. You now need to make sure that you compile this as a strong named assembly and copy the resulting DLL to the Global Assembly Cache (GAC). For more information on doing this see http://msdn.microsoft.com/en-us/library/dkkx7f79.aspx. Once this is complete you are ready to build your actions file that will surface this functionality in SharePoint Designer. The actions file for this example is shown in Listing 17-4.

LISTING 17-4: Custom Activity Actions File (Twitter.Actions)

```xml
<?xml version="1.0" encoding="utf-8" ?>
<WorkflowInfo Language="en-us">
<Actions Sequential="then" Parallel="and">
<Action Name="Tweet a message"
ClassName="CustomActivities.TwitterActivity"
Assembly="CustomActivities, Version=1.0.0.0, Culture=neutral,
PublicKeyToken=a62143cda0ae4f3f" AppliesTo="all" Category="Twitter Actions">
<RuleDesigner Sentence="Send a tweet message %1, by user %2 and password %3">
<FieldBind Field="TwitterMessage" DesignerType="TextArea" Id="1"/>
<FieldBind Field="TwitterUsername" DesignerType="TextArea" Id="2"/>
<FieldBind Field="TwitterPassword" DesignerType="TextArea" Id="3"/>
</RuleDesigner>
<Parameters>
<Parameter Name="TwitterMessage" Type="System.String, mscorlib" Direction="In" />
<Parameter Name="TwitterUsername" Type="System.String, mscorlib" Direction="In" />
<Parameter Name="TwitterPassword" Type="System.String, mscorlib" Direction="In" />
</Parameters>
</Action>
</Actions>
</WorkflowInfo>
```

Following are a few points to better understand what you are seeing in this .actions file.

You can see the Action Name and category, which affect how this action is displayed in the Actions drop-down menu inside SharePoint Designer and as shown in Figure 17-10.

Twitter Actions
Tweet a message

FIGURE 17-10

You can also see that there are configurable fields that can be inserted into the description. These are labeled as the Rule Designer Sentence followed by variables %1, %2, %3. Each of these variables will appear as links when you add the action to a workflow. These variables can then be configured with the default configuration tools SharePoint Designer makes available and you are used to using when you created your previous workflows (Figure 17-11).

FIGURE 17-11

Next the value of the Field attribute determines which parameter the configured value should be bound to. The Parameters section specifies parameter values that are to be bound to the action.

Once you have this .actions file complete, copy it to the %SPRoot%\Template\1033\Workflow folder.

You are not done yet, because you have to tell SharePoint that this new assembly you have added is safe. You need to open the web.config file for the web application on which you want to use this new action and scroll down near the bottom of the file. Here you will find a section called <System.Workflow.ComponentModel.WorkflowCompiler>.

Add a new line that describes your assembly. In this case the following line was added:

```
<authorizedType Assembly="CustomActivities, Version=1.0.0.0, Culture=neutral,
PublicKeyToken=a62143cda0ae4f3f" Namespace="CustomActivities" TypeName="*"
Authorized="True" />
```

Now perform an IISRESET and this new action will be ready to go! You should be able to see your new action surfaced inside SharePoint Designer.

EXAMPLE: BASIC WORKFLOW CREATION IN VISUAL STUDIO

For this basic example, you will be creating Sequential workflow. Some of the basic steps would be the same if you wanted to create a State Machine workflow but for these purposes just stick with Sequential.

Before you get starting building Sequential workflow for SharePoint, you need to be aware of and plan for a few issues. These are:

➤ Concurrent user task actions

➤ onTaskCreated issues

➤ onWorkflowItemChange listening issues

These are all relatively complex issues, but you should know some of the basics at work.

Issues arise with respect to concurrent user task actions when two users involved in a workflow take action on a task at the same time. For example, suppose I have a workflow that sends a task to a group of managers to approve a capital expenditure request. Two managers open the task and approve it at the same time (this has to be pretty exact). Assuming that a workflow task action takes 500 milliseconds to process, the second action would have to come in within that 500 milliseconds. For small-scale workflows that do not send out to groups or even multiple users at once, this will not pose any issues for you. However, for more enterprise-scale workflows, especially large-scale ones that are complex and can route to numerous users, this needs to be planned and accounted for.

For the onTaskCreated issue, you must first understand that when you create a task you ask for a task to be created, but the engine does not do so immediately. Rather it creates a request to create a task. The request to create that task will not be fulfilled until the workflow is serialized. This won't cause a problem in the majority of workflows, but it could if you need the task created in order to use the information in a condition. If I am checking this condition in a `while` loop that may immediately follow the CreateTask, the `while` loop will never be entered because the condition will not be able to see the task. For this reason Microsoft recommends not using the onTaskCreated event. You can find more information at `http://support.microsoft.com/kb/970548` and also on Rob Bogues's blog at `http://www.thorprojects.com/blog/archive/2010/02/07/ontaskcreated-delayactivity-and-persistonclose---how-you-can-force-the-creation-of-a-task.aspx`.

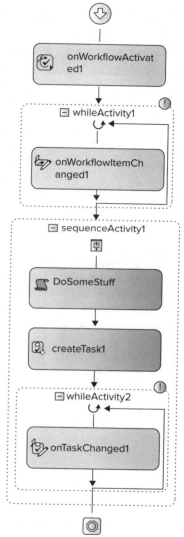

FIGURE 17-12

The onWorkflowItemChanged issue is a bit more involved. This problem is about how actively a workflow pays attention to events such as changes in workflow items. Suppose you created a workflow like the one in Figure 17-12.

Then suppose you set the workflow to watch the workflow item during the While activity but also have it go on its merry way to do other things, like the next watch item for onTaskChanged. In a sense the workflow is not paying attention anymore to the onWorkflowItemChanged event.

So how would this look in practice and what problem would it cause? Take the situation where you start a process on a document in a document library, then tell the workflow to watch for changes to that document, while at the same time you are assigning a task, processing some variables, collecting some information, and so forth. Then suppose you tell the workflow to watch for a change to that task you just assigned. Now the workflow is no longer watching the document for changes; it is just paying attention to the task. But someone is still working on the document, and when that event fires the workflow is watching the task and cannot process the item change event. At this point the workflow is no longer viable in this state. But don't fret; Rob Bogue has a solution for you, on his blog post at `http://www.thorprojects.com/blog/archive/2010/02/22/onworkflowitemchanged-and-workflow-event-delivery-problems.aspx`.

Though each of these potential workflow issues can cause serious effects, each needs specific situations to occur, and you can take these into account. Taking the time to do proper planning for both your workflow strategy and each individual workflow will help reduce the issues you run into along the way. Additionally, being well versed in best practices and keeping up on bugs will also help you be more proactive. To help you in this research, you'll find some good reference sites at the end of this chapter.

Throughout the previous sections, and even in previous chapters, you have been learning about different kinds of workflow, including different supporting technologies like event receivers. You have also read that there are pros and cons to each component. The big pro for creation of workflow with Visual Studio is also a con — the flexibility and power that come with it. It never fails that the more features, power, and flexibility a software company builds into a product, the more complicated it gets and the more time it takes to learn. Workflow is no exception to this. This chapter doesn't envision that the reader will walk away, jump right into Visual Studio, and create complex workflows. That may or may not happen. If you walk away from this book with one thing, it might be good if this were the advice to take a step back and properly analyze what you want to do and what you're trying to accomplish — then properly lay out a workflow strategy that may or may not involve creation of workflows inside Visual Studio 2010. With that understood you still need to walk a few steps in the workflow developer's shoes. This section will give you the opportunity to do so.

As you no doubt have gathered, building a workflow in Visual Studio 2010 is a little more complicated than doing so in SharePoint Designer. To better explain this difference, the walkthrough that follows will take a different format. Walking through a workflow tends to get more confusing the more steps it has, thus requiring more screenshots and descriptions of each screenshot. For this exercise you will be presented with some prerequisite information, as well as a screenshot of the entire workflow itself. There will be a reference table that describes each step that you see in that workflow. From this, I hope, you'll be able to understand the workflow and to reconstruct it on your own. This workflow as built has the following prerequisites:

➤ This workflow must be associated with a document library.

➤ The document library should have a column named Expense Approver that will be used by the workflow to determine who should get the approver task for the workflow.

➤ The task list content type Workflow Task should have a new list column associated with it, called Revision Status, which is a choice field with the following options: Pending Approval (default), Approved, Rejected, and Require More Info.

Once completed, this workflow will operate as follows:

1. The user creates a document, in this case a Word-based expense report. The user submits it by uploading it to a document library in SharePoint.

2. This causes the workflow to start off the insert event.

3. The workflow routes the document to the user's manager, which for simplicity's sake is determined by a Columns value in the document library.

4. The manager looks at the document and has the choice to approve, reject, or say that more information is needed.

5. If approved or rejected, an e-mail goes to the person who submitted the document.

6. If the manager selects Require More Info, the workflow will route the document back to the person who submitted it. Once this person has revised it, it can be resubmitted and will go back to the manager.

Once completed the workflow should look like Figure 17-13.

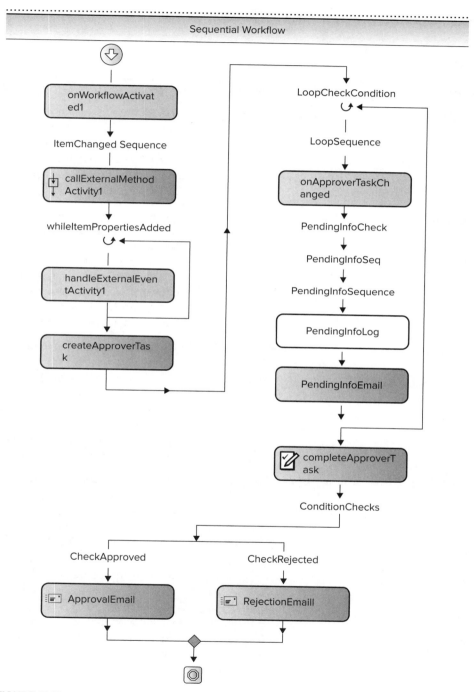

FIGURE 17-13

In tabular form, the information looks like that shown in Table 17-2.

TABLE 17-2: Workflow Components and Descriptions

COMPONENT TITLE	COMPONENT TYPE	USAGE
onWorkflowActivated1	onWorkflowActivated	Checks if the "Expense Approver" metadata field contains a value. If there is not a value, the workflow sets a Boolean variable to continue to check its value until it is filled or not null.
ItemChangedSequence	Sequence	This is the owner activity for callExternalMethodActivity1, handleExternalEventActivity1, and whileItemPropertiesAdded. This activity helps in grouping these three activities and limits the scope of the workflow listening to the WorkflowItemChanged event.
callExternalMethodActivity1	callExternalMethod	This activity subscribes to the InitializeEvent method raised by the Microsoft.SharePoint. Workflow.IListService interface on the workflow parent item. This subscription will be used by the handleExternalEvent1 activity to tap into the ItemChanged event.
handleExternalEventActivity1	handleExternalEvent	This event is fired each time the workflow parent is updated. Here the process checks to see if the "Expense Approver" field is set. If it is set, a Boolean variable is set to `False` so that whileItemPropertiesAdded does not continue to execute. If "Expense Approver" is empty, whileItemPropertiesAdded continues to wait for handleExternalActivity1.

COMPONENT TITLE	COMPONENT TYPE	USAGE
whileItemPropertiesAdded	While	This loop waits until the "Expense Approver" field is not null. This is required because the workflow is associated with the ItemAdded event and when a document is uploaded the first time this field is blank until the next screen appears asking the user to fill in metadata. By this time workflow is invoked and a Null exception is raised. It is driven by a Boolean variable, which is set by HandleExternalEventActivity1 after checking the "Expense Approver" field each time the document is modified.
CreateApproverTask	CreateTask	This activity creates a task for the approver mentioned in the "Expense Approver" field of the item.
LoopCheckCondition	While	Checks for Boolean variable "breakloop" to proceed. Continues execution of loop until this value is True.
LoopSequence	Sequence	Groups all components to be executed in the LoopCheckCondition loop.
onApproverTaskChanged	onTaskChanged	SharePoint workflow component that handles TaskChanged events. The code block checks if the "Revision Status" field of task is approved or rejected and sets the "breakloop" variable to True. It also sets Boolean properties (flags) for "Require More Info," "Approved," or "Rejected" based on the status of the revision field.

continues

TABLE 17-2 *(continued)*

COMPONENT TITLE	COMPONENT TYPE	USAGE
PendingInfoCheck	If-Else	This is the main If-Else condition.
PendingInfoSeq	If-Else Branch	This is the If-Else condition which checks the Boolean variable to decide if "Revision status" is set to "Require More Info."
PendingInfoSequence	Sequence	Groups together activities to be performed if "Revision Status" is "Require More Info."
PendingInfoLog	LogToHistory	This logs status to workflow history.
PendingInfoEmail	SendEmail	Sends e-mail to user who uploaded the document (CreatedBy) that some more information is required.
CompleteApproverTask	CompleteTask	This activity is used to complete a task.
ConditionChecks	If-Else	Main If-Else activity to decide if document was approved or rejected.
CheckApproved	If-Else Branch	Condition that checks if approved flag is set.
CheckRejected	If-Else Branch	Condition that checks if rejected flag is set.
ApprovalEmail	SendEmail	Sends approval e-mail to current item's CreatedBy user.
RejectionEmail	SendEmail	Sends rejection e-mail to current item's CreatedBy user.

Once you assemble the workflow shown with the components described, you will also need to ensure there is some actual code behind each component. The code is shown in Listing 17-5.

LISTING 17-5: Visual Studio Sequential Workflow (CodeSamples.VS2010.SQWorkflow.sln)

```
namespace CodeSamples.VS2010.SQWorkflow.Workflow1
{
    public sealed partial class Workflow1 : SequentialWorkflowActivity
    {
        public Workflow1()
        {
            InitializeComponent();
        }

        public Guid workflowId = default(System.Guid);
        public SPWorkflowActivationProperties workflowProperties = new
SPWorkflowActivationProperties();
        public bool isApproved = false;
        public bool isRejected = false;
        public bool RequireInfo = false;
        public bool breakLoop = false;
        public bool waitForItemPropertyUpdate = false;

        private void onWorkflowActivated1_Invoked(object sender, ExternalDataEventArgs e)
        {
            if (workflowProperties.Item["Expense Approver"] == null)
waitForItemPropertyUpdate = true;
            if (workflowProperties != null)
            {
                subscriptionID = new Guid();
                itemID = workflowProperties.ItemId;
                listID = workflowProperties.ListId;
            }
        }

        private void ApprovalEmail_MethodInvoking(object sender, EventArgs e)
        {
            SendEmail ApprovalEmail = (SendEmail)sender;
            ApprovalEmail.To =
GetUserEmail(workflowProperties.Item[SPBuiltInFieldId.Created_x0020_By].ToString());
        }

        private string GetUserEmail(string user)
        {
            if (string.IsNullOrEmpty(user)) return string.Empty;
            string userEmail = workflowProperties.Web.SiteUsers[user].Email;
            return userEmail;
            //return (string.IsNullOrEmpty(userEmail)) ? "test user email" : userEmail;
        }

        private void RejectionEmail_MethodInvoking(object sender, EventArgs e)
        {
            SendEmail RejectedEmail = (SendEmail)sender;
```

continues

LISTING 17-5 *(continued)*

```csharp
                RejectedEmail.To =
GetUserEmail(workflowProperties.Item[SPBuiltInFieldId.Created_x0020_By].ToString());
        }

        private void InfoRequiredEmail_MethodInvoking(object sender, EventArgs e)
        {
            SendEmail RequireInfoEmail = (SendEmail)sender;
            RequireInfoEmail.To =
GetUserEmail(workflowProperties.Item[SPBuiltInFieldId.Created_x0020_By].ToString());
        }

        private void LogActivity_MethodInvoking(object sender, EventArgs e)
        {
            LogToHistoryListActivity logger = (LogToHistoryListActivity)sender;
            if (isApproved) logger.HistoryDescription = "Document Approved";
            else if (isRejected) logger.HistoryDescription = "Document Rejected";
            else if (RequireInfo) logger.HistoryDescription = "Document required
more info";
            logger.HistoryOutcome = "Workflow Completed";
        }

        private void CheckDocRevisionStatus_Invoked(object sender,
ExternalDataEventArgs e)
        {
            string revisionStatus = (workflowProperties.Item["Revision Status"] !=
null) ?
                                    workflowProperties.Item["Revision Status"].
ToString() : string.Empty;

            isApproved = false;
            isRejected = false;
            RequireInfo = false;
            switch (revisionStatus)
            {
                case "Approved":
                    {
                        isApproved = true;
                        breakLoop = true;
                        break;
                    }
                case "Rejected":
                    {
                        isRejected = true;
                        breakLoop = true;
                        break;
                    }
                case "Require more info":
                    {
                        RequireInfo = true;
                        break;
                    }
                default:
```

```
                    break;
            }
        }

        private void createApproverTask_MethodInvoking(object sender, EventArgs e)
        {
            this.ApproverTaskID = Guid.NewGuid();
            this.ApproverTaskProperties.Title = string.Format("Please approve {0}",
workflowProperties.Item.Name);
            this.ApproverTaskProperties.StartDate = DateTime.Now;
            this.ApproverTaskProperties.DueDate = DateTime.Now.AddDays(3);
            string approver = workflowProperties.Item["Expense Approver"].ToString();
            this.ApproverTaskProperties.AssignedTo =
GetUserLoginName(Convert.ToInt32(approver.Substring(0, approver.IndexOf(";#"))));
            this.ApproverTaskProperties.Description = "Approver Task";
            this.ApproverTaskProperties.SendEmailNotification = true;
            this.ApproverTaskProperties.TaskType = 0;
        }

        private string GetUserLoginName(int userID)
        {
            return workflowProperties.Web.SiteUsers.GetByID(userID).LoginName;
            //return (string.IsNullOrEmpty(userEmail)) ? "administrator@demo3.
thorprojects.com" : userEmail;
        }

        private void onApproverTaskChanged_Invoked(object sender, ExternalDataEventArgs e)
        {
            SPListItem task =
workflowProperties.TaskList.GetItemById(ApproverTaskAfterProperties.TaskItemId);
            string revisionStatus = task["Revision Status"].ToString();

            isApproved = false;
            isRejected = false;
            RequireInfo = false;
            switch (revisionStatus)
            {
                case "Approved":
                    {
                        isApproved = true;
                        breakLoop = true;
                        break;
                    }
                case "Rejected":
                    {
                        isRejected = true;
                        breakLoop = true;
                        break;
                    }
                case "Require more info":
                    {
                        RequireInfo = true;
```

continues

LISTING 17-5 *(continued)*

```
                    break;
            }
        default:
            break;
    }

}

    public SPWorkflowTaskProperties ApproverTaskProperties = new
Microsoft.SharePoint.Workflow.SPWorkflowTaskProperties();
    public Guid ApproverTaskID = default(System.Guid);
    public SPWorkflowTaskProperties ApproverTaskAfterProperties = new
Microsoft.SharePoint.Workflow.SPWorkflowTaskProperties();
    public SPWorkflowTaskProperties ApproverTaskBeforeProperties = new
Microsoft.SharePoint.Workflow.SPWorkflowTaskProperties();

    public Guid subscriptionID = default(System.Guid);
    public Int32 itemID = default(System.Int32);
    public Guid listID = default(System.Guid);

    private void callExternalMethodActivity1_MethodInvoking(object sender,
EventArgs e)
    {

    }

    private void handleExternalEventActivity1_Invoked(object sender,
ExternalDataEventArgs e)
    {
        if (workflowProperties.Item["Expense Approver"] != null)
this.waitForItemPropertyUpdate = false;
    }


    }
}
```

Keep in mind that you can download all code and samples from the Wrox.com website. Once you have this code inserted appropriately, you can deploy this workflow by running a Deploy solution from the Build menu within Visual Studio.

You will now have created a workflow, deployed it, and tested it. Don't be frustrated if you had issues. As I said, there's is a learning curve with workflow development. But now you have had some exposure to the process and may at least understand what you don't understand.

WRAPPING UP WORKFLOW IN SHAREPOINT

You now have learned what SharePoint has to offer with respect to all things workflow. You've gone from the basic out-of-the-box experience to using SharePoint Designer and even diving into Visual Studio and banging out some code. I hope by this point you understand what your needs may be, and what's possible. You should put a fair amount of effort into this process to see just where you are now and where you think you will be in the near future. If you reach the point where what's offered meets some of your needs but not all, or you realize that you may be spending a lot of time in Visual Studio, you have to make a decision. That decision at its core (most of the time) is a "build or buy" one. Microsoft has empowered IT pros and developers with a tremendous number of tools to configure, assemble, and build just about anything they can dream up.

However, this assumes that you have the skill, time, and will to sit down and do what's necessary to accomplish your goals with the tools provided. What does your organization need, and is it willing to invest the time to train its developers on all the tools required? Will it invest the time to build, test, and deploy, and then continue to invest the resources to continually support its user base over time? If the answer is no, then you fall into the "buy" category, and that means that you will be shopping for a third-party tool that helps you accomplish your goals with respect to workflow and maybe even Business Process Management (BPM) without having to build it all yourself. Fortunately for you, many vendors out there specialize in helping companies like yours. These vendors range from those filling very basic needs to those that can handle huge enterprise BPM projects spanning groups, systems, and even organizations. Your job is to understand which ones fit your needs the best.

The first step in evaluating these vendors is to determine and document your requirements, needs, must-haves, and nice-to-haves. This will help you distinguish between vendors' offerings. Document the reasons why you are looking to buy rather than build. Do the out-of-the-box features work, so that you just want a better interface for design, management, and reporting? Does your organization need much more power in terms of functionality, system integration, and management? Answering these questions helps you correctly place yourself on the spectrum of workflow and BPM. Once you are correctly placed you can list the vendors that address your need level and are typically priced accordingly. If the basic functionality is close to enough but not quite, you probably are not going to be shopping for a high-end BPM platform or spending hundreds of thousands of dollars. Conversely if your needs are much greater than those provided, you're probably not going to get away with a low-end solution costing only a few thousand dollars. This section will get you started on this search by profiling a few of the top vendors out there and where they may fall in this grand spectrum.

Whether you feel that the real need to buy is to get a better design or authoring environment for you and your users, or you have seen the light and want to reap the benefits of a true BPM implementation, the following vendors will help you achieve your goals.

➤ **Bamboo:** http://store.bamboosolutions.com/sharepoint-workflow-conductor.aspx

➤ **Nintex:** http://www.nintex.com/en-US/Products/Pages/NintexWorkflow2010.aspx

➤ **K2:** http://www.k2.com

➤ **Global 360:** http://www.global360.com

Bamboo Workflow Conductor

Bamboo's Workflow Conductor provides a simple, yet powerful way to let the users who best know the existing processes create workflows that automate those business functions. Designing workflows in Conductor is a simple drag-and-drop experience that lets users create workflows that range from short and simple to large and complex, whichever suits the process at hand. Conductor even allows users to save workflows as templates that can then be reused across the farm.

Nintex Workflow 2010

Nintex Workflow 2010 adds a drag-and-drop workflow designer, connectivity, and advanced workflow features to the Microsoft SharePoint 2010 document management and collaboration platform, empowering business users and IT professionals alike to quickly and easily automate business processes; from a simple leave approval request, to complex integration across external applications and data sources

K2

K2 will give you process-driven applications — fast. It offers three software products to help you increase business efficiency and simplify work. K2's visual tools allow people of various technical and non-technical backgrounds to create applications that automate processes and streamline operations. And when something in the business changes, modifying the applications to keep up is easy.

K2 applications can be set up to manage simple business processes — such as document approval or inventory tracking — and they can be set up to pull together processes, people, services, information, and systems into a single application that helps drive business. Then what's been built can be used like building blocks to assemble new applications.

Global 360

Here is some information as well as the answers to questions about Global 360:

➤ **What makes Global 360 different?** Think of how much faster a new process will be adopted — and how often it will be adhered to — if it actually helps people get their work done. Forcing an unfamiliar, non-intuitive user interface on staff can hurt productivity more than it helps. This is why Global 360 spent over 18 months and $1 million to ensure that its applications were actually easy to use. Looking at "the other side" of BPM — the people side — is where Global 360 stands out. Its user-centric approach — from the initial assessment to how the technology gets implemented — delivers a solution that users love and truly changes how work gets done.

➤ **What is the Global 360 solution?** Global 360 is well respected in the BPM market. The technology is "high and right" in both the Forrester and Gartner BPM quadrants and Global 360 is the only vendor to lead in both case and process management. Global 360 has made a strategic commitment to leveraging and enhancing the Microsoft platform. Its solution is comprised of five key components:

➤ **Sophisticated business process analysis and optimization:** For continuous process improvement, Global 360 is built on the world's most popular modeling tool, Microsoft Visio. Business analysts and process owners can easily model, analyze, and improve their business processes. Using real data to provide a baseline, users can model the impact of process improvements and clearly understand process variances and cost drivers. Additionally the Visio Business Process Modeling

Notation (BPMN) models can be easily imported into the Global 360 process modeling environment for execution.

➤ **Visual process modeling environment:** This allows you to collaboratively design business processes, and connect to back-end systems without a single line of code. You can build everything you need — diagrams, forms, rules, services, and your data model — all in one place while developing a platform for ongoing process improvement.

➤ **Pre-built, persona-based user applications:** This makes it easier for people to get their work done. Because the process has to work for people and not the other way around, Global 360 spent over 18 months and $1 million to develop highly intuitive "userView" applications that deliver the information needed to help users get their jobs done.

➤ **Extensive process analytics and management dashboards:** These provide business insight and the ability to change on the fly. From simple, easily digested views of all process information to real-time reporting, managers can make smarter, faster business decisions. And if there is unexpected demand or changing workloads, they can simply and dynamically re-allocate work until service levels are brought back into balance.

➤ **Rich document repository:** Provided by the Global 360 repository or Microsoft SharePoint. Whereas some vendors allow you to add documents as attachments, Global 360 integrates documents as an integral part of the process. This enables rules to be applied to managing documents, audit trails to be established, and tasks to be assigned. From receipts and e-mails to voicemail messages, every "document" is treated as a full participant in the process.

For further study consider the following resources:

http://msdn.microsoft.com/en-us/vstudio/dd441784.aspx#Sharepoint

http://technet.microsoft.com/en-us/library/cc298653.aspx

Some Channel 9 Videos

http://channel9.msdn.com/learn/courses/Office2010/ClientWorkflowUnit/

Blogs:

http://www.wictorwilen.se/

http://philwicklund.com/default.aspx

http://www.thorprojects.com/default.aspx

http://www.mannsoftware.com/blog/default.aspx

Forum:

http://social.msdn.microsoft.com/Forums/en-US/category/sharepoint2010

SUMMARY

That brings us to the end of this workflow section of the book. I hope you've enjoyed your journey and have found the information in it to be useful. In this chapter you have learned about the new ability in SharePoint 2010 to import reusable workflow that was built with SharePoint Designer. You've also learned about the different pros and cons of taking this approach as well as different items to be aware of. You also learned about an approach to some workflow-like functionality through the use of event receivers and how those can play a role in your overall workflow strategy. Next you learned about the ability to create your own custom activities/actions for use inside SharePoint Designer. Lastly, you were able to see how you can create a custom workflow inside Visual Studio 2010 using Workflow Foundation. Workflow Foundation is at the core of all the workflows you build for SharePoint in Visual Studio and at some level all workflows that are hosted in SharePoint.

PART VII
Enterprise Search

18

Introduction to Enterprise Search

WHAT'S IN THIS CHAPTER?

➤ Understanding why search is more important and more complicated today

➤ A survey of SharePoint 2010 search product offerings and how to choose the right one for you

➤ A look at the search user experience, how to utilize it, and what information it provides to end users

Search has become a powerful and ubiquitous tool in business enterprises and personal life. Very few users in an enterprise have not had some experience with a search engine in one form or another. Search engines help us find such things as pictures of tree frogs, websites that sell office chairs, and the latest car-chase videos. They also help us answer questions like: Where do tree frogs live? How is the traffic on the Eisenhower? What is today's horoscope?

In short, search connects people to data that is timely and relevant to their current needs. In today's enterprises, the data is located on multiple systems that may or may not be under the control of the organization. Relevant data on those systems is in an increasingly abundant number of data formats. The corpus of content that our organizations are interested in is so large that end users can no longer simply browse for files or remember where all their documents are. In today's enterprise, search is becoming a business-critical system.

The SharePoint 2010 stack of search products offers search solutions that address nearly every search need that an organization may have, from the small-scale team and small business search all the way up to worldwide enterprises. With this broad range of search coverage and the depth of features offered by SharePoint comes a complex set of technical and conceptual components. You cannot simply "turn on" search and expect it to work. An effective search solution requires a lot of analysis and a lot of up-front configuration. Once in place, it will require constant monitoring and tweaking so that it does not grow stale and useless over time.

This chapter focuses on getting you up to speed with search and the SharePoint search products. It does not include any technical directions for configuring search components; that is saved for Chapters 19 and 20. Rather than jump into the technical side, this chapter introduces you to each of the moving parts involved in a search engine. Then it covers each of the SharePoint products that provide search capabilities. Finally, the chapter wraps up with a user's guide point-of-view discussion of the search user interface.

UNDERSTANDING SEARCH

When you come to a search product for the first time, it's important to understand how a search engine works. How do people use a search engine? What results do search users expect to see? How does the search engine gather results and present them to the end user? How much can I change the user interface to meet my organization's unique style and needs?

Often we think of search as a simple query/response model where the end user types in a set of keywords and the search engine displays results in a series of pages. Search Engine Optimization experts leverage this model to help get targeted entries higher in the search results page. The error in this model is that it does not take into account all the things a search engine can accomplish, nor does it allow for the variety of ways in which a person uses a search engine. This section begins with a discussion about search behaviors — a cursory look at how people use search engines and the kinds of results they expect to see. (Spoiler alert: People do more than search for a specific website.) The section then explains the many working parts that make up the search engine system — you cannot learn how to select and configure search until you first know how it works and how to use it.

Search Behaviors

Users approach search engines in a variety of ways and for a variety of purposes. The user who has forgotten where he uploaded a sales report uses search to find his document. The user who is writing a statement of work for the very first time uses search to find a set of sample documents to help him get going. The marketing manager who is getting ready to launch a product line will use search to find all content related to the product. The human resources specialist will use search to locate areas of expertise in the organization. In short, every user interacts with the search system in his or her own way and brings individual problems to the search. To be able to design and operate an effective search solution, it is helpful to distill these search behaviors into a few broad categories that the search manager can understand and manage.

> **Content search:** SharePoint is optimized for the content search approach. In a content search, the user searches to find results that are related to a specific search keyword or phrase. The search user is looking for a specific piece of content and may not know where it's located or may have forgotten. Content search answers a question like "Where is this year's benefits summary?" or "Where is the sales presentation that I uploaded yesterday?" It can also answer location-type questions like "Where is the Acme project team site?" or "Where are the corporate logos?"

➤ **Query search:** Sometimes we don't need a specific piece of content as much as we need to answer a question about a topic. In the query search approach the results are a collection of content and locations related to the search term in some way. This allows the search user to browse through a small set in a single location (the search results page) rather than haphazardly going through sites, file shares, databases, and other systems to answer the question. Some questions answered by the query search approach are "What do other statements of work documents look like?" or "Who's contributing the most documents on network operations?"

➤ **Research search:** Research search is a refinement of query search but is directed more to providing all information relative to a topic. More than answering a single question, the end user expects to browse and aggregate the information returned by the search engine. Perhaps the user is writing a report in response to an audit or is contributing to the company's annual report. In these and similar cases, the user may want to see people results that show most frequent contributors, a complete listing of all team and project sites related to the topic, presentations, reports, and other information that the searcher can then use to complete the audit report or annual report.

➤ **Application search:** Application search is a special situation used by developers who are building custom solutions. Many times, a developer may build an application that uses the search engine to provide data to the application. For example, a developer may build a Web Part that uses search against the company's CRM solution to display client information that is specific to the logged-in user.

In most organizations, you'll find all these search behaviors; some will be used more frequently than others. It is important to understand these categories of search behavior and how they are used in your organization, because each edition of SharePoint search products offers features that are optimized for each of these scenarios. This will not only affect your selection of a search product; it will also affect the operational maintenance and monitoring of your search solution. Knowing these behaviors will directly affect the success of your search solution.

I once consulted on a search project for a major food corporation where a senior vice president was campaigning to scrap the current search solution and bring in a new one, because he thought the current solution couldn't deliver relevant results. The problem was that this particular person frequently uploaded documents to team sites and promptly forgot where they were, or he had someone else upload documents and did not get a document link from them. When he came back to the system on the same day or within a couple of days he would search for the documents by entering the document's filename in the search box — a technique that should put the desired document at the top of the list. Consistently, the documents would not appear in the search results — not just on the first page, but not at all. When we examined his behavior against the search system, we found that the implementers of the search solution did not consider a user behavior in which the user would use search to find documents within a few days of uploading them. They assumed there would be a larger lag between uploading and searching and therefore set the crawl schedules at one-week intervals. When we changed the crawl schedule to every four hours, the VP began to find his documents every time he searched. Ultimately the problem was not the technology; it was the operational understanding of user behaviors.

Basic Understanding

The challenge to effectively learn search in the SharePoint product stack is to understand the basic components that make up a search solution. Although most users are quite familiar with using search engines on the Internet, this experience is limited to interactions with a small portion of the search system. A complete search system (Figure 18-1) includes five main components (crawl, index, query, user interface, and monitoring) and an application interface for developers.

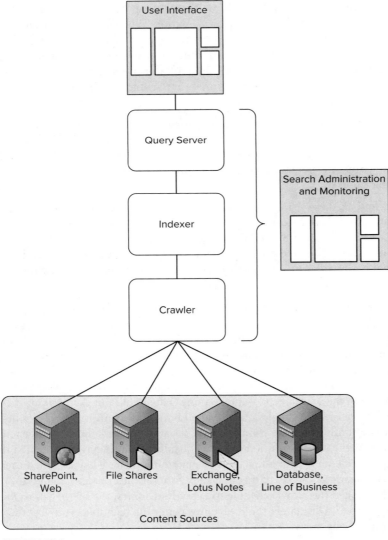

FIGURE 18-1

Search begins with the *crawler*. This is the component of the search engine that accesses content in its various forms and locations. In each location, the crawler is responsible for building the initial search index by reading, categorizing, and identifying metadata properties of the content stored in those locations. The crawler does not simply bounce from location to location without direction; rather, it follows a directed path identified by a set of *content sources*.

A content source in the search index identifies a location for the crawler to index and the parameters by which the crawler must perform its duties at that location. The settings defined in the content source help to limit the crawler so that it doesn't get out of control while roaming the content. These rules include limiting the number of hops that the crawler will follow, or limiting the crawler to a single server.

Beyond simple crawl settings, *crawl rules* allow you to set more restrictive controls on the crawler to include or exclude content. Unlike a filter that gathers all content together and then sifts out certain content for presentation, crawl rules force the crawler either to add entries to the index database or exclude them. In this way, the crawl rules affect the very content of the index and by extension what is available for the end users to view in search results.

In larger search systems where performance becomes an issue due to the quantity or size of content located in the content source, *crawler impact rules* and effective *scheduling* will aid in configuring the most efficient crawls. Each content source allows for its own crawl schedule, which is a powerful performance optimization technique allowing you to crawl frequently. The crawler impact rules allow you to increase crawl efficiency by defining batch sizes to limit the number of documents that are simultaneously crawled or to set a delay between documents for which the crawler needs a longer time.

Whereas the crawler gathers data from the content sources, the *indexer* is responsible for organizing the content. It takes the content from the crawler and determines how things are stored in the index databases. As it performs this organization it also continuously propagates the data to the index databases that are located on each *query server*.

Some aspects of the indexer are configured by search administrators to enhance the search experience or to improve the relevancy of search results that are presented to the end user. As the crawler works through content, it identifies metadata properties that it indexes. These *crawled properties* can be document properties in Word, PowerPoint, and other document files, columns in SharePoint lists or Excel spreadsheets, metadata tags in HTML files, and other identifiable fields associated with the content.

In many cases, you will want to utilize crawled properties in search scopes and as parameters in the Advanced Search form in the Search Center. Mapping a crawled property to a *managed property* allows for this kind of promotion. The managed property not only makes a crawled property available to search scopes and filters; it can also combine multiple crawled properties into a single managed property. For example, in many SharePoint instances, multiple SharePoint lists may have columns that refer to a vendor using column names like Vendor or Supplier. Managed properties allow you to combine these similar properties into one unit that will ensure search results contain all information relevant to a search query.

The query server is the final step in the search process. It processes requests and returns result sets to the web server for display in the user interface. Each query server contains its own copy of the index in order to respond most efficiently to search requests. This separation of indexes ensures that the crawler will not affect search performance as it interacts with content sources on the other end, and the other end will not affect the index. If any query or crawl operation becomes resource-intensive, it will not adversely affect the overall operation of the search system.

Although fully functional search systems provide the ability to index content from a variety of sources and formats, it is not feasible to index all information that may be relevant to an end user's search needs. Sometimes content is located on other systems that are indexed by other search engines, such as the Internet, which is serviced by engines such as Bing. Federated Search leverages open standards that will allow you to include search results from other search engines in your search results.

At the end of the search process, the *user interface* is the portion of a search system that all users are most familiar with. The user interface both accepts search criteria from the end user and presents search results back. The results presented in the user interface are sorted based on their *relevance*, which is a calculated *ranking* of each item based on the search terms and a variety of other criteria. Administrators are able to enhance the search experience by configuring *Best Bets* that will show specific search-result entries at the top of the results page above all others when specific keyword matches are made in the search criteria. Although the user interface is a rather passive presenter of information (the query server does the work of ranking, trimming, stemming, and sorting content), the interface is highly customizable in SharePoint.

With this basic understanding of the components of search in SharePoint, you will be better able to examine the many search offerings available in the SharePoint 2010 stack. Chapter 19 provides a more detailed look at each of these search components as well as in-depth discussions about configuring these features in SharePoint. The next section looks at each of these offerings in detail and follows that up with a discussion of the criteria that you need to consider when selecting a search solution.

PRODUCT OVERVIEW

Microsoft's search offerings seem to grow exponentially from one version of SharePoint to the next. In early versions of SharePoint, basic search was the only option. With MOSS 2007 and WSS, a selection between basic search and a more robust enterprise search offering was built into SharePoint Server. In the past few years, Microsoft has introduced stand-alone server products in free and licensed versions, and it has acquired FAST. With the release of the SharePoint 2010 stack, selecting a search solution is now a complex task that requires careful consideration of your organization's search needs. Therefore, you will need to understand what each search product brings to the table.

SharePoint Foundation 2010

SharePoint Foundation 2010 is an entry-level search offering that is integrated with the free version of SharePoint. This built-in offering limits the search capability to a single site collection within SharePoint Foundation and will only crawl SharePoint content — that is, lists, libraries, and web pages contained in the site collection. There is limited ability to configure the search system in SharePoint Foundation and the crawler is scheduled automatically.

The crawl server and the index server are combined and cannot be separated onto dedicated servers for redundancy or optimization purposes. On the other hand, the search capabilities can be separated onto a single dedicated search application server.

In most cases, SharePoint Foundation 2010 search will be insufficient to meet your requirements, not only because of the limitations in the technology, but also because Microsoft offers Search Server 2010 Express as a free download. When installing SharePoint Foundation 2010 as a collaboration solution, you should always download and install Search Server 2010 Express as well.

Search Server 2010 Express

Search Server 2010 Express is also an entry-level search offering, but it adds a number of important features that make search much more usable. This server is able to go beyond the boundaries of a single SharePoint site collection and can crawl a variety of external content sources such as SharePoint sites, websites, and file shares. Consider for a moment that most SharePoint Foundation 2010 installations are intended as collaborative environments for department- or project-level entities. Also consider that in most organizations the entire body of content that is relevant to the department or project is not usually contained within the SharePoint site: it is usually contained in SharePoint, file shares, other websites, databases, and possibly e-mail systems. The addition of Search Server provides your SharePoint Foundation installation with the necessary connectors to bring together the information from these disparate systems.

Similar to SharePoint Foundation, Search Server 2010 Express is very limited in its topology. You cannot deploy to multiple servers for redundancy or separate the index and crawl components for performance. Likewise, you are limited to 300,000 items in the index. For the most part, Search Server 2010 Express will fulfill your needs when you are adding search to a very small-scale solution or when your budget is extremely tight.

Search Server 2010

Search Server 2010 is the beginning of enterprise-level search solutions. As such, it is also the first product that requires a license to use. In the SharePoint stack, Search Server 2010 sits between Search Server 2010 Express and SharePoint 2010 as a stepping stone. In many cases, Search Server 2010 is deployed when your content overloads Search Server 2010 Express and requires a more substantial system. But it can also be used when SharePoint 2010 is not deployed or not available to provide search to your content.

Search Server 2010 provides most of the search capabilities that are found in the licensed SharePoint 2010 product with the exception of People Search, taxonomy, and social searching. This is an important point when making decisions about your search solution because it substantially impacts search-result relevance. One of the great advantages SharePoint Search has over many competing products is that it can produce highly relevant results that are better and more efficient because of the social searching capabilities it offers. Search Server 2010 does not benefit from these improved relevancy features.

This is not to say that Search Server 2010 results are not relevant. On the contrary, Search Server 2010 is able to leverage multiple content sources, Federated Search, crawled and managed properties, scopes, and other core search components to provide very relevant results. What it lacks is the ability to provide a search result that places a particular document at the top of the result stack because it was authored by your boss or because you tagged it in the SharePoint interface.

Search Server 2010 is freed from the topology restrictions that constrain Search Server Express and SharePoint Foundation. It can be scaled to multiple servers for redundancy and performance purposes, giving you the ability to index up to 100 million items. It is a robust search solution for the organization that does not use SharePoint. But if your organization is using SharePoint or is moving to SharePoint, you should strongly consider moving your search solution under the SharePoint umbrella.

SharePoint Server 2010

SharePoint Server 2010 is a complete search solution that provides a better search experience than its competitors. Like Search Server, SharePoint is able to index content from a variety of enterprise locations such as multiple SharePoint servers, file shares, web servers, Exchange, and Lotus Notes, and external line-of-business systems. It also provides the ability to tune, refine, and monitor search to improve the search experience. Finally, as noted earlier, SharePoint Server 2010 adds social-search capabilities and People Search.

SharePoint Server 2010 comes in a variety of editions, but the most important are the Standard and Enterprise editions. From a search point of view the difference between these editions is in the smaller details; the core search components are the same as well as the administrative components. In all editions, the search component is highly scalable, allowing you to separate the crawl from the index components and leverage multiple servers for each.

FAST Search Server 2010 for SharePoint

FAST Search Server 2010 is a new search product that provides advanced enterprise search capabilities. Where SharePoint Server 2010 can scale to index up to 100 million items, a FAST Search Server can be scaled to index more than a billion items of content (although Microsoft's published material lists it at 500 million plus).

Where FAST Search Server 2010 really shines is in the new features that it brings to the search experience. FAST adds Visual Best Bets, thumbnails, the ability to preview PowerPoint in the browser window, contextual search capabilities, and a variety of relevance-tuning options that take search from a generalized connection between users and content to a powerful search application that delivers timely and contextually relevant data to the right users. These new capabilities allow administrators and developers to create search applications such as research applications.

FAST Search Server 2010 is the high end of search products, but gains in productivity and expanded search experience will in most cases justify any costs that go with implementing this product.

WHICH PRODUCT IS RIGHT FOR ME?

In most organizations, the selection of a search product will come down to a decision between SharePoint 2010 search and FAST Search Server 2010 for SharePoint. The fact that you are reading this book suggests that you are looking at the entire SharePoint suite, rather than at search in isolation. That said, Search Server and FAST Server have stand-alone variants that are robust, fully featured search solutions in their own right.

For the purpose of this discussion, I will assume that your search decision will primarily fall between one of the enterprise products. The analyses presented here will also assist you if you are trying to decide between SharePoint Foundation (enhanced by Search Server 2010 Express) and full SharePoint Server.

Location Analysis

The first thing to consider when deciding your search solution, as well as when planning your selected solution, is to determine where the content and users are located geographically. In today's global environment content is often located not only in many different systems but also across the globe. In completing your analysis, you must consider both aspects of location.

The first aspect is to consider the system location of the content. That is to say, where are the physical files that your search solution will crawl and index? It is very rare to have a search solution where the entire body of content will lie within a single system. In most cases, content will reside in file shares, other websites, e-mail servers, remote and local databases, ERP systems, and other file repositories. In this step of your analysis you are less concerned with the kinds of content that you will search (that will be the focus of the next phase of analysis); rather, you need to understand where things are located geographically.

To develop a complete understanding of the content locations, it is most effective to develop an audit document or spreadsheet that will list all the content locations that contain files you want your search solution to service, as shown in Table 18-1. This spreadsheet should capture the kind or type of content location, such as database, e-mail, or file share, and it should capture the geographical location of the content.

TABLE 18-1: Search Content Location Analysis Worksheet

CONTENT	TYPE	CONTENT LOCATION	USERS	USER LOCATION
SAP	Line of business	New York	All	New York, Chicago, Munich
R&D team sites	SharePoint	Chicago	R&D, Engineering	Chicago, Munich
R&D shared drives	File shares	Chicago	R&D	Chicago, New York
Engineering shared drives	File shares	Munich	Engineering	Munich
Engineering project database	SQL Server	Munich	Engineering	Munich
Corporate website	Web	New York	All	New York, Chicago, Munich

The second aspect of location you'll be concerned with at this phase is user location. That is, who will need to search each of the content locations and where are they physically located? Using the same spreadsheet, you can add columns that indicate the users and their location for each content location that you already identified. At this stage, you should be concerned only with groups of users in a general sense. It would be overkill to identify Active Directory groups at this point. The goal is to get a geographical idea of where users are accessing search and what content they are interested in.

The audit of the content and user locations will not only help you begin the process of deciding which search product is right for you, but will also help you to design the topology of your search solution. The topology will be informed by performance and network factors that will become more evident as you complete the analysis. You need to keep two key considerations in mind as you identify content and user locations:

➤ **Crawl performance:** The crawler operates from the application servers out to the content locations and returns index information to the servers. Geographically dispersed content locations will increase the amount of time it takes for the crawler to send data back over the network to the application servers.

➤ **Query performance:** Similar to the crawler, the query engine resides on application servers that communicate with the user interface over the network. End users in geographically remote locations may experience less efficient search-query performance as a result.

When you have content and users that are geographically spread out, possibly worldwide, you need to consider ways to resolve the performance problems that come with large topologies. Generally speaking, you have three ways to resolve these problems based on your location analysis and performance needs:

➤ **Regional installation:** This is the best option when your content and users are located together in a small region. This solution focuses on a single installation of SharePoint Server 2010 that is scaled as content grows. Network performance is less of a concern in this scenario.

➤ **Central installation:** If your network provides acceptable throughput, for crawling and querying content you may deploy a central SharePoint Server 2010 installation that services all the remote locations. Although this is one of the easier-to-manage scenarios, you have to closely monitor your network performance and user load.

➤ **Distributed installation:** In scenarios where network performance is a concern or where the access requirements are regional, you may deploy many regional installations of SharePoint Server 2010 and tie them together only where it is needed. In the example presented in the Table 18-1 worksheet, the Engineering department in Munich has a database and file shares that need not be indexed and queried by anyone else in the organization. A regional installation allows the content to be indexed and queried for local usage, but frees the central installation of SharePoint from the responsibility for this local data.

The kind of installation you choose for your needs will affect your search solution decision, particularly if you are considering scenarios that will leverage SharePoint Foundation 2010 and Search Server 2010 Express. Because these two products are very limited in the scale of topology they support, they are only capable of regional-type installations, either as part of a larger distributed SharePoint Server topology or as a solution for smaller organizations.

When deciding between SharePoint Server 2010 and FAST Search Server 2010 for SharePoint, the key considerations will be how many users and locations you need to service. Both products are highly scalable in all three installation scenarios; however, extremely large organizations will benefit from many of the high-end performance and scalability features of FAST.

Content Analysis

Though content and user location is an important first step in your product decision, it is not the only step. The amount of content, the types of content, and the growth rate of content will also factor in deciding which search product can service your needs. Thus, it is necessary to dig a little deeper into each content location to identify some important characteristics.

In the content analysis phase, you will want to go beyond the storage medium, such as database, file share, or web, and look at the files and file types of the content located in each of those systems that the crawler must index (Table 18-2). The total set of files and the amount of space they consume is known as your search *corpus*. When managing a search solution it will be important to understand your corpus at all times as it grows. Understanding the growth rate of content in each location will also help you to configure and maintain a search configuration that will continue to be responsive as the system matures.

TABLE 18-2: Search Content Analysis Worksheet

CONTENT	TYPE	FILE TYPES	NUMBER OF FILES	SIZE OF CONTENT
SAP	Line of business			
R&D team sites	SharePoint	Lists, document libraries, pages	2,000	
R&D shared drives	File shares	Word, Excel, PDF	10,000	2 GB
Engineering shared drives	File shares	Word, PDF, CAD	5,500	8 GB
Engineering project database	SQL Server			
Corporate website	Web	Pages, video, images	450	500 MB

The first metric to keep in mind is that each Search Server product has a finite number of items that it can index. Your content audit should give you a very close idea of the size of your current corpus, which will be your starting point for a search solution; but, it is only the starting point. As time passes, the size of your corpus will change as business users create and remove files in each of your content locations. You will need to make sure that your search solution will be able to grow with the corpus over time. Table 18-3 summarizes the limitations of each search product.

TABLE 18-3: Search Scales

SEARCH PRODUCT	MAX ITEMS IN INDEX
SharePoint Foundation	10 million
Search Server 2010 Express	300,000 (with SQL Express) 10 million (with SQL Server)
Search Server 2010	100 million
SharePoint Server 2010	100 million
FAST Search Server 2010 for SharePoint	500 million +

One factor that can affect the number of items in your index is whether or not you will use Federated Search in your search results. Federated Search allows you to reduce the number of items in your index because it is a request that is passed to another search engine; the results from that request are integrated into the local search results. Let's take for an example an Engineering department site. This site will serve as a collaboration space for engineers who will use the search system to find files and information on local file shares and on SQL Server. Additionally, the engineers want to search content that is located on the corporate intranet site. The corporate intranet happens to be hosted on SharePoint Server 2010 and is being indexed by its own crawler. In this situation, you can use Federated Search to request search results from the corporate intranet rather than index the content on the engineering search server. In this example, the handful of web pages located on the intranet will probably not impact the overall size of the corpus on the engineering search server, but what if the engineers want to search content on an R&D file share that contains a few hundred thousand files? If that R&D file share is serviced by its own search engine, you can avoid duplication of indexes by using Federated Search.

The size of the corpus and of individual content sources becomes a factor when you are considering crawl performance and continuous propagation. Large file sizes and types will slow the crawler and will take longer to update the indexes. This affects how long it will take before new files can show up in search results. If the files you are crawling are very large, you will need to consider either the high-end capabilities of FAST or design a topology in which large content sources have dedicated crawlers.

All the search offerings from Search Server 2010 Express to FAST have the ability to handle multiple content sources and types of content in the index; therefore, the kind of content you are crawling will not typically affect your decision about which product to deploy. Where you'll need to make platform decisions is when you begin separating out crawl and query servers to account for frequently changing content, large quantities of content, and large content sizes.

Feature Requirements

The last factor to consider when deciding on a search solution is to examine the features you need in your solution. Up to this point, the location and content analyses have focused mainly on the performance aspects of search. From a performance point of view, the decision between products is rather straightforward: low performance needs Search Server 2010 Express, medium to high performance needs Search Server 2010 or SharePoint Server 2010, and high to extremely high performance needs FAST. Yet, there are many cases in which your performance needs are low but you need the higher-end products like SharePoint Server 2010 or FAST because they have features that the other products do not. When it comes to FAST, the search features alone can justify the choice and cost of deploying FAST.

When looking at features two major feature gateways will push your product decision one way or another. The first gateway is People, Social, and Taxonomy search. People Search allows the end user to query the MySite profiles of SharePoint users and view profile results. Social Search leverages the MySite and organizational information stored in user profiles to rank search results that make them more relevant based on user actions. For example, a document that is tagged by many users will rate higher in relevance than a similar document that has not been tagged at all. Finally, taxonomy integration leverages metadata and content tagging to refine search results. If these three capabilities, People, Social, and Taxonomy search, are required by your search solution, you can rule out SharePoint Foundation 2010, and both editions of Search Server 2010, because these features are only available in SharePoint Server 2010 and FAST.

The next gateway is Visual, Contextual, and Refinement search, and these are the features that separate FAST from SharePoint Server 2010. FAST allows the inclusion of Visual Best Bets and document thumbnails. If that is not enough, it includes a slide browser for PowerPoint files that allows the end user to browse through the slide deck within the search results page. Contextual search allows you to refine results based on a specific type of profile or audience. Lastly, FAST offers very powerful refinement options that substantially enhance the search experience. If search is an important tool for the end users in your organization, you should seriously consider deploying FAST even in cases where SharePoint Server can handle your performance needs.

Table 18-4 will help you examine the features that are available in each platform. The Microsoft Enterprise Search Center has many feature comparison tables that provide various looks at each server product and what they can do. The following table is extracted from the Search Model 1 of 4 – Search Technologies document that is available at `http://tinyurl.com/28fy8sx`.

TABLE 18-4: Feature Comparison

FEATURE	SHAREPOINT FOUNDATION 2010	SEARCH SERVER 2010	SHAREPOINT SERVER 2010	FAST SEARCH SERVER 2010 FOR SHAREPOINT
Site search	✓	✓	✓	✓
Visual Best Bets		Limited	Limited	✓
Scopes		✓	✓	✓
Contextual search				✓
Managed properties		✓	✓	✓

continues

TABLE 18-4 *(continued)*

FEATURE	SHAREPOINT FOUNDATION 2010	SEARCH SERVER 2010	SHAREPOINT SERVER 2010	FAST SEARCH SERVER 2010 FOR SHAREPOINT
Property Extraction		Limited	Limited	✓
Query federation		✓	✓	✓
Query suggestions		✓	✓	✓
Similar results				✓
Sort results				✓
Relevance tuning		Limited	Limited	✓
Shallow refinement		✓	✓	✓
Deep refinement				✓
Document preview				✓
Windows 7 Federation		✓	✓	✓
People Search			✓	✓
Social Search			✓	✓
Taxonomy integration			✓	✓
Rich web indexing				✓

USER EXPERIENCE

Now that you understand the basic concepts and components of search, the variety of search products available in the SharePoint stack, and the analyses necessary to select a search product, it is time to dig into the search experience in more detail. This chapter closes with a detailed look at the user experience provided by the search products. Chapter 19 digs deeper into the administrative and operational details of search, and Chapter 20 provides a deeper look at FAST.

Although significant feature differences exist between the search products in the SharePoint stack, the user experience is generally similar on all platforms. Where they differ is in the details, such as document thumbnails that appear only in FAST search results. For this reason, the following discussion and screenshots will not differentiate between the different product offerings. All the screenshots were taken on a system that has FAST Search Server 2010 for SharePoint deployed. Therefore, the search-results screenshots show things like document thumbnails and PowerPoint previews, which are not available in the other product lines. If you are unsure whether your edition of search has a feature that is shown here, consult Table 18-4.

In all the search products end users will interact with three key user interfaces to complete searches: the Simple Search Box, the Search Center, and the Advanced Search page. These three make up the input portion of the search interface where users enter their search criteria.

The Simple Search Box (Figure 18-2) is an element that is included in the master page definition for sites. Out of the box, it includes a drop-down that lists scopes along with a textbox where a user enters the search query. The scopes available in the Simple Search Box are defined by the site collection administrator in the site settings. A search scope is a filter that helps to refine the search results. Because the simple search is part of the master page, there are options for the developer to change or even remove this component from the page. If you are developing a master page for your SharePoint installation, it's very important before doing so to consider the user impact of changing this control.

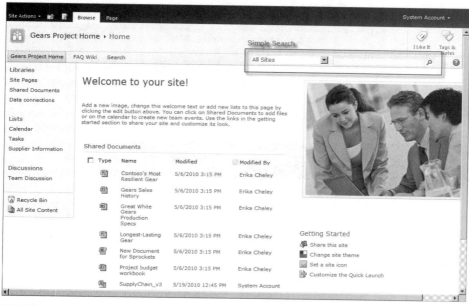

FIGURE 18-2

The Search Center (Figure 18-3) provides an interface that is familiar to any user who has ever interacted with Internet search engines. The tabs that appear across the top of the Search Center (All Sites, People, and Reports) are scopes similar to the drop-down in the Simple Search Box. Out of the box, the configured tabs are All Sites and People. Like simple search, the administrator may configure which tabs are available to the end user.

FIGURE 18-3

Advanced Search (Figure 18-4) provides a much more detailed search capability allowing the user to specify phrases, languages, and properties to search on. As an administrator or developer, the properties drop-down is an important component of the search page because the values presented in this control are managed properties. You learn more about configuring managed properties in Chapter 19.

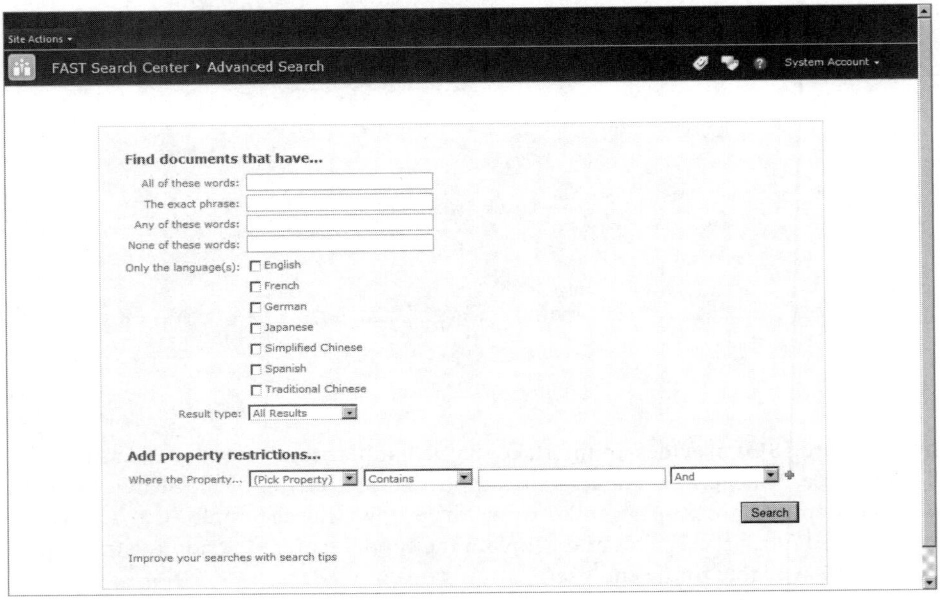

FIGURE 18-4

Once the user enters a query into one of the search interfaces, the query server returns the results to a search results page. The results page consists of a set of highly customizable connected Web Parts. These Web Parts work together to provide the user with a rich search experience that goes well beyond the simple display of search results. It will help your understanding of search to go through each of the major sections of the results page.

Search Refinement

Search refinements, or facets as they were once called, allow the end user to drill deeper into the search results based on tags and metadata found in the result set. By utilizing the search refinements that appear on the left-hand side of the results page as shown in Figure 18-5, the end user may switch from a general search in which he/she browses through pages of results to a more directed search where the end user may follow a guided path to a specific result set. Let's say an end user is doing a search for a project document related to the Gears project. She knows that the document she wants is a Word document. By using the refinement options, she can select all results from the result set that are Word documents. This works in a more research-oriented mode as well. For example, a user may be writing a statement of work and want to see some examples of other statements of work that have been written in the organization. If "statement of work" is a metadata property of all statement of work documents, the refinement bar will have an entry for statement of work that the end user may select.

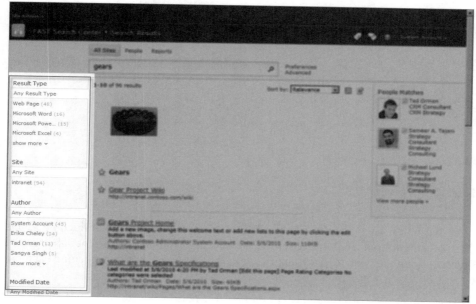

FIGURE 18-5

Best Bets

Best Bets are a configured set of keywords that have a specific entry associated with them as shown in Figure 18-6. These are created and configured by a site administrator to show a particular result at the top of the results pane. For example, an administrator may create a Best Bet for the search term "Annual Report" that will display a link to the most recent annual report for the company at the top of the search results. The assumption is that when an exact match occurs, the Best Bet represents the result that most users are looking for when they use that term.

For an administrator, Best Bets are often informed by the search usage reports that show common search terms and destinations. When a search term has large number of click-throughs on a single link, you have a good candidate for a Best Bet.

FIGURE 18-6

Thumbnails and Previews

Thumbnails and Previews are a feature of FAST search that are worth their weight in gold. FAST search will show a thumbnail image of the first page of each Word and PowerPoint document in the result set (Figure 18-7), making document recognition much easier and more efficient. The presence of thumbnails means that a user can find the document he is looking for without opening each one. This saves a lot of productivity over the life of the search solution.

PowerPoint is further enhanced with the option to preview the entire slide deck (Figure 18-8) in the results page. The user clicks the link and a browsing window opens in which the user scrolls through the slides. In most PowerPoint searches, users are typically looking for a single slide or set of slides, but they often cannot remember what slide deck the slides are located in. Like document thumbnails, PowerPoint preview saves a lot of lost productivity caused by opening search results, one after another, in search of a slide or two.

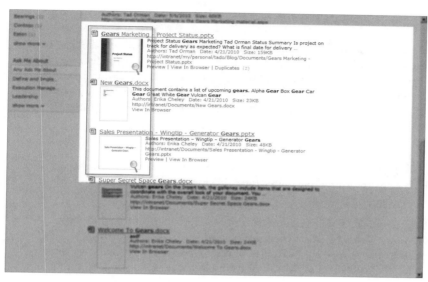

FIGURE 18-7

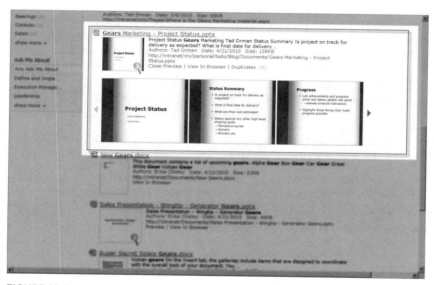

FIGURE 18-8

Similar Results and Duplicates

FAST also enhances the search experience by combining duplicate entries with a hyperlink that allows the user to view all the duplicates together in a results set. Likewise, FAST uses the metadata and other factors to identify similar results sets for individual results entries.

Sort Results

A powerful feature in the user interface is sorting. SharePoint Server 2010 allows the user to sort results by relevance and date modified, which can aid in many general document searches. But additional sorting is necessary for more specific searches. FAST provides the ability to sort based on metadata and on relevance ranking profiles. In this way a user can sort based on a single rank or on a property; providing a much more efficient way to browse through search results.

Query Syntax

Most users are familiar with entering keyword terms into a search box to query for results. SharePoint begins with basic keyword query syntax but adds more capability in the form of property, wildcard, and Boolean query syntax.

Keyword syntax is straightforward. The user enters a term or phrase into the search box, and the query engine delivers results based on the term or phrase. SharePoint allows the use of quotations around phrases to query for exact matches of a set of words. It also allows the use of the + and – operators for inclusion and exclusion of terms. For example, a search for "acme +project" will return results that have both keywords (acme and project) in the results. Alternatively, a search for "acme – project" will return results that have had any project items removed from the results.

Property filters allow the user to enter in a property name:value-type search. These are managed properties that are associated with content by the indexer and work in the same way as property searches using the Advanced Search page. The user enters the property name followed by a colon followed by the expected property value. For example: "author: Ken Schaefer" would return all content authored by Ken Schaefer. The limitation to property filter searches in SharePoint is that there's no easy way to know what properties are configured as managed properties, which the end user can put into the search box.

Wildcard search is a new feature in SharePoint 2010 that allows the user to enter an asterisk character at the end of a keyword. For example, a search for "ac*" could return results for academic, acme, and so on.

Another addition in SharePoint 2010 is Boolean syntax. Users may enter search terms using parentheses to organize the order in which search terms are utilized in the query. The user may also use AND, OR, and NOT to specify how matches are handled, as well as =, <, >, <=, and >= to refine the matches even more.

SOCIAL SEARCH

Social Search is a capability unique to SharePoint Server 2010 and FAST Search Server 2010 for SharePoint. SharePoint's profile and MySite capabilities are integrated with search to provide a search experience that combines traditional personal contact search with the best features of social networking. This allows the organization to begin identifying areas of expertise and locating the most active contributors of content and institutional knowledge.

People Search

Searching for people in organizations presents special challenges. In the past, solutions that provided People Search–like capabilities were nothing more than enhanced address books. The challenge for People Search (Figure 18-9) today is that users are accustomed to looking up people through social networks to gather much more than simple e-mail address and contact information. Today's social networks provide search users with visibility into people's activities, their expertise, and other information about the person. Organizations have struggled for years to find solutions that can offer the organization the same kinds of information the public social networks provide. SharePoint addresses all these challenges in its Social Search capabilities.

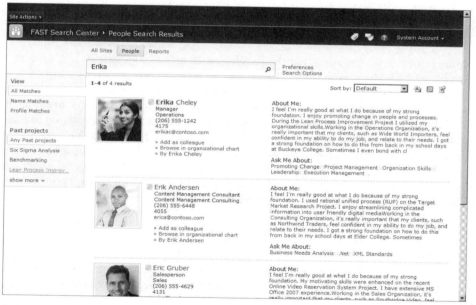

FIGURE 18-9

People Search is limited to the two SharePoint products (SharePoint Server 2010 and FAST Search Server 2010 for SharePoint) because it relies on the user profile capabilities of the SharePoint platform. User profiles combined with the MySite features of SharePoint provide an information-rich platform for personnel data that in many ways resembles a social networking site and which leverages many of the best features of those social sites, such as microblogging, personal profile information, and organizational information.

Search results in the People Search results page reflect much of the information that is stored in user profiles and on the MySite page (Figure 18-9). Personal pictures, About Me descriptions, and Ask Me About content are gleaned from the data entered into a person's MySite page and presented as part of the result, allowing search users to quickly browse important information about the person.

This is important to the search user who is looking for experts in a particular area or isn't sure if the person she is looking at is Erik from accounting or Erik from sales.

People Search also allows search users to locate content that is authored by a particular person. For example, a search user goes to a training course that was put together and presented by Sally Smith. Sally presented a PowerPoint slide deck that she uploaded to a SharePoint site that is indexed by the crawler. Perhaps the search user has forgotten the exact name of the training, or the particular PowerPoint slide deck isn't coming up in the search results. People Search provides a solution to this problem by allowing the search user to dig into content authored by a person through a hyperlink in the results pane.

One really neat feature in MySite, presented by People Search results, is a view into the organizational chart using the Silverlight-based organizational viewer. This is a dynamic, animated organizational browser that shows the organization chart from the selected person's position in the organization, in the form of sliding panes that show peers, subordinates, and superiors.

Despite the abundance of rich information that the People Search results page displays, it is highly dependent on profiles and MySite personal sites. If you plan to leverage this capability in any meaningful way, you must make a special effort to make sure that profiles are complete and imported into SharePoint. In most organizations, user profiles will be maintained in Active Directory. Active Directory allows the management of a great deal of contact and organizational information about each person in the organization. Similarly, SharePoint has the capability to maintain personnel information in its own profiles. The decision for most organizations is to determine which system will be the system of record that will be maintained with all the necessary information. If your organization determines that AD is the system of record, you will need to set up SharePoint to use the User Profile Synchronization Service (a topic beyond the scope of this chapter).

People results are also dependent on the content that individual users put into their MySite pages. If these users don't fill in the About Me and Ask Me About sections of their MySite personal site, that information will not appear in the search results. To effectively leverage People Search in SharePoint it is important to make MySite available to the users and to encourage them to fill in the information in their MySite profiles. Otherwise, many of the social-search enhancements that SharePoint offers are useless.

How Social Behavior Influences Relevance

SharePoint Search's relevance calculations take into account all aspects of social search, from content that people author, the relative location of people in the organizational charts, content entered into MySite personal profiles, and tags that people use on content. These additional capabilities that are found only in the SharePoint search products take search to a new level by presenting results in a context-oriented fashion that is personally relevant to the search user.

One of the key ways that SharePoint calculates relevance is through social distance based on the organizational chart. Content that is authored, modified, and tagged by people who are directly connected in the organization chart will appear before content of people who are many degrees away. SharePoint also takes into account any tagging or feedback that people close to the searcher have applied to content, which will also cause results to bubble up in relevance.

What if a person is far away on the organization chart from the search user, but the two are currently working together on a cross-departmental project? In the People Search results pane, each result entry contains a link to add a person as a colleague. By selecting this link, the search user places the person within his or her social network, which will in turn impact the relevance of search results.

SharePoint goes a step beyond the simple metrics of social distance and also factors in social frequency. This takes two forms, authorship and social participation. Authorship is a factor based on how much a person interacts with content in the system — the more content a user authors or edits, the higher the search relevance results. Not only does this place a particular user's content above others, it helps the organization identify centers of expertise. Social participation works in much the same way by factoring in the amount of tagging that a person does to content.

SUMMARY

Search in the enterprise using the SharePoint 2010 stack of products involves a lot of moving parts. The crawling engine gathers information about content from a variety of locations including SharePoint, databases and line-of-business systems, websites, file shares, Exchange, and Lotus Notes. The crawler communicates with the indexer, which organizes and stores the crawled content and properties in index databases. The query server pulls search results from the index databases in response to search queries, and the user interface accepts queries and presents results.

Selecting a search product in the SharePoint 2010 stack can be a daunting exercise because many search offerings are intended for different purposes, from entry level to full-featured enterprise-scale solutions. Deciding between products and when to migrate to higher levels requires that you complete regular audits of your users and the content that the system is crawling.

All the SharePoint search products provide a rich set of user interfaces that allows the user to submit search queries and view results. The search experience is greatly enhanced with features that allow for refinement of searches (previously known as search facets), the display of Best Bets and exact matches, and at the higher end thumbnails and previews.

After reading this chapter, you should have a good understanding of what search is, as well as what can be done with search in the SharePoint 2010 stack. The next chapter digs deeper into building your search solution so that it will successfully deliver relevant and timely results to your search users.

19

Administering and Customizing

WHAT'S IN THIS CHAPTER?

➤ Search administration configuration

➤ How to crawl content with crawl settings

➤ Enhancing the search results with query configuration

In any search server, many moving parts must be configured for your environment, and SharePoint search is no different. The search service application enables you to configure and tweak nearly every aspect of search, along with the tools to monitor the search health of your system. Success in large measure depends on your understanding of the content that your users will search. By understanding, I am referring to a deep and detailed knowledge of data locations, data formats, sizes of items, quantity of items, who uses the content, how often it is used, and where items should appear in search results relative to other results. It's not easy to become a search expert in your environment, but a well configured search system goes from being a useful tool to being a business-critical application.

This chapter addresses each of the search configuration interfaces in the order they appear in the search service application navigation bar. Although this order is generally the order in which you configure search initially, you will not always follow this specific flow when trying to configure or troubleshoot your search settings once your system has been in production for a period of time. On the other hand, the order of this presentation will help you understand the dependencies between search components: you must first crawl before you can query.

ADMINISTRATION CONFIGURATION

In SharePoint 2010, search is a service application that can be found on the Service Application Management page of Central Administration (Figure 19-1). All SharePoint search products use the base search service application, but FAST introduces two additional service applications for FAST content and FAST query. There is a great deal of consistency between the layout and pages of the search service application and the FAST service applications. It is essential that you learn the content of this chapter before moving on to the more advanced world of FAST.

Application Management
Manage web applications
Create site collections
Manage service applications
Manage content databases

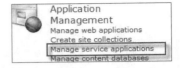

FIGURE 19-1

The left navigation of the search service application is divided into four major sections that represent the four major administration activities you will perform with search: Administration, Crawling, Queries, and Results/Reports. The Administration section provides farm-level and search service application-level settings for your search installation. Under normal circumstances you will configure these settings during the installation of search, and you will revisit them only when making major topological changes to your search infrastructure, such as scaling out servers.

Search Administration

The Base Search Administration page (Figure 19-2) that appears when you open the search service application provides statistical information about your search installation, a crawl history, topological information, and shortcut links to common search administration activities that you will perform. For the most part, you will use this page as a quick sanity check to see how things are going in your search application. You will also use this page if you ever need to change the default content access account. This is the account that the crawler will use to read content at all content sources when no other credentials have been provided through crawl rules.

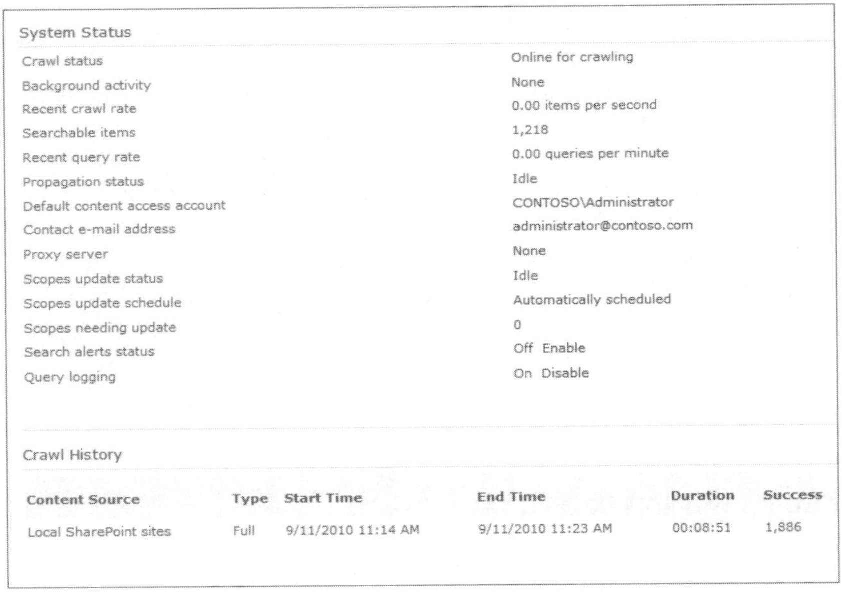
System Status
Crawl status
Online for crawling
Background activity
None
Recent crawl rate
0.00 items per second
Searchable items
1,218
Recent query rate
0.00 queries per minute
Propagation status
Idle
Default content access account
CONTOSO\Administrator
Contact e-mail address
administrator@contoso.com
Proxy server
None
Scopes update status
Idle
Scopes update schedule
Automatically scheduled
Scopes needing update
0
Search alerts status
Off Enable
Query logging
On Disable
Crawl History
Content Source
Type
Start Time
End Time
Duration
Success
Local SharePoint sites
Full
9/11/2010 11:14 AM
9/11/2010 11:23 AM
00:08:51
1,886

FIGURE 19-2

Farm Search Administration

The Farm Search Administration page (Figure 19-3) contains configuration settings that are specific to your SharePoint farm. Whether or not you work with these configuration settings usually depends on your infrastructure. If your crawler must move through a proxy server to get to Internet content or other content sources, you will configure the proxy settings here. You will also decide whether the crawler will continue to index content when the site name does not match the SSL certification registration. Finally, the time-out setting determines how long the crawler will attempt to make a connection to a content source.

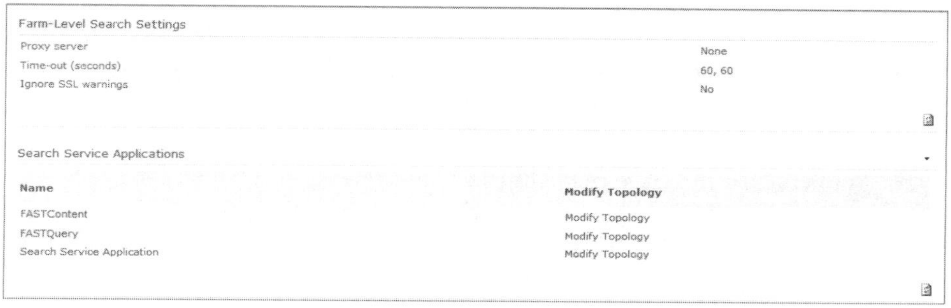

Farm-Level Search Settings	
Proxy server	None
Time-out (seconds)	60, 60
Ignore SSL warnings	No

Search Service Applications	
Name	**Modify Topology**
FASTContent	Modify Topology
FASTQuery	Modify Topology
Search Service Application	Modify Topology

FIGURE 19-3

Under normal circumstances, once you have set your farm-level configuration you will not need to revisit this page. Most of your configuration effort will occur in the Crawl and Query sections of the search service application.

CRAWLING CONFIGURATION

Crawl and Query are two sides of the same search coin, and you will often find that your work and/or troubleshooting occur on one side or the other. The crawl configuration is the side that determines what content will ultimately end up in your search index and therefore be available for search queries. To be successful with configuring crawl, you need to have an intimate understanding of the content that you want to crawl, how you want it crawled, and any rules or exclusions that you want to apply to the content as the crawler is doing its work.

Content Sources

A content source is an administrator-defined set of instructions that the crawl server uses to execute crawl operations and index search content. Each search service application can support many content sources, which are configured to search types of locations such as SharePoint sites, websites, file shares, line-of-business applications, and e-mail folders. The configuration and rules associated with content sources determine how content is introduced into the index. The content sources are the first step in the search process — gathering data.

How to Add a Content Source

Adding a content source to the crawl configuration is a straightforward process that involves identifying the type of content source and the location of the source, setting some parameters for the crawler, and establishing a schedule for the crawler to follow. The challenge to creating content sources is in understanding how each type of content source affects the crawler. There is also a bit of an art to selecting and building content sources for your search solution.

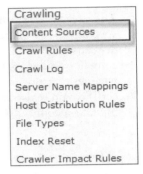

FIGURE 19-4

To begin adding a content source, open the SharePoint 2010 Central Administration site, then follow the links from Application Management ➪ Manage Service Applications ➪ Search Service Application ➪ Content Sources (Figure 19-4). The Content Sources link is located in the left navigation section under the Crawling heading.

The Content Sources link brings up a page that shows a listing of all defined content sources in this farm (Figure 19-5). You will visit this page frequently as you define content sources for your search solution, as well as when you are monitoring the performance of search in your environment. This page not only provides you with the link to create a new content source, but it also provides you with a lot of very important information.

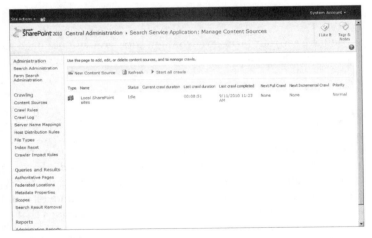

FIGURE 19-5

The content source list shows the status of the crawler for each content source. If the crawler is working, the status will read "Crawling Full" or "Crawling Incremental" to let you know what kind of crawl is being performed on that content source. You also get a feel for how long each crawl takes on this page, which will be important information when you begin considering performance scenarios that involve breaking up content sources.

The page also gives an immediate view into the scheduler by showing when the next full and incremental crawls are scheduled for execution. Finally, across the top of the list is a button to start all crawls, which will cause all defined content sources to execute their crawlers. Once you select this button, it is immediately replaced with Pause and Stop buttons. There is also a Create New Content source button, which you will click to begin the process of defining a content source.

 Out of the box, SharePoint defines a single content source called Local SharePoint Sites that includes all site collections defined in this farm. SharePoint does not create a crawl schedule for this content source. This means that SharePoint search is effectively turned off when it is installed.

The name (Figure 19-6) that you give a content source is an arbitrary identification, but you should keep in mind that the title you enter here will appear in the content sources list. In many cases, when you have only a handful of content sources defined in your farm, the names of the sources may not be an issue with you. On the other hand, if you have more than a few content sources, you will want to make sure that your names are descriptive. It is a very good idea to include text in the name that will help you to know, at a glance, what type of content source it is. The default content source, Local SharePoint Sites, is a great name for a content source because it not only tells you the type (SharePoint) of source; it also tells you the location (Local) of the content source. Months after you have defined your content sources when you are trying to troubleshoot a crawling issue, you will be thankful that your content source names are descriptive.

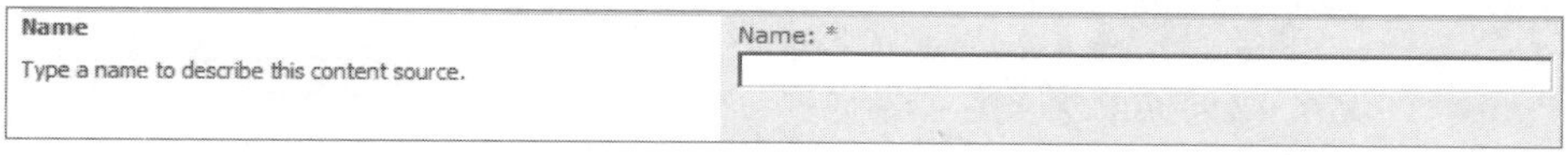

Name	Name: *
Type a name to describe this content source.	

FIGURE 19-6

SharePoint and the Search Server products support six types of content sources (Figure 19-7). Each type is discussed in detail later on. The content source type that is supported by all search products is the SharePoint Sites type, and it represents the most fundamental content source type that you will define.

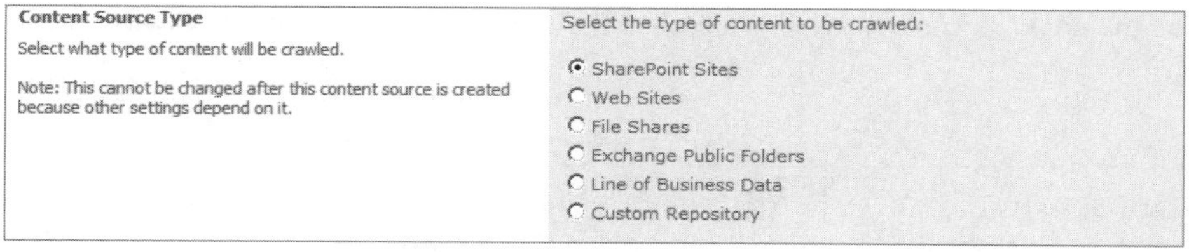

Content Source Type	Select the type of content to be crawled:
Select what type of content will be crawled.	⦿ SharePoint Sites
	○ Web Sites
Note: This cannot be changed after this content source is created because other settings depend on it.	○ File Shares
	○ Exchange Public Folders
	○ Line of Business Data
	○ Custom Repository

FIGURE 19-7

Although we have been referring to content sources in the singular, a single content source may be responsible for crawling many content locations. The start addresses (Figure 19-8) are a list of the starting URLs for each location defined as part of this content source. If you open the out-of-the-box

Local SharePoint Sites content source, you will likely have starting URLs for the entire set of site collections defined in your farm.

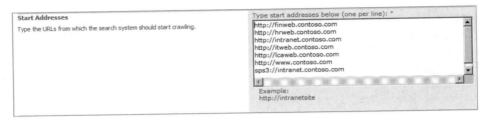

FIGURE 19-8

There is an art to defining content sources and start addresses because SharePoint imposes some limitations. The recommended maximum number of content source definitions is 50 per search service application. The actual maximum number of content sources is 500. The recommended maximum number of start addresses per content source is 100 but can go up to 500. The trick to configuring is that these two numbers should be in balance. If you have a lot of start addresses, you should have fewer overall content sources.

 A workaround to an extremely high number of start addresses is to create an index HTML page consisting of links to the start addresses. The single address of this index page is then entered as the start address of a Websites Content Source type. The crawler will follow the links to index the content. In this way, you can substantially reduce the number of start addresses.

The crawl settings (Figure 19-9) change depending on the content source type that you select. For the most part, the settings define the behavior of the crawler as it moves through each start address. In most cases, the default settings are to crawl all content under each start address; however, this is not often a desirable setting because you run the risk of crawling the world. You will want to use the crawl settings to strike a balance between amount of content crawled and crawl efficiency.

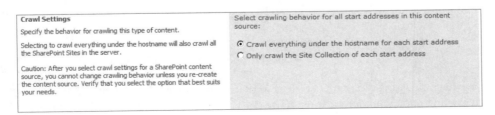

FIGURE 19-9

The Crawl Schedules section (Figure 19-10) allows you to either create a new schedule for both full and incremental crawls or to select a previously defined schedule. Like everything else in SharePoint search, there is an art to defining schedules. At the very least, you should define three schedules for each type of crawl: one each for high-, medium-, and low-frequency sites. Content sources that change a lot will need to be crawled with higher frequency than sites that consist mostly of static content.

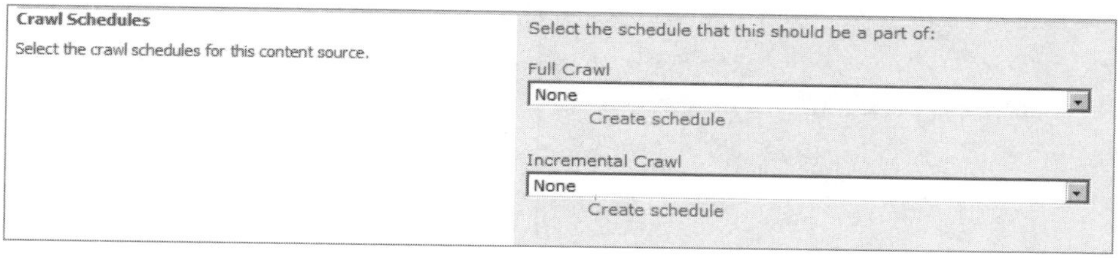

Crawl Schedules
Select the crawl schedules for this content source.

Select the schedule that this should be a part of:

Full Crawl
None
Create schedule

Incremental Crawl
None
Create schedule

FIGURE 19-10

An example of a high-frequency content source is a collaborative team site where users are uploading and editing documents, engaging in discussions, and adding list content many times a day. With high-frequency sites like a collaborative site, users will often want to search for content from the site within the same day in which it was added to the site. Therefore, it is necessary to have a crawler that is indexing this content multiple times throughout the business day. The schedule manager allows you to set up this kind of crawl, which will run frequently during business hours and less frequently at night. The tricky part is that you must define what the business day is in number of minutes.

At the other end are low-frequency content sources like document repositories or archives for reference documents such as a policies and procedures library. Because these are the types of content that typically do not change often, perhaps only once a year, you don't need to have a crawler using cycles to crawl this content frequently. Perhaps in the case of a site that holds mostly policies and procedures, it could be acceptable to set up a monthly crawl of the content.

I often get objections to setting up low-frequency crawls when content has been added to the site, but the next scheduled crawl will not occur for many weeks. Often this coincides with the release of annual enrollment documents. In these one-off cases is it often more efficient to coordinate with the SharePoint administrator to manually launch a crawl immediately after the new content is uploaded.

Once you have created the three basic crawl schedules for full crawls and three schedules for incremental crawls using the Manage Schedules page (Figure 19-11), you can select them from the drop-down lists for every content source that you define.

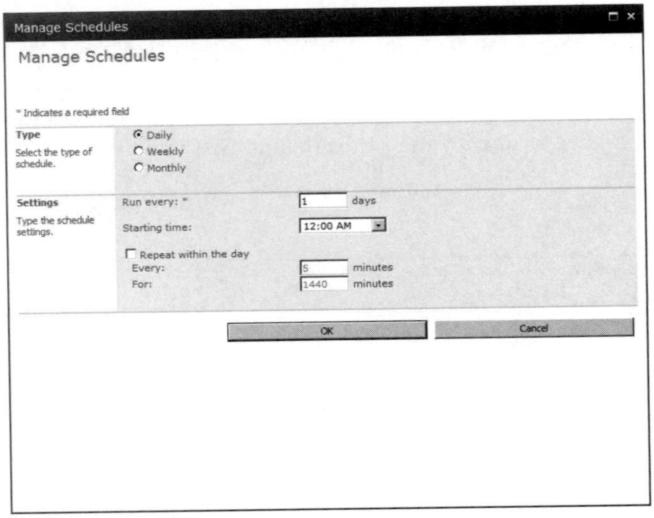

FIGURE 19-11

Deciding the schedules for incremental and full crawls depends on the frequency of content change and size of the content. You will want to balance thoroughness of the crawl with efficiency of performance. If you have a frequently changing content source like a team site, one you are crawling daily or many times a day, you will want to define those crawls as incremental in order to manage performance. Yet incrementally crawling with such a high frequency often introduces anomalies in the index that need to be resolved with a full crawl. Thus it is often necessary to define more frequent full crawls, such as weekly ones, to keep the indexes clean.

In the case of low-frequency sites, the deciding factor is more a function of the size of the content. In document repositories, the size of the content typically gets extremely large over time. As the size grows, so too does the time it takes to complete a full crawl. In these cases, you will find that you can eliminate full crawl schedules and rely on incremental crawls because the risk of introducing anomalies is lower and you can easily manage any needed full crawls on a manual basis.

In cases where you have many content sources using the same crawl schedule, or you click the Start All Crawls button on the Content Source List page, SharePoint uses the content source priority setting (Figure 19-12) to determine the order in which content sources are crawled. With this kind of setting, you will use your best judgment initially and then come back later when you have some solid usage statistics. Setting a priority will be a balance between the relative value of crawled content and the potential for crawl sources to slow down the crawler. You can use the crawl priority to put the faster content sources ahead of the slower.

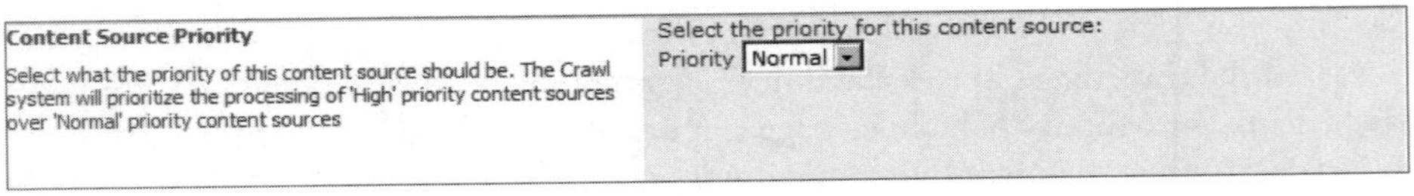

FIGURE 19-12

Although content source priorities helped in SharePoint 2007 installations, major architectural improvements in SharePoint 2010 may make this a less important component. In SharePoint 2010, you can separate crawl servers and content sources so that each crawler is responsible for a select set of content sources. This allows you to separate your high-priority content sources onto different crawl servers that can execute simultaneously. Each crawl server is responsible for indexing and propagating the content, independent of other crawl servers, which means that content from multiple crawlers indexing multiple sources will be available almost immediately on the query servers.

Content Source Crawl Settings

The Crawl Settings section of the content source configuration is different for each type of content source that you can define in SharePoint search. The crawl settings determine the depth and breadth of the crawl at each of the defined start addresses.

SharePoint Sites

The default crawl behavior for SharePoint sites (Figure 19-13) is to crawl everything under the hostname at each start address. Usually the hostname is defined with the web application, which means that the crawler will index every site collection and every site within the web application. This is the broadest and deepest SharePoint site crawl.

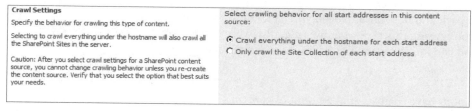

FIGURE 19-13

In many cases you want greater control over the crawling of SharePoint sites for scheduling, performance, or authentication reasons. For example, you may have a site collection whose content changes frequently, requiring more frequent crawls. You may also have a site collection with unique security requirements in which the default crawl account is not allowed read access to the content. In these cases you will use crawl rules and crawl schedules to control the crawl, but you will need separate content sources for these specialized cases. For these one-off content sources, you will need to use the crawl setting that limits the crawl to the site collection. Otherwise, you may risk crawling the entire web application with rules or a schedule that you do not intend.

Websites

Website crawls are a content source type where you can get yourself into a lot of trouble. When the crawler indexes a source as a website, it will follow all hyperlinked paths from the start page of the start address. For a small site that has only internal links, this may not be a concern; but, what if the site contains links to heavily linked sites like YouTube, Flickr, or Facebook? This is why the default setting limits a web crawl to the server on which the start address lives (Figure 19-14). With this limitation, if the crawler encounters a link that points to an external site, such as Flickr, it will not follow the link and index that content.

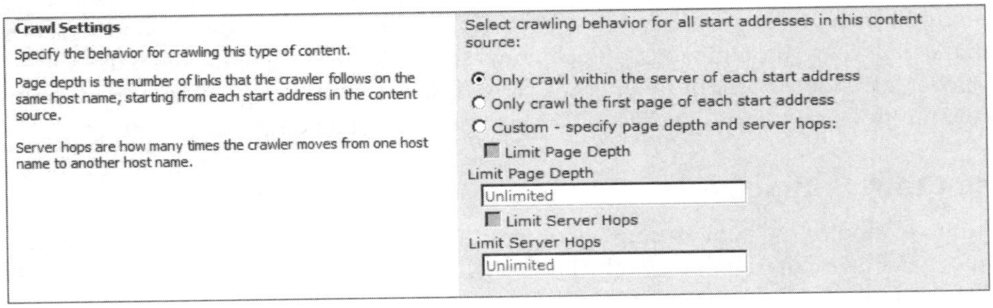

FIGURE 19-14

At times your web search requirements will go beyond the server. In these cases, you will use the custom web crawl settings, which enable you to control how many pages down in the hierarchy the crawler will go and how many servers it will follow links to. As stated before, if you do not limit the page depth and server hops, you potentially expose yourself to crawling the whole Internet.

When you use custom configuration, it is essential that you understand the content that is located at the configured path and how far and deep you really need to crawl. The first time that you conduct a crawl after configuring this type of crawl rule, it's a very good idea to keep a close eye on the crawl log so you can kill the crawl if it begins to index too much content.

File Shares

Most organizations have a substantial amount of content stored in file shares. In many cases the amount of content located on shared drives is so substantial that it is impractical to migrate that content onto the SharePoint servers. Setting up file-share content sources allows you to keep large amounts of binary content on the file shares yet still serve it up in search results.

As with a web crawl, you will need to make decisions about crawl depth when crawling file-share sources. In this case, you are only concerned with depth in the file structure; you will not need to worry about the crawler moving to other servers. As with every other content source, you will need to have a thorough understanding of the file-share structure and the content contained therein. By default, search will recursively crawl through every folder and subfolder within the start address (Figure 19-15).

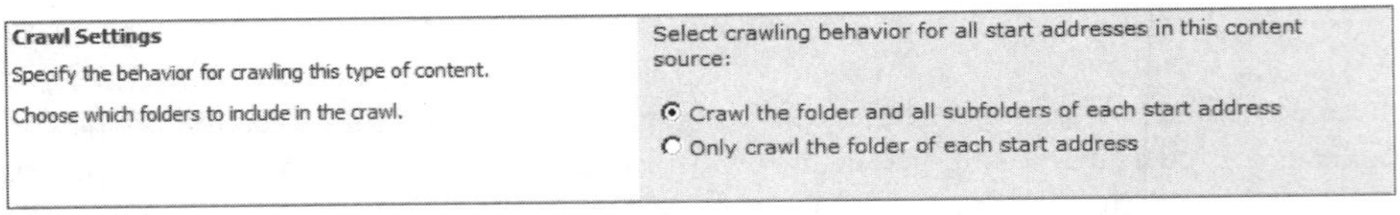

FIGURE 19-15

Exchange Public Folders

Exchange public folders are configured exactly the same way as file shares (Figure 19-16); even the crawl settings section contains the same options and the same instructions. The difference between the two is that exchange public folders are a part of the Exchange server product and are managed by it, whereas the file share content source is pointing to a network address that is managed by a file server. You will determine the depth to which the crawler accesses and indexes content within Exchange. The configuration that points the crawler to your Exchange server is the start addresses that you enter for the content source.

Crawl Settings	Select crawling behavior for all start addresses in this content source:
Specify the behavior for crawling this type of content. Choose which folders to include in the crawl.	⦿ Crawl the folder and all subfolders of each start address ○ Only crawl the folder of each start address

FIGURE 19-16

Line-of-Business Data

External data sources (Figure 19-17) allow you to search line-of-business data. Unlike the other content sources in SharePoint, setting up line-of-business data for search is not a task for the faint-hearted. The process begins by configuring your business data connectivity services by developing a custom Profile page for showing database results along with external data connections. Once configured in the Business Connectivity Services (BCS), you will configure and crawl the content source in the search service application. If crawling line-of-business content is something you need right away, you should read Eric White's post in the MSDN blog site at `http://tinyurl.com/22owsh8`.

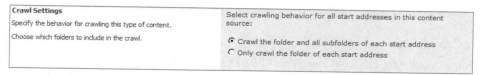

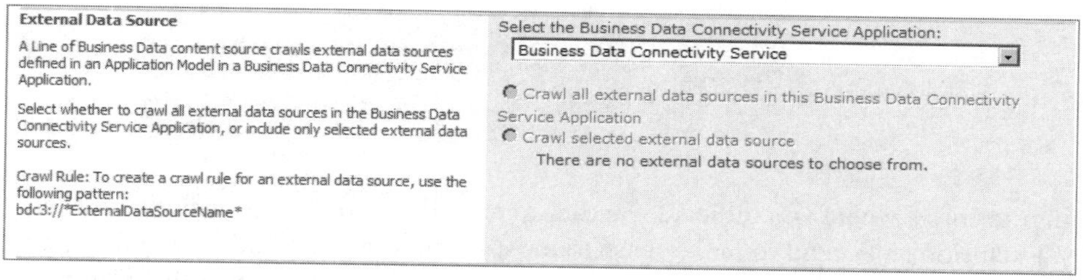

FIGURE 19-17

Crawl Rules

Crawl rules allow you to specifically include or exclude content that is located in the content source. Content sources by their very nature are an inclusive approach to indexing content; the only limitation to what the crawler indexes is in starting points and the depth of the crawl. Provided that the content resides within the context of the start address and is within the depth of the definition, the content will be indexed.

Consider a scenario in which you want to index a SharePoint site collection that consists of 10 subsites and you need to prevent the crawler from indexing a single subsite. Crawl rules allow you to configure an exclusion that will prevent the single site from being indexed.

 There is a critical difference between a crawl rule and a search scope (covered later in the chapter). A crawl rule prevents content from entering the index, whereas a search scope is a filter on the index content. If you create an exclusion rule in a search scope, the content remains in the index and is available to all other search scopes.

How to Add a Crawl Rule

To begin adding a crawl rule, open the SharePoint 2010 Central Administration site, then follow the links from Application Management ➪ Manage Service Applications ➪ Search Service Application ➪ Crawl Rules. In the Manage Crawl Rules page, click the New Crawl Rule button to add a crawl rule to the end of the crawl rules list.

The crawl rule path defines the URLs to which this crawl rule will apply. The path (Figure 19-18) can include as many URLs as you require, separated by semicolons. Crawl rule paths work much like the start address of a content source in that each path defines the starting point where the exclusion or inclusion rules will apply. You are able to refine the path by selecting the options to match the case of the path and/or to use a Regular Expression to define the path. Both of these options allow you to create rules that are very specific to your crawling requirements.

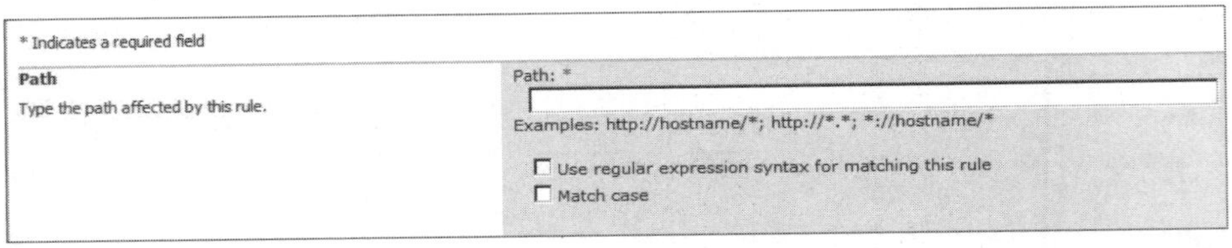

* Indicates a required field	
Path Type the path affected by this rule.	Path: * Examples: http://hostname/*; http://*.*; *://hostname/* ☐ Use regular expression syntax for matching this rule ☐ Match case

FIGURE 19-18

The crawl configuration is where you indicate whether to exclude content or to include content (Figure 19-19). Exclusion rules tend to make sense to most beginning search administrators, but inclusion rules tend to confuse beginners (and many seasoned administrators as well). The most common question that I hear is, "Doesn't the content source cover that?" Technically, the answer is yes, until you take a closer look at the inclusion options and consider the situations in which you will specifically add inclusion rules. The most common situation is to change the crawl account.

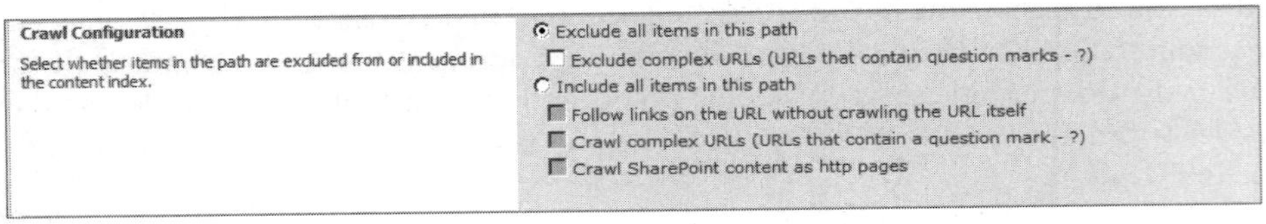

Crawl Configuration Select whether items in the path are excluded from or included in the content index.	⦿ Exclude all items in this path ☐ Exclude complex URLs (URLs that contain question marks - ?) ○ Include all items in this path ☐ Follow links on the URL without crawling the URL itself ☐ Crawl complex URLs (URLs that contain a question mark - ?) ☐ Crawl SharePoint content as http pages

FIGURE 19-19

In the search service application's farm-level settings you will establish a crawling account for the current service application. This is the account that the crawler will use to access all content in all defined content sources. If this account does not have at least read access to the content of the source, it will fail to index the data. In these situations, you may use an inclusion crawl rule to tell the crawler to use different account credentials to access content in a specified path. The Authentication section (Figure 19-20) allows you to define a variety of settings for crawling with different accounts.

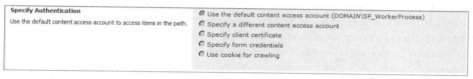

Specify Authentication
Use the default content access account to access items in the path.

- ⦿ Use the default content access account (DOMAIN\SP_WorkerProcess)
- ○ Specify a different content access account
- ○ Specify client certificate
- ○ Specify form credentials
- ⦿ Use cookie for crawling

FIGURE 19-20

Configuring Crawl Paths

The two most common search requirements for which you'll create crawl rules are to exclude sensitive content from the index and to include content using specific credentials. The crawl path is the uniform resource identifier (URI) that identifies the location of the excluded or included content.

The most basic approach to defining crawl paths is to enter the protocol and URL of the content. This approach requires that you create crawl rules for all content in the corpus that you want to exclude or include in the index. This can be a daunting task if you have a large number of search requirements that require crawl rules. To make the process of defining rules easier, SharePoint supports the use of wild cards in the definition of crawl paths. This allows you to define a path such as `http://mysitecollection/hrsite/*` to cover all content in the site.

Although the wild card is helpful in covering large amounts of data with little effort, it does not allow for a granular definition. At times you will want to crawl content within a location, such as a document library, but you will want to exclude a specific set of content based on some very detailed criteria. For example, consider a Human Resources site that may contain documents whose filenames begin with Social Security numbers. Because the site also contains documents that you want indexed, you cannot use a general wild-card crawl rule to exclude these files. This is where Regular Expression–based crawl rules come into play.

SharePoint 2010 allows you to define a crawl path using a Regular Expression. The details for defining Regular Expressions are out of the scope of this chapter, but a quick Bing search will provide you with nearly any Regular Expression pattern to match your needs. Using Regular Expressions to define the path enables you to specifically target content that the crawl rule will apply to. For example, if you want to exclude all content that contains a Social Security number in its path, you can use a Regular Expression to construct a path that will exclude this content.

Crawl Logs

Crawl logs are a very powerful tool and are essential not only to the initial setup of search but also to the daily operation of search. The crawl logs are your first point of reference to validate that the crawler is, in fact, indexing content into your search solution. It is also the first place you should look when you have situations where content is not appearing in search results. The logs will not only provide you with a glimpse into the content that is being added to your index, but it will also show you error messages when content is not added to the index.

Using the crawl logs is not a difficult task; the challenge is using them in the right way to help you identify and solve problems. The Crawl Log section provides five major sections to help you drill into the content of the logs in the most efficient way, depending on what you need. For day-to-day monitoring, the content source and hostname logs will provide you with basic crawling stats. For troubleshooting specific errors, the error message, content source, and hostname logs allow you to drill into specific crawl errors. Lastly, for drilling down to specific content, all the logs allow you to get to individual items to examine how they were indexed.

Content Source Report

The Content Source report (Figure 19-21) is the log that appears by default when you open the Crawl Logs page. This log shows all your content sources with statistics regarding the success or failure of the crawler to add content to the index. One thing to note about all crawl logs is that you can view them while the crawler is running. This is a handy technique when you are first setting up your search server or when you are adding content sources for the first time. After launching a full crawl on the content source, you can redirect to this page and then begin clicking the browser's Refresh button to see the statistics iterate as the crawler works.

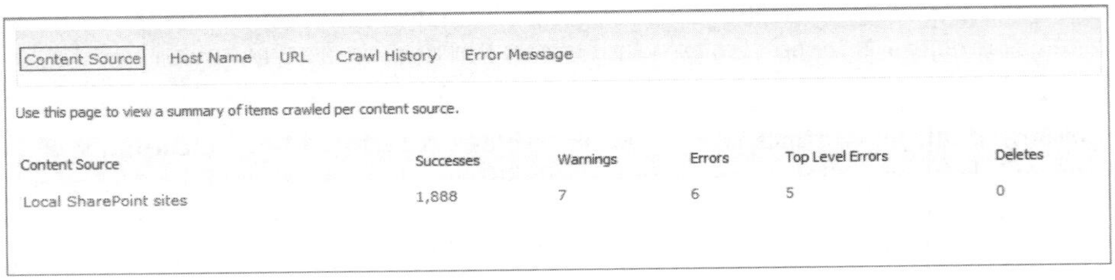

FIGURE 19-21

Hostname Log

The hostname log (Figure 19-22) is similar to the content source log; rather than display the crawl statistics for each content source, this log lists the statistics by hostname URL. This is a very useful log when you are troubleshooting missing data, and you know where the data should reside. By following the hostname, you can drill down into the errors to find problems with specific items, or drill into the successes to see that the content is in the index.

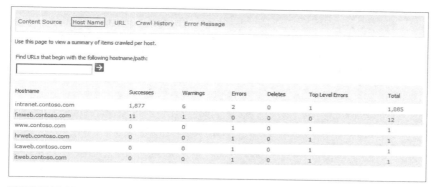

FIGURE 19-22

URL Log

The URL log (Figure 19-23) is the log in which you will spend most of your troubleshooting and validating time. When users report that they are not finding content in their search queries, this is your first stop. It's important always to check items to ensure that the crawler indexed the content. In my experience, most cases of missing content in search queries are either the result of a crawl error or not waiting for the crawl schedule to execute.

The URL log is itself a search form that allows you to search for and filter crawl results. Like the other logs, this report will update while the crawler is performing a crawl; therefore, it is a very useful tool for monitoring the crawler as it indexes content.

 Monitoring this log during the first full crawl of a content source is usually the time when I realize that I forgot to add a crawl rule to use a different account. I have many times watched the access-denied errors fill up a page while the crawler works.

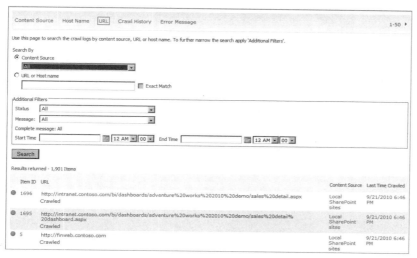

FIGURE 19-23

Crawl History Log

The crawl history log (Figure 19-24) is a useful tool for tracking trends and ensuring that crawls are running according to the expected schedule. This is a very useful tool for tweaking your crawl schedules based on the statistical results that you see over time.

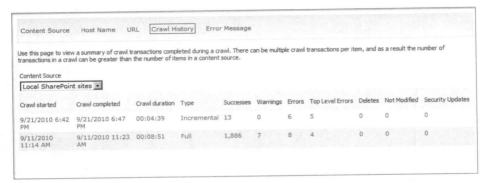

FIGURE 19-24

Error Message Log

The error message log (Figure 19-25) is useful for identifying substantial issues with your crawls. The error messages are sorted by frequency with the most frequently occurring errors at the top. This is where you'll find things like access issues, DNS issues, and time-out issues.

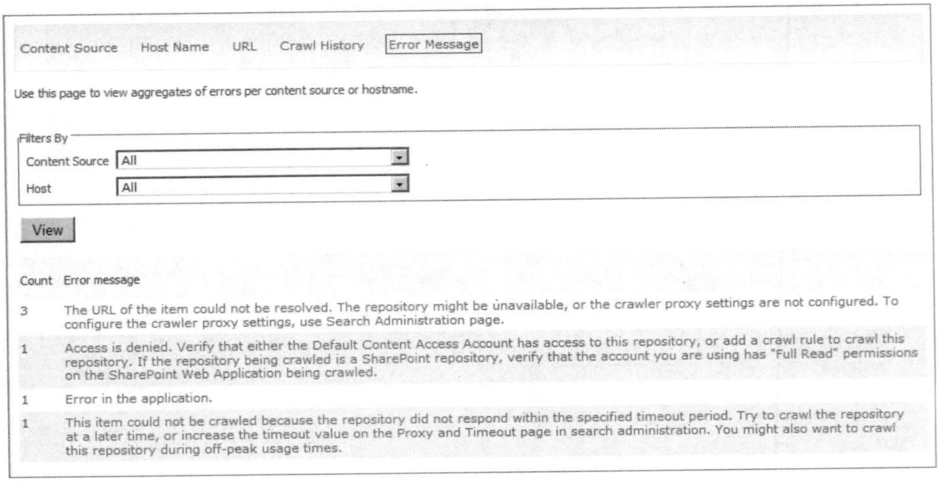

FIGURE 19-25

File Types

As the crawler indexes content in the content sources, it opens each item, reads the contents of the item, creates a text index of the content, and indexes crawled properties for the item. To complete this activity, the crawler uses an iFilter for each file type that provides it with instructions for opening, reading, and indexing content within the file type.

Out of the box, SharePoint includes iFilters for most common web-file formats, images, media, and office documents. This means that with no additional configuration your crawler will be able to index the majority of your content. The one glaring omission is the Adobe PDF iFilter. This filter does not come installed and is the one filter that nearly every search solution requires.

How to Add a PDF iFilter to Search

Adding the PDF iFilter is more than simply adding an entry to the File Type page in the search service application (Figure 19-26). To begin the process, you will first need to get the current 64-bit PDF iFilter from the Adobe website (http://tinyurl.com/a5gjyd) and install it on your SharePoint application server.

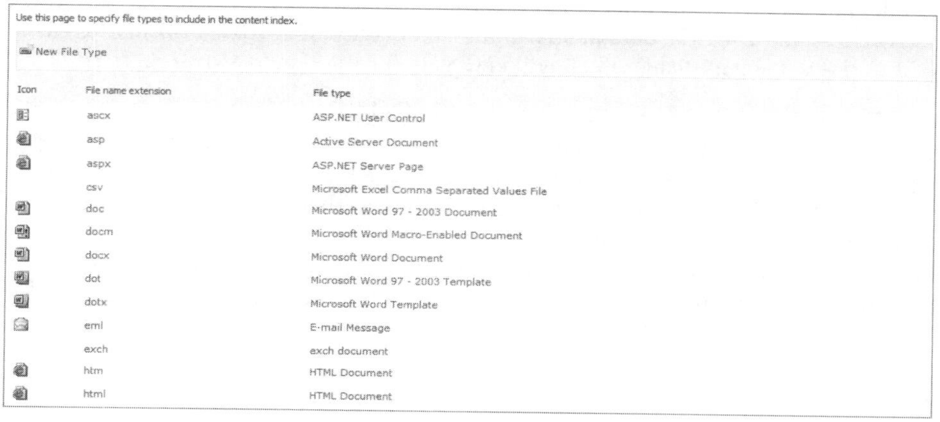

Use this page to specify file types to include in the content index.

New File Type

Icon	File name extension	File type
	ascx	ASP.NET User Control
	asp	Active Server Document
	aspx	ASP.NET Server Page
	csv	Microsoft Excel Comma Separated Values File
	doc	Microsoft Word 97 - 2003 Document
	docm	Microsoft Word Macro-Enabled Document
	docx	Microsoft Word Document
	dot	Microsoft Word 97 - 2003 Template
	dotx	Microsoft Word Template
	eml	E-mail Message
	exch	exch document
	htm	HTML Document
	html	HTML Document

FIGURE 19-26

The next step is to get an icon image and register it with SharePoint. This image will appear next to search results to indicate the file type for the end user. A quick Bing image search for 16x16 PDF image icons should yield a suitable gif image that you can download. Save the image to the TEMPLATE\images folder located in the SharePoint root folder. To register the icon, open the docIcon.xml file (Figure 19-27) located in the TEMPLATE\XML folder in the SharePoint root and add the following line in the mappings:

```
<Mapping Key="pdf" Value="pdf16.gif"/>
```

```
<ByExtension>
    <Mapping Key="accdb" Value="icaccdb.gif" EditText="Microsoft Access" OpenControl="SharePoint.OpenDocuments"/>
    <Mapping Key="accdt" Value="icaccdb.gif"/>
    <Mapping Key="accdc" Value="icaccdb.gif"/>
    <Mapping Key="accde" Value="icaccde.gif" EditText="Microsoft Access" OpenControl="SharePoint.OpenDocuments"/>
    <Mapping Key="accdr" Value="icaccde.gif" EditText="Microsoft Access" OpenControl="SharePoint.OpenDocuments"/>
    <Mapping Key="asax" Value="icasax.gif" OpenControl=""/>
    <Mapping Key="ascx" Value="icascx.gif" EditText="Microsoft SharePoint Designer" OpenControl="SharePoint.OpenDocuments"/>
    <Mapping Key="asmx" Value="icasmx.gif" OpenControl=""/>
    <Mapping Key="asp" Value="ichtm.gif" OpenControl=""/>
    <Mapping Key="aspx" Value="ichtm.gif" EditText="Microsoft SharePoint Designer" OpenControl="SharePoint.OpenDocuments"/>
    <Mapping Key="bmp" Value="icbmp.gif"/>
    <Mapping Key="cat" Value="iccat.gif" OpenControl=""/>
    <Mapping Key="chm" Value="icchm.gif" OpenControl=""/>
    <Mapping Key="config" Value="icconfig.gif" OpenControl=""/>
    <Mapping Key="css" Value="iccss.gif" OpenControl=""/>
    <Mapping Key="db" Value="icdb.gif" OpenControl=""/>
    <Mapping Key="dib" Value="icdib.gif"/>
    <Mapping Key="disc" Value="icdisc.gif" OpenControl=""/>
    <Mapping Key="doc" Value="icdoc.png" EditText="Microsoft Word" OpenControl="SharePoint.OpenDocuments"/>
    <Mapping Key="docm" Value="icdocm.png" EditText="Microsoft Word" OpenControl="SharePoint.OpenDocuments"/>
    <Mapping Key="docx" Value="icdocx.png" EditText="Microsoft Word" OpenControl="SharePoint.OpenDocuments"/>
    <Mapping Key="dot" Value="icdot.png" EditText="Microsoft Word" OpenControl="SharePoint.OpenDocuments"/>
    <Mapping Key="dotm" Value="icdotm.png" EditText="Microsoft Word" OpenControl="SharePoint.OpenDocuments"/>
    <Mapping Key="dotx" Value="icdotx.png" EditText="Microsoft Word" OpenControl="SharePoint.OpenDocuments"/>
```

FIGURE 19-27

After registering the image, you will need to register the file type with the system in the registry editor (regedit.exe). In the registry editor open the HKEY_LOCAL_MACHINE\SOFTWARE\Microsoft\Office Server\14.0\Search\Setup\ContentIndexCommon\Filters\Extension node, right-click the node, and add a new Key node: name the key node .pdf. This creates the registration with a default string. Double-click the default string and enter {E8978DA6-047F-4E3D-9C78-CDBE46041603} in the Value data field, which will complete the file type registration.

The last step is to return to the search service application and add a new file type for the PDF file type. You will need to restart the search service either from the command line or in the services application on your server. Once the service has been restarted, the crawler will know how to properly crawl PDF content. This does not mean that PDF content that was located in content sources will automatically appear in your search results because you installed the iFilter. To see indexed content for PDF files, you will need to first conduct a full crawl of all content sources that may contain PDF files. After the full crawl is complete, the indexed content will show up in search results.

Index Reset

Index reset (Figure 19-28) is the "do over" function in the crawl configuration. When you initiate an index reset, SharePoint removes all indexed content from the index. When the reset is complete you will need to conduct a full crawl of all content sources to refresh your search index.

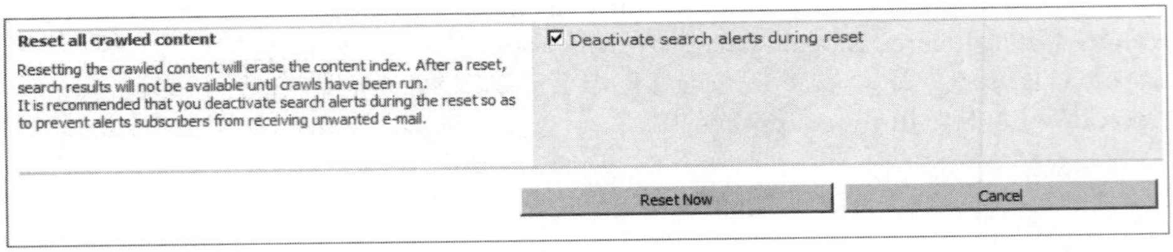

Reset all crawled content	☑ Deactivate search alerts during reset
Resetting the crawled content will erase the content index. After a reset, search results will not be available until crawls have been run. It is recommended that you deactivate search alerts during the reset so as to prevent alerts subscribers from receiving unwanted e-mail.	

	Reset Now	Cancel

FIGURE 19-28

Resetting your index may seem like an extreme measure, but in distinct situations it is called for. It is a recommended best practice to reset your index and recrawl your content after adding content sources to your server. This will ensure that the new content source does not introduce unnecessary noise into the index. Likewise, over time your index will begin to acquire extra noise that will ultimately impact crawl performance. Resetting your index will clear out unnecessary garbage. Lastly, sometimes content gets introduced into your index that you do not want to be there. Resetting the index ensures that the content is removed completely after you have created the appropriate crawl rules.

Crawler Impact Rules

Crawler impact rules (Figure 19-29) are performance enhancers that you utilize when you have large amounts of content or when content is of considerable size. When there is a large amount of content at the source, you can configure a number of documents that the crawler will request in batches. This reduces network traffic but can add a burden on both the crawl server and on the content source host. On the other hand, handling a large number of documents serially may be less burdensome on resources, but it will take considerably longer to execute.

In some cases, you will have content sources that host large files, such as file shares containing Computer-Aided Design (CAD) files. Setting a delay between crawl requests both gives the crawler time to index the large file as well as reduces the burden on the network and the host server. Whether batching requests or setting up a delay, crawler impact rules should be added with care and monitored closely for a period of time after implementing. Just as they can help search performance, they can also hurt it.

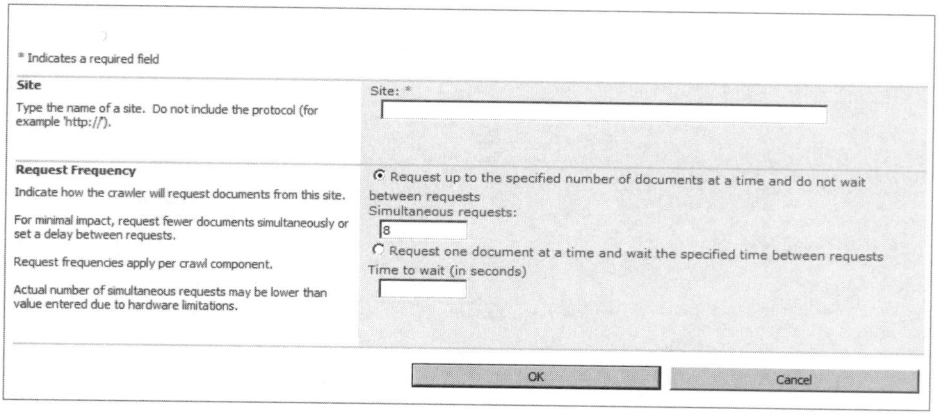

FIGURE 19-29

QUERIES AND RESULTS CONFIGURATION

The query side of SharePoint search is the side that most people think of when they think about search. The query server processes search requests and returns the results to the end user in the form of a rank-order listing. The way in which the server constructs the rank-order listing is governed by a very complex algorithm. The nature of the algorithm and the calculations that it performs are secret.

The question that naturally arises is this: if the algorithm is secret, how can you modify it to serve your own search needs? SharePoint provides a number of query configuration options that allow you to create configurations that will ultimately modify the way in which search results are returned by the search engine. These configuration settings combined with the information that we do know about the query algorithm will allow you to change the query and result configurations to make your search results more relevant to your end users.

Authoritative Pages

One of the factors the SharePoint query engine uses to rank the relevance of search results is to calculate the click distance of content from the start address of the content source. In practical terms, this usually means the root of the site collection or web server on which the content resides. The query server assumes that content closer to the top of the hierarchy is more relevant than content located further down in the hierarchy.

What if you want to be sure that content in a subsite dedicated to benefits data appears at the top of the search results before benefits-related data from other sites? For example, consider that there is a page in the root of the site collection that contains a news item about the annual benefits enrollment period, and that the actual benefits documents are located in the Human Resources team site. Immediately, the new item will appear to be more relevant than the actual benefits documents.

Authoritative pages (Figure 19-30) in SharePoint resolve this problem by promoting the relevance of links contained within specified URLs. This means that the configured Authoritative page is a preferred page from a relevance point of view. In SEO terminology, these are called canonical pages. By including the URL of `http://intranet.contoso.com/hr/benefits.aspx`, you influence the query server's ranking of benefits data. It is important to remember that you are influencing the query engine because click distance is only one factor. But when you carefully construct your authoritative pages, you will find that this is a powerful influence.

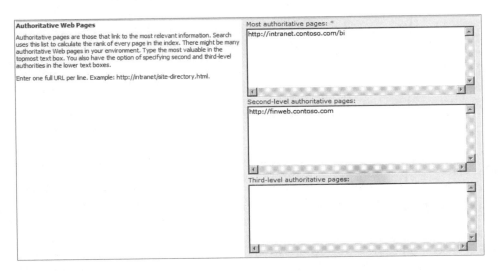

FIGURE 19-30

Not only can you make content more relevant by setting up authoritative pages, but you can also demote sites to make the content they hold less relevant in the search results. Unlike authoritative pages, which are specific pages with links to content, the non-authoritative sites (Figure 19-31) are websites.

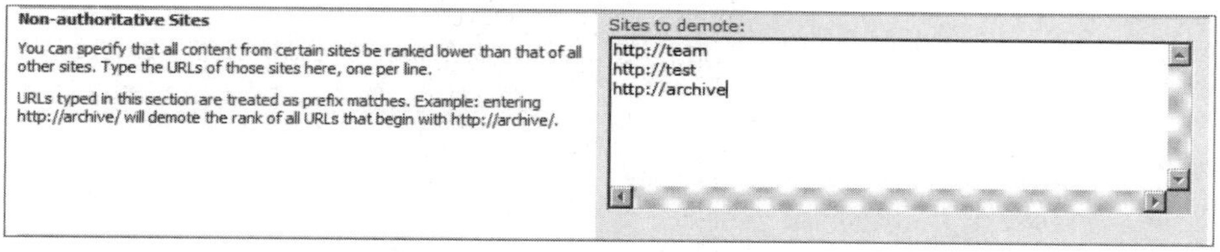

FIGURE 19-31

Federated Locations

Federated locations in SharePoint are external search engines that you configure to serve up search results along with the results that SharePoint serves in response to a search request. SharePoint passes the search query to all the configured federated locations, gathers the search responses from those locations, and returns the federated results along with the SharePoint results. The user interface in SharePoint includes a Federated Results Web Part. You configure this Web Part to display the results of the Federated Search.

Although federated locations are technically a query function, they will influence how you configure your search crawls. Many times it is impractical to crawl all the content that you need delivered in search results. This may be a factor of limited access to the content or of the corpus size, or it may simply reflect that some other search engine has already indexed the content for you. When you configure a content source, the crawler indexes all the content at the content source and saves the indexed results in your SQL server: more content means a bigger index, which means larger topologies. A federated location, on the other hand, stores no data at all in your SQL server; it is merely conveying search results from the federated location to the Federated Results Web Part. Leveraging federated locations will help you to minimize the size of your search topology and offer you the ability to serve up large amounts of search content to the end users.

Adding a Federated Location

The Federated Locations Management page (Figure 19-32) provides you with a listing of all federated locations defined on your search service application. It also provides the usage statistics for each location. This is a useful set of statistics because you can monitor it to see if the federated location is being used by the query server, and if so, whether your users are using the results. If either of these columns remains at 0 or a very low number for a long time, you may want to consider removing the federated location for performance purposes.

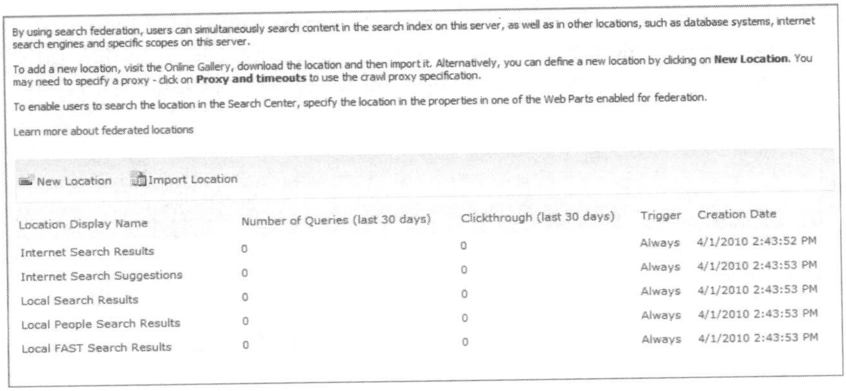

By using search federation, users can simultaneously search content in the search index on this server, as well as in other locations, such as database systems, internet search engines and specific scopes on this server.

To add a new location, visit the Online Gallery, download the location and then import it. Alternatively, you can define a new location by clicking on **New Location**. You may need to specify a proxy - click on **Proxy and timeouts** to use the crawl proxy specification.

To enable users to search the location in the Search Center, specify the location in the properties in one of the Web Parts enabled for federation.

Learn more about federated locations

📠 New Location   📥 Import Location

Location Display Name	Number of Queries (last 30 days)	Clickthrough (last 30 days)	Trigger	Creation Date
Internet Search Results	0	0	Always	4/1/2010 2:43:52 PM
Internet Search Suggestions	0	0	Always	4/1/2010 2:43:53 PM
Local Search Results	0	0	Always	4/1/2010 2:43:53 PM
Local People Search Results	0	0	Always	4/1/2010 2:43:53 PM
Local FAST Search Results	0	0	Always	4/1/2010 2:43:53 PM

FIGURE 19-32

You can add federated locations in SharePoint in two ways. The first way is to add the location manually and the second is to import a location definition. For most search installations you will probably want the imported locations available in the TechNet Search Connector gallery, but in some cases you may want to federate results with a non-public search engine. Perhaps your organization is running a stand-alone FAST server or has Google configuration installed. In these cases, you will need to manually add the location.

The location information (Figure 19-33) provides the query information with the basic configuration that it needs to communicate with the remote search engine. The location type tells the query server what kind of search server it is communicating with. The query template tells the query server how to pass search terms to the remote engine. And the More Results template tells the query engine what URL to expose when a user clicks the More Results link in the Federated Results Web Part.

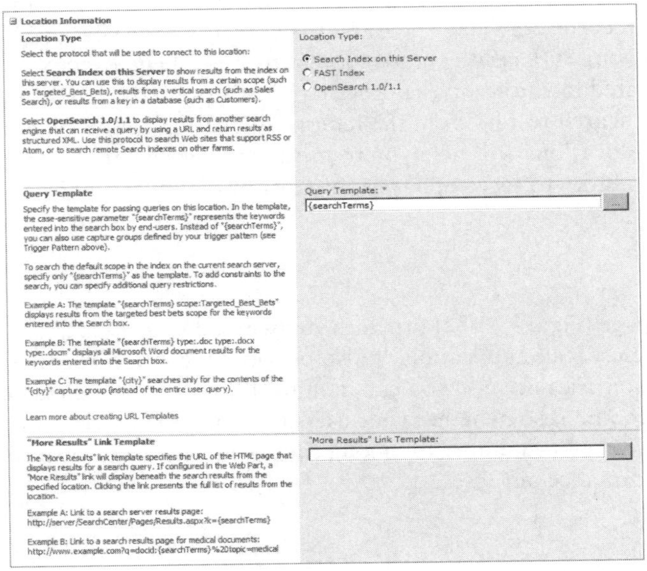

FIGURE 19-33

The Display Information section (Figure 19-34) is a set of XSL style sheets that define how federated results are displayed. Working with the contents of this section is generally a development task handled by someone well-versed in both search results and XSL.

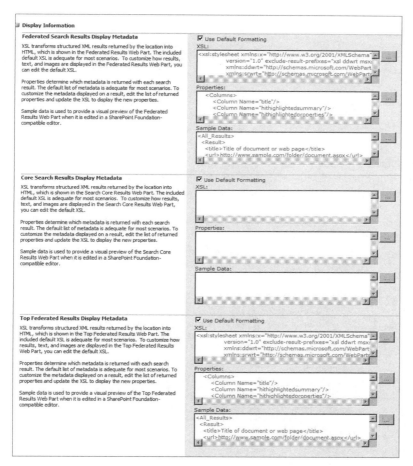

FIGURE 19-34

SharePoint allows you to control what sites can use this federated location in its Federated Results Web Part. You may need to utilize this functionality in some cases. For example, you may have a research and development department that has its own FAST server crawling confidential and trade secret information. You also have a research and development team site in your intranet and would like to serve federated results from the R&D server to users of the R&D team site. Using restrictions (Figure 19-35) on the federated location, you can ensure that non-R&D users of search will not see results that could potentially contain sensitive data.

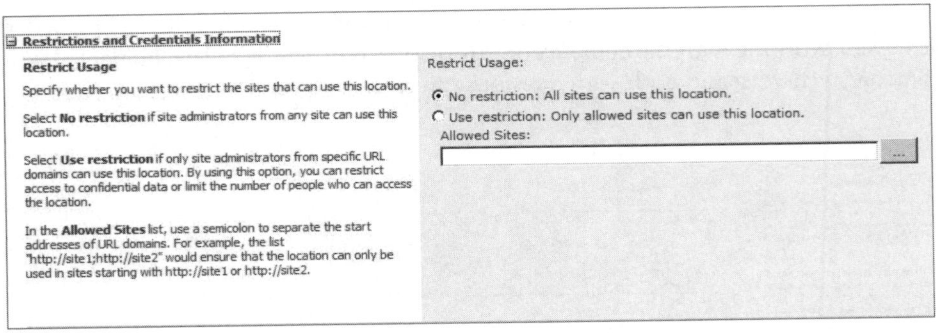

FIGURE 19-35

Lastly, when working with stand-alone search engines, you may need to provide specific credentials for making query requests. The Specify Credentials section (Figure 19-36) provides options for configuring nearly any type of security credential that an external search engine may require.

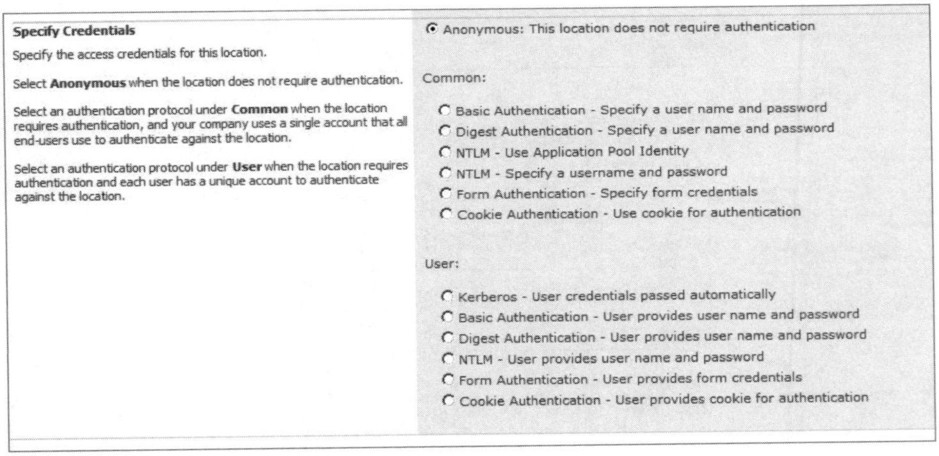

FIGURE 19-36

How to Import an Online Location

Microsoft provides a large number of preconfigured federated locations through its Federated Search Connector gallery at the TechNet Enterprise Search website (`http://technet.microsoft .com/en-us/enterprisesearch/default.aspx`) The link to the gallery appears just under the menu bar at the top of the Enterprise Search site (Figure 19-37).

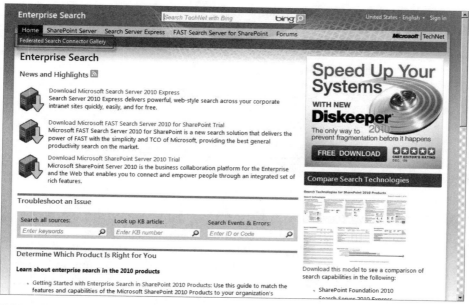

FIGURE 19-37

In the Federated Search Connector gallery, you simply select the search engine (Figure 19-38) that you would like to federate with and save the FLD file to a location on your local system. The FLD file is a federated location definition file that contains all the settings that you need to use these search engines.

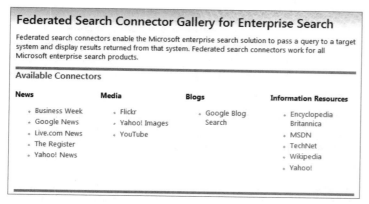

FIGURE 19-38

After you download the FLD file, select the Import Location button from the Federated Locations Management page and upload the FLD file (Figure 19-39). When the upload is complete, the location will appear in your configuration and you will be able to select the imported location in the Federated Results Web Part.

Use this page to import a new federated search location that you have downloaded or created. Once a new location is imported, it is added to the list of available locations. If the location requires authentication, you will need to re-enter your credentials after the location has been imported.

Location Definition File

Browse to the federated location definition file(.FLD) that specifies the location you want to import. If the location requires authentication, you will need to re-enter your credentials after the location has been imported.

You can download federated location definition files from the Online Gallery.

Federated Location Definition File

C:\Users\Administrator\Downloads\Wikipedia.FLD   [Browse...]

[OK]   [Cancel]

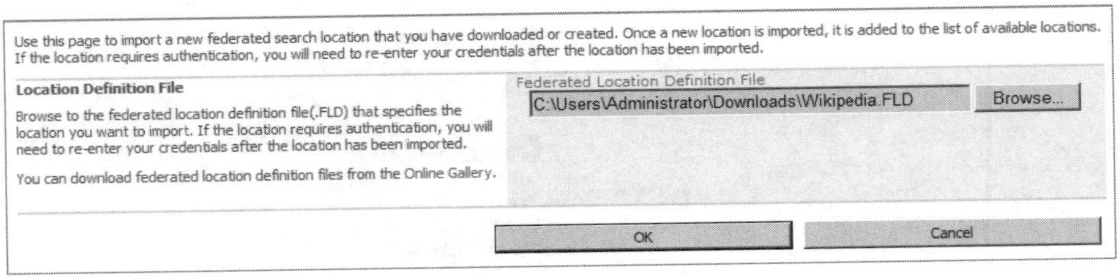

FIGURE 19-39

Adding Federated Results to the Search Center

Configuring the federated locations in Central Administration will not cause federated results to automatically appear in your end user's search results. For end users to see the results, you will need to configure the Federated Results Web Part on the search results page. Assuming that the search results Web Parts are located in the Search Center, open the Search Center and conduct a search. The content of the search is irrelevant because you only need the results page.

Once the results page is displayed use the site actions menu to edit the page. If this is the first time that you are editing the search results page, look around the Web Part zones at each of the search Web Parts. You will notice that the search results page consists of a number of connected Web Parts that perform very specific tasks in search. This gives you the flexibility to make substantial changes to the Search Center.

The Federated Results Web Part is located above the Core Search Results Web Part that is located in the bottom Web Part zone. This is the default location for the Web Part but is often the least optimal placement for this Web Part because it ensures that federated results will always appear above your local search results. If the search also produces a Best Bet match, you could have a situation where the core search results served by your SharePoint server are located "below the fold" on the web page, forcing your users to scroll down to get to the core results. In most cases, you will want to drag and drop the Federated Results Web Part to another zone (the right zone is the most common) or below the Core Search Results Web Part.

To assign a federated location to the Web Part, open the Web Part properties panel (Figure 19-40) by selecting the edit Web Part option in the Web Part menu. The federated Web Part is an extremely flexible Web Part with properties that allow you to modify nearly every aspect of the search results display. This section covers only the fundamental settings.

The Location Properties drop-down boxes contain a listing of the federated locations that are available to this site. To assign the location to this Web Part, simply select the location from the drop-down. You will also want to take a careful look at the display properties and make sure that the settings are best for this Web Part. The Web Part will look very different based on which zone you place the Web Part in. The bottom Web Part zone is wider and can accommodate more text per search entry. The right Web Part zone is much narrower, which requires that you set the character limits to smaller amounts to keep the Web Part from extending far beyond the bottom of the browser window.

If you make substantial use of the Federated Results Web Part in your search solution, you will want to consult TechNet and other online resources to learn about the other properties that are available in this Web Part.

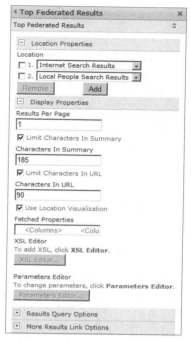

FIGURE 19-40

Metadata Properties

When the crawler indexes content from the content sources, it reads each piece of content and creates entries in the Properties database. The properties that the crawler defines while it indexes are the crawled properties. Crawled properties are used exclusively by the search server and are not exposed to the end user through the user interface. To make properties available to the end user, you will need to define managed properties.

Managed properties and the mapping of crawled properties to them is a very important concept for you to understand because it will directly impact your search results. When a user submits a search request, the keywords contained in that request are processed using managed properties. If a managed property does not exist, the query engine will not return metadata results for that term, and this will ultimately affect the page rankings in the content. In my field, for example, statements of work are a common content artifact and the term SOW is often used to refer to them. As the crawler indexes content on our servers it will at some point index the term SOW as a crawled property. To make search results for terms such as "SOW" and "statement of work" more relevant, it is important to map the crawled properties to a managed property.

The importance of managed properties does not end with search relevance. Managed properties are used in search scopes, advanced search, and search facets. The previous chapter discussed how to create search queries using property search syntax and how to follow facets that appear on the left-hand side of the search results page; all these features are directly related to defined managed properties.

The Metadata Properties page (Figure 19-41) in the search service application provides a list of managed properties along with the crawled properties they are mapped to. Out of the box, SharePoint contains managed property mappings for the most commonly used properties. What it does not have are the crawled properties that will be unique to the content in your index.

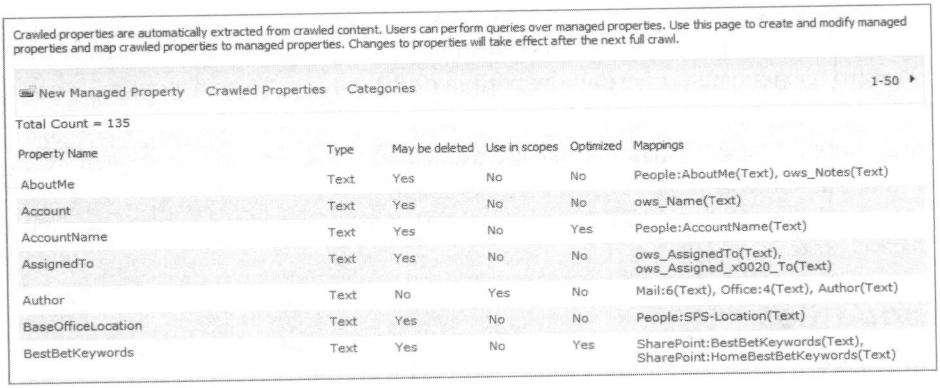

Crawled properties are automatically extracted from crawled content. Users can perform queries over managed properties. Use this page to create and modify managed properties and map crawled properties to managed properties. Changes to properties will take effect after the next full crawl.

New Managed Property   Crawled Properties   Categories   1-50 ▸

Total Count = 135

Property Name	Type	May be deleted	Use in scopes	Optimized	Mappings
AboutMe	Text	Yes	No	No	People:AboutMe(Text), ows_Notes(Text)
Account	Text	Yes	No	No	ows_Name(Text)
AccountName	Text	Yes	No	Yes	People:AccountName(Text)
AssignedTo	Text	Yes	No	No	ows_AssignedTo(Text), ows_Assigned_x0020_To(Text)
Author	Text	No	Yes	No	Mail:6(Text), Office:4(Text), Author(Text)
BaseOfficeLocation	Text	Yes	No	No	People:SPS-Location(Text)
BestBetKeywords	Text	Yes	No	Yes	SharePoint:BestBetKeywords(Text), SharePoint:HomeBestBetKeywords(Text)

FIGURE 19-41

The Crawled Properties (Figure 19-42) and Categories pages (Figure 19-43) will provide you with a listing of all crawled properties that exist in your index. You'll want to monitor these pages regularly to ensure that new business terms are being converted to managed properties as soon as the crawler begins identifying them. You will also spend a lot of time on these pages after you crawl your content for the first time. The goal in using these pages is to identify crawled properties that users will enter as search terms or that you will want to use for search scopes, facets, or advanced search properties, and then to map them to a managed property.

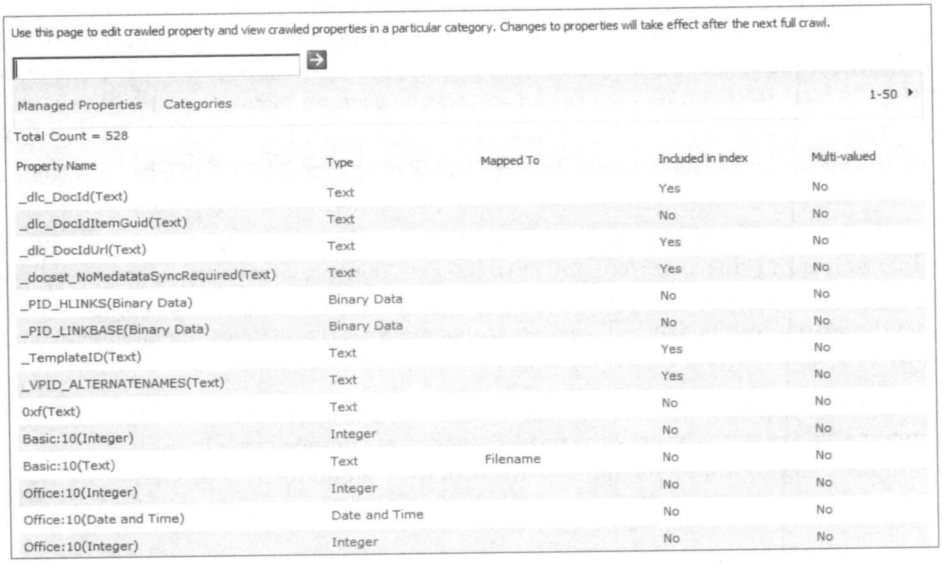

Use this page to edit crawled property and view crawled properties in a particular category. Changes to properties will take effect after the next full crawl.

[   ] →

Managed Properties   Categories   1-50 ▸

Total Count = 528

Property Name	Type	Mapped To	Included in index	Multi-valued
_dlc_DocId(Text)	Text		Yes	No
_dlc_DocIdItemGuid(Text)	Text		No	No
_dlc_DocIdUrl(Text)	Text		Yes	No
_docset_NoMedatataSyncRequired(Text)	Text		Yes	No
_PID_HLINKS(Binary Data)	Binary Data		No	No
_PID_LINKBASE(Binary Data)	Binary Data		No	No
_TemplateID(Text)	Text		Yes	No
_VPID_ALTERNATENAMES(Text)	Text		Yes	No
0xf(Text)	Text		No	No
Basic:10(Integer)	Integer		No	No
Basic:10(Text)	Text	Filename	No	No
Office:10(Integer)	Integer		No	No
Office:10(Date and Time)	Date and Time		No	No
Office:10(Integer)	Integer		No	No

FIGURE 19-42

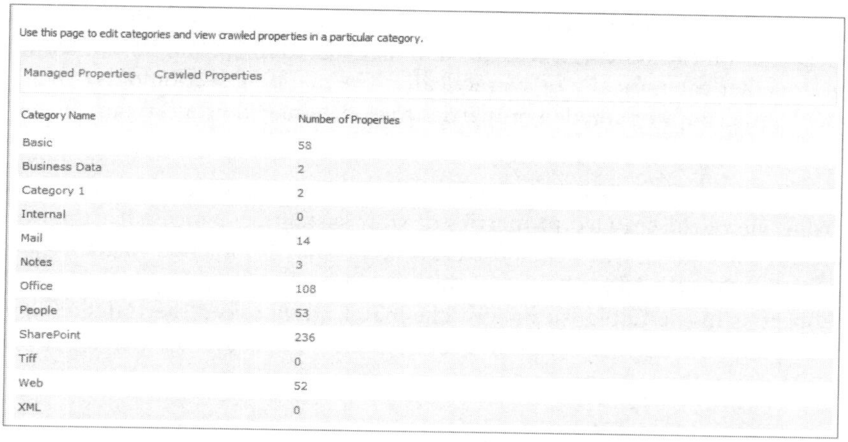

FIGURE 19-43

Add a Managed Property

From the Metadata Properties page (Figure 19-44), you can create a new managed property. Each managed property has a name and description. The name is the keyword phrase that the query engine will match against search terms entered by the end user. Therefore, you must carefully name the managed property.

You will also select a data type for the managed property, which tells SharePoint how to store the values associated with this managed property. Selecting a data type for the property requires intimate knowledge of the content of the crawled property and the content of your corpus. In many cases, you will be mapping more than one crawled property to this managed property and may have a situation where you have multiple data types associated with this property. In these cases, you can select the Multiple Value checkbox to accommodate the additional values.

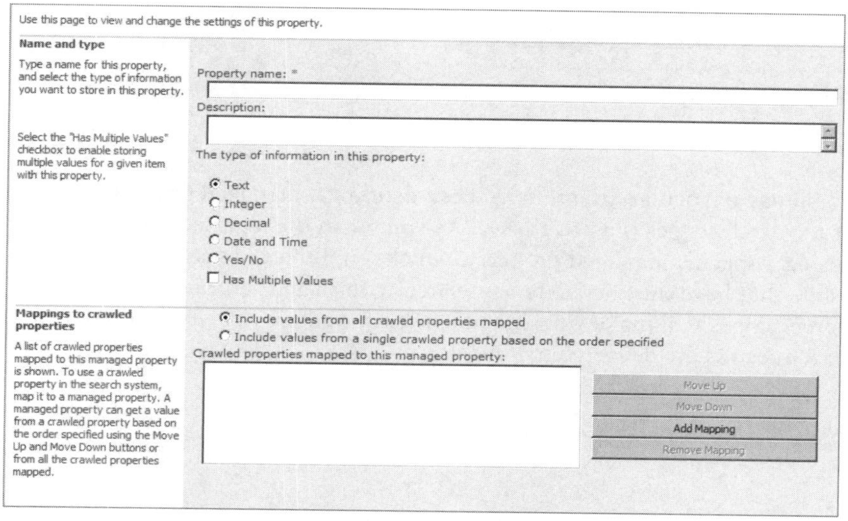

FIGURE 19-44

Many business terms in organizations are used in different ways or can be grouped together. As you monitor the crawled properties on the system, it will be commonplace to find groupings of crawled properties that either go together categorically or syntactically. The mapping section of the managed property is where you will add groups of crawled properties to this managed property and order them in relevance.

Clicking the Add Mapping button displays the crawled property selection dialog (Figure 19-45) where you can select from one of the crawled properties of your system. The nicest feature of this dialog is that you can select the category in which the crawled property is located to get a filtered set of properties in the dialog. Most of the time, you will be defining a managed property after viewing the crawled properties in the Categories page. The match-up between the Categories page and this dialog will make your life much easier as you set up your managed properties.

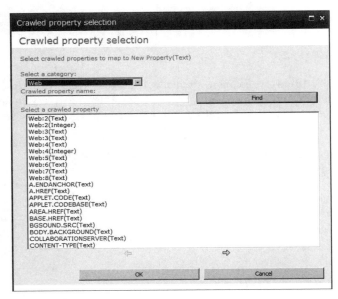

FIGURE 19-45

The last setting that you'll pay particular attention to when defining a managed property is whether to expose the property to search scopes (Figure 19-46). As you see in the next section, you can define a search scope using a specific managed property, which will limit the search results in the scope to only those results that have this metadata associated with them. Leveraging managed properties to define search scopes will make your life much easier and provide you with a great deal of control over how search results are delivered to your users.

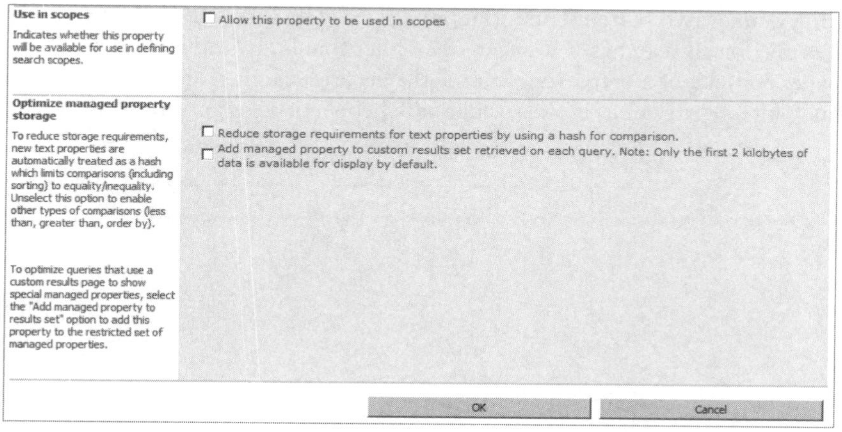

Use in scopes	□ Allow this property to be used in scopes
Indicates whether this property will be available for use in defining search scopes.	

Optimize managed property storage	□ Reduce storage requirements for text properties by using a hash for comparison.
To reduce storage requirements, new text properties are automatically treated as a hash which limits comparisons (including sorting) to equality/inequality. Unselect this option to enable other types of comparisons (less than, greater than, order by).	□ Add managed property to custom results set retrieved on each query. Note: Only the first 2 kilobytes of data is available for display by default.
To optimize queries that use a custom results page to show special managed properties, select the "Add managed property to results set" option to add this property to the restricted set of managed properties.	

OK	Cancel

FIGURE 19-46

Scopes

In their most basic form, search scopes are filters for search results. Impacting scope does not affect the relevance of the results that the Query engine returns; rather it impacts what the user sees rendered in the search results Web Parts by filtering out search results according to the rules of the scope. For this reason, scopes are often confused with crawl rules, which impact what content is indexed. When you define a search scope, the filtering that is defined for the scope is applied only when a search is conducted using that search scope. If the user conducts a search with any other search scope, the search results will be filtered in a different way.

I once helped a managing partner of a firm I worked for resolve this very issue. He was using a scope to filter out sensitive content that he did not want served in search results. He was very frustrated by the fact that the content appeared when using other search scopes. I pointed out that scopes do not prevent content from appearing in search results; they simply provide a filtered view of the content. To prevent content from appearing, he needed to apply a crawl rule. Further, because the content was already in the index, he needed to use the search result removal function to both create the crawl rule and clear the sensitive information out of the index.

It is easier to understand search scopes in the context of where they are used in search. The end user can select a search scope in three key places: in the Simple Search box, in advanced search, and as a tab in the Search Center. In each of these cases, the user selects the search scope and enters the search query. The query server gathers all the content that matches the search term and then applies security trimming rules to the content. Finally, the query server applies the scope rules to filter the results. In all cases, the query server begins the process with the entire set of search results that match the entered query.

Out of the box, SharePoint defines two search scopes (Figure 19-47). The first is the All Sites search scope that is the default scope for all searches. This is an open filter that allows all content to pass through to the results page. For lack of a better term, this is the generic search. The second scope is the People search scope, which filters the search results so that only people profiles appear in the results.

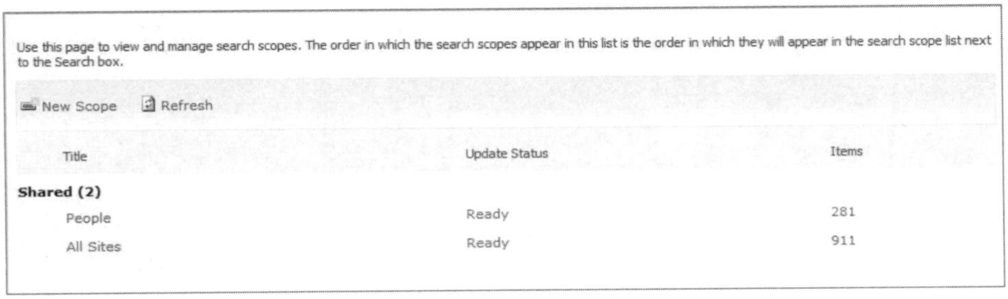

FIGURE 19-47

Adding a Scope

Adding a scope to your search server consists of two steps. First you define the scope, and then you apply rules to the scope. You define the scope in the new scope page (Figure 19-48) by giving the scope a name and a description. Keep in mind that the title you assign to the scope is the title that will appear in the drop-down lists or as a tab in the Search Center. You should carefully name the scope so that it conveys to the end user what the scope will do.

The scope definition also allows you to define a target results page. To understand how powerful this capability is, think about the processing of out-of- the-box search results. The query server responds to a search request by passing the search results to the default search results page. The default search page consists of a set of connected Web Parts that consume the search results and display them to the end user. Because the default results page is nothing but a Web Parts page with the search parts, you can create any number of variations of the results page in your own search results pages.

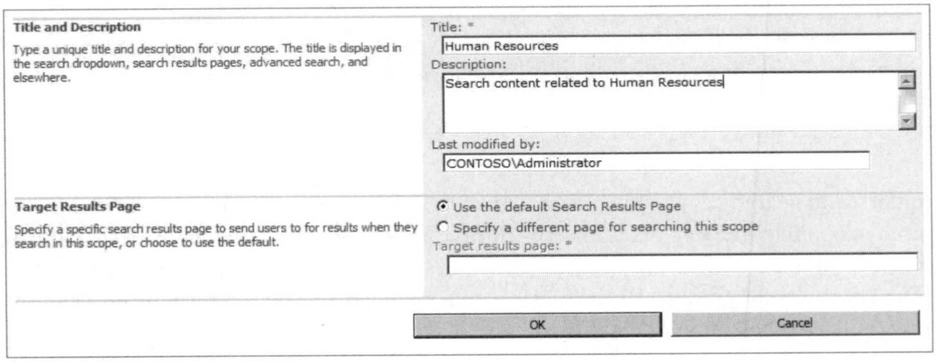

FIGURE 19-48

Once you add the search scope definition, it will appear in the Search Scopes page. This means that you can begin to utilize the search scope in your search solution by adding it to a site collection and exposing it to the Simple Search box, advanced search, and the search tabs. That said, the definition that you created is nothing more than a placeholder for scope rules. Until you add a rule to the scope, using it in search will have no effect on the search results. Initially, you can add rules to the scope by clicking the Add Rules link in the Search Scopes page (Figure 19-49). After you have defined rules, you can modify or add rules using the item drop-down menu.

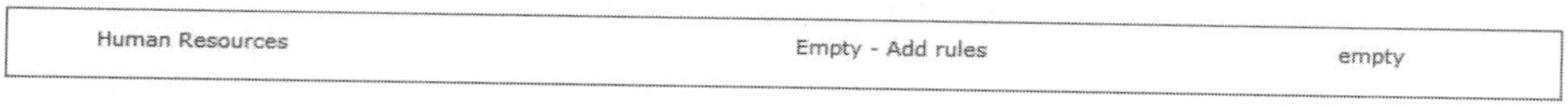

| Human Resources | Empty - Add rules | empty |

FIGURE 19-49

Each search scope can have multiple scope rules applied to it. The specific configuration of each rule (Figure 19-50) will depend on the type of rule that you are creating, but in essence each rule tells SharePoint how to filter the search results and what the filter does. You can use a rule to include all search results that match the rule or you can filter out and exclude all search results that match the rule. The configuration pane allows you to enter the filter information (how to conduct the filter) defined by rule type and the action (whether to include or exclude filtered results) by the rule behaviors. The next section details each of the rule types and how to configure them.

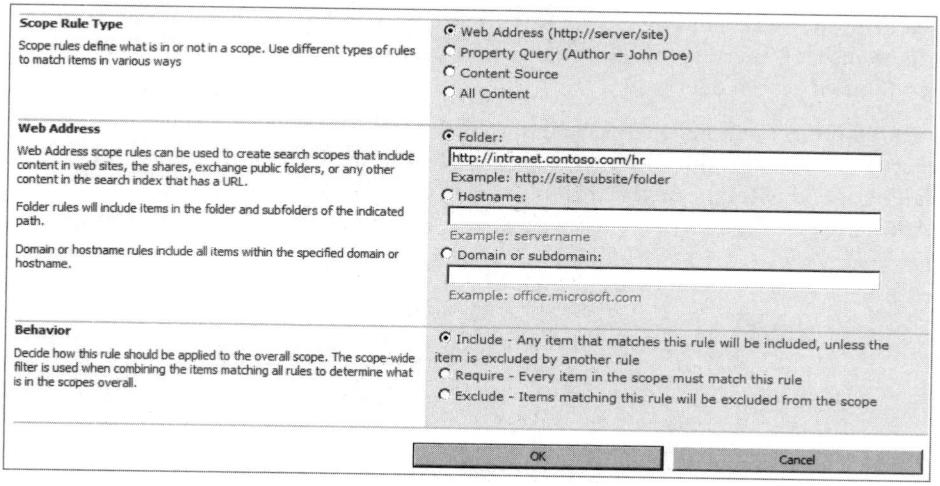

Scope Rule Type	
Scope rules define what is in or not in a scope. Use different types of rules to match items in various ways	● Web Address (http://server/site) ○ Property Query (Author = John Doe) ○ Content Source ○ All Content
Web Address	
Web Address scope rules can be used to create search scopes that include content in web sites, the shares, exchange public folders, or any other content in the search index that has a URL. Folder rules will include items in the folder and subfolders of the indicated path. Domain or hostname rules include all items within the specified domain or hostname.	● Folder: http://intranet.contoso.com/hr Example: http://site/subsite/folder ○ Hostname: Example: servername ○ Domain or subdomain: Example: office.microsoft.com
Behavior	
Decide how this rule should be applied to the overall scope. The scope-wide filter is used when combining the items matching all rules to determine what is in the scopes overall.	● Include - Any item that matches this rule will be included, unless the item is excluded by another rule ○ Require - Every item in the scope must match this rule ○ Exclude - Items matching this rule will be excluded from the scope
	OK Cancel

FIGURE 19-50

Scope Types

The four scope types that are available offer different configuration settings that affect the way in which the scope will filter the search results. As with everything in search configuration, a deep knowledge of the content will allow you to define scope types that maximize the efficacy of the search scope.

Web Address Rules

The web address rule (Figure 19-51) filters search results based on the URL associated with each item of content. SharePoint allows you to filter the URL from the very general domain down to the specific folder in which content resides.

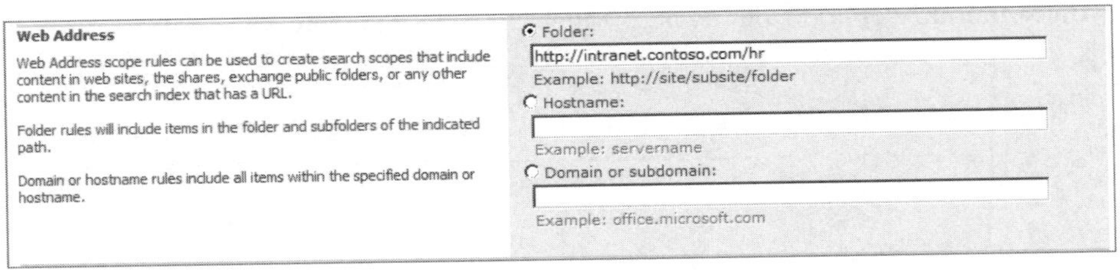

FIGURE 19-51

Property Query Rules

Property query rules (Figure 19-52) use managed properties to create a filter for the search results. The previous section discussed how to convert crawled properties into managed properties and how to make a managed property available to a search scope. In the property query rule, you select a managed property and then enter value criteria that the query server will match to filter the results. This type of search scope rule is no different than conducting a property-based query using advanced search or property search syntax, but it is a more top-driven search, meaning that the user does not have to go into advanced search to select the properties; instead you, the administrator, provide a pre-configured search query.

I worked on a search project at a major food manufacturer where we set up a property-based search scope that matched a "product" managed property with the value of a certain type of cookie product. This allowed end users to use the search scope to locate content and assets related to that particular cookie line.

FIGURE 19-52

Content Source Rules

The content source rule is the only direct method for mapping a content source to search results (Figure 19-53). To understand this, think about a search solution in which you create a content source that points to a set of file shares that contain documents and files related to policies and procedures. You have carefully constructed the content source from more than one start address; these map to file share locations all over your network. Now you want to be able to search just the policies and procedures documents in that content source alone without mixing it in with results from other content sources. To do this, you will need to use the content source rules in a scope. You can then create a custom search results page that will display only policies and procedures results; or you can add a policies and procedures tab to the search Web Part; or you can add the scope to one of the scope drop-down boxes.

Content Source	
	Local SharePoint sites ▾

FIGURE 19-53

All-Content Rule

The all-content rule is a catch-all rule that will include all index content in the search scope. Recall that, out of the box, SharePoint includes two scopes that specifically filter search results for people profiles and local SharePoint content. There is no search scope that will deliver all search results from all content sources. This crawl rule allows you to create that scope.

Scope Behavior

Scope behavior defines how SharePoint will apply the search scope rule to the search results. The "include" behavior (Figure 19-54) will show any results that match the rule criteria to the end user in the search Web Parts; however, the search results may be overridden by a rule that is lower down in the list. You may have a search scope rule that includes all policies and procedures documents from a content source but excludes those policies related to a specific plant by using a property-based rule.

The "require" behavior works the same as the "include" behavior except that the results delivered by the "require" behavior cannot be overridden by an exclusion rule. Finally, the "exclude" behavior filters out search results that match the rule. The "exclude" behavior is what most people think of when you talk about filters. For this reason, the default setting of Include tends to feel backwards to some administrators.

Behavior

Decide how this rule should be applied to the overall scope. The scope-wide filter is used when combining the items matching all rules to determine what is in the scopes overall.

○ Include - Any item that matches this rule will be included, unless the item is excluded by another rule
○ Require - Every item in the scope must match this rule
○ Exclude - Items matching this rule will be excluded from the scope

FIGURE 19-54

Search Result Removal

At times, despite best efforts, search results show up in a query that you never intended to be in a results set. In these cases, you usually realize immediately that you are missing a crawl rule that will prevent this content from being crawled; but what do you do when the content has already been crawled and is located in the index? The Search Results Removal page (Figure 19-55) is the "kill two birds with one stone" solution to this problem.

Search results removal will remove results that match the provided URLs from the index and ensure that the content will no longer appear in search results. It will also create a crawl rule for each URL that will prevent the content from re-entering the index at the next crawl. If the time comes when you would like to have those search results added back into the index, you simply remove the crawl rule and complete a full crawl of all content sources.

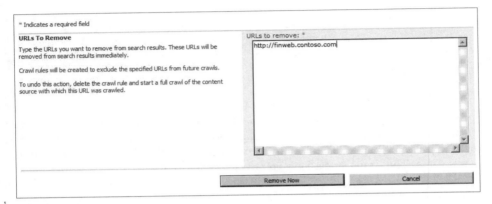

FIGURE 19-55

Though search results removal is a handy tool when you overlook content that should not be in the index, it is not always the best way to handle these situations. If the content that accidentally entered into the index is of an extremely sensitive nature, such as trade secrets or personnel data, you should create the crawl rules, then reset the index and conduct a full crawl. Resetting the index is a much more thorough way of dealing with sensitive content appearing in search results.

SUMMARY

Configuring a search server is initially a labor-intensive project that requires you to understand more about your organization's content than any other person in the organization. Armed with this knowledge, you will begin exposing the content to the crawler, which will lead to making it available to the query server to present in search results. Configuring search will become an iterative process where you crawl content, watch the search logs, tweak query settings, and test in the Search Center — and then go back and do it all over again. At times it can be frustrating and tedious, but a well-configured SharePoint search server will perform better and provide better results than any other search product on the market.

This chapter provided the foundational knowledge for successfully configuring your search server. There is a lot more to learn and Wrox has fantastic titles that will provide you with more in-depth discussion of these topics. But you now have the functional knowledge you'll need to begin tackling FAST search configuration, which is the subject of the next chapter.

20

FAST Search

WHAT'S IN THIS CHAPTER?

➤ What does FAST add to search?

➤ Tuning the crawler

➤ Advanced content processing

➤ Refining relevancy

➤ Search center enhancements

The previous two chapters have laid the groundwork for your understanding of enterprise search. This chapter introduces you to the advanced search capabilities provided by FAST Search Server for SharePoint. It is a basic overview of the most important components of the FAST product, but it is by no means a complete or deep instruction on this technology. Much of FAST is configured and administered through a complex set of XML files, Web Parts, PowerShell commands, and command line utilities. This gives you an overview of the topic.

FAST SEARCH CAPABILITIES

FAST Search Server 2010 for SharePoint adds new capabilities to enterprise search, as well as enhancing most of the capabilities that are included in the SharePoint Server 2010 enterprise search product. Everything from the crawler to the search experience is substantially improved with the FAST engine. FAST provides the architecture that allows for extreme scaling of the search engine to handle nearly infinite amounts of content while continuing to process and deliver content faster than any other search system.

Tapping into the advanced features of FAST requires more technical depth and a deeper understanding of your content and the search engine than were required to manage SharePoint

Server 2010 search. The sheer breadth and depth of configurability that FAST delivers to the search engine is greater than can be effectively delivered through a web user interface. Yet, FAST Search Server begins by leveraging the user interface of the SharePoint Search product. This allows you to gradually move into the FAST world with a common base of understanding. In other words, you do not have to relearn everything about the search engine.

One common misunderstanding at client sites is the myth that you can plug in a search engine and it will automatically "work." In reality, there is a direct correlation between the amount of effort required to configure the search engine and the quality and depth of results that the search engine returns. FAST is the flagship of search, and it requires the work and attention to detail due its position.

The Capabilities Themselves

Understanding what FAST Search Server 2010 provides above and beyond the SharePoint 2010 enterprise search product is an important starting point for planning and deploying your FAST installation. At the very least, a solid understanding of the capabilities and what they provide to the search experience will provide you with a way of organizing your search configuration efforts.

Advanced Crawl

FAST Search Server provides a level of crawl configuration flexibility that will make your head spin. But not to worry, the FAST search service applications provide content source configuration pages that look and feel identical to the content source pages found in the enterprise search service application. This enables you to begin using the FAST engine for crawling without worrying about the minutiae of crawl configuration. When you are ready to go beyond the Central Administration user interface, FAST allows configuration of every aspect of the crawler.

Contextual Search

FAST Search Server's contextual search capabilities provide a high level of control over how search results are presented to the end users of your system based on a variety of contexts. The contexts that follow allow you to serve different sets of search results for the same search query based on the user and other factors.

➤ **Relevancy tuning:** You can affect the location of items in search results by modifying the weighting value of individual items or all items within a site. By adding to (promotion) or subtracting from (demotion) the weighted value of the item or items, you effectively push the item up or down in the result set.

➤ **Synonyms:** SharePoint Server search provides support for one-way synonyms. When the user includes a synonymous term for a keyword in a query, the items for that keyword are returned in the result set. But when a user includes the actual keyword in the query, the synonymous items are not returned. FAST Search adds the capability for two-way synonyms, which means that both result sets will be returned.

➤ **Advanced Managed Metadata:** The previous chapter discussed crawled and managed properties in depth because managed properties are a critical concept to search. FAST Search Server expands on the capabilities and importance of managing properties by allowing you to apply stemming, refinement parameters, and priorities with each managed property.

➤ **Property extraction:** Property extraction is the capability to map specific content information to a search property. Using the property extraction rules, you can force the inclusion or exclusion of the content when the specified property is used in a query.

➤ **Rank profiles:** Search relevance is calculated using a powerful calculation that cannot be affected by SharePoint Server. FAST Search Server, however, provides access to rank profiles that control how content is ranked in search results.

Search Experience

Not only does FAST Search Server add capabilities to the underlying search engine, it also enhances and adds to the search user experience. The installation of FAST includes a new search center template that you can use to deliver a FAST-specific search interface to your end users. The high-visibility items that are included in the enhanced search center revolve around the visual search and conversational search capabilities.

➤ **Visual Best Bets:** SharePoint Search allows you to configure a Best Bet for a specific keyword. When the end user executes a query that uses the specified keyword, the user is presented with a set of links that usually appear at the top of the results page and that point to content associated with that keyword. Visual Best Bets work in the same way but present the user with an image rather than a text link. These are great for product, logo, or other types of searches that are best served with an image.

➤ **Document thumbnails:** A picture is worth a thousand words, and when a user is sifting through hundreds of documents to find a specific one, having a thumbnail of the first page of the document can often save a substantial amount of browsing. Having the thumbnail presented as part of the search results eliminates the need to click the link and open the document in Office to see what its contents look like.

➤ **Scrolling PowerPoint:** Research conducted by Microsoft has shown that in the case of PowerPoint searches, users most often look for a specific slide or set of slides in presentations. As with documents, opening many PowerPoint presentations to find one or a few slides can be a very time-consuming and frustrating process. FAST offers PowerPoint presentations in an embedded viewer that allows the user to browse through all the slides in the deck without leaving the search results page.

➤ **Sort results on managed properties:** SharePoint Server Search allows you to sort results only by relevance or date modified. FAST enhances the sorting of search results by allowing you to define managed properties as sorting fields.

➤ **Deep results refinement:** Similar to sorting results, SharePoint Server provides a limited set of facets that the user can select to refine a result set. FAST opens up the taxonomy to the refinement panel allowing you to configure any managed property as a refinement option.

➤ **Similar results and result collapsing:** When a user executes a search in the FAST Server Search Center, each result in the result set can include a link to show similar results, which will re-query the search engine with a request that is mapped to the individual search result. It also includes a link that allows the end user to collapse duplicates in the display.

Architecture and Administration

FAST Search Server 2010 integrates closely with SharePoint Server 2010. Architecturally, it is composed of the same basic components described in earlier chapters: crawler, index, and query. In fact, most of the administrative pages and tools work in FAST exactly as they did in enterprise search. This is good news when your enterprise search solution grows to the point that you need to scale up to FAST. You'll be able to leverage your knowledge of enterprise search to quickly put FAST into place, and you'll be able to continue to run the enterprise search solution while you scale into the FAST solution. Figure 20-1 shows schematically how it all works.

Although FAST shares an architectural heritage with enterprise search, it expands on its basic components (Figure 20-1). The result is a hybrid of the two search systems that distinguishes between content searches and searches for people. In this hybrid system, People Search continues to be serviced by enterprise search, but all content searches are serviced by the FAST engine.

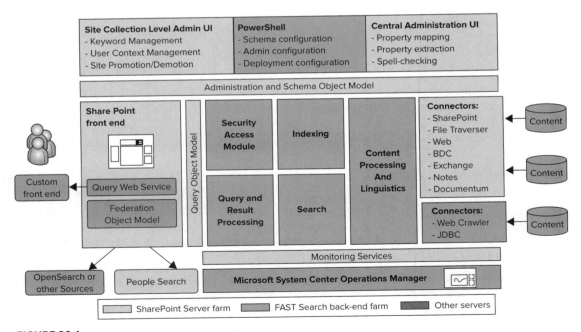

FIGURE 20-1

The hybrid approach to the search solution results in two search service applications for FAST: the FAST Content Search Service Application and the FAST Query Search Service Application.

The FAST Content Search Service Application handles all content crawling functions for the FAST server. FAST uses the same connectors that enterprise search uses to crawl and index content sources, and it includes additional connectors for high volume and Documentum searches. Like enterprise search the FAST Content SSA is able to crawl a variety of content sources.

The FAST Query Search Service Application handles all queries in the search system. It operates as a switchboard between content searches and People Search. If the query is for content, it passes the query to the FAST Search Server for processing. When the query is People Search, it passes the query to SharePoint Search.

PowerShell

If you haven't already started to learn PowerShell, you will need to learn it to accomplish most meaningful tasks in FAST Search Server. PowerShell is a command line environment that gives Windows many of the shell and scripting capabilities that UNIX users have enjoyed for many years. With it, administrators are able to automate and accomplish more tasks in Windows with a single interface.

PowerShell is built on the .NET Framework, which allows the capabilities of the shell environment to be extended with .NET class-based commands and compiled assemblies. The compiled assemblies are added to PowerShell as snap-ins that provide the user with access to a set of commands defined within the assembly. These commands are known as cmdlets.

Both SharePoint Server and FAST Search Server install a PowerShell snap-in that provides search-specific cmdlets. These snap-ins are Microsoft.SharePoint.PowerShell and Microsoft .FASTSearch.PowerShell. As would be expected, the FAST-specific snap-in provides more cmdlets and a greater ability to configure search than does the SharePoint Server snap-in.

As stated earlier, a cmdlet is a class-based command that performs an action in PowerShell. Cmdlets are organized around a verb-noun command model in which the noun identifies the object and the verb identifies the action to be taken on the object. The most basic example of this is the verb `Get` and the noun `Help` which results in a cmdlet of `Get-Help`, which you can use to access the PowerShell documentation.

Due to the substantial number of cmdlets provided by both snap-ins, it is not practical to show them all here. I encourage you to take the time to read up on both the SharePoint Search cmdlets and the FAST cmdlets in their respective TechNet library entries. You can read about the SharePoint cmdlets at `http://technet.microsoft.com/en-us/library/ee890087.aspx` and the FAST cmdlets at `http://technet.microsoft.com/en-us/library/ff393782.aspx`.

CRAWLING

Conceptually, the FAST Search Server crawler is no different than the SharePoint Server crawler. It is the portion of the search system responsible for accessing content at a defined content source and indexing the contents of each source item into the search index. Crawl parameters, crawl rules, and the other configuration options that were covered in the previous chapter apply and are used in the same way.

The key decision point between the FAST crawler and the SharePoint crawler lies in three specific capabilities: large-scale crawling, finding links in JavaScript, and advanced tuning. The FAST crawler is optimized for crawling and indexing large-scale content sources without any degradation in performance. Additionally, the crawler has the ability to follow links located within JavaScript code on a page — something that SharePoint Server cannot accomplish. Finally, you are able to configure nearly every aspect of the crawler.

Often, you'll scale up to FAST Search Server for one of these three reasons, not because you've maxed out the SharePoint Search Server. This tends to be true of FAST's other aspects as well; the need for advanced capabilities rather than simply growth will cause you to scale up.

Tuning the Crawler

The FAST crawler can be configured with the FAST Content Search Service Application, using the same approaches and configuration pages as SharePoint Server. Within Central Administration, you create and edit content sources (Figure 20-2) that provide the crawler with basic instructions for accessing and indexing content. Similarly, you can create crawl rules, monitor crawl logs, and define file types in exactly the same way you learned in the previous chapter.

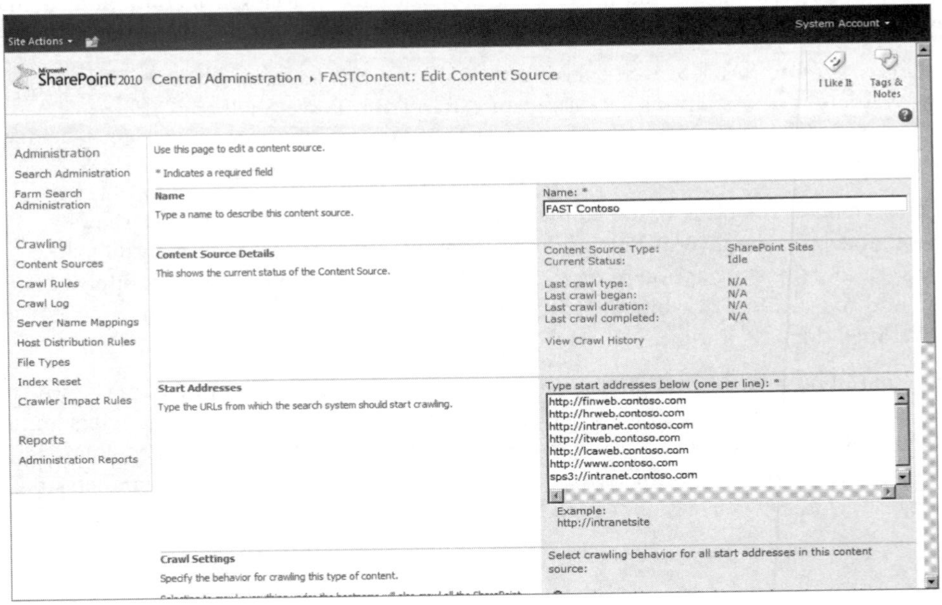

FIGURE 20-2

Leveraging the same configuration pages in Central Administration that you did for SharePoint Server makes the transition from SharePoint to FAST much easier and requires less of a learning curve. On the other hand, the configuration pages provided by Central Administration are substantially limited when compared to the vast array of configuration options available to the FAST crawler. Therefore, it is often in your best interest to abandon the Central Administration pages and get accustomed to working directly with the configuration files provided by FAST.

Advanced crawl configuration is accomplished in FAST with a set of XML-based configuration files. These files are located within the `etc` folder of the FAST root folder on the search server (this is usually `C:\FASTSEARCH\etc`). You can conceptually think of these files as you would content sources in the search service application, with the exception that the configuration files give you greater control over how the crawler behaves.

As with content source definitions, you should have one configuration file per content source. Because the format of the file is XML, it is valid to include all your crawl configuration in a single file. But once you begin scripting your configuration into the Crawler Admin Utility or PowerShell, you will wish you had separated them into individual configuration files.

FAST Search Server installs three sample configuration files in the `etc` folder. When configuring your own advanced crawler, it is best to begin by copying one of these files and modifying it to meet your needs. The sample configurations include a simple, an advanced, and an RSS configuration. All three files include copious comments that provide you with more than enough information to understand what each setting does for the crawler.

Crawler Administration Tool

FAST Search Server comes with a command line utility specifically designed to manage crawling in your farm. To use the Crawler Admin Utility you must be a member of the FASTSearchAdministrators group on the search server. The basic syntax for using the Crawler Admin Utility is crawleradmin -<switch>. Table 20-1 shows some of the more useful commands provided by the utility.

TABLE 20-1: Common Crawler Admin Utility Switches

SWITCH	DESCRIPTION
-f	Adds a content source to the collection
-G	Outputs the configuration of the content source collection
-d	Deletes a content source from the collection
-s	Suspends a crawl
-r	Resumes a crawl
--quarantine	Blocks crawling for specified number of seconds

continues

TABLE 20-1 *(continued)*

SWITCH	DESCRIPTION
--unquarantine	Unblocks the crawl
--refetch, --refetchuri, --refetchsite	Recrawls specified set of content
--status	Shows the status of the crawl
--sites	Displays a list of all sites being crawled
--statistics	Displays data about the crawler

CONTENT PROCESSING

At this point, it's probably a good idea to review how content is indexed by the crawler and processed by the indexer, because this is an important part of search to master. When the crawler indexes the content of a content source, it uses a search connector to understand how to access, read, and extract the content of the file. As it reads the content of an item, it converts the content into crawled properties that it stores in the index. The crawled properties are organized into categories based on the rules defined within the protocol handler or iFilter defined by the search connector.

Crawled properties do not participate in the search engine. It's important for you to understand this simple concept because many issues of missing content and bad search results begin with a misunderstanding of this basic principle. The crawler is not responsible for processing or presenting search results; it is responsible only for extracting and submitting content according to the configured rules. Therefore, there must be another process by which the results of the crawler's work is processed, formatted, and made available to the query engine.

The content processor is the part of the search engine responsible for mapping the crawled properties generated by the crawler into a form usable by the query engine. The content processor is part of the indexer and it does its work between the crawler and the index. When the crawler extracts a crawled property, it submits the data to the indexer, which sends the data through the processing engine. The result of content processing is the entry in the index database that is later used by the query engine when processing search requests.

The glue between the crawled property and the index database entry is the managed property. Managed properties map one or more crawled properties into a single managed property term. It is this managed property term that the query engine uses to process search requests.

Managed Properties

Managed properties in FAST Search Server are configured in exactly the way they are in SharePoint Server. The Managed Properties page provides you with a listing of configured managed properties as well as raw and categorized listings of crawled properties that you can analyze to determine mapping schemes.

The first major difference between the managed properties in SharePoint and managed properties in FAST is the location of the configuration page. Simply put, the link is not where you would expect it to be — it's not even close. Given that the link to managed properties in SharePoint Search is in the Query section of the navigation bar, you may think that the FAST Query Search Service Application (SSA) is the right place to find the link, and you are correct. The problem you'll face is that there is no link for managed properties in the navigation bar. Instead of a link under the Query section, the link is in the FAST Search Administration page. Therefore, to get to the page, go to FAST Query SSA ⇨ FAST Search Administration ⇨ Managed Properties.

The second difference between FAST managed properties and SharePoint managed properties is that FAST contains some additional options. FAST search provides the ability to apply stemming (Figure 20-3), the function that analyzes the root form of a word (for example, run, running, ran), to any text-based properties you define.

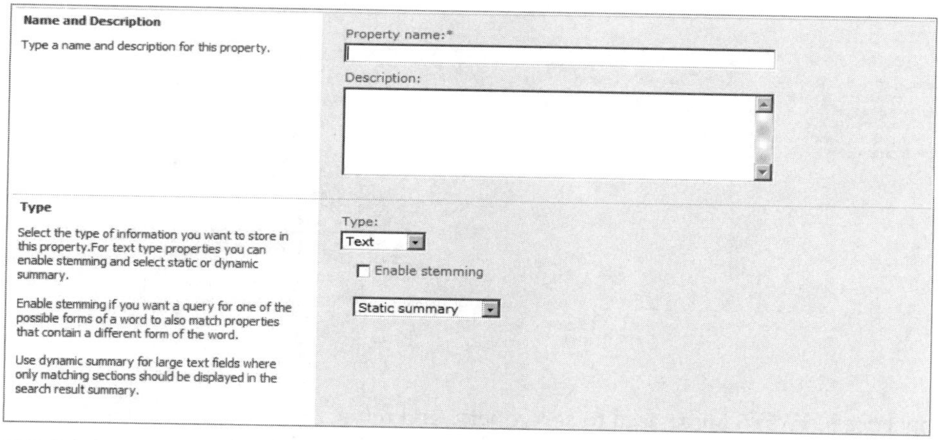

FIGURE 20-3

Stemming is a capability that has been a part of the SharePoint Search engine since SharePoint 2007; it just wasn't available at this low a level until FAST search. In SharePoint Search, stemming is applied to search results by the query engine. This means that the cost of stemming occurs at query time, which can affect performance depending on the search term that is being stemmed and the size of the result set.

As you recall, the mapping of crawled properties to managed properties is part of the content processing pipeline that affects actual entries in the index database. If a particular term is stemmed before it is entered into the index, the cost of stemming is paid up front and will not affect the performance of the query engine at all. To leverage this power and gain the full benefit of stemming at the managed property level, it is important to properly map crawled properties to the managed property in such a way as to maximize the benefit of stemming.

Although I am focusing here on stemming, the logic applies to the other FAST-specific properties (Sort, Query, and Refinement). That is to say, you must take special care and planning to map crawled properties because the work you do up front to map your managed properties will pay huge dividends in performance and search quality later on.

Within and across content sources, the crawler will often identify crawled properties that are simply variations of one another. For example, a crawler may go through a database and find a crawled property of **client**. Then it goes through a set of documents and defines crawled properties of **customer, cust_name,** and **cust**. In each case, the content refers to the same basic business concept: customer. From this content analysis, you would create a managed property called Customer and then map the four crawled properties to it (Figure 20-4).

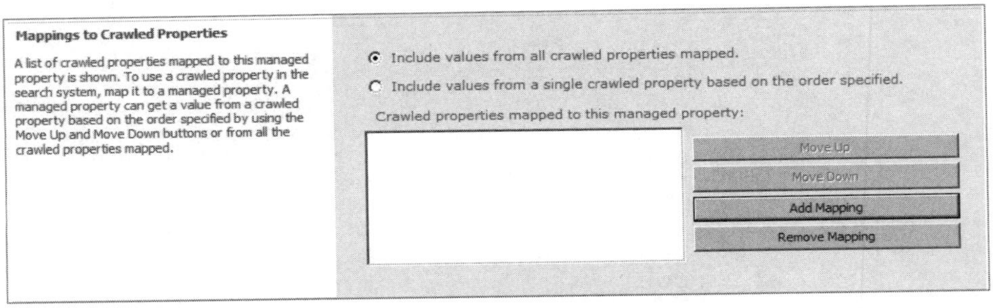

Mappings to Crawled Properties

A list of crawled properties mapped to this managed property is shown. To use a crawled property in the search system, map it to a managed property. A managed property can get a value from a crawled property based on the order specified by using the Move Up and Move Down buttons or from all the crawled properties mapped.

- ◉ Include values from all crawled properties mapped.
- ○ Include values from a single crawled property based on the order specified.

Crawled properties mapped to this managed property:

> Move Up
> Move Down
> Add Mapping
> Remove Mapping

FIGURE 20-4

Managed properties in FAST can be used to sort, query, and refine results in the search user experience. Later in this chapter, I cover how to configure the search Web Parts to allow users to sort, query, and refine using managed properties. Before you are able to configure the Web Parts, however, you must make each managed property available by enabling each taxonomy category (Figure 20-5). Enabling these categories is commonly referred to as taxonomy search refinement.

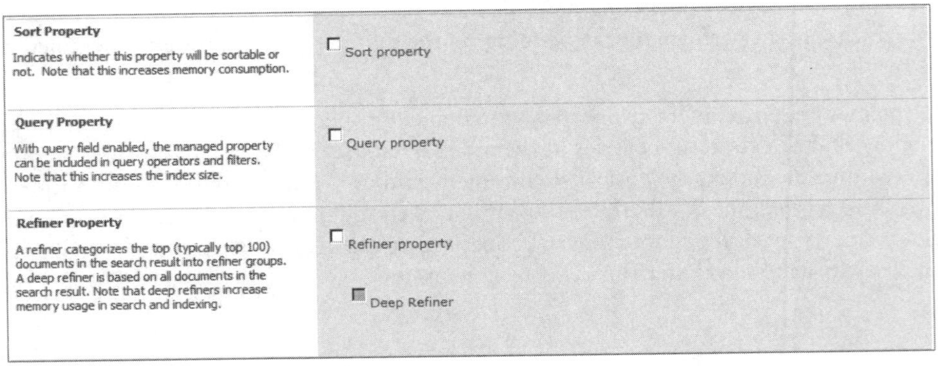

Sort Property

Indicates whether this property will be sortable or not. Note that this increases memory consumption.

☐ Sort property

Query Property

With query field enabled, the managed property can be included in query operators and filters. Note that this increases the index size.

☐ Query property

Refiner Property

A refiner categorizes the top (typically top 100) documents in the search result into refiner groups. A deep refiner is based on all documents in the search result. Note that deep refiners increase memory usage in search and indexing.

☐ Refiner property

☐ Deep Refiner

FIGURE 20-5

Finally, FAST allows you to prioritize a managed property by setting a mapping value between 0 and 7 (Figure 20-6). The priority that you configure for a managed property will directly affect the relevance of search results matching this managed property compared with results marching other managed properties. This allows you to make managed properties related to specific business concepts more relevant in search results than properties that may be related to content not important to the business. For example, you may have documents and web pages related to company team sports that result in crawled properties pertaining to team names, ranks, schedules, and so forth, which you'll map to managed properties that you can push lower in search results.

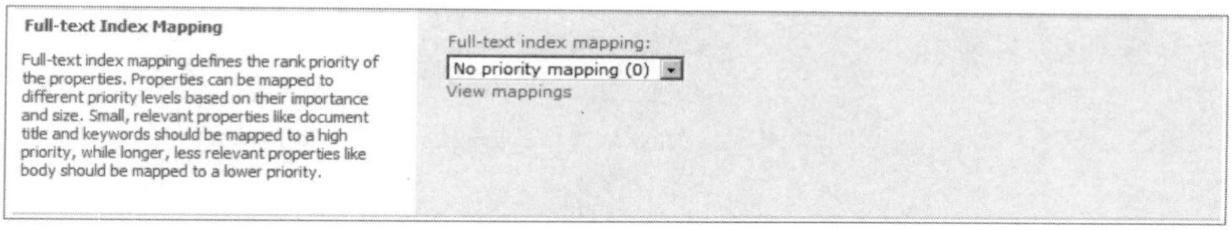

Full-text Index Mapping

Full-text index mapping defines the rank priority of the properties. Properties can be mapped to different priority levels based on their importance and size. Small, relevant properties like document title and keywords should be mapped to a high priority, while longer, less relevant properties like body should be mapped to a lower priority.

Full-text index mapping:

No priority mapping (0)

View mappings

FIGURE 20-6

Property Extraction

Mapping crawled properties to managed properties is an "after the fact" approach to managing content: you must crawl the content first to find the crawled properties, then analyze them, and finally map them to managed properties. Property extraction is a more proactive approach to indexing content. The property extraction process finds and extracts specific information from the content and maps it to one of a set of predefined extractors.

Out of the box, FAST includes extractors for companies, locations, and person names. Using special XML files that are located in the FAST root folder on the server's filesystem, you can add more extractors to meet your business needs (consult the MSDN documentation for instructions).

When you define a term in the extractor, you either set it as an inclusion or exclusion to the extractor. Inclusions define terms that the extractor should recognize and map to the extractor (Figure 20-7). Exclusions define terms that the extractor should ignore.

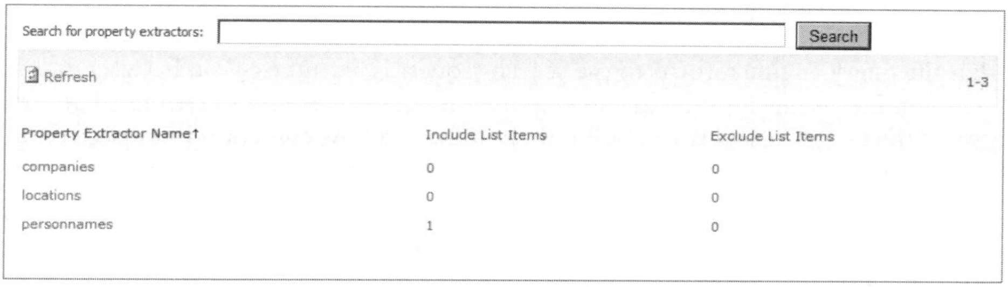

Search for property extractors: [   ] [Search]

Refresh   1-3

Property Extractor Name↑	Include List Items	Exclude List Items
companies	0	0
locations	0	0
personnames	1	0

FIGURE 20-7

Adding a term to the extractor (Figure 20-8) is a very straightforward process. You click the numbered link next to the extractor to either include or exclude a term based on your business need. This brings up a list of all inclusions or exclusions defined for the extractor. You can then use the Add Item button to enter a term into the list. Once added, that term will be mapped to the extractor on all subsequent crawls. This is why it's a good idea to reset your index after making substantial changes to the configuration of your search engine.

Search include list:		Search
🖼 Add Item 📄 Refresh		1-1

Include List Items ↑

Kenneth Schaefer

FIGURE 20-8

RELEVANCY TUNING

I think that the most important capability offered by FAST Search Server is the ability to tune relevancy at the site-collection level. This is where you are able to materially affect the quality of search results in your organization in ways that are not available in any of the other SharePoint Search offerings. Before we dig into relevancy tuning in FAST, it is important to review what relevancy is and how it relates to search queries.

The main function of the query engine is to strike a balance between recall and precision. Recall is a factor of quantity whereas precision is a factor of quality. To better understand this differentiation, consider a search request that returns a result set. When the query engine makes the request for content it makes that request to the entire index of content. The amount of content that the index returns to the query is the level of recall. In other words, returning all items in the index is 100 percent recall; everything else is a percentage of the whole.

Returning all items in the index for every search request would not yield quality results and it would not enhance performance. As a result, the query engine will return only items that are relevant to the search request. If the returned result set contains only items that are relevant to the search request, you have 100 percent precision. If some items in the result set are not relevant, you have some factor of diminished precision.

The result set that the query engine returns to the search request is an intersection between recall and precision. The configurations for crawling and content processing are those settings that affect the balance between the two. These settings will impact what and how content is delivered to the query. Relevancy tuning, on the other hand, affects the ordering of content in the returned result set.

FAST Search Server uses a complex calculation to apply a ranking score to each item in the search result set. The ranking score determines the item's location in the search set; higher ranking items appear toward the top of the set and lower ranking toward the bottom. FAST Search Server's relevancy tuning capabilities allow you to modify aspects of an item's ranking score in order to move it up or down in the result set.

FAST and SharePoint use six factors to calculate ranking scores (but only FAST Search allows you to tweak the score):

➤ **Quality:** This is a static score that is based on the content itself and reflects the item's level of importance. This score is calculated at the time of indexing.

➤ **Authority:** This is a score that reflects the frequency of matches between the search query and the link text of a document. For example, if a document is stored at a URL of `<site>/Benefits%20Documents/Dental%20Benefit.docx` and the user types in the keyword Benefit, the authority of the item will be boosted by the two exact matches of the string Benefit that occur in the URL. Authority is also affected by search results that have been clicked on in previous queries. If a person makes a query for Benefit and clicks the link to the Dental Benefit document, and then another person executes the same query for Benefit, the Dental Benefit document will be given additional ranking points because of the previous click-through.

➤ **Freshness:** This is a calculation that is based on the difference between the last modified date of the document and the date of the search query. The smaller the difference between the two, the higher the ranking value that is added to the document.

➤ **Proximity:** When a query consists of more than one word, the proximity score reflects the frequency with which these words in the query occur together in the document. For example, if a person searches for Dental Plan, a document containing the phrase Dental Plan will get a higher score than a document that contains the words Dental and Plan in different places. The number of times that the phrase Dental Plan occurs in the document will also add ranking to the document.

➤ **Context:** This score is based on where query terms are found in the document. Managed properties allow you to set Full Text Index Mapping; this is the configuration that impacts the context quality of the document. Therefore, only managed properties that are part of the full-text index are considered in this calculation.

➤ **Managed property boosts:** Once again, I can't emphasize the importance of managed properties enough. FAST allows you to use any managed property to increase or decrease the ranking score of an item. In SharePoint Search many people do not like the fact that PowerPoint documents are rated higher than Word documents. Using a managed property in FAST, you can boost the value of Word documents to be above that of PowerPoint documents.

There is an important distinction to understand here from a troubleshooting point of view. If you are looking at a result set and you find that there is missing content or content that should not be there, you have a problem with the recall/precision equation and you need to look at the content processing pipeline. If you are looking at a result set and the content is not in the right order, you have a problem of ranking. I have seen many clients lose time trying to fix the wrong thing.

To discuss all the techniques and tools to tune each of the relevancy categories would fill many pages. It's a relatively advanced topic and requires deep knowledge of your content and the PowerShell environment. This is something that you should look into after you have mastered all other aspects of search. In the remainder of this section I cover the site settings that are available to you and that also affect the ranking score of documents in the result set. These are modifiers that are applied at query time when the query engine is returning a result set.

The site collection-based ranking techniques are all located in the Site Collection Administration section of Site Settings. It is important to remember that some items in Site Collection Administration are specific to SharePoint Search and some items are specific to FAST Search (Figure 20-9). The techniques discussed in this section rely on the FAST settings.

FIGURE 20-9

Keywords

Before digging into the specific ranking techniques for site collections, we must review keywords because many of the refinement settings are tied to keywords. A keyword (Figure 20-10) is a word or phrase that matches the word or phrase entered by a user in a search request. By capturing a match for specific words or phrases, you can configure search to respond to common business terms, acronyms, or important business concepts. The most common two responses that you will configure for keywords are synonyms and Best Bets (Best Bets are covered later in this section).

---

* Indicates a required field

Keyword Phrase

The keyword phrase is the word or phrase that users type in the search box.

When you have saved a keyword, you can add best bets, visual best bets, document promotions and demotions to improve the search result for this keyword.

Keyword phrase: *
| Annual Enrollment |

Synonyms

When users search for the keyword, results from all synonyms will also be displayed in the search result. Separate multiple synonyms by using semicolons.

When users search for a two-way synonym, results from this synonym will be displayed in addition to results from the keyword and all other synonyms.

When users search for a one-way synonym, only results from this synonym will be displayed.

Two-way synonyms:
| Benefits; Health Insurance; Dental Plan |

One-way synonyms:
| |

Keyword Definition

The keyword definition will be displayed on the search result page when users search for the keyword.

Keyword definition:

Content related to the annual enrollment process.

FIGURE 20-10

When the user includes a synonymous term for a keyword in a query, the items for that keyword are returned in the result set. But when a user includes the actual keyword in the query, the synonymous items are not returned. For example, suppose you create a keyword for the phrase Annual Enrollment and create a one-way synonym for Benefits. What this means is that if a user types the word Benefits in a search query, he will get results that include matches for Benefits and matches for Annual Enrollment. If the user executes a search for Annual Enrollment, he will get matches for Annual Enrollment only. FAST allows you to set up two-way synonyms so that a search for Annual Enrollment will also return matches for Benefits.

After creating a keyword, you will be able to configure synonyms by editing the keyword from the Keywords page. The drop-down item menu (Figure 20-11) on the items page will also give you access to configure the other FAST relevancy refinements that are linked to the keyword.

FIGURE 20-11

Document Promotions and Demotions

FAST Search Server allows you to promote and demote documents (Figure 20-12) that match a keyword. What a promotion does to the specified document is add or subtract 1,000 rating points to the document within the result set returned by the keyword. For example, suppose that you are analyzing the result set for Annual Enrollment documents and you see that the document called "Summary of Annual Enrollment Changes" is at the bottom of the first page, but you want it at the top. By setting a document promotion for this document, it will likely push the document to the top of the results page. Similarly, you may find that last year's document is also on the listing; by applying a demotion you can push it down in the set.

* Indicates a required field	
Title	
Enter a title for the document promotion. The title will not be displayed in the search result.	Title: * United Health Care Changes
Document Promotion	
Add a URL for the document that you want to promote.	URL: * pso.com/hr/enrollment%20documents/2011/uhc%20changes.docx
User Context	
Add one or more user contexts for which the document promotion should apply. Leave blank if the the document promotion applies for any user context. To create a new user context, go to the user context page.	User context: Add Remove
Start and End Date	
In the start date box, type the date that you want this document promotion to appear in the search results. In the end date box, type the date that you want this document promotion to no longer appear in the search results. Leave blank if the document promotion should take effect immediately with no expiry.	Start date (leave blank for immediate start): 11/1/2010 End date (leave blank for no expiry): 12/6/2010

FIGURE 20-12

Many of the relevancy refinements in FAST can have start and end dates assigned to them. If the date values are left blank, the refinement will begin immediately and run indefinitely. Yet at times having a start and end may be a desired factor of the refinement. For example, perhaps you want to boost Annual Enrollment specific documents only during the annual enrollment period, after which you want documents to be listed according to their natural ranking.

Site Promotions and Demotions

Site promotions and demotions (Figure 20-13) work exactly the same as document promotions and demotions, by adding or subtracting 1,000 document ranking points. Unlike document promotions/demotions, the site promotions/demotions are not tied to a keyword, and they apply to all documents contained within the site.

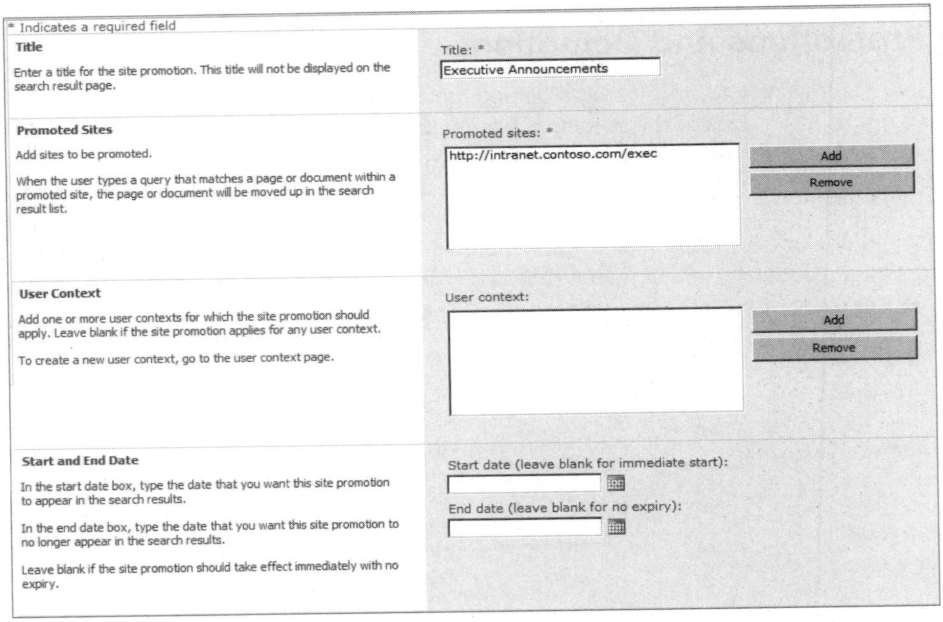

FIGURE 20-13

Each promotion/demotion that you create can be mapped to more than one site. This is helpful when certain documents are located in a variety of content sources. For example, suppose you are a major food manufacturer and you want to promote all documents related to a new line of cookies. You may have documents about the research and development of the cookies, marketing brochures and materials about the cookies, logos and product images, and other documents. All these may be stored in various team sites, file shares, or other sources. By creating a single site promotion for the cookie line and then mapping each of the site URLs to this promotion, you can apply the promotion to all documents for this cookie rather than creating a keyword and adding a document promotion for each and every document that you have.

User Context

FAST Search Server allows you to define promotions, demotions, and Best Bets according to user context. The user context is a specific group that is configured (Figure 20-14) in site settings to which the promotion/demotion or Best Bet will apply.

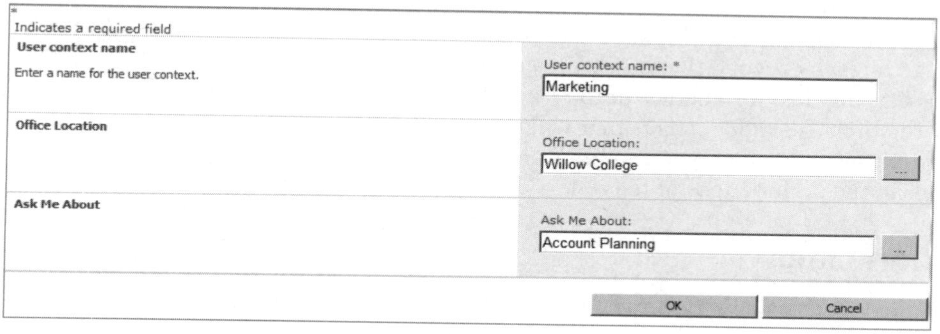

FIGURE 20-14

User context is a power refinement-tuning mechanism because it means that different users will be able to see different result sets for the same search term based on the user's context. For example, a human resources employee may need to see a different set of search results for the term Annual Enrollment than another employee of the company. In this case, creating a user context for the human resources employee and applying that context to promotions, demotions, or Best Bets will provide the human resources employee with a better search experience.

FAST SEARCH EXPERIENCE

FAST Search Server adds a number of enhancements to the search experience by expanding on the existing search Web Parts and by adding new Web Parts to the system. The enhancements that FAST brings to the search experience are ones that allow you to provide richer and deeper search results to the end user. FAST adds a new search center template to SharePoint, appropriately called the FAST Search Center. This template contains a preconfigured search experience that mirrors the one that comes with SharePoint Server but includes the new FAST-specific Web Parts.

Search Core Results

The FAST Search Core Results Web Part (Figure 20-15) adds the ability to display similar results, document previews for PowerPoint, and document thumbnails for Word, as well as specific settings pertaining to these FAST-specific capabilities. Similar Results is a link that shows with each item in the search results page. When the user clicks the link, FAST will re-query the index using the search terms associated with the Similar Results link. This capability is disabled by default but is easily enabled by checking the box in the Display Properties of the Search Core Results Web Part.

Document previews and thumbnails are enabled by default in FAST search, but you may find that you want to tweak things like the size of the preview or the number of previews and thumbnails that the result set displays. Most users do not progress in search results beyond the first few pages of the result set. Considering this, it is inefficient to return document previews and thumbnails for documents that will appear further down in the result set. Therefore, you can limit the number of previews and help the performance of the results display.

Search Action Links

The Search Action Links Web Part displays the sorting drop-down box and links to RSS and Search from Windows. By default it is located at the top of the results page above the results display. FAST Search allows you to hide or display the links individually by selecting or deselecting the checkboxes at the top of the Search Action Links properties pane (Figure 20-16).

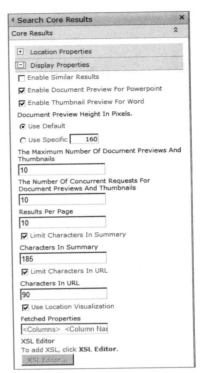

FIGURE 20-15

More importantly, the Search Action Links Web Part is where you enable the sorting of search results based on managed properties. As you recall from the earlier discussion of managed properties, FAST includes a selection to make the managed property available for sorting. The managed properties that have sorting enabled will appear in this Web Part, but are not enabled by default. To allow users to sort on the managed property, you select the enabled checkbox in the Web Part properties pane and then select a sorting direction for the property.

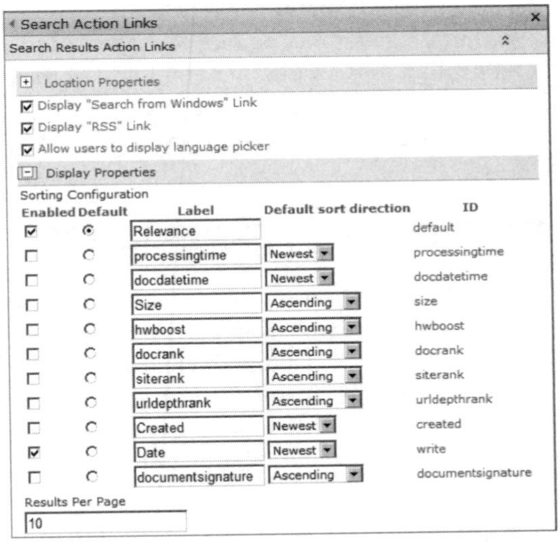

Visual Best Bets

Best Bets are a functionality available in SharePoint Search. When you configure a keyword, you can associate a set of links that you want to appear whenever a user executes a search using the specified keyword. The SharePoint Search Best Bets are simply a set of links that appear within the Search Best Bets Web Part (Figure 20-17), but sometimes a Best Bet is better served with an image. For example, if you set up a keyword for

FIGURE 20-16

Company Logo, you may want to have a Best Bet that points to the logo usage guidelines document, but you may also want to have the logo itself show up at the top of the results. FAST adds the Visual Best Bet Web Part to your search center so that you can accomplish this requirement.

FIGURE 20-17

Visual Best Bets, like Best Bets, are contained within a keyword. In the keyword drop-down menu (shown earlier in Figure 20-10) you were given the option to add Best Bets and Visual Best Bets directly to the keyword definition. You may also select the keyword details option to see a summary view (Figure 20-18) of the keyword, which includes a listing of all Best Bets and Visual Best Bets assigned to the keyword. The summary screen also provides you with links to add, edit, or remove Best Bets and Visual Best Bets.

Keyword	Edit Keyword
The keyword phrase is the word or phrase that users type in the search box.	Keyword phrase: * **Gears**
You can add synonyms to a keyword. When users search for a keyword, results from both keyword and synonyms will be displayed in the search result.	Two-way synonyms:
	One-way synonyms:
The keyword definition will be displayed on the search result page when users search for the keyword.	Keyword definition:
Best Bets	
Best bets are the recommended results for this keyword. Best bets will be displayed on the search result page in the order listed.	Add Best Bet Title Gear Project Wiki Remove Edit
Visual Best Bet	
Visual best bet is rich content (like images or html snippets) that will be displayed on the search result page.	Add Visual Best Bet Title Gear Image Remove Edit
Document Promotions	
A promoted document is moved to the top of the search result list.	Add Document Promotion
Document Demotions	
A demoted document is moved to the bottom of the search result list.	Add Document Demotion

FIGURE 20-18

To add a Visual Best Bet to a keyword, you must provide a unique title and a complete URL that points to the image you want to display in the Visual Best Bet (Figure 20-19). As with promotions and demotions, you can specify a user context for the Visual Best Bet and set the start and end dates.

The one key difference between Best Bets and Visual Best Bets (besides the visual part) that you need to be aware of is that the Visual Best Bet is not a link, as opposed to the Best Bet, which is a link to specific content. This means that in most cases, you will want to add a matching Best Bet that links to the content relevant to the keyword.

 Not only does FAST allow you to set start and end dates for a Visual Best Bet; FAST also adds the ability to set start and end dates, as well as apply a user context to Best Bets.

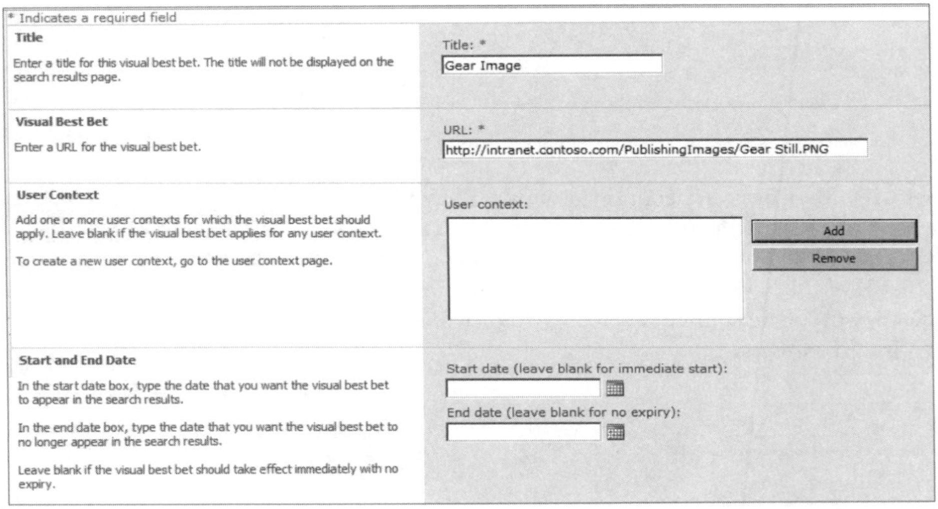

* Indicates a required field

Title

Enter a title for this visual best bet. The title will not be displayed on the search results page.

Title: *

`Gear Image`

Visual Best Bet

Enter a URL for the visual best bet.

URL: *

`http://intranet.contoso.com/PublishingImages/Gear Still.PNG`

User Context

Add one or more user contexts for which the visual best bet should apply. Leave blank if the visual best bet applies for any user context.

To create a new user context, go to the user context page.

User context:

| Add |
| Remove |

Start and End Date

In the start date box, type the date that you want the visual best bet to appear in the search results.

In the end date box, type the date that you want the visual best bet to no longer appear in the search results.

Leave blank if the visual best bet should take effect immediately with no expiry.

Start date (leave blank for immediate start):

End date (leave blank for no expiry):

FIGURE 20-19

Refinement Panel

In the search world, refining results based on content metadata is a concept referred to as faceted search. In SharePoint, facets are displayed in the Refinement Panel Web Part and are referred to as refiners. Out of the box, SharePoint Search provides refiners for document properties that are extracted during content processing and stored in the index. The default set of refiners that SharePoint handles are Result Type, Site, Author, Modified Date, and Companies.

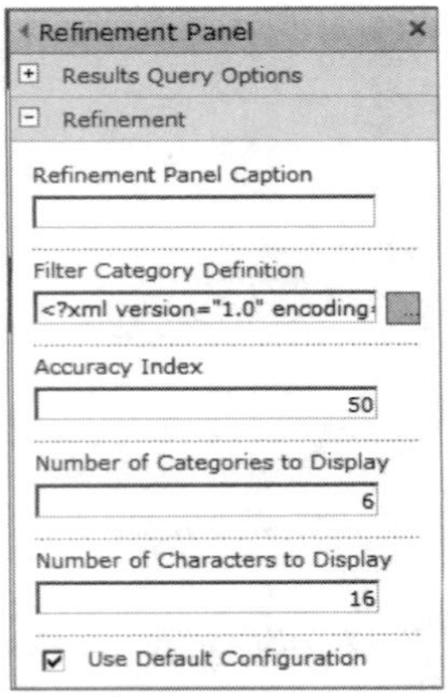

FAST Search Server allows you to add managed metadata and tags as refiners in the Refinement panel (Figure 20-20); this is known as taxonomy refinement. The Filter Category Definition property of the Web Part contains an XML document that defines the facets available to the Refinement Web Part. This chapter does not provide an in-depth discussion of the XML contained in this property, but when you get to

◄ Refinement Panel ✕

⊞ Results Query Options

⊟ Refinement

Refinement Panel Caption

Filter Category Definition

`<?xml version="1.0" encoding:`

Accuracy Index

50

Number of Categories to Display

6

Number of Characters to Display

16

☑ Use Default Configuration

FIGURE 20-20

the point where you are ready to begin adding properties to the panel, it will be much easier to copy the text into an IDE that has color coding, such as Visual Studio, for easier editing of the configuration.

 One thing to remember when you work with the filter categories is that they work with managed properties that have been enabled as refiners. If you have not enabled refinement on the managed property, it will not work as a refiner.

SUMMARY

Unfortunately, a short chapter such as this one cannot sufficiently explain all the different aspects and configurations available in the FAST Search Server product. It is a very capable search platform that gives you a great deal of control over the search engine and search experience. The downside is that it requires a deep and technical knowledge to work with all the different options.

This chapter wraps up the section on enterprise search. At this point, you should have a solid understanding of the components of a search engine and how those components are exposed in the SharePoint 2010 stack of search products. You should also be able to configure a SharePoint Search engine that will provide high quality and high performance search results to your end users.

21

Wrapping It All Up

You have come to the end of this book on SharePoint 2010. We hope you've taken several steps forward on your journey into the marvelous world of SharePoint. If you are truly serious about being successful in deploying and using SharePoint, with all its power and benefits, this book should be just the beginning. You should never stop learning, growing, trying new things, reading up on what others are doing, and networking with others who are also on the SharePoint path.

Each author has a few parting words designed to give you insight into what you should be doing now in the area of that author's particular subject. As you read in the introduction, this book was not designed or intended to be a full-on educational deep dive. Rather, the intent was just to get you started and give you enough information for a solid head start. The rest is up to you. Where you go from here depends on the needs of your organization and your personal topic or niche preferences. If you find Business Connectivity Services amazing and fun, then by all means dig into every aspect of BCS and take that part of your SharePoint implementation to the fullest. If it's one of the other major areas that intrigues you, go for that.

PARTING ADVICE FROM THE AUTHORS

Here are your authors, speaking on the six major areas that make up the Six-in-One approach of the title. In the order of presentation in the book, these are branding, development, Business Connectivity Services (BCS), the social networking side of SharePoint, workflow, and search. Several of the authors have also given you websites where additional information can be obtained.

SharePoint Branding

 Making SharePoint Server 2010 not look like SharePoint can be quite a challenge, but now that you understand the components of what is involved to brand it, you have a head start. As you start determining what you would like to change, you should evaluate each of the pieces and make a plan. You should make sure that your plan allows for user acceptance testing and a phased approach to your solution.

When it comes to SharePoint, many pieces must be considered in your branding plan. The master pages and themes are just the starting points. You will also need to keep in mind all the different pieces that you'll need to change with your CSS. You can examine more in-depth ideas about branding SharePoint in the Wrox book *Professional SharePoint 2010 Branding and User Interface Design* (by Randy Drisgill, et al.). Just make sure that you allow for the addition of new style sheets and branding as you move forward with your implementation. Some of these future customizations could include custom-developed solutions or third-party solutions that have been purchased to further expand the functionality of your sites.

— CATHY DEW

SharePoint Development

This book has just scratched the surface of SharePoint development. Because SharePoint is built on ASP.NET and the .NET Framework, you have an extensive toolset available for you to create custom SharePoint solutions.

Luckily, Microsoft has provided extensive online documentation for SharePoint 2010. The SharePoint Server 2010 SDK is your best source for detailed information regarding any of the topics covered in Chapters 7 and 8 of this book. You can find this information on the Microsoft Developer Network (MSDN) site. A good starting point is to visit http://msdn.microsoft.com/sharepoint or http://msdn.microsoft.com/en-us/library/dd776256(office.12).aspx.

Wrox Press also has several books to help get you going. You can start out by reading *Beginning SharePoint 2010 Development* by Steve Fox. Once you have a handle on SharePoint development, you can dive deeper by reading *Professional SharePoint 2010 Development* (by Tom Rizzo, et al.).

If you already feel comfortable with ASP.NET development and are trying to branch out into SharePoint development, Microsoft has provided handy online documentation just for users like you. Take a look at this starting point in MSDN: http://msdn.microsoft.com/en-us/library/ff829215.aspx.

Many bloggers in the SharePoint community post helpful content on a regular basis. There are too many of them to list here, but as you use public search engines to find solutions to your SharePoint development problems, keep an eye out for bloggers who provide helpful answers. Many bloggers alert their users of new content via Twitter, so try to take advantage of Twitter as well. Users frequently use the #SharePoint or #SP2010 tags to advertise their content.

Last but not least, remember that SharePoint development requires a new skill set and a detailed knowledge of the product. Just as you probably spent more than a week learning ASP.NET development, object-oriented programming, design skills, or whatever else you focus your energies on, keep in mind that learning the nuances of SharePoint development also takes time. Stick with it and you'll find you can build great things.

Whereas Microsoft initially advertised SharePoint 2007 as a collaboration platform, with the release of SharePoint 2010 Microsoft is trying to raise public awareness about the number of high-profile companies that use SharePoint for their public-facing sites. You can find a list of many public-facing

SharePoint WCM sites on the WSS Demo site at http://www.wssdemo.com/Pages/websites.aspx. These sites may give you an idea of the kind of unique look and feel that can be generated on the SharePoint WCM platform.

A number of books have been published about SharePoint 2010, and like this one they contain information about publishing sites. However, the book that covers the topic of SharePoint WCM in the most in-depth way was written for SharePoint 2007 by Andrew Connell, and is called *Professional SharePoint 2007 Web Content Management Development: Building Publishing Sites with Office SharePoint Server 2007*. Although various concepts such as Visual Studio development and the use of the Ribbon were different for SharePoint 2007, many of the fundamental concepts have remained the same between versions of SharePoint. In light of that, this book is still a good reference for building WCM sites. Andrew Connell has published a number of helpful articles through the years regarding web content management in SharePoint on his blog and on MSDN. You can find a list of his WCM-oriented blog posts at http://www.andrewconnell.com/blog/category/67.aspx.

Microsoft has extensive online documentation regarding the development of SharePoint WCM sites. You can find a good starting point on the MSDN site at http://msdn.microsoft.com/en-us/library/ms573556.aspx.

Randy Drisgill has published a set of "starter" master pages you can use as a starting point for building your own publishing site master page. You can download the starter kit from Codeplex at http://startermasterpages.codeplex.com/.

— BECKY BERTRAM

Business Connectivity Services

Now that you have learned about the possible BCS solution types, you should have an idea of how BCS can be used in your own environment. Perhaps you will be building a simple solution, creating an External Content Type (ECT) using SharePoint Designer. If that's the case, you may want to consider a book on SharePoint Designer 2010. A good one, for starters, from Wrox is *Beginning SharePoint Designer 2010* (by Woodrow W. Windischman, et al.). Perhaps you will be building an intermediate solution that takes advantage of workflows or custom InfoPath forms — both of which are deep areas that should be looked into. If you are surfacing BCS data in Office applications, you may want to consider looking into OBA (Office Business Applications) and specifically creating custom Office solutions using Visual Studio 2010, because that provides the support for advanced integration opportunities.

Overall, it is important to understand the concept of Composites and to know what building blocks you have at your disposal. It may be tempting to jump directly into the BCS before understanding the out-of-the-box Web Parts, workflow actions and conditions, and list capabilities, but those concepts are often key components of a successful BCS solution and should not be overlooked.

— RAYMOND MITCHELL

The Social Networking Side of SharePoint

Social computing inside SharePoint 2010 replaces traditional search for finding documents hidden inside the corporation. This functionality relies solely on user participation, which is also the reason this aspect of SharePoint can fail so easily. What are you doing to make social computing accepted within your organization? Is your system prepared for a high adoption rate? Does your user base know how to use SharePoint? Does your internal team understand how to administer and maintain not just the SharePoint infrastructure but also the social content that will be accumulated over time? This book discusses these items and also offers several links from both Microsoft and the community so that the reader can dive into areas to learn more about a given subject.

The chapters in this book contain several links, and the following section contains more of the important ones related to social computing. Whether it be planning for an initial launch of My Site personal sites to understanding how the pesky User Profile Synchronization works, plenty of resources are available to make social computing work effectively for your organization.

Planning for My Site websites and determining users and user permissions:

`http://technet.microsoft.com/en-us/library/cc262500.aspx#section3`

Planning Terms and Term Sets (SharePoint Server 2010):

`http://technet.microsoft.com/en-us/library/ee519604.aspx#section3`

Configuring profile synchronization (SharePoint Server 2010):

`http://technet.microsoft.com/en-us/library/cc678863.aspx#Section3`

Rational guide to implementing SharePoint Server 2010 User Profile Synchronization (UPS):

`http://www.harbar.net/articles/sp2010ups.aspx`

Planning for Availability (SharePoint Server 2010):

`http://technet.microsoft.com/en-us/library/cc748824.aspx`

SharePoint Server 2010 Performance and Capacity Test Results and Recommendations:

`http://www.microsoft.com/downloads/details.aspx?FamilyID=fd1eac86-ad47-4865-9378-80040d08ac55&displaylang=en`

— ANDREW CLARK

Workflow and SharePoint

Workflow can be as simple or as complicated as you make it — I hope that idea has come through in the workflow chapters of this book. Those chapters have taken you from out-of-the-box workflows and figuring out how to make those work for your situations, to building custom workflows in Visual Studio. In order to take the next steps — using custom workflows with SharePoint Designer or developing workflows with Visual Studio — you may have to pick more of a focus. These two paths can differ quite significantly. Choose a path that best fits your needs and your organization's needs and start the journey. Both these paths have a wealth of resources available to help you. Following are some places for additional information.

For SharePoint Designer, there is usually some very good content at End User SharePoint:

```
http://www.endusersharepoint.com/
```

Microsoft sites have a wealth of information:

```
http://office.microsoft.com/en-us/sharepoint-designer-help/
```

```
http://channel9.msdn.com
```

You will also find some specific books out or coming soon at this site:

```
http://www.wiley.com/WileyCDA/WileyTitle/productCd-0470643161.html
```

If you plan on digging into SharePoint Workflow by building workflows in Visual Studio, here are two useful sites:

```
http://www.wiley.com/WileyCDA/WileyTitle/productCd-0470617888.html
```

```
http://www.wiley.com/WileyCDA/WileyTitle/productCd-0470617896.html
```

Visual Studio walk-throughs on MSDN:

```
http://msdn.microsoft.com/en-us/vstudio/dd441784.aspx
```

Hands-on labs:

```
http://www.microsoft.com/downloads/en/details.aspx?FamilyID=c010fc68-b47f-4db6-
b8a8-ad4ba33a35c5&displaylang=en
```

For workflow in general you may benefit from materials on `http://www.wfmc.org/`. These may not focus on technology specifically but may help you organizationally and with methodology.

Some SharePoint community members you will want to get to know and learn from are:

David Mann at:

```
http://www.mannsoftware.com/blog/default.aspx
```

Rob Bogue at:

```
http://www.thorprojects.com/blog/default.aspx
```

Asif Rehmani at:

```
http://blog.sharepointelearning.com/
```

There are literally hundreds of options out there for you to keep learning and growing in SharePoint and workflow. All you have to do is get started.

— Chris Geier

SharePoint and Search

Enterprise search is the glue that connects the parts of SharePoint. Whether you use SharePoint for enterprise content management, collaboration, business intelligence, or websites, search is a key information delivery technology. It acts as the magnifying glass when you are seeking out specific information. It is also the line of store windows when you're browsing through content and aren't sure of exactly what you need. When it is done right, search is a very powerful weapon in your arsenal. When done poorly, it can be a horrible experience that receives nothing but criticism from your user base.

The challenge you face is getting from out-of-the-box to the highly capable search solution. Many organizations subscribe to the myth that search should "just work" once you turn it on. The reality is that search requires a lot of upfront research and configuration. Although the level of effort required for search diminishes after the initial setup, it continues to require constant monitoring and updating to keep up to date with changing content needs, increasing content volume, and changing user behavior.

Successful search implementations begin with the content. Content is the central purpose of search; therefore, it stands to reason that you must know as much as possible about the content of your organization — where it is, how much you have, who uses it, how they use it, and how frequently it changes. You must understand the answers to these questions at all times, not only when you are setting up search but also as you maintain it over time. Understanding content is so important to search that you can often camouflage your technical shortcomings with an in-depth knowledge of your content.

Once you understand content, you can tackle the technical part. This book gives you a solid foundation to work from. At a minimum, you should be able to identify content sources, crawl content, monitor crawl logs, create and map managed properties, and set up search scopes. To take search to the next level, you will want to begin learning about the search Web Parts and building a good functional knowledge of their purpose and how they all work together to create the search experience. If you don't know XSL, you will need to learn it. The whole look and feel of the user experience is built upon a skeleton of XSL.

If you are using FAST, you have a lot of work ahead of you. Chapter 20 was a very brief look at the functionality FAST brings to the table. To be truly successful with FAST, you must become proficient with PowerShell and be comfortable working with XML configuration files. There is no safe web interface for you here, nor do you want it. But there is great power here.

Finally, use the tools and resources that are readily available. Microsoft has developed an exemplary set of documentation and training materials for all aspects of SharePoint, but the search-specific resources are indispensable. Here are some links to resources:

Microsoft Enterprise Search Center:

```
http://www.microsoft.com/enterprisesearch/
```

Microsoft Enterprise Search Blog:

```
http://blogs.msdn.com/b/enterprisesearch/
```

Other books to read:

Professional SharePoint 2010 Development:

http://www.wrox.com/WileyCDA/WroxTitle/Professional-SharePoint-2010-Development.productCd-0470529423.html

Professional SharePoint 2010 Administration:

http://www.wrox.com/WileyCDA/WroxTitle/Professional-SharePoint-2010-Administration.productCd-0470533331.html

Professional Microsoft Search: FAST Search, SharePoint Search, and Search Server:

http://www.wrox.com/WileyCDA/WroxTitle/Professional-Microsoft-Search-FAST-Search-SharePoint-Search-and-Search-Server.productCd-0470584661.html

— Ken Schaefer

General SharePoint Resources

Now that you have some simple advice on each topic, you should also be working to collect your arsenal of great resources that you can use to keep up on the latest developments. You should be out there in the community networking and conversing with your peers, learning from each other, and finding new ways to improve your implementation and get more value. To that end this section should provide you with some recommended resources to get you started.

Online Microsoft Resources

There is a wealth of information about SharePoint on the Internet, but some key places are worth mentioning. This is not meant to be a complete list, but the resources listed here are some of the core resources that have stood the test of time. The first may seem obvious, but it is frequently ignored: Microsoft's SharePoint homepage (http://sharepoint.microsoft.com). Here you will find general information about the product as well as links to several other online resources.

For developers there really is no better place to get started than MSDN (http://msdn.microsoft.com/SharePoint). Called the SharePoint Developer Center, this site provides links to technical resources regarding SharePoint. Though most of the content is geared toward developers, a number of other resources are hosted at MSDN that are not specific to developers.

For the server administrators/IT pros of the world, TechNet (http://technet.microsoft.com/SharePoint) is where you want to go. There you'll find information on product updates and patches, guidance on server planning and deployment, and links to many other helpful resources.

For general technical information and to keep up with all things SharePoint, consider subscribing to the product team blogs. Two blogs in particular are the main SharePoint team blog (http://blogs.msdn.com/SharePoint) and the SharePoint Designer team blog (http://blogs.msdn.com/SharePointDesigner).

Another great resource is the Microsoft Events homepage (http://www.microsoft.com/events). Here you'll find webcasts, videos, virtual labs, podcasts, and in-person events. At the time of this writing more than 50 free videos (not including recorded webcasts) were available for SharePoint 2010, so this is definitely a resource you don't want to miss out on.

Chances are good that at some point in your journey with SharePoint you will have a question. When you do have questions (or feel ready to answer some questions), be sure to head to *the* definitive place to ask a SharePoint question: the SharePoint forums on MSDN (http://mssharepointforums.com). Several topics are used to categorize questions and there's a search to review existing questions.

These official channels are a wonderful help. There are other great resources — too many to list here. One thing I recommend is to listen to and participate in the SharePoint community. If there is a great new resource out there, the community will let you know!

Learning from the Community

One of the greatest things about SharePoint is its community. Whether it's online via social networking or in person at a conference or free event, countless users, developers, and administrators are participating in daily conversations about SharePoint.

Social Media

Name your social network and you'll find SharePoint there. Here are a few examples of how SharePoint is making waves in the social-media world.

On Twitter you'll often find people asking questions or discussing trending SharePoint topics. When a new service pack comes out it's not uncommon for people on Twitter to discuss any questions or issues that might be related to the service pack. You'll find everyone from a brand-new SharePoint user to members of the SharePoint product team in Redmond on Twitter and talking about SharePoint — it's definitely not a tool to be ignored!

On Facebook a number of groups and pages are dedicated to SharePoint. If you become a fan of SharePoint, you may even find some new friends to talk SharePoint with! You'll also find user group sites and notices of SharePoint events. LinkedIn also has a number of SharePoint-related groups that you can join to network with other members of the community.

Events

A number of great opportunities exist to network in person as well as online, including dozens of SharePoint and Office-related user groups worldwide. You can search for a user group near you at http://www.technicalcommunity.com.

Each year national and regional conferences provide opportunities to learn from experts. Although it does not take place every year, Microsoft sponsors an event just for SharePoint that draws thousands of attendees. At the conferences you'll have the opportunity to learn from industry experts, network with other SharePoint users, and meet vendors with custom products built on top of SharePoint. Though many conferences require a fee, there are also a number of free events in the form of SharePoint Camps and SharePoint Saturdays. You can learn more about SharePoint Saturday events and get a list of upcoming events at http://www.sharepointsaturday.org.

There are even social SharePoint events like "SharePints" (http://www.SharePint.org) where you can meet with fellow SharePointers and discuss (perhaps over a beverage) your deepest philosophical SharePoint questions.

Microsoft Most Valuable Professionals

Although many evangelize SharePoint in the community, roughly 200 individuals worldwide are nominated and selected to be SharePoint MVPs. Microsoft has MVPs for a number of products including SharePoint. You can find a listing of MVPs by product specialization at `https://mvp.support.microsoft.com/communities/mvp.aspx`. Recognized as community leaders, MVPs participate in many events including Q&A with SharePoint Experts chats (`http://msdn.microsoft.com/chats`).

LinkedIn

You can participate in many professional and technical groups through the LinkedIn site. These groups allow you to connect with other like-minded individuals as well as participate in discussions, ask questions, and find out who's doing what in the SharePoint community. To get started simply sign up for a LinkedIn account and browse to `http://www.linkedin.com/groupsDirectory` to start searching for groups.

Twitter

Twitter is a major source of tips, links, and of course people you need to connect with and know. Many people in the SharePoint community are active on Twitter and are constantly sharing helpful information. This is also a good place to find out about upcoming events, ask questions, get advice, and even make some friends. Getting started is very simple. Just browse to `www.twitter.com` and sign up. Next set up a search for a topic that interests you and start following the conversation. To get you started here is a short list of some good people to start following — all co-authors of this book:

- ➤ @catpaint1
- ➤ @sharepointac
- ➤ @beckybertram
- ➤ @idubbs
- ➤ @Iwkid

FINAL WORDS

We hope that after reading this book you feel you've gained the knowledge necessary to get well under way on your SharePoint journey. This final chapter was designed to give you that next piece of advice, and where you go from here. SharePoint provides many features or specialty areas that you can get interested in and really dig into. Additionally, a vast number of resources are available that will allow you to go out and learn more about your chosen area. If we were to attempt to cover them all, you might need a forklift to carry this book around. One key piece to keep in mind — the SharePoint community is one of the best around. The people who participate regularly are open and always willing to answer questions, share information, and help those who are seeking it. Don't be intimidated or afraid to get out there and start interacting.

INDEX